VIRGINIA VALLEY
RECORDS

VIRGINIA VALLEY RECORDS

Genealogical and Historical Materials
of Rockingham County, Virginia
and Related Regions
(With Map)

By

JOHN W. WAYLAND

HARRISONBURG, VA.

SPECIAL CONTRIBUTORS

DAVID A. HEATWOLE, Dale Enterprise, Va.
REV. J. R. ELLIS, Lynnwood, Va.
JOSEPH K. RUEBUSH, Dayton, Va.
HENRY W. SCARBOROUGH, Philadelphia, Pa.
GEN. C. C. C. CARR, Chicago, Ill.
MRS. NELLIE D. TUFTS, Camden, Ark.
CHARLES M. ZIRKLE, Clifton Forge, Va.
PROF. ALCIDE REICHENBAUGH, Collegeville, Pa.
DR. JESSE D. BUCHER, Bridgewater, Va.
P. C. KAYLOR, Pleasant Valley, Va.
MRS. PHILIP SPENCE, Wytheville, Va.
JASPER N. KEESLING, New Castle, Ind.
MISS PAULINA S. WINFIELD, Broadway, Va.
HON. CHARLES E. KEMPER, Staunton, Va.
MILO CUSTER, Bloomington, Ill.
MRS. JOHN S. MACY, Indianapolis, Ind.

GENEALOGICAL PUBLISHING CO., INC.
BALTIMORE   1973

Originally Published
Strasburg, Virginia, 1930

Reprinted
Genealogical Publishing Co., Inc.
Baltimore, 1965

Reissued
Genealogical Publishing Co., Inc.
Baltimore, 1973

Library of Congress Catalogue Card Number 64-20826
International Standard Book Number 0-8063-0372-7

Made in the United States of America

PREFACE

THIS volume is largely a source book of genealogical and historical materials, compiled from the public records of Rockingham County, Augusta County, Greenbrier County, Wythe County, Montgomery County, and other counties of Virginia, with valuable contributions from various other parts of the United States.

In 1912, when the author's History of Rockingham County, Virginia, was published by the Ruebush-Elkins Company, Dayton, Va., a number of valuable materials were left over. During the eighteen years since that date many other documents of interest and value have been collected. All these, with various important contributions by numerous friends in different sections of the country, are now presented in this volume.

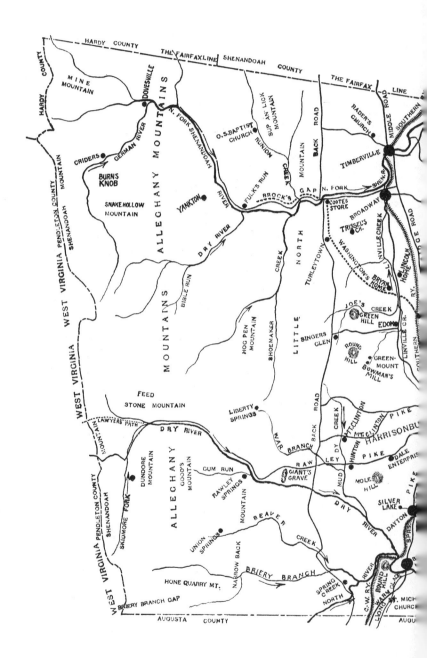

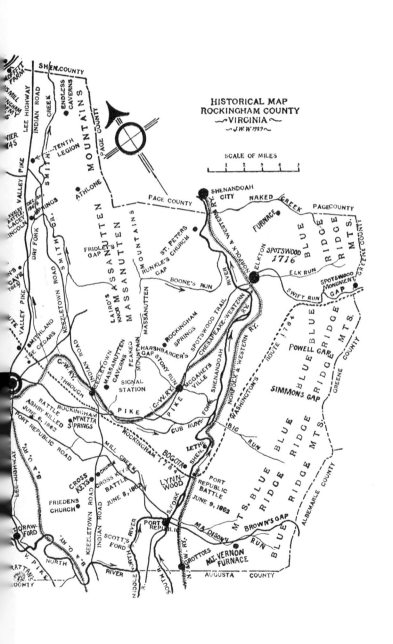

HISTORICAL MAP
ROCKINGHAM COUNTY
~VIRGINIA~
~J.W.W 1929~

SCALE OF MILES

CONTENTS

MARRIAGES IN ROCKINGHAM COUNTY
FROM 1795 TO 1825

The following lists have been compiled from records in the county clerk's office at Harrisonburg.

On pages 444-448 of Wayland's History of Rockingham County is a list of marriages from 1778 to 1794. The lists below are a continuation.

James Boyles	Rosanna Boon	January 4, 1795
Martin Cuntraman	Margaret Stolts	January 13, 1795
James Williamson	Kezia Thomas	January 15, 1795
Jacob Hickam	Catharina Comer	January 25, 1795
John Reagan	Elenor Kyle	January 26, 1795
Frederick Armintrout	Barbara Monger	February 3, 1795
John Kilburn	Mary Erwin	February 24, 1795
Jacob Miller	Margaret Hemphill	March 4, 1795
James Boyles	Rosanna Boon	March 8, 1795
Thomas Hopkins	Sarah Erwin	March 10, 1795
William Morrison	Margaret Nickoles	March 24, 1795
Daniel McCartney	Sarah Price	April 7, 1795
Ezekiel Green	Anne Lokey	April 14, 1795
James Ervin	Grace Shanklin	April 15, 1795
Thomas McKinsey	Margaret Thomas	April 24, 1795
Jacob Cokenhour	Susanna Rader	April 26, 1795
Henry King	Elizabeth Smith	April 27, 1795
Robert Shanklin	Margaret Rader	April 28, 1795
Jacob Marks	Mary Cherryholmes	May 2, 1795
John Miller	Nancy Wisehart	May 25, 1795
John Messeck	Sarah Teagy	June 5, 1795
John Cable	Elizabeth Smith	June 8, 1795
Charles Chestnut	Elizabeth Robertson	June 9, 1795
George Bell	Nancy Ervin	June 12, 1795
James Messeck	Mary Tounsley	June 22, 1795
Henry Moyers	Sarah Bryant	June 22, 1795
Dennis O'Bryan	Nancy Green	June 22, 1795
Archibald Rutherford	Jean Burges	June 23, 1795
Zachariah Fields	Ann Hamilton	June 25, 1795
Jacob Passinger	Catharine Cash	July 10, 1795
John Long	Mary Whitsell	July 20, 1795
Thomas Brill	Mary Headrick	August 3, 1795
Isaac Hammer	Susanna Bowman	August 11, 1795
Philip Awrey	Elizabeth Circle	August 29, 1795
Michall Joseph	Mary Bowland	September 14, 1795
Abraham Huffman	Dolly Tenkle	September 23, 1795
John Davice	Sarah Ewin	September 24, 1795
Frederick Coniker	Rachel Wiseman	September 28, 1795
Johnston Guinn	Polly Pry	September 29, 1795
Benj. Agle	Mary Boshang	October 15, 1795
James Campell	Amelia Harrison	November 5, 1795
William Woodford	Hannah Mass	November 6, 1795
Christian Bowars	Elizabeth Andres	November 26, 1795
John Vance	Jane Green	December 4, 1795
Michael Waren	Esther Shanklin	December 9, 1795
John Crotzer	Eleoner Waron	December 10, 1795
John Graham	Sarah Dehart	December 24, 1795
John Caplinger	Betsy Roler	December 29, 1795

John Keplinger	Betsy Roler	December 29, 1795
John Hall	Elesebeth Gragg	January 2, 1796
Jacob Cash	Elizabeth Sellers	January 5, 1796
Michael Circle	Rebeca Daugherty	January 6, 1796
John Rader	Susanna Curry	February 12, 1796
Daniel Oliver	Sarah Mole	February 27, 1796
Abram Christman	Polly Johnson	March 1, 1796
John Christman	Ann Harrison	March 10, 1796
David Mynes (?)	Elizabeth Kiney	March 17, 1796
George Berry	Margaret Green	April 20, 1796
John Bowman	Eve Steet	April 25, 1796
Archebald Hopkins	Margaret Shanklin	May 12, 1796
John Book	Barbara Miller	May 24, 1796
Peter Pasinger	Hannah Snider	May 30, 1796
Frederick Fickner	Magdalene Earhart	June 2, 1796
John Layburn	Jane McDowell	June 8, 1796
Solomon Huffman	Elizabeth Finkle	June 10, 1796
	(Tinkle?)	
Peter Beard	Mary Eavy	June 18, 1796
John Mathias	Barbarey Dispanet	July 5, 1796
Charls Youst	Polly Brock	July 5, 1796
John Pitt	Elisabeth Matthews	July 22, 1796
Benjamin Webb	Sarah Hamilton	August 2, 1796
George Monger	Frances Hestant (?)	August 2, 1796
Peter Moore	Sally Sheltman	August 24, 1796
Daniel Finn	Mary Erwin	September 8, 1796
John Herrington	Sally (?) Boshang	September 19, 1796
John Carrell	Deborah Rader	September 27, 1796
Samuel Leaney	Mary Harrison	September 28, 1796
Moses Norman	Mary Higgins	October 3, 1796
John Pence	Mary Ewin	October 6, 1796
Robert Fairbearn	Mary Jackson	October 7, 1796
Christian Sidel	Susanah Bowen	October 8, 1796
Jacob Hoover	Elizabeth Shoemaker	October 18, 1796
George Eary	Mary Cougler	October 20, 1796
Joseph Byerly	Kathren Landis	November 8, 1796
John Twitwiler	Mary Strough	November 21, 1796
Stephen Dorsey	Patience Proctor	November 24, 1796
Elijah Moore	Leday Reeves	November 28, 1796
John Howman	Catherine Simmers	December 6, 1796
Benjamin Groos	Hannah Swagget	December 10, 1796
Jacob Yankey	Mary Shrum	December 19, 1796
Samuel Coffman	Katy Orabough	December 20, 1796
Abraham Pupp	Sevile Miller	December 25, 1796
Augustine Bowman	Rachel Dunlap	December 26, 1796
Casper Pasinger	Eve Snider	December 26, 1796
Robert Jackson	Mary Gum	December 26, 1796
Danel Brunk	Magreat Grace	January 1, 1797
Charles Kyle	Jean Kyle	January 6, 1797
David Farquer	Mary Magaughey	January 11, 1797
William Orabough	Mary Stoutlemire	January 21, 1797
Jacob Trumbo	Polly Hughes	February 6, 1797
Jacob Stoutlemire	Barbara Orabough	February 18, 1797
Gabriel Smith	Susanna Yeates	February 27, 1797
Adam Smelcer	Mary Kretzinger	February 28, 1797
Adam Curry	Phebe Hickman	March 13, 1797
John Cuntriman	Christena Sitley	April 6, 1797
George Ryen	Mary Riner	April 6, 1797
John McCara	Hannah Bell	April 16, 1797
Michael Pickle	Elizabeth Witzel	April 17, 1797
John Green	Susanna Winter	April 24, 1797

Henry Staulp	Catharina Hoe	April 24, 1797
Michael Crowbarger	Elizabeth Thompson	April 29, 1797
Peter Hauver	Modalana Aedir	May 7, 1797
John McNeil	Patience Beard	May 10, 1797
Samuel Wiseman	Polly Bowger	May 10, 1797
Ezekiel Logan	Margaret Harrison	May 22, 1797
Mathias Moyers	Mary Collens	May 23, 1797
Christian Kite	Agness Hestant	June 6, 1797
Jacob Sheets	Mary Martin	June 6, 1797
Jacob Showalter	Sophia Softly	July 24, 1797
Martin Nave	Elizabeth Deran	July 24, 1797
George Crowbarger	Susanna Sipe	August 1, 1797
George Ruebush	Elizabeth Wheelbarger	August 1, 1797
Charles Beggs	Dorotha Trumbo	August 1, 1797
	Ferdinand Lair, Preacher	
John Bower	Magdelena Andes	August 2, 1797
William Baily	Lucy Croohed	August 11, 1797
John Headrick	Molly Kester	August 28, 1797
Gorden Rogers	Francis Downey	August 30, 1797
Christian Laundis	Madelena Byerly	September 2, 1797
Peter Leonard	Elizabeth Bowers	September 9, 1797
Joseph Showwalter	Lydia Ronk	September 12, 1797
Peter Bish	Phebe Blazea	September 12, 1797
Benjamin Ralston	Margaret Henry	September 12, 1797
John Haney	Margaret Miller	September 15, 1797
George Leonard	Susanna Rodes	September 17, 1797
John Davis	Sarah Dokertey	September 19, 1797
John Keplinger	Caty Wheelbarger	October 10, 1797
John Stults	Madalana Caplinger	October 11, 1797
William Mitchel	Eve Nestreete	October 16, 1797
Henry Martin	Elisabeth Pitt	October 25, 1797
Abraham Whitzel	Magdalin Keller	November 5, 1797
Chrisley Beamand	Ann Ewbler	November 7, 1797
Joseph Aldorphats	Margaret Seevely	November 9, 1797
George Brunk	Nelly McCue	November 9, 1797
John McKee	Jenny Berry	November 9, 1797
Even Reece	Charlotte Mae	November 20, 1797
Philip Spitzer	Eve Holsinger	November 21, 1797
Edwin Nichols	Elizabeth Kring	November 21, 1797
William Woods	Ruth Beazer	November 25, 1797
John Harrison	Ann Tallman	November 25, 1797
Thomas Campbell	Ann Blain	December 2, 1797
Clemens Ewin	Jane Stuart	December 5, 1797
William Smith	Dianna McDonough	December 19, 1797
William Dunnavan	Keaty Gay	December 20, 1797
John Saylor	Betsey Kysor	December 26, 1797
Martin Buck	Mary Smith	December 31, 1797
John Cole	Keaty Wolfe	January 1, 1798
Robert Huston	Sarah Herron	January 8, 1798
George Summers	Elizabeth Haney	January 18, 1798
Jacob Fillinger	Elizabeth Sanger	January 28, 1798
John Leonard	Sophia Krim	January 29, 1798
Daniel Bowman	Ceny Zimmerman	February 8, 1798
Jacob Wyant	Mary Gay	February 9, 1798
Jacob Fox	Mary Ashenfelter	February 17, 1798
Joseph Yunt	Elizabeth Bowman	February 23, 1798
David Fisher	Rachel Peters	February 26, 1798
Jacob Everheart	Keaty Stagleather	April 9, 1798
John Shumaker	Barbara Countraman	April 10, 1798
George Wolfe	Catharine Armontrout	April 16, 1798
John Birer	Elizabeth Bowman	April 17, 1798

John Kysor	Peggy Null	April 23, 1798
Peter Staman	Madalena Swich	April 23, 1798
Phillip Miller	Cloe Boshong	April 24, 1798
John Roller	Susanna Wheelberger	April 26, 1798
Jacob Harshbarger	Barbara Boshong	May 15, 1798
Edward Ervin	Polly Stuart	May 22, 1798
Martin Crotzsinger	Elizabeth Snider	May 22, 1798
Mickeal Kline	Elisebeth Byŕer	May 22, 1798
Philip Deeds	Mary Bush	May 25, 1798
Michael Kline	Elizabeth Byer	June 2, 1798
Jacob Roop	Martha Price	June 12, 1798
John Long	Elizabeth Comer	June 12, 1798
Jacob Perky	Elizabeth Lemon	June 25, 1798
Henry May	Keaty Sites	June 25, 1798
Joseph Garver	Catharina Leedy	June 26, 1798
Joseph Garvens	Catharine Lady	July 24, 1798
William Michael	Keaty Louck	July 26, 1798
John Brown	Magdalena Andis	August 2, 1798
Martin Grimsley	Mary Strickler	August 20, 1798
Abraham Haynes	Aseneth Rose	August 25, 1798
Wm. Read	Elizabeth Snodden	August 26, 1798
Lewis Stephens	Elizabeth Wolfe	September 11, 1798
James Boyd	Isabella Watson	September 15, 1798
Michael Stultz	Betsey Whitmore	September 24, 1798
George Pence	Christina Crowbarger	September 25, 1798
David Louderback	Margaret Hoard	September 25, 1798
Joseph Yunt	Elisabeth Bowman	September 30, 1798
Morris Moris	Rebecca Porter	October 1, 1798
Leonard Painter	Catherine Funk	October 9, 1798
Abraham Funk	Sarah Allford	October 15, 1798
Isaac Burner	Barbara Shrum	October 22, 1798
Joseph Hicks	Ann Kyle	October 23, 1798
Andrew Smith	Elizabeth Rotherford	November 13, 1798
John Brant	Mary Catharine Kale	November 15, 1798
Martin Depoy	Mary Young	November 18, 1798
John Miller	Catharine Miller	November 19, 1798
Lewis Long	Catharine Hestant	November 19, 1798
Jacob Rush	Catharine Everheart	November 19, 1798
Gedean Dun	Mary Keys	November 22, 1798
Martin Coffman	Sarah Whitehouse	December 7, 1798
John Simmons	Rosanna Kratzer	December 10, 1798
John Holesclaw	Elizabeth Beerry	December 11, 1798
Jacob Fisher	Mary Painter	December 27, 1798
Fits Morris	Betsey Smith	December 28, 1798
Jesse Web	Nancy Boyles	December 31, 1798
Warner Peters	Eve Joseph	January 5, 1799
James Craig	Elizabeth Shettman	January 10, 1799
Nathan Smith	Catharine Morrison	January 16, 1799
John Harner	Sarah Harshman	January 21, 1799
Samuel Gilmore	Elener McQuillim	February 4, 1799
David Roalston	Susanna Matthews	February 7, 1799
Frederick Eppart	Elisabeth Snider	February 8, 1799
Marcus Adler	Barbara Moyers	February 12, 1799
Henry Hammer	Mary Beesley	February 14, 1799
Henry Pence	Keaty Munger	February 16, 1799
Job Ingram	Elizabeth Higgins	February 18, 1799
Abraham Wisekop	Macdelane Wisler	February 19, 1799
George Smith	Edith Thomas	February 19, 1799
Abraham Painter	Madelena Carns	February 24, 1799
Christian Beerry	Keaty Frank	February 25, 1799
Thomas Oliver	Mary Morris	February 25, 1799

Jacob Claypole	Margaret Baker	March 5, 1799
Thomas Oliver	Mary Morris	March 5, 1799
Thomas Holton	Martha Ireland	March 15, 1799
David Marks	Mary Kyle	March 16, 1799
William Dyer	Margaret Riddle	March 19, 1799
Mathew Roalston	Jean Shanklin	March 21, 1799
Jacob Grove	Catharine Crim	March 25, 1799
Conrod Custer	Elizabeth Christman	March 26, 1799
John Shoemaker	Barbara Conrad	March 26, 1799
David Berry	Polly Black	April 6, 1799
Jacob Bierly	Madalena Landis	April 7, 1799
John Shoemaker	Barbara Cuntryman	April 10, 1799
John Rogers	Sarah Messick	April 16, 1799
Peter Stults	Julina Keplinger	April 23, 1799
William McCoy	Elizabeth Harrison	May 6, 1799
Joseph Showalter	Ann Burkholder	May 13, 1799
Philip Shaver	Elizabeth Stonetraker	May 15, 1799
	(Stonebraker)	
David Marks	Mary Kyle	May 16, 1799
David Byer	Sary Moyers	May 16, 1799
Jacob Roop	Martha Price	June 12, 1799
Jacob Moyers	Catherine Bloss	June 18, 1799
Peter Bowman	Margaret ———	July 2, 1799
Martin Laborn	Betsey Bear	July 23, 1799
John Boyer	Mary Passinger	July 29, 1799
James Pummel	Rachel Davis	August 10, 1799
James Harshman	Rodah Burk	August 14, 1799
William Philips	Agnes Dever	August 21, 1799
John Baker	Magdalene Dove	August 22, 1799
William Missamore	Peggy May	August 22, 1799
George McCoy	Rebecca (free negroes)	August 31, 1799
Anthony Nicely	Margaret McCall	September 10, 1799
John Dyce	Elizabeth Harrison	September 10, 1799
David Louks	Peggy Smith	September 17, 1799
John Higgs	Susannah Cukel	September 17, 1799
Daniel Funkhouser	Mary Whisler	October 9, 1799
John Alford	Margaret Alford	October 10, 1799
Henry J. Gambill	Margaret Burns	October 10, 1799
James Salvage	Ellener Muncy	October 11, 1799
Abraham Cherryholmes	Elizabeth Heaggy	October 14, 1799
Jacob Burkholder	Mary Coffman	October 15, 1799
Adam	Patty (free negroes)	October 20, 1799
Andrew Sellars	Hannah Hagy	October 21, 1799
David Thomson	Susanna Skelton	October 25, 1799
Robert Mathews	Nancy Green	November 2, 1799
Charles Lofland	Mary Probyman	November 7, 1799
George Bloss	Keaty Grey	November 11, 1799
John Hite	An Pebeles	November 12, 1799
George Wright	Sarah McCall	November 30, 1799
Adam Trowerbough	Catherine Pence	December 3, 1799
Nicholas Shaver	Hannah Coughgar	December 5, 1799
Samuel Hemphill	Clarenda Lolferd	December 17, 1799
Benjamin Britten	Betsey Grace	December 24, 1799
David Bowman	Catherine Frons	December 25, 1799
	Benj. Bowman, Preacher	
Jacob Lingle	Elizabeth Hansbarger	January 1, 1800
Adam Trouerbough	Catherine Pence	January 1, 1800
Ebenezer Etherton	Perces Bowyes	January 15, 1800
John Horn	Catharine Pence	January 18, 1800
Jacob Stultz	Cathrine Caplinger	January 21, 1800
Jacob Rinehart	Barbarah Runkle	January 23, 1800

Jno. Hauk (Hank?)	Nancy Runnion	February 4, 1800
William Keplinger	Modalena Keplinger	March 6, 1800
James M. Long	Betsy Scotthorn	March 18, 1800
Michael Passinger	Barbara Wooleaven	March 21, 1800
John Ervin	Esther Herring	March 25, 1800
Isaac Day	Catherine Ferin (?)	May 6, 1800
Nicholas Leib	Mary Mongar	May 13, 1800
John Propps	Elizabeth Doide	May 20, 1800
Daniel Doide	Catharine Moyers	June 5, 1800
William Shannon	Ealanor Ragan	May 22, 1800
Thomas Ashenfelter	Catharine Shumaker	June 22, 1800
Adam Fulk	Mary Desponey	June 22, 1800
John Landis	Jenney Branaman	July 8, 1800
John Boyd	Elizabeth N. Burgys	July 17, 1800
Jacob Donaven	Rosannah Fell	July 21, 1800
Conrod Brown	Elizabeth Epler	July 24, 1800
William Turner	Catharine Maricha	August 5, 1800
Danel Jackson	Barbara Barrick	August 5, 1800
Charles Fox	Rosannah Ackletree	August 8, 1800
Archibald Huston	Martha Williams	August 12, 1800
David Rapp	Ann Muncy	August 12, 1800
David Camran	Elizabeth Hunrichouson	August 16, 1800
Benjamin Lewis	Margaret Hite	September 2, 1800
Michael Helbert	Elizabeth Beam	September 2, 1800
Leonard Spencer	Susanah Twitchete	September 9, 1800
William Chipley	Abigail Herring	September 23, 1800
Feilding Harrison	Ann Zuina	October 1, 1800
Martin Whetzell	Catharine Shaver	October 13, 1800
Abraham Brock	Caty Willhelm	October 13, 1800
Bird Rogers	Mary Ann Truman	October 21, 1800
Martain Whitzel	Catharine Shaver	October 21, 1800
John Ervin	Easter Herring	October 21, 1800
Daniel Rudy	Polly Beare	October 25, 1800
Martin March	Mary O'Roark	October 26, 1800
John Vass	Mary Carthrea	November 3, 1800
Lewis Schothorn	Ann Tallman	November 4, 1800
Henry Pence	Rebecca Dundore	November 10, 1800
Aaron Thomas	RosannaParrot	November 11, 1800
Jacob Rinehart	Barbarah Runkle	November 11, 1800
Aron Homan	Rosanna Parrot	December 9, 1800
John Hottinger	Mary Orebaugh	December 9, 1800
John Kayler	Katy Hains	December 11, 1800
Stephen Losh	Sally Dashner	December 15, 1800
William Cave	Mary Smith	December 25, 1800
Jacob Coffman	Sarah Gum	December 29, 1800
John West	Elizabeth March	January 12, 1801
Lewis Fridley	Susannah Bradshaw	January 17, 1801
Caleb Chandler	Mary Spankler	January 20, 1801
Daniel Curry	Abaigail Herring	January 22, 1801
Robert Erwin	Niomey Herring	January 22, 1801
Richard Furguson	Clara Moore	January 22, 1801
Joseph Fawcett	Lucretia Keys	January 24, 1801
Jacob Kyger	Barbara Shaver	January 25, 1801
Andrew Scote	Pheby Laird	February 4, 1801
John Brown	Mary Woolf	February 9, 1801
David White	Mary Koontz	February 17, 1801
Adam Carpenter	Caty Sellers	February 18, 1801
David Spears	Barbara Bowyess	February 26, 1801
Charlie Chrisman	Catherine Custer	March 2, 1801
Alexander Curry	Elizabeth Crafford	March 4, 1801
Alexander Curry	Elizabeth Curry	March 11, 1801

Hugh Kyle	Sarah Crafford	March 19, 1801
David Pence	Dolly Hammer	April 2, 1801
John Coffman	Rachel Shoemaker	April 7, 1801
John Margal	Solamee Steel	April 12, 1801
Henry Fisher	Elizabeth Gains	April 13, 1801
Elisha Little	Nelly Harris	April 14, 1801
John Runkle	Lydia Shoort	April 17, 1801
John M. Smith	Catherine Pence	May 5, 1801
William Johnston	Rebecca Nicely	May 13, 1801
John Fulk	Christina Kyle	May 18, 1801
John Bowers	Clare Hankings	May 26, 1801
Jesse Harrison	Rachel Harrison	May 26, 1801
Adam Disponey	Mary May	June 4, 1801
Henry Earhart	Elizabeth Stoutemire	June 9, 1801
Anderson Moffett		
George Faught	Christena Yeagly	June 17, 1801
Thomas Gilmore	Mary Grace	June 18, 1801
John Sipe	Caty Tutwiler	June 27, 1801
John Haynes	Mary Grenner	July 21, 1801
Martin Burkholder	Elizabeth Krotzer	July 21, 1801
John Barrick	Elizabeth Shumaker	July 23, 1801
Philip Tussing	Catharine Hottinger	July 26, 1801
Daniel Burns	Mary Kaite	July 29, 1801
Christian Sellars	Elizabeth Snider	July 30, 1801
Samuel Miller	Mary Brumback	August 4, 1801
John Baker	Elizabeth Laush	August 5, 1801
Frederick Pupp	Mary Ketner	August 11,1801
Anderson Moffett		
Bethewel Sampler	Elizabeth Beaver	August 11, 1801
Edwd. Thompson	Susanah Earhart	August 15, 1801
John Lightner	Elizabeth Reader	August 17, 1801
John Smith	Jane Hart	August 20, 1801
John Lokey	Susanna Layton	September 8, 1801
Adam Frensler	Barbara Hoover	September 8, 1801
John Shireman	Abagail Gilbert	September 9, 1801
Henry Billhimer	Catharine Cook	September 15, 1801
William Pence	Christina Sellars	September 15, 1801
Christian Crotzer	Catherine Roads	September 22, 1801
William Young	Elizabeth Burgiss	September 29, 1801
John Shurley	Ann Scott	October 1, 1801
Jacob Rust	Susanah Palser	October 20, 1801
John Grumby	Easter Twichet	October 25, 1801
Joseph McMullen	Catharine Knestrick	October 29, 1801
Abraham Joseph	Mary Rawly	October 30, 1801
Tobias R. M'Gahey	Mary E. Conrod	November 12, 1801
John Graey	Mary Ann Trumbo	November 17, 1801
Robert Glass	Christina Storm	November 26, 1801
Abraham House	Judeth Fitzwater	December 1, 1801
James Rogers	Sally Black	December 1, 1801
David Long	Hannah Yontz	December 1, 1801
Joshua King	Hannah Chrisman	December 1, 1801
Peter Pence	Elizabeth Henton	December 3, 1801
John Lokey	Susana Layton	December 8, 1801
John Roadcap	Marinda Watson	December 12, 1801
Stephen Clemmers	Betsey Frane	December 15, 1801
Christian Crotzer	Catharine Roads	December 22, 1801
William Crossby	Caty Moss	December 24, 1801
Thos. Haskins	Sarah Covington	December 26, 1801
William Cochran	Eliza Fulton	December 31, 1801
Andrew Trumbo	Catrine Davis	January 5, 1802
Jacob Tinkle	Elizabeth Magell	January 5, 1802

Joseph Grove	Barbara Whitemore	January 9, 1802
Israel Petterson	Margaret Stulty	January 9, 1802
Henry Bowers	Nancy Fleming	January 19, 1802
Daniel Harshman	Elizabeth Fultz	January 20, 1802
Hezekiah Woods	Juriah Rice	January 26, 1802
John Lingh	Mary Cook	February 4, 1802
Jacob Earhart	Catharine Cool	February 16, 1802
Jacob Hansicher	Eve Parrote	March 2, 1802
Charles Christman	Catharin Custer	March 2, 1802
Frederick Young	Nancy ——ller	March 2, 1802
Jacob Youtzler	Sophia Tafflemire (?)	March 9, 1802
Wm. Deckey	Mary Asher	March 11, 1802
William Short	Sharlotte Garrott	March 12, 1802
Jacob Dove	Sarah Wetzel	March 16, 1802
Mathew Thomson	Eliza Shanklin	March 30, 1802
Henry Neaf	Barbara Burkholder	March 30, 1802
Benjamin Mefford	Nancy Saxton	April 25, 1802
Peter Thomas	Elizabeth Shank	April 27, 1802
John Earley	Christiana Byerly	April 28, 1802
George Eppert	Catharine Busby	April 28, 1802
Alexander Reed	Mary Foster	May 3, 1802
Jacob Heater	Mary Grove	May 6, 1802
Conrod Weaver	Rebecka Semers	May 15, 1802
Thomas Lawson	Sarah Twitchett	June 8, 1802
William Crawford	Nancy Smith	June 22, 1802
Daniel Kite	Magdelen Pickler	June 25, 1802
Joseph Brown	Nancy Smith	July 20, 1802
John Proud (?)	Nancy Reed	July 26, 1802
Nathaniel Alger	Ammen	July 29, 1802
Henry March	Catharine Mathews	August 4, 1802
Andrew Stult	Agness Shurly	August 10, 1802
Isaiah Curry	Abbigal Hall	August 10, 1802
John Taylor	Elizabeth Grady	August 12, 1802
John Koontz	Mary Shiery	August 16, 1802
George Bush	Catharine Maggort	August 17, 1802
Richard Kyle	Sarah Harrison	September 20, 1802
John Nisewanger	Rosana Peters	September 28, 1802
James Rains	Zuriah Davis	September 30, 1802
Peter Lower	Magdelene Snider	October 8, 1802
Jacob Brunk	Barbara Menick	October 14, 1802
Henry Monger	Catharine Fultz	October 19, 1802
Adam Melizer	Susana Orbough	October 26, 1802
Henry Harrison	Susanna Tallman	October 27, 1802
Henry Kring	Nancy Harrison	November 2, 1802
Patrick Henry McAtee	Jane Harrison	November 3, 1802
Daniel Ragen	Melinda Harrison	November 18, 1802
John Breaker	Elizabeth McCann	November 19, 1802
Luke Black	Peggy Rader	November 23, 1802
Daniel Hoof	Elizabeth Grim	November 28, 1802
John Proud	Nancy Reed	November 30, 1802
George Rosenbarger	Marget Zerkel	November 30, 1802
George Day	Catherine Brinkman	December 9, 1802
John Smith	Elizabeth Travis	December 30, 1802
Charley Lew Moore	Margaret Click	January 4, 1803
Stephen Porter	Lydia Moore	January 12, 1803
George Carns	Barbara Pence	January 13, 1803
Robert McCann	Margaret Evins	January 24, 1803
Henry Good	Magdalena Kneepp	January 25, 1803
John McLaughlin	Elizabeth Houdishell	February 1, 1803
William Wheeling	Carlile	February 4, 1803

John Herdman	Sarah Rolestone	February 7, 1803
James Henry	Elizabeth Green	March 1, 1803
Martain Miller	Easter Bowman	March 8, 1803
John Fauver	Elizth. Ogan	March 10, 1803
William Mes—	Barbara Cline	March 15, 1803
Windle Swaggart	Margaret Peters	March 18, 1803
George Bowman	Margaret Miller	March 20, 1803
Andrew Lair	Ruth Hinton	March 22, 1803
Henry Shoemaker	Nancy Cownrad	March 22, 1803
Jared Erwen	Sally Herron	March 24, 1803
Philp Apburt	Marget Woods	March 24, 1803
John Burkholder	Rosanna Blain	March 31, 1803
George Hice	Magdalene Miler	May 10, 1803
George Rader	Elizabeth Eater	May 15, 1803
Elijah Hooks	Anne Allen	May 17, 1803
William Kite	Elizabeth Harnsbarger	May 19, 1803
Peter Nye	Susanah Waggy	May 24, 1803
Daniel Connerly	Mary Smith	May 26, 1803
David Miller	Elenor Clark	June 16, 1803
David Usher	Rebecca Erwin	July 1, 1803
William Beever	Barbara Nickle	July 4, 1803
Peter Sprinkle	Polly Martin	August 4, 1803
Anderson (a free negro)	Peggy (a free negroe)	August 5, 1803
Christian Orebaugh	Elizabeth Hinegardner	September 15, 1803
Thomas Robertson	Sarah Zirkle	September 16, 1803
Hugh Kyle	Sarah McCartney	September 20, 1803
George Bright	Fanny Bowman	September 20, 1803
Hugh Kyle	Sarah McCartney	October 3, 1803
William Lokey	Racel Bowers	October 12, 1803
Adam Bloss	Judy Sours	October 13, 1803
John Crumer	Sophia Whistman	October 13, 1803
Adam Bloss	Tudy Jones	October 27, 1803
John Stell	Elizabeth Larey	October 27, 1803
Jacob Rohr	Deborah Travis	November 4, 1803
Mathias Link	Margaret Robertson	November 4, 1803
James Lokey	Margaret Harrison	November 10, 1803
Nicholas Albert	Christena Huffman	November 15, 1803
Frederick Poinesbuck	Hannah Morrel	November 15, 1803
Jacob Martz	Frankey Lokey	December 3, 1803
William Rogers	Sarah Cross	December 5, 1803
John Rush	Sarah Young	December 6, 1803
James Smith	Elizabeth Miller	December 8, 1803
Mathew Blain	Mary Ray	December 8, 1803
Josiah Crawford	Anna Ogan	December 12, 1803
Jacob Showalter	Sarah Bowers	January 1, 1804
Samuel Bowman	Susanna Kratzer	January 3, 1804
William Green	Sarah Smith	January 17, 1804
Nicolas Olbart	Christena Huffman	January 24, 1804
Jacob Sprinkle	Polly Sheltman	January 25, 1804
Jacob Barrick	Elizabeth Put	January 31, 1804
Robert McCann	Margaret Evans	January 31, 1804
Robert Hill	Eve Waggy	February 7, 1804
John Moyers	Christina Wiseman	February 14, 1804
Robert McClought	—— Tutwiler	February 20, 1804
Peter Shaver	Barbary Bowman	February 26, 1804
Jacob Strove	Susanna Pifer	February 26, 1804
John M'Clining	Amelia Dickey	February 28, 1804
Peter Holsinger	Catharine Taylor	February 28, 1804
Peachy Harrison	May Stuart	February 29, 1804
John Baxter	Margaret Stuart	February 29, 1804
Christian Thos. Reed	Sophia Henes	March 6, 1804

Thomas Callehan	Hannah Green	March 7, 1804
George Moss	Mariah Metts	March 20, 1804
Samuel Haines	Elizabeth Summers	March 20, 1804
Samuel Hite	Nancy Rollens	March 20, 1804
Matthias Miller	Susannah Carns	March 26, 1804
George Oughts	Elizab Zimmerman	March 27, 1804
Jacob Wolf	Elizabeth Hufman	April 2, 1804
James Rice	Ann Hopkins	April 3, 1804
Abraham Bolton	Rosanna Miller	April 5, 1804
Samuel Miller	Elizabeth Quinn	April 12, 1804
Samuel West	Mary Limer	April 17, 1804
Joseph Thornton	Sarah Kelley	April 19, 1804
Benjamin Kite	Susanna Kite	April 25, 1804
Samuel West	Mary Limer	April 27, 1804
Benjamin Brown	Frances Woodford	April 28, 1804
James Rice	Ann Hopkins	April 30, 1804
Lewis Lemmon	Elizabeth Armentrout	May 1, 1804
James Hazel	Mary Clark	May 3, 1804
Reuben Harrison	Perthena Harrison	May 16, 1804
Christian Fry	Widow Catherina Bowman	May 22, 1804
John Bowman	Catharine Minick	May 27, 1804
William Pence	Rachel Zirkel	May 31, 1804
Phenais Kirkland	Margaret Hite	May 31, 1804
Henry Shank	Francis Martin	June 23, 1804
Fielding Woodard	Catharine Joseph	June 30, 1804
Adam Ruble	Elizabeth Groves	July 29, 1804
Philip Long	Margaret Long	August 8, 1804
Archibald Rolston	Elizabeth Henton	August 16, 1804
Solomon Pirkey	Ally McCauslin	August 20, 1804
John Young	Elizabeth Barkley	August 30, 1804
James Grigs	Margaret McCoy	August 30, 1804
Elijah Eliot	Elizabeth McCoy	August 31, 1804
George Hulvey	Mary Nave	September 3, 1804
Adam Mensey	Polly Clark	September 7, 1804
Benjamin Olinger	Elizabeth Hiesland	September 11, 1804
Jacob Myer	Chatherina Bowman	September 18, 1804
John Randal	Polly Thorp	September 25, 1804
John Goshun	Nancy Hoover	September 26, 1804
Michael Trout	Hannah Thompson	October 6, 1804
Jacob Joseph	Hannah Higgins	October 17, 1804
Cornelius Calahan	Margaret Helsey	October 22, 1804
John Eppert	Sally Miften	November 8, 1804
Elias Houff	Margaret Evilsizer	November 8, 1804
	(by publication)	
William Sprinkle	Mary Ferrel	November 10, 1804
Henry Rupe	Elizabeth Price	November 15, 1804
Wm. Byre	Nancy Garrett	November 20, 1804
Peter Crup	Christian Snider	November 20, 1804
William Brown	Caty Traver	November 22, 1804
James Ragley	Mary Smith	December 3, 1804
John Dearmin	Rebeckah Piercey	December 5, 1804
William Rogers	Sarah Crose (?)	December 5, 1804
Joseph Strickler	Hannah Lyons	December 7, 1804
Thomas Cummings	Mary Bowers	December 18, 1804
Andrew Spitzer	Elizabeth Brewer	January 1, 1805
	(by publication)	
Joseph Arumford	Matlena Martz	January 1, 1805
William Colwell	Elizabeth Howard	January 2, 1805
Christopher Cummings	Mary Evens	January 8, 1805
George Miller	Mary Ann Pirkey	January 8, 1805
Peter Whetsel	Peggy Lewnbarger	January 10, 1805

Michael Irick	Francis Brown	January 13, 1805
George Beaver	Ann Callihand	January 18, 1805
Henry Spitser	Elizabeth Holsinger	January 21, 1805
John Good	Mary Nisewanger	January 22, 1805
Charles Fridley	Peggy Armintrout	January 22, 1805
Conrod Readhfer	Ann Showalter	January 24, 1805
Conrod Marca	Catharine Widick	January 24, 1805
Thomas Moore	Betty Hite	February 5, 1805
John Light	Jane Hooke	February 5, 1805
Jacob Holeman	Pheby Dunkenson	February 10, 1805
Peter Eversole	Mary Roof	February 19, 1805
John Deeds	Barbara Armintrout	February 21, 1805
Christian Bear	Polly Grove	February 26, 1805
Hugh Stultz	Elizabeth Hively	February 26, 1805
Jacob Sugars	Mary Freed	February 29, 1805
John Koontz	Catharine Koontz	March 5, 1805
Sampson Turley	Catharine Shoemaker	March 19, 1805
James Burns	Eve Comer	March 20, 1805
John McCoy	Elizabeth Miller	March 20, 1805
William Hopkins	Ann Rolston	March 28, 1805
John Branarman	Magdalin Burkholder	April 2, 1805
Jacob Howser	Barbara Eversole	April 11, 1805
Henry Pence	Margaret Abright	April 30, 1805
James Bowers	Polly Turkeyhiser	May 4, 1805
James Erwin	Mary Devier	May 4, 1805
Richard Jackson	Mary Stephenson	May 7, 1805
Henry Keisle	Polly Ryne	May 14, 1805
Christopher Merche	Molly Widick	May 15, 1805
Jacob Hansbarger	Catharine Hansbarger	May 16, 1805
John Whitmer	Francis Hansford	May 20, 1805
Daniel Good	Martha Whitmore	May 20, 1805
John Kyger	Elizabeth Harshman	May 31, 1805
Nicholas Carns	Mary Painter	June 10, 1805
Jacob Souaer	Polly Robison	June 10, 1805
Treanch Dove	Suzanna Whetzel	June 11, 1805
Benjamin Tallman	Lidia Harrison	June 18, 1805
Charles L. Moore	Polly Reeves	June 20, 1805
Isaac Black	Gracy Woodford	June 24, 1805
Adam Pence	Elizabeth Peterfish	June 25, 1805
Davis Dunivan	Margaret Twitchet	June 27, 1805
William Henton	Mary Lincoln	June 27, 1805
Jacob Wetsel	Polly Pelse	July 2, 1805
Samuel Richardson	Margaret Rankin	July 9, 1805
Abraham Messick	Polly McDonald	July 11, 1805
Frederick Martin	Polly Sowerbeer	August 11, 1805
Hugh Baker	Sarah Ong	August 15, 1805
Michael Zimmers	Elizabeth Nicewander	August 20, 1805
Moses Thomas	Gracy Davis	August 25, 1805
Samuel McInter	Barbara Black	August 27, 1805
John Rutherford	Elizabeth Joseph	September 5, 1805
Michael Correll	Ruth Tarpen	September 8, 1805
David Campbell	Nancy Lewis	September 12, 1805
Joseph Mauzy	Christena Kisling	September 12, 1805
Joseph McKey	Elizabeth Berry	September 24, 1805
Edward Erwin	Polly Brollon	September 25, 1805
James Nichols	Betsy Ewin	September 26, 1805
William Taylor	Hephzeih Turley	October 9, 1805
William Brisbin	Hannah Harrison	October 17, 1805
Joseph Black	Polly Weigel	October 25, 1805
Daniel Runnion	Peggy Orebaugh	October 29, 1805
Isaac Long	Barbara Miller	November 5, 1805

James Quinn	Mary Snodden	November 14, 1805
James Beesley	Sarah Rains	November 19, 1805
George Parrott	Mary Shaver	November 19, 1805
Peter Cook	Polly May	November 20, 1805
Daniel Bright	Nancy Mesick	November 21, 1805
Byrd Hawkins	Polly Trout	November 21, 1805
Abraham Ransborough	Elizabeth Miller	November 23, 1805
Andrew Campbeil	Catharine Byrd	November 26, 1805
Philip Carthrea	Elizabeth Turley	November 28, 1805
Leonard Herron	Anna Erwin	December 3, 1805
Henry Neishwonger	Barbara Wisler	December 3, 1805
John Shiery	Mary Pain	December 12, 1805
George Shaver	Hannah Sites	December 19, 1805
John Harmon	Rachel Rader	December 19, 1805
Jacob Markwood	Nelly Mackfall	December 24, 1805
John Sheetz	Nancy Shemaker	December 26, 1805
Samuel Newman	Polly Moffett	January 2, 1806
Michael Nave	Rebeckak Boyers	January 21, 1806
James Anderson	Mary Blain	January 34, 1806
George Mesick	Celia Rogers	February 13, 1806
Henry Burgess	Margaret Harrison	February 20, 1806
John Cave	Elizabeth Thomas	March 16, 1806
William Boils	Polly Gregg	March 18, 1806
Thomas Mury	Sarah Erwin	April 16, 1806
Adam Lamb	Sarah Keplinger	April 22, 1806
Adam Shank	Elizabeth Eagle	May 6, 1806
John Dundore	Jane Martin	May 6, 1806
Conrod Sellers	Mary Laymans	May 11, 1806
David Clemer	Martha Wilson	May 11, 1806
Simon Snider	Mary Pence	May 22, 1806
William Beland	Jane Gallehan	May 26, 1806
Jacob Wiseman	Caty Smally	June 5, 1806
John Harrison	Ruth Harrison	June 12, 1806
John McKinney	Jane Herdman	June 19, 1806
George Koogler	Elizabeth Gilmore	June 24, 1806
Lewis Luntz	Polly Albright	July 10, 1806
John Blakey	Mary Hook	July 23, 1806
William Rice	Milly Gaines	July 24, 1806
Benjamin Nigh	Polly Beaver	July 26, 1806
James Peters	Betsey Lockhart	July 28, 1806
Isaac Fleming	Francis Philips	August 13, 1806
Abednago Larey	Sarah Henton	August 19, 1806
John Meats	Polly Smith	August 21, 1806
John Click	Sarah Scott	September 16, 1806
John Eaton	Christian Moyers	September 16, 1806
Adam Lash	Catharine Fridley	September 16, 1806
John Carr	Margaret Holsinger	September 23, 1806
William Cochran	Deborah Custer	October 28, 1806
Peter Armantrout	Sarah Snider	November 4, 1806
Daniel Webb	Elizabeth Feester	November 11, 1806
Vincent Sandy	Catharine Andrew	November 13, 1806
James Beard	Mary Crummey	November 13, 1806
Jacob Cool	Mary Woodley	November 17, 1806
David Norman	Catharine Seglar	November 18, 1806
Samuel Gay	Mary Ireland	November 20, 1806
George May	Catharine Cook	December 2, 1806
Henry Welch	Jane Scott	December 4, 1806
Thomas Porter	Margaret Herring	December 11, 1806
Benjamin Bryan	Piercy Lair	January 1, 1807
John Ragen	Sarah Samples	January 8, 1807
Thomas Green	Elizabeth Kizer	January 15, 1807

James Tate	Rebecka Baxter	January 18, 1807
Timothy Dunnaven	Mary Dunnaven	January 22, 1807
George Hansbarger	Jane McMon	January 23, 1807
George Sites	Rebeccah Matthews	January 26, 1807
Dennis Swanson	Sarah Freeholder	January 29, 1807
William Vance	Nancy Burnsides	February 4, 1807
Richard Carryer	Catharine Bowman	February 12, 1807
Voluntine Wolf	Nancy Hyndaker	March 4, 1807
Joseph Rife	Nancy Chawk	March 8, 1807
Reuben Rawley	Elizabeth Bargahizer	March 10, 1807
William Cooper	Phebe Harrison	March 12, 1807
Lewis Veil	Elizabeth Bailey	March 14, 1807
James Hoard	Anne Brandown	March 17, 1807
George Argabright	Susannah Tinkle	March 19, 1807
Henry Trout	Caty Culp	March 24, 1807
John Addimson	Sarah Harris	March 24, 1807
Cable Larick	Elizabeth Turley	April 2, 1807
Daniel Miller	Anne Hoover	April 14, 1807
Michal Howard	Lydia Harrison	April 16, 1807
John Seek	Nancy Whislow	May 19, 1807
David Loak	Elizabeth Whitehouse	May 24, 1807
David Wallace	Mary Cahoon	June 4, 1807
Alexander Akins	Rebecka Bright-	June 14, 1807
Charles L. Moore	Dorcus Robertson	June 16, 1807
Camp Gains	Polly Beason	July 7, 1807
George Sheetz	Mary Driver	July 28, 1807
Bastan Rader	Sally Fulton	August 4, 1807
Joseph Norford	Catharine Brinker	August 6, 1807
George Long	Elizabeth Bodey	August 10, 1807
Christopher Stultz	Elizabeth Click	August 11, 1807
Joseph Higgins	Catharine Robertson	August 14, 1807
Aaron Moffett	Catharine Carrier	August 18, 1807
John Cale	Elizabeth Jones	August 18, 1807
Elliot Rutherford	Rachel McCulley	August 21, 1807
Jacob Treavey	Mary McCartney	August 25, 1807
William Smith	Mary Desson	August 25, 1807
Jacob Rhoads	Catharine Helfrey	August 27, 1807
Peter Dovell	Elizabeth Kysor	August 28, 1807
George Baker	Margaret Crawford	September 1, 1807
George Faflinger	Elizabeth Parrott	September 2, 1807
Frederick Shoemaker	Rachel Shaver	September 8, 1807
Joseph Hicks	Cecelia Harrison	September 8, 1807
John Jenkins	Catharine Sheets	September 10, 1807
Christopher Camer	Babara Craft	September 12, 1807
Henry Kapel	Nancy Tiller	September 15, 1807
Henry Logan	Levenah Haynes	September 22, 1807
Jacob Howell	Bridget Eaton	September 22, 1807
George Smalts	Catharine Rader	September 24, 1807
Samuel Sulenbarger	Betsey Scott	October 1, 1807
Isaac Miller	Margreat Lair	October 8, 1807
John Peoples	Mary Eyeman	October 15, 1807
William Ewin	Elizabeth Bryan	October 15, 1807
John Snapp	Elizabeth Cook	October 20, 1807
Jacob Coc—	Francis Shank	October 20, 1807
Felty Bear	Christiana Rickey	October 27, 1807
Alexander Newman	Peggy Dunlap	October 29, 1807
Robert Black	Mary Shickle	December 3, 1807
Michael Howdershell	Barbara Rader	December 8,1807
John Butcher	Elizabeth Rohr	December 9, 1807
Martin Speck	Elizabeth Rader	December 10, 1807
Samuel Donaven	Elizabeth Lair	December 22, 1807

Andrew Cofman	Elizabeth Conrod	December 27, 1807
Andrew McCartney	Susanna Treevy	December 31, 1807
Peter Raderbaugh	Mary M. Shaver	January 5, 1808
Noah Fidler	Mary Hinton	January 26, 1808
William Hannah	Mary Hudlow	January 26, 1808
Matthais Miller	Mercy Painter	January 26, 1808
Benjamin Vance	Hannah Sites	February 2, 1808
William Barks	Lovelis Grimsly	February 2, 1808
David Nicely	Mary Wi——ley	February 9, 1808
Jacob Pickering	Hannah Miller	February 10,1808
Jesse Shanklin	Edith Hening	February 16, 1808
Jacob Akerd	Elizabeth Barnhart	February 20, 1808
John Cohenan	Catharine Seager	February 25, 1808
Luke Rice	Urdilla Gains	March 8, 1808
John Olobaugh	Sarah Ketner	March 10, 1808
John Clemmens	Anne Rogers	March 15, 1808
William Blain	Elizabeth Berry	March 22, 1808
Jacob Moyer	Sarah Yount	March 22, 1808
Abraham Zilpers	Christina Woolback	March 30, 1808
Solomon Messerly	Mary Palsley	April 6, 1808
William Loak	Elizabeth Shoup	April 7, 1808
Adam Fultz	Elizabeth Bolton	April 19, 1808
Michael Finley	Ruth Ewin	April 26, 1808
Henry Devers	Anne Moore	May 5, 1808
Timothy Roark	Mary Loar	May 15, 1808
Benjamin Curry	Jane Ervin	May 26, 1808
Samuel Parrott	Polly Sites	June 7, 1808
John Layton	Grace Philips	June 12, 1808
George Irick	Anny Woodford	June 21, 1808
George Cushingberry	Lucy Tate	July 6, 1808
John Pickering	Anne Brown	August 10, 1808
Adam Pence	Elizabeth Nail	August 16, 1808
Daniel Pickering	Hannah Dunlap	August 17, 1808
John Vana	Rebecca Trump	August 25, 1808
Henry Kyser	Mary Layman	September 5, 1808
Henry Bingham	Mary Amon	September 15, 1808
David Cummings	Mary Armentrout	September 20, 1808
John Tallman	Elizabeth Harrison	September 21, 1808
John Cowen	Mary Pickering	September 24, 1808
John Gilman	Ann Brumfield	September 27, 1808
David Smith	Susan Martin	September 29, 1808
George Miller	Rachel Shoemaker	October 5, 1808
Thomas Beard	Elizabeth Kepler	October 8, 1808
Peter Mintee	Catharine Miller	October 18, 1808
George Bible	Betsey Dustimer	October 26, 1808
Benjamin Van Pelt	Polly Ragan	November 2, 1808
Michael Moyers	Elizabeth Loar	November 3, 1808
Daniel Pretzman	Polly Tingley	November 10, 1808
Andrew Orebaugh	Hannah Fay	November 15, 1808
Christian Shoemaker	Eve Cherryholmes	November 17, 1808
Jacob Step	Elizabeth Kite	November 23, 1808
David Lincoln	Catharine Bright	December 6, 1808
Jacob Moore	Margaret Benson	December 8, 1808
Jacob Mefford	Susanna Hudlow	December 21, 1808
Adam Keplinger	Elizabeth Hoffman	December 29, 1808
Michael Ritter	Margaret Finley	January 23, 1809
John Conrod	Mary Nicholas	January 26, 1809
Larkin Rains	Hannah Martin	January 31, 1809
John Burgess	Prisscetta Rawlings	January 31, 1809
Rody Tate	Catharine Dean	February 2, 1809
George Barnhart	Magdoline Simmers	February 5, 1809

Simon Kratzer	Hester Bear	February 16,1809
Solomon Vance	Lucy Harnsford	February 19, 1809
John Clemmons	Peggy Cromer	February 21, 1809
Peter Snyder	Ann Blatch	February 21, 1809
Wilson Loyd	Susanna Clemmons	March 9, 1809
George Trout	Polly Miller	March 16, 1809
Enos Alger	Elizabeth Bollen	March 19, 1809
John Byer	Margret Deaver	March 28, 1809
Abraham Harrison	Grace Harrison	April 2, 1809
Benjamin Harrison	Elizabeth Koontz	April 4, 1809
James Devier	Martha Newman	April 6, 1809
John Mallowry	Hannah Ewin	April 13, 1809
Christian Haase	Susanna Bowman	April 20, 1809
Nathaniel Offutt	N. Watson	April 30, 1809
James Long	Sally Bryant	May 12, 1809
Abraham Eversole	Barbara Dovel	May 17, 1809
Daniel Hott	Polly Wyer	May 18, 1809
Isaac Fridly	Betsey Sellars	May 30, 1809
John Henton	Polly Sites	June 6, 1809
John Long	Elizabeth Utz	June 7, 1809
Daniel Smith	Frances Duff	June 13, 1809
George Newman	Margaret Devers	July 6, 1809
Andrew Spitzer	Caty Grady	July 13, 1809
Charles Eary	Rosana Hammer	August 3, 1809
George Deets	Mary Wideck	August 18, 1809
Stephen Matheny	Susanna Argebright	August 28, 1809
George Whelekel	Polly Brinkman	August 31, 1809
Joseph Blain	Susanna Burkholder	September 7, 1809
Moses Cummins	Catharine Sheelds	September 19, 1809
Henry Good	Christina Widick	September 20, 1809
Walter Davis	Rebecca Herring	September 21, 1809
Abraham Caplinger	Elizabeth Nisewanger	September 21, 1809
Henry Sheetz	Eve Wolf	September 21, 1809
John Tate	Sally Bryan	September 28, 1809
William Sprinkle	Sally Ireland	October 5, 1809
Odin Whitehouse	Elizabeth Turner	October 7, 1809
James Moody	Barbara Arnold	October 18, 1809
Joseph Greer	Mary Blain	October 31, 1809
Noah Bowers	Phebe Harrison	November 2, 1809
Jacob Hortinger	Catharine Price	November 13, 1809
Reuben King	Ann Sipe	November 21, 1809
Joshua Catling	Elizabeth Williams	November 21, 1809
Henry Wills	Sally Houf	November 23, 1809
John Carpenter	Sally Warner	November 23, 1809
George Crawford	Sally Roalston	November 27, 1809
William Philips	Elizabeth Hogshead	November 28, 1809
Ezekiel Harrison	Ann Bell	December 5, 1809
Phillip Lamb	Polly McDaniel	December 12, 1809
Andrew Stoneburner	Susanna Turner	December 12, 1809
John Kessler	Betsey Ashaufelter	December 18, 1809
Benjamin Bowman	Catharine Wine	January 1, 1810
William Sites	Ester Henton	January 16, 1810
Philip Ritchy	Sally Wright	March 1, 1810
Manual Roadcap	Elizabeth Chencholmes	March 5, 1810
Jacob Hill	Katy Butt	March 6, 1810
Thomas Hoard	Poily Pain	March 12, 1810
William Rutlege	Elizabeth Drawbond	March 20, 1810
Job Smith	Betsy Rader	March 22, 1810
Paul Shoemaker	Susanna Lamb	March 23, 1810
John Hennings	Sally Grandle	March 28, 1810
David Dufflemoyer	Barbara Long	April 12, 1810

William Harrison	Mary McClure	April 17, 1810
James Brown	Patsy Scott	April 19, 1810
John Lowe	Sarah Messerly	May 1, 1810
Henry Gilmore	Barbara Koogler	May 15, 1810
Joseph Sipe	Frances Paisley	June 10, 1810
Isaac Sybert	Peggy Anderson	June 21, 1810
Daniel Zirkle	Anne Philips	June 22, 1810
Robert Crawford	Sarah Henton	July 9, 1810
John Ashward	Catharine Cocker	July 22, 1810
John Reader	Abby Carrier	July 22, 1810
George Smith	Keziah Williamson	July 26, 1810
Simeon Fry	Mary Smith	July 26, 1810
John Mittenberger	Betsey Blous	July 30, 1810
Samuel Lambert	Catharine Hisey	August 7, 1810
Solomon Mathews	Eliza Cutter	August 13, 1810
Samuel Henry	Sally Stuart	August 23, 1810
David Showalter	Agness Linville	August 24, 1810
Adam Wyant	Mary Gowl	August —, 1810
Jacob Whistler	Magdalena Lass	September 4, 1810
Gasper Stoutlemyer	Catharine Trout	September 6, 1810
Andrew McGuire	Sarah Wells	September 18, 1810
Yearly Taylor	Nancy Tate	September 18, 1810
Henry Moyers	Milly Claybough	September 20, 1810
Jesse Ray	Mary Howdershell	September 24, 1810
Jacob Vanpelt	Susanna Summers	September 25, 1810
Gabriel D. Yancey	Mary S. Bell	September 27, 1810
Thomas Frost	Elizabeth Mulliner	September 30, 1810
Jacob Dehart	Nancy Harrison	September 30, 1810
James Patton	Susanna Hapher	October 3, 1810
Henry Emble	Peggy Kyser	October 5, 1810
Conrod Miller	Mary Boman	October 22, 1810
John Hoop	Sally Koontz	October 23, 1810
George Conrod	Susannah Miller	October 25, 1810
Williams Evans	Rebecca Harrison	October 25, 1810
John Bowman	Elizabeth Dundore	October 25, 1810
John Neff	Magdalena Drawbond	October 30, 1810
Theodorius Jordan	Martha McVay	October 30, 1810
Philip Olinger	Elizabeth Kips	November 3, 1810
John Wooden	Gemima Gladwell	November 3, 1810
George Fulk	Catharine Fawley	November 8, 1810
Jacob Shirley	Sally Cook	November 22, 1810
Michael Summers	Mary Shultz	November 22, 1810
William Stinespring	Catty Shankes	November 23, 1810
John Bish	Anne Campbell	November 23, 1810
Jacob Helbert	Mary Loyd	November 27, 1810
Adam Gowl	Eve Fultz	November 27, 1810
David Homan	Lydia Thomas	November 28, 1810
Abraham Steep	Molly Shuler	November 28, 1810
Reuben Harrison	Barbara Hansbarger	November 29, 1810
Frederick Long	Mary Newman	November 31, 1810
David Snyder	Agness Matthews	December 4, 1810
Jacob Koogler	Polly Rush	December 27, 1810
Jacob Runkel	Elizabeth Fey	December 27, 1810
James Kook	Jane Campbell	———, 1810
John Rohr	Catherine Miller	January 3, 1811
Michael Newman	Peggy Smith	January 3, 1811
Henry Liens	Lucy Wooden	January 15, 1811
Henry Moredeck	Betsey Whistleman	January 28, 1811
John Lokey	Eve Long	January 31, 1811
Samuel Snelling	Francis Staunton	February 4, 1811
Adam Harnsbarger	Sally Miller	February 7, 1811

Jacob Welchhons	Caty Pence	February 14, 1811
Simeon Burket	Eve Rader	February 20, 1811
Philip Sowders	Eve Fulk	February 24, 1811
John Markey	Nancey Underwood	February 28, 1811
Aaron Back	Elizabeth Hammer	March 12, 1811
John Tusinger	Susanna Price	March 17, 1811
Michael Miller	Elizabeth Trout.	March 17, 1811
John Firebaugh	Elizabeth Whitmore	March 18, 1811
Richard Custer	Elizabeth Trumbo	March 28, 1811
George Eavilsizer	Eve Wise	April 11, 1811
Jacob Ewin	Susanna Price	April 16, 1811
Henry Wolf	Mary Strayer	April 18, 1811
Andrew Moore	Caty Zimmerman	April 18, 1811
Jesse Thompson	Peggy Harry	April 23, 1811
John Baugher	Rachel Hall	May 2, 1811
George Dunlap	Betsey Philips	May 15, 1811
Israel Eblenand	Barbara Harnest	May 19, 1811
Daniel Warner		May 25, 1811
William Shyry	Rebecca ————	May 28, 1811
Garland McCallester	Polly Ockletree	May 30, 1811
Jacob Shoemaker	Mary Elger	June 3, 1811
Philip Miller	Sally Flucke	June 6, 1811
Samuel Dodds	Frances Hennings	June 18, 1811
George Mowrey	Nancey Johnston	June 23, 1811
John Hess	Mary Blows	June 27, 1811
Reezon Hammon	Nancy McWilliams	July 1, 1811
David Beard	Ruth Roalston	July 2, 1811
Peter Shickle	Margaret Rader	July 4, 1811
Samuel Miller	Mary Loker	July 4, 1811
Joseph Rogers	Jane Dunlap	July 18, 1811
Henry Wideck	Rachel Brockney	July 23, 1811
David Coffman	Sarah Moore	July 23, 1811
Michael Kite	Caty Dufflemoyer	July 25, 1811
Andrew Harper	Rebecca Vance	August 1, 1811
George Kelly	Mary McGinnis	August 4, 1811
Michael Lore	Caty Miller	August 13, 1811
———— Showalter	Patsy Stultz	August 15, 1811
Frederick Woolfe	Polly Hoops	August 16, 1811
Patrick Murray	Elizabeth Clifton	August 25, 1811
Nathan Lee	Mary Baker	September 1, 1811
Evan Henton	Peggy Burnsides	September 5, 1811
Jacob Hoover	Elizabeth Lamb	September 12, 1811
Christian Utsler	Nancey Self	September 13, 1811
Jacob Orebaugh	Rachel Fry	September 17, 1811
Jonathan Irick	Polly Boston	September 24, 1811
Benjamin Long	Elizabeth Garber	September 24, 1811
John Bowers	Darcus Lecky	September 26, 1811
John Beard	Hetty Roalston	October 8, 1811
Jacob Miller	Susanna Good	October 15, 1811
William Thompson	Elizabeth Price	October 17, 1811
John Crummy	Elizabeth Kelly	October 24, 1811
Levi Lucas	Elizabeth Utsler	October 24, 1811
James Tuiter	Nancy King	October 26, 1811
Jacob Cremar	Susanna Eyman	October 29, 1811
Nelson Kimbrough	Jane Hennings	October 31, 1811
Jesse Wine	Polly Breedlove	November 5, 1811
Abraham Quick	Madalene Moore	November 15, 1811
Christian Coffman	Catharine Lincoln	November 19, 1811
Moses Cummins	Ann Brinker	November 21, 1811
Henry Messersmith	Susanna Andrew	November 28, 1811
William Campbell	Lidia Nible	December 3, 1811

Jacob Ettinger	Hannah Trump	December 5, 1811
John Lamb	Nancy Erwin	December 5, 1811
Robert Hutchinson	Elizabeth Ott	December 9, 1811
Andrew Keesinger	Nancy Kayler	December 10, 1811
John Bowman	Susanna Wine	December 10, 1811
Jacob Roalston	Nancy Beard	December 10, 1811
Abraham Sheetz	Nancy Nave	December 10, 1811
Jacob Koontz	Maria Graham	December 12, 1811
George Cook	Nancy Beesly	December 12, 1811
Frederick Kyle	Sophia Redfern	December 12, 1811
Peter Irick	Peggy Bowlin	December 19, 1811
Jacob Kessler	Elizabeth Funk	December 24, 1811
John Sellers	Catharine Miller	December 24, 1811
Andrew Treevy	Catharine Higgins	December 26, 1811
John Kessler	Susanna Scantling	December 27, 1811
Daniel Ludwick	Catharine Kessler	December 29, 1811
Henry Moyers	Sarah Bryan	December 31, 1811
John Neff	Barbara Andis	December 31, 1811
George Graves	Mary Hoover	December 31, 1811
Adam Simons	Margaret Dove	January 2, 1812
Henry Cowen	Magdalene Layman	January 9, 1812
John Billhimer	Betsey Robertson	January 21, 1812
Willis Skelton	Hannah Locke	January 23, 1812
Henry Shaver	Susanna Strickler	February 6, 1812
Willis Swanson	May Breedlove	February 7, 1812
William Deberty	Mary Gilmore	February 8, 1812
Thomas Roalston	Magdalene Baker	February 11, 1812
Jacob Bear	Sarah Beever	February 20, 1812
John Beever	Susanna Bear	February 20, 1812
Henry Camer	Hannah Lincoln	February 23, 1812
John Taylor	Barbara Robertson	February 30, 1812
Jesse Roalston	Jane Hinton	March 3, 1812
Daniel Holsinger	Polly Smith	March 17, 1812
John Ketner	Elizabeth Long	March 17, 1812
Joseph Williams	Peggy Tinder	March 18, 1812
Joseph Mallowy	Elsy Tate	March 19, 1812
Joseph Miller	Betsey Thomas	March 24, 1812
John Nigh	Sarah Redford	March 24, 1812
George Bougher	Anney Hansbarger	April 9, 1812
George McKemper	Matilda Graham	April 13, 1812
Stephen Smith	Lucinda Smith	April 21, 1812
Peter Filch	Sally Roberts	April 21, 1812
Jacob Rife	Catharine Miller	April 28, 1812
Michael Dougherty	Sarah Robertson	May 1, 1812
Valentine Dougherty	Mary Ann Kelley	May 1, 1812
Frederick Kessler	Barbara Trobaugh	May 12, 1812
Stephen Hansbarger	Elizabeth Baker	May 13, 1812
John G. McWilliams	Milly Tanner	May 19, 1812
Samuel Roach	Nancy Davis	June 7, 1812
Henry Cline	Betsey Cook	June 24, 1812
Lewis Genner	Margaret Haga	June 25, 1812
Alexander Miller	Ann Matthews	June 25, 1812
Daniel McGuire	Lidia Hutchinson	June 30, 1812
Philip Weaver	Nancy Stokesberry	July 9, 1812
John Caine	Susana Keeling	July 9, 1812
Jacob Spitzer	Christina Harmon	July 21, 1812
John Hammer, Jr.	Elizabeth Snyder	August 6, 1812
James Lineback	Susana Wise	August 6, 1812
Henry Showalter	Mary Billhimer	August 10, 1812
Conrad Spitzer	Mahala Pitt	August 11, 1812
Henry Eyman	Mary Bryan	August 13, 1812

Earnest Cool	Peggy Matheny	August 13, 1812
Archibald Hopkins	Elizabeth Gordon	August 27, 1812
Joseph Sparke	Catharine Dalton	September 9, 1812
Solomon Bowers	Mary Harmon	October 6, 1812
Peter Harry	Prudence Chandler	October 6, 1812
John Bennet	Hannah Hoke	October 6, 1812
Philip Shoemaker	Barbara Lamb	October 9, 1812
Anthony Nisely	Rachel Hulvey	October 9, 1812
James Foley	Phebe Koontz	October 14,1812
Isaac Hunter	Elizabeth Kiger	October 15, 1812
Solomon Ve——	Sarah Reedy	October 28, 1812
Charles Campbell	Elizabeth Summers	October 28, 1812
James Fulton	Mary Huddle	November 5, 1812
Absolum Painter	Sarah Thompson	November 10, 1812
Henry Sheetz	Susy Welt	November 10, 1812
James Burnsides	Charlotte Miller	November 12, 1812
Henry Highdecker	Catharine Feazle	November 17, 1812
John Grub	Rebeckah Highdecker	November 17, 1812
Robert Gray	Isabella Waterman	November 18, 1812
John Baker	Sally Turner	November 18, 1812
James McCampbell	Nancy Davis	November 19, 1812
Smith Kysor	Phebe Philips	November 29, 1812
Abraham Bushong	Christina ——	December 3, 1812
Augustus Pol——	Elizabeth Hank	December 10, 1812
James Banks	Delila Rains	December 16, 1812
David Armentrout	Barbry Layman	December 17, 1812
John Swartz	Hannah Erhenwhelter	December 22, 1812
Miller Bowman	Phebe Harrison	December 24, 1812
Daniel Zetty	—— Cherryholmes	December 24, 1812
William Smith	Christina Sites	December 29, 1812
John Strickler	Sally Peterfish	January 19, 1813
James Evilsizer	Polly Roop	January 19, 1813
Solomon Ritchie	Elizabeth Baker	January 21, 1813
Jacob Muntz	Polly Stokesberry	January 21, 1813
Reuben Brackey	Susanna Eary	February 2, 1813
James Cr——	Catharine Spangler	February 10, 1813
Henry Rader	Catharine Propts	February 11, 1813
Samuel Payne	Juliana Eubank	February 14, 1813
Paul Custer	Delilah Johnson	February 18, 1813
John Decker	Sally Hartman	February 23, 1813
Shadrick	Lucy ——	February 25, 1813
Thomas Batcheler	Polly Higgins	February 25, 1813
Terrence Fitzgerald	Elizabeth Bourn	March 2, 1813
John Loop	Elizabeth Sh——	March 2, 1813
Joshua Catling	Tracy ——	March 8, 1813
Joseph Linville	Peggy Parrott	March 9, 1813
John Stanforth	Mary Brown	March 16, 1813
George Kite	Susanna Long	March 23, 1813
William Dunlap	Mary Bridges	March 23, 1813
Henry Conrod	Sally Hansbarger	March 25, 1813
James Stanforth	Esther Shaver	March 30, 1813
Richard Fletcher	Nancy Ragan	March 31, 1813
Henry Peterfish	Polly Kite	April 3, 1813
William Clyfton	Mary Murry	April 21, 1813
Henry Andis	Rebeckah Rader	April 22, 1813
Jacob Shaver	Elizabeth Stanforth	May 1, 1813
Charles Clark	Phoebe Keys	May 5, 1813
Philip Reedy	Susanna Showalter	May 8, 1813
George Bontz	Catharine Pirkey	May 13, 1813
William Mathews	Hannah Bricherton	May 18, 1813
Hugh Bruffy	Ann Ireland	May 20, 1813

John Overholt	Lady Deppoy	June 10, 1813
Daniel Ettinger	Eliza Burnsides	June 10, 1813
John Graham	Susanna Nisewanger	June 11, 1813
Arthur Davidson	Barbary Rawley	June 22, 1813
Joseph Houston	Polly Albright	July 1, 1813
Abraham Pifer	Lydia Fry	July 20, 1813
Jacob Elgard	Susanna Fent	August 3, 1813
John Letrick	Elizabeth Peary	August 9, 1813
Norton Gum	Sarah Shoup	August 17, 1813
Gasper Moyers	Rachael Shoemaker	August 17, 1813
William Bellas	Elizabeth Trump	August 17, 1813
Allen Dever	Nancy Turley	August 18, 1813
Elzy Breedwell	Betsey Tidd	August 20, 1813
James Blain	Becky Magill	August 21, 1813
Benjamin Hensley	Nelly Meadows	August 22, 1813
Joseph Strawsnider	Elizabeth Eyman	August 23, 1813
Peter Henebarger	Elizabeth Bear	August 26, 1813
John Carn	Barbara Eater	August 26, 1813
Simon Graves	Maria Yancey	August 28, 1813
John Chippy	Darcus Williams	September 7, 1813
George Bungaman	Grace Lokey	September 9, 1813
Henry Deeds	Peggy Crist	September 23, 1813
Abraham Rader	Catharine Beam	September 28, 1813
Abraham Nave	Catharine Ollebough	October 5, 1813
Thomas Loker	Mary Cowan	October 12, 1813
Daniel Brillhart	Catharine Shultz	October 26, 1813
Jeremiah Ragan	Rachel Ragan	November 10, 1813
Thomas Dean	Polly Lash	November 11, 1813
Jacob Snider	Peggy Roberts	November 16, 1813
William Paul	Jane Lock	November 25, 1813
Samuel Burkholder	Elizabeth Good	November 25, 1813
Jacob Cowan	Susanna Pickering	December 9, 1813
Jacob Leamon	Mary Armentrout	December 16, 1813
George Kice	Malinda Burnsides	December 21, 1813
John Rader	Caty Turner	December 21, 1813
John Argenbright	Polly Miller	December 29, 1813
Joseph Mohoy	Dorothy Coffman	December 30, 1813
Jacob Stoner	Catharine Trout	——, 1813
John Sheetz	Polly Hansford	January 13, 1814
George Mauk	Polly Turner	January 17, 1814
Westly Harrison	Peggy Custer	January 18, 1814
Michael Corns	Elizabeth Miller	January 22, 1814
John Armentrout	Margaret Kysor	January 28, 1814
Michael Butt	Betsy Arnold	February 3, 1814
George Rumsay	Susanna Losh	February 10, 1814
Bannett Like	Sally Lock	February 17, 1814
John Hinchy	Mary Barley	February 24, 1814
Jacob Pence	Lucinda Graves	March 3, 1814
Peter Dairey	Polly Ransbottom	March 15, 1814
Christian Swartz	Polly Bergehiger	March 17, 1814
Gideon Overshiner	Barbara Campbell	March 17, 1814
James Westfall	Eleanor Brown	March 20, 1814
George Moyers	Caty White	March 22, 1814
John Miller	Margaret Cook	March 25, 1814
James Cline	Jane Hansbarger	March 30, 1814
John Harry	Barbara Allbright	April 7, 1814
Daniel Shickle	Elizabeth Driver	April 21, 1814
John Chrisman	Catharine Warren	April 21, 1814
Benjamin Housdin	Elizabeth Turner	April 26, 1814
James Morris	Sally Morris	April 26, 1814
David Garber	Solomia Zate	April 26, 1814

Jacob Arnold	Caty Lantis	April 26, 1814
William Hevener	Leonah Custer	April 26, 1814
Gabriel Custer	Louis Slater	May 17, 1814
Michael Moyer	Ann Cromer	May 24, 1814
Solomon Ritchy	Mary Smith	May 31, 1814
William Graves	Jane Prollinger	June 2, 1814
Jacob Varner	Rhody Rittentrout	June 8, 1814
Henry Long	Mary Shular	June 8, 1814
Jesse Grigory	Mary Argabright	June 8, 1814
Henry R. Brown	Sally Nicholas	June 8, 1814
George Shular	Delitha Doval	June 8, 1814
John Lock	Mary Snider	June 9, 1814
James Nickle	Rachael Sheridan	June 23, 1814
Philip Evilsizer	Anna Hough	July 14, 1814
Noah Higgs	Elizabeth Brinks	July 19, 1814
Frederick Huddle	Magdalena Byrd	August 8, 1814
Ephriam Salvage	Frances Strickler	August 11, 1814
William Ready	Nancy Smelser	August 16, 1814
Daniel Layman	Barbara Armantrout	August 29, 1814
William Jinkens	Rebecca Dunlap	August 30, 1814
Jacob Ammon	Christena Argabright	September 4, 1814
John Brilhard	Any Cammel	September 4, 1814
Andrew Bare	Lydia Waren	October 20, 1814
Jacob Burkholder	Elizabeth Nisewanger	October 25, 1814
William Quinn	Nancy Quinn	October 27, 1814
John Lineabaugh	Anna Wise	November 8, 1814
Ale—— Walters	Rachel Decker	November 8, 1814
Thomas Henton	Betsy Strayr	November 11, 1814
Jacob Fink	Sally Laund—	November 16, 1814
Mathew Dyer	Rebecah Lincoln	November 25, 1814
John Fink	Christena Smith	December 10, 1814
William Houston	Nancy Harrison	December 15, 1814
Rueben Moore	Martha McWilliams	December 21, 1814
Daniel Bazle	Mahala Higgs	November 21, 18?
Abraham Bowers	Elizabeth Loker	
Phillip Bowers	Catharine Kipps	
John Bowers	Sophia Miller	
William Brown	Mary Alger	
Isaac Long	Elizabeth Shuler	
George Renland	Betty Miller	
John Smith	Barbara Driver	
John Step	Polly Haga	December 28, 18?
Daniel Garber	Elizabeth Shank	January 10, 1815
Abraham Louderback	Barbara ———	January 10, 1815
Henry Bushnell	Sally Laird	January 17, 1815
John Driver	Mary Stoutemire	February 9, 1815
Henry Movers	Margaret McKinsey	February 10, 1815
Philip Bushong	Betsey Brane	February 14, 1815
Charles Beard	Margaret Berry	March 2, 1815
David Fulk	Sally Swecker	March 4, 1815
John Summers	Rebecca Keister	March 7, 1815
Daniel Wise	Elizabeth Leedy	March 9, 1815
Patrick Rains	Sally ———	March 9, 1815
George Showalter	Nancy Coffman	March 14, 1815
Joseph Weller	Elizabeth Stephen	March 29, 1815
Alexander Trout	Ann Mary Armentrout	March 30, 1815
John Swern	Christina Weaver	April 11, 1815
Paul Chamerline	Catherine Peterfish	April 15, 1815
John Turner	Jane Stephenson	April 15, 1815
George Bear	Polly Knight	April 16, 1815
William Barrick	Sally Fifer	April 16, 1815

Samuel Liggett	Hannah Bryan	April 18, 1815
Joseph Fifer	Catharine Drawbend	April 18, 1815
Jacob Miller	Madgalene Sanger	April 20, 1815
John Bryan	Esther Westfall	April 28, 1815
Nathaniel Hord	Mary Gilmore	May 13, 1815
Christian Boody	Elizabeth Frysinger	May 18, 1815
Jesse Harrison	Matilda Herring	May 23, 1815
Stephen Taylor	Betsey Glovier	June 6, 1815
Charles Stockard	Elizabeth Walters	June 24, 1815
Samuel Brillhart	Susanna Whitsel	June 27, 1815
Christian Pixler	Elizabeth Heston	July 2, 1815
John Bible	Sally Branner	August 8, 1815
John Runnian	Mary Price	August 8, 1815
Zack Bruston	Elizabeth Strock	August 24, 1815
Samuel Hinegardner	Fanny Showalter	August 24, 1815
John Bridges	Catharine Arnold	August 25, 1815
Abraham Philips	Elizabeth Dunlap	August 29, 1815
John Sites	Margaret Barnhart	September 8, 1815
Samuel Hoober	Anna Hoober	September 19, 1815
Thomas Sterlings	Mary Harrow	September 21, 1815
Austin, a free man of Colour	to Abigail a free woman	September 23, 1815
David Hughes	Rebecca Stutzer	October 3, 1815
Richard Ragan	Phebe Sampler	October 4, 1815
Adam May	Catharine Branner	October 5, 1815
John Rush	Barbara Ruff	October 12, 1815
Andrew Price	Polly Ritchy	October 19, 1815
Jehu Loker	Elizabeth Layman	October 24, 1815
Jacob Bowers	Susanna Andis	October 24, 1815
Reese Allstadt	Elizabeth Evilsizer	November 2, 1815
Meredith Jones	Mariah Graham	November 3, 1815
Jacob Fogle	Sally Cummins	November 7, 1815
Peter Holsinger	Elizabeth Layman	November 13, 1815
Tobias Beam	Lydia Roads	November 14, 1815
Seth Alger	Polly Mitchum	November 14, 1815
Henry Bear	Anne Nisewanger	November 16, 1815
Lewis Huff	Sally Deeds	November 21, 1815
John Beery	Anne Nickhart	November 23, 1815
Christian Bitter	Hannah Price	November 28, 1815
Thomas McGuire	Polly Whitmore	November 30, 1815
George Shultz	Hannah Trace	December 5, 1815
Daniel Flory	Catharine Yount	December 12, 1815
Jacob Hoover	Eleanor Bryan	December 28, 1815
John Mcadows	Mary Harnes	January 2, 1816
Joshua Tate	Susanna Hynicker	January 18, 1816
John Gladwell	Jane McKee	January 25, 1816
Michael Stover	Phebe Dickey	January 30, 1816
Thomas Logan	Elizabeth Rodgers	February 6, 1816
George Berry	Polly McGuire	February 8, 1816
Joseph Sellars	Catharine Moyers	February 21, 1816
John Carrier	Sarah Simers	February 22, 1816
Abraham Smith	Polly Scott	February 27, 1816
Charles Blain	Sally Gainz	March 5, 1816
Peter Effinger	Harriet Graham	March 6, 1816
Anthony Roads	Ann Good	March 7, 1816
St. Clair Shiflet	Elizabeth Self	March 7, 1816
John Mauk	Margaret Hansbarger	March 14, 1816
Peachy H. McWilliams	Polly Ragan	March 19, 1816
Samuel Miller	Barbara Senger	March 19, 1816
Michael Clinepelter	Christina Simmers	March 19, 1816
Jeremiah Hansbarger	Elizabeth Miller	March 21, 1816
John Waggoner	Elizabeth Oneil	April 2, 1816

MARRIAGES FROM 1795 To 1825

James Waggoner	Elizabeth Oneil	April 2, 1816
John Holliday	Ann Waren	April 2, 1816
Martin Mungar	Susanna Hefferman	April 4, 1816
John Bowers	Sally Kayler	April 4, 1816
David Frank	Elizabeth Stout	April 10, 1816
Joseph Strock	Fanny Westpall	April 16, 1816
Henry Cook	Polly Teisler	April 17, 1816
Eli Harry	Sally Ragan	April 17, 1816
John H. Rolston	Mary Hopkins	April 18, 1816
John Fye	Christena Long	April 22, 1816
David Whitmore	Elizabeth Frank	May 7, 1816
John Neese	Nancy Miller	May 12, 1816
John Fisher	Polly Weaver	May 19, 1816
Philip Long	Sally Hashlaw	May 21, 1816
Josiah Welcher	Betsy McGuirre	May 23, 1816
Jehu Gum	Ann Shoup	May 28, 1816
William Pickering	Bethiah Bartz	June 11, 1816
Joseph Long	Nancy Grady	June 17, 1816
Henry Durrow	Julian Wetsel	June 18, 1816
Henry Chrisman	Catharine Rader	July 4, 1816
Jacob Shank	Polly Floyd	July 16, 1816
John Chrisman	Eleanor Rolston	July 23, 1816
William Smith	Elizabeth Chrisman	July 25, 1816
Benjamin Solomon	Jane Turley	August 7, 1816
Grovey French	Mary Coleman	August 7, 1816
Christopher Newel	Charlotte Lilly	August 8, 1816
Daniel Arnold	Catharine Hansbarger	September 3, 1816
John Coffman	Jane Kyle	September 3, 1816
Joshua Evilsizer	Francis Dodds	September 26, 1816
David Summers	Margaret Howard	October 2, 1816
Joseph Moore	Phebe Moore	October 5, 1816
John H. Deck	Mary Stark	October 15, 1816
Seth Elger	Sally ————	October 24, 1816
Adam Rader	Christina Miller	November 16, 1816
William Shanks	Hannah Cravens	November 19, 1816
William Higgans	Nancy Harrison	December 19, 1816
John Morris	Margaret Graham	December 26, 1816
Jonathan Breeden	Nancy Meadows	January 2, 1817
Christopher Merclia	Catharine Blows	January 9, 1817
Jacob Weatherhols	Betsy Fawley	January 23, 1817
Jacob Rife	Caty Garber	February 6, 1817
George Hinecker	Mary Overholt	February 17, 1817
David Fleak	Pegg Vanpelt	February 18, 1817
Daniel Fulk	Sally Sowders	February 20, 1817
Daniel Getts	Christena Frexter	February 24, 1817
Martin Baxter	Sally Jinkens	February 26, 1817
George Evers	Peggy Miller	February 28, 1817
Henry Ritchey	Elizabeth Miller	March 6, 1817
Peter Pence	Elizabeth Harshman	March 13, 1817
Westley Calhoun	Jane Musick	March 13, 1817
Reuben French	Sally Coleman	March 25, 1817
George Overholt	Polly Stephens	March 27, 1817
Samuel Jewett	Francis Underwood	April 3, 1817
Meshaac Samuels	Elizabeth Noland	April 10, 1817
Kenly Berry	Caty Foster	April 17, 1817
Thomas Jones	Ellin McCracken	April 24, 1817
Daniel Beaver	Mary Huston	June 19, 1817
Thomas Turner	Polly Baker	July 3, 1817
Sylvester K. Fuller	Elizabeth Carpenter	July 10, 1817
Patrick Dougherty	Mary Lary	July 22, 1817
Martin Edwards	Hannah Kyser	August 7, 1817

Michael Koontz	Mary Brillhart	August 10, 1817
John Lamb	Susanna Turner	August 15, 1817
Joseph Moyers	Polly Sellarz	August 21, 1817
Mathias Pifer	Susanna Still	August 28, 1817
Nathaniel Britton	Nancy Funk	September 9, 1817
Daniel Landis	Caty Wooden	September 18, 1817
Robert Craig	Hannah Chrisman	September 30, 1817
William Rolstone	Catharine Chrisman	September 30, 1817
John Snyder	Mary Baker	October 14, 1817
Anthony Ocker	Elizabeth Ocker	October 21, 1817
Abraham Baker	Mary Riggleman	October 22, 1817
Reheboam Matthews	Elizabeth Robertson	October 23, 1817
Jacob Robertson	Margaret Cowan	December 9, 1817
Daniel Vantrump	Christina Bowers	December 22, 1817
Abraham Shultz	Elizabeth Young	January 13, 1818
Samuel Coots	Emily Graham	January 13, 1818
Philip Parritt	Barbara Ann Snyder	February 19, 1818
Joseph Loker	Charlotte O'Kean	March 5, 1818
John Whisler	Mary Fifer	March 12,1818
Henry Crider	Betsy May	March 18, 1818
William Hinkle	Hannah Trout	March 31, 1818
Thomas E. Wyatt	Catharine Funk	April 9, 1818
Abraham Peery	Elizabeth Wanger	April 14, 1818
William Hopkins	Esther Keatzer	April 16, 1818
Ephriam Rinker	Ann Brock	April 21, 1818
Joseph Wanger	Barbara Beery	April 28, 1818
George Acre	Betsey Ong	May 12, 1818
Bernard Huffman	Peggy Spitzer	June 4, 1818
David Irick	Ann Bear	June 4, 1818
David Swartz	Eleanor Berry	June 18, 1818
Valentine Snyder	Catharine Martz	June 18, 1818
Andrew Burnsides	Sarah Higgins	June 25, 1818
Jacob May	Sally Orebaugh	July 2, 1818
Reuben Dove	Catharine Dove	July 9, 1818
David Berry	Betsey Foster	July 21, 1818
Lewis Bowers	Elizabeth Pates	July 24, 1818
Barnett M. Annon	Nancy Luan	July 27, 1818
George Lore	Magdalene Butt	August 4, 1818
Abraham Hisley	Elizabeth Newman	August 5, 1818
Joseph Ransbottom	Catharine Albright	August 11, 1818
Christopher Shultz	Jerusha Harrison	August 11, 1818
Isaac Fleming	Sally Hiscr	August 12, 1818
Elisha Morris	Phebe Williams	August 19, 1818
Daniel Kyser	Lucy Turly	August 27, 1818
Elijah Hooks	Phebe Reeves	September 15, 1818
William Beard	Margaret Miller	September 17, 1818
Hugh Donaghe	Elizabeth Barley	September 22, 1818
Jacob Bish	Polly Kelley	September 24, 1818
Joseph Coffman	Abigail Lincoln	October 6, 1818
George Cambill	Rachael Nicely	October 22, 1818
James Hopkins	Elizabeth Bryan	October 29, 1818
Henry Spices	Polly Dillimore	November 3, 1818
George Caplinger	Catharine Feister	November 17, 1818
Samuel Leigh	Franey Shoemaker	December 31, 1818
John Martz	Ann Robertson	January 19, 1819
Sebastian Martz	Catharine Snyder	February 16, 1819
Adam Painter	Catharine Long	February 18, 1819
Henry Fowler	Susanna Linebarger	February 19, 1819
Jacob Shickle	Eve Gowl	February 23, 1819
Isaac Richy	Catharine Baker	March 2, 1819
Henry Baker	Elizabeth Eppard	March 18, 1819

James Westfall	Elizabeth Ettinger	March 30, 1819
Joseph Fry	Elizabeth Peery	April 22, 1819
Nicholas Long	Jemimah Short	April 22, 1819
Jacob Miller	Nancy Moyers	April 27, 1819
Samuel Heaton	Polly Bowers	April 29, 1819
Joseph Cromer	Mary Harnsbarger	May 20, 1819
William Rolston	Eleanor Herdman	May 21, 1819
John Kiblinger	Sally Kyger	May 25, 1819
Hugh Dover	Maria Blain	May 27, 1819
William Vanpelt	Mary Rodgers	June 10, 1819
William Southard	Elizabeth Sheetz	June 10, 1819
Michael Minick	Elizabeth Weller	July 20, 1819
Jonathan Horn	Catharine Vance	July 28, 1819
Martin Marshall	Margaret Snider	July 29, 1819
David Edwards	Eliza Bolington	July 29, 1819
David Puls	Betsey Palsel	August 3, 1819
James Dougherty	Sarah Robertson	August 10, 1819
Joseph Clyne	Isabella Pence	August 26, 1819
Garland Shifflet	Peachy Selz	September 2, 1819
Michael Feazle	Elizabeth Ettinger	September 7, 1819
Jacob Orts	Sally Hanan	September 21, 1819
Peter Fifer	Nancy Turner	September 21, 1819
Jacob Kyser	Catharine Harshman	September 24, 1819
Jacob Wanger	Rachel Floyd	September 25, 1819
George Hoof	Hannah Bear	October 12, 1819
John Kratzer	Hannah Bryan	October 21, 1819
Abraham Snyder	Mary Ann Yancey	October 21, 1819
Jacob Hammer	Ann Teen	October 21, 1819
James Hamilton	Dianna Custer	October 26, 1819
Benjamin Smith	Jerusha Solomon	October 28, 1819
Robert Hines	Sally Smith	November 9, 1819
William Sellers	Perthena Harrison	November 18, 1819
Joseph Snell	Mary Sharfey	November 18, 1819
Peter Stumbough	Deborah Craig	November 18, 1819
William Smith	Frances Bradwell	November 25, 1819
William Kenney	Ann C. Smith	November 29, 1819
Henry Bear	Eleanor Vance	November 30, 1819
John Bent	Sally Horn	December 17, 1819
Daniel Dovel	Eve Shular	December 21, 1819
Henry Miller	Susanna Harnsbarger	December 23, 1819
Henry Bush	Rebecca Mildew	December 26, 1819
Robert Blackwell	Eve Josnet	December 26, 1819
Andrew Coffman	Mary Charlton	December 28, 1819
George McCoy	Nancy Givens (negroes)	January 1, 1820
George Weaver	Rosanna Garney	January 13, 1820
William Sites	Melinda Hite	January 13, 1820
George Philips	Martha Kenney	February 15, 1820
John Philips	Rosanna Hillard	February 15, 1820
Benjamin Norman	Sally Huffman	February 15, 1820
Samuel Hisey	Susanna McCullock	February 26, 1820
Benjamin Kofman	Elizabeth Hoover	February 29, 1820
John Wise	Elizabeth Orebaugh	March 1, 1820
Benjamin Powell	Catharine Powell	March 9, 1820
Joseph Bywater	Phebe Clarke	March 16, 1820
William Jones	Mary Snyder	March 21, 1820
Jacob Good	Catharine Brunk	March 23, 1820
John Harshman	Susanna Pence	March 23, 1820
John Pukel	Sally Devany	March 24, 1820
Johnson Caplinger	Rebecca Seever	March 27, 1820
Arnal Delaney	Mary Burk	April 10, 1820

William Jordon	Margaret Kyser	April 12, 1820
Joseph Huling	Susanna Murray	April 13, 1820
William Crawford	—— Pool	May 7, 1820
Abram Bear	Anna Hoover	May 16, 1820
John Harrell	Nancy Rogers	June 1, 1820
Abednago Samuels	Margaret Nowlands	June 13, 1820
Samuel Summers	Polly Carnes	June 20, 1820
Joseph Sampson	Hannah Short	June 25, 1820
Benjamin Waid	Elizabeth Weaver	June 29, 1820
Henry Thomas	Catharie Rife	July 25, 1820
Harmon Houck	Eveline Sprinkle	July 27, 1820
George Price	Ann Miller	August 3, 1820
Lewis Garrison	Elizabeth Right	August 6, 1820
John Hall	Elizabeth Smith	August 13, 1820
John Swartz	Susanna Jordan	August 15, 1820
John Brown	Polly Deger	August 15, 1820
David Baldin	Mary Byer	August 17, 1820
David Spitzer	Mary Crumley	August 24, 1820
John Markey	Sally Nipple	September 12, 1820
Uriah Woods	Polly Schmucker	September 14, 1820
Reuben Holt	Elizabeth Shaver	September 21, 1820
Thomas Nance	—— Silby	September 21, 1820
Michael Correll	Phebe Fridley	September 28, 1820
Charles Snelling	Jane Mooney	September 28, 1820
John Koontz	Polly Thompson	September 28, 1820
Henry Stall	Sally Crim	October 3, 1820
Fredrick Cline	Polly Kofman	October 10, 1820
Sylvester Fuller	Eliz Graham	November 6, 1820
Daniel Crut	Elizabeth Bish	November 9, 1820
Jacob Houck	Martha Rhodes	November 19, 1820
Shelton Slodger	Deborah Smith	December 7, 1820
Edmond Bridges	Catharine Minnick	December 15, 1820
Christian Lore	Phebe O'Roark	December 21, 1820
James Michie	Elizabeth Graham	January 4, 1821
William Ship	Mary Getts	January 4, 1821
William Clarke	Milly Grubs	January 25, 1821
George Rinehart	Christena Blose	February 2, 1821
John Cravens	Reehannah Chaplain	February 15, 1821
Dewalt Bish	Mary Drawbond	February 20, 1821
John Uffner	Ann Woods	February 22, 1821
Andrew Getts	Betsey Getts	February 25, 1821
Jacob Bailey	Phebe Henton	March 8, 1821
Jacob Strickler	Delitha Rosenbarger	March 18, 1821
John Long	Susanna Rumsey	March 20, 1821
Martin Miller	Nancy Sanger	March 27, 1821
John Kenney	Elizabeth E. Duff	April 10, 1821
James Pickering	Polly Loker	April 12, 1821
William Thompson	Jennie Beam	April 19, 1821
James Wilson	Hannah Rader	April 25, 1821
George Cline	Christina Garber	May 15, 1821
William S. McDowell	Eliza F. Carthrea	May 15, 1821
John Gordon	Nancey Waren	May 29, 1821
Jacob Beaver	Barbary Miley	June 14, 1921
Philip Koontz	Polly Crumley	June 28, 1821
James Dilworth	Charlotte Wartman	July 5, 1821
Dennis Jenkins	Elizabeth Mowry	August 9, 1821
William Gray	Fanny Fox	August 13, 1821
John Guile	Mary Driver	August 27, 1821
Jonathan Dun	Miriah Thornhill	October 4, 1821
Conrod Blose	Margart Rinehart	October 25, 1821
Lewis Long	Nancy Bougher	December 6, 1821
Jesse Roach	Mary Ann Chapline	December 13, 1821

John Doherty	Hannah Turkeyhizer	December 25, 1821
Thomas Walters	Polly Woods	December 27, 1821
Gabriel Pain	Mary Bontz	February 14, 1822
Thomas Meadows	Elizabeth Breeding	February 19, 1822
James Scarf	Sally Bloses	March 14, 1822
Andrew Pumfrey	Mary Trusinger	April 2, 1822
Joseph Nance	Elizabeth Hupp	April 4, 1822
William Miller	Lucinda Woods	April 11, 1822
Daniel Arnold	Elizabeth Wise	April 16, 1822
———— Cummins	Eleanor Gar——	April 23, 1822
Peter Brumfield	Elizabeth Harshbarger	May 5, 1822
Hiram Garress	Nancy Jatlet	May 8, 1822
John Staunton	Ann Laburn	May 14, 1822
Jonathan Croft	Sally Herd	May 17, 1822
Peter Whitmore	Polly Ruebush	May 22, 1822
Henry Thornhill	Susan Harris	May 30, 1822
Joel Smith	Harnet, Ann	June 20, 1822
John Rinehart	Elizabeth Sellars	June 20, 1822
Richard Breeding	Ann Braskney	June 27, 1822
George Gilmer	Eliza F. Grattan	July 9, 1822
John Price	Elizabeth Rinehart	August 8, 1822
Isaac Yost	Mary Liggett	August 15, 1822
Abraham Martz	Ruth Pitt	August 20, 1822
Benjamin Strickler	Margaret Phelps	September 12, 1822
John Samuels	Mary Hensley	September 26, 1822
Wilson Fowler	Lucinda Nickols	October 3, 1822
Pierce Perry	Sally Holsinger	October 10, 1822
Brewer Reeves	Mary Ann Corn	October 31, 1822
John Freed	Lucy Biller	November 11, 1822
David McGuire	Polly Buran	November 16, 1822
Abraham Hutwool	Susanna Helbert	December 12, 1822
Allason Breeding	Elizabeth Bolton	December 22, 1822
John Brumback	Betsey Thomas	January 2, 1823
Timothy O'Roark	Rebecca Pheleps	January 3, 1823
William Pugh	Phebe Tusing	January 9, 1823
Henry Hammer	Christena Gibbon	January 9, 1823
Benjamin Fishburn	Sarah Rice	February 4, 1823
Abraham Shrimp	Elizabeth Fansler	February 13, 1823
Conrad Long	Maranda Genther	February 13, 1823
Jacob Davis	Catharine Hoof	February 18, 1823
William Hisey	Lydia Baker	February 20, 1823
Jacob Fawley	Susannah Price	February 20, 1823
Michael Ritter	Jacob (?) Bowers	February 23, 1823
John Altaffer	Elvira Harrell	February 23, 1823
Phelep Bible	Polly Fawley	February 23, 1823
James Dever	Matilda McWilliams	March 7, 1823
John McCullock	Sally M. McCray	March 10, 1823
Jacob Bowers	Madalena Harshbarger	March 18, 1823
Samuel Driver	Elizabeth Wombler	April 4, 1823
Boony Yeager	Susie Short	April 8, 1823
Benjamin Long	Elizabeth Moore	April 10, 1823
Michael Helbert	Barbara Etinger	April 17, 1823
John Wise	Anny Burner	April 18, 1823
John Fawley	Mary Hawke	May 8, 1823
Jacob Flory	Catharine Stoner	May 15, 1823
John Fresler	Elizabeth Hoover	June 10, 1823
Israel Shaver	Polly Cummins	June 12, 1823
Christian Garber	Fanny Rife	June 22, 1823
Abraham Deal	Philipdina Gowans	August 14, 1823
Jacob Kafman	Rebecca Earback	October 4, 1823
Joseph Tucker	Polly Grimsby	November 6, 1823

Jacob Sprinkle	Eliza Ann Cole	November 6, 1823
George Arien	Barbara Young	November 25, 1823
Larkin Norman	Margaret Miller	November 25, 1823
Joseph Argenbright	Polly Miller	November 28, 1823
Joshua Sheets	Lydia Sherfick	December 2, 1823
John Arely	Betsey Miller	December 21, 1823
Abednago Lary	Nancy Bridges	January 6, 1824
Henry Fultz	Fanny Hollingsworth	January 22, 1824
Henry Carrier	Delilah Harmon	January 22, 1824
Samuel Glen	Jane M. Black	February 9, 1824
Samuel Coffman	Eve Zimmerman	February 10, 1824
Henry Plaugher	Elizabeth Messick	February 12, 1824
Jacob Fawley	Peggy Price	February 25, 1824
Anthony Huffman	Caty Cline	February, 1824
Robert M. Cartney	Rachel Kiser	February, 1824
Samuel Flory	Elizabeth Young	March 11, 1824
Jeremiah McKee	Any Beam	March 23, 1824
George Fultz	Nancy Strickler	March 25, 1824
Christian Eversoul	Christina Hoover	April 15, 1824
Mathias Tate	Salley Rumsey	April, 1824
Christian Richey	Margaret Reese	April, 1824
William Baggott	Hannah Quick	May 9, 1824
Anthony Boar	Emily Bridges	May 13, 1824
John Lofftus	Syntha Sandy	May 16, 1824
Thomas Hegs	Malinda Short	May 18, 1824
Joseph Bierley	Sally Bierly	May, 1824
William McCausland	Harriet Kyle	June 10, 1824
Thomas Poage	Eliza Ervin	June 19, 1824
Nathaniel Woods	Catharine Walters	June 24, 1824
Samuel Hulings	Catharine Martz	June 27, 1824
Jonathan Hulon	Lydia Orebaugh	July 1, 1824
Elijah Bowin	Polly Tankenly	July 18, 1824
Joel Minick	Hannah Huber	July 22, 1824
Michael Voland	Katherine Semer	August 2, 1824
Thomas Cotrell	Rebecca O'Kane	August 19, 1824
Jacob Croft	Patsey Shotwell	August 19, 1824
Henry Cup	Ann Baker	August, 1824
Thomas Burton	Susan Cline	August, 1824
John Mason	Polly Miller	September 12, 1824
David Ongst	Anna Sharfey	October 5, 1824
Michael Harris	Jane H. Smith	October 27, 1824
James Philips	Nancy Alford	October, 1824
Jacob Garver	Litia Stoner	November 25, 1824
George Cline	Nancy Grimsley	December 15, 1824
James Riddle	Ruth Gilmore	December 21, 1824
Henry Gasing	Elizabeth Mooney	December 22, 1824
Abraham Strickler	Susanah Hollingsworth	December 26, 1824
Reuben Kyser	Peggy Strickler	December 30, 1824
George Haugh	Christina Haines	December, 1824
John Lowny	Mary Huston	December, 1824
Thomas Miller	Peggy Kyser	December, 1824
David Sechrist	Ann Adams	January, 1825
John Pence	Anna Roller	January, 1825
Jacob May	Elizabeth Rains	January, 1825
——— Henton	Elizabeth Sellers	February 3, 1825
John Whitt	Rebecca Stottinger	February 17, 1825
Joshua Gilmore	Synthia Bridges	February 22, 1825
Thornton Devin	Polly Summers	February 24, 1825
David Wambler	Any Long	March 17, 1825
John Philips	Rachael Hinkle	March 17, 1825
Michael Miller	Mary Langes	March 24, 1825

William Hawk	Cyrena Peal	March 24, 1825
James Rankin	Easter Beard	March 24, 1825
John Steffy	Anna Bower	March 29, 1825
Daniel Brower	Wancy Lants	March 31, 1825
Jacob Roudabush	——— ———	March, 1825
Felix Landis	Elizabeth Kite	March, 1825
James Welch	Louisa Moore	April 6, 1825
John Guyer	Peggy Miley	April 7, 1825
John Moffett	Sarah Summers	April 11, 1825
John Garrison	Sarah Eigenburg	April 17, 1825
Paul Allen	July Ann Stall	April 21, 1825
John Sanger	Elizabeth Flory	April 26, 1825
Jonathan Bateman	Margaret Utsler	April 26, 1825
James Miller	Elizabeth Kyle	April 27, 1825
Jacob Shaver	Sarah Alford	April, 1825
Samuel Rodes	Catharine Bowman	May 15, 1825
Isaac Hawks	Mary Ludwick	May 26, 1825
Peter Stall	Hannah Huffman	May 31, 1825
Henry Hostates	Patsy Harrison	May 31, 1825
David Fadely	Anna Baker	May 31, 1825
Emanuel Armentrout	Mary Argebright	May, 1825
George Haines	Margaret Haugh	May, 1825
John Adams	Polly Long	June 1, 1825
William Hammer	Ann Graves	June 16, 1825
John Waring	Harriet Rice	July 6, 1825
William Winborough	Julian Mauzy	July 7, 1825
Andrew May	Peggy Smith	July 18, 1825
Michael Brock	Keniah Turner	August 23, 1825
John Fisher	Barbara Hudlow	July, 1825
Henry Beery	Catharine Wise	July, 1825
John Koontz	Mary Palmer	August 1, 1825
John Souverine	Betsey Bowman	August 8, 1825
Michael Flory	Sarah Hedrick	August 9, 1825
Fountain Dear	Betzy Munnick	August 11, 1825
William Haton	Hannah Cupp	August 16, 1825
Henry Early	Sarah Showalter	August 18, 1825
William Reese	Eliza Wine	August, 1825
John Landes	Catherine Burklcy	September 5, 1825
John Brown	Elizabeth Zimmerman	September, 1825
John Witmor	Elizabeth Altorpher	September, 1825
Benjamin Bierly	Susanna Whitmore	September, 1825
David Thompson	Dolly Pifer	September, 1825
Rueben Allen	Jane Koontz	October 18, 1825
John Shoemaker	Barbara Zetty	October 18, 1825
Otway Sterling	Catharine Yakle	November 1, 1825
Steevy Shackey	Anna Jordon	November 9, 1825
George Wise	Stanah Bear	November 9, 1825
Benjamin Denton	Tabitha Jackson	November 10,1825
Washington Lewis	Harriet Duff	November 10,1825
Samuel Armentrout	Sophia Armentrout	December 5, 1825
Michael Kindle	Catharine Rinker	December 8, 1825
Daniel Hoof	Elizabeth Miley	December 29, 1825
Samuel Huffman	Margaret Roller	December, 1825
Samuel Arnold	Sally Burner	January 23, 1—
Jacob Blose	Elizabeth Ammon	January 2, 18—
George Clarke	Susan Lee	November 28, ——
John Doval	Sallie Shular	June 22, 182-
Jacob Durrow	Mary Doman	December 12, 182-
Henry Y. Gainer	Elisabeth L. Lee	November 13, 182-
Henry Hansbarger	Polly Bear	November 14, ——
Jacob Kennedy	Amanda Craven	December 6, ——

Terry Louderberry

Thomas Meadows
Christian Oler
William Oler
Conrad Sanger
George Shaver
John Short

Jemima Bryan
(Free people of color)
Elizabeth Breeding
Molly Kite
Paticy Runkle
Caty Flora
Ann Paine
Sarah Long

August 6, ——

October 4, 18—
May 16, ——
November 7, 18—
February 27, 182–
September 6, 182–
August 1, 182–

The following persons were recorded as having been married by Rev. John Brown during the years from July 1800 to December 31, 1823.

John Pence
Peter Shlosser
Charles Frye
David Bolton
Christian Eagle
Michael Renhard
George Saftly
David Geisser
Henry Horner
John Souther
John Wedig
John Thuma
John Sehler
Leonard Tudwiler
Jacob Whittmor
Jacob Kyle
John Blacker
Peter Etrich
Christian Kensly
John Earman
John Petefish
Frederick Arnd
William Spangler
Peter Gigger
William Bailey
Peter Michael
Henry Kyle
Philip Lindsay
John Brightman
John Detemore
John Shank
George Sour
Henry Balser
John Trent
John Aply
Adam P. Fifer
Robert Blakly
William Tamoo
Joseph Cupp
Garland Heggason
George Hartman
John Titman
John Campbill
Henry Patrum
George Snyder
William Earman
Martin Backer

Sally Zeller
Mary Deams
Peggy Zellers
Barbara Fridley
Christena Cook
Delilah Frye
Anna Seavely
Lidia Hill
Elizabeth Pence
Catharine Alstat
Polly Drourbough
Magdalena Brown
Rachel Sipe
Mary Shank
Polly Cupp
Caty Moffard
Susana Rohler
Catharine Blacker
Caty Argebright
Barbara Sehler
Margarath Monger
Caty Harmans
Susanna Boyer
Rebecca Fisher
Magdalena Hannah
Mary Ham
Betsey Pirkey
Sally Gillmore
Matheldy Long
Nancy Long
Susana Hoffman
Elisabeth Hofner
Elizabeth Hauk (Hank?)
Frances Garrison
Elizabeth Donough
Catharine Fisher
Sara Kampbell
Polly Derrow
Barbara Roots
Mary Blackly
Elizabeth Boyer
Mary Ann Rocby
Patsy Beard
Susana Monger
Mary Blacker
Polly Messerly
Elizabeth Sehler

John Batman	Jane Marcks
William Smith	Sarah Batman
Adam Deterick	Polly Pfifer
Fredrick Croan	Sara Fleshman
John Branden	Elizabeth Linsey
William Hartman	Elisal Livingston
George Miller	Elisabeth Fessel
William Kiser	Barbara Wise
Philip Hollwy	Magdalen Bernhard
Isaac Long	Catherine Will
Peter Reubush	Susan Huffman
Simon Stoufer	Catharine Wyand
Valentine Pence	Catharine Smith
William Zimmerman	Margaret Wildbarger
Peter Kellor	Mary Ruebush
Henry Sheetz	Polly Rees
Jacob Wyand	Anna Hernsbarger
Tobias Tanner	Elizabeth Wagner
Anna Cline	Jacob Jones
Frederick Han	Barbara Pence
Philip Delicat	Magdalena But
Jacob Pence	Mary Tanner
Jacob Huff	Elizabeth Lamry
Henry Miller	Barbara Armentrout
Henry Freasner	Barbara Cook
Henry Detemore	Elizabeth Miller
John Neble	Elizabeth Mayer
Daniel Nonemaker	Christina Shoe
Henry Ettinger	Elizabeth Pence
John Hop	Catharine Stoutmier
John Wolf	Barbara Royers
Henry Weldbarger	Sara Welsh
Michael Karbel	Elizabeth Uniah
Casper Maffer	Catharina Jones
Michael Kannely	Mary Bowers
Zebulon Harrison	Mary Tollman
John Stoutemier	Elizabeth Noland
John Tark	Elizabeth Shurey
George Armentrout	Elizabeth Michall
Matthew Leeb	Elizabeth Monger
Joseph Seafley	Elizabeth Harvey
Valentine Cook	Catharine Kraft
John Backer	Mary Spater
Henry Oloebaugh	Catharine Paulus
Peter Kepler	Elizabeth Ergebright
Jacob Rush	Elisabeth Ward
George Long	Sara Stambough
George Muleissen	Elizabetht Cline
John Kiser	Mary Cline
Charles Chandler	Peggy Weaver
William Armentrout	Sally Sellers
Jacob Zach	Lidia Gigger
Henry Shlosser	Caty Dage
John Showalter	Betzy Weaver
Mathew Long	Margareth Deck
Samuel Filsto	Christina Deck
William Krekenbarger	Susana Spater
Henry Shultz	Elizabeth Bab
George Hollny	Elizabeth Brown
Jacob Pence	Polly Smith
Daniel Beam	Mary Caufman

George Price
William Garriot
Jacob Rush
John Magert
Henry Propst
Jacob Freas
Tobias Roubush
Jacob Lingle
Henry Yeagely
John Smelzer
John Michael
William Bear
Jacob Paul
John Sellars
Sebay Burges
Jacob Koontz
Fielding Jollett
William Pifer
Philip Wanderlik
William Hiser
Peter Cline
Jacob Hoffman
Adam Deater
Joseph Farthlely
John Fisher
William Brett
Samuel Nible
Benjamin Whitmore
Samuel Hamaker
Henry Amend
Henry Harnesberger
George Fletcherand
John Krukelbarger
Jacob Keblinger
William Smith
John Painter
Jeremiah Kyle
John Warran
Daniel Boon
George Ruebush
Benjamin Smith
Emanuel Hoover
John Hollingsworth
John Leedy
John N. Reed
Henry Swisher
Stephen Conrad
Samuel Whitmore
Peter Brown
David Herring
George Shlosser
Cornelius Cain
George Gigger
Jacob Pifer
Abraham Boon
John P. Gun
George Kiser
Peter Rohler
George Cup
Christoffel Armentrout
John Andrew

Sophia Baudern
Barbara Nicholous
Caty Dondoahr
Elisabeth. Eppert
Elizabeth Gegger
Catharine Snider
Catharine Megel
Mary Mongar
Margaret Snider
Christina Blosser
Magdalena Mandel
Elizabeth Neble
Elizabeth Hoffman
Catharine Brown
Barbara Pifer
Nancy Cline
Ann Stoutemier
Elizabeth Willhelm
Elisabeth Lootz
Rebecca Beckerton
Christena Royer
Elisabeth Byerly
Elisabeth Holevz
Catharine King
Polly Long
Mary Newcomb
Christena Juty
Sara Falls
Elisabeth Croan
Eve Tanner
Sally Galaday
Molly Miller
Polly Weldbarger
Elisabeth Nicholores
Nancy Bulger
Sally Lanise
Elisabeth M. K. Kyle
Eve Shambaugh
Polly Sehler
Susan Thinkle
Elisab Welsher
Barbary Seller
Mary Strahl
Eve Kiser
Elizabeth Brown
Mary Hafner
Mary Cook
Catharine Allborphes
Elisabeth Hoffman
Mahaly Grady
Catharine Hudlow
Ann Keblinger
Sarah Pence
Betsey Maghead
Mary Sehler
Elisabeth Taylor
Susana Byerly
Elisabeth Safly
Sally Thinkle
Ann Deeds
Caty Hannah

George Keller	Catharine Beard
Nicholas Perkey	Rhoda Allen
William McD'aniel	Elizabeth Messerley
Henry Hafner	Margareth Sour
George Perkey	Anna Gigger
John Hoffman	Catharine Bohler
John Patrum	Polly Monger
John Long	Elizabeth Shultz
John May	Catharine Myler
William Dayley	Jane Adams
Henry Pence	Lucy Gygger
John Blakly	Elizabeth May
Adam Armentrout	Susana Whitmore
Peter Moyer	Catharine Bagerly
Abraham Monger	Polly Grove
Jacob Whittemore	Nancy Allorphes
William Morris	Eliza Pallmer
Michael Shank	Catharine Wysel
John Dover	Eliza Gilmore
John I. Rife	Ann Cline
Frederick Hoffman	Ann Rohler
Jacob Sour	Mary Ann Zellar
Abraham Swisher	Nancy Roads
George Wyler	Mary Raines
John Rush	Mary Nicholas
Peter Kayler	Sally Gigger
David Sipe	Maria Kiser
John Kruger	Elizabeth Early
Christian Detamore	Mary Dorman
William Hess	Elisabeth Welsh
William Stutzer	Elisab Dillon
John Brendel	Ann Zuikhel
Paul Beard	Elizabeth Mandd
John Koogler	Barbary Rush
John Link	Barbary Hernsbarger
Abraham Deal	Mary Wetzel
Peter Ogler	MargarethPirkey
Mathew Weldbarger	Sara Earman
Peter Boyer	Rachel Hodlow
Henry Drawbough	Eve Noll
George Wysel	Susan Tudwiler
John Cline	Susana Near
John Miller	Catharine Pence
Jacob Faber	Elisabeth Warner
George Magennett	Susan Armentrout
David Whitmor	Catharine Maye
John Pence	Mary Miller
Jacob Sipe	Catharine Argenbright
Samuel Harrison	Ester Huck
David Krekenberger	Mary May
John Pfaidly	Barbara Beard
Henry Voges	Catharine Arnds
Paul Rohler	Elizabeth Martin
William Redehers	Elizabeth Jackson
George Michel	Elizabeth Huie
Peter Rawhoof	Catharine Brown
Henry Landis	Elisabeth Backer
Michael Mowzey	Grace Laird
David Love	Susana Swartz
Adam Firebaugh	Elisal Kerchhof
Martin Near	Ann Woods

Forkner Philips
Daniel Miller
Adam Pence
Valentine Homan
John Wise
Andrew Hodlow
Abraham Sleed
Jacob Ruebush
Andrew Legoa
Ludwig Shol
David Wise
Henry Garber
Jacob Wizel
Charles Pence
Ephriam Hernsbarger
Daniel Cup
John Wise
Jacob Huttle
John Ewing
John Hudlow
George Hine
John Landes
Andrew Vilemmer
Jacob Widy
Daniel Thinkle
Michael Earman
Jacob Neble
Maurice Ziliwit
Joseph Cline
Isaac Thompson
James Cahon
Joseph Shuar
Abraham Boon
George Horner
Christian Sehler
Jacob Kroah
Jacob Shryer
Peter Beard
John Powell
John Smith
Henry Cup
John Pirkey
Jacob Argebright
George Earman
Jacob Shoe
Jacob Weyman
Jones Michel
Jacob Lamb
Christian Gigger
John Drohrbough
Adam Michel
Thomas Beck
Joseph Allen
Philip Slutter
Henry Hoffert
John Barker
Daniel Smith
Jacob Unruh
Fredrick Ott
Thomas Curry
John Smith

Sarah Johnson
Elizabeth Teshlern
Catharine Zellers
Amelia Backer
Mary Voght
Elizabeth Boyers
Mary Grim
Magdalena Wizel
Pfifer Mary
Magdalena Hanyel
Apeloma Lamb
Susana Ergebright
Catharine Ruebush
Mary Dondoah
Reb Mower
Elizabeth Belcher
Polly Lamb
Ann Hammen
Catharine Moffort
Martha Jackson
Mary Cambell
Ehster Wise
Sara Swartz
Mary Deal
Catharine Petefish
Cath Messerly
Virginia Early
Jane Plaud
Sara Hartman
Anna Huck
Mary Freasner
Magdalena Pley
Mary Earman
Rebecca Michel
Elizabeth King
Mary Zesh
Sara Pearce
Esther Beard
Sara Ewing
Catharine Kepler
Susana Backer
Ann Medlebarger
Catharine Long
Sara Ergebright
Eva Wagner
Catharine Markwood
Susana Keller
Susana Wise
Rebecca Gigger
Elisal Tafelmier
Magal Armentrout
Eva Brak
Amelia Weig
Eve Miller
Elizabeth Michel
Margareth Rush
Christina Stonebecker
Elizabeth Beard
Catharine Beard
Elenor Zuitchel
Elisabeth Marten

John Freas	Mary Midy
Jacob Brill	Magdalena Hatresh
Daniel Johnston	Mary Fisher
Jacob Butt	Susana Pence
William Evans	Rebecca Boyers
Henry Baamgartner	Elizabeth Herzoy
Christian Mesner	Elizabeth Long
Jacob Wagner	Catharine Bander
Jones Stevens	Margaret Firebaugh
Peter Thinkle	Catharine Sehler
John Boyer	Barbara Phery
Jacob Swisher	Sarah Harry
Henry Swab	Ehster Fall
John Kellor	Susana Sour
John Karn	Barbara Weber
John Wisekup	Susana Nigh
James Brandue	Ann Britton
Henry Ewily	Mary Beyerly
Fredrick Stambough	Sara Brak
Samuel Harry	Mary Thomson
George May	Nancy Berks
Isaac Bolton	Mary Firebaugh
Thomas Bear	Catharine Neble
Benjamin Hauf	Caty Allbughs
William Campbell	Nancy Robertson
Christian Kerbough	Caty Shlosser
Abram Funkhouser	Catharine Kaufman
Daniel Whitmor	Susana Cup
Ewen Hoops	Christena Kensor
Ubuck Sehler	Rebecca Early
Jacob Bushong	Catharine Cline
John Shultz	Susan Argebright
Jacob Hershbarger	Magdalena King
Jacob Aply	Eve Kerbough
Fredrick Cup	Elizabeth Backer
George Sprenkle	Hannah Barby

Obviously the records are defective in some particulars; also names in a few cases are repeated under different dates. Possibly one date may indicate when the marriage license was issued; the other when it was returned to the clerk's office.

LANDOWNERS OF ROCKINGHAM COUNTY IN THE YEAR 1789

Lists compiled from original manuscripts in the county clerk's office.

The number preceding the name indicates the militia district of the citizen; the number following shows the number of acres of his land.

These lists supplement those on page 449 of Wayland's History of Rockingham County.

List by Ralph Loftus, Commissioner

1 Alce, Adam	180	6 Bowman, Joseph	152
3 Aylor, John	44	6 Brumfield & Company	79
3 Aylor, Henry	140	6 Brumfield, David not Com. &c.	320
4 Alford, John	180	6 Brannaman, David	220
4 Aldorpha, John	15	6 Bowers, Andrew	153
4 Amond, Mathias	1180	6 Bear, John	114
5 Argabright, Martin	508	6 Burkholder, Peter	543
5 Argabright, Adam	140	7 Bible, Adam	356
5 Apler, John	146	7 Baker, Michael	581
(With Hickes)		7 Bags, John	220
5 Auker, Peter	125	7 Bible, Adam, Jr.	113
1 Black, Henry	280	1 Crawford, Johns	363
1 Blain, William	130	1 Coul, William	384
1 Boyd, William	97½	2 Crawford, Geo.	800
1 Bowyer, Wm. A.	155	2 Calhoun, James	175
2 Bowers, Thomas	100	2 Campbell, Thomas	457
2 Berry, David	478	2 Coffman, Jacob	406
2 Berry, Benj.	901	2 Cromer, Martin	180
2 Baxter, George	1196	2 Currys, Robt. & John	350
2 Brannamon, Abraham	200	2 Crisman, Mary	300
2 Beery, Abraham	157	3 Cooglar, George	195
2 Blain, John	307	3 Cloverfield, Ann	120
3 Butt, Windle	557	4 Campbell, Elisabeth	128
3 Black, Frederick	302	4 Cathrea, John	890
4 Byerel, Joseph	326	4 Campbell, Robert	206
4 Brown, Peter	158	4 Caller, Ludwick	169
4 Baker, John	100	5 Currys, James	
4 Beard, James	1365	5 Cravens, Robert	539
5 Burges, Henry		5 Coonrod, Peter	
5 Broombaker, Henry	421	5 Cravens, William	251
5 Brown, Michael	55	6 Casner, George	235
5 Boshong, Jacob	223	6 Click, Margaret	200
5 Bradey, Coward		6 Coffman, Jacob	180
5 Black, John	134	6 Custard, Jacob	275
6 Briant, William	100	6 Crest, Andrew	135
6 Briant, Morgan	100	6 Chennington, William	83
6 Briant, Cornelius	100	6 Contryman, Henry	278
6 Briant, John	100	6 Coffman, David	288
6 Briant, Thomas, Sr.	954	6 Crisman, George	375
6 Bowman, Jacob, Sr.	240	6 Crumbaker, Peter	186
6 Bowman, Susanna	128	6 Cring, John	324
6 Bowers, Laurence	100	7 Custard, Conrad	169
6 Bear, Jacob	127	7 Counce, Polser	100

7 City, Peter	220
7 City, Christian	54
7 Crumbaker, Abraham	95
7 Custard, Richard	93
7 Caplinger, Christian	134
7 Custner, Jacob	134
1 Douglas, Joseph	975
1 Davison, Arther	200
1 Dever, William	575
1 Dever, John	319
1 Dever, Hugh	506
1 Dunn, James	325
1 Davies, John	1380
2 Davison, Josiah	980
2 Dunlap, Robt.	230
2 Doke, James	400
3 Deck, Hyerenomus	256
4 Doddman, Christian	120
4 Doubt, Mathias	195
4 Deck, Henry	165
4 Deck, Jacob	70
4 Donaghe, Hugh	734
5 Dictim, Joseph	230
5 Dever, James, Land Co.	1283
5 Dundore, Catharine	250
5 Dyger, Gasper	70
5 Dickinson Dan'l & Nath.	220
6 Davies, William	130
6 Dunlap, William	230
7 Doup, Henry	308
7 Despenny, Joseph	189
1 Cruin, Benjamin Revd.	200
1 Cruin, Francis	470
1 Cruin, Samuel	147
1 Cruin, Benjamin	150
1 Cruin, Henry	356
2 Cruins, John, Sr.	875
5 Cuins, Henry	1101
5 Cuins, John, Jr.	
1 Fulton, Thomas	200
3 Fowler, William	150
3 Fifer, Augustine	393
4 Fisher, Abraham	514
4 Frazier, John	182
4 Fall, Martin	228
5 Flickinger, Christian	74
6 Ford, Michael	88
6 Forsythe, Abraham	150
7 Fitzwater, Thomas	171
7 Fitzwater, William	214
7 Fulk, John	270
7 Feezle, Michael	293
1 Guin, James	480
2 Gordon, Thomas	340
2 Green, Zekiel	155
2 Gilmore, James	175
2 Gilmore, Sam'l. Thos. & Alex.	50
2 Green, Francis	703
3 Green, Daniel	100
3 Grattan, Jr.	2047
3 Gray, Jacob	110

3 Gartin, Uriah	405
5 Graham, John & Jas.	
5 Guin, John	78
5 Guin, Patt	106
5 Guin, Randolph	100
5 Guin, James	186
5 Gay, Samuel	
6 Green, James & Jos.	350
6 Gum, Norton	100
6 Gum, Sarah	275
6 Grattan, John	915
1 Heart, Silas	704
1 Henry, Henry	442
1 Henry, John	150
1 Hamilton, Gawin	952
2 Hopkins, John Jr.	301
2 Hopkins, Jn., Sr.	419
2 Hopkins, Arch, Jr.	586
2 Hopkins, Arch, Sr.	1551
2 Hinton, Joseph	446
2 Herdman, John, Sr.	390
2 Herdman, John, Jr.	572
2 Hinton, Ebenezer & Benj.	466
2 Hinton, Benj. & Ralston	130
2 Hinton, Benj.	62
2 Harrison, Jess, Jr.	285
2 Harrison, Daniel	78
2 Higins, William	164
2 Harrison, Jess, Sr.	544
2 Heaten, Jonas	22
3 Hening, William	516
3 Hulvey, Coonrad	275
3 Huffman, Valentine	286
3 Herring, Bethuel	278
3 Huston, John	100
3 Herring, William	400
3 Harnsberger, Stephen	298
4 Huston, Mary	392
4 Huston, George	703
4 Huston, Nathan	275
4 Hook, Robert Sr.	400
4 Hook, James	200
4 Hudlow, Jacob	350
4 Huston, John	297
4 Hudlow, George Jr.	350
4 Hudlow, John	150
4 Houlder, Michael	680
4 Hook, Robert Jr.	170
4 Hook, William	327
4 Hanna, Joseph	496
4 Hay, Alexander	320
5 Harrison, Robt. & Ruben	
5 Hicks, John	
5 Herring, Leonard	230
5 Harrison, Benjamin	1024
5 Harrison, Robert & Ruben	1620
5 Harrison, Thomas	860
5 Hemphill, Samuel	653
5 Hinton, James	22
5 Hair, Samuel	1
6 Headrick, Charles	260

6 Harris, John	200
6 Howman, John	150
7 Honiker, Hedrick	75
7 Humble, Conrod	91
7 Hearter, George	136
2 Johnston, John	300
6 Johnston, John, Poages Tract	130
1 King, Thomas	244
2 Knowland's	279
4 Kyzer, Valentine	211
4 Kiplinger, John	400
4 Kiplinger, Philip	220
4 Keester, Philip, Sr.	217
4 Keester, Philip	52
4 Knowles, William	135
4 Kirkhoof, Stophel	125
6 Kesler, Woolery	550
7 Kester, Paul	245
1 Loftus, Ralph	246
2 Linvil, Benjamin	300
3 Laird, David Augusta	282
5 Love, Daniel's Exro.	278
5 Lenachan, Dennis	
6 Lincoln, John, Sr.	200
6 Lincoln, Jacob	425
6 Lear, Mathias	237
6 Lincoln, John, Jr.	15
7 Lear, Ferdinand	146
1 Malcolm, John, Jr.	150
1 McDowell, Thomas	198
1 Miller, John	748
1 Miller, Henry	671
1 Magill, James	438
2 Mathews, Townsend	345
2 McCartney, James	136
3 McMurry, Barnabas	100
3 Morris, Morris	300
4 McCreery Williams	175
4 Machall, John	1282
4 Miller, Leonard	351
4 Mefford, John	100
5 McWilliams, Samuel	
5 Mitchel, James	
5 McClain, Charles	
5 Miller, Samuel	410
5 Miller, Isaac	370
5 Miller, Samuel's Exrs.	636
5 Martin, James	
5 Mathews, Solomon	75
6 Masberger, Martin	95
6 Masberger, John	95
7 Marshall, Elisabeth	100
7 Miller, Abraham	412
7 Moyer, Michael	45
4 Nicewonger, Christian	91
6 Noffsinger, Jacob	236
3 Oat, Francis	50
5 Oliver, Jerimah	150
2 Palcer, Peter	130
3 Poss, Nicholas	120
4 Painter, Leonard	140

4 Perkey, John	200
5 Peebler, Lewis	195
6 Peery, Nicholas, Sr.	240
6 Peery, Nicholas, Jr.	145
7 Parrott, Joseph	131
7 Parrott, Samuel	120
7 Price, David	160
1 Rice, John	861
1 Rader, David	180
1 Ralston, James	250
2 Ralston, David	451
2 Ralston, David, Jr.	48
3 Ragin, Richard	99
3 Roler, Peter	1033
3 Rudok, Cornelius	502
4 Rust, Valentine	140
4 Rodearmer, Barbara	320
5 Reeves, Bruer	
6 Rimil, Philip	174
6 Rife, Jacob	231½
6 Robison, William	304
6 Robison, Riley	50
6 Rodes, Henry	150
6 Robison, Widow	305
6 Rodes, Christian	137
6 Ruddle, Cornelius	704
7 Ruddle, John	335
7 Runion, John	213
7 Ruddle, Stephen	490
7 Rineheart, Adam	125
7 Ruddle, George	54
1 Smith, John	435
1 Smith, Benjamin	230
1 Stephenson, William	280
1 Smith, William	858
1 Smith, Henry	1053
1 Shipman, Isaiah	430
1 Smith, Joseph	582
2 Shanklin, Elisabeth	250
2 Samples, Robert	299
2 Shanklin, Thomas	853
2 Spitler, Jacob	207
3 Steward, Francis	230
3 Sanger, Jacob	268
3 Shanklin, Edward	575
3 Snowdon, William	467
3 Sayer, Lewis	175
3 Smith, Abraham	100
4 Sively, Catharine	84
4 Shoukerman, Henry	120
4 Snap, John	629
4 Scott, Jacob	325
4 Safely, Valentine	300
4 Smith, Jacob	112
4 Srum, David	306
4 Snider, Henry	350
4 Surface, Martin	228
4 Shirea, Michael	37
4 Shirea, Jacob	203
5 Scott, Thomas	
5 Shipman, Jonathan	

5 Stephenson, Caster	879	4 Turk, Thomas	164
5 Shanklin, Andrew	255	5 Tiffney, Hugh	
5 Smith, Benjamin	955	5 Turner, John	
5 Smith, Margaret	173	6 Trout, Michael	170
5 Sulivan, Thomas		6 Thomas, John	683
5 Sheltman, Phelix	6	6 Thomas, Reece	433
6 Smith, John	208	7 Trumboe, Jacob	420
6 Sights, "Johin"	270	1 Vicars, Elias	200
6 Shaver, Nicholas	441	2 Vance, Handle, Sr.	170
6 Shoemaker, Peter	190	6 Vance, Handle & John	250
6 Shank, Henry	250	1 Wagey, Philip	80
6 Shank, Adam	100	1 Weldon, Edward	215
6 Spears, George	445	1 Walker, Thomas	900
6 Strock, Joshua	190	3 Wise, Michael	100
7 Shoemaker, George	500	3 Wise, John	237
7 Shoemaker, Simon	234	4 Wilberger, Mathias	250
7 Stults, Peter	159	4 Witmore, Jacob	196
1 Taylor, John	400	5 Wolwine, Mrs.	
2 Teeter, Abraham	150	5 Winger, Henry	500
2 Thomas, Evan	379	6 Whistler, Henry	225
3 Tanner, John	140		
4 Troubough, William	291	7 Witsel, Martin	369
4 Tutwiler, Leonard	328	7 Witsel, Henry	104

List by Reuben Moore, Ccmmissioner

8 Josiah Harrison's Company		13 Beesley, Jeremiah	244
9 Ezekiel Harrison's Company		13 Bear, Jacob, Jr.	450
10 Richard Ragan's Company		13 Bear Henry	450
11 John Rush's Company		13 Bear, Adam	194
12 Casper Hains' Company		14 Berry, Mallekiah	159
13 Henry Miller's Company		14 Bush, William	75
14 Michael Rorick's Company		14 Brier, Edward	150
8 Armontrout, George	150	8 Counce, Martin	165
8 Acort, Jacob	150	8 Counce, Peter	246
9 Andrews, Andrew	600	8 Counce, Phillip	90
9 Airhart, George	360	8 Cummins, Moses	320
10 Armontrout, Peter	174	8 Cowen, Henry	100
10 Armontrout, John	353¾	9 Carn, Nicholas	341
10 Alstott, John	50	9 Crumpacker, John	323
10 Armontrout, Phillip	173	9 Caplinger, Christian	115
10 Armontrout, George	140	9 Crim, Peter	516
11 Armontrout, Henry	147	10 Crow, Walter	759
11 Armontrout	357	10 Crotzer, Joseph	641½
11 Argabright, Jacob, Sr.	336	10 Conrad, Joseph	150
12 Ammon,Cristophel	238	10 Conrod, Jacob	120
8 Beaver, Matthias	386	11 Coffelt, Vollentine	193
8 Bird, Abraham	163	11 Craig, John	1314
8 Bird, Andrew	270	11 Carpenter, George	449
8 Butcher, James	200	11 Carpenter, John	110
9 Bear, John, Sr.	836	12 Conrad, Stephen	377
9 Bowman, John	270	12 Cook, Henry	188
10 Bowyer, Ingle	334	12 Carsh, Matthias	680
10 Bell, Laurence	200	12 Conrad, Peter	890
10 Bright, John	238	12 Conrad, George	844
11 Bruster, James	265	14 Comer, Cristophel	120
12 Black, Henry	90	8 Dilling, William	145
12 Barnett, Agness	250	8 Dunkerson, Thomas	228
12 Brannamore, Anthony	401	10 Dickey, Robert	191
12 Brannamore, Peter	426	10 Dippoy, Isaac	400
12 Boyer, John	140	12 Deck, Michael	281
13 Bloss, Adam	160	13 Davis, William	841

9	Eator, Henry	194
9	Easterly, George	130
10	Ellett, Robert	237
10	Eversole, Jacob	310
8	Funk, Peter	60
9	Foland, Frederick	200
9	Fulmore, Ludwick	84
9	Fry, Crisley	170
9	Fifer, Adam, Sr.	602
10	Fought, Adam	469
11	Fulwiler, Jacob	70
12	Frye, Crisley	144
13	Fudge, Mary	244
14	Fulce, John, Sr.	420
14	Fulce, George	90
9	Grove, Cristian	480
10	Grub, Danniel	163
11	Gilmore, Peachy	490
14	Griggsbe, John	100
8	Helfrey, John	131¼
8	Henton, William	8
8	Harrison, Reuben	1204
8	Harrison, Zebulon	575
8	Holsinger, Michael	290
8	Harrison, Josiah	280
8	Hoof, John	264
8	Harrison, John	155
8	Harrison, Matthew	900
8	Henton, Mary, wd.	63
8	Hulings, Catharine	81
9	Hennigan, Michael	180
9	Hauber, Michael	160
9	Hartinger, Conrod	80
9	Hoover, Jacob	516
9	Heasting, Jacob	225
10	Harrison, Nathaniel	200
10	Harrison, John	938
10	Harrison, Hannah	300
10	Hagay, Godfrey	730
10	Harned, David	795
10	Howard, Christophel	280
10	Herring, Leonard	318
10	Harpole, Jacob	100
10	Harmon, George	190
12	Hammer, John	100
12	Haines, Frederick	230
12	Hartman, John	411
12	Haines, John	157
12	Haines, Jonas	240
12	Headrick, John	625
12	Haines, Casper	217
12	Haines, Peter	217
12	Hufmon, George	138
12	Hufmon, Michael	137
13	Hashmon, Peter	110
13	Hansbarger, Adam	350
13	Hansbarger, Conrod	155
14	Hashmon, Danniel	250
14	Hoard, William	200
10	Jammison, Andrew	
11	Jones, Gabriel	1004

11	Iler, Peter	110
8	Kephart, Henry	250
9	Ketner, Jacob	200
9	Knave, Henry	118
9	Kesler, John	135
9	Kips, Michael	205
9	Konkle, Jacob	220
10	Kessle, George	810
10	Kisore, Isaac	84
10	King, Sammuel	79
11	Kiger, Christian	200
11	Kislinger, Jacob	615
12	Kislinger, Peter	235
12	Kaylor, Michael	150
12	Kirtley, Francis	824
12	Kisling, Henry	9
14	Kite, William	260
14	Kite, George	75
14	Kisore, Michael	566
14	Kite, John	70
14	Kite, John, Sr.	280
14	Kite, Phillip	60
8	Lokey, Thomas	530
8	Lokey, James	266
10	Lear, Joseph	366
10	Lard, James	256
10	Lear, Joseph	407
11	Lard, David	445
11	Lewis, Thomas, Sr.	2050
12	Lingle, Jacob	333
13	Lingle, Paul	257
13	Loins, Robert	280
14	Lung, Henry	200
14	Louderback, Matthias	100
14	Louderback, Joseph	160
14	Long, Barbara	100
8	March, Saboston	515
8	McDole, William	452
8	Moore, Thomas, Sr.	1070
9	Miller, David	276
9	Moore, John Quaker	1088
9	Miller, Abraham	188
9	Minnick, John	100
10	Mole, Edward	216
11	Miller, Peter	260
11	Mann, George	195
11	Miller, Peter, Sr.	95
11	Mallow, George, Sr.	359
11	Michael, William	237
11	Miltebarger, Nicholas	240
12	Michael, Frederick	133
12	Monger, John	274
12	Monger, Henry	340
13	Miller, Henry & Elisabeth	1215
13	Miller, Catharine	390
13	Meadows, Francis	400
14	Moier, Jacob	430
11	Monger, David	160
8	Newman, Walter	100
9	Nestrick, John	235
9	Nestherod, Frederick	83

11	Nicholas, Henry	79	
11	Nicholas, Peter, Jr.	71	
11	Nicholas, Barbary	100	
11	Nicholas, Jacob	30	
11	Nicholas, Peter, Sr.	125	
13	Nall, William	44	
14	Null, George	250	
14	Null, Henry	695	
9	Oreboh, Andrew	281	
9	Oreboh, Adam	274	
12	Osmus, Peter	111	
14	Oler, John	184	
14	Oler, William	260	
14	Oler, Henry	187	
8	Phillips, John, Sr.	540	
8	Phillips, John, Jr.	357	
8	Pickerel, William	150	
9	Painter, Chrisley	279	
9	Pup, Cristian	100	
9	Pup, Henry	164	
9	Pitner, John	415	
11	Pence, George	703	
11	Perkey, Jacob	360	
11	Pence, John, Sr.	179	
11	Perkey, John	515	
11	Perkey, Henry	515	
11	Pence, Adam	135	
11	Price, Augusteen, Sr.	531	
11	Price, Augusteen, Jr.	192	
11	Price, Frederick	195	
11	Pence, Jacob	105	
12	Price, Henry	178	
12	Peterfish, Conrod	266	
12	Peterfish, John	34	
12	Pence, William	238	
13	Peters, Jacob	270	
14	Price, Danniel	417	
8	Rickerboher, Adam	114	
8	Rorick, Fellomon	100	
8	Ramboe, Jacob	54	
8	Reeves, John	400	
9	Reader, Anthony	345	
9	Reader, Adam	245	
9	Reader, Mathias	350	
9	Roland, Richard	115	
9	Reader, Michael	84	
9	Roller, Peter	108	
10	Ragan, Richard	736	
10	Ragan, Jeremiah	479	
10	Rutherford, Ellett	434	
10	Rutherford, Joseph	384	
10	Robison, John	251½	
10	Roadcap, Peter	199	
11	Rush, John	443	
11	Rush, Charles	553	
12	Rape, Jacob	300	
12	Runkle, Peter	389	
12	Rhinehart, Ludwick	55	
13	Roach, Reuben	150	
14	Runkle, Ludwick	120	

14	Runkle, Jacob	100	
14	Rorick, Michael	172	
14	Rutherford, Robert	180	
8	Sircle, Ludwick	932	
8	Sircle, George	250	
8	Stephen, Ludwick	249	
8	Smith, Conrod	235	
8	Slusser, Henry	280	
9	Stolph, Henry	225	
9	Shoemaker, Henry	60	
9	Stolph, John, Sr.	165	
10	Sellers, Michael	106	
10	Scorethorn, Ann	107	
10	Shulce, Charles	312	
10	Sheets, George	193	
10	Smith, David	120	
10	Smith, Jane, Sr.	500	
10	Smith, Benjamin	500	
10	Smith, Jane, Jr.	383	
10	Smith, Danniel (Exct.)	88	
10	Smith, William, Jr.	165	
10	Smith, Vollentine	155	
10	Swhing, Godfrey	210	
10	Sheltman, John	30	
10	Smith, Benjamin	323	
11	Shaver, George, Sr.	210	
11	Snider, Conrod	249	
11	Spotts, Jacob	84	
11	Swisher, John	676	
12	Sink, Danniel	43	
12	Sellers, John	394	
12	Sellers, Adam	1154	
12	Sellers, Peter, Sr.	396	
13	Smith, Briton	157	
13	Smith, Jacob	60	
13	Smith, John	200	
13	Smith, Mary	400	
14	Strickler, John	230	
14	Shuler, Matthias	300	
14	Slaughter, Robert	430	
8	Taylor, Notiff	234	
8	Tallman, Benjamin	170	
8	Tallman, William, Sr.	74	
9	Thomas, John	155	
9	Trumboe, Jacob, Jr.	150	
9	Trout, Felty	350	
10	Toreman, Andrew	173	
12	Tousler, Henry	225	
14	Tofflemire, Michael	188	
10	Vanpelt, Tunis	148	
8	Woodley, Jacob	300	
9	Wine, Adam	222	
9	White, Alexander	350	
10	Wearren, Michael	433½	
10	Wolf, Vollentine	400	
10	Wise, John	215	
10	Williams, Robert	156	
11	Weaver, George	590	
13	Williams, Edward	300	

ABSTRACT OF CHURCH RECORDS

Linville Creek, Smith Creek, Brock's Gap, &c., 1756 to 1844

These records, very full for the early years, antedate the county records of Rockingham (first a part of Augusta) by 22 years. Augusta County was organized in 1745; Rockingham, from Augusta, in 1778. These old church records begin in 1756.

The Linville Creek Baptist Church organized August 6, 1756, in accordance with the confession of faith adopted by the Baptist Association at Philadelphia, 1742; reprinted 1743.

Charter members: Rev. John Alderson; his wife, Jane Alderson; Samuel Newman; his wife, Martha Newman; John Harrison; William Castle Berry; his wife, Margaret Castle Berry.

John Thomas, baptized prior to August 6, 1756; his brother, James Thomas, baptized August 7, 1756; both received into full communion and fellowship by the charter members.

Rees Thomas and Mary States, belonging to Pennsylvania churches, were admitted to transient communion.

The foregoing 11 joined in the first communion, August 7, 1756.

August 6, 1756, Samuel Newman was called to be church clerk and was also put upon trial as a deacon. He probably wrote the minutes and the various historical notes in connection.

Samuel Newman and his wife, members of Montgomery Church, Philadelphia County, were the first members of any Baptist church to settle hereabouts. They came evidently (not definitely stated) in or about 1744.

Soon afterwards John Harrison, Sr., "being convinced of his Duty to come to the holy Ordinance of Baptism, went for it somewhere towards New York, to a Place called Oyster-Bay; but was received then a Member of no particular Church; But by a Certificate of his Baptism, was recommended to be received, or associated into any Church of that Order, where God in his Providence should shew most convenient for him. In all this While, there was no Minister of that Denomination came here."

The next Baptist family, whereof the head was a member, was that of Rees Thomas, who settled on Linville Creek.

The next was Sister Mary Newman, wife of Jonathan Newman, "belonging to the Church of Christ in Southamton, in the County of Bucks."

Rees Thomas belonged to the church of the same order in Cumry Township, Lancaster County.

About this time Mr. Samuel Eaton, the first Baptist minister in orders, visited these parts "and preached at old Mr. Harrisons, the only Disciple he knew to be in the Place."

The next "in Order" was Mr. Benjamin Griffith, who came on purpose to visit the aforesaid Brother Samuel Newman. "The next after him was our Reverend Brother (John Alderson) whom God at last was pleased to send as his Instrument, to settle this Church."

"His first Visit was to Rees Thomas, and on Linvils Creek, the Forest, and North River, where the People were much affected, and prepared to receive further instructions from his Mouth. The next in Order was again Mr. Samuel Eaton, he visited only the inhabitants of Smiths Creek."

"Then God was pleased to visit the Inhabitants of Smiths Creek, Linvils Creek, and North River of Shenandoah, the Places where now the Church is built, by Mr. John Gano, a faithful Servant of his, who was received by the Love and Likeing of almost all sorts of People. After him the Revrd. Mr. Alderson visited again his second Time; and then began to conclude to come and Settle; and bought Land, and then came, and through the Grace of God, was instrumental in gathering the Church, by whom also She was constituted, and the first Pastor of the Church of Christ, at Smiths and Linvils Creeks, in Frederick and Augusta County's."

"Thus was the Labours of those Gentlemen aforenamed, for the Space of Eleven Years, from the First Setler, as above named, and about one Year before the Consititution of the Church."

(Note by J. W. W.—Thus the year when Samuel Newman came is fixed as about 1744.)

William Castle Berry and his wife, of Newbritain Church, came and settled on Muddy Creek, Augusta County.

"Our Revd Pastor Mr. John Alderson, and Mrs. Jane Alderson his Wife, being both Members of Newbritan Church in the County of Bucks, moved their Residence, and came to us the same Spring before we were Constituted."

The church covenant, prayers, hymns, etc., are included in the record.

October, 1756, at a general meeting by "the three congregational Churches of Christ, baptised on personal Profession of Faith; in Fairfax & Frederick Counties, in Virginia; it was agreed that the said Churches do Annually Meet at some one of their several Meeting-Houses, to hold Communion and Fellowship together, on the second Sabbath of June in each Year hereafter, to begin with the Church of Christ at Smiths Creek in June the Second Sabbath 1757."

The next member added at Linville Creek was Mary Barrot, wife of Authur Barrot, she being brought up in Quakerism; received in April, 1757.

Next was Catherine Harrison, wife of Jeremiah Harrison; received second Sunday of May 1757; third communion; present Rev. Malachi Bonam of East Jersey.

Next communion, 2d "Sabbath" in June 1757, by appointment of the three churches aforesaid in annual meeting; present Rev. Alderson, Rev. John Garret, minister in Fairfax County, also of Mill Creek, Frederick County. Public worship on three successive days.

During these meetings the following persons were received as members of the church, at "the North River of Shannandoah, and Linvils Creek": Wife of George Nicholas (she a zealous Presbyterian of good report); "The other a Gentleman of no mean Character, a Man in Authority both civil and military; Cornelius Ruddell, by Name, who had often opposed the Truths we profess publickly."

Ruddell was formerly a Church of England man.

Next yearly meeting set for Catockton Church, Fairfax County, second Sunday in June 1758.

Second Saturday in July (1757), at a Linville Creek church meeting, it was agreed that the members lay by them in store, as they may be blest, some moiety to be given quarterly at the church meeting, for the use of the church, as she shall think proper and as her occasions may call, for the glory of God "and for the Assisting travailing Ministers, when they come to Visit, or are called."

The day following (2d Sunday in July 1757) was held the 5th communion.

August 1757, 2d Saturday, it was enacted that the collecting for church use begin at the next monthly meeting. Non-members were also to be given an opportunity to contribute. John Thomas and William Castle Berry were appointed to "lift the Collection." A letter was to be sent to the Catocton Church; also to be read at Mill Creek—a letter of love, desiring correspondence.

August 1757, 2d Sunday, Mary Denham, wife of Joseph Denham, was baptized and received into membership; the 6th communion. Mary Denham had been brought up a Quaker.

"About this Time arose certain of the Favourers of that Scriptureless Practice, Infant Sprinkling, and, in a disorderly manner, called one Alexander Miller to their Assistance, to go Ridicule & Slander our Ministers, and our Church Officer, who at that Time did officiate the Office of Deacon by the Churches Appointment, which said Miller had before ridiculously aspersed our Rev. Brother of being a Baptist.

"Accordingly, on Wednesday the 21st of Septem. 1757, the said Miller and a rude Assembly with him, in a disorderly Manner, without Leave, or previous Notice given to the Church, or Persons by him accused, opened our Meeting House, and assumed our Pulpit, and there slanderously, falsely, and contrary to Christian Rule & Order (did) dispitefully use our Minister, and Brother, the Deacon, with approbrious Speeches, of Spite & Malice, entirely untruth, and unknown to the said parties; and of which we are fully convinced, neither of them were guilty of the Errors by him charged, neither in Thought, Word, or Deed, which said Irregular and disorderly Practice of his, has since occasioned Animosities in the Neighbourhood, and he the said Miller, hath been thereby instrumental, in the Hands of Satan, to disturb the Churches Peace, and the Peace of the Neighbourhood, this being a Time of noted Peace with us, in the Midst of Difficulties elsewhere."

(Note by J. W. W.—Alexander Miller was probably Rev. Alexander Miller, a noted Presbyterian minister of the neighborhood. The charges were evidently directed against Rev. John Alderson and Deacon Samuel Newman. The "Difficulties elsewhere" were likely those in connection with the French and Indian War, which was then in progress.)

"The Wednesday following this riotous Action, it pleased God to permit the Heathen (Indians) to fall on our Settlements, and disordered the whole worse than they had done themselves, the Week before. A just Retaliation for such unheard of Proceedings and Measures they had taken &c. The aforesaid Proceedings, together with the Indian Troubles, hindered our Church Meetings, from that Time, till the first Saturday in January 1758; at which Time the kind Providence of God enabled us to regulate so many of the Disorders that attended us, as that with Comfort and Peace, we could proceed." . . .

January 1758, 2d Sunday, 7th communion.

"After this Time, the Spring coming on, the Indian Troubles continued, and all Opportunities of Meetings were taken from us; and not only so, but the whole Neighbourhood forced either to go into Forts or over the Mountains, to escape their Rage, in the month of June following."

"During which Time of Troubles, divine Providence seemed entirely against us, and the whole Neighbourhood; and some Disorders happened in these Troubles amongst our own Members. . . .

"These Disconveniences continued, and got no better, till the Summer of the Year 1759, when it pleased God to make our Armies victorious in the North Part of our Continent, which drew the Enemy from us, so that the Forts that harboured them to our Hurt fell into our Hands without Blood shed."

(Note by J. W. W.—The defeat of General Braddock, near the site of Pittsburgh, in July 1755, exposed all the Virginia frontier to invasions by the Indians and French. Fort Seybert, about 25 miles northwest from Linville Creek, was captured by the Indians in 1758, probably in the summer. From 1755 to 1758 the Indians devastated the frontier settlements. But in November 1758 the English captured Fort Duquesne (Pittsburgh), and in September 1759 they took Quebec, the key to Canada. Thenceforth the Virginians had relief.)

"And when the Summer of 1759 was ended, and the Enemy not permitted to break in upon us, in the Month of September the Church assembled together, on Saturday the 22d, and by the good Hand of God with us, setled the Disorders of her Body, so that on Sunday, the 23d, the Lords Supper was celebrated in its usual Solemnity and was our Eighth Communion since Constitution. At this Time there were two Members added viz. Jeremiah Ozban & Mary Ozban his Wife; and all our Members were together save two; one by reason of Distance and Cumber; the other disobedient and disorderly, refused to come, who having walked disorderly & riotous, was by the Church set aside, and not to be allowed Communion, nor may Act as a Member thereof, till Satisfaction given, viz. Cornelius Ruddell."

"From the Time last noted, by Reason of the Length of the Way, the Difficulty of Winter, the Troubles of removing back from our Flights caused by the Enemy, and great Affliction of the Small-Pox raging in the Land, we had not an Opportunity to meet in Church Order nor hold Communion till the 10th of August 1760, when it pleased God, of his great Mercy to permit some few of us to meet," . . . 9th communion since constitution; next appointed for 2d Sunday of October following.

A small number met in October as appointed; 10th communion.

"From which Time till the fourth Sabbath of May 1761, Disappointments of one Kind or another happened, that we could not come together, at which Time it pleased God to grant us a good Time . . . and an Addition of a new Member to our Body viz. one Philip Fegans."

Appointed Friday for fasting and prayer; Saturday for church business; and Sunday following (last Sunday of August 1761) for ordinances of the Gospel.

A few met on Friday for fasting and prayer. On Saturday a goodly number attended and 5 offered for baptism: Thomas Porter, Jeremiah Harrison, John Ozban, his wife Elizabeth Ozban, and Esther North, wife of John North. John North, having been baptized elsewhere, was admitted to transient communion; and Sarah Thomas, wife of James Thomas, was also admitted. James Thomas was already a member. On Sunday (last in August 1761) was held the 11th communion.

Second Sunday in May 1762, Sarah Porter, wife of Thomas Porter, was admitted to membership; 12th communion.

Saturday before 2d Sunday of August 1762, Thomas George and his wife were baptized.

"The Day following, being the Day appointed for the Ordinance of the Lords Supper, there was a great Congregation of People gathered, which by the good Hand of God with us, was awed with a profound Silence, and behaved with Reverence." The 13th communion.

The 2d Sunday in November (1762) was appointed for next communion. Rev. John Alderson was chosen as messenger to the association; Samuel Newman was ordered to draw the association letter.

The said appointment was "frustrated." But on December 25 the 14th communion was celebrated. March 1763, 2d Sunday, was set for the next meeting.

"But the Church was disappointed for lack of Wine for its Use, but the Association Letter was read, and the Church of Smiths Creek, a Branch of North Shanandoah, in Frederick County, was received into Fellowship with the Association of the associate Churches, of the same Faith and Gospel Order at Philadelphia, October 12, 1762. Then the Church proceeded to her Business, in her own Body, and called Thomas George and John Thomas to Officiate in the Office of Ruling Elders upon Trial."

"The Church then took it under their Consideration, the Circumstance of our Meetinghouse, and according to Circumstances all the Male Members subscribed each Twenty Shillings, to carry on that good Work. And our Widows, heads of Families, each ten Shillings; and some others, to the amount of twelve pounds, five shillings."

The 5th Sunday of May (1763) was appointed for the next communion.

On the said Sunday (following a business meeting on Saturday) the 15th communion was held, Rev. David Thomas of Fauquier being present.

The next appointments, August (4th Sunday and Saturday preceding) 1763, were "by the barbarous Enemy the Indians disappointed; the Church being scattered, and no Communion celebrated, nor other Meeting in its stead. But at a publick Meeting at Linvils Creek, the Church was called on to meet as a Church for Business, on the last Saturday of September next, being the 24th Day, which they did at the Dwelling house of Samuel Newman; where they recalled that Brother to the Office of an Elder, and continued the Call of the other two." . . .

On May 26, 1764, Sister Jane Rodgers, a member of the church at Cumm, Berks Co., Pa., was provided lodging at Samuel Newman's. John Alderson and Samuel Newman were requested to look after her. Her son-in-law, Thomas Evans, was reported as having mistreated her.

The next business meeting of the church was held on Saturday, April 20, 1765; "And as Samuel Newman and Martha his Wife were moving away to some Parts of North or South Carolina, sued for Letters of Dismission, which was granted. And likewise Phillip Fegans sued for a Letter of Dismission, to the same Place, or Places, as Providence may direct, which was likewise granted by the Church. And, as Mary Barrot is by her Husband moved away; but came first and desired, That when the Church should sit on Business, they would please to send her Dismission by Samuel Newman; which was also granted."

On this date (April 20, 1765) Thomas Porter was made church clerk. John Thomas and Thomas George were dismissed from trial of ruling elders. Thomas Porter and John Ozban were called to trial in their stead; and Thomas George was put on trial as deacon in room of Thomas Porter.

Saturday before 2d Sunday of May was appointed to be a day of examination "on the Ground of the Points of Faith, and the Day following for the Sacrament Day.

"Met the Saturday before the second Sabbath in May (1765), according to Appointment, but was not examined; being detained by a Person who offered himself for Baptism, but was not admited, by Reason of some Difference between him and a certain Person in the Neighbourhood. For which Reason the Church was pleased to

appoint our Rev. Brother Mr. John Alderson and Thomas George, to
see if they could make up this Matter.   Next Day was the Sacrament
administered.   This is the 16th Communion since Constitution."

On the 2d Sunday of June (1765) were added two members, viz.
Joseph Thomas and a Negro man called Joe.   Appointed 2d Sunday
of August for next communion "at Linvils Creek Meeting-House."

On 2d Sunday of August John Ray and Thomas Evans were
admitted to membership.

"And then was admitted into transient Communion a Person of
Quality viz. Silas Hart by Name. . . . Then the Church appcinted
to meet the fourth Saturday in September next, and every Male
Member to pay seven Shillings for Mr. Aldersons Journey to the
Association in Philadelphia."

Met 4th Saturday in September (1765).   19th communion.

Met 2d Sunday in April, 1766.   Nicholas Fain was received into
transient communion, "and Joseph Thomas excommunicated, for
scandalizing a young Woman, and refusing to obey the Calls of the
Church." . . . 20th communion.

Met 3d Sunday in May (1766).   Silas Hart was received into
full communion by a letter from Penypack Church in Pennsylvania.

(Notes by J. W. W.—Silas Hart was a "person of quality."   He
was a magistrate and perhaps sheriff of Augusta County.   In 1778,
when Governor Patrick Henry appointed 17 justices for the new
county of Rockingham, the name of Silas Hart was first on the list.
Hart lived in that part of Augusta County that became Rockingham.
He was first sheriff of Rockingham.   John Thomas, another member
of the Linville Creek Church, was also one of the first 17 magistrates.

(In 1790 Silas Hart wrote his will.   He died in 1795.   In his
will he proposed to endow a foundation for the education of Baptist
ministers.   This was 29 years before the first Baptist theological
seminary (the one at Hamilton, N. Y.) in the United States was
founded.   The laudable provision of Brother Hart's will was not
sustained by the courts, owing to the indefinite form of statement of
the name of the trustee.   The case was in the courts for many years,
finally going to the U. S. Supreme Court.   In that august body no
less a jurist than Chief Justice John Marshall wrote the final
decision.   This decision was rendered in 1819, the very year in which
the theological seminary at Hamilton, N. Y., was established.)

On the 3d Sunday in June, 1766, Benjamin Alderson and Ann his
wife were baptized and admitted to membership at Linville Creek.
The 22d communion was held.

The last Sunday in July was appointed for preparing a letter to
the association.   On that date Grace Lockard, wife of Daniel
Lockard, was baptized.

Communion was held on the last Sunday in August (1766).
Ann Mace was baptized.

"An Yearly Meeting held in our Meeting-House on Smiths
Creek, the Second Sabbath in June 1767."

Communion the second Sunday of October 1767.

At a business meeting the last Saturday in May, 1768, Thomas Porter was appointed to warn John Ray to appear before the church to give satisfaction for some offences; Mr. John Alderson to warn John North to appear; and likewise James Thomas to warn John Thomas to appear at the meeting house on Smith Creek the last Saturday in June next.

"Met according to Appointment the last Saturday in June 1768, and the Church went upon Business within her own Body, and John Ray was censured in the highest Degree next to excommunication, for certain Offences committed, and is suspended from Communion with the Church untill Reformation and Repentance, by him had; and then appointed to meet at Linvils Creek the first Saturday in August next" (1768).

Met accordingly and a letter was prepared for the association.

The association was held at Smith Creek the 2d Saturday in August, 1768.

At a business meeting the 1st Saturday in March, 1769, John Alderson, Jr., was baptized.

In June 1769 was held a meeting of fasting and prayer.

On the 2d Saturday in August (1769) a letter was sent to the association. "Then the Church apointed to hold a Meeting the Second Saturday in September Anno Domini 1771, and also agreed and enacted that they would admonish Disorderly Members according to Church Discipline & Gospel Rule."

In 1771 were baptized Isaac Morris and Ruth his wife, Samuel Nicholas, and Curtis Alderson.

In 1772 were baptized Mary Henton, wife of Evan Henton; Ann Needham, wife of John Needham; Hester Wright; Susannah Ray, wife of John Ray; Mary Alderson, wife of John Alderson, Jr.

Also there were received into the church by letters Joshua Lewis, from New Valley Church; David Pergrin and wife Mary, from Great Valley Church, Pa.; and Thomas Woolsey, from a church in "New York Government, and now ordained for the Ministry by Order of this Church, by the Rev. Mr. Jno. Alderson."

On July 11, 1772, Joshua Lewis was to be "called out orderly on Tryal of his Gifts to preach the Gospel, and to give him a Certificate to go to Greenbriar or else where called."

August 8, 1772, a letter was ordered for the association. Andrew Davison, Hannah Alderson (wife of Thomas Alderson), Hannah Harrison (wife of John Harrison), Ann Dedrage, and Catherine Waren (wife of Timothy Waren), were baptized.

Sept. 12, 1772, David Pergrin was to warn Thomas Evans to appear at the next monthly meeting to give his reason why "he hath absented himself from his Place in the Church."

April 10, 1773, Isaac Moris was called to exercise his gifts as a ruling elder till further orders.

"2dly That the Church seek Mr. Jno. Jarard to suply us in our destitute Condition when Convenient for him."

"3dly that we are to hold our next Church Meeting at Brother Thomas Evans on the second Saturday in May, next."

On 2d Sunday in August (1773) a letter was ordered for the association. "And that Thomas Woolsey is to be dismist, and Ruth Morris is to be dismist. Ordered also that Brother Jno. Alderson junior preach at the Association, on the Tryal of his Gifts to exercise amongst us, and that a Collection be made for the Charges of the Deligate to go to the Association."

On 2d Saturday in September (1773) . . . "any Member, or Members, may have their Children brought before the Church and the Minister, to take them in his Arms, and beg a Blessing for them."

"3dly that Brother Jno. Thomas as a Delegate is to go & enquire of Silas Hart, what is his Reason for his Long Absence from the Church, and to make Report at the next Meeting."

Curtis Alderson was to inquire likewise of Sister Esther North, wife of John North.

Jeremiah Ozburn was to notify Ann Mace to attend the next meeting.

"6thly, That Mr. Jno. Alderson sn. is to be summoned to appear at our next monthly Meeting, to vindicate the Charges alledged against him."

"At a Meeting held the 11th of June 1774, the Church entered on Business, and Ordered, 1st, That our Revd Brother Jno Alderson be noticed, That he, with two other Members of this Church go and make faithful Enquiry concerning the Reproach, alledged against him by two Men in Frederick Town, in Maryland, and that before the Meeting that is to be held before the next Association."

David Pergrin and John Thomas were appointed to go to Maryland with Mr. Alderson.

Isaac Morris was dismissed by a letter to the church at Great Bethel.

"5thly, That the Church meet again on the Saturday before the Second Sabbath in next Month at the Forest."

(Note by J. W. W.—The Forest was—and is—the region between Timberville and Mt. Jackson, Forestville being the center thereof.)

July 9, 1774, some members of the church met together to act in behalf of the church, "but the Inconstancy of the Members hath so much abounded, that we are scarcly able to hold Meetings." . . .

August 6, 1774, "This Day met togethe.· the Members of our Church, living on Smiths Creek, in Order to examin into an Affair between Jno. Conner & Susannah Ray, the wife of Jno. Ray." . . .

John Alderson, Jr., and Hannah Harrison were appointed to examine the persons named.

August 13 (1774) John Conner was suspended for unseemly behavior with Sister Sarah Porter. Sarah Porter was also suspended.

Esther North, wife of John North, was suspended for inconstancy.

Rev. John Alderson, Sr., was also suspended.

August 12, 1775, "At a Monthly Meeting held at Linvils Creek, it was agreed 1st, That a collection be made, for the Use of the Association which was 10 10." (Probably 10 shillings and 10 pence.)

"2dly, That Brother Jno. Alderson jun. be sent to the Association, and be presented to the Trial of his Qualifications for Ordination."

"3dly, That Brother Jno. Alderson jun. & Brother David Pergrin be sent as Delegates to the Association, and a Collection be made for defraying their Charges."

About the last of October 1775 John Alderson, Jr., was according to regular order ordained minister at Linville Creek by Rev. John Marks.

The 2d Saturday in November 1775 monthly meeting and communion were held at Brother John Needham's house. John Needham and Ann Bland were baptized.

March 9, 1776, met at Thomas Evans's. Abraham Elger offered by letter and experience, but agreed to wait longer till better satisfied with his life.

John Thomas was to go to Brother Hart and hear his reason for absenting himself from church meetings. John Needham to John Conner. The same to John Ray. John Alderson to Sister North, continued. James Thomas to Ann Mace, continued.

May 10, 1775, Sarah Porter excommunicated.

Second Saturday in August, 1776, it was agreed that Ann Mace be continued a member; John Ray to continue suspended, and Thomas Alderson to warn him to the next meeting of the church; John Conner to be continued under consideration.

Also agreed "That the Church do meet, by Order, the last Saturday in this Month, at Brother Thomas Evans, to know whether the Accusation, Laid against him by Sister Ann Dedrage, be Matter of Fact, or not."

"Church met at the Big Spring Nov. 9th, 1776, and Jno. Ray was sentenced to be excommunicated, & likewise Jno. Conner; agreed to be executed the Day following. Agreed that Abraham Elger be received."

(Note by J. W. W.—The Big Spring was probably what is now known as Lacey Spring, one of the heads of Smith Creek, about midway between New Market and Harrisonburg. Lacey Spring seems to be a misnomer, applied by some accident. No Laceys, it is said, have ever lived thereabouts. Lincolns have lived there for more than a hundred years. "Lincoln Spring" would seem to be a much more fitting name.)

December 7 (1776) the said Elger gave in his letter and was received. "Brother Lincoln was deligated to go & acquaint Brother Hart of the Times of our Stated Meetings."

(Note by J. W. W.—This was probably John Lincoln, one of the five sons of "Virginia John," who bought land on Linville Creek in or about 1768. "Virginia John" had five sons: Abraham, Isaac, Jacob, Thomas, and John. Abraham and Thomas went to Kentucky;

Isaac to East Tennessee; John late in life to Ohio. Jacob lived and died on Linville Creek. His son David located at the Big Spring about 1820. For many years John Lincoln was the mainstay of the Linville Creek Baptist Church, as will appear.)

January 11, 1777, the church met.

February 9, 1777, met and sent David Pergrin and Abraham Elger to John Thomas to learn his reason for absence and to excite him to his duty. Pergrin and Thomas Alderson were sent to Brother Evans, "to know how it is with him, & make Report accordingly."

"3dly, That Brother Jno. Alderson (Jr.?) be deligated to the Seperate Church, for a Correspondence with them."

Wednesday, March 13, 1777, "Called a Meeting, upon the Accompt of the Revd Jno Alderson sn, who gave as Grounds to hope that the Lord hath restored him by a sound Repentance, and we received him into his Place, in the Church."

(Note by J. W. W.—And now comes a period of ten years without an entry. It is possible that the records from 1777 to 1787 have been lost. More probably the war of the Revolution and the subsequent years of disorder interrupted the life of the community to such a degree that no regular meetings were held for a long time. Benedict, in his history of the Baptists, published in 1813, speaks of a great revival among Virginia Baptists that began in 1785 and continued spreading until 1791 or 1792. This may imply that for some years preceding 1785 the work of the churches was neglected.)

Saturday, December 15, 1787, "At a Church Meeting held at the House of Brother Jno. Lincoln's, Brother Anderson Moffett being present, was called as a help, and chosen Moderator, and Brother John Thomas Clerk. . . . A Motion was made by Brother Lincoln, viz. Whether this church should continue and keep their Constitution, or join Brother Moffetts Church Bodily, and dissolve its own Constitution? . . . It was answered that we think it best to keep our Constitution yet for a while."

Next meeting was appointed for Saturday before 3d Sunday in February (1788) at Mr. Zebulon Harrison's house on Smith Creek.

Mr. Moffett was engaged to supply the church at business meetings.

"Then a Motion was made, whether this Church will join with the Smiths Creek Church (i. e. the s'd Brother Moffets Church) in a certain Resolution, of making a Contribution to hire a Hand to Work on Brother Moffetts Place, or for him, the better to enable him to attend upon the Business of preaching the Gospel &c. at the different Places that he may be called to? It was agreed that we will join in such a Contribution."

(Note by J. W. W.—Rev. Anderson Moffett (1746-1835) was pastor for many years of the Smith Creek church, located at or near New Market. At this time (1787) he was probably living on a farm between New Market and Mt. Jackson. About 1800 he located on a splendid plantation on the Shenandoah River, a mile or two west of

New Market, just in the edge of Rockingham County, where he died and where his grave may be found today.)

Saturday before 3d Sunday in February 1788 the church met at the house of Mr. Zebulon Harrison. John Lincoln was chosen clerk. It was agreed that each member would join in the contribution aforesaid. Also, that "our old Church Book should be transcribed into one new cover'd Book, that is to say our Constitution & Introduction preceding s'd Constitution, and the Register of all our Church proceedings from Time to Time, both what is contained in s'd old Book, and other Papers, and it is appointed and agreed, That Brother Thomas & Lincoln do the same as well as they are able, and that they carefully examine the same by the Original & make it exactly agreeable to and with the Sense of s'd Original."

"3dly, agreed that our next Church Meeting be held at Brother Lincoln's House, on the Saturday before the 3d Sabbath in April next and we will send Word to our Revd Brother Moffett, of the same."

"4thly, agreed that Letters, or some sure Word, be sent to Brother Silas Hart & James Thomas & his Wife, acquainting them of our next Church Meeting and other Things that may be thought Necessary."

Saturday before 3d Sunday in April (1788) met at Brother Lincoln's. Brother Moffett continued moderator; Brother Lincoln chosen clerk.

John Thomas and John Lincoln reported that they had transcribed the old church book according to instructions.

Mary Lincoln, wife of John, was received into the church.

Brother Moffett was earnestly requested to engage to preach at the Baptist meeting house on Linville Creek one Sunday in every month, in summer at least; but could not as yet consent.

Bro. John Runyan called to officiate as a deacon at the next communion. Brethren Thomas and Lincoln to provide bread and wine.

Saturday before the 3d Sunday in May, 1788, met at the church on Linville Creek. Bro. Moffett continued moderator; Bro. Lincoln clerk.

Bro. Moffett would not yet make a stated engagement, but said he would preach at Linville Creek as often as he could.

James Thomas and wife Sarah were given a letter to join some other church of the same faith and order. Bro. Lincoln to write the same.

Sunday (3d in May 1788) Rev. Moffett preached to a large concourse of people at the meeting house. Mary Lincoln, wife of John, was baptized and admitted to membership. Communion.

Saturday before 5th Sunday of June, 1788, Bro. Moffett moderator and Bro. Lincoln clerk.

Bro. Lincoln was instructed to draw up a paper for members of the church, her friends and neighbors, to subscribe money to pay a hand to work on Bro. Moffett's plantation "for the Space of one whole Year, the better to enable him to attend on the Business of preaching the Gospel at this Place."

Brethren Thomas and Lincoln were to prepare a letter to be sent to the association (to meet at Buckmarsh in August). Bro. Lincoln appointed messenger to the said association.

Bro. Runyan to officiate as deacon at next communion.

Brethren Lincoln and Thomas were instructed to insert (record) in the church book every item of past business and interest—to collect any or all loose pieces of paper bearing records and transcribe into the said book; supplementing from memory; and to write a "short Historicle Account of what hath happened to this Church."

Saturday before 2d Sunday in August (1788), business meeting. Association letter and subscription paper were read and approved.

Bro. Lincoln was appointed to visit the members on Smith Creek and inquire into the reason of their absence; and Bro. Thomas to visit Bro. Hart for the same cause.

Saturday before 2d Sunday in September (1788) met at "the old Meetinghouse." Brethren Lincoln and Thomas reported that they had visited the members and heard their excuses, which were deemed sufficient. Bro. Hart's bad state of health and old age recognized as justifying him for absence.

Minutes of "our Association" and circular letter and minutes and circular letter of Philadelphia Association were all read.

Bro. Lincoln was appointed "to take Subscriptions to the Proposals for printing by Subscription An Abridgment of Dr. Gills Exposition of the old & new Testaments."

John Lockard offered and was received into fellowship. He was baptized the 1st Sunday in October following.

Saturday before 2d Sunday in November (1788) met at the old meetinghouse. Appointed next meeting for Saturday before 2d Sunday in December at Mr. Jacob Lincoln's house.

"The 4th Sabbath in Nov. 1788, The Revd Mr Wm Mason pay'd us a Visit at Linvels Creek, & preach'd us a most excellent Sermon at the Meetinghouse, as he had also done the Day before at the cross Roads (New Market), & the Evening following he preach'd at Brother Lincolns House . . . & then he return'd for Home."

Saturday before 2d Sunday in December (1788) met and continued Bro. Moffett as moderator and Bro. Lincoln as clerk.

Saturday before 2d Sunday in April, 1789, met at the old meeting house in Linville Creek. Bro. Moffett moderator, Bro. Lincoln clerk.

Brethren Thomas and Lincoln were asked to write Bro. Hart and solicit him to contribute something towards the support of the church.

The same brethren were asked to write a letter to Mr. John Stinson, "who, we are inform'd, has been legally baptized according to Scripture," inviting him to come and join this church.

"Agree'd that we seek . . . a greater intercourse & reciprocal Union & Communion with our Sister Church on Smiths Creek."

Saturday before 5th Sunday in May (1789), Bro. Lincoln was appointed "to attend at the Meeting of Business of our Sister Church on Smiths Creek next Saturday & invite the Members of s'd Church to come and commune with us the Second Sabbath in June, at this Place, & Appointed Brother Runyan to officiate as Deacon at s'd Communion, & Brother Lincoln to provide the Elements."

Saturday before 2d Sunday in June (1789) met and agreed "that the Members now present from our Sister Church on Smiths Creek be and are invited to set with us in a Church way," and hereafter whenever present.

Saturday before 2d Sunday in August (1789), Bro. Moffett continued moderator, Bro. Lincoln clerk.

Bro. Lockard appointed messenger to the association to be held next Saturday at Broad Run, Fauquier County; "and also Brother Aron Solomon on Condition he will comply." Association letter read. "The Business of Building a new Meeting-house was then discoursed upon, and the Church appointed Brother Lincoln to have a Subscription Paper for that Purpose against our next Meeting."

September 12, 1789, Bro. Lincoln reported that, upon conversing with the people at large in the neighborhood, he found it expedient to drop the drawing a subscription paper for building a new meeting house, but instead to repair the old one upon the same plan, viz by subscription.

At a called meeting at the house of Bro. John Lincoln, Thursday, October 1, 1789, a letter was presented to the church by Bro. Lincoln to be sent to our district association at Water-Lick, beginning on Saturday the 3d inst. Letter agreed to. Bro. Lincoln to bear the letter, as messenger.

"The old Catocton Association was divided last August into two District Associations; containing about twelve Churches each, the Upper District (being that which we fall into) still retaining the old name of the Catocton Association; and the lower, the Chapawamsick Association."

Saturday before 2d Sunday in November (1789), Bro. Ashbruck, a preacher of our order, from North River Church, being present, according to an appointment of his, was invited to a seat among us.

Considered the matter of making contribution to Bro. Moffett towards paying a hand he has hired to work on his place. Bro. Lincoln reported that he had been informed by Mr. Custer that $7 of the old subscription was unpaid. Agreed that when said money was paid it should be applied to the above use.

Members of the sister church on Smith Creek were invited to communion on 5th Sunday, instant.

Fifth Sunday, November, 1789, communion. "Was present with our beloved Brother Moffett, our Beloved & reverend Brother James Ireland, who also assisted in administering s'd Sacrament . . . the two Revd Brethren partaking with us."

Saturday before 2d Sunday in December (1789), "Brother Lincoln inform'd the Church, Brother Moffett being present & acting as Moderator, Brother Wiley also being present & acting as a Member with us, of some of the Exercises of his Mind respecting the expediency of his promoting & holding prayer Meetings &c. on Smiths Creek with his fellow Members & Neighbours as often as might appear convenient to him & them on Sabbath Days, upon which Matter he desir'd the Advice of the Church. After Brother Moffett stated the Matter again to the Church, he agreed it was a necessary Undertaking, & the Church agreed, that it might be or was expedient to hold such Meetings."

Saturday before 2d Sunday in April, 1790, agreed to make a contribution to Bro. Moffett for his supplying this place with the ministry of the Gospel. Non members welcome to subscribe with us.

Agreed that we contribute something to Bro. Stone tomorrow, if he should come here.

Saturday before 2d Sunday in May (1790), Bro. David Thomas was present; invited to act as moderator.

Margaret Thomas, daughter of Evan, offered and was received; baptized by Rev. David Thomas.

Bro. Lincoln appointed to provide the elements for communion at the yearly meeting, to begin 2d Saturday of June.

Saturday, June 12, 1790, rain; meeting late. "None of the Ministers that was appointed by the Association attended the Yearly Meeting but Brother Ireland, though Brother Moffett attended it on his own Appointment, and both preach'd Saturday and Sunday, and according to Appointment, on Sunday the Lords Supper was administered."

Saturday before 2d Sunday in August (1790), letter to association read; Bro. Lincoln appointed messenger.

Saturday, October 9, 1790, Brother John Munro being present, upon invitation opened the meeting.

Gave Bro. Munro a call to officiate tomorrow. Accepted.

Being informed by Bro. Munro that Bro. James Johnston, a minister of our order, "of respectability," had no charge, Bro. Lincoln was appointed to write him and invite him to visit us.

Saturday before 2d Sunday in November (1790), three members paid off their subscriptions and got credit. Bro. Lincoln informed the church that he had advanced some money to Bro. Stone in behalf of the church, which they agreed to repay him, except what he is willing to let stand.

Second Sunday in February, 1791, Patience Brumfield was received for baptism.

Saturday before 2d Sunday in March (1791), Bro. Moffett moderator. Amelia Smith received for baptism.

Sunday, March 13 (1791), Patience Brumfield, wife of David, and Amelia Smith, wife or widow of John Smith, were baptized.

Saturday before 2d Sunday in April (1791), Bro. Moffett moderator, Bro. Lincoln clerk.

Considered a subscription by church and the people at large for the support of Bro. Johnston, should he become our preacher.

Brethren Thomas and Lincoln to prepare the elements for the May communion.

Second Sunday in May (1791), communion. Present Bro. Moffett, Bro. James Johnston, Bro. Josiah Ozburn, ministers.

Saturday before 3d Sunday in June (1791), Bro. Johnston present, applied for transient membership, not having obtained his dismission from Buckmarsh Church; was received. He was chosen moderator.

Easter Henton, widow of John Henton, presented a letter of dismission dated November 23, 1766, from a church of Christ at Cumry Township, Berks County, and Province of Pennsylvania. Amelia Bowen, wife of Francis, presented a letter of dismission dated May 28, 1791, from the United Baptist Church of Christ at Mill Creek, Shenandoah County, Va. Both received.

Dinah Talman, wife of Benjamin, received for baptism.

Agreed to ask Bro. Moffett to attend here 2d Sunday in July to administer baptism.

Saturday before 2d Sunday in July (1791) Elener Gum, widow of Norton Gum, was received for baptism.

Brethren Johnston, Lockard, and Harrison, or any two of them, appointed messengers to Ketocton Association; Bro. Lincoln to prepare our letter to said association.

Next day (2d Sunday in July, 1791) Dinah Talman and Elener Gum were baptized by Rev. Moffett.

Saturday, August 13, 1791, Bro. James Riggs, member of a sister church, being present, was invited to a seat in our church meeting.

Letter to the association was read. Brethren Johnston and Lockard agreed to go as messengers to the association. A collection of ten shillings was made to send by our messengers to the association, which money said messengers may apply to such uses in the association as may appear to them necessary.

Agreed to adopt some plan to obtain church fellowship, or rather membership if possible, with certain Baptists living on and about the North and Dry Rivers of Shenandoah. Brethren Johnston, Thomas, and Lincoln asked to draw up a plan setting forth the conditions on which we will receive those Baptists into church fellowship or membership with us; the plan to be submitted to us for approval; and the said brethren and Brother Lockard or any two of them to carry said plan to Brother Silas Harts, and there with said brother to meet the aforesaid Baptists the Saturday before the first Sabbath in September next, to have this matter investigated with them; and nominated Bro. Hart and Bro. Riggs to give the necessary notice; Bro. Lincoln to write Bro. Hart about it.

(Note by J. W. W.—The Baptists sought for affiliation may have lived in Brock's Gap or in the vicinity of Bridgewater and Mt. Crawford. There is a north river of Shenandoah, with a Dry River affluent, in each of the aforesaid regions. But Silas Hart probably lived on Muddy Creek, which is southwest of Linville. Going to his home from Linville would have been going away from Brock's Gap; but it would have been going towards (nearer) Bridgewater and Mt. Crawford. North River is today the name of a postoffice near Mt. Crawford; and there are old Baptist churches at Bridgewater and Mt. Crawford. A century or more ago there was also a Baptist church at Dayton, near Bridgewater.)

Sunday evening, August 28, 1791, minutes of our last association were read, and a plan to be sent to certain Baptists, as above mentioned; which plan was agreed to by the church.

Saturday, September 10, the circular letter from our association was read and looked upon as very satisfactory and good.

Bro. Johnston presented his letter of dismission from Buckmarsh Church, dated last May, giving him a very good recommendation, both as a Gospel preacher and as to his good and orderly standing as a member; and he was gladly received into full fellowship.

"Brother Johnston made report that himself and all the other Brethren appointed, excepting Brother Hart, had attended last Saturday at the North River, at the house of Michael Kingery, a house fixed upon by those Baptists living in that Neighbourhood, to meet us at, but as but a Part of those Baptists, by reason of the badness of the Weather, met with us, we could not bring the Matter in Hand so fully to bear as might otherwise have been the Case; nevertheless, as many as did meet with us did, on their own Parts, agree to our written Plan, and other Proposals made to them concerning Church Fellowship &c."

Bro. Lincoln to provide the elements for October communion, and to try to inform Bro. Runyan of the appointment, that he may officiate as deacon.

Appointed Thursday before 2d Sunday in October for a day of fasting, humiliation, and prayer.

Saturday, October 8, 1791, Bro. Johnston was ordained as pastor of this church, with imposition of hands, etc., by Rev. John Monroe and Rev. Anderson Moffett.

October 9, Sunday, communion; administered by Brethren Monroe and Moffett.

Saturday, November 12, 1791, Elener Gum was excommunicated for alleged misconduct.

Bro. James Riggs presented a letter of dismission from a church on the waters of Peters Creek, dated Nov. 11, 1788, and was received upon the same.

"The Case of black Members or Slaves was consider'd, that is, whether they should be admitted to a Seat among us on Days of Business, when meeting with us on those Days; Resolved that they should."

Resolved that Mr. John Stevenson be considered as a member of this church in full fellowship.

"It was moved & put to Vote, whether the Right Hand of Fellowship should be given to a Member, or Candidate, when receiv'd upon Experience or Letter, by all the Members of the Church present, or by the Modr or Minister only, in the Name & Behalf of the whole Church. Answer'd by the Minister or Moderator only."

Francis Bowen offered experience and was received.

Brethren Lincoln and Lockard were appointed "to enquire of the Trustees, for repairing this Meetinghouse, how they have transacted therein, as soon as a convenient Opportunity shall offer."

Sunday, November 13, 1791, Francis Bowen was baptized and came under imposition of hands by our lately ordained Brother James Johnston.

Meetings Dec. 10, 1791, and January 7, 1792.

Saturday, February 12, 1792. resolved that "certain of our Members living near the Centre of our Bounds do meet with other Members living about the North & Dry Rivers, at Brother Riggs's, the Saturday before the 1st Sabbath in March next, to set with them there, to hear and receive Experiences upon the Authority of the Church."

Saturday, March 10, 1792, Bro. Johnston reported that he was the only member from about the center of this church that attended the meeting last Saturday at Bro. Riggs's; that he did attend according to appointment; met with a few members in that neighborhood set upon business; that Mary Webb offered and was received upon experience and was baptized the day following.

Saturday, May 12, 1792, after two short discourses by Br. Ozburn and Johnston proceeded to business.

"Invited a certain Brother Woods (a Member of Brother Countz Church) to a Seat with us, who accordingly accepted."

(Note by J. W. W.—Rev. John Koontz's church was at or near Mill Creek, now Page County. "Brother Woods" was perhaps Jesse Woods or Wood, who was clerk of Koontz's church in 1798.)

"Resolved unanimously, that the publick Worship of God, at this Place, when Brother Johnston is to preach, begin at eleven O'Clock as nearly as can be ascertained, for the future, both in Summer and Winter."

Sunday, May 13 (1792), Benjamin Talman was baptized, "& then was celebrated the Sacred Ordinance of the Lords Supper with its usual Solemnity, being as we suppose our largest Communion since our Revival, Br Johnston Administrator."

(Note by J. W. W.—See note following items of March 13, 1777.)

Saturday, June 9 (1792), Brethren Talman and Lincoln were nominated for deacons, one to be chosen.

Bro. Lincoln was appointed to write the letter to our next association, which is to be held at Long Branch, Fauquier County; and Br. Johnston, Talman, & Lincoln, or any two of them, were nominated as messengers.

Ruth Brigs came forward and related her experience, but was put off as to her reception for awhile.

Saturday, August 11, 1792, Br. Talman and Lincoln put on trial for deacon. Ruth Brigs received for baptism. Letter to association was read; collection taken to send with messengers to association. Members present, or most of them, signed a subscription paper to Bro. Johnston. The same to be presented also to non-members.

Sunday, August 12, Ruth Brigs baptized, and came under imposition of hands of Br. Moffett and Johnston.

Saturday, Sept. 8, 1792, Bro. Johnston reported on association, among other things that the minutes were to be printed before we could receive them.

Saturday, October 13, our messengers to the late association reported they had laid out 6/2 more than was contributed to bear their expenses. This amount was now laid on the table by contribution and delivered to said messengers.

Bro. Lincoln presented to the church a subscription paper for repairing the meetinghouse, which was approved and subscribed to by the members present; and it was concluded to present it to some of the nearest livers to said meetinghouse, though non-members, for their subscriptions.

Sunday, October 14, communion.

Saturday, Nov. 10 (1792), the church agreed to allow the deacon or deacons 3 shillings for elements, &c., for each of the two last communions, it being all the deacons "would wish to have, according to the present standing &c of the Church."

"Resolved that for the future it shall be the Duty of the Church and each Member thereof, that is able to come out on Days of Business, to meet at 11 O'Clock in the Morning at latest, in the Winter Season."

"The Expediency of Society Meetings was spoken of, but was laid over till next Meeting."

Saturday, Dec. 8, 1792, "The Subject of Society Meetings of our Members on such Lords Days as we have no publick preaching in our Bounds agreeable to our Faith was resumed, and after considerable Debate on said Subject agree'd to postpone the Appointment of such Meetings for the . . . Present . . . Notwithstanding, as Brother Talman is of Opinion that good might be done by the Appointment of such Meetings & holding them at Times in his Neighbourhood, we have no Objection to his making a Trial therein."

Nominated Bro. Talman to deal with Sister Margaret Harrison for her non-attendance so frequently of late on our church meeting days, and excite her to her duty. Sister Margaret Thomas to deal with Bro. Bowen and wife for the same. Bro. Lincoln with Bro. Thomas for the same.

Saturday, Jan. 12, 1793, Bro. Absalom Graves presented letter of dismission from "the Church of Christ on Rapedan River, in Culpeper County, and was received into the Fellowship of this Church."

"The Brethren and Sister appointed last Meeting to deal with certain Brethren and Sisters for their none attendance of late at Church Meetings, made their Report which was prity satisfactory."

"Other Members that were absent last Church Meeting were inquired of to give their Reasons for their thus being absent, which Reasons when given were such as were unanimously put up with."

"Society Meetings were again spoken of, but nothing decisive determined upon respecting them."

Saturday, Feb. 9, 1793, Rozanah Garretson, wife of John, member of Mill Creek Church, presented letter of dismission from that church, "but on account of some jealousy on the Mind of one of the Members Respecting her Walk since she hath been living in the Bounds of our Church, her reception was postponed till next Church Meeting."

The advisability of receiving "old Brother Wm Davis" was considered.

Saturday before 2d Sunday in March (1793), Sister Lucinda Rice, wife of John, presented letter of dismission from Crooked Run Church in Culpeper County and was received.

The case of Rosannah Garretson considered. Jealousies not yet removed. She not present with her letter. Nothing done.

Saturday, April 13, Bro. Johnston moderator.

Saturday, May 11 (1793), a lecture by Bro. Moffett, moderator.

Mr. Hopkins Doll offered for membership on experiences, but was not received.

Bro. Ezekiel Harrison's house was pitched upon for a general communion of this church with Bro. Moffett's church, 2d Sunday in August.

Sunday, May 12, communion; Bro. Moffett assisting in the administration with Bro. Johnston.

Saturday, June 8 (1793), Jonathan Latham and Kisandren his wife presented letter from church at Chopanamsick, Stafford County, and were received.

Br. Johnston, Lincoln, and Riggs nominated (any two) for messengers to next association; a collection to be taken for expenses. Bro. Lincoln to write the church letter to the association.

"Agree'd to send a Query to s'd Association concerning a Plan for our Associations holding a Correspondence with other Associations viz. By printing so many Copies of the Minutes of our Association as to furnish each Church belonging thereto with one, and each Church belonging to every other Association on the Continent, that will respond with us, with one."

Upon application of Bro. Lockard, Bro. Lincoln was appointed to write a letter of dismission for Sister Grace Fine, who hath been removed out of the bounds of our church for some years past.

Saturday, August 10 (1793), Mr. Hopkins Doll again related experience, but was not received.

(Note by J. W. W.—"Mr. Hopkins Doll" was probably "Mr. Hopkins's Doll," a slave woman.)

Letter to association was read and approved; Br. Johnston, Lincoln, and Riggs "finally inserted as our Messengers."

Letters of dismission prepared for Sister Webb and Sister Smith.

Saturday, Sept. 7 (1793), aforesaid letters delivered: also a "particular Recommendation for Sister Amelia Smith."

One pound and one penny had been collected for messengers' expenses to the association. Their expenses were 14 shillings and one penny. The balance, 6 shillings, was left in Bro. Lincoln's hands to be laid out by the church's order.

The 3d subscription paper to Bro. Johnston was presented to the church and subscribed to by the members present.

Saturday, Oct. 12 (1793), Mary Woods, formerly Mary Cox, being present, was "conversed with" by Bro. Johnston about joining this church; to which "she appear'd to have no great Objection," as soon as she could obtain a new letter of dismission from the Ragged Mountain Church, Culpeper County. She had lost her old letter.

"The Members present nam'd the Sums of Money or Property they would be willing to Subscribe towards building a House for Brother Johnston, on Brother Ezekiel Harrison Land which is set on a separate Piece of Paper, & to be inscribed in these Minutes hereafter."

Saturday, Nov. 9 (1793), Bro. Johnston informed the church that our sister church on Smiths Creek had appointed a fast, or day of humiliation and prayer, hoping this church will join; place proposed Bro. Ezekiel Harrison's house; time next Thursday; agreed.

Bro. Lincoln to write a letter of dismission for Bro. Absalom Graves and wife.

Saturday, Dec. 7 (1793), agreed that Bro. Johnston disappoint his preaching at Linville tomorrow on account of being requested to preach the funeral of Mrs. Phebe Harrison on Smith Creek, "who departed this Life in the 108 Year of her Age."

Saturday, Jan. 11, 1794, agreed to draw a subscription paper for raising money or property to build a dwelling house for Bro. Johnston on the land of Bro. Ezekiel Harrison, said paper to be presented to members and non-members.

Saturday, Feb. 8 (1794), Bro. Johnston, having been furnished with the minutes of the Culpeper Association for the use of this church, read them.

Saturday, March 8 (1794), met and read a subscription paper drawn by Bro. Lincoln (as agreed upon in January), which was approved but not signed, on account of a change that appeared to have taken place in the mind of Bro. Johnston.

Met Saturday, April 12 (1794).

Saturday, May 10, Bro. Moffett being present was chosen moderator for the time being.

Reported to the church that a member, viz. Margaret Harrison, was aggrieved, but was loath to bring it forth. The church agreed that she should bring it forward at the present moment for certain reasons. Accordingly she came forward and made known her grievance which was against "Mr. Moor's Joe (who is a Member of this Church) for propagating, as she says, a scandalous Report as a

Truth, against a Member of Sister Harrisons Family," . . . Accordingly said Joe was laid under the censure of the church.

Absalom Lynn and wife Jenny related their experience and were joyfully and unanimously received by the church. Next day (Sunday) they were baptized. Communion. Rev. Anderson Moffett present, assisting in the administration.

Saturday, June 7 (1794), Bro. Latham's mulatto woman called Sucky related "a very agreeable & satisfactory" experience and was received for baptism. She was baptized the next day.

Queries to our last association respecting a division of the association we unanimously oppose, till the bounds be fixed upon and the association submit the plan to all the churches concerned.

The query from Back Lick concerning the form of an oath was laid over till next meeting.

Saturday, July 26 (1794), query considered. The question put, is the present form of administering and taking an oath faulty or not? Yes.

"Brother Joe being now present, had a hearing concerning the Charges brought against him by Sister Margret Harrison, and which was the Cause of his Suspension, and upon hearing his Relation, the Church was of Opinion that there was as much Cause for her being suspended as him, and upon it being put to Vote, Whether he should be restor'd or whether she should be suspended, and he continued suspended; a Majority was for suspending her with him, which was according done."

(Note by J. W. W.—This is an interesting sidelight: a Negro slave being treated to even-handed justice in a trial with a white woman of one of the leading families.)

"Appointed Brother Latham and Talman, & Sister Hannah Harrison (if she can go) to wait upon s'd Sister Margret Harrison, in Order, if possible, that her Grievance against Brother Joe may be done away, & that Matters of Dispute or Difference may be amicably setled between them."

Br. Lincoln and Latham appointed our messengers to the next association, Bro. Lincoln to write the letter.

Saturday, August 9 (1794), Bro. Latham being the only member that waited on Sister Margaret Harrison reported; but Sister Harrison being present herself was interrogated. "She came to so far as to forgive s'd Brother Joe his Fault against her, or that which she view'd as a Fault in him; and agreed that he might keep his Place in the Church, as well as herself, and that she would not neglect her Duty in the Church on this Account; but this she undertook on Condition that said Joe shall not have the Previledge of her Wench Dine, as his Wife."

Upon this the said two contending members were both restored from under suspension to full Previledge in the Church.

Saturday, Sept. 13 (1794), agreed to read a very small pamphlet, set forth by the church of Christ at Difficult, concerning contribution, &c.

Received Sister Margaret Briton into transient communion, she being a member at Buckmarsh.

Bro. Lincoln ordered to prepare a letter of dismission for Bro. John Thomas (on his request), to be delivered this fall, if applied for.

The matter of laying on hands on baptized persons was "some little debated," but action deferred till next church meeting.

Saturday, Oct. 11 (1794), printed minutes of our last association came to hand; read; 4 copies distributed among the members; one deposited with the clerk.

Bro. Johnston expects shortly to remove; applied for letter. Bro. Lincoln to prepare letter. Bro. John Thomas appointed to write one for Sister Ruth Brig.

The messengers to late association reported their expenses 21/6. Paid.

Action on laying on of hands further deferred.

Saturday, Nov. 8 (1794), Bro. Lincoln moderator pro tem. Bro. Johnston removed from us. Church now destitute of a pastor. Bro. Moffett called to supply one Sunday each month; a reasonable contribution promised.

Saturday, Dec. 13 (1794), Bro. Latham moderator pro tem. Call to Bro. Moffett continued; Br. Talman and Lincoln to raise money for Bro. Moffett. Goal 6 pounds.

"Agree'd to Pay Tom or Jem (who are black Members of the Church) six Shillings if either of them will sweep the Meetinghouse & make Fires when necessary for one year."

Saturday, April 11, 1795, Bro. Latham moderator, Br. Talman and Lincoln reported contributions for Bro. Moffett:

Bro. Talman & wife	1 pound
Bro. Lincoln & wife	1 pound
Bro. Latham & wife	10 shillings
Bro. Bowen & wife	10 shillings
Bro. Lynn & wife	6 shillings
Bro. McFarland & wife	5 shillings
Sister Hannah Harrison	10 shillings
Sister Margaret Harrison	10 shillings
M. Thomas	9 shillings
E. Henton	10 shillings
Bro. Lockard	4 shillings
Sister Brumfield	3 shillings
—— Briton	3 shillings

(Note by J. W. W.—Although Linville Creek was (and still is) in the midst of German settlements, none of the above names appear to be German—unless possibly Bowen or Brumfield.)

Saturday, June 13 (1795), Sister Henton was asked why she was absent last April; answer, sickness. Excused. Also, Bro. Bowen, likewise.

Saturday, August 8 (1795), Bro. Latham moderator. Bi-monthly business meetings agreed upon, except in extraordinary cases.

Bro. Latham nominated our messenger to the Ketocton Association, next week. Members present contributed 11/9 towards his expenses.

Saturday, Nov. 7 (1795), Bro. Latham moderator; he informed the church that he expects his mulatto woman Sucky, who is a member of the church, shortly to remove out of its bounds; letter requested and given.

Sunday, Nov. 8 (1795), communion; Bro. Moffett officiated.

Saturday, March 12, 1796, Bro. Lincoln reported he had prepared a letter for Sucky; also for Bro. Latham & wife and Bro. Lynn & wife; signed by himself and Bro. Talman, and delivered.

Met Saturday, May 7 (1796). May 8 communion.

Saturday, June 11, business meeting.

Saturday, Aug. 13, Bro. Lincoln appointed messenger to our association. Our return to the association was 20 members.

October 8 (Saturday), Bro. James Ireland present, having come to visit us and preach, chosen moderator.

Letter presented by Rhoda Jeffreys, wife of ———— Jeffreys, from the Baptist Church of Christ on Lost River; received.

Sunday, Oct. 9 (1796), communion; Br. Ireland & Moffett administering.

Saturday, May 13, 1797, proportioned each member's share in a subscription paper to Bro. Moffett. Agreed to hold future meetings monthly, April to October or November, July only excepted.

Saturday, June 19 (1797), business meeting.

Saturday, August 12, Bro. Talman appointed messenger to association; 12 shillings made up for his expenses. Our return to the association 21 members.

October, 1797, business meeting on Saturday; and on 4th Sunday of same month communion, Bro. Thomas Bridges preaching and assisting Bro. Moffett in administering.

April 7, 1798, church meeting.

Saturday, Aug. 11 (1798), Bro. Lincoln appointed messenger to next association.

Saturday, Dec. 8 (1798), Bro. Thomas Yates gave in his letter from F. T. Church and was received.

Aug. 8, 1801, Bro. Lincoln stated that he and two other members were aggrieved measurably with a fellow member, but not having taken Gospel steps they all forbore to mention particulars.

Saturday, Sept. 11, 1802, Bro. Lockard brought forward a letter of dismission from Ketocton Association to join Culpeper Association.

Br. Lockard and Lincoln reported conference with Sister Nansy Green. She was laid under censure and cited to appear at the next church meeting.

Bro. Lincoln appointed our messenger to the Culpepper Association.

Saturday, Oct. 9 (1802), Bro. Lockard reported that he had noticed Sister Green to attend this meeting. She plead a willingness, but was unable by reason of indisposition of body.

Bro. Lincoln reported he had attended the association (Culpeper) when this church was received into it.

Saturday, Nov. 13 (1802), Sister McKinsy is to notice Sister Green to attend meeting next April.

"Appointed Brothers Talman, Lincoln, and Lockard and to meet with any Members of the Methodist Class, on Linvils Creek, that may be properly authorised to meet with them, to consult on a plan for building a new meeting-house. Br. Lockard to inform said Class of said Appointment, and if they concur, are to fix on time and place for both Bodies to meet on said Business, and notice our Brethren thereof."

(Note by J. W. W.—This is an interesting instance of an early attempt at sectarian co-operation. Probably it did not lead to material results. An old Methodist church stood on the hill just east of Linville Creek, close to Wenger's Mill and not far from the old Lincoln homesteads.)

Saturday, Sept. 10, 1803, church letter to the association (to begin Friday before 1st Sunday in October) was read and approved.

Oct. 8 (1803), Bro. Moffett "being present was chosen Moderator." Nancy Harrison, wife of John, received for baptism. Rachel Britton received on letter from Hill-Town Church, Bucks Co., Pa. Hannah Lincoln, daughter of John, received for baptism.

Sunday, October 9, Rachel Lincoln received for baptism. After sermon Nancy Harrison, Hannah Lincoln, and Rachel Lincoln were baptized by Bro. Moffett. Communion.

Saturday, Nov. 13 (1803), church collections now and last meeting amounted to 30 shillings.

Saturday, April 9, 1804, letter of dismission and recommendation granted our beloved Sister Ann Harrison, who expects to remove from our bounds.

Br. Talman & Lockard to press Bro. Moffett to preach at D. Brumfield's on 2d Sunday of May.

Saturday, June 9 (1804), Bro. Lockard moderator. Bro. Giles Turley presented letter from Little River Church, Loudoun County, and was received.

(Note by J. W. W.—Turleytown, not far from Linville Creek, was probably founded by Giles Turley. See Wayland's History of Rockingham County, pages 204, 243.)

Saturday, Aug. 11 (1804), Br. Lockard & Yates appointed our messengers to the association, Br. Turley & Lincoln to write the letter.

N. B. On Saturday before the 2d Sunday in April 1803 Bro. John Lockard was called by the church to exercise his spiritual, or ministerial, gift on trial, either by praying, opening up & explaining a hymn or psalm, exhorting, or even preaching; & at a future meeting this call was continued till the church should otherwise ordain.

Sept. 8 (1804), business meeting.

Saturday, Oct. 13, Bro. Lockard moderator. Sister Claria Yates, wife of Abner, was received on letter from F T Church in ———— County, Va. Said Abner received for baptism.

"Agreed to send for Brother Moffette to attend at Br. Turleys or Lincolns, to preach & administer the Ordinance of Baptism, & the Lords Supper if practicable the 4th Sunday instant." . . .

Saturday, Oct. 27 (1804), met at Bro. Lincoln's. Bro. Moffette, being present, was chosen moderator. Mrs. Terry came forward & related her experience and was not received. Delphe, a black woman of Mr. McKinsey's, came forward and was received for baptism.

Next business meeting appointed at the schoolhouse on Linville Creek, Saturday before 2d Sunday in December.

Br. B. Talman & John Lincoln, who had been put on trial as deacons some years before, were solemnly set apart and ordained by prayer and laying on of hands by Bro. Moffette.

The church unanimously agreed to make a contribution for Bro. Moffette at our next meeting.

Sunday, Oct. 28 (1804), Mrs. Hoy, Abner Yates, and Delphe were baptized by Bro. Moffette.

Saturday, Dec. 8 (1804), collection for Bro. Moffette amounted to $4.50; $4 more promised.

Saturday, March 9, 1805, Bro. Lincoln requested to be relieved as writing clerk; Bro. Giles Turley made writing clerk.

"We as a Church agree that it is necessary to try to have a meetinghouse built at or near this Place, viz Linvils Creek old meeting-house, for the worship of God."

Saturday, April 13 (1805), Bro. Lockard moderator. Bro. Ezekiel Harrison and wife being present took their seats amongst us.

Upon motion of Bro. Harrison, the church decided that it was highly necessary to offer a subscription generally for building a meeting-house near Linville Creek. Br. John Lincoln, John Lockard, & Giles Turley appointed to draw up a subscription paper.

Bro. Elijah Elliott granted letter of dismission.

Saturday, May 10 (1805), Bro. Lockard moderator. Subscription paper approved, but held over till June meeting for further consideration.

Saturday, June 8 (1805), Bro. David Coffman, being present, was invited to a seat among us. Subscription paper approved; to be handed out to the public for their approbation.

Saturday, Aug. 10 (1805), Bro. Lockard moderator. Br. Lockard and Yates appointed our messengers to the Culpeper Association (to begin Friday before 1st Sunday in October). Bro. Lincoln to prepare a letter.

Saturday, Sept. 7 (1805), Bro. Lockard moderator. Lucy Rice, wife of John, discontinued as a member "for Transgressing the order of this Church by Joining the Methodist Society."

Sister Brumfield to notify Sister Talman to our next meeting to show cause for absences. Bro. Lincoln submitted letter; approved for the association.

Saturday, Oct. 12 (1805), Sister Brumfield not present—no report concerning Sister Talman. Bro. Lockard is "about to Travel to the Western City," and applies for letter of recommendation.

Saturday, April 12, 1806, Bro. Lockard appointed to wait upon Sister Brumfield and inquire her findings regarding Sister Talman.

The church agreed to continue the subscription paper for raising money to build a meeting house.

Saturday, May 10 (1806), Bro. Lockard reported seeing Sister Brumfield; no satisfactory answer; Sister Brumfield continued.

Saturday, June 7, Sister Talman being present signified her desire to continue her membership; granted, on condition she fill her place as an orderly member.

John Miller received for baptism. Bro. John Stevenson granted letter of dismission.

Sunday, June 8, John Miller baptized by Bro. Moffett.

Saturday, Aug. 9 (1806), Br. Lincoln, Talman, & Turley appointed messengers to Culpeper Association (to begin Friday before 1st Sunday in October); Bro. Lincoln to prepare letter to association.

Bro. Lockard, being about to move his place of residence, is granted a letter of dismission.

Phebe Burnsides received by letter.

Business meeting Saturday, Sept. 12 (1806).

April 11, 1807, Bro. John Lincoln moderator. "At the Request of the Dover and Goshen association for Materials to furnish the writing a History of the Baptists, we agree to furnish such things as come unto our knowledge and appoint Brother Lincoln to collect such as he may think most suitable for that purpose."

"Agreed that the Church in general meet at the Union meeting in New Market the second Sunday in May on purpose of Communing at that place instead of appointing one in our own Church."

Saturday, May 16 (1807), met at Linville Creek and appointed Saturday before the 2d Sunday in June for next business meeting, at the school house.

August 8, 1807, Bro. Lincoln moderator. Br. Lincoln, Talman, & Turley appointed messengers to the Culpeper Association (to be held at the meeting house upon Robinson in Madison County, beginning Friday before the 1st Sunday in October). Bro. Lincoln to prepare the letter to the association.

Sister Talman discontinued as a member.

Saturday, Sept. 19 (1807), Bro. Lincoln read a chapter and made some remarks. Letter to Culpeper Association read and approved.

Saturday, Nov. 7 (1807), Bro. Lincoln moderator.

Saturday, April 9, 1808. Bro. Samuel Hindun being present, preached a short discourse. Business session. Next business meeting appointed at the old school house.

Saturday, May 7 (1808). Br. Samuel Hindun and William Buck being present, Bro. Hindun chosen moderator. Business session. Appointed next meeting at Bro. John Lincoln's, Saturday before 2d Sunday in June.

Rebeckah Dunlap offered her experience to the church.

Saturday, June 11 (1808), met at Bro. John Lincoln's. Bro. Samuel Hindun preached a short discourse. Business session. Bro. Anderson Moffett moderator. Elizabeth Dunlap related her experience and was received. John Homan Aaron (John Homan's Aaron?) also related his experience "and in the Judgment of Charity was Recd."

Bro. John Miller, intending to move, was granted a letter.

Sunday, June 12 (1808), Rebeckah Dunlap, Elizabeth Dunlap, and Homan Aaron were baptized by Bro. Hindun.

Also was received into this church Bro. Peter Biann, "formerly a Member of Coffman Church."

Friday, June 17 (1808), Bro. John Lincoln moderator. The church unanimously agreed to call Bro. Samuel Hindun to the pastoral care of the church. Bro. Lincoln notified Bro. Hindun.

Bro. Hindun accepted the call to attend this church once a month on the 1st Saturday and Sunday. The church agree to support the preaching to the best of their abilities.

Mr. Dunlap's woman Ede came before the church, related her experience, and was received for baptism.

Saturday, Aug. 16 (1808), Bro. Hindun moderator. Bro. Lincoln appointed to write a letter to the association.

Saturday, Sept. 3 (1808), Bro. Hindun moderator. Bro. Lincoln submitted letter for association, which was read and approved. Br. John Lincoln and Giles Turley appointed messengers to association. Bro. Benjamin Talman, about to remove, was granted a letter.

Next business session appointed to meet at Mr. Jacob Lincoln's.

Saturday, Oct. 8 (1808), met at Mr. Jacob Lincoln's; Bro. Samuel O. Hindren moderator. Bro. Benja. Dawson being present was invited to a seat. Bro. Ezekiel Hanson also.

John Runyon came forward and related his experience, which was acknowledged. Nancy Hawk also informed the church of a work of grace wrought in her soul, which was acknowledged. Anne Runyon and Elizabeth Dundore were received for baptism. The above named persons were baptized on Sunday, October 9.

(Note by J. W. W.—Jacob Lincoln, brother to Deacon John Lincoln, and one of the five sons of "Virginia John," had been an officer in the Revolutionary army. He lived on the east side of Linville Creek, in a substantial brick house built there about 1800 and still standing. In this house the meetings of 1808 above chronicled were no doubt held. Nancy "Hawk" may have been Nancy Hank. There were Hanks in the vicinity.)

Saturday, Nov. 5 (1808), the church met at the house of Mr. Crotzer (Kratzer); Bro. Lincoln moderator. It was agreed that a public collection be made quarterly on Sunday after preaching for the support of the pastor of the church, to begin November 6.

The next (December) meeting was appointed for Mr. Crotzer's Saturday before 2d Sunday.

(Note by J. W. W.—Mr. Kratzer probably lived at the site of the present village of Linville, about 3 miles south of Jacob Lincoln's.)

Saturday, Dec. 3 (8?), 1808, church met according to appointment; Bro. Hendren moderator. Bro. Ezekiel Hamson (Harrison?) and wife invited to a seat.

Saturday, February 4, 1809, met according to appointment at Bro. Giles Turley's; Bro. Samuel O. Hindren (Hinton?) moderator.

Lewis, a man of color, came forward and was received for baptism; baptized the next day.

Saturday, March 4 (1809), met at Bro. Lincoln's; Bro Hendren moderator. Lewis was received into full fellowship.

Agreed to alter the stated time of public preaching from the first Sunday to the third. Next meeting to be held at the house of Mr. Kroatz (Kratzer?).

John Pack, a man of color, was received for baptism; baptized the next day, March 5.

Saturday, April 15 (1809), John Peck was given the right hand of fellowship.

"Resolved by the Church that Lewis a man of Colour be suspended from communion on the third Lords day in this Month and that Brother John Peck cite him to attend at the next Church Meeting to give Satisfaction Respecting his Conduct."

Saturday, May 20 (1809), business session at Bro. John Lincoln's. Case of Lewis continued.

Sunday, May 21 (1809), preaching at Mr. Kratzer's.

Saturday, June 17, business meeting at Bro. John Lincoln's; Bro. Hendren moderator. The case of Brother Lewis was taken up. After discussion he was restored to full fellowship.

Mrs. Trumbo related her experience and was unanimously received. The next business meeting was appointed for Saturday before the 3d Sunday in August, at the new meeting house.

Saturday before 3d Sunday in August (1809), met according to appointment; Bro. Abner Yates moderator, Bro. Lincoln clerk.

Bro. Lincoln appointed to write letter to association; Br. Lincoln and Turley messengers. Association to be held at F T meeting house in Culpeper County, Friday before 3d Sunday in September.

September business meeting to be held at Bro. Lincoln's.

Saturday, October 14 (1809), Bro. Abner Yates moderator. A contribution of 1 pound 14 shillings was made up to reimburse our messenger for money paid to the last two associations and for elements for two communions.

Agreed to give Bro. John Peck a letter of dismission.

Saturday, Nov. 18 (1809), business session at Bro. Lincoln's; Bro. Lincoln moderator.

December business meeting was held at Bro. Turley's; Bro. Lincoln moderator.

Saturday, February 16, 1810, business meeting at Bro. Turley's; Bro. Lincoln moderator.

Saturday, April 14 (1810), business session at Bro. Lincoln's; Bro. Lincoln moderator.

Saturday, May 19 (1810), at the new meeting house; Bro. Lincoln moderator.

Saturday, June 16, at Bro. Lincoln's; Bro. Lincoln moderator. Bro. Lincoln to forward a letter to Bro. Booten, inviting him to preach at the new meeting house, Linville Creek, as soon as convenient.

Bro. Lincoln to prepare a letter to the Culpeper Association, to be held at Ferry Run, beginning Friday preceding the 1st Sunday in September.

Saturday, August 18 (1810), at new meeting house. Letter to association read and approved.

Saturday, Sept. 15 (1810), business session. Appointed next church meeting for Saturday before 3d Sunday in October.

Saturday, Dec. 15 (1810), at Bro. Lincoln's; Bro. Lincoln moderator. Next session to be held at Bro. Turley's, Saturday before 3d Sunday in January, 1811.

Saturday, April 20, 1811, Bro. Lincoln moderator.

(Note by J. W. W.—The entries in the old record during this period are only occasional and very brief.)

Saturday, May 13 (1811), Bro. Lincoln moderator. The church agreed to hold communion the 2d Sunday in June, Bro. Hindren attending.

Saturday, July 20, Bro. Lincoln moderator. He was appointed to write the letter to the association.

Saturday, Aug. 17 (1811), Bro. Lincoln moderator.

"Brother Lincoln prepared a letter to the Culpeper association to be held at Smiths Creek, Shanadoah County, to begin the friday before the first Sunday in Septr, which was Read and approvd of. Brethren John Lincoln Giles Turley and Abner Yates appointed our Messengers to the said association."

Saturday, Sept. 14 (1811), business session.

Saturday, Oct. 19, church meeting at Bro. Lincoln's.

Saturday, Nov. 16 (1811), at Bro. Lincoln's; Bro. John Runyon moderator.

Saturday, Dec. 14, at Bro. Lincoln's; Bro. John Runyon Sr. moderator. Brother Elijah Skidmore also present.

Next church meeting to be held at Bro. Turley's, Saturday before the 3d Sunday of February, 1812.

Saturday, November ——, 1812, Bro. John Runyan Jr. moderator, Bro. Abner Yates clerk. Sister Hester Trumboe and

Sisters Betsy & Rebeckah Dunlap applied for letters of dismission. . . .
Next business meeting to be at Bro. Turley's on Saturday before 3d Sunday in December.

December 19 (1812), met at Sister Caldwell's house, sometime Bro. Turley's; Bro. John Runyan Jr. moderator, Bro. Lincoln clerk. The matter of granting letters to Sisters Betsy & Rebeckah Dunlap was again agitated, but laid over till next church meeting, which was appointed for Saturday before 3d Sunday in February, 1813.

This meeting failed on account of excessive inclement weather.

Saturday, April 17, 1813, met at Bro. Lincoln's. Bro. Abner Yates moderator; Bro. Lincoln clerk. The Dunlap sisters stated that they had given up the idea of requesting letters of dismission.

Bro. Lincoln requested to write to Elders Mason & Sims asking them, if convenient, to attend at our meeting-house in June.

Saturday, May 15 (1813), at the meeting-house. Bro. Lincoln stated that he had written Br. Mason and Sims.

"Elders Mason & Sims attended at our meeting-house last thursday in May & first Lords day in June, & preached, the latter time especially to a very large and respectable congregation, but no communion held for want of a table."

June 19 (1813), Bro. A. Yates moderator, Bro. Lincoln clerk. No particular business.

Saturday, July 17, Bro. Abner Yates moderator, Bro. Lincoln clerk. Bro. Lincoln to write letter to the association, which is to be held Saturday before 3d Sunday in August.

Saturday, Aug. 14 (1813), Bro. Runyan moderator, Bro. Lincoln clerk. Association letter read and agreed to; Bro. Lincoln unanimously chosen messenger to the association.

Appointment for Saturday before 3d Sunday in September (1813) "fell through on account of excessive rain."

Saturday, Oct. 16 (1813), Bro. Runyan moderator, Bro. Lincoln clerk. Another session on Saturday, November 20.

Saturday, April 16, 1814, met at our meeting-house; Bro. Yates moderator. Edith, a black member, was arraigned; confessed to some of the faults charged against her, professed hearty sorrow, and the church forgave her.

Friday, May 14 (1814), met for business. Appointed another meeting for Saturday before the 3d Sunday in June.

Saturday, June 18, Bro. Yates moderator. Resolutions passed regarding absence from church meetings, looking towards a stricter enforcement of rules relating thereto.

Saturday, Aug. 20 (1814), Bro. Yates moderator, Bro. Lincoln clerk. Letter for association read; Bro. Lincoln appointed messenger. A letter to be sent to Bro. George Trumboe.

Anderson Runyan was received for baptism. "Mrs. Dunlaps Edith to be cited to appear before the next church-meeting to answer for her gross misconduct, or more probably to hear her sentence of excommunication."

Saturday, Sept. 17 (1814), Elder Hershberger being present was chosen moderator.

Edith was excommunicated.   Another black female member, Delph, was arraigned for adultery.   After "mature consideration & some debate" the case was laid over to next meeting.

Anderson Runyan, having been baptized in Brock's Gap the last Sunday in August by Elder Hershberger, was received into fellowship; "also John Runyan junior of junior, & Esther his sister, & Jacob Runyan, having been baptized by the same Administrator, at the same place."

Mary Beaver, wife of Matthias, was received for baptism.

Appointed communion at the union meeting to be holden at our meeting-house the last Saturday & Sunday in next month (October); and our next business meeting to be held at said Matthias Beaver's house on Linville Creek.

Saturday, Oct. 8 (1814), met at Mr. Beaver's.   Elder Hershberger preached, then acted as moderator.

"Received Samuel Price and his ancient mother Hannah Price into the fellowship of the church, he having related his experience in Aug. last to the said Elder & a part of the Church at old Br. Runyan's on Saturday & was, with some others, baptized on Sunday; and she . . . was baptized some time afterwards."

Also received Hannah Bare, daughter of John Bare.   She and Mary Beaver were baptized.

"Excommunicated the aforesaid Delp." . . .

Sunday, Oct. 30 (1814), at a union meeting Elders Jones, Harshbarger, & Booten all preached or exhorted both days (Saturday and Sunday).   Communion on Sunday.

Preceding communion John Tussing & his brother Philip Tussinger, Hannah Price & Mary Price, daughters of Samuel Price, were received into full fellowship.

"This was a happy season for our little church."

Saturday, Nov. 12 (1814), met at Bro. Lincoln's.   Eld. Harshbarger present; Bro. Solomon present invited to a seat.

On motion of Bro. Lincoln, the church unanimously gave their call to Bro. Harshbarger to supply her a part of his time, which he agreed to do monthly, Saturday and Sunday.

Next church meeting to be at Bro. Hawks, in Brock's Gap.

Saturday, Dec. 24 (1814), met at Bro. John Runyan's Sr.   Our pastor present.   Daniel Runyan & wife Margaret, Jacob Price, & Katherine Williams, wife of Peter, all previously baptized by Elder Harshbarger, were received into fellowship.

On the evening of the above day, after preaching at Bro. Hawks, Susanah Tusinger, wife of John, was received for baptism.   On Sunday the church gave the right hand of fellowship to Eve Price, wife of Andrew.

Saturday, January 21, 1815, at our meeting-house; Eld. Harshbarger moderator; Bro. Lincoln agreed to write to Bro. G. Trumbo again; also to Sisters Betsy Bowman, Burnsides, & Briton.   Bro. Harshbarger to see & converse with Bro. & Sister Turley.

March 25 (1815) met at Bro. Lincoln's. Bro. Harshbarger reported a conference with Bro. & Sister Turley, who acknowledged themselves faulty for not attending church meetings, but alleged several reasonable excuses; professed an intention of being with us soon; and requested a letter to join Salem Church.

Saturday, April 22 (1815), at the meeting-house; Eld. Harshbarger present. Next church meeting and preaching to be in Brock's Gap.

Saturday, May 27, at the house of old Bro. Runyan; Eld. H. present. "Old brother Trumboe, who lives on the south Fork of Potomack, being present, related in a very humble & affecting manner his reasons for his long absence from church meetings & worship, at the same time expressing his great attachment to the church & sincere desire to attend her meetings more frequently for the future; his reasons &c. were considered to be sufficient & satisfactory to the church."

Rebecca Bealer was received for baptism.

There were present at this meeting 23 members.

Sunday (May 28, 1815) Elder P. Sperry being present preached, immediately after Eld. Harshbarger. Susanah Tusinger, Lissy Runyan, and Rebecca Bealer were baptized.

Saturday, June 24 (1815), at Linville Creek meeting-house; Eld. Harshbarger moderator. Bro. Lincoln, clerk, appointed to write letter to next association. Susanah Tusing, Lissy Runyan, & Rebecca Bealer were received into fellowship.

(Note by J. W. W.—It may now be observed that the membership of the Linville Creek Baptist Church is being made up of German people along with the English, Scotch-Irish, etc.)

Saturday, Aug. 26 (1815), business session at Bro. Lincoln's. Bro. Harshbarger present. Br. Lincoln, Runyan, Yates, & Philip Tussenger were nominated as messengers to the association.

Next church meeting to be held at Sister Hawk's in Brock's Gap; also preaching there on Sunday.

Saturday, Sept. 23 (1815), Eld. H. present. Bro. Lincoln appointed to write Bro. Turley & wife & excite them to their duty. Next business session at the meeting-house.

Saturday, Oct. 21, Bro. Hershbarger reported that he had conversed with Sister Trumbo who, because of the great distance from this church, wishes a letter of dismission to join the South Branch Church. Granted.

Sister Betsy Bowman, who lives nearer the center of Salem Church than this, personally applied for a letter to join Salem. Granted.

Bro. Beaver to deal with Sisters Mary Beaver & Hannah Bare before next church meeting and excite them to their duty.

Next church meeting to be at Sister Hawk's and preaching on Sunday at Jacob Trumbo's.

Saturday, Nov. 25 (1815), business meeting at Sister Hawk's. Bro. Beaver reported good promises from the absent sisters.

Sister Rebeckah Bealer was inquired of respecting her neglecting the two last church meetings, who says her father would not consent to her attending them.

Hannah Price, daughter of Samuel, having been visited by Sisters Hawk and Anne Runyan, . . . was excluded from fellowship.

December appointment not attended.

Saturday, January 27, 1816, met at Bro. Lincoln's. A subscription paper for Eld. Hershbarger was agreed upon, to be presented to members and the general public.

A subscription had been made up at last church meeting among the members only of about $20, to be paid Bro. H. as soon as convenient for past services.

Saturday, Feb. 23 (1816), at Bro. Lincoln's. A subscription paper for Bro. Harshbarger was read and approved.

At a meeting at Bro. Price's Saturday, April 26, it was unanimously agreed upon motion of Bro. Hershbarger to hold communion at Bro. Lincoln's the 4th Sunday in June; church meeting on Saturday preceding at the same place.

May meeting failed on account of rain.

Saturday, June 22 (1816), business session at Bro. Lincoln's. Bro. Harshbarger to visit Sister Mary Beaver & excite her to her duty. Bro. & Sister Turley being present applied for a letter to join Salem Church. Granted.

Communion on Sunday; 24 communicants.

Saturday, July 27 (1816), Br. Harshbarger & Beaver appointed to visit delinquent Sisters Beaver & Bare and excite them to their duty. Bro. Lincoln to visit or write Sister Hannah Carrier for like purpose, and also to write association letter.

Saturday, Aug. 24, met at Bro. Samuel Price's. Association letter read and approved; Br. Beaver, Jacob Price, and Lincoln appointed messengers.

Sister Rebecca Ginkins (Jenkins?) being about to remove to the state of Ohio was granted a letter.

Members returned to the association 38: 4 dismissed by letter, 1 excluded, & 1 dead (dismissed by letter, Sisters Trumbo & Bowman, Bro. Turley & wife; excluded, H. Price jun.; dead, Sister Brumfield).

September 21 (1816) business session at the meeting-house. Appointed next church meeting at Bro. John Tusinger's "high up in Brocks gap."

At the October meeting little was done except appointing the next at Bro. Lincoln's.

Nov. 23 (1816) at Bro. Lincoln's; some of the members paid up their subscriptions to Bro. Hershbarger.

Saturday, Dec. 21, at Sister Hawk's. Anne Runyan, daughter of John, was received for baptism; likewise Madeline Runyan, wife of Daniel. Next day both were baptized.

Next meeting appointed for Bro. Samuel Price's. No record.
Saturday, April 26, 1817, met at Bro. Lincoln's.

Saturday, May 24, met at the church; Bro. Lincoln moderator;
Bro. Harshbarger absent.

"Brother Yates having previously undertaken, brought forward
a new walnut table for the use of the Church, for which he was
allowed $3.25, to be paid him by her members in a reasonable time."

Saturday, June 21 (1817), at the meeting-house; Bro. Hershbarger present.

Saturday, Aug. 23, at Bro. Price's; Bro. Harshbarger present.
Association letter, previously prepared by Bro. Lincoln, was read &
approved; Br. Jacob Price and John Tussing appointed our messengers. $1 contributed for the fund. Bro. Lincoln paid over $1 to
Bro. Harshbarger, it having been put into his hands by Bro. Trumbo,
to be disposed of as the church should direct.

Saturday, Sept. 27 (1817), at Sister Hawk's; business session.

Contributions at different times to pay for communion table
furnished by Bro. Yates:

Bro. Anderson Runyan _____	1 shilling	
Bro. Daniel Runyan _____	9 pence	
Bro. John Lincoln & family ____	7 shillings	6 pence
Sister Price _____	1 shilling	6 pence
Bro. Beaver _____	1 shilling	6 pence
Bro. John Tussing & Saml Price _	1 shilling	6 pence
Bro. Runyan 2d & Sister Hawk __	1 shilling	9 pence
Bro. Jacob Price _____	9 pence	
Bro. Jacob Runyan _____	9 pence	
Bro. Philip Tussing _____	9 pence	
Bro. Lincoln, to pay Bro. Yates _	1 shilling	9 pence

"N. B. This last pays for a pamphlet the property of the
Church. It is the 3d annual report of the Baptist Board of Missions
&c."

Saturday, Nov. 8 (1817), church meeting at Bro. Lincoln's.

Saturday, Dec. 13, church meeting at Bro. Lincoln's. Minutes
of last association read. Next church meeting at Sister Hawk's.

Saturday, Feb. 7, 1818, church meeting at old Bro. Runyan's;
Bro. Lincoln moderator.

No minutes of the meeting at Sister Hawk's, but the following
reported from that meeting:

Bro. Runyan the younger (or 3d) made claim of $6 against Bro.
John Tussing.

Br. Runyan 2d & Saml Price appointed to investigate and make
report to the church.

Today (Feb. 7) Bro. Runyan 3d makes report, Price & Tusing
being absent. The church unanimously agreed that Tusing should
pay Runyan $6 with interest.

Bro. Tusing cited to appear at the next church meeting to answer for certain statements; and Bro. Price cited to answer for his non-attendance today.

Saturday, March 7 (1818), Bro. Lincoln moderator. Br. Tusing & Price being present made their several excuses and were acquitted. Then Bro. Tusing obtained a rehearing on the $6. All witnesses being heard on both sides, it was agreed by a majority that Bro. Tusing should pay to Bro. Runyan $2.75; upon which each party at length appeared to be satisfied.

No minutes made of the April meeting.

Saturday, May 9 (1818), at the meeting-house; Bro. Hershbarger present. Sister Rebecca Bealer being present was convicted of certain charges and excluded from fellowship.

No minutes for June meeting.

August 8 (1818), met at Nansy Hawk's. Widow Dunlap admitted to membership. Appointed Br. Anderson Runyan, Samuel Price, John Runyan, & John Lincoln our messengers to the next association, & contributed about 6 shillings to send by them.

Saturday, Sept. 12, at Linville Creek, Bro. Runyan moderator.

Sister Dunlap's coloured woman Edith professed repentance; but her reception was deferred.

Next church meeting at Bro. Price's.

(Note by J. W. W.—Now comes a hiatus of 25 years, 1818 to 1843. About 1820 John Lincoln and his family, who had been the mainstay of the Linville Creek Church for 40 years, moved to Ohio. Following the hiatus in the old minutes we find

THE CONFESSION OF FAITH OF THE REGULAR BAPTIST CHURCH CALLED BROCKS GAP

"The members composing the old regular baptist church called Linvels creek, met at Brocks Gap meeting house the 18th of February in the year of our lord 1843 and mutuly agreed that they would in future be known by the name of the old school Baptist Church called Brocks Gap, and in evidence of their christian love and affection gave each other the right hand of fellowship, and adopted the following as a summary of the leading doctrines they believe."

Then follows their confession of faith, covering several pages, signed by

Brethren	Sisters
Jacob Trumbo	Elisabeth Trumbo
Adam Tusing	Lydia Tusing
Samuel Price	Susan Price
David Price	Mary Price
John Heeps	Catharine Heeps
Christian Biller	Hannah Biller
Jacob Fawley	Sarah Fawley
Anderson Runyon	Sarah Runyon
Levi Heps	Dorothy Heps

John Hulve
James May
Philip Tusing
John Bosey
John Minnich
Samuel a Collered man

Margaret Hulve
Hannah Henester
Elisabeth Thomas
Melvina Peterson
Mary Bull
Margaret Painter
Sarah Riggleman
Katharine Tusing
Leane Runyon
Katharine S. Kinkle
Nancy Biller
Barbary Turner
Margaret Dwyer

October 15, 1842, church meeting at Brock's Gap; Christopher Keyser moderator; Jacob Trumbo clerk.   Confessions of faith of Smith Creek and Linville Creek read.

December 18, 1842, Christopher Keyser moderator; Jacob Trumbo clerk.   Coloured brother Samuel cited to appear at the next meeting.   Moved that we get a church book.   Christopher Keyser and Levi Heps appointed a committee to revise the constitution of the Linville Creek Church by next meeting.

Sister Dyer requested to attend and show cause for long absence. Brother Keyser elected pastor.

February 12, 1843, Brother Samuel's case was laid over till next meeting.   The revised confession of faith of the Linville Creek Church was adopted.   Reference concerning Sister Dwyer laid over till next meeting.   Keyser moderator; Trumbo clerk.

April 15, 1843, meeting; same officers.

June 17, 1843, Bro. Samuel restored to favor; case of Sister Dyer laid over again, but she was to be cited by Sister Hennester. Bro. Levi Heps to write letter to next association; $1.25 to be raised towards printing the minutes.   Keyser moderator; Trumbo clerk.

August 19, 1843, letter to association read and approved.   Levi Hep moderator; Jacob Trumbo clerk.

October 14, 1843, Bro. Charl Woods and Sister Catharine Woods his wife of the Hawksbill Church were received by letter.   Mrs. Ruddle was received for baptism.   Keyser moderator; Trumbo clerk.

December 16, 1843, Ann Hepps was received for baptism.   Bro. Keyser re-elected pastor.   Keyser moderator; Trumbo clerk.

February 17, 1844, Br. Philip Tusing and James May to be cited by Brother ————.

(Note by J. W. W.—Here the record, as I have it, ends abruptly. Acknowledgment is gratefully made to Mr. Henry W. Scarborough of Philadelphia for a copy of the church minutes.)

ROCKINGHAM MEN IN SERVICE AGAINST THE INDIANS, 1774

In the Revolutionary convention at Williamsburg, Monday, June 24, 1776, as shown by the journal, Mr. Richard Lee, from the Committee of Public Claims, reported that the committee had, according to order, had under their consideration a claim of Capt. Joseph Haynes, Lt. Daniel Smith, and Ensign John Smith, to them referred; and that it appeared to them that the said Joseph Haynes, in the month of June, 1774, received orders from Col. Abraham Smith of Augusta to raise as many men as the short notice would admit and march to the North Fork of the South Branch of Potowmack River, to protect the inhabitants of that place, who at that time were threatened with an invasion by the Indians; that the said Haynes, within six days after receiving the orders, marched with 30 men to the place aforesaid, leaving his ensign to proceed with the remainder that were enlisted as soon as they could be convened, who two days after joined him with twelve men; that the said Col. Smith, thinking these 42 men, with the officers, would be a sufficient reinforcement for the garrison, ordered the captain not to enlist any more till he should receive orders for so doing from the county lieutenant; that the captain applied to the county lieutenant for permission to recruit eight men, who were then ready to enlist under him, to complete his company, that he might be entitled to a captain's pay, who told him not to enlist any more without further orders, and assured him that he should draw full pay as captain, notwithstanding his company was not complete; that the commissioners have allowed the said Joseph Haynes lieutenant's pay, the said Daniel Smith ensign's pay, and the said John Smith serjeant's pay, for 38 days, the time they were in service on the South Branch, and the same for the number of days they served on the expedition against the Shawanese, which last mentioned time there were 49 privates enlisted, two of whom were returned as deserters, and one as a spy, as appears by the roll; and that they had come to the following resolutions thereupon; which he read in his place and afterwards delivered in at the clerk's table, where the same were again twice read and agreed to.

Resolved, That the said claimants have been already allowed by the commissioners full pay, agreeably to law, for the time they served on the Shawanese expedition.

Resolved, That the following additional allowance be made to the said claimants for the 38 days they were on duty on the South Branch of Potowmack River, to wit: To the said Joseph Haynes, as captain, 2s.6d. amounting to 4l. 15s. to the said Daniel Smith, as lieutenant, 1s. 6d. per day, amounting to 2l. 17s. and to the said John Smith, as ensign, 3s. 6d. per day, amounting to 6l. 13s. being the difference between the allowance made them by the commissioners and this committee for the said services.

SOME ROCKINGHAM PETITIONS ON FILE IN RICHMOND

Pay for a Slave

1778

At a Court of Oyer & Terminer held for Rockingham County for the Trial of Will a negro man Slave belonging to George Keezell accused of feloniously murdering Hans Cloverfield Miller of the said parish & County.

The said Negro Will being brot. to the Bar & found guilty of the Crime wherewith he stands charged, is ordered to be hanged by the Neck untill he is dead &c. the Court in Consequence of the said Sentence do value the said Slave to two hundred & twenty-five pounds Curt. Money which is ordered to be certified to the next Session of Assembly

by the Court

Petr. Hog C. C. R.

I do assign all my Right & Title of the within Certificate to Josiah Davidson & desire the Money may be levied in his Name for Value received as Witness my hand this 28th Sept. 1778.

gorg Kes ——— (illegible)

Test Petr. Hog

To the Honourable the Speaker and House of Delegates

The Petition of George Keezle: Humbly sheweth; That at A Court of Oyer and Terminer Held for the County of Rockingham for the tryal of Will, A Negrow man Slave: the Property of your Petitioner; Who was accused of Murder; and being found Gilty; was sentenced by the Court to be Hanged by the Neck untill he is Dead; But the Night Preceeding the Day appointed for his Execution; The said Negro made his Escape from Goal; But was afterwards; Retaken: at which time He making an obstinate Resistance; some of the party then Present shot him through the Body of which wound He Died; before the Sheriff Could be Brought to Hang him.

His head; agreeable to the Sentence pronounced by the Court; was Dissected from his body and fixed on A pole at the Cross Roads.

The Court in Consequence of Said Sentence Did Vallue the Said Slave to two Hundred and twenty five Pounds Current money which your Petitioner Prays may be allowed him and as in Duty bound Shall Pray &c.

George Keezell

George Keezles Petn Oct. 29, 1778
refd. to Claims
£225 Allowed reported Novr. 5th

A SOLDIER PRAYS RELIEF

To the Honourable Speaker and Gen. Delegates

The Petition of John Willson of the County of Rockingham most humbly Sheweth

That your Petitioner in the Year 1774 went out in the Expedition against the Indians—And the unhappy Contest with Britain Breaking out soon after Your Petitioner entered himself Volunteer in the Glorious cause of Liberty, and Continued a Soldier in the American Service till the Conclusion of peace—In which Service he recd. four different Wounds in four different Battles (Viz) At Brandy Wine at Germaintown—Monmouth and Gilford—in which last Battle the Wound so fractured his left Arm—with many former Fatigues—Particularly at the Building of the fort at West Point—in which Fatigue, by the fall of a Log, by which two Men were killed, Your Petitioner's Back was so much Bruised and Weakened, that ever since Yr. Petitioner is incapable of getting his living, by honest industry—Also Yr. Petitioner being arrived in his Sixtieth Year, Implores yr. Honours would take his deplorable Condition in serious consideration and allow him a Small annual Pension, that he may not become troublesome to the County in which he resides—And your Petitioner as in Duty bound will ever pray &c.

The foregoing petition was presented in 1782.

In 1784 Benj. Harrison, George Baxter, and Archd. Hopkins signed a statement declaring that John Wilson had enlisted in the Continental Army, in Virginia's quota of troops, in 1776, and had continued in service as a soldier to the end of the war, by different enlistments, with very short intermissions; that he had received many wounds in different engagements—Brandywine, Germantown, Monmoth, Gilford; all of which made it difficult for him to get a living; . . . asks for the same bounty in lands that was being given other soldiers of the Virginia Line for equal services.

On January 17, 1782, John Crawford, postmaster, certified (certified by Php. Clayton) that John Wilson had received no pay for his 18 months service in the Southern Army.

Dr. W. Foushee declared over his signature that Wilson did not appear to be disabled from his wounds.

"FIFTEEN BAD WOUNDS"

To the Honourable the General Assembly of Virginia:

The Petition of James Gilmer of the County of Rockingham most Humbly Sheweth That your Petitioners Son Samuel Gilmer being enlisted as a Soldier in the Service of this State and was so unfortunate to be in Colo. Bufords defeat at the Hanging Rock in Carolina in the Year 1780 at which time he received Fifteen bad Wounds Ten of which was in his head out of which came five Bones, and returned Home to your Petitioner (who is very Ancient and in

low circumstances) in a very Miserable Condition being almost
naked, your Petitioner truly commiserating the unhappy Siuation of
his Son, employed a Doctor to cure his Wounds, also hired a Woman
to take care of and to nurse him by whose Care and Assistance under
Divine Providence he recovered for which your Petitioner payed
Forty Shillings to each of the said persons vizt. the Doctor and the
Nurse for their trouble and likewise Cloathed him from head to foot,
your poor Petitioner therefore prays to be reimbursed the Money he
has expended upon the Cure of his said Son, and further to be
Allowed Such Compensation for Cloathing and finding him four
Months Board as may be thought just and reasonable.

And your Petitioner as in Duty Bound Shall pray
Signed by:

Henry Henry	Thos. Gordon
Wm. Boyd	Archibald Hopkins
Thos. Peel	John Hopkins
William Henry	Ephraim Hopkins
Robert Boyd	Ephraim Love
George Smith	

Presented November 2, 1784
referred to Claims
November 8, 1784 Allowed £15
Reported

ANOTHER REVOLUTIONARY SOLDIER

Francis Meadows of the 8th (6th?) Virginia Regiment who was
taken at Charles Town & made his Escape; Alledges that his time of
Service is Expired. he is Permited to pass, untill a Place of Rendezvous is Appointed, when his enlistment will be Enquired into

Given under my hand this 5th (?) Sept. 1780

JAMES WOOD, *Colo. Com.*

The Auditor of Accounts Richmond:
Sir, On Settling my Accts. for pay and land please deliver the
Certificates &c. unto Capt. John Hopkins

his
Francis X Meadows
mark

(Appended to above:)
February 26th 1786
This Day Came Francis Meadows Before me one of the Justices
of the Peace for the County of Rockingham And Signd. And
Acknowledg the Above order

Benja. Harrison

Certified By me
26 Feby. 1787

I do certify that Francis Meadows inlisted about the first of
January 1777. Seventy seven and continued in service in the
original 10th Virga. Regimt. Capt. Lamm's compy. till the capture
of Charles town, his term of service being then expired, he made his
escape from the British.
Given under my hand Mar. 10th, 1787.

L. Hawes formerly L. Co.
1st Vir. Regiment

This claim has not been settled
Audrs. Office 14 Novr. 88   I. Pendleton

To the Honble the Speaker and Gent. of the House of Delegates:

The Petition of Francis Meadows Humbly Sheweth that sometime in the year 1777 he inlisted into the Virginia line on Continental
service and Continued till the Capture of Charles Town where he was
made a Prisoner, from whence he made his Escape and came to the
Albemarl Barracks (there being no place of Rendevous nearer) that
when he came to the said Barracks he applied to Colo. James Wood
who was Commanding Officer at that Place and obtained a furlough
till he should be called into Service, but his time of service for which
he inlisted being expired he was not again calld into Service till the
Army was disbanded and consequently could not obtain a discharge to
enable him to draw his pay & depreciation.

He now prays that you will direct the Auditor of Public
Accounts to Settle his Accounts and give a Certificate for the same Or
grant him such other relief as you in your Wisdom may think mete.

Presented Nov. 15, 1790
Referred to Claims
    Reasonable
    Congress
reported 8th Dec. 90

TOBACCO WAREHOUSE PROPOSED, 1784

To the Honourable the Speaker & the Gentlemen of the House of
Delegates The Petition of Sundry of the Inhabitants of Rockingham
County Humbly Sheweth,
    That the great Scarceity and the large demands for Cash at this
juncture is become most alarming; None, or at least Comparitively
speaking few, of the good Citizens in the said County being able to
pay their publick Dues required by Government; As they hold little
Or no property that will Command Cash at this day; Or at least in
no wise Addequate To the Demands; Cattle and Horses being our
former Staple Comodity of Trade; Which at this day there Appears
so small Ademand for; that Monies Arising from the Sale will In no
wise enable the people at large to pay their just dues; Tobacco at
this Day Being the Only property which Appears to Command Cash

in this State, Some Few of the People in sd. County have this last Season planted their Ground with Tobacco; and made A tolerable Experiment perhaps One hundred Hogsheads; And, finding a Soil and Climate to answer the purpose perfectly well for Makeing Tobacco

The People, almost in General, with proper Incouragement; would wish to Make Some quantity More the Insueing Year; But the long distance from Inspection will, Certainly, Deter great Numbers; as it must be Attended With Great Expence To waggon Tobacco so far, and then possably might not pass Inspection; and Consequently the loss of two or three Hogsheads might be almost the ruin of Some poore Families; And least the Building the necessary ware House and providing Other things Necessary for the purpose of Inspection, at publick Expense, Should be thought Burthensome, Or, Grivouse to Any—

James Diviers in the town of Harrisonburg in sd. County, Purposes, to Build the sd. Warehouse and provide all things nessery thereto at his own Expense; on his own Land in Sd. Town; on his being allowed the Usual benafit Allowed to Other Owners of Warehouses

Therefore your Petitioners Pray that the Honourable House In their wisdom would Grant That A ware House for the Inspection of Tobacco may be Established at the Towne afore Said, And Your Petitioners as in Duty bound Shall Ever Pray &c.

Aug. 18th, 1784

John Sheltman	Peter Vannaman
Sam Black	John Collins
John Peregern	Dennis Lionhan (?)
Robt. Scott	William Rees
John Mitchell	Henrich Selzer (?)
Francis Mara	George Waver
Conrad Leaveston	John Reves
John Apler	Dvd. Harned
James Charlton	Danl. Hoowtser (?)
James Blain	Townsend Matthews
Charles McClane	George Argabrite
Michel McCluer	Henry Burgess
Richd. Ragon	Ephraim Hopkins
John Flek (?)	Jas. Divier
Josiah Davisson	Hugh Divier
Sovoick (?) Stratton	Wm. Deviers
Saml Anderson	Nicholas Smyth
Charles Donnelly	John Hay
Robt. Harrison	George Bond
Isaha Shipman	James Mitchell
Reuben Harrison	Arther Davison
John Shipman	John Ewin
James Coyle (?)	Hy. (?) Ewin

Michl. Mullan
Ben. Smith
Jno. Smith
Roger Dyer
John Guin
Edward Collins
George Kisel
Soln. Matthews
Thos. Fulton
Wm. (?) Ergebright
Joseph Douglass
John Ervin (?)
Uriah Garton
Jno. Robinsone
James Bruster
Ellet Mather (?)
Wm. Cravens
Josiah Harrison
Joseph Smith
Andrew Erwin
William Hind
William Dunnavan
Ezekiel Harrison
John Bryon
Robert Curry
Benj. Harrison

George Baxter
Wm. Smith
Isaac Hinkle
George Chrisman
Geo. Huston
Stephen Coonrod
Josiah Harrison
Benjn. Smith
John Rerh (?)
Jno. Shipman
Jacob Kirlin
Robert Hook
Wm. Hook
John Edde
John Grattan
John Hopkins, Jr.
William Nall
Reuben Harrison
Jeremiah Beesly
Brewer Reeves
John Divire
Jere Cravens
Robt. Cravins
John Hemphil
Thos. Reed
Peter (?) Bryan (?)

The foregoing petition was presented Nov. 20, 1784, and referred to "Props."

No evidence has been found that a tobacco warehouse was established in Harrisonburg in conformity with this petition.

A New County Asked For

On October 11, 1792, an interesting petition was presented to the General Assembly from Rockingham and Shenandoah, as follows:

To the Honorable the Assembly of Virginia The Petition of a number of the Inhabitants & Freeholders of the Counties of Shenandoah & Rockingham

Humbly Sheweth, That your Petitioners from the situation of those parts of their Respective Counties in which they live, Experience great and many Inconveniencies and difficulties in attending the Courts of the same. Also a great delay in the Administration of Public Justice, owing in a great measure to the largeness of the Counties in which they live, and the multiplicity of business therein Added to the distance of thirty five or forty miles which Your Petitioners have to travel over mountains and rivers, which at many times in the year are not only difficult and dangerous, but Impossible to pass over, which obliges many of your Petitioners to remain at home,

Contrary to their Interest and Inclination, and to the great delay of Public Justice among them, They not being able to get their Witnesses frequently to Court for reasons before mentioned—

From Inconveniencies and a wish to promote the Publick good, Your Petitioners are Constrained to apply to your Honorable body to redress their grievances by passing an Act of Assembly for forming a new County out of the Upper Or south end of Shenandoah, or the lower or North end of Rockingham Counties (those parts of each County to be taken off to be as follows) to begin on the Top of the Blue Ridge in the line which divides Culpeper from Shenandoah Counties, so that leaving the Culpeper line at Right Angles it may Cross the Road leading from Winchester to Staunton in the County of Shenandoah at a place known by name of Jumping Run—and then the Course Continued unto the Top of the Mountain on the line between Shenandoah and Hardy County then up the Fork Mountain along that line, and the line between Rockingham and Pendleton County so far, that leaving the same at right Angles, a line will pass through the County of Rockingham at a place known by name of the big spring—and from thence the Course Continued Unto the Top of the Blue Ridge & then down the same to the Beginning—

And that all within the sd. bounds may be formed into a new County and a Court house be Erected for the same at the Village of Newmarket, which from its being situated on the Main Road leading from Winchester to Staunton, Also being directly Opposite the only passable Gaps with any kind of Carriage; over the Branch of Masenutting Mountain—Renders it a place truly Eligible and one by nature Rendered Convenient for Your Petitioners to travel Unto, at all seasons of the Year, without difficulty or danger.

Your Petitioners therefore pray that Your Honorable body will take into Consideration their Local grievances, as well as their Remote Situation, and if you in your Wisdom shall think fit to comply with the Prayer of our Petition, it will not only be the means of furthering Publick Justice amongst the Litigants; but also, of preventing of Oppression and delay—

And your Petitioners as in duty bound shall ever pray &c.

The foregoing petition is written in beautiful straight lines and uniform letters, as plain today after 136 years as a print from copper plate; and was probably the work of Col. Jacob Rinker of Shenandoah, so long prominent as surveyor, justice, and writer of deeds.

Attached to the body of the petition are 14 different sheets of paper, sewed and pasted together; the whole forming a huge sheet 66 inches from top to bottom and 16 inches from side to side; and on it are written the names of 572 men and women, some of whom lived in Rockingham, some in Shenandoah. Some of the names are well written, clear, legible, with letters elegantly formed; others are almost faded out, and many are in irregular scribbling. No less than 79 are written in German script, and a half-dozen or so are written in a mixture of German and English. A few of the petitioners made their marks.

Among the signers who are rather well known are (were) the following:

Taverner Beale (S)	Andrew Byrd (R)
Jno. Jordan (S)	Darkis Robinson (R)
Anthony Reader (R)	John Sever (S)
John Neff (S)	Jacob Rinker (S)
Jese Dehaven (R)	Martin Shank (R)
Lewis Rinehart (S)	George Prince (S)
Mounce Byrd (S)	Daniel Smith (R)
William Sehorn (S)	Coonrod Brinker (S)
Jacob Trumbo (R)	John Rousch (S)
William Marshall (S)	George Ruddell (R)
Wm. Byrd	Barnerd Peal (R)
Paul Hinkle (S)	Jacob Rambo, Jr. (R)
Davis Allen (S)	George Munger (S)
John Kagy (S)	John Huff (S)
Jacob Stiegel (S)	Martin Coffman (S)
John Bar (R)	Henry Dove (R)
Philip Lung (S)	James Dwyer (R)
Thomas Moore (S)	Isaac Dehaven (R)
Daniel Rouch (S)	Isaac Samuels (S)
Jacob Roush (S)	Jacob Custer (R)
Jackson Rembow (R)	Daniel Strickler (S)
Johannes Roller (R)	John Beery (R)
John Pennybacker (S)	George Rader (R)
Peter Rufner (S)	

By the use of the letters (R) and (S) after these names an effort is made to locate these persons in either Rockingham or Shenandoah County.

In spite of the arguments adduced and the numerous signatures appended, this petition was rejected. In 1831 Page County was established, partly from Shenandoah and partly from Rockingham, but on different lines from those proposed in 1792.

TO REPAIR SWIFT RUN GAP ROAD, 1794

To the Onarable Speaker and the Members Composing the House of Assembly of Virginia; your pertitiners from the County of Rockingham, having but one publick Merchent Road Over the blew Ridge none (known) by the name of Swift Run Gapp, to which Cheaf of there produce is carried to Alexander, Fredeburg, and the Sity of Richmond; your pertisiners prayer is that you pass an Act to Empower the Court of Rockingham to Leavy on the Tithable persons of sd. County not Exseading the sum of —— to Repair and ceap in Repair the road Over swift run gapp from Peter Hershmond in sd. County to Daniel Wolferd in Orange County; And that the Court of Rockingham shall appoint Commissiners to Agree with some person to seay that the Moneys is laid Out to the best Advantage for the said road, and your petitiners shall ever pray—

Among the 125 signers of this petition were:

Francis Kirtley	Richard Reagan
Jacob Bear	Michael Waren
Thos. Rice	John Harrison
Jacob Miller	Smith Lofland
Joseph Kennerly	Benj. Smith, Jr.
George Bell	Benj. Smith, Sr.
John Smith	Francis Stewart
William Fearill	William Pence
Conrad Harnsberger	Isaac Peters
John Wren	Jacob Good
David Garvin	Wm. Bryan
Layton Yancey	A. Waterman
John Yancey	George Good
Peter Wine	Thos. Harrison
James Rains	Reuben Harrison
Martin Lamb	Robert Harrison
Peter Harshmand	John Epler
Adam (?) Hansbarger	Isaac Kisor
Landen Veach	George Krisman
Charles Lewis	Jacob Krisman
Adam Sellers	John Kring
Peter Conrad	Edward Shanklin
Henry Thornhill	Abram Miller
James Taylor	James Harrison
Jacob Nicholas	Joseph Cravens
John Wayt	John Cline
S. W. Williams	John Gwinn
John Henry	Teater Kipling
John Graham	(Kiplinger? Kissling?)
Jeremiah Reagan	

The foregoing petition was filed Nov. 19, 1794. It was reported as reasonable.

In 1801 several petitions were presented asking that the Swift Run Gap road be made a turnpike. Other petitions relating to this turnpike were filed in 1802 and 1803.

CALL FOR A CONSTITUTIONAL CONVENTION

In 1797 five petitions were presented to the General Assembly from Rockingham County expressing a desire for a convention to reform the state constitution.

HARRISONBURG IN 1798

To the Honourable the speaker and members of Boath Houses of the General Assembly of Virginia

The Petition of the subscribers Humbly Sheweth that the Town of Harrisonburg in the County of Rockingham has nearly one Hundred acres laid of in lotts, publick square, Streets & Alleys on a very rough and Rockey piece of Ground and Containing as many as eight streets four Alleys and all being built on at this time except two Streets.

Many parts of the Publick Square streets & Alleys are Quite Impassible for Carriages on account of rocks as allso several Bridges are much Wanting across a small Watercourse leading threw sd. Town which obstruction will require much labour and Expence to remove and as the Aforesd. Labour and Expense doth Intirely fall on the Citizens of sd. Town Neever the less each Tithable in Town must work as many as from six eight an Ten days p. anum on Country roads This Last Grievance they Humbly pray your Honourable body to remove them from by takeing their cas in to Consideration and by enacting a Law relieve all the Tithables in sd. Town from working on High ways in the Country Authorizing the Trustees of the sd. Town of Harrisonburg to Appoint Over Seers with Powers to call on the Tithables in sd. Town to work under them in Opening & repairing the Streets Alleys &c. as Also Giveing Those Trustees an Additional power to regulate the General Police of said Town

And they In duty Bound will ever Pray.

J. Shipman	C. Lofland
Philip Grymes	John Pence
Jeremiah Kyle	A. Mason (?)
Edwd. McDonough	Antoni Sainsbery (?)
H. L. Gambill	James Burges
G. McWilliams	George Sites
Wm. Dunovan	James Kyle
John Owens	John Messeck
Fleet (?) Smith	John Turner
Thomas Scott	Jos. Cravens
Thos. Herron	Saml. Chandler (?)
Henry Burgess	John Graham
William Sprinkel	John Rogers
Abrm. Yost	Michl. Lindsay
Wm. Ireland	Robt. S. Shanklin
James Cochran	Michael Klein (?)
Thos. Sulavan (?)	Jacob High (?)
James Martin	Philip Wolff
William Messick	Adam Fareburn (?)
John Peeling (?)	Jacob Bibler (?)
James Godwin (?)	Jacob Dunnavn
Chas. Rogers	Archd. Rutherford
Jeremiah Richey	Solomon Gladdin
Alex. Graham	Wm. Cochran Jr. (?)
Yohanes Smith	Charles Kyle (?)

A. Waterman   James Basley (?)
Frederick Spangler   Elihu Messeck
James Mason (?)   Georg (?) Roland

This list of subscribers gives a good idea of the heads of families and other men in Harrisonburg in 1798.

The petition was presented Dec. 10, 1798; reported reasonable.

Lawyers and Court Days

In November 1798 a petition was drawn praying certain changes in the court days for Rockingham and Augusta, signed by sundry inhabitants of the said counties and especially the attorneys practicing law in those counties. Following is the list of names appended to this petition. It is of special interest as containing (in all probability) the names of all the lawyers and court officials of Rockingham and Augusta in 1798.

Alex. St. Claire   Anthony Rader (?)
Jacob Kinney   Jno. Wayt
Jno. Coalter   S. (?) Blackburn
W. Howwe (?)   James Bell
John Bowyer   J. (?) Heiskell
James Allen   John Fackler
David Parry   Joseph Bell
R. Grattan   Philip Grymes Jun.
J. Shipman   W. (?) Bowyer
S. W. Williams   Francis Erwin
H. L. Gambill   Abraham Stilby
D. Lee   C. Lofland
Gabriel Jones   John Koontz
Ezl. Harrison   Geo. Hewton (?)
Gaw. Hamilton   John Ewin
Wm. Dunlap   Jno. Taylor
John Smith   B. (?) Fawcett
A. Waterman   And. Shanklin
Matthew Harrison   Robert Stuart
Andrew Correll (?)

It was filed Dec. 26, 1798; three days later was reported reasonable.

Beginnings of Keezletown

In September, 1923, Hon. Geo. B. Keezell loaned the writer (J. W. W.) an interesting old document—an article of agreement between his grandfather, George Keezell, and a number of his neighbors for the development of a town in East Rockingham on Keezell's land.

Following is a copy of the said document:

The conditions on which George Keesle proposes to lay out 100 acres of the plantation where he now lives into lotts for a town;

(viz) one half acre of an in lot; & one half acre of an out lot; the first purchase of which; the purcher is to pay twenty shillings in the old way for the two half acre lotts; and also shall be subject to pay four shillings in silver as a yearly rent for said lotts; and shall build and improve on said lots within three years after purchasing; or forfit to the proprietor forty shillings per year every year he shall neglect to build after the said three years first allowed.

The said George Keesle obligates and obliges himself to make a sufficient title for said lotts to the purchasers as soon as they shall have paid the purchase money.

Know all men by these presents that we the subscribers are each of us held firmly bound unto George Keesle in the just sum of ten pounds silver currency to be paid to the said Keesle his certain attorny heirs executors administrators or assigns for the which payment well and truly to be made and done we bind our selves our and each of ours heirs executors & administrators jointly and severally and firmly by these presents.

In Witness whereof we have hereunt set our hands and seals this first Day of May —, 1781. The condition of the above obligation is such that if the subscribers or purchasers of lots shall comply with the conditions above proposed then the above obligation to be void otherwise to remain in force.

Sealed & Delivered in Presence of

	David (?) Harison (Seal)
	Thomas Lownsdale (Seal)
(Signed by)	* * * * * * * * * * (Seal)"
Jn. Harrison (?) (Seal)	Michael Hudlow (?) Seal
Cornelius Cain (Seal)	John Altstatt (Seal)
Abm Lincoln (Seal)	John A. * * * * * * *
Engle Boyer (Seal)	* * * * * * * * * *
Thos. Hewit (?) (Seal)	* * * * * * * * * *
Charles McClean (Seal)	* * * * * * * * * *
Thomas Lincoln * * *	David Laird
John Rife (Seal)	David Laird
John Armentrout (Seal)	David Laird
Mourice Byrd (Seal)	Gottlieb Hoffman (?)
And. McKinley (Seal)	* * * * * * * *
Martin Greider (Seal)	John A. * * * * * (Seal)

Some of the names are not now legible.

Shortly after the beginnings of Keezletown were made as indicated in the foregoing plan, one or two petitions were presented to the General Assembly of the state praying that the town be chartered by law. These petitions are preserved among the archives at Richmond. One of the reasons emphasized in these petitions for claiming such recognition for Keezletown was its location on the main road through the Valley from north to south.

However, it was ten years from the time Mr. Keezell launched his project for a town until the said town was actually chartered; but by Act of Dec. 7, 1791, "Keisell's- Town" was legally established.

"VOCHERS" IN THE SEVERAL MILITIA COMPANIES OF ROCKINGHAM COUNTY IN 1788

All men, including servants and slaves, herein listed were above 16 years of age.

"VOCHERS" IN CAPTAIN BENJAMIN SMITH'S COMPANY, No. 1

Benj. Smith, 1 slave, 2 horses
Joseph Smith, 4 slaves, 3 horses
John Rice, 2 horses
John Frain, 1 horse
John Rice, 5 slaves, 7 horses
Joseph Hinton, 4 horses
Anthony Curtner, 2 horses
William Bradey
Wm. Freehoulder, 3 horses
Adam Alce, 3 horses
James Rigs, 4 horses
James Ralston, sons Robert and John, 7 horses
Mitchell Reed, 3 horses, apprentice Charles Stewart
Elias Vioars, apprentice Jas. Malcolm
Arthur Davison, 5 horses
Daniel Chesnut, 1 horse
Robt. Warnock
Philip Wagey, son John, 3 horses
Thomas Fulton, 8 horses
Henry Black, son John, 1 slave, 7 horses
Edward Weldon, 3 horses
John Morrow
John Crawford
James Crawford, 7 horses
Thomas King, 4 horses
Wm. Dever, 3 slaves, 6 horses
Isaiah Shipman, sons William and Isaac, 3 slaves, 3 horses
David Shipman, 2 horses
John Shipman, 3 horses
Wm. Smith, 3 slaves, 4 horses
Henry Smith, 2 slaves, 7 horses
John Malcom, 3 horses
Benjamin Garvin, 3 horses
Silas Heart, 3 slaves, 14 horses, "and a Carriage having 4 wheels named a Chatilow"

Isaac Shockey, son Abraham, 4 horses
William Moor
Hugh Dever, 2 slaves, 6 horses
Alexander Gilmore, 2 horses
Umphra Salts, 3 horses
John Chism, 1 horse
John Dever, 2 slaves, 6 horses
George Bell
John Smith, 4 slaves, 7 horses
Sarah Reeds, 4 horses
John Davies, 2 slaves, 5 horses
Robert Davies, 5 horses
James Davies, 4 horses
Francis Erwin, 2 slaves, 14 horses
Samuel Erwin, sons John and Samuel, 6 horses
Benjamin Erwin, 6 horses
Rev. Benj. Erwin, 5 horses
James Todd, 3 horses
George Coagler, 5 horses
John Sheets, 2 horses
James Magill, Jr., 7 horses
James Magill, Sr., 1 slave, 10 horses
Stephen Eastin, 3 slaves, 4 horses
Morris Morris, son Morris, 6 horses
James Guin, 3 slaves, 5 horses
Christian Venice, 2 horses
James Humrickhouser &
Father-in-law Peter Brunner, 2 horses
Joseph Douglas, 6 horses
William Goul, 2 horses, apprentice Chas. Tresler
Thomas Chantril, 2 horses
Thomas Gilmore, 2 horses
William Boyd, son Robert, 6 horses
Thomas McDowel, 5 horses
Gawin Hamilton, 3 slaves, 16 horses
John Miller, 1 slave, 8 horses
Christian Kinsor, son Philip, 5 horses

Philip Castin
Michael Joseph
Moses Joseph, son Abraham
"David Rader above 16 years having one creature"
Ralph Lofftus, 6 horses
Wm. Blain, 6 horses

Adam Quickle, 1 horse
Henry Miller, 3 horses
Peter Moyer, 1 horse
Samuel Smallridge
Michael Kisnor
John Coonrod

"VOCHERS" IN CAPTAIN JOHN HERDMAN'S COMPANY No. 2

William Higgins, sons John and Thomas, 6 horses
Owen Williams, 4 horses
John Clough, 3 horses
John Ewins, Sr., 2 slaves, 8 horses
Thomas Shanklin, sons Thomas and James, 2 slaves, 11 horses
James Doak, 3 horses
Moses Samples, 2 horses
Wm. Wretchford, 3 horses
James McCartney, 2 horses
Hugh Ferguer, 3 horses
John Johnston, son John, 6 horses
James Blain, 1 horse
John Herdman, Jr., 2 slaves, 8 horses
John Herdman, Sr., 1 horse
Henry Henry, son Hugh, 5 horses
Benjamin Berry, 3 horses
Thomas Gordon, son Thomas, 2 slaves, 8 horses
John Church, 1 horse
Robert Samples, 3 horses
Samuel Gilmore, 1 horse
Thomas Campbell, 3 horses
John Lock, 5 horses
John Henry, 3 horses
Elisabeth Shanklin, son Robert, 4 horses
Elisabeth Harrison, 10 horses
Mathew Harrison, 2 horses
John Hopkins, son William, 8 horses
Jane Hopkins, son John, 2 slaves, 13 horses
John Boyd, 1 horse
George Baxter, sons Joseph and George, 1 slave, 9 horses
John Steel, 1 horse
Archibald Hopkins, Jr., son Rob't B., 1 slave, 3 horses

Abraham Teeters, 4 horses
Benjamin Linvil, 3 horses
Zekiel Green, son Zekiel, 3 horses
James Calhoon, 5 horses
Evan Thomas, son Esekillas, 6 horses
Abraham Branaman, servant Coonrod Helmer (hireling), 5 horses
Mary Crisman, sons Jacob, Joseph, Abraham, 7 horses
Peter Placer, sons Peter and David, 7 horses
Handle Vance, sons Christian and Solomon, 11 horses
William Vance, 2 horses
John & Rob't Curry, 11 horses
John Flack, 1 horse
Jesse Harrison, servant William Saxton, 3 horses
Town's End Mathews, son Robert, 4 horses
Ezekiel Mathews
Benjamin Hinton, 6 horses
Ebenezer Hinton, 2 slaves, 7 horses
Adam Dickey, 1 horse
Abraham Beery, 3 horses
William Ralston, 1 slave, 4 horses
David Ralston, son James, 8 horses, apprentice Samuel Mahoney
David Ralston, Jr., 6 horses
John Cromer, 1 horse
Martin Cromer, 2 horses
Jacob Coffman, son Benjamin, 9 horses
John Blain, 4 horses
Robert Blain, 2 horses
Robert Dunlap, son William, 5 horses
Thomas Bowen, 7 horses

Francis Green, grandson Francis Bowen, 7 horses
Arch Hopkins, Sr., son Ephriam, 3 slaves, 13 horses
Joshua Davison, 2 slaves, 7 horses
William Henry, 1 horse
Jacob Spitler, son Daniel, 6 horses
David Broomfield, 1 horse

Thomas McKinzey
David Berry, sons John and George H., six horses
James Gilmore, 4 horses
Gad Gilmore, 1 horse
David Gilmore, 1 horse
William Hank, 2 horses

"VOCHERS" IN URIAH GARTIN'S COMPANY, No. 3

Henry Hansberger, 5 horses, apprentice Joseph Davies
Adam Wise, 7 horses
Rhonomus Deck, 4 horses
Geo. M. McClure
Richard Pursell, 1 horse
John Montgomery, 2 horses
Lewis Sryer, 3 horses
Andrew Bogan, 4 horses
David McClure, 1 horse
James Lockheart, 1 horse
Edward Ferrol, son Christian, 3 horses
John Grattan, son Robert, 5 slaves, 11 horses
Michael Loudermilk, 1 horse
Jacob Smellcer
Cornelius Cain
Jacob Sanger, sons Adam and Peter, 4 horses
Francis Beard, 2 horses
William Fowler, 5 horses
Stephen Hansberger, 5 horses
John Fairburn, 3 horses
Barnabas Murray, 3 horses
John Huston, son Robert, 6 horses
Randolph Guin, 1 horse
Godfrey Bowman, 4 horses
Capt. Uriah Gartin, 2 horses
George Smelcer, 1 horse
John Young, 1 horse
Francis Stewart, son James, 7 horses
Bethuel Herring, 9 horses
John Black, son Frederick, 4 horses
Coonrod Rowler, 3 horses
Adam Butt, 3 horses
John Spar, 2 horses
Abraham Smith, 2 horses

Henry Broombaker, son Henry, 7 horses
Col. Benj. Harrison, sons John, Benjamin, James, 2 slaves, 7 horses
Philip Hains, 1 horse
Leonard Herring, 8 horses
Abagail Herring, 1 slave, 1 horse
William Herring, son Alexander, 8 horses
John Syzer, 3 horses
Edward Shanklin, sons Joseph and Samuel, 9 horses
Andrew Shanklin, 1 slave, 5 horses
Francis Oat, 2 horses
Daniel Guin, 2 horses
John Messerley
Thomas Killburn, 1 horse
Henry Kinger, 7 horses
Christian Hoover
Henry Bowman, 1 horse
Jennet Cummis, 3 horses
Peter Moyers, 4 horses
Philip Swatsil, 2 horses
Robert Harrison, 3 horses
Michael Wise, 3 horses
John Wise, 6 horses
Coonrad Hulvey, 7 horses
John Butt, 3 horses
George Snowden, son William, 12 horses
Mathias Geerheart, 3 horses
George Eeley, 3 horses
Michael Coonce, 2 horses
Handle Shunk, 2 horses
Henry Snider, sons Henry and Michael, 4 horses
Hindle Butt, 5 horses
Henry Butt, 2 horses

Christopher Heeton, 1 horse
Peter Roler, sons Peter and John, 6 horses
George Sanger, 3 horses
John Argabright, 2 horses
Valentine Huffman

James Alexander
Tilman Crockt
Joseph Byerly, 3 sons not named, 6 horses
Samuel Miller, 1 horse

"Vochers" of Captain George Huston's Company

William Troubaugh, sons Jacob, Michael and William C., 6 horses
John Fraizer, 3 horses
John Aldorpha, 1 horse
John Lemmons, Jr., 2 horses
Anthony Aldorpha, son Joseph, 3 horses
Catharine Sivela, son Joseph, 4 horses
Mary Hudlow, 1 horse
Wm. Crawford, 4 horses
John Witmor, 1 horse
Robert Hooks, son James, 4 horses
William Hooks, 4 horses
John Snap, son Joseph, 2 slaves, 9 horses, apprentice Jos. Thorn
Thomas Barclay
George Messersmith, 3 horses
Frederick Prinkman, 2 horses
John Weaver, 1 horse
John Stoop, 1 horse
Robert Hooks, Sr., sons Elijah, George, 8 horses
Mary Huston, son Arch, 1 slave, 6 horses
Capt. Geo. Huston, 2 horses
Nathan Huston
John Kiplinger, 6 horses
Thomas Hanna, 4 horses
Peter Peck, 3 horses
Jacob Cook, son Jacob, 5 horses
Jacob Argabright, 2 horses
John Huston, 2 horses
Luke Metheny, 2 horses
Arch Metheny, 2 horses
Henry Deck, 1 slave, 4 horses
Jacob Surface, 1 horse
Gideon Viah, 2 horses
George Painter, 3 horses
Peter Brown, 2 horses
John Surface, 1 horse

William Bell, 4 horses
Jacob Rodearman, 4 horses
John Miller, 1 horse, apprentice Henry Utt
Valentine Kizer, 5 horses
George Hudlow
Martin Rhine
George Knave, 2 horses
Abraham Tanner, 2 horses
Michael Fifer, 2 horses
Philip Keister, 2 horses
Philip Shirea, 4 horses
Peter Keister, 1 horse
John Baker, 2 horses
Samuel Baker
John Kiplinger, 3 horses
Christian Deadm, 3 horses
John Alford, son Benjamin, 3 horses
John Alford, Jr.
John Newil, 4 horses
John Hoop, 2 horses
Christian Nicewanger, 2 horses
Leonard Tootwiler, son John, 4 horses
William Ireland, 4 horses, apprentice Adam Bowyer
Joseph Hannah, 4 horses
Jno. Carthera, 5 slaves, 9 horses
David and J. Kyle, 1 horse
John Skinner, 2 horses
Daniel Fisher, 4 horses
Benoni Cushoe, 4 horses
John Shipman, 2 horses
Jacob Lemmons, 2 horses
John Cody, 4 horses
John Milteberger, 2 horses
John Cartherea, 1 slave, 7 horses
Abraham Fisher, 5 horses
John Lemmons, Sr., 2 horses
Frederick Moyers, 4 horses

Joseph Long
Jacob Scott, 4 horses
Elisabeth Campbell, 2 horses
Peter Cook, 2 horses
James Beard, sons James and William, 3 slaves, 8 horses
Peter Shalley
John Shank, 1 horse
John Shirea, 4 horses
Mathias Willberger, sons David and Henry, 3 horses
Jacob Pacinger, 2 horses
Christian Sailer, 2 horses
Mathias Doubt, 5 horses
William Robison, son John, 2 horses
Philip Kiplinger, son Peter, 4 horses
Lewis Fillinger
Charles Shults, 2 horses
Stophel Cline, 1 horse
Jacob Gray, son Adam, 4 horses
Adam Miller, 3 horses
Frederick Keister, 2 horses
John Mackley, son Jacob, 3 horses
Benjamin Yearly, son Samuel, 5 horses

Valentine Safely, son George, 2 horses
Valentine Huffman, sons George, Christian and Abraham, 8 horses
John Mackalls, 10 slaves, 8 horses
Gausper Mefford, sons John and Gausper, 4 horses
Peter Lowry, 3 horses
James Hook, 3 horses
Martin Surface, 2 horses
George Surface, 1 horse
William Ore, 1 horse
Leonard Miller, 2 horses
Ludwick Caller, 3 horses
Jacob Miller, 1 horse
Jacob Deck, 3 horses
Leonard Painter, 1 horse
Nicholas Smith
Jacob Witmore, sons Martin and Jacob, 4 horses
Philip Keeister, Sr., son John, 3 horses
Jacob Hudlow, 5 horses

"VOCHERS" IN CAPT. ROBT. HARRISON'S COMPANY, No. 5

Thomas Herring, 2 horses, apprentice Thomas Loftland
Thomas Scott, 2 horses
James Martin
James Curry, 1 horse
John Graham, 1 horse
Dennis Lerachan, 1 slave, 5 horses
John Hall
William Price
John Crummey, 1 horse
Jemima Oliver, 2 horses
William Donnovan, 2 horses
Henry Burges, 1 horse, apprentice Jacob Cool
Anthony Sourbeer, 1 horse
James Mitchell, 1 horse
Robt. Rutherford, son Elliott
Andrew Shanklin, 1 slave
Samuel Gay, 2 horses
John Braden, 1 horse
Charles McClain

James Hinton
Smith Lofftus
Brewer Reeves, 2 slaves, 1 horse
Samuel McWilliams, 1 horse
Hugh Siphney, 2 horses
John Turner
John Hicks, 2 horses, apprentice James Brown
Jonathan Shipman, 3 horses
John Apler, 1 horse
Samuel Hair, 1 horse
James Brown, 2 horses
James Guin, 3 horses
Joseph Dictim, son Richard, 9 horses
Benjamin Smith, 1 slave, 7 horses
Martin Argabright, 1 horse
John Guin, servant Wm. Lowry, 5 horses
Phelix Sheltman, son John, 3 horses
Adam Argabright, 3 horses
John Hemphill, 1 horse

Christian Dundore, 7 horses
Catharine Dundore, 1 horse
George Dundore, 3 horses
Samuel Hemphill, son Robert, 7
    horses
Robert Crawford, 2 horses
John Martin, apprentice Geo. Hegey
Thomas Harrison, 2 slaves, 6 horses
John Miller, 3 horses
Christian Miller, 1 horse
Jacob Miller, apprentice Jonathan
    Hooden
Michael Miller
Abraham Miller
Abraham Branaman, 3 horses
Samuel Miller, 6 horses
Isaac Miller, servant Chas. Knowles,
    7 horses
Michael Muller
John Stone
Jacob Boshong, 5 horses
Daniel Love, 2 slaves, 3 horses
Powel Shoemaker
John Black, son Samuel, 4 horses
Robert Cravens, 4 horses
Daniel Harrison, 2 horses
Jacob Wickle, 2 horses
Lewis Peebler, 2 horses
Jacob Peebler, 2 horses
Daniel Dickinson, 1 horse, apprentice
    Sam'l Chanley
Jacob Wickle, 2 horses
Lewis Publer, 2 horses
Frederick Hanes, 3 horses
Robert Gibson, son James, 3 horses
Henry Erwins, 5 slaves, 6 horses
    "and a two wheeled carriage"
John Erwins, Jr., 1 slave, 1 horse
Frederick Spangler, 1 horse
James Gamble, 1 horse
John Cline, 3 horses
Coonrod Cline
Christian Flickinger
Jacob Spitler, 2 horses
Arch Saylor, 4 horses
"John & Wm. Taylor refused to give
    in themselves or 4 horses as they
    were in Georgi the 9th of March"
Margaret Smith

Christly & P. Shoemaker
Wm. Cravens
Albert & Reuben Harrison, 5 slaves,
    8 horses
Henry Stone, 2 slaves, 11 horses
Christian Stone, 9 horses
George Hoover, 10 horses
Pursley Hoover, son Thomas, 19
    horses
Jacob Berier, 2 horses
Henry Roleman, 2 horses
Jacob Gilespey, 4 horses
Leonard Props, son George, 12 horses
Laurence Hoover, 4 horses
Christian Rullman, son Jost, 1 slave,
    15 horses
Henry Swadley, 13 horses
Rev. Peter Mitchel, 1 horse
Zachariah Rexrole, son John, 5 horses
Zachariah Rexrode Jr., 3 horses
Henry Props, 4 horses
Michael Props, 4 horses
John Miller, 2 horses
Michael Props Jr., 4 horses
Peter Hoover, 12 horses
John Spinner, 2 horses
Frederick Props, sons John and Jacob,
    7 horses
Jacob Cowger, 1 horse
Frederick Keester, 12 horses
James Keester, 5 horses
Robt. Davison, 7 horses
John Davison, 2 horses
John Moral, 4 horses
Burton Blizzard, 6 horses
Mathew Patten, son Ab, 5 slaves, 17
    horses
William Patten, 1 horse
Stophel Dancer, 1 horse
George Duncle, sons George and
    John, 9 horses
John Duncle, servant John Carlock,
    1 slave, 9 horses
William Herring, 1 horse
Peter Vindwender, 3 horses
Samuel Moral, 5 horses
James Blizzard, 3 horses
Mathias Dice, son George, 12 horses
William Blizzard, 5 horses

John Blizzard, 3 horses
James Dyer, sons Wm., John and James, 1 slave, 19 horses
Philip Fisher, 2 horses
Thomas Hall, son David
Thomas Blizzard, son John, 3 horses
Lewis Wagoner, Jr., 7 horses
Lewis Wagoner, Sr., 3 horses
Lewis Wormstorf
Rodger Dyer, 1 slave, 9 horses
Jacob Haviner, son Nicholas, 9 horses
Frederick Haviner, 8 horses
Sophia Props, 3 horses
Patt Sanit, 6 horses
Jacob Seeker, 5 horses
Laurence Hushare, 2 horses
Jacob Coyle, 1 horse
George Coyle, son George, 2 slaves, 9 horses
Philip Kyzer, 3 horses
Henry Kiplinger, 4 horses
Gabriel Coyl, sons Andrew and Samuel, 3 horses
Gabriel Coyle, Sr., 2 horses
George Coyle, 2 horses
Charles Hedrick, sons Jacob, John, Frederick and Charles, 14 horses
Jacob Coonrod, 16 horses
Domnick Donally, 7 horses
John Skidmore, son Elijah, 9 horses
John Skidmore, Jr., 1 horse
George Kiplinger, 4 horses
George Hammer, 14 horses
William Clifton, 2 horses
Michael Harole
Jacob Harper, son Henry, 8 horses
Charles Powers, sons Isaac and John, 9 horses
Michael McClure, 1 horse
George Dice, 7 horses
John Harpole, 7 horses
George Vindevender, 2 horses
Adam Harper, 3 horses
John Harper, 2 horses
Wm. Harper, 1 horse
Francis Evick, 9 horses
George Evick, 5 horses
Jacob Friend, son Jonas, 7 horses
Jacob Vindevender, 5 horses

Valentine Castle, sons Henry and Peter, 6 horses
George Bible, 3 horses
Philip Bible, 2 horses
Henry Ine, 2 horses
Anthony Fountain, 1 horse
Geo. Vitesel, 3 horses
Peter Phenimon, 1 slave, 9 horses
Sammeywell Richards, 2 horses
John Smith, 2 horses
Thomas Collick, 7 horses
John Fisher, 2 horses
Thomas Cock, 3 horses
Thomas Bland, sons John and Henry, 6 horses
Lewis Bush, 1 horse
Michael Bush, 5 horses
Leonard Bush, 6 horses
Samuel Skidmore, 2 horses
William Laurence
Joseph Skidmore, 5 horses
Andrew Cookhold, 2 horses
Martin Stratton, 1 horse
William Peterson, 2 horses
Joseph Brigs, son Charles, 3 horses
John Phereis, son Robert, 6 horses
Adam Kiplinger, 6 horses
Christopher Smith, 1 horse
Henry Crook, son John, 3 horses
Jacob Fisher, 3 horses
George Waldrim, sons Philip and Thomas, 4 horses
Amis Skidmore, 1 horse
Joseph Orbaugh
Jacob Harper, Jr., 4 horses
James Skidmore, 3 horses
James Graham, 2 horses
Saraiah Stratton, 5 horses
Thomas Bland, sons John and Henry, 6 horses
Peter Wirech, son John, 3 horses
John Wolf, 5 horses
Joseph Bennet, 4 horses
Peter Ferrol, 7 horses
Thomas Webb, 1 horse
Jacob Root, 6 horses
James Wagh, 3 horses
Joseph Summerfield, 4 horses
John Neelson, 5 horses

John Lambard, son John, 6 horses
Isaac Hincle, 4 horses
Joseph Wilson, 4 horses
Isaac Coberly, 1 horse
James McCally
John Carpenter, 3 horses
Robert Minnis, 8 horses
James Cunningham, sons William
and James, 4 horses
William Cunningham, 2 slaves, 4
horses
Reden Blunt, sons Siras and Andrew,
5 horses
Wm. Everman, 4 horses
George Wilkinson, 4 horses
Yost Hincle, 8 horses
Philip Teeters, sons John and Samuel, 7 horses
John Shull, 4 horses
Gabriel Murphy, 1 horse
Cornelius Thompson, 2 horses
James Thompson, 1 horse
Andrew Johnston, 11 horses
Samuel Gregg, 2 horses
Peter Shull, 5 horses

Abraham Hinckle, 5 horses
Samuel Redmond, 1 horse
Geo. Negley, 4 horses
Geo. Teeters, son Jacob, 7 horses
Paul Teeters, 2 horses
John Mitchel, 4 horses
Jacob Carr, 7 horses
Philip Harper, 7 horses
Jacob Harper, 13 horses
Philip Harper, Sr., 1 horse
Rebecca Teeters, son Abraham, 7
horses
Lewis Full, 2 horses
William Greeg, Sr., 4 horses
William Greeg, Jr., 5 horses
Leonard Miller, 2 horses
Isaac Wood, son John, 3 horses
Thomas Gilespey, 2 horses
James Woods, 2 horses
Johnston Phereis, 5 horses
John Stuttler, 3 horses
John Carpenter, 3 horses
George Loagh, 2 horses
Adam Loagh, 8 horses
John Teeters, 2 horses

Capt. Josiah Harrison's Company, No. 9

Michall Holsinger, 1 tithable, 3
horses
Danniel Fraley, 1 tithable, son William, 3 horses
Michael Hennisee, 1 tithable, 1
horse
John Armstrong, 1 tithable, 1 horse
Amos Hilyard, 1 tithable, 1 horse
Conrod Smith, 1 tithable, 4 horses
Josiah Harrison, 1 tithable, 4 horses
Daniel Helfrey, 1 tithable, 5 horses
Ludwick Stephenson, 1 tithable, 1
slave, 5 horses
Jacob Moss, 1 tithable, 2 horses
George Phillip, 1 tithable, 3 horses
John Deen, 1 tithable, 6 horses
John Phillips, 1 tithable, son John,
6 horses
John Hepler, 1 tithable, 6 horses
Michael Keller, 1 tithable, 3 horses
Martin Counce, 1 tithable, 2 horses

Adam Rickerboher, 1 tithable, 3
horses
John Lokey, 1 tithable, sons Thomas
and James, 5 horses
Jacob Perkley, 1 tithable, 2 horses
Joseph Sampson, 1 tithable, 1 horse
Wm. Smith, 1 tithable
Isaac Black, 1 tithable, 1 horse
Wm. Erwin, 1 tithable
Sabaston Marts, 1 tithable, sons John,
Samuel and Henry, 10 horses
John Reeves, 1 tithable, son John, 1
slave, 7 horses
Abraham Phillips, 1 tithable, 3 horses
Thos. Dunkeson, 1 tithable, 1 slave,
4 horses
Jacob Caster, 1 tithable, son Henry
John Lawford, 1 tithable, 2 horses
Elijah Russel, 1 tithable, 3 horses
Henry Kephart, cleared of poll tax,
4 horses

Christopher Kephart, 1 tithable
Henry Angle, 1 tithable
Geo. Armontrout, 1 tithable, 3 horses
Frederick Armontrout, 1 tithable
Conrod Keller, 1 tithable, 3 horses
John Harmon, 1 tithable, 2 horses
Allexander McFarling, 1 tithable, 1 horse
Jacob West, 1 tithable, 1 horse
Wm. Dilling, 1 tithable, 3 horses
Thomas Lewis, 1 tithable
Henry Sly, 1 tithable, 2 horses
John Colwell, 1 tithable, son David
Zebulon Harrison, son Reuben, 1 slave, 6 horses
John Power, 1 tithable
Thos. Lokey, 1 tithable, 6 horses
Wm. Pickeren, 1 tithable, 4 horses
Jacob Woodley, 1 tithable, son John, 1 slave, 13 horses
Thomas Wells, 1 tithable
Moses Cummins, 1 tithable, 4 horses
Peter Counce, 1 tithable, son Peter, 5 horses
Andrew Bird, 1 tithable
Andrew Bird, Sr., 1 tithable, 4 slaves, 9 horses
Wm. Ruddell, 1 tithable, 2 horses
George Springer, 1 tithable, 2 horses
John Springer, 1 tithable, 1 horse
Mathias Beaver, 1 tithable, 6 horses
Jacob Acort, 1 tithable, 2 horses
James Rogers, 1 tithable, 1 horse
Ezekiel Harrison, 1 tithable, 3 slaves, 7 horses
John Shaver, 1 tithable
John Edwards, 1 tithable
Martin Crider, 1 tithable, son Crisley, 3 horses
Josiah Harrison, Jr., 1 tithable, 1 horse
Arther Fulkner, 1 tithable
William Eaten, 1 tithable, 1 horse
Laurence Bell, 1 tithable, 5 horses
Peter Henton, 1 tithable, 4 horses
Reuben Harrison, 1 tithable, sons Joseph and Reuben, 3 slaves, 9 horses

Benj. Faulmon, 1 tithable, son James, 6 horses
Wm. Faulmon, 1 tithable
Fellimon Rorick, 1 tithable, 4 horses
Wm. Henton, 1 tithable, 2 horses
Henry Cowen, 1 tithable, 2 horses
Andrew Hullings, 1 tithable, 1 horse
James Flemmons, 1 tithable, 2 horses
John Harrison, cleared of poll tax, 4 horses
Even Phillips, 1 tithable, 4 horses
John Hoof, 1 tithable, sons George, John, Jacob, Frederick and Henry, 7 horses
Ludwick Sircle, 1 tithable, 2 slaves, 7 horses
John Sircle, 1 tithable, 2 horses
Charles Harvey, 1 tithable, 2 horses
Ignatius Turley, 1 tithable, 4 horses
Jacob Saltser, 1 tithable
William Williams, 1 tithable
Sammuel Allen, 1 tithable, 1 horse
Wm. McDowell, 4 slaves, 9 horses
Jacob Ramboe, 1 tithable, 4 horses
Matthias Selser, 1 tithable
Solomon Matthews, 1 tithable, 7 horses
William Fowler, 1 tithable, 1 slave, 2 horses
Smith William, 1 tithable
Thos. Moore, Sr., 1 tithable, 4 slaves, 7 horses
Reuben Moore, 1 tithable, 1 slave, 7 horses
John Moore, 1 tithable, 4 horses
Thos. Moore, Jr., 1 tithable, 4 horses
John Brown, 1 tithable
John Frittz, 1 tithable
Sammuel Dailey, 1 tithable, 1 horse
Philip Counce, 1 tithable, 5 horses
(Geo. Fridley above 16 with Philip Counce)
William Williams, 1 tithable
John Swick, 1 tithable

CAPTAIN TRUMBOE'S COMPANY, No. 10

Henry Shoemaker, 1 tithable, 3 horses

Matthias Hill, 1 tithable, 1 horse

Christian Grove, 1 tithable, son Jacob, 6 horses

George Sites, 1 tithable

Samuel Kerril, 1 tithable

Mical Grove, 1 tithable, 1 horse

Andrew Bear, 1 tithable, 1 horse

Nicholas Carn, 1 tithable, 6 horses

Cornelius Collins, 1 tithable, 1 horse

John Bear, 1 tithable, 3 horses

Henry Good, 1 tithable, sons Jacob and Philip, 5 horses

Geo. Arehart, 1 tithable, son John, 6 horses

John Campher, 1 tithable, 1 horse

Peter Smith, 1 tithable, 1 horse

Michael Kipps, 1 tithable, son George, 5 horses

Catherine Polon, 2 horses

John Bowman, 1 tithable, 7 horses (George Bowman his father)

Adam Oreboh, 1 tithable, 4 horses

John Hefler, 1 tithable, 4 horses

Chas. Goarden, 1 tithable, son Charles

William Blythe, 1 tithable, 1 horse

John Cook, 1 tithable, 4 horses

Peter Cook, 1 tithable, 1 horse

John Cook, Jr., 1 tithable, 1 horse

Mical Cook, 1 tithable, 1 horse

Andrew Oreboh, 1 tithable, 5 horses

John Thomas, cleared of poll tax, 5 horses

Richard Roland, clear levy, 5 horses

Conrod Hartinger, 1 tithable, 2 horses

Andrew Andis, 1 tithable, 8 horses

Henry Hartinger, 1 tithable, 1 horse

Peter Andis, 1 tithable, 1 horse (Jacob Hartinger above 16 with Peter Andis)

Abraham Miller, 1 tithable, son Daniel, 3 horses

Jacob Miller, 1 tithable, 2 horses

John Nestrick, 1 tithable, 6 horses

Adam Wine, 1 tithable, 3 horses

George Minnick, 1 tithable, 1 horse

John Minnick, 1 tithable, son John, 3 horses

Jacob Ketner, 1 tithable, 1 slave, 6 horses

Henry Eater, 1 tithable, sons John and Joseph, 5 horses

Christian Smith, 1 tithable, 2 horses

Frederick Nesslerod, 1 tithable, 2 horses

Christopher Caplinger, 1 tithable, 1 horse

Jacob Trumboe, 1 tithable, 5 horses

John Fracksler, 1 tithable

Abraham Cup, 1 tithable, 1 horse

Crisley Cup, 1 tithable, 4 horses

Adam Cup, 1 tithable, 2 horses

Henry Cup, 1 tithable, 4 horses

Henry Carn, 1 tithable

Benj. Thomas, 4 horses

Henry Hank, 1 tithable

John Fifer, 1 tithable, 4 horses

Phillip Hinkle, 1 tithable, 3 horses

Henry Stolph, 1 tithable, 6 horses (Geo. Moiers above 21 with Henry Stolph)

John Shutter, 1 tithable, 2 horses

Jacob Shutter, 1 tithable, 1 horse

Vollentine Trout, 1 tithable, 4 horses

Adam Moier, 1 tithable, 1 horse

Anthony Reader, 1 tithable, son John, 1 slave, 9 horses

Peter Fifer, 1 tithable, 1 horse

Martin Roop, 1 tithable, sons Martin and George, 4 horses

Michael Hauber, 1 tithable, sons George and Peter, 7 horses

John Stolph, 1 tithable, sons Adam, Jacob, Peter and John, 8 horses

Frederick Shover, 1 tithable, 1 horse

Adam Rader, 1 tithable, 3 slaves, 10 horses

Mathias Reader, 1 tithable, son George, 7 horses

John Bear, 1 tithable, sons Henry and Adam, 10 horses

Peter Weaver, 1 tithable

Christley Painter, 1 tithable, 7 horses

John Moore, Sr., 1 tithable, son Thomas, 1 slave, 9 horses

Peter Boyer, 1 tithable

George Ruddell, 1 tithable, sons George and John, 3 horses

Peter Funk, 1 tithable, 3 horses

John Crowder, 1 tithable

Ludwick Fulmore, 1 tithable, 2 horses

Cristian Fry, 1 tithable, son Cristian, 3 horses

George Hiney, 1 tithable, 4 horses

John Crumpacker, 1 tithable, 3 horses

Jacob Kunkle, 1 tithable, 1 horse

John Searphos, 1 tithable, 3 horses

Adam Fifer, 1 tithable, sons Adam and Jacob, 4 horses

David Miller, 1 tithable, 2 horses

John Pitner, 1 tithable, sons John and Adam, 5 horses

Henry Knave, 1 tithable, son Matthais, 5 horses

CAPTAIN JOHN RUDDELL'S COMPANY, No. 11

John Caplinger, 1 tithable, 2 horses

John Nave, 1 tithable, 2 horses

Abraham Crumparker, 1 tithable, son Joel, 1 horse

Christian City, 1 tithable, 2 horses

Abraham Miller, 1 tithable, 6 horses

John Teter, 1 tithable, 1 horse

Peter City, 1 tithable, son Peter, 5 horses

George Shoemaker, 1 tithable, son George, 5 horses

Joseph Parrott, 1 tithable, 4 horses

Samuel Parrot, 1 tithable, 3 horses

Mical Lam, 1 tithable, 2 horses

Henry Lam, 1 tithable, 3 horses

Jacob Lam, 1 tithable, 2 horses

Nicholas Lam, 1 tithable, 1 horse

William Lam, 1 tithable, 1 horse

John Fulk, 1 tithable, 6 horses

Adam Bible, 1 tithable, sons John and Ludwick, 7 horses

Adam Bible, Jr., 1 tithable, 3 horses

Peter Stulce, 1 tithable, son Mical, 3 horses

George Ruble, 1 tithable, 3 horses

John Ruble, 1 tithable, 1 horse

Thos. Cunningham, 1 tithable, 1 horse

John Hites, 1 tithable, 2 horses

Paul Custard, 1 tithable, 7 horses

William Cherrinton, 1 tithable, 3 horses

Peter Bloom, 1 tithable, 2 horses

Richard Custard, 1 tithable, 3 horses

Wm. Cherryhomes, 1 tithable, son Greenberry, 5 horses

Wm. Cherryhomes, Jr., 1 tithable, 1 horse

Mical Baker, 1 tithable, 10 horses

Wm. Fitzwatters, 1 tithable, 5 horses

John Fitzwatters, 1 tithable, 1 horse

Thos. Fitzwatters, 1 tithable, 2 horses

Henry Doup, 1 tithable, son Frederick, 8 horses

John Colp, 1 tithable, 2 horses

Nicholas Weatherholt, 1 tithable, 2 horses

Geo. Caplinger, 1 tithable, 3 horses

Henry Wetsle, 1 tithable, son John, 2 horses

Peter Wetsle, 1 tithable, 2 horses

Joseph Despenny, 1 tithable, sons Jacob, John and Adam, 6 horses

George Harter, 1 tithable, son Philip, 2 horses

George Liewes, 1 tithable, son George, 2 horses

Adam Harter, 1 tithable, 4 horses

Michael Moier, 1 tithable, 3 horses

Henry Counce, 1 tithable, 5 horses

John Marter, 1 tithable, 3 horses

George Doup, 1 tithable, 3 horses

Martin Wetsle, 1 tithable, 1 slave, 9 horses

Jacob Misely, 1 tithable, 1 horse

Christian Caplinger, 1 tithable, 4 horses
James Scott, 1 tithable, 2 horses
Colsen Shaver, 1 tithable, 3 horses
Danniel Baker, 1 tithable, 1 horse
Henry Marter, 1 tithable, 2 horses
Colsen Counce, 1 tithable, 4 horses
John Counce, 1 tithable, 3 horses
Ferdinand Lear, 1 tithable, 4 horses
Simon Shoemaker, 1 tithable, son Samuel, 5 horses
Frederick Honniker, 1 tithable, 1 horse
(Henry Dove above 16 years with Frederick Honniker)

John Reynels, 1 tithable, 4 horses
John Beggs, 1 tithable, 7 horses
Jacob Trumboe, Sr., 1 tithable, 4 horses
John Hatwell, 1 tithable, 1 horse
John Ruddell, 1 tithable, son Moses, 1 slave, 6 horses
John Runyen, 1 tithable, son Jacob, 5 horses
John Runyen, Jr., 1 tithable, 1 horse
Mical Ferle, 1 tithable, 2 horses
David Price, 1 tithable, 2 horses
Edward Walters, 1 tithable, 3 horses
Tobias Hauk, clear of poll tax, 1 horse

Captain George Crisman's Company, No. 12

Catherine Lear, 1 slave, 2 horses
Michael Airmon, 1 tithable, 1 slave, 2 horses
John Perry, 1 tithable, 1 slave, 1 horse
William Robison, 1 tithable, 1 slave, 6 horses
Isaac Jackson, 1 tithable, 1 horse
Henry Colp, 1 tithable, 3 horses
John Sites, 1 tithable, 1 horse
Christian Roads, 1 tithable, 2 horses
Michael Colp, 1 tithable, 4 horses
Anthony Roads, 1 tithable, 1 horse
Frederick Rodes, 1 tithable, 1 horse
Nicholas Shaver, 1 tithable, 1 slave, 7 horses
John Sites, 1 tithable, 3 horses
Jacob Miller, 1 tithable, 4 horses
Wollery Kesler, 1 tithable, son John, 6 horses
Joseph Kesler, 1 tithable
Jacob Cofman, 1 tithable, son Crisley, 4 horses
Henry Contraman, 1 tithable, 5 horses
Reece Liewes, 1 tithable, son John, 1 horse
John Lincoln, 1 tithable, son Michael, 2 horses
Henry Whistler, 1 tithable, 6 horses
James Grace, 1 tithable, 4 horses

Peter Crumbaker, 1 tithable, 3 horses
Jacob Vossinger, 1 tithable, 4 horses
David Branamon, 1 tithable, 4 horses
John Clecker, 1 tithable, 1 horse
Aron Solomon, 1 tithable, 1 horse
Christian Sights, 1 tithable, 3 horses
Geo. Spears, 1 tithable, son John, 3 slaves, 9 horses
Michael Trout, 1 tithable, 8 horses
Joseph Rogers, 1 tithable
James McCoy, 1 tithable, 5 horses
John Whitehouse, 1 tithable, 1 horse
John Rimil, 1 tithable, 3 horses
Phillip Rimil, 1 tithable, 4 horses
Elias Rimil, 1 tithable, 2 horses
Frederick Crawn, 1 tithable, 1 horse
Collins Baits, 1 tithable, 2 horses
Hantel Vance, 1 tithable, 4 horses
John Vance, 1 tithable, 1 horse
William Cook, 1 tithable
Wm. Achins, 1 tithable, sons James and Alex.
William Freeman, 1 tithable, 2 horses
John Brian, 1 tithable, 3 horses
Thos. Briant, 1 tithable, son William, 6 horses
John Hanks, 1 tithable
Bartholomew Wickert, 1 tithable
Jacob Lincoln, 1 tithable, 5 horses
Jacob Furr, 1 tithable, 2 horses

Cornelius Briant, 1 tithable, 1 horse
Joshua Strock, 1 tithable, 3 horses
Jacob Bear, 1 tithable, sons Philip
and Abraham, 7 horses
Henry Fox, 1 tithable, 1 horse
Jacob Bowman, Sr., 1 tithable, 3
horses
John Snither, 1 tithable
Andrew Bowers, 3 horses
Jacob Rife, 1 tithable, 5 horses
Jacob Thomas, 1 tithable
Jacob Whitehead, 1 tithable
David Rife, 1 tithable, 1 horse
Cristophel Heahtell, 1 tithable, 1
horse
Matthias Lear, 1 tithable, 8 horses
Peter Taylor, 1 tithable, 3 horses
John Grim, 1 tithable, 4 horses
Peter Auker, 1 tithable, 3 horses
Joseph Thompson, 1 tithable
Jacob Bowman, Jr., 1 tithable, son
Jacob, 6 horses
John Bear, 1 tithable, 3 horses
Henry Rodes, 1 tithable, 4 horses
Margaret Click, 4 horses
John Rogers, 1 tithable
Laurence Bowers, 1 tithable, 4 horses
John Leble, 1 tithable
Cutlop Howman, 1 tithable, 4 horses
Thos. Lincoln, 1 tithable, 3 horses
John Lincoln, Sr., 1 tithable, 3
horses
Peter Briant, 1 tithable, 4 horses
Thos. Briant, 1 tithable, 1 horse
Wm. Briant, 1 tithable, 5 horses
John Wiseman, 1 tithable, 2 horses
Henry Sites, 1 tithable
Thos. Briant, Jr., 1 tithable, 6 horses
John Masberger, 1 tithable, son
Martin, 4 horses
John Thomas, 1 tithable, sons Reese
and John, 8 horses
Reece Thomas, 1 tithable, 6 horses
Jehu Gum, 1 tithable, 3 horses
David Cofman, 1 tithable, 5 horses
Jacob Borders, 1 tithable
Riley Robison, 1 tithable, 2 horses
Nicholas Perry, 1 tithable, 5 horses
Wm. Dunlap, 1 tithable, son Wil-

liam, 7 horses
John Lauk, 1 tithable, 3 horses
John Briggs, 1 tithable, 2 horses
John Smith, 1 tithable, 2 horses
Robt. Windleborough, 1 tithable
Andrew Crist, 1 tithable, sons Jacob
and John, 5 horses
Morgan Briant, 1 tithable, 2 horses
Henry Shank, 1 tithable, 3 horses
Adam Shank, 1 tithable, 3 horses
Benj. Savage, 1 tithable, 1 horse
Peter Sights, 1 tithable, 3 horses
John Cring, 1 tithable, son Henry,
1 slave, 7 horses
Geo. Crisman, 1 tithable, son
Hughe, 4 slaves, 17 horses
Zachary Shekleford, 1 tithable, 1
slave, 1 horse
James Green, 1 tithable, son James,
4 horses
Joseph Green, 1 tithable, 1 horse
Thomas Riddle, 1 tithable, 4 horses
John Ferrel, 1 tithable, 2 horses
William Davis, 1 tithable, son Wil-
liam, 2 horses
Mical Ford, 1 tithable, 1 horse
Geo. Cashner, 1 tithable, 4 horses
Arnold Ford, 1 tithable, 4 horses
Martin Shoemaker, 1 tithable, son
Peter, 4 horses
William Ralston, 1 tithable
John Harris, 1 tithable, 2 horses
James Webb, 1 tithable, sons Asa
and Jeremiah, 2 horses
Aden Webb, 1 tithable
James Brooke, 1 tithable, 1 horse
Norton Gum, 1 tithable
Abraham Forsith, 1 tithable
Joseph Thompson, 1 tithable, 1
horse
Pattrick Cumberford, 1 tithable, 3
horses
Joseph Scott, 1 tithable
Joseph Bowman, 1 tithable, 6 horses
John Rubert, 1 tithable (Andrew
Crest above 16)
Jacob Hufft, 1 tithable, 1 horse
John Jorden, 1 tithable, James

Doherty, 1 tithable, 1 slave, 14 horses

Andrew Arehart, 1 tithable, 1 horse

Thomas Bennett, 1 tithable

Edmond Ong, 1 tithable

Dennis Brian, 1 tithable

Robert Shepton, 1 tithable, 1 horse

Captain Richard Ragan's Company, No. 13

Phillip Dede, 1 tithable, 1 horse

Geo. Calebship, 1 tithable, 3 horses

Ingle Boyer, 1 tithable, 3 horses

John Armontrout, 1 tithable, 6 horses
(John Leonard above 16 years with John Armontrout)

John Harrison, 1 tithable, son William, 6 horses

Isaac Kiser, 1 tithable, 2 horses

Cristian Miller, 1 tithable, 3 horses

Frederick Fraley, 1 tithable, 1 horse
(William Scott above 16 with Frederick Fraley)

Peter Wheland, 1 tithable, 3 horses

George Hagay, 1 tithable, 2 horses

Loughlin Doil, 1 tithable

Isaac Wiseman, 1 tithable, son Samuel, 2 horses

John Sheltman, 4 horses

Richard Ragan, 1 tithable, son Danniel, 7 horses

Sammuel Harned, 1 tithable, 1 horse

Jeremiah Ragan, 1 tithable, 1 slave, 8 horses

Danniel Ragan, 1 tithable, 1 horse

Thomas Harrison, 1 tithable, 1 horse

John Harrisson, 1 tithable, 1 slave, 5 horses

Jane Smith, Sr., 6 slaves, 17 horses

Elihu Messick, 1 tithable, 4 horses

John Dunnaphen, 1 tithable, 5 horses

John Shep, 1 tithable, 2 horses

Geo. Dashner, clear poll tax, 4 horses

John Benson, 1 tithable, 4 horses

George Sheets, 1 tithable, son Danniel, 2 horses

Robert Ellott, 1 tithable, son David, 6 horses

John Ellott, 1 tithable

Sammuel King, 1 tithable, 1 horse

Sammuel Critchett, 1 tithable, 4 horses

Joseph Lear, 1 tithable, 6 horses

Jacob Custard, 1 tithable, 6 horses

John Lockhart, 1 tithable, 1 horse

John Boggs, 1 tithable, 1 horse

Walter Crow, 1 tithable, 2 slaves, 7 horses

Philip Armontrout, 1 tithable, 4 horses

John Bright, 1 tithable, 7 horses

Passle Forkeson, 1 tithable above sixteen

Ellett Rutherford, 1 tithable, 1 slave, 7 horses

Joseph Rutherford, 1 tithable

William Kiser, 1 tithable, 1 horse

Isaac Wiseman, Jr., 1 tithable

Jacob Wiseman, 1 tithable

Peter Van Pelt, 1 tithable, 6 horses

Michael Dashner, 1 tithable

Peter Armontrout, 1 tithable, 5 horses

Philip Armontrout, Sr., clear of tax, 1 horse

Peter Keldon, 2 horses

David Smith, 1 tithable, 4 horses

Nathaniel Harrison, 1 tithable, 4 horses

Joseph Hall, 1 tithable, 5 horses

William Herring, 1 tithable, 3 horses

Mical Brown, 1 tithable, 1 horse

George Brown, 1 tithable

Robert Dickey, 1 tithable, son James, 4 horses

Robert Dickey, Jr., 1 tithable, 1 horse

David Taylor, 1 tithable, 6 horses

Charles Shulce, 1 tithable, son Adam, 4 horses

Thomas Cammil, 1 tithable, 4 horses

Michael Wearin, 1 tithable, sons Michael and Thos., 4 horses

Christophel Howard, 1 tithable, sons Adam, Stophel and Phillip, 11 horses

Isaac Dippoe, 1 tithable, son Jacob, 4 horses

Conrod Dippoe, 1 horse

Joseph Rutherford, 1 tithable, son Thomas, 1 slave, 6 horses

Godfrey Swinge, 1 tithable, 2 horses

John Grabill, 1 tithable, 1 horse

Peter Carn, 1 tithable, 2 horses

John Williams, 1 tithable

James McKibbens, 1 tithable, 1 horse

Archibald Rutherford, 1 tithable, 5 horses

Richard Fisher, 1 tithable, 1 horse

George Kessle, 1 tithable, 4 horses

John Alstoff, 1 horse

Andrew Jameson, 1 tithable, son Jacob, 6 horses

Adam Bonds, 1 tithable

William Lewis, 1 tithable

Matthias Sowermilk, 1 tithable, William Felix, 1 tithable, 4 horses

Joseph Denny, 1 tithable, 3 horses

Danniel Olliver, 1 tithable, 2 horses

Adam Stanton, 1 tithable

Thos. Clark, 1 tithable

George Carpenter, 1 tithable, 7 horses

James Lard, 1 tithable, 3 slaves, 9 horses

Adam Fought, 1 tithable, 5 horses

Reese Williams, 1 tithable, 1 horse

Edward Mole, Clear of levies, 3 horses

Geo. Armontrout, 1 tithable, 2 horses

Mary Armontrout, 3 horses

Polson Everholt, 1 tithable, son Charles, 2 horses

George Harmon, 1 tithable, 1 horse

David Harned, 1 tithable, 5 slaves, 15 horses

John Mall, 1 tithable

John Wise, 1 tithable, 2 horses

Shephard Armstrong, 1 tithable, son William, 3 horses

Danniel Grub, 1 tithable, 3 horses

Henry Kiser, 1 tithable, 3 horses

George Fridley, 1 tithable, son John, 3 horses

Danniel Mogganet, 1 tithable, 2 horses

Henry Armontrout, 1 tithable, son John, 3 horses

Cristian Miller, 1 tithable, 3 horses

Jacob Harpole, 1 tithable, 3 horses

William Linsey, clear poll tax, 1 horse

Danniel Farra, 1 tithable

Joseph Davis, 1 tithable, 4 horses

William Stone, 1 tithable, son William, 3 horses

Samuel Lander, 1 tithable

Henry Eaton, 1 tithable, 1 horse

Jacob Saday, 1 tithable, 4 horses

Peter Rodecap, 1 tithable, 4 horses

Jacob Eversole, 1 tithable, 8 horses

Joseph Crothers, 1 tithable, son Joseph, 8 horses

(John Krotzer above 16 with Joseph Crothers)

William Gray, 1 tithable, 1 horse

Edward McKenney, 1 tithable, 2 horses

George Clark, clear Co. levy, 1 horse

Joseph Conrod, 1 tithable, son John, 1 horse

Joseph Scorethorn, 1 tithable, 1 horse

Michael Sellers, 1 tithable, son Jacob, 4 horses

John Robison, 1 tithable, 4 horses

George Henton, 1 tithable, 2 horses

Christian Brewins, 1 tithable

Wm. Woodford, clear levy, son William, 1 horse

Captain John Rushe's Company, No. 14

Cristophel Wetsle, 1 tithable, 1 horse

Laten Yancey, 1 tithable, 1 horse

George Shaver, 1 tithable, son Jacob, 3 horses

John Shaver, 1 tithable, 1 horse

George Shaver, Jr., 1 tithable, 1 horse

Peter Iler, 1 tithable, son Peter, 4 horses

Vollentine Coffelt, 1 tithable, son Henry, 6 horses

John Rush, 1 tithable, 6 horses

(Jacob Nicholas above 16 with John Rush)

Adam Harmon, 1 tithable, son Jacob, 2 horses

Chas. Smith, 1 tithable, 3 horses

Michael Mallow, 1 tithable, 4 horses

George Mallow, Sen., 1 tithable, 3 horses

Christian Kizer, 1 tithable, son Frederick, 5 horses

Julius Pattrom, 1 tithable, 1 horse

Augustine Price, 1 tithable, son Peter, 8 horses

Conrod Price, 1 tithable, 3 horses

Frederick Price, 1 tithable, 3 horses

Augusteen Price, Jr., 1 tithable, 5 horses

Peter Miller, 1 tithable, 4 horses

William Michael, 1 tithable, 3 horses

George Mallow, 1 tithable, 4 horses

Jacob Pence, 1 tithable, son John, 5 horses

George Pence, Jr., 1 tithable, 1 horse

Charles Rush, 1 tithable, 1 slave, 4 horses

Peter Nicholas, Sr., 1 tithable, 1 horse

Christophel Kerrickhoof, 1 tithable, 3 horses

Jacob Helmontall, 1 tithable

John Wineberry, 1 tithable, 4 horses

John Headrick, 1 tithable, 5 horses

Michael Helmontall, 1 tithable, 2 horses

Peter Nicholas, 1 tithable, 3 horses

Conrod Snider, 1 tithable

Martin Snider, 1 tithable, 3 horses

John Nicholas, 1 tithable, 1 horse

Barbary Nicholas, 1 slave, 2 horses

Henry Nicholas, 1 tithable, 2 horses

Francis Wallgrave, 1 tithable

Jacob Argabright, 1 tithable, son Jacob, 10 horses

Nicholas Pick, 1 tithable

Frederick Armontrout, 1 tithable, sons George, John, Cristophel, Charley, Augusteen and Frederick, 12 horses

John Craig, 1 tithable, 3 slaves, 9 horses

Henry Pence, 1 tithable, 4 horses

Jacob Leigh, 1 tithable, son Jacob, 8 horses

Thos. Carr, 1 tithable, 4 horses

Henry Perkey, 1 tithable, 5 horses

Sammuel Beard, 1 tithable, son Sam, 3 horses

Robert Beard, 1 tithable

Thomas Liewes, 1 tithable, son Thomas, 8 slaves, 12 horses

William Cammil, sons William and James, 7 horses

Robert Cammil, 1 tithable

Roger Mallery, 1 tithable, 1 slave, 1 horse

William Jacks, 1 tithable

Cristophel How, 1 tithable, 4 horses

Cristophel Manness, 1 tithable

Gabriel Jones, 1 tithable, 16 slaves, 6 horses and a "too" wheel chair"

Adam Shillinger, 1 tithable, 3 horses

Jacob Kessling, 1 tithable, 4 slaves, 7 horses

Margaret Smith, 1 horse

James Bruster, 1 tithable, son James, 4 horses

Sammuel Erwine, 1 tithable, 2 horses

Jacob Perkey, 1 tithable, son Henry,

2 slaves, 6 horses

George Weaver, 1 tithable, 1 slave, 5 horses

Conrod Plum, 1 tithable, 2 horses

John Pence, Sr., 1 tithable, 2 horses

John Perkey, 1 tithable, 3 horses

Adam Pence, 1 tithable, 5 horses

John Pence, Jr., 1 tithable, 7 horses

George Main, 1 tithable, sons Jacob and John, 5 horses

Henry Miller, clear poll tax, 3 horses

Peter Miller, 1 tithable, son Henry, 3 horses

Peachey Ridgeway, 1 tithable, 12 slaves, 16 horses

Charles Taylor, 1 tithable, 3 horses

Jacob Fulwiler, 1 tithable, 1 horse

Henry Armontrout, 1 tithable, 4 horses

Jacob Evilsizer, 1 tithable, 3 horses

Jacob Spotts, 1 tithable

(Geo. Armentrout above 16 with Jacob Spotts)

John Bush, clear Co. levy, 1 horse

Rudolph Cagey, 1 tithable, 2 horses

George Pence, 1 tithable, sons John and Henry, 8 horses

Ludwick Boyer, 1 tithable, 1 horse

James Welsh, 1 tithable

David Lard, 1 tithable, 3 slaves, 9 horses

John Swisher, 1 tithable, 5 horses

Jacob Womert, 1 tithable

CAPTAIN STEPHEN CONRAD'S COMPANY, No. 15

Teter Kesling, 1 tithable, 5 horses

Adam Sellers, sons Cristian, Henry and Peter, 9 horses

Peter Sellers, 1 tithable, 3 horses

John Peterfish, 1 tithable, 2 horses

Conrod Peterfish, 1 tithable, 3 horses

George Hufmon, 1 tithable, son Peter, 5 horses

Michael Hufmon, 1 tithable, son Jacob, 4 horses

Casper Haines, 1 tithable, son Frederick, 6 horses

Geo. Price, 1 tithable, 2 horses

Stephen Conrod, 1 tithable, 4 slaves, 9 horses

Peter Conrod, 1 tithable, 2 slaves, 4 horses

Henry Thornhill, 1 tithable, 1 horse

Henry Monger, 1 tithable, 3 horses

Peter Weyhunt, 1 tithable, 3 horses

Michael Kealor, 1 tithable, son George, 3 horses

Danniel Sink, 1 tithable

Henry Cook, 1 tithable, 2 horses

Conrod Boyer, 1 tithable

William Pence, 1 tithable, 3 horses

Danniel Price, 1 tithable, 1 horse

Henry Dauger, 1 tithable, 1 horse

Michael Deck, 1 tithable, 3 horses

Anthony Branamon, 1 tithable, son John, 5 horses

Frederick Haines, 1 tithable, 4 horses

Cristian Lega, 1 tithable

Peter Branamore, 1 tithable, 3 horses

John Hardmon, 1 tithable, son John, 5 horses

(Henry Kisling above 16 with J. Hardmon)

John Monger, 1 tithable, son Martin, 5 horses

John Headrick, 1 tithable, son William, 1 slave, 6 horses

John Fye, 1 tithable, son Charles, 5 horses

Jacob Rape, Polser Dickout, 1 tithable, 2 horses

John Hammer, 1 tithable, son John, 2 horses

Elisabeth Black, 2 horses

Henry Trusler, 1 tithable, 3 horses

John White, 1 tithable

Adam Price, 1 tithable, 5 horses

Cristian Deck, 1 tithable, 1 horse

Abraham Louderback, 1 tithable, 1 horse

John Boyer, 1 tithable, 5 horses

John Michael, 1 tithable, 2 horses
Frederick Michael, 1 tithable, son William, 3 horses
Matthias Carsh, 1 tithable, son Matthias, 8 horses
Jacob Carsh, 1 tithable
George Carsh, 1 tithable
Peter Runkle, 1 tithable, 5 horses
Nicholas Fogle, 1 tithable
Peter Haines, 1 tithable
Jonas Haines, 1 tithable
John Haines, 1 tithable, 5 horses
Christophel Ammon, 1 tithable, 4 horses
Levy Derry, 1 tithable, 1 horse
Jacob Lingle, 1 tithable, 4 horses
Bolen Lee, 1 tithable
David Tople, 1 tithable, 2 horses
Cristian Yootsler, 1 tithable

George Caylor, 1 tithable, son Michael, 2 horses
Thos. Barnet, 1 tithable, 1 horse
Ludwick Rinehart, 1 tithable, 3 horses
William Reece, 1 tithable, sons James and John, 6 horses
Danniel Link, Sr., 1 tithable, 3 horses
Conrod Baker, 1 tithable
Francis Kirtley, 1 tithable, Samuel Garrison, 1 tithable, 11 slaves, 9 horses
John Sellers, 1 tithable, sons Jacob and John, 8 horses
Peter Sellers, Sr., 1 tithable, sons John and Jacob, 7 horses
Henry Brill, 1 tithable
Henry Kesling, 1 tithable

CAPTAIN JOHN PETERSES COMPANY, No. 16

William Nall, 1 tithable, 7 slaves, 12 horses
Adam Hansbarger, 1 tithable, 1 slave, 5 horses
John Dunnaway, William Airy (above 16 with A. Harnsbarger)
Mary Fudge, Cristian Fudge, Conrod Fudge, above 16, 7 horses
Wm. Davis, 1 tithable, 3 slaves, 6 horses
William Davis, 1 tithable, 3 slaves, 16 horses
John Smith, 1 tithable, 3 horses
Edward Williams, 1 tithable, 6 slaves, 6 horses
Mary Smith, 2 horses
Bruten Smith, 1 tithable, 3 horses (Jacob Magort above 16 with B. Smith)
Peter Hashmon, 1 tithable, 2 horses
John Rogers, 1 tithable, 1 horse
David Garvin, 1 tithable, 2 horses
Paul Lingle, 1 tithable, 8 horses (John Magort above 16 with P. Lingle)
Peter Wien, 1 tithable, 3 horses
Jacob Smith, 1 tithable, 3 horses

John Harvey, 1 tithable, 2 horses
Micagah Smith, 1 tithable, 2 horses
Francis Williams, 1 tithable, 1 horse
John Page, 1 tithable, 1 slave, 1 horse
Jacob Bear, 1 tithable, sons Jacob and Henry, 4 slaves, 13 horses
Henry Miller, 1 slave, son Jacob, 1 slave, 12 horses
Conrod Hansbarger, 1 tithable, 1 slave, 7 horses
Wm. Painter, 1 tithable, son William, 1 slave, 4 horses
John Raines, 1 tithable
Reuben Raines (above 16), 1 horse
James Raines, 1 tithable
Reuben Roach, 1 tithable, 1 horse
Thomas Burriss, 1 tithable, 1 slave
Timothy Conoly, 1 tithable, 1 horse
Francis Meadows, 1 tithable, 1 horse
Francis Meadows Jr., 1 tithable, 2 horses
James Meadows, 1 tithable
Robert Loin, 1 tithable, 1 horse
Thomas Team, clear of Poll tax, 1 horse

Jeremiah Beesley, 1 tithable, 2 slaves, 6 horses

Benj. Harvey, 1 tithable, 1 horse

Shadrick Butler, 1 tithable, 1 horse

Sander Veach, 1 tithable, 1 horse

Bowlin Curtless, 1 tithable, 1 horse

Martin Crawford, 1 tithable, 1 horse

Jacob Boyer, 1 tithable, 1 horse

John Crawford, 1 tithable, 1 horse

John McDonald, 1 tithable, 1 horse

Wm. Ferril, 1 tithable

James Maiden, 1 tithable

Reuben Roberts, 1 tithable, 3 horses

Isaac Smith, 1 tithable, 3 horses

Wm. Smith, 1 tithable, 1 horse

Silas Veatch, 1 tithable, 3 slaves, 1 horse

Geo. Argabright, 1 tithable, 4 horses

Ludwick Sliker, 1 tithable, 1 horse

Jacob Peters, 1 tithable, 1 horse

Christian Peters, Mathias Meadows, 1 tithable, 2 horses

John Standley, 1 tithable, 1 horse

CAPTAIN MICHAEL RORICK'S COMPANY, NO. 17

Wm. Oler, 1 tithable, 2 horses

John Fulce, Sr., 1 tithable, son Philip, 3 horses

Geo. Bowers, 1 tithable, 1 horse

John Fulce, 1 tithable, 4 horses

Saboston Fulce, 1 tithable, 1 horse

John Oler, 1 tithable, 2 horses

Joseph Louderback, 1 tithable, 2 horses

Henry Oler, 1 tithable, 4 horses

Michael Tofflemire, 1 tithable, 3 horses

Michael Rorick, 1 tithable, 7 horses

John Handback, 1 tithable, 2 horses

Elisabeth Null, 8 horses

Adam Bloss, 1 tithable, 3 horses

David Monger, 1 tithable, son John, 2 horses

Phillip Moier, 1 tithable, 3 horses

Danniel Price, 1 tithable, son Jacob, 10 horses

Ludwick Runkle, 1 tithable, son Jacob, 3 horses

William Turner, clear Co. Levy, 2 horses

Ludwick Malmon, 1 tithable, 3 horses

Henry Null, 1 tithable, sons Henry, Charles and Cristian, 10 horses

Jacob Moier, 1 tithable, sons Jacob and Michael, 1 slave, 1 horse

Sammuel Short, 1 tithable, 4 horses

John Griggsbe, James Breeding, 1 tithable, 4 horses

Phillip Kite, 1 tithable, son Henry, 4 horses

Michael Kiser, 1 tithable, 4 horses

Christian Straubs, 1 tithable

Jacob Kisor, 1 tithable, 2 horses

Danniel Hashman, 1 tithable, 4 horses

George Bloss, 1 tithable, 4 horses

Zackeriah Lee, 1 tithable, 3 horses

Marcus Stowers, 1 tithable, 1 horse

David Snider, 1 tithable, 1 horse

Casper Snider, 1 tithable, 4 horses

Jeremiah Brian, Clear of Levy, son Edward, 4 horses

Matthias Long, 4 horses

Wm. Bush, 1 tithable, 1 slave, 3 horses

Ludwick Long, 1 tithable

George Aulse, 1 tithable, 2 horses

George Kite, Sr., 1 tithable, sons John and George, 7 horses

William Hoard, 1 tithable, 2 horses

Sarah Hoard, 1 slave, 5 horses

Wm. Kite, 1 tithable, son Martin, 7 horses

John Kite, 1 tithable, son Philip, 5 horses

Adam Kite, 1 tithable, 3 horses

Joseph Crims, 1 tithable, 1 horse

David Fulce, 1 tithable, 1 horse

Cutlip Airy, 1 tithable, 2 horses

John Strickler, 1 tithable, son John, 5 horses

Mallikiah Berry, 1 tithable, son —ary, 3 horses

Cristophel Comer, 1 tithable, 3 horses

Robert King, 1 tithable, 1 horse

Zacceriah Wattson, 1 tithable, 6 slaves, 18 horses

Henry Long, 1 tithable, 1 slave, 6 horses

Nicholas Long, 1 tithable, 5 horses

Frederick Bodey, 1 tithable, 1 horse

Matthias Shuler, 1 tithable, sons John and Jacob, 2 horses

Mical Shuler, 1 tithable, 3 horses

Abraham Heasting, 1 tithable

Henry Rineinger, 1 tithable, 2 horses

David Hinemor, 1 tithable

Daniel Boher, 1 tithable, 7 horses

Barnet Kisemer, 1 tithable, 2 horses

Jacob Ewley, 1 tithable, 4 horses

WASHINGTON IN ROCKINGHAM

In 1784 Gen. George Washington spent several days in Rockingham County on his way home from the Ohio Valley. He came down
through Brock's Gap, crossed the county to Lynnwood, east of the
Shenandoah River; spent a couple of days with Thomas Lewis and
Gabriel Jones; then went on home by way of Swift Run Gap.

The following paragraphs from his journal give many interesting particulars of the great man's sojourn hereabouts. He had
received the surrender of Cornwallis at Yorktown just three years
before. Five years later he was inaugurated first president of the
United States.

SEPTEMBER 29, 1784

"Proceeding up the So. Fork of the So. Branch (of Potomac)
about 24 miles—bated our Horses & obtained something to eat ourselves at one Rudiborts. Thence taking up a branch & following
the same about 4 miles thro' a very confined & rocky path, towards
the latter part of it we ascended a very steep point of the So. Branch
Mountain, but which was not far across, to the No. Fork of Shanon-
doah;— down which by a pretty good path which soon grew into a
considerable road, we descended until we arrived at one Fishwaters
in Brocks Gap, about Eight Miles from the foot of the Mountain—12
from Rudiborts—& 36 from Colon. Hites. This gap is occasioned
by the above branch of Shannondoahs running thro' the Cacapehen
& North Mountains for about 20 Miles and affords a good road,
except being Stony & crossing the Water often.

SEPTEMBER 30, 1784

"Set out early—Captn. Hite returning home—and travelled 11
or 12 Miles along the River, until I had passed thro' the Gap—then
bearing more westerly by one Bryan's—the Widow Smith's—and one
Gilberts, I arrived at Mr. Lewis's about Sundown, after riding about
40 Miles—leaving Rockingham Ct. House to my right about 2 Miles.

OCTOBER 1, 1784

"Dined at Mr. Gabriel Jones's, not half a mile from Mr. Lewis's,
but separated by the South Fork of Shannondoah; which is between
80 and a hundred yards wide & makes a respectable appearance
altho' little short of 150 miles from its confluence with Potomack
River; and only impeded in its navigation by the rapid water & rocks
which are between the old bloomery and Keys's Ferry; and a few
other Ripples; all of which might be easily removed—and the navigation, according to Mr. Lewis's account, extended at least 30 Miles
higher than where he lives.

"I had a good deal of conversation with this Gentleman on the Waters and trade of the Western Country; and particularly with respect to the Navigation of the Great Kanhawa and its communication with James & Roanoke Rivers.

"His opinion is that the easiest & best communication between the Eastern & Western Waters is from the North Branch of Potomack to Yohiogany or Cheat River; and ultimately that the Trade between the two Countries will settle in this Channel. That altho James River has an easy & short communication from the Mouth of Carpenters or Dunlaps Creek to the Green briar, which in distance & kind of Country is exactly as Logston described them, yet, that the passage of the New River, above Kanhawa, thro' the Gauly Mountain from every acct. he has had of it, now is, and ever will be attended with considerable difficulty, if it should not prove impracticable.

"The Fall he has understood, altho' it may be short of a Cataract, or perpendicular tumble, runs with the velocity of a stream descending a Mountain, and is besides very Rocky & closely confined between rugged hills. He adds, that from all appearance, a considerable part of the Water with which the River above abounds, sinks at or above this Rapid or Fall, as the quantity he says, from report, is greatly diminished, however, as it is not to his own observations, but report these accts. are had, the real difficulty in surmounting the obstructions here described may be much less than are apprehended; wch. supposition is well warranted by the assertion of the Fish.

"Mr. Lewis is of opinion that if the obstructions in this River can be removed, that the easiest communication of all would be by the Roanoke, as the New River and it are within 12 Miles, and an excellent Waggon Road between them—and no difficulty that ever he heard of, in the former, to hurt the inland Navigation of it.

October 2, 1784

"I set off very early from Mr. Lewis's who accompanied me to the foot of the Blue Ridge at Swift Run Gap, 10 Miles, where I bated and proceeded over the Mountain—dined at a pitiful house 14 Miles further where the Roads to Fredericksburgh (by Orange Ct. House) & that to Culpeper Court House fork.—took the latter, tho' in my judgment Culpeper Court House was too much upon my right for a direct course. Lodged at a Widow Yearlys 12 Miles further where I was hospitably entertained."

The general's route through Rockingham on this tour may be definitely followed. He came out of Brock's Gap at or near Cootes's Store, thence continued by way of the present Turleytown and Cherry Grove, crossing Linville Creek at Miss Kate Pennybacker's (the old Bryan place); thence by Linville (site of present village), George W. Liskey's (Smithland— "Widow Smith's"), Peale's Cross Roads (Gilbert's), and so on, probably by the Lawyer Road, to Jones's and Lewis's.

Gabriel Jones, "The Lawyer," lived at Bogota, now the home of Dr. A. S. Kemper, about two miles below Port Republic. Thomas Lewis lived just across the river at Lynnwood, on the ground where the battle of June 9, 1862, was fought. The old house in which Thomas Lewis entertained Washington is still standing.

George Rockingham Gilmer, governor of Georgia, in his famous book, "Georgians," relates an amusing story of Washington crossing the Shenandoah. Gilmer's mother was Elizabeth Lewis, daughter of Thomas. As Washington, in the dusk of the evening, was crossing (fording) the river he met a young man in the stream. It was Thomas M. Gilmer, coming back from a visit to Elizabeth Lewis. Why he was coming back so early in the evening has not been explained.

"How do I go to get to Mr. Lewis's?" asked Washington. Young Gilmer, thinking it was some resident of the community who was teasing him about Elizabeth, answered pertly, "Follow your nose."

The general did so and arrived shortly. Just when young Gilmer learned that he had been rude to the "Father of His Country" is not stated; but he probably found it out the next time he went to see the young lady—possibly before.

WASHINGTON IN 1756

In all probability Washington passed through what is now Rockingham County in 1756. Washington Irving, in his life of Washington, states that in the autumn of 1756 Colonel Washington, after a tour of inspection of the frontier forts, came up from the southwest (Catawba Country) in seven days to Augusta County court house. The latter was then at Staunton, as it is today.

One may be almost certain that Washington proceeded on down the Valley from Staunton, through Harrisonburg (site) or Keezletown (site), New Market (then Cross Roads), Strasburg (Stover Town), and Stephens City to Winchester (Frederick Town). Washington at this time had his headquarters at Winchester, where he was building Fort Loudoun, the main fort in the long line by means of which he was trying to protect the Virginia border against the Indians and the French.

There is a tradition that Washington surveyed the Fairfax Line, part of which is still preserved as the county line between Rockingham and Shenandoah.

It is possible that Washington ran parts of this line in laying off lands for Lord Fairfax after 1748. In this year he was first employed by Fairfax. But there is no evidence in Thomas Lewis's journal of the survey of the Fairfax Line (1746) that Washington was in the company. The four surveyors, two for Fairfax, two for the king, are named. Besides, Washington was only 14 years old in 1746.

THE BROCK'S GAP MYTH

Another popular tradition in Rockingham gives an interesting though unreliable account of the naming of Brock's Gap, to the effect that it was named after the well known British general, Sir Isaac Brock, the "Hero of Upper Canada."

Various particulars are added, for example that General Brock was leading a force (perhaps from Winchester) to the relief of Fort Seybert, on the South Fork of the South Branch of the Potomac, and enroute camped in the Gap, thereafter "Brock's Gap."

Certain facts make the tradition faulty. Fort Seybert was captured by the Indians and probably destroyed in 1758; so says Kercheval. The old minute book of the Linville Creek Baptist Church shows that the Indian raids broke upon the region in 1757 and continued for several years. General Brock was not born until the year 1769, and he did not serve in America till 1802.

It seems much more probable that Brock's Gap got its name from some early settlers therein or thereabout by the name of Brock. Records show Brocks in or near the Gap as early as 1748 and 1752. See Wayland's History of Rockingham County, page 21.

From Washington's journal quoted above it will be seen that the name Brock's Gap was familiar in 1784, when Washington came down through the Gap. In 1784 Gen. Brock was only 15 years old—was not a general; and he did not come to America until 18 years later.

AN INCIDENT OF THE WHISKEY REBELLION

The meeting of the Synod of Virginia, at Harrisonburg, in the month of September, 1794, was signalized by an effort of the military to put down the freedom of debate in an ecclesiastical body. The Synod, at that time, was composed of the Presbyteries of Hanover and Lexington, in Virginia; Redstone, in Pennsylvania; Transylvania, in Kentucky; and Ohio, north of the Ohio River.

In Pennsylvania, in the bounds of one of these Presbyteries, that popular outburst, commonly known as the Whiskey Insurrection, had taken place; and the insubordinate, commonly called the Whiskey Boys, were many of them members of Presbyterian congregations. The part of the armed force, raised in Virginia to quell the insurrection, was encamped at Harrisonburg at the time of the meeting of the Synod. The town and country were excited. The proceedings of Synod were closely watched. Mr. Hoge (Moses Hoge, D. D., born in Frederick County, Va., 1752; died at Hampden-Sidney, 1820), after conference with some of his brethren, proposed—"That the Synod prepare an address to the people under their care, inculcating upon them the duty of obedience to the laws of their country."

Mr. Graham opposed the resolution as uncalled for, and as prejudging in an ecclesiastical court the case of a people that felt themselves aggrieved politically by the practical working of a law of Congress, that pressed as tyrannically upon them as the Stamp Act upon the colonies. The proposition was lost by a small majority.

The military were enraged, and threatened personal violence. Tar and feathers were hastily provided. An officer of high grade residing in Rockingham sent to the Synod a demand of the yeas and nays on the question, and the reasons for the decision. This was refused by the Synod as an assumption of power. The popular rage increased, and the inflamed soldiery were scarcely restrained from violence by the remonstrances of Dr. Hoge, who rushed amongst them, and entreated them to respect themselves, and refrain from acts that could only be detrimental, and bring disgrace upon themselves.

So great was the influence acquired by his proposed resolution, and his earnest remonstrances, that a general demand was made for him to deliver them a sermon previously to their march westward. He took for his text,—"Render therefore unto Caesar the things that are Caesar's; and unto God the things that are God's," and left upon his audience an impression of delight with the boldness, clearness, simplicity, and piety of the man.

(From "Sketches of Virginia," First Series, by W. H. Foote; pages 560, 561.) Published 1850.

SOME INTERESTING TRADITIONS OF ROCKINGHAM COUNTY

By David A. Heatwole

Authentic history generally concedes that the settlement of our Virginia Valley by the whites commenced in the year 1732, more than a century after the first English settlement in Virginia. But traditional history reaches far beyond that period and relates for facts many incidents and bloody affairs that took place between contending tribes of Indians. Tradition also informs us that a tribe of Indians known as Catawbas dwelt in the Valley of Virginia; and what is now known as Rockingham county was then included as part of their territory or hunting ground. We are also informed that the tribe or nation lived long in peace and quiet prosperity, undisturbed and unmolested by other tribes or nations and that they were a wealthy people. Not only were their hunting grounds well stocked with all kinds of game that afforded flesh for food and hides and pelts for clothing, but their great chief and all his warriors were loaded down with gold and silver ornaments, which was a clear indication that somewhere in their hunting domain were rich mines of these precious metals.

This ornamental wealth, possessed by the Catawba tribe, tempted other tribes to look upon their wealth with an earnest desire to dispossess them of the source thereof, which was located somewhere inside of their boundaries. But the location of these valuable mines was kept a profound secret by the Catawba Indians, and the invasions of other tribes were always watched with a suspicious eye.

We are informed that this quiet and rich tribe of Indians did not live always in peace and prosperity. Their domains were invaded by an army of Delaware Indians who came across the mountains from the Wapatomaca, the old Indian name of the great South Branch, and attempted to drive out these Catawbas and thereby get possession of their hunting grounds and rich mines of gold and silver.

Tradition relates that the Catawbas were aware of the intended invasion of their enemies and were prepared to meet them in defense of their homes and hunting grounds. And we are told that a great battle took place between these two tribes at or near where the North Mountain Road now crosses War Branch. Here these Indians met in deadly combat, and a bloody battle was fought. The Catawbas knew full well upon this battle depended their future possession of their hunting grounds, their homes, and their valuable mines of gold and silver; and they went into the battle for victory or death; whilst the Delawares came across the mountains with a full determination to conquer their enemies and drive them away and get possession of their wealth, which they so much desired. Both armies fought bravely, but at length the Delawares gave way and the battle turned in favor of the Catawbas.

The chief of the Delawares (who was mortally wounded) and twenty-four of his brave warriors a remnant of a powerful army, left the field of battle and attempted to make their escape over the mountains by the same route by which they had entered the valley; but their victorious enemies followed and pressed them so hard that they compelled them to enter the western chain of mountains some where near the place now known as Rawley Springs. Here the Catawbas discontinued their pursuit, and it is supposed that the twenty-four Delawares made their flight up a small stream now known as "Gum's Run."

From the fact that at this day, about three miles above Rawley Springs, can be seen a grave marked with head and foot stones, and from time almost immemorial known as the "Old Indian Grave," here no doubt the wounded chief died and was buried by the remnant of his faithful followers who made their escape across the western mountain.

The statement in regard to the gold and silver mines known to the Catawba Indians, which they guarded with such jealous care, and by which they became so rich in ornaments, may be considered by the present generation as a myth or a legendary tale; but we have authentic history which certainty in part corroborates tradition that both gold and silver did exist in this region before the settlement of the valley by the whites.

He who has lived his three score and ten years and will take the trouble to look up his old Adams' Geography will find therein a statement in reference to the mineral wealth of Virginia, and that in Rockingham County lumps or nuggets of gold were found on the surface of the ground about two miles west of Harrisonburg, on the farm now owned by Daniel J. Myers.

And it is also known that in other parts of the county silver has been found in considerable quantities; and besides these facts there are striking evidences in different parts of the county that clearly indicate that mining operations had been carried on many years before the whites settled in the Valley of Virginia.

A recent tradition informs us that a man by the name of Jones, in one of his hunting rambles in the mountains of West Rockingham wounded a deer and was following its trail by the blood running from the wound, and in his pursuit of the deer he accidentally noticed some kind of ore lying on the ground which attracted his attention. He hastily picked up some of the lumps and put them into his shot pouch, and continued the pursuit of the deer until he captured his prize. And after he returned home he examined his find more carefully and it is said he melted some of this ore and moulded it into bullets and shot away the greater part of them before he discovered that he was shooting away bullets of gold. And it is further stated in this tradition that the man Jones, soon after he learned the value of his discovery, took sick and died before he disclosed to any one the location of his find.

Although there has been much speculation as to where Jones did his hunting and considerable time and thought have been spent in searching for this mineral wealth, as yet no one has been so fortunate as to find the place where Jones got his gold.

(Note by J. W. W.—The foregoing narrative came into my hands in 1912.)

The following paragraphs appeared in the *Shenandoah Herald* (Woodstock, Va.), date of May 31, 1918.

How a Testament Saved a Life

When the Stonewall Brigade, in 1861, was encamped near Fairfax C. H., Sergeant Holland, of Co. I, 33rd Va. Regiment, was accidently shot. The ball struck a testament which he carried in his left breast pocket. The ball glanced and passed through his elbow. Dr. Hay, father of ex-Congressman Hay, amputated his arm. He remarked "Those little books have saved many lives." Sergeant Holland replied, "Yes, Doctor, and many souls."

Mr. Holland afterwards became a prominent Lutheran minister. At one time, he was County Supt. of Schools of Rockingham County.

(Note by J. W. W.—Mr. G. W. Holland was county superintendent of schools in Rockingham from 1870 to 1872.)

REV. MR. ELLIS'S NARRATIVE

In 1912, when the manuscript for the History of Rockingham County was being prepared for the printer, the author wrote Rev. J. R. Ellis, Lynnwood, Va., asking him to contribute an account of the Episcopal Church in the eastern part of the county. Mr. Ellis did so. A condensed sketch was included in the book then published. The complete narrative, as prepared by Mr. Ellis, is presented herewith.

THE EPISCOPAL CHURCH IN EAST ROCKINGHAM

The Episcopal Church was long regaining a foothold in Rockingham County—and indeed in the upper part of the Valley—after the Revolutionary war. That it had a foothold at that time seems to be true. The house near Port Republic in which three generations of Kempers lived, and which has but recently passed out of the family, is known as "Madison Hall" from the fact that it was the home of Bishop Madison, a cousin of the President. Three miles away is "Lynnwood," now occupied by Mr. John F. Lewis, in which have lived seven generations of that name. They have always been Episcopalians despite the fact that until but recently there was no Episcopal Church near them; and through them the Church goes back to the Revolutionary times. There is no other neighborhood in the county known to the writer of which this may be said. The church at Harrisonburg was built in comparatively recent times. But the good folk of Lynnwood and Lewiston and Mapleton and now Avonfeld (the recently built home of Mr. S. H. Lewis) have, with some of their family connections, stoutly maintained their loyalty and allegiance to the church of their forefathers with a spiritual lineage which antedates the Revolution.

Services were held there now and then by the ministers from Staunton and Harrisonburg, as opportunity presented itself. Good Dr. Wheat, who was afterward the Rector of the Parish for some time, has been known to walk from Staunton, twenty miles away, in order that these devoted people might have a Prayer Book service. Rev. O. S. Bunting, then Rector of Emmanual Church, Harrisonburg, in his report to the Council in 1885, says: "Since last Council a Mission Church has been established at Lynnwood, twelve miles east of Harrisonburg, on the Shenandoah River. Services had been held here by the Rector one Sunday afternoon in the month during the longer days of two seasons when, in October last, Rev. G. Moseley Murray assumed charge in connection with his work at Luray. Since then the Mission has been organized, a Sunday School established, and services held two Sundays a month in a country-schoolhouse." This was the beginning of the work of this Church in the foothills of the Blue Ridge in East Rockingham known as the work among the mountain folk, which has since assumed large proportions. It is to these people Rev. Mr. Bunting refers in his report, when he says:

"The work is in a community for the most part destitute; the congregations are large and interest increasing. There is a class of twelve awaiting confirmation." Rev. Mr. Murray went with zeal and energy to the task of putting up a church building. He was helped gladly and willingly by the people in the accomplishment of this long-cherished object. In two years the church was built and ready for consecration. In his Council Address in 1887, Bishop Randolph, now of the Diocese of Southern Virginia, has this to say of its consecration:

"On April the 6th, Grace Memorial Church at Lynwood, Rockingham county, was consecrated. The Rector, the Rev. G. Moseley Murray, the Rev. Dr. Wheat, and the Rev. O. S. Bunting, of Harrisonburg, assisted in the services. The church is Gothic in form, and both the exterior and interior are comely and graceful. The seating capacity is for two hundred persons. In addition there is a gallery for colored people, which is always well filled. The cost of the building is $1,200—a specimen of economical construction. It stands upon the field of the battle of Port Republic, and upon the spot where the fight was hottest and the carnage the greatest. Nature heals the ravages that man has wrought in the earth, and the grass grows green upon the mounds of buried cities and from the blood of battle-field. The gospel of peace that comes from the Lord of Nature heals the wounds of human passion, and survives the desolations of the wrongs and strifes of men. This little valley was once covered with the pall of the smoke of battle and echoed with the cries of combat and the thunder of artillery. Today it is peaceful, and consecrated to the gospel of peace, and the hills around it echo to the hymns of redemption. I cannot speak too warmly of the fidelity and enthusiasm of the minister of this parish and his people in their work among the poor."

In 1888 Rev. James C. Wheat, D. D., succeeded Rev. Mr. Murray and had charge of this work for several years; but resigned in 1895 when Rev. John S. Douglas was elected Rector. He in turn was succeeded by Rev. C. E. A. Marshall, and he in turn by Rev. William H. Darby.

The work of the Episcopal Church in Rockingham County outside of Harrisonburg has been confined almost exclusively of late years to those referred to by Rev. Mr. Bunting as "for the most part very destitute"—the people in the foothills of the Blue Ridge, a section known locally as East Rockingham. To these the three Rectors last named ministered most devotedly and earnestly. The Rev. Mr. Marshall gave much time to a Mission in historic Brown's Gap, which, with the services in the country schoolhouse under Rev. Mr. Murray, and at Grace Church, as well, was kept up largely by the Misses Lewis and Miss Eleanor Wheat as they grew into womanhood, from the three houses, Lynwood, Lewiston and Mapleton. The Sundays when the Rector was absent or when the Parish was vacant, these ladies were found at schoolhouses or church, doing faithful work among the people in the foothills. The devotion of the people

of the foothills to the Prayer Book and its teaching—especially their
desire to bring their children to the Church for Baptism—gives proof
that these labors were not in vain. (It may be noted that this work
was begun many years before the work in the Ragged Mountains was
inaugurated by Rev. Mr. Neve.)

During the rectorate of Rev. Mr. Darby a small church was
built—tho not consecrated—near Island Ford, on a small plat of
ground bought of W. H. Hickle. It was called St. Stephen's, and
was afterwards moved to Berrytown. Lynnwood Parish was set apart
at this time, also, as separate from Rockingham Parish, the
boundaries "to be Page on the northeast, Greene and Albemarle
counties on the southeast, Augusta county on the southwest, and a
straight line extending from Good's Mills in Augusta county to Page
county on the northeast."

In 1905 Rev. Mr. Darby resigned the Parish and was succeeded
by the present incumbent (1912). His predecessors had worked the
two Parishes of Luray and Lynnwood from the ends, spending two
weeks of each month at either place, Luray or Lynnwood, but he
thought it wise to work from the middle, so he lived at Elkton for the
first five years of his ministry while he had the two Parishes. This
enabled him to cover the fifty miles of mountain territory and to meet
his appointments, which sometimes numbered ten, more readily. In
1910 his labors were restricted to Lynnwood Parish in Rockingham
county. Meantime, schools had been established and the work was
progressing.

In the fall of 1905, a small lot of land was purchased at Berrytown of Mr. White Shifflett by Miss Eleanor Wheat, the paid Missionary of the Diocese, who had given much of her time to teaching these
people, and upon this was built in 1906 a two-story building for a
schoolhouse. In this the first school was begun. It succeeded well
from the beginning. The pioneer teacher, Miss Lizzie Meade (great-
granddaughter of Bishop Meade), took with the people, and she was
joined the second year by her sister, Miss Maxwell Meade. They did
splendid work and commended themselves and the work to the
children and their parents. Other teachers have come and gone; all
have done their part so well that now (1912) a three-room up-to-date
schoolhouse has been built to accommodate the large number of
children applying for admission to the school.

Meantime, in 1908, St. Stephen's Church was moved to the
schoolhouse lot, from its location near Island Ford Depot. More
land was added to the lot and in 1910, when the Settlement House
was built, the Church was remodeled and put in its present attractive
shape. This improvement in 1910 was accomplished through the
generosity of the many friends of the Church, but Mr. W. H. Baker
of Winchester was the largest donor, he taking over the church as a
memorial to his wife—it having been consecrated in 1911 as St.
Stephen's Church, a Memorial to Mrs. W. H. Baker.

The success of the St. Stephen's School aroused the interest of
others interested in the education of these children; and other schools

were started at Lynnwood, Rocky Bar, and Sandy Bottom or Wauken's Hollow. All of these have been kept up except the first-named, which was abandoned for want of proper support by the parents of the children; so that nearly two hundred children were in these schools during the session of 1911-12.

It may not be amiss to add that the Settlement House is so called because it accommodates not only the Rector and his family, but the teachers at St. Stephen's as well; and is a gathering place at times for the people of the neighborhood—is a house settled indeed among the people for their help and uplift.

It is well to add that these people are kindhearted, tractable and responsive, and what is needed is a truer conception of their lives and characters. When this is had, the Christian Church will be more ready and willing to remove the neglect from which they are suffering, a neglect not theirs, but ours.

AN OLD REGIMENTAL BOOK

Mr. Joseph K. Ruebush of Dayton, Va., well known book dealer, publisher, and antiquarian, has loaned the writer (J. W. W.) an old book—what is left of it—that is of unusual interest as a source of history and genealogy for Rockingham County a century and more ago. In size it is 8¼ inches from left to right, and 13 inches from top to bottom. It still contains 29 leaves, nearly all of which are written full. At least 10 leaves have been torn out, as shown by the ragged stubs remaining.

This old book was bound by Frederick A. Mayo, Staunton, Va., who "neatly executed all kinds of Blank Books." His card is printed in English and in German.

On the first page of this book is written, "Regimental Book for the years from 1813 to 1824. Thos. C. Fletcher." Under Fletcher's name is that of George Mauzy.

The first ten or twelve pages are missing. The "Amount Brought forward" on the first page that remains is $93.50. To this amount are added various items, to wit:

To Peter Fitch, who was employed as an express, $7.00.

To Andrew McClelan, for 4 days attendance at the battalion and regimental courts martial, $12.00.

To Henry J. Gambill, for services in attending the several battalion and regiment courts martial and for making out list of fines as required by law, $56.00.

To the same for advertising the list of delinquent muster fines for 1813, as returned by the sheriff, $4.00.

It was ordered that the aforesaid several claims be paid out of the fines for 1814.

It was ordered that the respective companies enroll the following persons—Henry Snyder, Henry Hulvey, Jacob Baker, Peter Fitch, George Pence, John Ellinger, Samuel Garber, Leonard Null, Jacob Whitmore, Conrad Mellebarger, Samuel Glyn, Jacob Snell, and Joseph Erman, "it appearing to the court that they have so fair recovered as to be able to do Militia Duty."

The minutes were signed by William Beard, major and commandant.

JUNE 8, 1815

At a regimental court martial held for the 58th regiment of the militia in Rockingham County, June 8, 1815, for the trial of sundry privates of the said militia who refuse to march or perform their respective tours of duties in the service of the state agreeable to the calls of the governor of the 24th and 26th of August, 1814, present:

George Huston, colonel and president of the said court

Adam Harnsbarger, major and commandant of the 2d battalion in said regiment

Captains Robert Erwin, Robert Hooks, Jacob Keplinger and John Mallow

The court being duly organized, was qualified according to law and proceeded to business as follows:

Ordered that Henry J. Gambill be appointed clerk or judge advocate to this court, who thereupon took an oath faithfully to perform the duties of the said office. Ordered that John Rush, Jr., be appointed provost martial to this court and that he give his attendance accordingly.

Commonwealth against Joseph Miller, a private in Capt. R. Magill's company—the said defendant not appearing, altho solemnly called (and it appearing that he had notice hereof), it is considered by the court that for such his contempt he be fined in the sum of $56, that being the pay of a private in the army of the United States for seven months, for failing to march or perform a tower of duty under the call of August 26, 1814; and it is further considered by the court that if the said defendant shall fail to make payment of the said fine, and shall have no goods & chattles whereof distress can be made, he shall be imprisoned by the sheriff for one callender month for every 5 dollars of such fine.

Commonwealth against Henry Harshbarger, a private in Capt. Robert Magells company; also against Martin Miller, a private in the same company; the said defendants appeared in court and being fully heard in their defence, it is considered by the court that for such their contempt the said Hershberger be fined $24, being the pay of a private in the army of the U. S. for 3 months, failing to perform a tower of duty . . . . and that the said Martin Miller be fined in in the sum of $40, being the pay of a private in the army of the U. S. for 5 months. . . . .

Mathias Cash, a private in Capt. A. Harnsbarger's company was fined $8 for failing to march &c. in room of John Crawford "who he had hired as a substitute."

Christian Telkerd (?), a private in Capt. H. Perkey's company was fined $8 for not marching under the call of the 26th August, 1814.

Reuben Rawley, a private in Capt. Luke Rice's company, was fined $16 for failing to march &c. under the call of Aug. 26, 1814.

Henry Hansbarger, a private in Capt. Luke Rice's company, was fined $24 for a like offence.

William Nair, a private in Capt. J. Snapp's troop of cavalry, was fined $40 for failing to march under the call of Aug. 26, 1814.

John Byerly, a private in Capt. Reuben Harrison's company, was fined $24 for failing to march under the orders of Aug. 24, 1814.

Benjamin Wenger (?), a private in Capt. R. Harrison's company, was fined $8 for failing to march agreeably to the Genl. Orders of the 24th August, 1814.

John Blosser, a private in Capt. R. Harrison's company, was fined $40 for the same offence.

Jacob Blosser, a private in Capt. R. Harrison's company, was fined $24 for failing to march under call of Aug. 24, 1814.

Jacob Early, a private in Capt. R. Harrison's company, was fined $32 for failing to march under the call of Aug. 26, 1814.

Jacob Ferrell, a private in Capt. R. Harrison's company, was fined $16 for failing to march under the call of Aug. 26, 1814.

Daniel Whisler, a private in Capt. R. Harrison's company, was fined $24 for failing to march under the call of Aug. 26, 1814.

It will be recalled that it was in August and September, 1814, that the British advanced upon Washington and Baltimore, and it is possible that the general calls of August 24 and 26 were made to gather troops for the defence of those cities.

Anthony Roads, a private in Capt. R. Harrison's company, was fined $24 for failing to march under the call of Aug. 24, 1814.

Frederick Young, a private in Capt. R. Harrison's company, was fined $8 for failing to march under the call of the same date.

John Showalter, a private in Capt. R. Harrison's company, was fined $8 on the same charge.

Christian Garber, a private in Capt. R. Harrison's company, was fined $16 on the same charge.

Gabriel Heatwool, a private in Capt. R. Harrison's company, was fined $40 for failing to march agreeably to the orders of Aug. 26, 1814.

It will be observed that Capt. Reuben Harrison's company was hard hit with refusals. The explanation is probably to be found in the fact that a number of the men enrolled in his company were Mennonites and Dunkers, whose religious traditions were opposed to military service.

It was ordered that John Rush, Jr. be allowed the sum of $6 for his services in attending the court martial.

Henry J. Gambill was allowed $38 for his attendance as clerk or judge advocate and for making out and certifying the lists of the fines assessed by the court.

The minutes of this date (June 8, 1815), were signed by Geo. Huston, Lt. Col. commanding the 58th Regt. Va. Militia.

The total amount of the fines at this session of the court was $480. The list was delivered to Daniel Ragan for collection and a copy was sent to the auditor by mail about the last of June—which is said to have miscarried; and another copy was forwarded by post Nov. 17, 1815.

"The whole amount is collected, so Ragan says, and shall be paid when the Assembly meets."—H. J. Gambill, Nov. 17, 1815.

November 3, 1815

At a court martial held for the 1st battalion and 58th regiment Virginia militia in Rockingham County on Friday, Nov. 3, 1815, were present John Vigers, major commanding the said battalion in the absence of the major, and captains Jacob Spader, Samuel Lynn, and Lt. Elisha Hooks of riflemen and Jacob Hansbarger, lt. of cavalry.

The major commanding laid before the court a list of delinquents returned by Capt. Luke Rice, which delinquents were severally called, and not appearing, it was considered by the court that they severally make their fines in the payment of 75 cents each for such their non attendance at the said muster, unless good cause be shown for said delinquency at the next regimental court of inquiry.

The same was voted for, according to the record, by Capt. John Vigers, Capt. Samuel Lynn, Capt. Jacob Spader, Capt. R. Loftis (for Lt. Hansbarger), Capt. Eugene Erwin, and the minutes were signed by John Vigar, captain.

November 4, 1815

At courts martial held for the 2d battalion and 58th regiment Virginia militia in Rockingham County on Saturday, Nov. 4, 1815, were present Adam Hansbarger, major of said battalion, captains Henry S. Pirkey, John Armentrout, John Miller, and Lt. Jacob Hansbarger, lt. of cavalry, and Lt. Andrew Wilson, lt. of riflemen.

The major laid before the court a list of delinquents returned by Capt. Henry S. Pirkey, which delinquents were severally called, and not appearing, it was ordered that they make their fines in the payment of 75 cents each for such their non attendance at the said musters, unless good cause be shown for such their neglect at the next regiment court of inquiry.

Signed by Adam Hansbarger, major.

November 20, 1815

At a court martial held for the 58th regiment of the militia of Rockingham County on Monday, Nov. 20, 1815, were present Joseph Mauzey, colonel of the said regiment, Adam Hansbarger, major of the 2d batalion, and captains Henry S. Pirkey, Ralph Loftus (of cavalry), Jacob Spader, Samuel Lynn, John Armentrout, and lieutenants Andrew Wilson (of riflemen) and John Miller.

On the motion of John Working, and for reasons appearing to the court, it was ordered that he be exempted from militia duty.

On the motion of Joseph Earmon, and for reasons appearing to the court, it was ordered that he be exempted from militia duty.

John Earman the same.

At this time were present also Eugenia Erwin, captain of riflemen in 1st battalion, Samuel H. Lewis, captain of artillery, and Capt. John Vigers.

On the motion of Peter Shank, and for reasons appearing to the court, it was ordered that he be exempted from militia duty.

On motion of William Cave, late lieutenant, who was fined for non attendance at the training in 1812, and for reasons appearing to the satisfaction of the court, it was ordered that the fine be remitted.

On motion of Charles Youst, and for reasons appearing to the court, it was ordered that he be exempted from military duty.

Thomas Lewis, deputy for Charles Lewis, late sheriff, returned a list of delinquents for the year 1813 which was examined and allowed by the court and ordered to be certified. .

The court proceeded to make the allowances for the year 1815, as follows:

To Nathan Chandler, late adjutant, for 4 days attendance, $24

To John Yancy, the present adjutant, for two days attendance, $12

To Eli Lightner, for 3 days attendance as a drummer at the training, $6

To Andrew McClelan, for 3 days as provost martial to the court, $9

To Henry J. Gambill, for his attendance as clerk on the several battalion and regiment courts and for making out the list of fines in 1815, $48

To the same for advertising the list of delinquent muster fines this day allowed by the court (for 1813), $4

To Philip Boston, late provost martial, for his attendance on the business of the court during the last year, 4 days, $12

To William Pener (?), late captain, for a fife furnished his company some time ago, $1

It was ordererd that the aforesaid several allowances, totaling $116.00, should be paid out of the fines of 1815, according to law.

The record was signed by Joseph Mauzy, commander of the 58th regt.

Next follows a list of fines assessed in the 58th regiment in Rockingham County for non-attendance at musters in 1815.

The number after each name indicates the musters missed, for each of which the fine was 75 cents.

FIRST BATTALION

Delinquents Returned by Capt. Luke Rice

Allen Dever (4), William Robinson (1), Henry Berry (2), Henry Detmore (3), Earnest Cool (3), John Bridges (3), Daniel Losh (1), Peter Huff, (2), Anthony Niely (3), Isaac Waggy (4), John Calhoon (4), John Miller (2), Adam Howdyshell (3), John Dinkle (1), John Robinson (2), Henry Hansbarger (3), Reuben Rawley (2), John Robinson Sr. (1), Charles Weaver (1), Edmund Price (1), Jacob Bargerhiser (1), Caleb Larrick (1).

RETURNED BY CAPT. JOHN VIGAR

James Dever (2), Michael Ritter (1), Jacob Koogler (1), Joseph Sheffer (1), Christly Miller (6), George Hisey (1), Martin Miller (6), John Click (6), Abraham Smith (4), William Carsey (4), Joseph Miller (6), Bernard B. Moppin (1), Henry Brown (3), John Dearman (1), Michael May (2), John Warren (6), James Morrison (1), Henry Nisewander (3), James Nickel (1), Peter Fetrick (Tetrick?) (2), Abraham Whitmore (6), Henry Hershbarger (6), Jacob Snell (6), Philip Hisey (1), Henry Moredock (2), David Frank (2), Jacob Miller (5), Joseph Snell (5), James Davies (1), George Newman (1), Lemuel Taylor (1), John L—— (2), Daniel Fetrick (1).

RETURNED BY CAPT. SAMUEL LYNN

John Brown (2), Robert Ward (2), Daniel Yount (2), John Rust (2), Jacob Whitmore, Sr. (1), John Kesler (1), John Bateman (1), Jacob Rust (2), John Pence, Sr. (1), Abraham Rinehart (2), Samuel Decker (1), Andrew Hudlow (1), John Yount (1), George McNett (1), Jacob Spitser (1), John Dundore (1), Daniel Hant (1).

RETURNED BY CAPT. JACOB SPADER

David Groves (3), John Sailor (1), Joseph Wagoner (1), Jacob Farrol (6), Joseph Argebright (1), Peter Moyer (1), Christian Garber (6), Jacob Roemer (5), Matthew Haney (1), Daniel Wine (6), Daniel Brannaman (6), Jacob Early (6), Benjamin Winger (6), Jacob Miller (6), Gabriel Heatwool (6), Frederick Young (6), Abraham Winger (4), Jacob Blosser (6), John Blosser (6), Solomon Messerly (2), Daniel Flora (6), Daniel Whisler (6), Anthony Rodes (6), John Showalter (6), Henry Early (6), John Flora (6), Samuel Miller (6), Stephen Rodecap (6), Jacob Rodecap (6), Christian Heatwool (6), Samuel Garber (6), Michael Wine (5), Jesse Williams (1), John Brown (1), Peter Blosser (3), Jonas Blosser (3), David Blosser (3), John Allebough (2), Isaac Miller (1), Jonas Gladden (1), David Greere (3), John Greere (1).

RETURNED BY CAPT. RALPH LOFTUS

Lewis Byrd (1), William Hogshead (1), Garland McCollester (1), John —— (1), Valentine —— (1), Abraham Hambleton (1), John Clarkson (2), John Carthrae (2), George Moss (1), Reuben Matheany (2), James Newman (2), Alexander Newman (1), Benjamin Vance (2), Jacob Pence (2), George Miltenbarger (2), William Carthrae (1), Charles Chandler (2), John Stuple (1), George Detimore (1).

RETURNED BY CAPT. EUGENED ERWIN

Joseph Shank (2), David Whitmore (2), James Erwin (1), William Erwin (1), Silas Hogsett (1), John Long (1), Simeon Fry (2), Michael Wise (1), Jacob Shank (1), George Secrist (1), Philip Lindsey (1), John Brown (1), John Pipher (1).

SECOND BATTALION
Delinquents Returned by Capt. John Miller

John Lawson (1), Honorias Powel (2), Andrew Burnsides (2), St. Clair Kirtly (3), Henry L—— (5), Zecheriah Crawford (2), James Rains (1), ...

(Next leaves are torn out.)

A List of Muster Fines assessed in the 58th Regiment of the Militia in Rockingham County for the year 1816.

First Battalion
Delinquents Returned by Capt. John Vigers

Michael Ritter (2), Jacob Koogler (1), Reuben French (1), Christly Miller (5), Abraham Smith (4), George Hisey (1), Stephen Matheny (1), Martin Miller (5), John Click (5), William Carsey (1), Adam Howdyshell (1), Joseph Miller (5), Henry Brown (3), Henry Nisewanger (5), Abraham Whitmore (5), Martin Frank (1), Henry Harshbarger (5), Jacob Snell (5), Jeremiah Lamb (1), Philip Hisey (1), Henry Moredock (2), David Frank (3), Samuel Sheetz (1), Jacob Miller (5), Joseph Snell (5), Martin Speck (1), Daniel Tetrick (5), Henry Dinkle (1), Jacob Shoe (2), Edmund Price (3), Earnest Cool (3), Peter Huff (5), Isaac Waggy (5), Caleb Larrick (2), John Miller (1), Francis Humes (4), Philip Denton (2), William Bridges, Jr. (5), Emanuel Shereman (4), James Crawford (1), Joseph Sharfick (2), Daniel Flora (4), Henry Gilmore (2), Robert Walker (2), William U. Dever (2), David Whitmore, cooper (1), Isaac Flemins (1), John Brown (1), Thomas Gilmore (1), William Frank (1), John Bridges (1), Allen Dever (1).

Returned by Capt. Eugenea Erwin

John Amon (4), James Erwin (6), Joseph Frank (3), Simeon Fry (3), John B. Keith (1), Benjamin Solomon (1), David Whitmore (6), Joseph Waggoner (4), John Halterman (1), Joseph Miller (1), John Roller (1), David Fadely (2), Abraham Richards (1), George Rice (4), Michael Simmers (3), John Argebrite (1), John Coleman (3), Cornelus Cain (2), Henry Detamore (1), Mayberry Curry (1), Jacob Shaver (1), Israel Shaver (1).

Returned by Capt. R. A. Loftus

James Fulton (1), William Hogsett (1), Reuben Matheny (1), Jacob Roots (1), James O. Stephens (1), Richard Robertson (1), Charles Carthrae (1), John Robertson, Sr. (1), Jacob Arnold (1), John Stuple (1), Abraham Hamilton (1), Charles Weaver (1).

Returned by Capt. Jacob Spader

David Grove (6), Jacob Farrell (6), Henry Hansbarger (5), Jacob Neible (1), Christian Garber (6), John Greer (1), George Long (1),Adam Howdyshell (6), Matthew Haney (5), Daniel Wine (6), Daniel Brannaman (6), Jacob Early (6), Benjamin Winger (6), Gabriel Heatwool (6), Frederick Young (6), Abraham Winger (3), Jacob Blosser (6), John Blosser (6), Solomon Messerly (3), Daniel Florey (1), Daniel Whisler (6), Anthony Rhodes (6), John Showalter (6), Henry Early (6), John Florey (6), Samuel Miller (6), Stephen Rodecap (6), John Rodecap (6), Christian Heatwool

(6), Samuel Garber (6), Michael Wine (6), Jesse Williams (1), Henry Winkle (1), Jacob Showalter (2), Jacob Messick (1), Peter Blosser (5), Jonas Blosser (6), David Blosser (5), Isaac Miller (6), Anthony Showalter (1), John Wright (2), Jacob Beel (2), Martin Beel (2), David Garber (4), John Thomas (5), John Rumsey (4), David Heatwool (1), Jacob Miller (1).

Returned by Capt. S. H. Lewis

Daniel Beaver (2), Isaac Beaver (2), John Blakely (3), William Caldwell (2), Thomas Clayter (2), Charles Davis (4), William R. Head (1), Robert Morton (2), Henry Marshall (2), William Marshall (4), Thornton Maddox (1), Philip Blume (2), Jonathan Rush (3), John Stevenson (2), Joel Taylor (3), Larkin Taylor (1), John Black (5), Benjamin Cash (1), Samuel Caldwell (1), Daniel Pretzman (1), Daniel Hott (2), William Bateman (1).

Returned by Capt. Samuel Lynn

Archibald Brown (2), John Bateman (1), Abraham Rinehart (1), Daniel Yount (5), John Yount (5), Robert Ward (3), John Alford (3), John Brown (3), James Bateman (1), Jacob Deal (1), Stephen Tinder (2), John Dundore (1), Hail Snow, alias Hayland (2), Thomas Allen (1), Adam Trobough (1).

Second Battalion
Delinquents Returned by Capt. Thos. Bryan

Elisha Morris (3), Echilles Roach (2), Ezekiel Crawford (1), Zecheriah Crawford, Sr. (2), Philip Lamb (1), James Rains (2), John Pence (1), John Crawford (1), William Smith (1), Henry Lee (4), George Bougher (1), Stephen Shiflet (1), Zecheriah McDaniel (1), Israel Eblin (1), John Self (1), Jonathan Welch (1), Zecheriah Crawford, Jr. (1), James Rodgers (1).

Returned by Capt. John Yancey

George Baker (1), Nicholas Leap (1), Benson Rains (4), George Seigfried (1), Mark Seigler (2), Christian Utsler (1), James Lilly (1), Jacob Bloss (1), Henry Balser (1), John Cline (1).

Returned by Capt. S. H. Lewis

William Gillaspy (2), Jacob Delkard (2), Reuben Gardner (1), Henry Utsler (1), George Weaver (1), George McNutt (1).

Returned by Capt. John Armentrout

Jeremiah Vanpelt (1), Christopher Comer (1), Michael Kite (1), Reuben Kite (2), Jacob Croft (1), Benjamin Hansen (?) (1), John Dovel (1), David Huffman (1), Henry Pence (1), Joseph Strickler (1), John Jones (1), John Runkle (1), William Dovel (1), Reuben Fulse (1), John Heastan (1), Mathias Long (1).

Evidently the companies of Yancey, Lewis and Armentrout were made up in East Rockingham—those of Yancey and Lewis around McGaheysville, Port Republic, and Grottoes; that of Armentrout farther down, between Elkton and Shenandoah and Newport.

Returned by Capt. R. A. Loftus

Henry Hammer (1), Charles Airey (2), John Hammer (1), Philip Pirkey (1), George C. Cook (3), Jonathan Rains (1), James O. Stephens (1), John Pence (1), John Royer (1), Jacob Hammer (1), Jacob H. Peterfish (1), Jacob Rush (1).

Returned by Capt. Henry S. Pirkey

Charles Lewis (1), Jacob Harshbarger (1), William Rush (1), Daniel Judy (2), Christian Royer (1), Henry Deads (1), Peter Kyger (2), George Berry (1), Henry Sipe (1), Jacob Sites (1), Joseph Good (1), Nicholas Pirkey (1), John Bowyer (1), Andrew Spitzer (1).

October 25, 1817

At a court martial held for the 1st battalion of the 58th regiment of the militia of Rockingham County, at the house of Richard Patton, on Saturday the 25th October, 1817, were present John Vigar, major commandant of said battalion; Capt. Eugeno Erwin (of riflemen); Lt. Peter Harry (commandant); and Ensign Joseph Cline (commandant).

The major commandant laid before the board a list of delinquents returned by said Capt. Vigars for non attendance at his musters held in the year 1817, which delinquents were severally called, and not appearing, or not having a reasonable excuse, they were fined $1 each, to be paid unless good cause be shown at the next regimental court of inquiry.

The same was done regarding Capt. Eugeno Erwin, Capt. Peter Harry, Capt. Joseph Cline, and Capt. Ralph A. Loftus.

The minutes were signed by John Vigar, captain.

October 27, 1817

At a court martial held for the 2d battalion of the 58th regiment, at the house of John Maggott, on Monday, October 27, 1817, were present Maj. John Yancey, Capts. John Armentrout and John Rush (of riflemen); John Argebright, lt. commandant; Jacob Pirkey, ensign commandant; and Wm. D. Clarke, lt. of artillery.

Henry J. Gambill, clerk, being absent, the court appointed William Herron as clerk protempore.

The major laid before the board a list of delinquencies returned by Capt. John Armentrout for non-attendance at his respective musters in 1817, and the delinquents were fined $1 each, &c.

The same for Capt. John Rush, Capt. John Argenbrights, Capt. Jacob Pirkey, Capt. Samuel Lewis, and Capt. Ralph A. Lofftus.

The minutes were signed by John S. Yancey, major 2d battalion.

November 7, 1817

At a court martial held for the 58th regiment, Friday, November 7, 1817, were present Joseph Mauzy, colo. commandant of said regiment; John Yancey, major 2d battalion; capts. John Armentrout and John Rush (of riflemen); John Argenbright, lt. commandant; Jacob Porkey, ensign commandant; John Smith, ensign commandant; and Layton Yancy, cornet (commandant) of cavalry.

The members of the court being qualified proceeded to business as follows: Present, Capt. John Vigers, Capt. Eugene Erwin (of riflemen), and Lt. Wm. D. Clarke (of artillery).

On motion of Frederick Young and for reasons appearing to the court, it was ordered that the fines assessed against him for 1816 be remitted, and the sheriff have credit for the same.

On motion of Walter Liskey and for reasons appearing to the court, it was ordered that he be exempted from militia duty.

Thomas C. Fletcher & John Carthrea, Jr., deputies for George Huston sheriff, returned a list of delinquents in the muster fines for 1816, which was examined and allowed by the court and ordered to be certified.

The court proceeded to make the following allowances for the year 1817:

To Edward Stephens, for 4 days service as adjutant to this regiment, $24

To Peter Harry, for 2 days attendance as adjutant to the regiment, $12

To Peter Harry (capt), for musick supplied at his company muster held in April, 1817, (to wit) a drummer & fifer @ 125 per day, $2.50

To Eugene Erwin, for musick employed (to wit) a fifer 6 days at his musters @ 125 cents, $7.50

To Capt. Samuel Lewis, for musick employed at his respective musters held in 1817 (to wit) a drummer & fifer 6 days each @ 125 per day, $15.00

To Capt. Joseph Cline, for musick employed at his 2 company musters (to wit) a drummer & fifer 2 days, each @ 125 cents each, $5

To the same, for musick employed at 2 company musters held in 1817, @ 1 dollar per day, $2

To Andrew McClelan, for 3 days attendance as provost martial to the regiment, $9

To Henry J. Gambill, clerk, for his services 4 days in attending the several battalion and regiment courts martial and for making out the list of muster fines as required by law, $40

To the same, for advertising the delinquent muster fines for 1816, as returned by the sheriff and allowed this day, $4

To Capt. John Vigers, for the expenses of repairing a drum for the use of his company, $3.50.

A total of $124.50

It was ordered that the sheriff pay the aforesaid several allowances out of the fines of 1817.

The minutes were signed by Joseph Mauzy, commandant 58th regt.

A list of muster fines assessed in the 58th regiment of the militia in Rockingham County for the year 1817:

FIRST BATTALION

Delinquents returned by Capt. Joseph Kline

Jacob Lineweaver (3), John Greer (1), Jacob Ferrill (5), Henry Harnsbarger (5), Christian Garber (6), Daniel Wine (6), Daniel Branaman (6), Jacob Early (6), Benjamin Wanger (6), Gabriel Heatwool (6), Abraham Wanger (3), Jacob Blosser (6), Daniel Whisler (6), Anthony Roads (6), John Showalter (6), Henry Early (6), John Flory (4), Samuel Miller (6), Stephen Roadcap (6), John Roadcap (6), Henry Hulvey (1), Samuel Garber (6), Michael Wine (6), Jesse Williams (1), Henry Winkle (1), Peter Blosser (6), Jonas Blosser (6), John Allebough (1), Anthony Showalter (2), Leonard Tutwiler (1), John Wright (1), David Garber (5), John Thomas (6), Harrison Corben (1), David Heatwool (6), Thomas McGuire (1), Jacob Miller (6), Henry Eaglebarger (5), Henry Lineweaver (1), David Groves (6), Samuel Weaver (5), Conrad Sanger (6), Joseph Bierer (5), John Kline (1), John Sharfey (5), Jacob Spader (1), Samuel Kline (2), Joseph Kaufman (1), John Rimel (2), John Bierly (3), David Blosser (3), Joseph Fry (3), Jacob Flory (1), Samuel Showalter (2).

The figures after the names indicate the number of musters missed by the respective men. The fine at this time was $1 for each absence.

It seems probable that Capt. Joseph Kline lived in Harrisonburg (see Wayland's History of Rockingham County, page 188), and that his company was made up largely of the German farmers and tradesmen round about, many of whom evidently had scruples against military service.

LIST RETURNED BY CAPT. PETER HARRY

John Brower (5), John Bateman (1), James Bateman (1), John Dundore (1), Stephen Tinder (Finder?) (3), Daniel Yount (6), John Ritermon (2), Daniel Whitmore (1), Dabney Freeman (1), John Hafner (2), William Smith (1), James Shepherd (1), Jacob Waserman (4), Samuel Adams (1), James Cunningham (2), Jacob Kyger (2), John Miller Iron Works (5), Leonard Null (1), William Scantling (4), John Redheffer (1), Abraham Boon (1), James Smallwood (2), Thomas Johnston (2), Henry Rowland (3), Thomas Allen (1), Samuel Butler (1), Abraham Deal (1), Robert Hook (1), Jacob Huffman (1), Jacob Keplinger (1), Joseph Patterson (1), Nicholas Pirkey (1).

Capt. Harry's company was probably made up in southeast Rockingham, in and around Port Republic.

Returned by Capt. Eugeneo Irvine

John Amin (1), James Erwin (6), Simeon Fry (4), John B. Keith (3), John Long (1), George Rice (6), John Shoemaker (1), Jacob Shaver (2), Samuel Sheetz (1), Michael Wise (1), George Argebrite (1), George Baker (1), Dickeson Burrows (1), John Davies (1), Jacob Detamore (1), Henry Detamore (1), Joseph Frank (1), William Fisher (1), James Gladden (1), William Keyser (1), Joseph Miller (1), Israel Shaver (1), Michael Zimmers (1).

Capt. Irvine's company was probably located around Bridgewater and Spring Creek.

Returned by Capt. Ralph A. Lofftus

James Newman (1), John Harry (1), Benjamin Cravens (1), Thomas Rice (3), John Clarkson (5), Lewis Byrd (3), George Richards (1), James Fulton (2), Joseph Hannah (3), John Carthrae (5), James Magill (3), Reuben Matheny (6), Alexander Newman (2), John Hannah (3), Joseph Hottell (2), Richard Robertson (4), John Robertson, Jr. (6), John Robertson, Sr. (6), Jacob Long (5), John Cline son of George (4), Henry Miller forge (5), Joseph Makoy (1), Peter Winebranner (4), John Calhoon (6), William Robertson (6), Charles M. Carthrae (3), Frederick Crow (1), Jacob Roots (1), Garland McCollester (1), Peter Cook (1), Jacob Arnold (1).

It is difficult at this time to locate Capt. Loftus's company with any certainty. Some of the names sound like Augusta County names (Scotch-Irish), for example, Fulton, Hannah, Robertson, McCoy, and others. In recent years the Hannas have lived around Mt. Solon and the Fultons in the same or a neighboring community. The Miller Iron Works were at Mossy Creek. Both Mt. Solon and Mossy Creek are in Augusta County, but not far from the Rockingham line. The Crows and Carthraes are now thought of as belonging in southeast Rockingham, at or near Port Republic. This place is near the Augusta line. At a guess one might say that Loftus's company was perhaps made up of men who lived at rather widely separated places in southwest and southeast Rockingham, near the Augusta line.

Returned by Capt. John Vigars

Michael Ritter (3), Walter Davies (1), James Dever (2), Christly Miller (6), Abraham Smith (4), George Hisey (1), Philip Tetrick (2), Stephen Matheny (2), Martin Miller (6), John Click (6), Adam Howdyshell (1), Henry Brown (2), Samuel Matheny (1), Henry Nisewanger (6), Abraham Whitmore (6), Martin Frank (2), Henry Hershbarger (6), Jacob Snell (6), Philip Hisey (1), David Frank (1), Jacob Miller (6), Joseph Snell (6), James G. Davies (1), William Bridges (6), John Brown (2), Martin Speck

(3), Daniel Tetrick (6), Henry Dinkle (2), Allen Dever (2), Edward Rice (1), Benjamin Wiltshire (2), Edmund Price (2), Thomas Oaks (3), Earnest Cool (2), Thomas Robertson (1), Daniel Laush (2), Peter Huff (3), Isaac Waggy (5), John Miller (1), Luke Rice (5), Philip Denton (2), Emanuel Shearman (1), Joseph Sharfick (6), Jacob Stoner (6), Thomas Gilmore (4), Daniel Flora (6), Peter Bird, Jr. (1), Andrew McGuire (1), John Whissleman (1), David Whitmore (6), Samuel Finley (1), Reuben Dever (3), Enoch Dunn (5), Jacob Kagy (1), Henry Sheets (3), Wedon Wiltshire (1), Thomas Faulkner (2), Robert Hooks (2), John Cravens (2), Joseph Miller (6), Henry Black (1), John Stanforth (1), Joseph Shaffer (2), John Flora (2), John Johnson (2), David McGuire (1), Reuben Sandy (1), James Lee (1), Jacob Michael (2), David Miller (1).

It is reasonable to conclude that the "conscientious objectors" to military service did not attend any of the musters, unless compelled to do so. They, on this assumption, paid their fines habitually, and they may usually be recognized in these lists by the 6's after their names. But obviously there was at this time (1817-1818) much indifference towards musters on the part of many others, not "conscientious objectors." Evidently a number of the farmers and business men thought that their day at home was worth more than the dollar fine; so they paid the fine in many instances and went about their ordinary business.

It is possible that Capt. Vigars, in the foregoing list, was reporting delinquents for two companies. Just where these companies were located is not certain. The names seem to have a wide distribution. Some appear to suggest Dayton and Rushville, some Mt. Crawford and Cross Keys, some Harrisonburg and Massanetta (Taylors) Springs, some Hinton and Whitmer's Shop, etc.

SECOND BATTALION

Delinquents Returned by Capt. John Argebright

Zecheriah Crawford, Sr. (4), Zecheriah McDaniel (2), Philip Lamb (2), Zecheriah Crawford, Jr. (5), Israel Eblin (3), John Crawford (3), John Embra (4), Jonathan Dean (1), Henry Hansbarger (3), Ezekiel Crawford (5), John Self, Jr. (1), Jacob Maiden (1), James Rains (2), Adam Alexander (1), Frederick B. Shover (1), Jonathan Welch (2), Benjamin Hensley (1), John Meadows (1), John Almon (1), Achilles Roach (2).

Returned by Capt. John Armentrout

John Runkle (1), Henry Dufflemyer (2), Paul Long (1), Joshua Snyder (1), John Jones (1), Christian Boody (1), Lewis Boody (1), Christopher Comer (2), William Dovel (2), Reuben Fultz (1), Benjamin Kite, Jr. (1), Jacob Croft (2), Mathias Long (1), Nicholas Long (1), Simeon Lucas (1), William Pence (1), Samuel Short

(2), Joseph Strickler (1), Berry Yeager (1), James Kibbon (1), Thomas Night (2).

The companies of Capts. Argebright and Armentrout were almost certainly in East Rockingham, that is, around McGaheysville, Island Ford, Elkton, Bear Lithia Spring, Shenandoah, Furnace, Grove Hill, Ingham, and Newport. Some of the places last named are now in Page County.

List Returned by Capt. John Rush

William Long (1), Jacob Conrad (1), George Eppert (1), George Airey (1), Lewis Long (1), Benson Rains (2), John Cline (1), Henry Kisling of Jacob (2), Samuel Sullenbarger (1), John Cave (1).

Evidently Capt. Rush's company were located, partly at least, in East Rockingham. But inasmuch as he had a company of expert riflemen it is possible that they may have been selected from a rather wide area.

Returned by Capt. Ralph A. Lofftus

Henry Hammer (1), George Deck (2), John Hammer (1), Philip Pirkey (1), George C. Cook (6), Bennet Rains (1), Jacob H. Peterfish (2), Emanuel Hansbarger (1).

Returned by Capt. Jacob Pirkey

George Berry (5), Charles Lewis (3), Philip Lamon (2), George Sampson (2), Jacob Pirkey Mill (1), Henry Secrist (1), Thomas Bountz (1), Jacob Alstot (1), George Durrow (1), George Michael (1), Jacob Sites (1), Andrew Spitzer (1), George Bontz (1).

Returned by Capt. Samuel H. Lewis

John B. Middleton (5), Jacob Delkerd (6), Henry Utzler (3), William Clasby (1), Lewis Clasby (1), Samuel Fitz (1), Reuben Gardner (1).

All three of the foregoing companies were evidently from southeast and southwest Rockingham—Yancey, Island Ford, Goods Mill, Lynnwood, Port Republic, Grottoes, etc. Judging from the brevity of these lists in comparison with some of the others, it seems reasonable to conclude that East Rockingham was much more warlike than West Rockingham. Many facts support this conclusion. The Lewises, for example, were of the famous Augusta family, of whom came Gen. Andrew Lewis and Col. Charles Lewis of colonial and Revolutionary fame. Capt. Samuel H. Lewis (1794-1869), later general of militia, lived at Lynnwood, ancestral home of the Lewises, and later (1862) a famous battlefield of the Civil War (battle of Port Republic). See Wayland's History of Rockingham County, page 127.

The next pages of the old book are torn out. On them were evidently the minutes of a court martial signed by John S. Yancey, major 2d battalion.

November 23, 1818

At a court martial held for the 58th regiment on Monday, Nov. 23, 1818, were present Joseph Mauzey, colonel of said regiment; John Yancey, major of 2d battalion; and captains John Viger, Eugene Irwin, Samuel H. Lewis, Jacob Perkey, John Rush, Joseph Cline, John Argenbright, Layton Yancey, and Jacob Strole.

On motion of Robert Hooks, who was fined for disobedience of orders at the battalion court held for the 1st battalion, in the sum of $5, for reasons appearing to the satisfaction of the court it was ordered that the said fine be remitted.

On motion of Francis C. Diver and for reasons appearing to the court, the said Francis Dever was exempted from militia duty.

Peter Blosser and John Byers the same.

James M. Bush, deputy for George Huston, late sheriff, returned a list of delinquents in the muster fines for 1817, which was examined and allowed by the court and ordered to be certified.

The court proceeded to make the following allowances for services in the year 1818:

To Peter Harry, adjutant to the regiment for 6 days, $36

To John Humes, for 3 days attendance at the training of the officers, as fifer, $6

To John Vigers (major commandant), for musick employed to attend his battalion muster, being the 1st batallion, to wit a drummer & fifer $125 each, $2.50

To Eugene Erwin, for musick employed at his 4 company musters, to wit a fifer @ $125 per day, $5.00

To Samuel H. Lewis, for musick employed at 2 company musters, to wit a drummer and fifer 2 days each, $5.00

To Joseph Cline, for musick employed at his company muster, to wit drummer 2 days & fifer 3 days, at $1 per day each, $5.00

To John Argubright, for expenses in repairing a drum for his company, $1.25

To Henry J. Gambill, for his services as clerk in attending the battalion and regiment courts, and for making out the list of muster fines as required by law, $32.00

To the same for advertising the delinquent muster fines as required by law for 1817, $4.00

To Andrew McClelan, provost martial to the court, for 3 days services, $9.00

It was ordered that Thomas C. Fletcher be appointed clerk of this court martial for this regiment in the room of Henry J. Gambill resigned, and that he qualify as the law directs.

Minutes signed by Joseph Mauzey, commandant 58th regt.

A List of Muster Fines assessed in the 58th Regiment, 1818

First Battalion

List of Delinquents Returned by Capt. John Vigers

Thomas Robertson (2), George Hisey (1), Peter Bird, Jr. (1), John Whisselman (1), Jacob Koogler (1), Michael Ritter (2), Abraham Smith (5), Peter Tetrick (2), Martin Miller (6), John Click (6), Adam Howdyshell (1), Samuel Matheny (1), Henry Nisewanger (6), Abraham Whitmore (6), Henry Hershbarger (6), Jacob Snell (6), Philip Hisey (2), David Frank (2), William Bridges, Jr. (1), David French (3), Jacob Miller (6), Joseph Snell (6), Martin Speck (1), Daniel Detrick (6), Henry Dinkle (1), Allen Dever (2), Edward Rice (2), Edmund Price (3), Thomas Oaks (1), Isaac Waggy (4), John Miller (2), Luke Rice (1), Philip Denton (3), Joseph Sharfick (6), Jacob Stoner (6), Thomas Gilmore (4), Henry Gilmore (1), Andrew McGuire (1), David Whitmore (?) (5), Samuel Finly (2), Robert Hooks (1), Joseph Sheffer (3), John Flora (6), Reuben Sandy (6), James Lee (2), Jacob Hansbarger (1), Samuel Burgess (6), Christly Miller (6), John Gordan (5), Anthony Nicely (5), Robert Travis (2), John Robertson (1), John Brower (3), Jonathan Life (5), Samuel Taylor (3), Enoch Dunn (2), Daniel Andrew (3), Samuel Lambert (2), Samuel Weaver (5), Benjamin Wiltshire (1), Reuben Dever (4), Henry Sheetz (2), William Root (1), Thomas Williamson (1), William Paul (1), Philip Tetrick (1), Robert Jones (1), Staunton Taylor (1), James Ervin (1), John Faro (1), William Ervin, Jr. (1).

See note on Capt. Vigar's long list for 1817. This list (1818) suggests the same localities as those named in the note under the 1817 list—Dayton, Rushville, Mt. Crawford, Cross Keys, Harrisonburg, Massanetta (Taylors) Springs, Hinton, Whitmer's Shop—also Bridgewater, Paul's Mill (Ottobine), Beaver Creek, Spring Creek, etc.

List Returned (1818) by Capt. Eugeneo Irvine

John Kyser (1), John Amon (1), George Baker (?) (2), James Baker (?) (1), Henry Brown (?) (1), Jacob Detamore (3), Henry Detamore (2), David Fadely (1), James Gladden (1), Jacob C. Irvine (1), William Kyser (1), Solomon Messerly (3), Jacob Pifer (1), Peter Roubush (1), Peter Roller, Jr. (1), George Roubush (1), Jacob Shaver (1), Israel Shaver (1), Benjamin Solomon (2), Samuel Sheetz (2), Michael Wise (1), Joseph Waggoner (3).

Rollers, Kisers, Wises, Shavers, and Irvines have long been residents of the rural communities around Bridgewater, Mt. Crawford, and Pleasant Valley.

List Returned by Capt. Layton Yancey

Benjamin Smith (1), Thomas Rice (3), John Clarkson (4), Joseph Hannah (2), James Magill (3), Alexander Newman (1), John Hannah (2), Richard Robertson (2), John Robertson (2), Frederick Crow (4), Peter Winebranner (3), William Marshall (2), Joseph Hottell (3), Jacob Long (2), Henry Miller (2), Joseph

Makoy (1), John Calhoon (3), William Robertson (2), Hugh Dever (1), John Dever (1), John Miller Iron Works (1), Charles Carthrae (2).

These names have a sound of rather wide geographical distribution. The Yanceys have long been associated with McGaheysville; the Hannahs (Hannas) with Mt. Solon (Augusta County); the Crows with the Goods Mill section; the Longs have been at various places in Rockingham; so have the Devers, the Millers, and the Smiths. Millers Iron Works were at Mossy Creek, three miles above Bridgewater, just over the Augusta line.

List Returned by Capt. Samuel H. Lewis

Strother Scantling (3), John Blakey Jr. (1), Daniel Beaver (5), William Bailey (2), Henry Blooz (?) (3), Samuel Barnes (?) (5), Lewis Carthrae (4), Charles Davies (5), Samuel Golliday (1), Frederick Ford (1), William Hinckel (?) (1), Charles Lewis, Jr. (1), William Marshall (3), Robert Morton (3), John Swaney (1), William Scantling (1), Robert Blakely (1), John Dundore (2), Thomas Cliffton (4), John Clarke (2), John Murray (2), Jonathan Rush (3), Andrew Armstrong (1), William Alexander (1), William Carthrae (1), John Fisher (1), Andrew Hudlow (2), William Harper (1), Joseph Harper (1), Henry Marshall (1), Thomas Collins (1), James McCausland (2), James Harris (1), Thomas Holt (1), Winston Vier (1).

Many of these names sound like "Tuchahoe" (Eastern Virginia). East Rockingham, extending up to the crest of the Blue Ridge, naturally had a larger proportion of East Virginians than the sections farther west.

Strother, Blakey, Bailey, Ford, Marshall, Clarke, Winston, and Via (Vier) are all familiar family names in Albemarle and adjacent counties just across (east of) the Ridge.

Second Battalion
List Returned by Capt. John Argenbright

George Bougher (1), Henry Hansbarger (2), Ezekiel Crawford (3), Zecheriah McDaniel (1), Zecheriah Crawford, Jr. (2), (next 4 names illegible), Edmund Bush (2), James Rogers (3), Jacob Huber (1), Reuben Harrison (1), Jacob Argenbright (1), David Switzer (2), Henry Bush (1), Jacob Meadows (1).

Returned by Capt. Jacob Pirkey

George Berry (5), John Ragan (5), Peter Weaver (3), George Plumb (1), Philip Lamon (1), George Utsler (1), Christian Utsler (1), Charles Williams (2), Samuel Todd (2), John Smith (3), James Staunton (2), Richard Austin (1), Isaac Keys (1).

Returned by Capt. Saml. H. Lewis

William Bateman (2), Jacob Delkerd (2), John B. Middleton (3), Henry Utsler (1).

Returned by Capt. John Rush

William Long (2), George Eppert (2), George Hartman (3), John Hartman (1), Benson Rains (4), St. Clair Williams (2), Julius Wetsel (1), Jacob Hansbarger (1), Archibald McCollum (2).

Returned by Capt. Layton Yancey

Philip Pirkey (1), George Cook (3), Jacob H. Peterfish (2), Peter Cook (2), John Royer (1), Henry Deck (1).

Returned by Capt. Jacob Strole

Henry Dofflemyer (2), Philip Long (2), John Armentrout (1), Christian Folts (1), Reuben Fultz (1), Benjamin Kite, Sr. (1), Jacob Croft (3), James Kibbon (3), Mathias Long (1), Nicholas Long (2), Daniel McGuire (1), Simeon Lucas (1), Jacob Nepple (1), Christian Ohler (1), William Ohler (1), George Price (1), John Runkle (3), John Short (2), Samuel Short (2), David Sipe (1), Martin Strickler (1), David Strickler (1), Joshua Snider (1), John Hord (1), James Scarff (2), Richard Jones (2), Martin Welfly (2), Berry Yager (1), Jonathan Kroft (1).

It is evident that Capt. Jacob Strole had succeeded Capt. John Armentrout in the region between Shenandoah and Newport, now in Page County.

List Returned by Capt. Joseph Cline

Christian Garber (5), George Long (2), Daniel Wine (5), Daniel Brenaman (5), Jacob Early (5), Benjamin Wanger (5), Jacob Blosser (5), John Blosser (5), Daniel Flora (5), Daniel Whisler (5), John Showalter (5), Henry Early (5), Samuel Miller (5), Stephen Roadcap (5), Samuel Garber (5), Michael Wine (5), Jessee Williams (5), Henry Winkle (5), John Shepherd (1), Jonas Blosser (5), John Ollebough (1), Anthony Showalter (1), David Garber (4), John Thomas (4), John Miller (2), David Heatwool (5), Thomas McGuire (1), Jacob Miller (5), Henry Lineweaver (2), David Groves (5), Conrad Songer (5), Joseph Byerly (5), John Cline (1), John Sharfey (4), Abraham Miller (1), Jacob Spader (3), Samuel Cline (2), Joseph Coffman (1), David Blosser (5), Joseph Fry (5), Jacob Witsel, Jr. (1), Jacob Flora (5), Samuel Showalter (4), Mathias Ely (4), Abraham Heatwool (5), Thomas Dean (3), Abraham Hartman (1), Martin Garber (5), Eilliam A. Coffman (4), Abraham Blosser (5), Martin Miller (3), Benjamin Williams (4), William Spangler (4), Andrew Spitzer (4), William Daniels (3), Henry Thomas (5), Michael Simmers (2), John Cline (Miller) (1).

Evidently Capt. Cline had only five musters in 1818. One might reasonably inquire how it was possible for him to have any.

William Spangler, of Capt. Cline's company, was fined for contempt to the court marshal held for the 1st battalion of said regiment in 1818, $10.00.

October 25, 1819

At a court marshal held for the 1st battalion of the 58th regiment on Monday, October 25, 1819, were present John Viger, captain commandant of the battalion; Capt. Joseph Klyne, Capt. Charles Lewis, Lt. James Newman (of cavalry), Ensign Elisha Hooks (of rifle company), Lt. Nicholas Pirkey (of infantry).

A list of delinquents returned by Capt. Viger for non attendance at his musters for 1819 were called, and not appearing, and not having a reasonable excuse, were fined 75 cents each for each absence.

The same was done with regard to delinquents in the companies of Lt. Adam Reader (in Capt. Viger's company), Capt. Joseph Cline, Capt. Samuel H. Lewis, Capt. Charles Lewis, Lt. James Newman (of Capt. Layton Yancey's company), Capt. Eugenu Erwin, Ensign Elisha Hooks (list of Capt. Erwin's Co.), Lt. Nicholas Pirkey (list of Capt. Deal's Co.).

The minutes were signed by John Vigar, captain.

October 26, 1819

At a court martial held for the 2d battalion of the 58th regiment on Tuesday, Oct. 26, 1819, were present John Yancey, major; captains John Rush, Layton Yancey, Jacob Strole, Charles Lewis; and Jacob Argabryht, ensign of John Argabryte's company.

Delinquents returned by Capt. John Rush for non attendance at his musters in 1819 were fined 75 cents for each absence. The same was done with regard to delinquents reported by Capt. Jacob Strole, Capt. Layton Yancey, Capt. Samuel Lewis, Capt. Charles Lewis, Capt. Jacob B. Ergebrit, and Capt. Jacob Pirkey.

Capt. Jacob Pirkey was also present.

The minutes were signed by John S. Yancey, commandant 2d battalion.

The next three leaves of the book are torn out—so much of them as to render most of the records valueless. On the fragments of one leaf may be found the names of the following persons:

Lt. Adam Reader, of Capt. John Viger's company; Jacob Stoner, Thomas Gilmore, Daniel Florey, Andrew McGuire, David Whitmore, James Fulton, John Florey, John Myers, Isaac Miller, George Weaver, John Blakely, Jr., William Coldwell, ———— Grayham, ———— Marshill, ———— Cash, ———— Carthrae, ———— Detamore, ————Ervin, ———— Foley, ———— Fadely, Thomas Faulkner.

Some of the last were in Irvine's company.

The next full page continues a list of men who were absent from musters:

William Kyser (1), John B. Keyth (3), Solomon Messerly (2), Adam Pipher (1), Jacob Pipher (1), William Pipher (1), Peter Roler, Jr. (1), Jacob Shaver (2), William Roof (1), Israel Shaver

(1), Benjamin Solomon (1), Samuel Sheets (1), Joseph Shaver (3), George Stembough (1), John Tidman (1), David Wise (1), Michael Wise (1), Abraham Wise (1), Joseph Waggoner (2), Benjamin Williams (1).

These men evidently belonged to the company of Capt. Eugene Irvine, and lived around Bridgewater, Mt. Crawford, Centerville, and in Wise Hollow.

The following were reported by Elisha Hooks, ensign in Capt. Irvine's company:

James Byer (1), David Fleming (1), John B. Keyth (2), John Shoemaker (1), Jacob Shaver (1), Joseph Waggoner (1).

Reported by Nicholas Perkey, Lieutenant Commandant in Capt. Deal's Company

Henry Eglebarger (3), Terry (?) R. Brown (1), Thomas Coleman (1), Jacob Deal (3), John Earman (3), John Fogle (1), Jacob Kablinger, Sr. (3), Henry Keller (3), Jacob Wydick (3), Daniel Yount (1), John Yount (3), Philip Baker (2), Jacob Kablinger, Jr. (1), Jacob Spitzer (1), David Stoafer (2), Stephen Tinder (2), Samuel Whitmore (1), Jacob Whitmore (1), Abram Deal (1), David Deal (1), John Perkey (1).

Second Battalion
Reported by Capt. John Rush

Elijah Breeding (1), Henry Body (1), Jacob Coonrod (2), John Hall (1), Jerebemon Harshman (1), Willis Jackson (1), William Long (2), George Mauzey (1), John Meadows (1), Edmond Prue (Price?) (2), Samuel Sullenbarger (2), David Switzer (1), Julius Whetsel (1), Edmund Shifflett (1), James W. Geer (1).

Reported by Capt. Jacob Strole

Henry Dofflemire (1), John Armontrout (1), Christian Boady (1), John Horde (1), Reuben Kite (1), Jonathan Crofft (1), James Kibben (2), Matthias Long (2), Nicholas Long (1), Daniel McGuire (3), Christian Ohler (1), John Runkle (1), John Short (2), George Shular (2), Martin Strickler (1), Joshua Snyder (3), David Strickler (1), John Smith (2), James Scarff (2), Martin Welfley (1), Berry Yager (2), Nathan Turner (1).

Reported by Capt. L. Yancey

George Cook (2), Jacob Rush (1), Bennett Raines (2), Jacob H. Peterfish (2), Emanuel Hansbager (1), Lewis Carthrae (2), Henry Deck (1), David Irick (1), Martin Marshell (1), Thomas Yancey (1).

Reported by Capt. Jacob Pirkey

George Berry (3), George Youtsler (2), John Ragan (3), George Mourey (4), Christian Youtsler (5), Joseph Good (1),

Zachariah Crawford (4), Jevus (?) Keller (1), Isaac Kees (1),
Joseph Mauzey (2), Philip Laman (1), George Burker (?) (1),
Wm. Colley (1), Samuel Moore (1).

Reported by Capt. S. H. Lewis

John B. Middleton (3), Jacob Delkerd (1).

Reported by Capt. Charles Lewis

James McCausland (3), John Hall (1), James Bateman (1).

Reported by J. B. Ergabrght, Ensign

Elisha Morris (?) (1), John Dean (1), Israel Eblen (2), Jacob
Maiden (1), Zachary Berry (2), Zachary McDaniel (1), James
Rogers (1), William Michael (1), John Crafford (1).

November 6, 1820

At a court martial held for the 1st battalion, 58th regiment, at
the house of Richard Patton on the 6th November, 1820, were present
Eugene Erwin, major commandant; captains Joseph Klyne, Philip
Deal, Elisha Hook, and Adam Reader; John Nicholas, cornett of
cavalry.

Andrew McClelan, provost martial to this battalion, failing to
appear, Jacob Leneweaver was appointed provost pro tem.

The major laid before the court a list of delinquents returned
by Capt. Joseph Klyne for non attendance at his musters for 1820.
They were fined $1 each for each absence.. The same action was
taken on lists returned by Lt. David Lincoln, Capt. Adam Reader,
Capt. Philip Deal, Lt. Nicholas Perkey, Capt. Elisha Hook, Capt.
Layton Yancy, and Capt. Charles Lewis.

It was ordered that Charles Patton, Barnett Gaines, & Joshua
Sherfey, who were enlisted in Capt. Wm. McMahon's troop of cavalry, be fined $3 each for three delinquent muster fines for contempt
of the battalion of militia in the 58th regiment.

The minutes were signed by Eugenia Irvine, major 58th regiment.

November 7, 1820

At a court martial held for the 2d battalion of the 58th regiment
militia, Nov. 7, 1820, at the house of John Maggert, were present
John Yancey, lt. col. commandant; captains John Rush, Jacob
Pirkey, Layton Yancey, Jacob Strole, Charles Lewis, and Jacob Argebright.

The colonel laid before the board a list of delinquent muster
fines returned by Capt. Rush for non attendance at his musters in
1820. Each delinquent was fined $1 for each absence. The same
was done as to lists returned by captains Layton Yancey, Jacob
Perkey, Charles Lewis, Jacob Strole, and Jacob Argebright.

The minutes were signed by John S. Yancey, lt. col. 58th regt.

November 11, 1820

At a court martial held for the 58th regiment at the house of Peter Nicholas, Saturday, Nov. 11, 1820, were present John Yancey, "Left Colo," Eugene Erwin, "Majr," John Rush, "Capt," Jacob Pekey, "Capt," Joseph Klyne, "Capt," Philip Deal, "Capt," Capt. Charles Lewis, "Capt," Capt. Jacob Argabright, and Layton Yancey, "Capt."

The court being organized proceeded to business as follows:

On motion of John Roberts (?), for the remission of his three muster fines for the year 1819, for reasons appearing to the court it was ordered that they be remitted and be certified to the Auditor of Public Accounts.

Present, Elisha Hooks, captain.

On motion of Wm. Michael, and for reasons appearing to the court, he was exempted from militia duty.

On motion of Jacob Kublinger, Sr. for the remission of three muster fines for 1819, and for reasons appearing, the said fines were remitted.

On motion of James McCausland, and for reasons appearing, his six fines for 1819 were remitted.

Present, Adam Reader, captain.

On motion of Jacob Kiblinger Jr for remission of one muster fine for 1819, and for reasons appearing, the said fine was remitted.

On motion of Jacob Spader for remission of two muster fines for 1819, and for reasons appearing, the said fines were remitted.

On motion of Edward Rice (?) for the remission of two muster fines for 1819, and for reasons appearing, the said fines were remitted, &c.

Here, at the end of the book, four or five or more leaves are torn out, only small stubs remaining.

Inside the back lid of the book are some memoranda, among them the following: "Gaines & Patton, 12"; "David (?) Kemper, 10"; "Thos. C. Fletcher"; "Round sum"; "Capt. Huttle (?) Bounds"; "Capt. Deals Bounds"; "make out for Capt the Bounds of his company and send to him"; "Thomas C F"; etc.

SONS OF TEMPERANCE IN ROCKINGHAM

A strong leather-bound book, its leaves yellow with age, contains the records of the Marshall Division No. 3, Sons of Temperance, during the first four years of its existence, 1844 to 1848. The organization had its beginning in this wise:

About the first of January, 1844, William G. Stevens of Harrisonburg wrote a letter, making certain inquiries about the Order, addressing it to "Any officer of the Order of the Sons of Temperance, Washington City." After a few days an answer came, dated January 9, and signed by John D. Clark. In accordance with directions given by Mr. Clark, a petition, signed by Wm. G. Stevens, Jacob R. Stevens, J. M. Conrad, Joseph T. Rohr, Wm. McK. Wartmann, John W. Bear, Littleton W. Gambill, and Chas. D. Gray, was sent to the Grand Division of New York, praying for a charter. Following out the purposes in hand, J. M. Conrad and Jacob R. Stevens, as a special committee, went to Washington City and were there initiated into the Order, in the Timothy Division, and empowered to perform the services of initiation at Harrisonburg. A charter in the meantime had been issued, not by the Grand Division of New York, but by that of New Jersey, according to a rule of the Order that required a new chapter to receive its charter from the nearest Grand Division.

Before the Harrisonburg chapter, under the name, "Marshall Division No. 3 of the Sons of Temperance of the State of Virginia," was organized, Henry T. Wartmann took the place of Joseph T. Rohr, and hence became one of the eight charter members.

On the evening of March 11, 1844, the organization of the new division was completed by the rites of initiation, the election of officers, the appointment of a committee to report bylaws, etc. The application of Joseph H. Shue, "24 years of age, a Book Binder, and Post Master," was received; and he was elected to membership at the next meeting. These first meetings were held in the office of Chas. D. Gray.

Beginning with the preliminary entries, from which the foregoing account has been prepared, the old book contains the "Constitution," blanks for "Amendments" and "By-Laws," a roll of membership signed by 153 men, and minutes of weekly meetings, until nearly 400 pages are filled. The last entry is under date of October 24, 1848. One of the questions under consideration at this time was the proposed establishment of a college by the Sons of Temperance of Virginia—a plan that was emphatically disapproved in the report adopted.

Some of the other well known names on the role of membership are the following: Alg. S. Gray, Geo. O. Conrad, St. Clair Kyle, Jacob E. Harnsberger, P. Liggett, Jacob N. Liggett, John H. Graham, Morgan Switzer, and John G. Effinger.

After the Civil War the Sons of Temperance were succeeded by the Friends of Temperance.

THE ALDERSONS IN ROCKINGHAM AND GREENBRIER

In the abstract of the records of old Linville Creek Baptist Church, beginning on page 48, Rev. John Alderson, father and son, are prominent. The following items concerning the Aldersons, with records of marriages performed by Rev. John Alderson, Jr., in Rockingham (Augusta) and Greenbrier, have been supplied by Mr. Henry W. Scarborough of Philadelphia.

Rev. John Alderson, Sr., went from the New Britain Baptist Church, Pa., to Linville Creek in the spring of 1756. (See page 49.) Rev. John Alderson, Jr., it is said, located in Greenbrier County, Va., now West Virginia, in 1777. It is probable that Rev. John Alderson, Sr., located in Greenbrier at or about the same time.

In 1911 Rev. Robert B. McDanel preached a historical sermon at the old Greenbrier Baptist Church at Alderson, W. Va., on the 130th anniversary of the said church, and stated that the church had been organized on Nov. 24, 1781, by 12 members, namely, John, Mary, and Thomas Alderson, John Kippers, John Shepherd, John, Catherine, Joseph, and Lucy Skaggs, and Bailey, Ann, and James Wood.

In 1777 Rev. John Alderson had taken up 1750 acres of land on the south side of the Greenbrier River. At the same time his brother-in-law, William Morris, took up a tract of the same number of acres on the north side of the same river. John Alderson's home was near the present Alderson Hotel. He had made two missionary trips to the Greenbrier Valley before he located there.

The church organized in 1781 was the first of any denomination in what is now southern West Virginia. It was a member of the Ketockton Baptist Association. In 1911 it had 506 members.

ALDERSON MARRIAGE RECORDS, 1776 To 1798

Marriages performed by Rev. John Alderson, Jr., at Linville Creek, now Rockingham County, and in Greenbrier County, Va.; the latter now in West Virginia. The following items are made up from a typewritten copy of Rev. John Alderson's marriage register furnished Mr. Henry W. Scarborough of Philadelphia in 1924 by Prof. Garnett Ryland from the original manuscript at the University of Richmond.

1776

January 4, James Sconce (?) and Elisabeth Miller; William ———— and Catherine ————; January ————, Philip Custer (?) and Elisabeth Levi (?); Peter Sho—— (?) and Elisabeth Lee

February 13, Henry ———— and Rebecca Harden, of or in Dunmore County

March ————, Holton Muncey (?) and ————

April 1, George Reuble and Catherine ————; April 2, Adam Rader and Clare Ruddel; April 22, Michael Lime and Magdalan Harter; April 23, Joseph Rambo and Sarah Warren; April 23, Evin Phillips and Elisabeth Dever

May 16, ———— Dorman and ————; May —, —— King and ————; May 21, William Tyrie and Elisabeth Prise, both of Dunmore; May 23, Nathan Wiatt and Sarah Smith; May 23, James Hall and Ann Cristy

The last or the next to the last marriage above was of or in Dunmore County, now Shenandoah.

"On the Day of Setlement with the Curiot was June ye 4, 1776. David Rader with Ruth Henton."

June 25, James Prise and Catherine Smith

July 26, Joseph Rodgers and Catherine Funk

August 13, Jacob Teganfus and Christenah Brilian

September 17, Jacob Cortner and Catherine Panter

November 13, Bennedick Alsie (?) and Elisabeth Williams, from Dunmore

1777

January 16, John Jackman and Hannah George; January 28, John Mitchel and Annmary Jacobin

February 3, Jacob Vandeverter and Elisabeth Bibl (?); February 21, Isaac Strickler and Susanah Brubaker

March 3, names illegible; March 22, William Evens and Mary Fleming

April 15, William Vance and Barbara Crider; April 28, Daniel Branermon and Mary Durst

May 12, Peter Perseful (?) and Margaret Selser; May 19, Barefoot Runyan and Margaret Rambo

August 11, Edward Millon and Mary White; August 17, James Jamason and Martha Crow; August 18, Carlile Hance and Hannah Waring

October 21, John Petty and Margaret Hundly; in Greenbrier

December 25, George Lee and Martha George

1778

February 10, Alexander Hoseck and Sarah Tolle; February 23, William McGuire and Mary Shirley

March 19, Dennis Neel and Ann Ibbet

April 2, Robert Raburn and Sarah McGuire; April 10, William Loctridge and Sarah Linsy; April 30, John Woods and Abigail Estel

May 4, William Hogan and Sarah Sullavan

June 1, John Baughman and Catherine Shirley; June 21, David Kuke (Cook?) and Sarah Pullin

July 14, Oziah Barns and Jane Flemings

August 7, John Ewins and Esther Cook

"June 4, 1776; Received from John Alderson three pounds five shillings, being the amount of ten marriage fees.—Alex. Balmain, Clk., Curate of Augusta Parish."

December 22 (1778), Walis Estel and Jane Wright

1779

January 14, Jesse Jarrat and Sarah Cambel; January 18, David Rees and Grisile Lagua; January 19, John McCalester and Anna Loagua; January 28, David Rodgers and Elisabeth Palintine (Ballentine?)

February 2, George Clandennan and Jamminah McNeel; Abraham Baker and Sarah Smith

March 5, John Sopes and Margaret Miller; March 12, John Clarke and Elisabeth Cortner

June 8, John Gilkason and Nansy Davis; June 16, Jacob Chapman and Margaret Burns; June 22, John Dankadys and Rhobachah Lewis

July 14, John McGuire and Elisabeth Cottel; July 14, Patrick Murphy and Elisabeth Spenser

August 21, Charles Smith and Elisabeth Rosety; August 24, Jacob Man and Mary Kisaner

September 5, John Oncel Blare and Esther Davis; September 16, Joseph Riffe and Margaret Carpenter

October 8, Samuel Clark and Margaret Burgan; October 8, Edward Barrat and Susan Griff

November 8, James M———— and Sarah Gilkason; November —, James ———— and Sarah Nash

December 20, ———— Perrigen and Susanah Burgan

1780

January 4, Jacob Price and Wereford (Weneferd?) Hillary; January 10, James Kitchen and Jane Pattason

February 14, Daniel McMullan and Nelly Keenany

March 1, Thomas Spenser and Mary Evison; March 3, Philip Haman and Christen Kuke (Cook?); March 20, Valantine Smathers and Barbara Wimer

April 18, Owen Jarrot and Mary Doran; April 19, Thomas Shelton and Elisabeth Cavender

May 2, John McMullan and Fransinah Gully; May 9, James Williams and Sibna Wilson; May 11, John Wallis and Jane Miller

June 13, William Hunter Cavindish and Jane Murphy; June 15, William Dun and Hannah Welch; June 15, Richard Homes and Martha Heard

July 5, James Christy and Sarah Scarborough; July 7, Samuel Jamison and Rhobacah Ward; July 13, George Frazer and Rosana Reyley; July 21, John Crane and Esther Kirk

August 23, James Howard and Hannah Geffers

September 3, John Lee and Margaret Garrat; September 28, Henry Davis and Martha Crage

October 10, Mathew Creed and Elisabeth Carlile; October 12, Cornelius Miller and Ann James; October 19, Richard McCalester and Margaret Nicholas; October 19, Henry Howard and Isbill Griffin; October 19, Thomas Bird and Margaret Tolbart

November 20, William Cooper and Fanny Esthel

December 5, William Mary Ellit and Elisabeth Philson; December 5, Simon Acers and Mary Smith; December 12, Thomas Cuper and Ann Roack; December 22, William Shanks and Sarah Hanby; December 26, Robert Boid and Mary Glass; December 26, William Oharra and Margaret Tincher

1781

January 2, Gordan Griffin and Catherine Kichener; January 11, Michael Keeney and Catherine Lewis; January 30, Brice Miller and Elisabeth Bradshaw

February 6, James McNut and Sidny Evens; February 6, Littleton West and Elinor Gallaway; February 17, William Jeffers and Susanah Johnson; February 17, Joseph West and Agnes Carpenter; February 18, James Williams and Catherine Nicholus; February 25, Antony Sebrok and Nancy Tuckwell

March 1, David Cutlip and Jane Burris

April 9, David Jamison and Hannah Richards; April 12, Richard Wilson and Mary Rogers

June 4, ———— Hutcheson and Rhobecka Hutcheson; June 11, John Davis and Elisabeth McFarlen; June 14, George Alderson and Sarah Osburn; ————, John Fenton and Mary Ann Fairs; June 15, Daniel McDowel and Euphamia Huston

July 2, Thomas Cooper and Margaret Hilyard

August 28, David Trimble and Lucy Lacy

October 5, William Harris and Sarah Persival; October 10, Edward Moss and Barbara Boyer; October 29, Edward Pemberton and Mary Anderson; October 29, John Kirny and Mary Samson

November 23, John Clapole and Rebecca Osburn; November 27, Moses Turpen and Magdilia Black; November 29, William Comer and Mary McCarty

December 19, Joseph Edwards and Agnes Ramsy; December 24, Charles Hines and Margaret Dickson

1782

January 9, Charles Wimer and Lettis Hannah; January 23, John Russel and Susanah Day; January 23, William Gilliner and Hannah Aclen (by license); January 30, Edward Barret and Easter Burnsides

February 5, James Oharra and Elisabeth Davis; February 9, James Kelly and Agnes Caperton; February 11, John Cincaid and Elisabeth Gilaspy

March 3, Richard and Mille; March 19, Walter Davis and Ellener Harbart

April 5, Robard Bogs and Sarah Fluston; April 5, Joseph Hanes and Barbara Rife; April 16, James Knox and Margaret Johnson; April 25, Peter Woods and Jael Kavanaugh; April 29, Angel Conner and Mattie Flemmen

May 1, James Hoogens and Jane Cook; May 9, Isaac Anglin and Nancy Dier; May 15, John Snodgrass and Elny Murphy; May 23, David Mordah (Murdock?) and Margaret Tomson; May 28, Robert Nicol and Margaret Gray

July 14, Timothy Sweet and Catrien Nurf; July 15, James Stiles and Jane Harwood; July 23, William Doderidge and Rebecca Doharty; July 30, James Sconce and Lidea Britton

August 9, William Sconce and Margaret Murley; August 13, John Shoumaker and Elisabeth Youlekem; August 22, William Toney and Leah Gatlift; ————, Thomas Fulton and Susanah Kisenyer; ————, Samuel Estell and Jane Tase

September 1, Benjamin Johnston and Lidea Ford; September 1, George Owens and Mary Cotton; September 14, George Stuart and Christin Holshople; September 17, Isaac Fisher and Rachel Riggs; September 19, Isaac Poulton and Ann Green; September 26, Samuel Black and Mary Donaly

October 22, William Baly and Jane Johnson; October 29, Richard Mullen and Elisabeth Lewis; October 31, James Harris and Mary Edwards

November 14, John Erwin and Jane King; November 18, John Frier and Elisabeth Biggs; November 20, George Dickson and Vorona Venbebber; November 26, John Curry and Isblla Ellison

December 17, Ase Ellison and Elisabeth Kilpatrick; December 20, George Stevenson and Elener Clendenen

1783

January 9, Robert Johnson and Martha Raulston; January 30, John Gibson and Sarah Stevenson

February 10, John Dunbar and Elisabeth Osbun; February 11, Isaac Burgan and Mary Tacket; February 25, William Maddry and Elisabeth Man

June 18, William Hicks and Hannah Garrad

July 29, Jacob Kissinger and Sarah Fulton

September 9, James Walker and Catherine Miller; September 9, James Gilkason and Elisabeth Currens; September 22, Charles Friend and Rachel Tacket; September 30, David Lodinback and Kezia Ward

October 20, Ralph Gyates (Ralph G. Yates?) and Jennet Wiley

November 27, Joseph Williams and Elisabeth Raulston

December 9, Adam Man and Mary Maddy; December 9, Garrat McCallester and Susannah Crage; December 9, Abraham Dewit and Catherine Barns; December 27, Abraham Noetel and Mary McDannal

1784

January 22, Alexander Reed and Rebecca Mitchel

May 6, William Booton and Matilda Sturgess; May 13, John Carlile and Rosanah Souards; May 24, William Wiley and Karanhapouch Gatliff

June 19, William Canafax and Elisabeth Miller; June 19, Joshua Townsen and Elisabeth Caperton

September 6, William Adams and Sarah Sturde; September 14, Thomas Wyate and Rachel Burnside; September 21, Daniel Nicholus and Rebecca Sturde

November 9, Luke West and Rosey Acars

December 6, William Haze and Lovine Gully; December 7, Willis Morris and Elisabeth Garrat; December 14, Joseph Hickenbottom and Mary Reed; December 16, James Stephens and Mary Man; December 30, Ambrus Jones and Martha Crage

1785

January 17, William Butcher and Margaret Donnaly; January 18, Andrew Cissiner and Saveney Nestor; January 19, Edward Price and Elisabeth Newhouse; January 25, Mitchel Porter and Penelope West

February 8, George Parker and Anny Maddy; February 8, Paul Long and Elisabeth Maddy; February 8, Thomas Nickell and Joane Reiburn

March 8, Martin Turpen and Nancy Fleming; March 8, Jeremiah Carpenter and Elisabeth Hamm; March 8, Mosely (?) Childris and Elisabeth Jeffries

April 7, Robert Ervin and Barbara Nicol; April 18, Robert Johnston and Catherine Doren; April 24, David Garrat and Susanah Hicks

May 24, John Lewis Jr. and Rachel Viney

June 8, Samuel Dunbar and Debrough George; June 21, Samuel Kincaide and Mary Tincher; June 29, Peter Venbebber and Eleaner Venbebber

July 1, James Bales and Rebecca Bracken; July 3, Math Forbs and Easther McMullen; July 6, John Keppers and Rebecca Patterson; July 8, Simon Cooper and Margaret Tincher; July 22, Peter Venbebber and Sarah Yolkecome

August 8, John Maddy and Barbara Miller

September 21, James Shannaday and Jane Williams; September 21, Hough Caperton and Rhodeiea Sturgen

October 13, John Curry and Mary Johnston

November —, James Fleming and Mary Kinder; November 5, Thomas Trimble and Abigal Gatliff; November 10, Joseph Miller and Margaret Best; November 21, Mark Lacey and Agnes McDonald

December 14, William Sprowl and Jane Hamelton; December 29, Levi Low and Sarah Kincaed

1786

January 10, James Bailey and Nancy Tharp

February 14, John Scaggs and Kitty Hicks; February 21, James Wilson and Leucresta Sturgen; February 21, Henry Green and Sarah Henderson; February 21, William Jones and Sarah Reburn

March 2, William Carteron and Jane Miller; March 2, William Holly and Prudence Castile; March 9, Richard Hicks and Jane Skags

May 3, David Scarbrou and Elisabeth Anderson; May 6, Thomas Williams and Elisabeth Nickolus

June 18, Aaron Turpen and Jane Barns

July 3, William Lacey and Martha Blankenship

October 3, George Doughaty and Juda Holshopel; October 6, Thomas Spencer and Elisabeth Perkins; Oct. 6, James Hayns and Ann Ellison; October 10, Samuel Peepels and Sarah Tincker; October 17, Travis Booton and Ruth Estele; October 17, John Canterbery and Nancy Lowe

November 30, Simon Shramm and Barbara Belew

December 18, George Lewis and Leah Viney

1787

January 23, Obadiah Hammonds and Elisabeth Skaggs; January 30, Joseph Sawyers and Elisabeth McDade

March 8, William Johnston and Elisabeth Hicks; March 15, Nimrod Tackete and Ann Howard

April 17, David Miller and Ruth Burditt; April 19, William Trimbel and Mary Fleming; April 30, Isaac Paul and Massy Eleson (?)

May 7, Ezekiel Parsons and Elisabeth Kesener

July 3, William Daghaty and Lidia Tacket

September 3, Hugh Paul and Ann Kilpatrick; September 13, William Drawdy and Ruth Ellison; September 19, Griffith Garten and Hanna Miller; September 25, Peter Dick and Barbara Null

October 30, John Fauster and Clairy Burdit

November 5, John Ellis and Anne Paul; November 8, Alexander Wilson and Mary Dickson; November 15, John Hansford and Jean Morris; November 25, John Claston and Bridgit Martin (or Williams); November 26, William Slavin and Nancy Ingram

1788

February 9, Samuel Ramsy and Elisabeth Griffith; February 28, Robert Tincher and Nancy Dickson

March 18, Solomon Turpin and Mary West

April 24, David Keeny and Peninah Bails

May 1, John Peck Forde and Jane Frogg; May 15, Henry McDaniel and Hannah Bryant; May 22, Levi Morris and Margaret Garret

June 26, John Lacy and Sarah Porter; June 30, Abraham Henderson and Ann Blanton

July 5, Edward Goand and Nelly Needham; July 19, Peter Likins and Mary Garrat

September 15, Davis Alderson and Leah Carrol

November 10, James Claypole and Elener Butler; November 12, Benjamin Morris and Nancy Garrat

1790

March 25, William Dickens and Feaby Lewis

April 2, Daniel Javen and Martha Thompson; April 29, Moses Wilson and Martha Rickey

May 3, Adam Man and Polly Flinn; May 30, Daniel Jones and Isbel Hunter

August 9, Jeremiah Roach and Elisabeth Null

September 1, Nicholus Null and Ruth Ellis

October 24, William Griffits and Mary Lewis; October 26, Cothel Lively and Sally Meddy

November 1, Nathan Robinet and Sarah Burnsides; November 4, Robert Hews and Elisabeth Tincher; November 8, James Smith and Sarah Piper; November 22, George Hews and Margaret Johnston; November 25, John Humphries and Jane Ward

December 11, Joseph Black and Esther Dison; December 13, William Cook and Jane Young; December 23, William McGinstery and Elisabeth Hail; December 23, Robert Renick and Polly Hamilton; December 28, Henry Hedrick and Betsy Comber

1791

January 10, Ezekel Mathews and Jane McSparvin; January 11, John Williams and Martha McMillen; January 13, Adam Eyhole and Mary Britan; January 18, Hugh Williams and Jane Bell; January 27, Edward Farlo and Lettece McM———; January 31, John Paterson and Elisabeth Mullin

February 7, Ezkial Jenkins and Anna Ford; February 24, Michel Miller and Elisabeth Smith; February 24, Andrew Wilson and Janey Hutchison

March 2, Duncan Graham and Anna Parsons; March 3, Grigsby Foster and Martha Handly; March 5, Andrew Boggs and Susanah Bowen; March 6, Aron Ewing and Elinor Bartley; March 6, Robert Harvie and Esther Bartley; March 6, Griffith Evins and Martha McNiel; March 8, John Lowance and Sarah Holly; ——— Patrick Murphy and Ann Miller

April 29, John Lewis and Rebecca Sowards

June 28, Louther Smith and Barbara Loudeback

August 1, Robert Louis and Betsy Morris; August 4, Francis Watkins and Anna Donnaly (Kanawha County); August 12, Aron Newman and Catharine Blair

September 9, James Kennedy and Rachel Scarbrough; September 13, Joseph Dicson and Nancy McClung; September 16, Jacob Fodge and Christina Darcks; September 27, Andy Showens and Betsy McGuire

October 24, William Kinder and Talitha West

November 22, Thomas Kincaid and Hannah Vine (Viney?)

December 1, Boyd Miller and Mary Story; December 1, Thomas Masterson and Jane McClung; December 17, James Cash and Pheby Lacy

1792

January 19, David Jacocke and Lilly Smith

February 7, Thomas George and Catron McCoy; February 15 Rubin Bootan and Mary Dick

April 17, Ephraim Claypole and Lucy Arbough

May 31, Thomas Holaday and Elisabeth Ballentine

"This is to Certify to home it May Concern that we the Subscribers have Reason to believe from all Sircumstances that James Parsons is Ded. Givin under our hands this 3 Day of March 1791.

"Richard George, Robert Reed, Alexander Hosick, Benjamin Reed, James Chambers, Angel Connel, Jacob Kilyon."

1794

September 11, Alexander Porter and Mary Mathews

October 2, John Patterson and Betsy Carroway

November 12, Elijah Cornwell and Ruth Swobe; November 20, Robert McDowell and Mary Harbert; November 27, Bedford Foster and Lissy Cornwell; November 27, Hatis Legg and Elizabeth Cornwell

December 9, Joseph Phillips and Phebe Thomas; December 11, John Hinchman and Sarah Vincon

1795

January 1, William Legg and Susanah Vincon; January 1, James Fauster and Elisabeth Humphress; January 6, Mathew Leech and Polly Gullett; January 22, John Jordan and Catherine Blare; January 22, John Lewis and Elizabeth Edwards; January 22, Moses Shepherd and Mary Holly; January 29, Moses Massy and Rebecca Lewis; January 29, Adam Fifer and Catherine Myars; January 30, Jacob Althair and Susanah Fleshman

February 12, William Taylor and City Alsup; February 25, William Carrol and Catherine Shoemaker

March 10, Henry Carraway and Margaret Smith

April 19, John Groves and Catherine Seivers

May 5, John Morehead and Jane Nicholus; May 7, Nicholus Kerns and Laney Vanordal; May 7, Thomas Blare and Nancy Callison; May 12, Samuel Blare and Peggy Vaughob; May 21, William Williams and Mary Watts

June 30, Charles Arbuckal and Esther Shiles

September 1, John Lovese (?) and Mary Cambel; September 3, Isaac Garrat and Magt. Macey; September 15, James McCoy and Betsey Hines

October 20, Robert Sampels and Maryann Walker; October 20, Jonathan Mathews and Hannah Macy

November 17, Jacob Ellis and Margaret Griffith; November 26, James Griffith and Susannah Davis

December 29, Esom Leach and Jane Handly; December 31, Enoch Fauster and Margaret Wallis

1796

January 28, Isaac Lewis and Helana Blake

"March the 19, 1791, This day setled with John Flin and Ballance Due to him Three Gallons and three Quarts Whisky"

February 16 (1796), George Swobe and Nancy Givin; February 16, Edward McClung and Sarah Viney; February 25, John Hanna and Eliz. Smith

March 6, Cpt. Maddies Nagros; March 10, William Butler and Taccy Gray

April 19, Thomas Smithson and Margaret Alderson

May 3, Jesse Carpenter and Jenny Rite (?)

June 7, Thomas Feamster and Mary McClung

July 12, William Lewis and Dinah Viney

August 9, Henry Miller and Barbara Arbaugh; August 30, Joseph McMullen and Jane Arbaugh

September 13, Henry Newhous and Elizabeth Claypole

October 27, John Withers and Elisabeth Smith

November 15, James Phillips and Elisabeth Lewis (?); November 24, Joseph Scaggs and Anna Lewis

1797

February 2, William Wiley and Mary Nicholus

April 5, John Byrnsides and Elizabeth Alexander

May 13, John Keen and Neomia Keen

August 24, John Carter and Catherine Hite (?)

September 21, George Nikle and Margaret Neilson

December 27, Charles Birdit and Elizabeth Legg

1798

January 2, Telison Shewmate (or Shoemaker) and Elizabeth Birdit; January 9, Samuel Ingels and Elizabeth Scaggs; John Prichet and Mary Taylor

March 4, Samuel Canterbery and Jane Dicks

May 5, Edmond Meddows and Sarah Calloway; May 29, John Perry and Jane Nelson

Anent the Greenbrier and other West Virginia records, Mr. Henry W. Scarborough of Philadelphia makes the following observations:

"The History of Monroe County, West Virginia, shows that James Christy, whom the Rev. Mr. Alderson married to Sarah Scarbrough on July 5, 1780, was the first pastor of the Rehobeth

Methodist Church about two miles from Union, now Monroe County, West Virginia; and he and his brothers-in-law, William Scarbrough and James Scarbrough, were among the five trustees, as is shown by said history. They were the children of Robert Scarborough, my ancestor, mentioned by you in the History of Shenandoah County and who settled somewhere on the banks of the North Branch of the Shenandoah River, as is shown by a deed on record in Philadelphia and by his letter, as being about a mile from the Quaker meeting on Holman's Creek and about an equal distance from a mill, probably Neff's Mill. I do not believe that this marriage record has been published anywhere and I would think that even the marriages performed at Greenbrier would be of great historical use, because probably most of them were persons who had removed from the Shenandoah Valley or eastern Virginia."—Date April 26, 1928.

A LETTER FROM INDIANA, 1855

Deer Creek, Henry County, Indiana
January 13, 1855

Dear Brother & Sister:

I embrace the present opportunity of addressing you a few lines to inform you that we are all well at this time and have been ever since we have been here, hoping that when this reaches you it may find you enjoying the same blessing.

We arrived at Uncle Philips on the 15th of November and found them all as well as usual, but Johnathan and Sarah. Jonathan has not been able to do anything all winter, and Sarah has been sick for a good while, but is nearly well again.

We got along very well but had a very tiresome trip. We got on the cars at Green Spring depo at 5 o'clock in the evening and got to Benwood, four miles below Wheeling, at four o'clock next morning, a distance of 208 miles. We then crossed the river and got on the cars and dragged along that day and night till 12 o'clock, and got to Xenia, a distance of 175 miles, which distance we expected to have made by ten o'clock that day, and then we would have got to New Castle that night at 9 o'clock; but we met a train that had run over a very large bull and overset the cars and tore both of his horns off in the cow catcher and broke all of his legs, and we had to walk about a quarter of a mile around that train to change cars; and all of the baggage of about five hundred passengers had to be carried that distance.

That occurrence and my boxes getting broke to pieces threw us back one day. We nor the children got scarcely any sleep atall. They were so tired and sleepy that wherever we stopped they would drop down like dead flies.

We are all very well pleased with the country so far, and would not exchange it for 500 Rockinghams. Unkle Philip has been like a father to us, and the rest of the neighbors have been very kind. They have brought us more milk and butter and other things than we can make use of, and that is more than the folks would do there if people were half starving. No person would believe the difference in the hospitality of the people of Virginia and the people here. We have got more meat and bread stuff together now, and got it paid for, than we would have had in Virginia in a whole year.

Lydia says you must tell Ann that she wants her to leave the hills and rocks and briers and come to the land of mud. We have had a great deal of wet weather all winter, and you may judge that we have some of the mud. I bought my wheat at $1.00 and corn at 30 cents per bushel and my pork at $3.50 and beef at $5.00 per hundred that me and the boys worked for. Groceries are as cheap and some things a goodeal cheaper here than they are there. We can get the best kind of molasses for 35 cents pr gallon.

I would have written to you a good while ago but I have not been about a great deal yet, and had but little of importance to write.

Philip can pretty near walk, and he is as saucy as a pet pig. Lydia wants you to let her know how your little girl comes on, and whether she can walk or not. Unkle Philip says he would like to see Unkle John and all the rest of them, but the way he is situated it is impossible for him to go to Virginia at this time, but it suits them better to come to see him. Tell Mag to come out here and take a peep at the hoosier boys.

I have taken a lease on Unkle Philips 80 acres of land in Delaware County. He gives me a better chance than any person else here would. I now only lack about $50.00 to get into a stock of hogs with to give me a start and put me in the way of making money, but I believe that ever since you first knew me you will be ready to acknowledge that no person was more diffident in asking favors than myself. Indeed I have always considered it as more pleasing to an honest mind to confer than to receive a favor; but circumstances compel me to solicit the loan of that amount until next Christmas, by which time I will be able to turn the hogs into money again an return it to you again. If you can send me the required amount let me know as soon as possible, as it is the best time from now on till spring to buy stock hogs.

I forgot to tell you what it cost me to get out here. I kept a correct account of the distances and expenses. The distance from Turley Town to Uncle Philip Branners is 567½ miles; and my expenses were $79.04; so you can give a pretty near guess what I had left when I got here.

Dont fail to write to us as soon as you get this and let us know how you are all coming on.

No more at present but remain your affectionate brother and Sister

ANDERSON MOORE
LYDIA MOORE

Philip Bible
Barbara A. Bible

Appended to the foregoing letter are the following lines and names, in the same handwriting:

Mr. John Bible:

We all join in sending our love to you and to inform you that we have all got into hard work and it agrees with us very well. We grow and fatten on it fine. We want you to write to us and let us know what you are doing and how you are coming on. We are living in a log cabin. A person cant be a hoosier till he lives in a log cabin a while. Write to us and let us know when you are coming to the west. No more but Remain Yours Affectionately

ISAAC N. M. MOORE
PHILANDER J. A. MOORE
HIRAM W. A. MOORE
GEORGE A. MOORE
PHILIP P. A. MOORE

John Bible Esq.

(Note by J. W. W.—The five Moore boys were probably sons of Anderson and Lydia. This letter has been supplied by Miss Paulina S. Winfield of Broadway, Va., who found it among the papers of her father, Captain John Q. Winfield.)

A LETTER FROM INDIANA, 1856

Delaware County, State of Indiana

January 13, 1856

I have seated myself to write you a few lines about my trip homeward. I had an awful cold time. On Monday night I got very cold until I got to Winchester, then we got along very well to Harpersferry and up to Martinsburg. There the snow had drifted some and the wind was blowing and blocking up the road in places. They put an engine to the snowplough to open the road; two to the train, one to draw and one to push in order to get along up grade to Piedmont.

There they changed hands. The conductor was of the opinion that they could get along without the snowplough. The engineer started the train again, getting along badly by getting fast in the snow sometimes. He tugged us to the next station; ran on the siding; waited until they could send two hands back eight miles on foot to bring snowplough and engine up to open the track until we got on the west side of the mountains. There the snow was not so deep; and being mostly down grade we got along tolerably well. Leaving the plough and one engine we got to Wheeling at twelve o'clock on Wednesday night.

The river being froze tight, they took us down to Belair, four miles, in an open sleigh at four in the morning. I never have been so cold in my life before. The train started at five. We made the connections through to Richmond (Indiana) until sunset. Being no evening train on the Chicago road, I was compelled to lay over until Friday morning. I came on to Middletown. My friends welcomed me home. The snow being only four or five inches deep, the roads well patted down, I walked home and found them threshing wheat.

The weather has moderated some yesterday and today. I heard some old settlers say it has been colder than it has been for thirteen years. Last Tuesday night it was said the thermometer was 28 degrees below zero. It is not much travel on the road now on account of the severity of the weather; it being a good many accidents on the road now. I would not advise any person to travel by railroad until they can get more of the ice off the road. Providence smiled upon our trains not to have any serious accidents. The trains don't make regular connexion now. I have just been 24 hours longer crossing the mountains than I ought to have been; but we can be thankful to both the engineers and conductors for getting through as well as we did.

Wheat has come down to $1.25; corn from 30 to 37 cents; pork is come down some.

The health is tolerable good again, I believe. I have not been about much yet. Yesterday I have been to David and Andrew Bowers. They said they were well. I am told Mr. Coffman's family has increased by a young daughter. We are well. I have nothing much more to write now.

I haven't told you yet that fatherinlaw Sowerwine has sold his farm to Mr. Martin Roadcap for $10,500. He has some notion of going to Iowa to look at the country. Please write to me.

Nothing more. Yours respectfully,

WM. D. BOWMAN

To Mr. Moses Bowman and friends.

(Note by J. W. W.—The foregoing letter was handed me recently by Miss Paulina S. Winfield of Broadway, Va. Mr. Bowman probably rode in the stage coach from Rockingham to Winchester, a distance of about 60 miles, inasmuch as the railroads had not been extended above Winchester and Strasburg in 1856.)

A LETTER FROM CHICAGO, 1911

3101 Washington Boulevard,
Chicago, Ills.,
Oct. 28, 1911.

John W. Wayland,
Charlottesville, Va. (Forwarded to Harrisonburg)
Dear Sir:

A few days ago while at the Newberry Library in this city, I was so fortunate as to find in the Pennsylvania German Magazine of January 1909, your very interesting article on "The Pennsylvania-Germans in the Valley of Virginia" and, needless to say, read it with the greatest care, attention, and pleasure, having therein a personal interest which, with your permission, I shall attempt to explain.

Among the prominent Pennsylvania-German families named is that of the Koontzes, of whose origin and date of immigration to the Valley I have been seeking information for years, but with results of a very unsatisfactory character. The older records of the courts of Rockingham County having been, unfortunately, destroyed during the Civil War, so far it has been impossible for me to find so much as a family Bible, a record of births, marriages, and deaths, or even records of transfers of property—of which there must have been quite a number.

Colonel John Koontz, my great-grandfather, was for many years a very prominent and active man in the affairs of Harrisonburg and Rockingham County; member of the legislature for several terms; colonel of the 31st regiment of Virginia Militia, which he marched to and commanded at Norfolk, Va., in the War of 1812-15; the proprietor of the place known for years as "The Big Springs"—now Lacey Springs—ten miles north of Harrisonburg, on the Valley Pike;

and yet his family of ten sons and two daughters (the latter married at Harrisonburg) have disappeared from the face of the earth as completely as though they had been swallowed up in an opening made by an earthquake, without leaving a paper or a record of any kind behind them.

The natural inference is that some one . . . concealed or destroyed such papers and records as may have been left in his former home. Of all this large family, my grandfather Lieutenant Jacob Koontz, 20th Infantry U. S. Army, who died while in service at Norfolk, May 6, 1815, is the only one of whom I have been able to obtain any record or history. From the fact that you wrote of the Koontzes as you did it seemed to me that possibly you might have some information concerning them which would be very interesting and valuable for me to possess. This is my excuse for writing you upon a subject mainly of personal interest to myself, a liberty which I hope you may pardon. . . .

In Hening's Statutes of Virginia, Vol. XV, there is a statute passed January 23, 1798, appointing John Koontz, Thomas Harrison, John Waterman and ———— Spangler a commission to report upon the feasibility of making the Shenandoah River navigable. In the same volume is a statute passed December 29, 1797, appointing John Koontz, John Waterman and ———— Spangler trustees to establish a form of government for the town of Harrisonburg.

I am of the opinion that John Koontz did not come to Virginia until after the close of the Revolutionary War, but that he was there very soon after and taking a prominent part in public affairs is plainly shown by the statutes above cited. I take it for granted that he came from Lancaster or some of the other counties of Pennsylvania so largely populated by the Pennsylvania-Germans, but have no written evidence of the fact. If he could be traced back to any one of the towns or counties of Pennsylvania it is more than likely that much information in regard to him could be obtained from the registers of the Lutheran churches. . . .

Yours truly,

C. C. C. CARR,
Brigadier-General,
U. S. Army, retired.

P. S. Could one possibly find at the University of Virginia a file of the *Rockingham Register,* published at Harrisonburg? I have looked in vain for one both in Washington and Richmond. I have thought seriously of offering a cash reward for the privilege of reading that of the years 1830-1831.

Notes by J. W. W.—Camillo Casatti Cadmus Carr was born in Harrisonburg March 3, 1842, son of Dr. Wattson Carr and Maria Graham, his wife. He was educated at Wheeling (now West Virginia) and Chicago. In 1862 he left school at Chicago and joined the 1st Cavalry U. S. Army. He was made 1st lieutenant in June 1864. He was wounded at Todd's Tavern, Va., and in the battle of

Cedar Creek. After the close of the Civil War he served many years against the Indians in the West, gradually rising in rank until he was made brigadier-general in 1903. He contributed to military journals and translated an important book on cavalry service from the French. His wife was Marie C. Camp of Washington City. He died July 24, 1914.

Gen. Carr's mother was Maria Graham, whose interesting reminiscences of early days in Harrisonburg are referred to several times in Wayland's History of Rockingham County.

It is only fair to observe here that the Koontzes who are living in the vicinity of Lacey Springs and at other places in Rockingham County are probably descendants of some of the twelve children of Col. John Koontz, Gen. Carr's great-grandfather. Why he could not find them or get any information from them is rather singular.

In regard to the *Rockingham Register,* it may be a matter of interest that files of this famous old paper, covering mainly the period from 1866 to 1906, were presented to the writer by the publishers in 1911 while he was preparing his history of Rockingham County. Later he had these papers bound (three parallel files in some periods), and the most complete files were placed in the Virginia State Library at Richmond and in the Congressional Library at Washington. The third file is in the possession of the State Teachers College at Harrisonburg.

A LETTER FROM IOWA, 1913

A few months after the History of Rockingham County was published (1912) the author received a long letter from Mr. W. P. Dunlap, a prominent resident of Iowa. Parts of this letter follow.

Maquoketa, Iowa, January 11, 1913

. . . I am glad my friend, John E. Fultz, gave you my address. . . . I am the oldest child of John Wallace and Agnes Phillips Dunlap, born July 7, 1833, one mile east of the New Erection Church, north of Harrisonburg; on the same farm and in the same house my father was. I believe the farm is now owned by the Suters.

My grandfather's name was William Dunlap. My father was his only child. They sold that farm to Peter Good, and bought and sold several others; finally bought the Brightwell farm near Ottobine Church, adjoining Capt. Peter Paul's, Judge (John) Paul's father's farm.

In regard to the horse you spoke of, Rubycon, I don't remember ever seeing him, but do remember other thoroughbred horses he had—Diomed, Paul Clifford, Byron, & Gallitin, all thoroughbreds; and American Hiatoga, a fine black pacer, a splendid saddle horse.

My father was colonel of the 145th regiment of militia at Harrisonburg for a number of years in the forties and fifties. In the fall of 1857 my father, mother, and their seven children (I being the oldest) started from Ottobine for what was then the wild West, with a two-horse wagon and a big old Virginia family carriage for father, mother, and sisters to ride in; and after 56 days' travel we landed on the wild prairies in Clinton County, Iowa, now one of the finest farming countries in the United States.   There were nine of us when we arrived here.   Now there are but three of the nine living, two brothers and myself.   (My brothers are) Asbury N. and John W., who was elected last fall to his second term in the state legislature on the Democratic ticket.

After being here some four years I married a lady that was born in the state of New York, but raised here.   We went to farming and raising fine horses and shorthorn cattle and continued in the business for near forty years, until I retired and moved in to Maquoketa.   We had four children, two sons and two daughters.   One son and one daughter are dead; the other son and daughter are married, have families, are in business, and live in Maquoketa.

In the fall of 1907 my wife and self started to Jamestown, and to make a visit to my old home in the Valley.   She was taken sick and died in Norfolk, Va., November 10, 1907.   This sad affair ended our trip, and I returned home with the remains.

Being somewhat of an inventor, as you will see from cuts on back of letter, I have invented and patented several useful articles now in use, which have made me some money.

After reading your letter and seeing you have got out a history of Rockingham County, it reminds me of many incidents that occurred when I was a boy or young man, and especially one thing.   In the early fifties I commenced driving a six-horse team for my father, hauling flour and other produce to Winchester, and goods back for the merchants anywhere in the Valley or southwestern Virginia.   I remember one incident that occurred, and often wonder if there is any person now living in Harrisonburg that was present at the time and remembers the circumstance.   When A. B. Irick and Mr. Henneberger started the first bank in Harrisonburg I hauled the iron safe up from Winchester.   It weighed 4100 pounds.   We took the hind wheels off the wagon and unloaded and put it in a little one-story stone building south of the spring.   If I am not mistaken, Mr. Henneberger told me there was $80,000 in gold and silver in it at the time. . . .

W. P. DUNLAP.

On page 388 of Wayland's History of Rockingham County, Virginia, may be found various items concerning the old bank referred to by Mr. Dunlap; also other banks of the county.

In the early fifties Winchester was the nearest point to Harrisonburg on the railroad.   In 1850, when President Fillmore sent a messenger to Staunton by stage and horseback to invite Hon. A. H. H. Stuart to become a member of his Cabinet, the messenger went by stage from Staunton 93 miles to Winchester to telegraph his report to Washington City.

The little stone house (the Waterman house), where Mr. Dunlap unloaded the safe, is still to be found at the southwest side of the public square in Harrisonburg, though it has been considerably transformed by remodeling. A quaint old iron safe, perhaps the identical one that Dunlap hauled up from Winchester, heavy with gold and silver coin, is still preserved in Harrisonburg.

A LETTER FROM ARKANSAS, 1913

Dear Mr. Wayland:

I've been thinking for some time that I would write to you and tell you some of the little stories of Harrisonburg which have been handed down in my family.

The very name of the town is so sacred and beautiful to me, and so closely is it identified with the ever-living memory of my mother, that when I visited there a few years ago it seemed a kind of homecoming. I have enjoyed reading your book, especially the earlier part where familiar names crop up on every page. My mother's name was Elizabeth Strother Smith, the second daughter of Judge Daniel Smith. She was born (1814) in Wheeling, now West Virginia, and her family removed to Rockingham when she was such an infant that during the greater part of the journey she was carried in a kind of sling put around the neck of a faithful old man servant, who rode on horseback. I think it was done as a relief to my grandmother, who was always more or less of an invalid.

I do not know where their first home was situated, but know that the house afterwards called "Waverly" was built about 1821; because mother always told us of the new red shoes she had "when they first went to the new house, and that she was seven years old."

Her grandmother was Elizabeth Strother, who married James Duff. They kept a hotel in Harrisonburg in the 20's. Grandmother Duff was always considered a very superior person by the children of the family, because upon one occasion she "danced the minuet with General Washington." This story was generally brought to a climax by the entreaties of the children for her to show them the various fancy steps and low bows, with much lifting of scanty skirts, which characterized the dance.

Grandfather Duff was a jolly old man who, evidently, did not believe in "giving the young folks a chance"; for mother said when the grown-up granddaughters visited him they had to receive their beaux in the family living room; and as a gentle hint, when it was time for them to depart, Grandfather Duff had a way of taking off his coat and unbuckling his suspenders, which caused the beaux to make their exit in short order.

Waverly was about four miles in the country, and here my mother, who was considered rather tomboyish by my Aunt Margaret (Mrs. M. H. Effinger), and who was very fond of reading and altogether a typical young lady of that period, led an ideally happy life.

She must have been an original child, and full of sentiment. One time she conceived the idea of flying. Why couldn't she use her arms for wings, she thought. She studied the motions of the birds, as they flew by; and finally she planned her initial trip. She selected the hour when the family were at dinner, thinking how surprised and pleased they would be to see her flying gracefully across the yard.

When the time came she climbed to the top of a high gate post, "to get a good start," and then spread out her little arms. To use her own words, "I felt exactly as if the ground flew up and hit me."

Another time, after reading in the Bible, St. Matthew 17:20, she went to a quiet spot to think it all out carefully; and then raising her hand and pointing to the mountains said, "Be thou removed," &c. And after that for years it was a source of secret regret that her faith had not been sufficient for the occasion.

She had many playmates among the German or "Dutch" neighbors, and one of the joys of my childhood was to hear her call over the names of the Allebaugh children. She told us of the Lincolns, but always pronounced the name "Linkhorn." All the neighbors kept geese, and upon one occasion several persons compared notes and found that many of their geese had mysteriously disappeared. One old lady, being asked if she had missed any, said, "Why no; because every evening I go down to the meadow and drive up my number."

There was a boy named Joseph Baxter who used to figure in my mother's stories, to our great amusement. Upon one occasion she was in her father's study, amusing herself with pen, ink, and paper—a kind of forbidden fruit, I imagine—when she began to let her fancy have full play and wrote a letter to her mother in the character of "Mrs. Joseph Baxter," "Mr. Baxter" being represented as a brilliant and prominent lawyer. The letter closed with cordial invitations for the family to visit her, "Mr. Baxter sending his kindest regards," &c.—signed "Your affectionate daughter, Elizabeth Baxter."

Finally the epistle was twisted up in a tight twin knot and thrown up on the very top row of the book shelves. Some months later, during a vigorous siege of house-cleaning, for which my grandmother was noted, the fatal letter was found, and furnished an unlimited subject for teasing on the part of the family; and the hated nickname of "Elizabeth Baxter" was a household word.

My mother was a beautiful brunette girl. Her father used to say, "Yes, Elizabeth is black, but she is comely." She met my father during a visit to Staunton. He was then a young law student from Washington College (now Washington and Lee), named Christopher C. Scott, of Halifax County, Va.

I have often heard my mother tell of visiting Collicello. She loved Cousin Robert Gray and Cousin Isabella. How familiar the names look in your book; and how delighted I was to know that Cousin Algernon Gray, whose name possessed a perfect fascination for me, as a child, should have lived such a chivalrous and beautiful life. I remembered hearing about the blind boy, Jouett Gray.

Gus Waterman always figured as the harum scarum boy who made the most audacious speeches to the girls, and then took on such an innocent expression that he usually escaped reproof. The Herrings and Chrismans are also familiar names. I was brought up to call them all "Cousin."

I am sure my mother must have often been a visitor to the beautiful old Kenney house shown in your book, for she often told us about Mrs. Elizabeth Kenney, whom she called "Aunt Betsey." I was so sorry not to have met Mr. John Kenney during my visit to Harrisonburg, but he happened to be out of town. I wonder if he cares whether an old lady of sixty living away off in Arkansas calls him "Cousin John" or not?

I was intensely interested in visiting the old part of the cemetery in your town. How I wish the spirit would move you to collect data and write the story of those whose names were carved upon the stones there, so many years ago! How I would have enjoyed Mrs. Effinger's reminiscences if they had been put down in black and white.

Perhaps I have presumed upon your good nature in writing this long letter, but I had the impression that you would be interested in some of the things of which I have spoken. Thanking you again for your kindness in letting me know about your book, I am

Yours sincerely,

(MRS. A. A.) NELLIE D. TUFTS.

Camden, Arkansas, March tenth, 1913.

Notes by J. W. W.—Waverly, the old home of Judge Daniel Smith, was near Dayton, a short distance east of the Harrisonburg and Warm Springs Turnpike. Collicello, the home of the Grays, is in Harrisonburg, not far from the Waterman School. The old Kenney home, referred to by Mrs. Tufts, stood at the west side of the courthouse square in Harrisonburg, on part of the lot now occupied by Denton's furniture store.

The book to which Mrs. Tufts refers is Wayland's History of Rockingham County, Virginia. On pages 352, 353 of that book will be found a sketch of Judge Smith, with his portrait.

A LETTER FROM CLIFTON FORGE, 1925

Clifton Forge, Va., Nov. 11, 1925.

Dr. Jno. W. Wayland,
    Harrisonburg, Va.

Dear Sir:

You have "increased my years and prolonged my days" since you have started me to live over my boyhood days. . . . Naturally after the war the feeling was more or less bitter against anything Northern. I remember that in 1866 or 1867 there came to Harrisonburg a Northern Methodist preacher by the name of Pierce. No one would receive him or have anything to do with him. Finally a widow, Mrs. Bamber, who lived on Main Street near the Lutheran Church, took him into her house to give him shelter. This so enraged her son Joe that when Pierce began preaching on the street he threw a stone and either cut his head or knocked him down. Any way the mayor, J. L. Sibert (Jake), sent Joe to jail for a few days—and there came near being a riot! Many sided with Joe. It is hard to understand such feelings now.

I do not think that I ever saw Prof. Jos. Salyards; but I do know I wanted to go to his New Market school. But I did read his magnum opus, "Idothea, or the Divine Image." I can't recall one sentence now, but it was, it seems to me, equal to Milton or Dante. But he was a poor Southern man and could not attain the prominence he would have had if he had lived in the North. Did you know he wrote a story of Indian life & wars? I do not know what name he gave it, but the publisher killed it by calling it "Big Foot Sam, or the Prairie Thunderbolt"! I remember reading it, and considering it first class. Something like Cooper.

I was reasonably acquainted with Prof. Howard Johnson of Romney, who wrote the appreciation of Salyards in your book. I met him when he visited his father, Col. Jake Johnson, at Franklin, W. Va. He and his brother Jim were born blind.

In 1866 there were a good many Irish people in Harrisonburg— Sullivan, the postmaster, Kavanaughs, Scanlons, Kellys, Toomeys, Carneys, Conners, Dwyers, Ragans, &c. The postoffice then was, I think, in the first building south of the old Presbyterian Church, just across Main Street from the Shacklett Corner. In the same room was the telegraph office during the war when Newton Burkholder was the operator. I remember being in the office and, it seems to me now, that the messages were received on narrow strips, or ribbons, of paper; that the dots and dashes were perforated in the paper and read from the paper instead of being taken by sound, as now.

Scanlon and Kavanaugh had a hotel directly opposite where the Federal Building now is. It was considerably second class, but lived on the bar room patronage. The two principal hotels were Hill's Hotel and The American. The American was across the Main Street from the present First National Bank. Hill's Hotel was immediately opposite the Masonic Hall. I think that the printing establishment is on the Hill Hotel lot. Capt. Jno. N. Hill was very popular. The stages stopped at his hotel, and there was as much diversion from the arrival of the stages as from a railroad train now. They came in a gallop and with a flourish. How well I recall seeing them come up the Pike from the North, and down from the South! Fine horses. fine drivers, and fine people.

I remember an anecdote told about the stage. I do not know whether it happened with one of the Valley stages or not, and I will not vouch for its truth. It was said that once as the stage pulled up in a gallop and stopped suddenly before the hotel, one of the horses dropped dead. Some one remarked, "What a sudden death!" "No," said the driver, "not sudden. He died back here a half mile, but I did not let him down."

Capt. Jno. M. Locke ran the American Hotel for a while, and then Jacob P. Effinger ran it, but somehow it never succeeded like Hill's. One of Capt. Hill's sons was Dr. William Hill. I suppose you knew him. . . .

I went to school with Jake Yost, Winfield Liggett, Henry Strayer, Dewitt Coffman, L. G. Henneberger. The last two were in the Navy. Also Elverton Shands, Herbert Coffman, Jno. Taliaferro, and many others. Some became prominent, and some did not. I think you will find our family listed in the Funk Family History, as my mother was nearly related to the Funks on her mother's side. She was a Coffman from New Hope, Augusta County, & related to the Harrisonburg Coffmans. Evidently the name was originally Kauffman.

I want to mention more particularly one of my school mates, Dr. W. E. Dold, Bellevue Hospital, New York. We were desk mates at R. M. Academy. He was a fine fellow. Later studied medicine; went to New York; I think he is still living. A younger sister, Bessie, married Chas. G. Maphis of U. Va. They were married one day before I was—on Oct. 15, 1890.

There are several things I cannot satisfy my mind about. Lieut. L. C. Myers, who has been connected with the First National Bank of Harrisonburg for at least 50 years, had a store in Edom in either 1864 or 1865. How he got there or how he left I cannot recall.

Another thing. I remember I went to school at Edom to William S. Rohr, whom you mention in your book. It must have been a summer school, & he must have been reading law at the time.

L. C. Myers ("Curg" Myers, as he was called) was a son of old Squire Myers, a justice of the peace & a good citizen.

There are many, many little things that come back to me since reading your history.

Chas. M. Zirkle.

A BRIEF HISTORY
OF THE
VALLEY NORMAL SCHOOL
Bridgewater, Virginia
By
Professor Alcide Reichenbach, Ursinus College, Collegeville, Pa.

and

Doctor Jesse D. Bucher, Bridgewater, Virginia

The Graded School of Bridgewater, which had been in existence for several years prior to the year 1873, was closed early in March of that year, by direction of the County Superintendent, on account of too low an average attendance to obtain aid from the Peabody fund. Later, it was determined by leading patrons to place a limited number of pupils for a select school in the spring, under the management of Mr. Jesse D. Bucher, County Surveyor, who had taught the primary pupils, during the five months' session of the Graded School, under the former management; but Mr. Bucher was then suffering from a severe attack of rheumatism, so that the plan was abandoned.

During the summer, Mr. Bucher, having recovered his health, was elected to take charge of the free school pupils and to organize a primary and an advanced department. Miss Laura O'Ferrall, sister of Judge Charles T. O'Ferrall, later Governor of the State, was elected primary teacher. This arrangement was not entirely satisfactory to those patrons who wanted their boys to study the ancient classics at home, as long as possible. With the Rev. Joseph S. Loose, County Superintendent, as leader, several patrons decided to employ an additional teacher to conduct a Classical School. Accordingly, on the 27th of July, the Superintendent drafted a subscription paper for the purpose, which was signed by the following named patrons: Clement Irvine, Joseph S. Loose, E. J. Armstrong, A. L. Lindsey, P. Herring, J. H. Lindsey, Henry M. Argabright.

In September, after a year's study and travel in Europe, Mr. Alcide Reichenbach, a Swiss by birth, opened correspondence with Superintendent Loose, which resulted in his journeying to the home of the latter, who introduced him to the good people of Bridgewater. A public meeting was called, at which Mr. Reichenbach addressed the audience on education in Germany. After the address he was elected Principal of the Classical School of Bridgewater, by the people present, and he was to cooperate with the two teachers already chosen to teach the free school pupils. The subscription paper was handed to the Principal, who carefully preserved it to the time of writing his part of this sketch.

After his election the Principal sought to become fully acquainted with Mr. Bucher, whom he found to be a man of a genial turn of mind and a practical teacher, who had had four years training in

Normal School work in Pennsylvania, with whom he could most heartily cooperate. Mr. Bucher felt that he could do likewise and, seeing that Mr. Reichenbach too had been trained to teach in Normal Schools, proposed to the latter that they together establish the first Normal School for white teachers in Virginia. Mr. Reichenbach, taking Mr. Bucher by the hand, said: "I am your man." This compact was the initiatory step toward establishing the Valley Normal School. It was not a selfish bargain nor a visionary scheme, although almost insuperable obstacles were in the way; but it was a deep conviction that the greatest educational need in the Valley was the training of teachers for the public free schools. Looking to the Lord for wisdom and guidance, these two men proceeded to perform a most difficult task.

The new school was opened on the 29th of September, 1873, with three teachers and forty-nine pupils on the roll, about half a dozen reporting to the Principal and the rest being almost equally divided between the other two teachers. Miss O'Ferrall later on also took charge of the pupils in instrumental music.

The Principal taught ancient and modern languages and mathematics; the other teachers taught the branches required by law. The patrons closely watched the new management and soon declared that they had a good school. This was true for those early days of free schools, but the Principal was not satisfied with his work. Four years' experience had not qualified him to teach so many branches, but the patrons decided otherwise.

Professional work for teachers was delayed till July 13, 1874, when the first six weeks' Summer Institute was opened. County Superintendent Loose was scheduled for lectures on school government; Principal Reichenbach, for theory and practice of teaching; County Surveyor Bucher, for instruction in writing, vocal music, arithmetic, surveying, and supervision of the Model School; and Professor A. L. Funk was added to the teaching corps to instruct in grammar, geography, history and elocution. The Institute closed August 21st, with 68 for the first catalogue,—18 ladies, 30 gentlemen and 20 children in the Model School. This was really the close of the first year; and as work was begun for teachers, professionally, it was thought proper to say that the Valley Normal School was established in 1873-4. The catalogue issued for that year gives no account of the school from September 29, 1873, to June, 1874; but it adds to the report of the Institute, a full announcement of teachers and courses of study, and gives other information, for the second year.

In September, 1874, the Valley Normal School opened for the second year's work, under more favorable auspices. Professor A. L. Funk's services were secured for the whole year. Teaching was, therefore, begun in four rooms, and during the winter the school was transferred to a new building, which added much to the comfort and convenience of pupils and teachers. Fuller courses of study were pursued and more pupils were enrolled. Instead of giving prominence to the ancient classics, however, a teachers' department of two grades was organized and carried on with a classical department of three grades. The Summer Institute for 1875, including the Model School, had an attendance of 85, as against 68, the previous summer. The attendance in the Model School was the same for both years, but the attendance of teachers rose from 48 to 65. Three instructors were added to the teaching corps; namely, Professor T. S. Denison, Professor S. H. Owens of Richmond and Miss Laura O'Ferrall, who was elected Principal of the Model School. Teachers were in attendance from West Virginia and Ohio. Virginia was represented by teachers from six counties. The Institute awakened wide-spread interest and elicited the hearty support of the Hon. W. H. Ruffner, State Superintendent of Public Instruction, as well as of the present Lieutenant Governor J. Taylor Ellyson, then editor of the Educational Journal of Virginia. Much of the success of the Valley Normal School and especially of the Summer Institute was due to the official recommendation of these distinguished educators.

The third year the courses in the Valley Normal School were changed from grades to years. Most prominence was given to the teachers' courses, one of which covered two years and the other four years. In the former, the public school branches were supplemented by methods and practice of teaching; in the latter, branches were added for high school teachers of that time, besides a full list of professional studies as then pursued. Catalogues of German and American normal schools were freely consulted in arranging these teachers' courses. The ancient classics were subordinated to the studies for teachers, but not abandoned, because of the regard of the instructors for patrons who wished to send their boys to college, later on. There were three courses leading up to the teachers' courses; namely, a primary course of three years, an intermediate course of three years, and a grammar and scientific course of two years. The corps of teachers of the previous year was retained and another teacher, Mrs. Marie Reichenbach, was added, to teach French and drawing. The attendance again increased and more satisfactory teaching was done.

The summer Institute for 1876 enrolled 71 teachers; and 23 pupils attended the Model School. Professor L. P. Slater and Miss Virginia Paul, sister of Judge John Paul, were added to the regular corps of instructors, but Professors T. S. Denison and S. H. Owens did not return, nor did the Rev. J. S. Loose. The Hon. W. H. Ruffner, Professor S. T. Pendleton, Major Jed. Hotchkiss, and the Rev. E. E. Higbee, President of Mercersburg College, delivered lectures. Supt. Ruffner spent a week at the school. As eight counties were represented, this time, in Virginia alone, instead of one Superintendent examining the teachers at the close of the Institute, a board of examiners consisting of the Superintendents of the schools of Rockingham, Augusta and Highland counties, was appointed.

The fourth year the self-sacrificing and excellent instructor, Professor Jesse D. Bucher, was very much missed in the Valley Normal School, as he was elected Principal of Oakland Business

School,; Doe Hill, Highland Co., Va.; but he served as instructor in the Summer Institute of 1877. Miss Virginia Paul was elected to the position made vacant by the resignation of Professor Bucher, and she also taught in the Summer Institute, the following summer. Mr. Rockingham Paul, twin brother to Miss Virginia Paul, also became an instructor, at the beginning of the scholastic year, and Miss M. A. Brown took charge of the instruction on the piano, whilst Miss Laura O'Ferrall retained the instruction on the organ. The Valley Normal School now had seven regular instructors, whereas the beginning was made, four years before, with three. Decidedly better teaching could now be done and tangible results were shown by the end of the year. Three classes were graduated—one from the business course and two from the teachers' courses. Six students in the first-named class completed the business course. The commencement program, dated June 8, 1877, shows that Verdie Brown, J. H. Fauver, Anna Hoff and Gertie Jenkins were graduated from the teachers' course covering two years; and J. B. F. Armstrong, Cyrus H. Cline and Rockingham Paul, from the teachers' course covering four years. Certificates were granted instead of diplomas, on the ground that the instructors held that the union of a public and a private school should not assume the privileges of chartered or state institutions to issue diplomas and confer degrees. The term graduation was used in this modified sense. When the commencement was reported to State Superintendent Ruffner, he said in his reply to the Principal: "You have graduated the first white teachers in Virginia."

The Summer Institute for 1877 opened July 16th. Besides the regular instructors, the lecturers were the Hon. M. A. Newell, Superintendent of Public Instruction of Maryland and Principal of the State Normal School, at Baltimore; the Rev. Professor W. B. McGilvary of Richmond and the Rev. S. N. Callender of Mt. Crawford. The same board of examiners served again at the end of the session. The attendance of teachers was 53, a marked decrease if compared with former years. There were natural reasons for it; a large deficit in the school fund of the State, at that time, discouraged most teachers too much to continue further study. Lower salaries seemed to be a certainty.

Principal Reichenbach had hoped for increased appropriations for school purposes and had planned to diminish still more the classical studies or even to abandon those that could not legitimately be incorporated into the teachers' courses. The instructors still taught too many branches and were over-worked. More specialization was needed to bring the school up to the standard of an excellent Normal School. When, however, the announcement came from Richmond that the deficit in the school fund, in 1877, was already between $300,000 and $400,000 and was still increasing, thus amounting to nearly half of the teachers' salaries for that year, the Principal was thunder-struck. Furthermore, the Peabody fund was also no more available. Instead of teaching fewer branches, it was evident that the instructors must teach more. The Principal, whose health began to fail, very reluctantly resigned and left Virginia, after the close of the Summer Institute of 1877, contrary to the wishes of the good people of Bridgewater. The Associate Principal at this Institute, Professor A. L. Funk, was elected Principal of the Valley Normal School, for the ensuing year. Professor George H. Hulvey took charge of the classical department.

The following year Professor Hulvey became Principal and under his management prominence was again given to the classical department. He was remarkably successful in making his students proficient in Latin and Greek, as well as in other studies pursued by them. It seems that the name, Valley Normal School, was dropped with the departure of Principal Hulvey, or soon thereafter.

Other Summer Institutes were opened at this time and before, in various places in Virginia, so that special schools for teachers gradually became popular. The movement at Bridgewater no doubt suggested the establishing of the Shenandoah Valley Institute, at Dayton, and the opening of a Brethren's Normal, at Spring Creek, which, by transfer, later became Bridgewater College.

This brief history gives statistics of the Summer Institute only, in order to avoid making the reading tedious. A summary of statistics by scholastic years, collected from corrected catalogues and other sources, follows:

1873—September 29th, opening day, enrolled _____ 49
　　　　Estimated additions to June, 1874 _____ 75
　1874—Summer Institute, exclusive of Model School _____ 49
1874-5, including Summer Institute, 1874 _____ 204
1875-6, including Summer Institute, 1875 _____ 208
1876-7, including Summer Institute, 1876 _____ 210

The last two catalogues were issued in April, thus making it impossible to include the institute following; hence the Institute of each summer of the preceding year was inserted. By substituting the Institutes of 1876 and 1877, respectively, for the last two above, in order to obtain uniform statistics, the figures appear as follows:

1875-6, including Summer Institute, 1876 _____ 209
1876-7, including Summer Institute, 1877 _____ 187

To the above brief history of the Valley Normal School, it is only just to add Professor Alcide Reichenbach's present view of the educational activities, at Bridgewater, Virginia, from 1873 to 1877. Being still engaged in teaching and having taught pedagogy to the senior class at Ursinus College, Collegeville, Pennsylvania, for a number of years, he should be competent to judge fairly and intelligently, in regard to the above-named educational activities.

First of all, he regards the Valley Normal School as having been simply a pioneer in normal school work, in Virginia. Judged from modern standards, the methods pursued were in part crude and the results following were imperfect. The old and the new were not properly blended and a few things were attempted, ahead of the times; nevertheless the institution was true to its name—a school of high moral tone, especially designed for teachers, awakening in them the spirit of the true teacher and enabling them to teach better than formerly. No man blazing a new path will please every observer. The Principal was much surprised that notes of disapproval were so rarely heard, and then only from the uninformed as to actual facts. The people of Bridgewater and all others who sustained any relations to the Valley Normal School deserve the highest praise for their unanimous support of the school as well as for their loyalty to every instructor in the institution. Without such sympathy and such self-sacrifice, on the part of the patrons, and without such devotion to the welfare of the pupils, on the part of the instructors, the Valley Normal School never could have existed. Nowhere else, either in Europe or in the United States has Professor Reichenbach found a people so sympathetic, so hospitable and so loyal, as he found in Virginia. These sterling virtues may well be cherished as educational factors, in her schools for all time.

April 3, 1909.

THE HARVESTER

A Letter Written in 1928 to Hon. Andrew Price,
State Historian of West Virginia

Dear Mr. Price: I have just finished reading your interesting article in the current *Times* in which you note that "Steven McCormick invented a new plow that got first prize and that is where the McCormicks broke into the implement business."

I happen to know something about where the McCormicks got their big boost in the business. I think it might interest you.

Just after the Civil War a man came into the neighborhood where I was raised, from somewhere in New England. He was called a carpet bagger. He was a school teacher. He settled at a village called Montezuma, near above Bridgewater, Virginia. He was a genius and in his spare moments he worked on the model of some kind of a machine. He made the model of a reaping machine with vibrating cutter bar and guards that have not been improved on very much to this day.

After he had his model completed he went among his neighbors and solicited aid to get it patented, as he was a poor man financially.

Among the rest, Mr. Young appealed to a neighbor by the name of Milton Irvine. Mr. Irvine as well as all his neighbors was very hard up at the time and the $60 that it took to get a patent was hard to get. Mr. Irvine had a cottage in the mountains at a place called Union Springs where he spent part of the hot summer with his family and friends. Mr. Irvine was an Elder in the Presbyterian church. In his official capacity he had visited Rockbridge County and he had met Silas McCormick whom he had invited to come down and spend some time with him in his mountain home. Mr. McCormick accepted and he came down with his daughter.

In a general way Mr. Irvine told McCormick of Young's machine. McCormick sent for Mr. Young, who brought his model. McCormick immediately sent it away and secured a patent but he got it in the name of McCormick.

McCormick then built six machines. Mr. Irvine got one of them. They were very heavy. It took four horses to draw it. It had a reel to knock the wheat on to a table of slats. When enough wheat had been cut, the machine tender with a foot lever would drop the rear of the table and with a rake would draw off the wheat. Men following would gather it up and tie it. It was rather crude, but I notice there has been but very little improvement on the reel and vibrating cutting bar and guards.

Isaiah Young died very poor, but he was a good clean man. He had the good will of every one who knew him.

I have sometimes thought it would have been a better investment for Silas' grandson to have erected a monument over Isaiah Young's grave at Montezuma than to have wasted the money he did on that other business.

I have read in a book where McCormick had spent sleepless hours on his original machine. No doubt he did, on improvement on the original. But the original idea was dug from the brain of a carpet bagger by the name of Isaiah Young.

In later years friends of Young wanted him to bring suit against McCormick for his patent, or interest in it. Young declined saying he would invent a corn harvester. He made a model of one but it was not a success.

This all happened near your former home, but you were not yet born.

I am quite sure that this story could be referred to by people who are yet living in that neighborhood.

I can well remember how the old cradlers would come across the mountains from the west to take advantage of the big wages paid through harvest—$1.50 to $2.00 per day—for swinging a cradle steadily in the boiling hot sun from daylight to dark. They kicked and complained that the machine would destroy their picnic.

How shallow was their foresight, we just then began to live.

Yours very truly,

H. F. CROMER
Cheat Bridge, W. Va.

Notes by J. W. W.—A copy of the *Pocahontas Times,* of March 8, 1928, published at Marlinton, W. Va., containing the foregoing letter by Mr. Cromer, was brought to my attention by Isaiah Young's daughter, Mrs. James R. Shipman, of Bridgewater. The letter is reproduced here as a matter of interest in connection with a subject of much importance and no little controversy.

At Port Republic, December 28, 1911, William Groves, who operated there a small foundry, told me that his father, Michael Groves, invented the notched sickle for McCormick's reaper.

Michael Groves died in West Virginia in 1891, aged about 75.

William Groves stated that at the time his father invented the notched sickle for McCormick he (Michael Groves) was working with the McCormicks at their furnace at Vesuvius, Rockbridge County, Va. William Groves also said that Holbrook made the McCormick sickles in his shop at Port Republic. This shop he further stated was washed away in the flood of 1870.

Cyrus H. McCormick obtained his first patent on his reaper in 1834. On January 31, 1845, a patent was secured which applied to the reverse angle of the serrations on the sickle, the form of the guard, and a better divider. In 1846 he arranged to have 100 machines manufactured in Cincinnati; and in 1848 he built his factory in Chicago.

MONUMENTS AND TABLETS IN ROCKINGHAM COUNTY

There are in Rockingham County at least sixteen monuments and tablets that mark places of general historical interest. There should be many more, of course. A bare catalog follows, arranged chronologically.

In 1876 the Ladies Memorial Association erected a monument in Woodbine Cemetery, Harrisonburg, in grateful remembrance of the Confederate soldiers who lie buried there. It contains an appropriate inscription on each of its four faces.

In 1898 a monument, composed of two massive stones, one granite, the other limestone, was reared on the spot, a mile and a half south of Harrisonburg, in Chestnut Ridge, where Gen. Turner Ashby fell mortally wounded on June 6, 1862.

All of the buildings at the State Teachers College, Harrisonburg, are in a sense monuments to illustrious men and women whose names are therein enshrined. In one of them, Harrison Hall, is a bronze tablet to the man whose name has there been adopted and whose diligent and accurate scholarship should ever be an inspiration to all students—Gessner Harrison, a native son of Harrisonburg, for many years a distinguished teacher in the University of Virginia. This tablet was presented in 1917 or 1918 by Gessner Harrison's son, Robert L. Harrison, of New York City, at the solicitation of President Julian A. Burruss.

In 1921 the Colonial Dames of America in the state of Virginia marked the trail across the Blue Ridge that was likely followed into what is now Rockingham County in 1716 by Alexander Spotswood, the Tubal Cain of Virginia, and his "Knights of the Horseshoe." At the summit of the pass in Swift Run Gap they built a massive pyramid of native stones and into its southwest front set a tablet of marble. Its story is simple but epic. This monument stands within a few rods of the line between Rockingham and Greene, on the side of Greene.

The beautiful and distinctive bronze statue, on a granite base, that attracts all who pass the intersection of Liberty Street and Main, near the southwest end of Harrisonburg, commemorates all the sons of Rockingham and Harrisonburg who lost their lives in the World War. It was erected in 1924 by Rockingham Post No. 27 of the American Legion, the auxiliary of the Legion, and other patriotic citizens.

In 1926 three Rockingham County battlefields of the Civil War were marked by handsome bronze tablets fixed on massive stone bases. Harrisonburg, Cross Keys, and Port Republic were all commemorated in this manner. The marker at Harrisonburg, which is dedicated to General Turner Ashby of Fauquier and all enlisted men from

Rockingham County, stands just southwest of the city at the mouth of the old Port Republic Road, not far from the spot where Ashby fell.

The one that helps to keep alive the memory of Cross Keys is near Victory Hill school house and Mill Creek Church. The battle here was fought on Sunday, June 8, 1862, between Ewell, with part of Jackson's army, and Fremont.

The marker for Port Republic stands about two miles below the village, near the Episcopal church at Lynnwood, and only a few rods from the old coal hearth on the shelf of the mountain whereon one of the Federal batteries stood and rained its iron and fire until the Louisiana Tigers, after repeated trials, captured it. This was on June 9, 1862.

The three markers last above mentioned were constructed and put in place by the Virginia Battlefield Markers Association, under the untiring leadership of Veteran R. M. Colvin of Harrisonburg.

At the southwest approach to the county and city court house in Harrisonburg are two beautiful bronze tablets, placed there in 1927 by the Daughters of the American Revolution. One of these honors Charles Watson Wentworth, Marquis of Rockingham, British Prime Minister, after whom Rockingham County was named in 1777.

The other is dedicated to the memory of Thomas Harrison, patriot, who gave the land for the county court house and other public buildings in 1779. Harrisonburg was named after him.

Already within the year 1928 the Department of Archives and History of the State Conservation and Development Commission of Virginia has erected four markers in Rockingham County: one near Kaylor's Park, to call attention to the place where Ashby fell; one at Lacey Spring, to tell of Rosser's attack on Custer, December 20, 1864; one at the river bridge just above Mt. Crawford, to recall the engagement there on March 1, 1865, a final brush with Sheridan as he was passing through the Valley on the final campaign; and one at the county line a mile above New Market, to commemorate the surveying of the Fairfax Line in 1746.

In April, 1928, Bridgewater College rededicated its oldest academic building as a memorial hall, and placed just inside the door of the front entrance a bronze tablet to the first board of trustees, forty men "who builded better than they knew."

On August 30, 1928, a tablet was unveiled at Dayton to the men of that community who participated in the World War.

THE KILLING OF LIEUTENANT MEIGS, 1864

Written about 1925 by P. C. Kaylor

In the fall of 1864 Sheridan's army was encamped around Harrisonburg and Dayton, having closely followed the retreat of Early's Confederate forces from Fisher's Hill. At Harrisonburg Early had left the Valley Pike, on the southeast side, thereby permitting Sheridan's cavalry to go up the Valley as far as Staunton and Waynesboro unmolested.

Early passed Port Republic and went into camp near Weyer's Cave and Grottoes, later going to Rockfish Gap near Waynesboro, where he awaited the arrival of the brigades of Kershaw and Rosser from east of the Blue Ridge.

Reinforced by Kershaw and Rosser, Early determined to attack Sheridan. He called a council of his lieutenants and it was decided to send two trusted scouts to Bridgewater to see if it was possible to obtain information of the expected move of Sheridan, and also to locate his position.

On the morning of October 3, 1864, a man from North Carolina named Campbell and one from East Virginia named Martin, members of Rosser's brigade, were detailed to perform this duty. Inasmuch as they were not familiar with the roads in that section, an officer in the 1st Va. said he would get a man that lived there and knew every pig trail to accompany them. Forthwith he sent for B. Frank Shaver, Co. I, 1st Va.

Shaver, born and reared on the farm now owned by Q. G. Kaylor, had little more than reached his majority when Virginia called for troops. He volunteered in the cavalry and developed at once into a fearless and adventurous soldier. He took to scout duty as naturally as a duck takes to water. He was a splendid type of physical manhood—more than six feet in height, of dark complexion, with black hair and beard.

Shaver had never met Martin and Campbell until this trip. When informed of his task he was pleased. He said, "I would like to go home and see the folks and get a good square meal." He also remarked that he had received a letter from his sister Hannah stating that they had a Federal guard with them, and that he would probably have a Yankee brother-in-law when he returned home. Imagining that this guard had probably spoken to some of the family about the Federal movements and that this would be an ideal place to get information the trio started.

Arriving at Bridgewater and learning nothing of Sheridan's movements, they decided to go through the picket posts to Shaver's home, having learned where the several pickets were stationed.

From Bridgewater they came to the home of Squire John Herring, and there Mr. Herring confirmed the fact that there were three picket posts on the road that extends from Dayton to the Mennonite Church on the Valley Pike. One was where the road leaves Dayton; the second was on top of the high hill at the Leedy place; and the third was at the Mennonite Church.

The three scouts decided to go between the picket posts to Shaver's home; so leaving Mr. Herring's they went northeast by the Byrd farm (now owned by Sam Will) and by the Grove farm (now the home of Grove Heatwole). They crossed the road that leads from Dayton to the Mennonite Church near the home of Jacob Flory and soon entered a piece of timber which extended the entire distance from Flory's to the old Swift Run Gap Road. From this wood they had full view of the Warm Springs Pike.

A halt was made at the far edge of the timber, and a close observation of the surrounding country was made. About half a mile to their left (northwest) they saw a picket, stationed where the Swift Run Gap Road leaves the Warm Springs Pike. Apparently no one was between them and this picket. They passed out of the timber through a gap in a new rail fence into the Swift Run Gap Road. Turning to the right (eastward) they started up the hill along the new fence, which extended about a hundred yards to the Smith and Wenger corner, with the intention of following the road until it turned north. Here they would leave it and go due east through the timber to the top of the high hill west of the Shaver home.

A few moments after coming out into the road they were surprised by three Federals, who came up from under the hill at the point where the said road (old Swift Run Gap Road) is now crossed by the Chesapeake-Western Railroad. The three scouts would gladly have ridden on, but the Federals came up in a gallop calling on them to halt.

Shaver, Martin, and Campbell continued in a walk, and agreed to fight it out if the Federals rushed them before they came to the end of the new fence. Seeing that thy would be overtaken before they could make a dash for the timber, they drew their pistols. The Federals were now upon them. The scouts wheeled their horses and commenced firing. The little battle was soon over, and a Federal officer, Lieut. John Rodgers Meigs, of Sheridan's staff, lay dead in the road, about one-half mile from the Warm Springs Pike. One Federal soldier was captured. The other made his escape by jumping off his horse, climbing the fence, and running into the timber.

The only Confederate injured was Martin, who was shot through the groin. He was about to fall from his horse, but was caught by Campbell. He implored his comrades to take him out of the Federal lines at once, fearing the consequences if caught there.

The Federal prisoner was soon relieved of his weapons, given Meig's horse to lead, and ordered to keep his mouth shut. The little party galloped back down the Swift Run Gap Road (the same road that Meigs had come up) and crossed the Warm Springs Pike into the woods. The picket stationed there did not realize the situation until the little party was past and in the wood, going west as fast as their horses could take them. The picket then fired but without effect.

When the scouts were near the Abe Paul home (north of Dayton) Shaver and Campbell removed the pistol belt from around Martin and decided to leave him at the home of Robert Wright near Spring Creek. There Dr. T. H. B. Brown of Bridgewater rendered him medical attention. Shaver and Campbell returned with their prisoner to the camp of the 1st Va. near Milnesville (now Centerville); and Campbell, leaving Shaver and their prisoner, went on to Rosser's camp, near Burketown.

The Federal soldier that made his escape, not knowing that his opponents in the fight were Confederate soldiers, because they were wearing raincoats or capes, reported to Sheridan's headquarters that Lieut. Meigs had been shot by citizens.

To administer a gentle rebuke to the neighborhood, Sheridan ordered that the houses and barns that did not have a Federal guard and the town of Dayton should be burned. The torch was at once applied to a number of houses, thereby creating what is known as the "Burnt District." It is thus referred to by Gov. O'Ferrall in his book, "Forty Years of Active Service," page 128.

Among those who lost their homes in the "Burnt District" were Daniel Garber, Mrs. Catherine Miller, Jonas Blosser, William Shaver, George Hall, Selima Sunafrank, Benj. Wenger, Abraham Blosser, Reuben Swope, Mike Harshberger, Noah Wenger (barn only, the fire at the house having been put out), Joe Harshberger, Nevel Rogers (this was the Judge Smith place, a large brick house, with mahogany doors), Rev. John Flory, John Herring, Esq., Mrs. Sophia Groves (two dwelling houses, barn, and all outbuildings), Michael Shenk, William Byrd and son, Abe Garber, David A. Heatwole (barn), Abraham Paul (barn), and Joseph Coffman (barn).

The following day residents of Dayton were warned of the impending destruction and moved their property and families into the surrounding lots and fields, where they spent the night, waiting to see their homes go up in flames. In the meantime news of the burnings that took place the same evening that Meigs was killed and the information that Dayton was to be destroyed as soon as the women, children, and old men were moved out, had reached the Confederate forces.

The late T. R. Sandy, at that time a young man and a Confederate soldier, was at the home of his father, William Sandy near Friedens Church, badly wounded in both legs, but beginning to use crutches, when some Yankees came and took two horses from the field and threatened to take him prisoner, but he begged off. That night his father came home from up near Sangerville at about midnight on his best horse.

T. R. told him that the Yankees would surely take the horse in the morning and would probably take him also, so the family agreed it would be best for T. R. to take the horse and leave that night, which he did. He took with him his brother George, a boy of about 12, to open fences and gates as far as Stemphleytown.

He had to go across country, through fields and woods, because every road had picket posts. These had to be dodged. His father had informed him where the pickets were. In order to reach a ford in Cook's Creek just below Dayton, on the Joseph Coffman farm, he had to pass by the residence. Grazing around the yard were a number of Federal cavalry horses, loose, but saddled and bridled. The noise made by these horses enabled him to get by with his horse without being detected. He crossed the ford and reached Stemphley-town without being molested. There he left his brother George with his uncle, David Snell.

By this time it was three o'clock. The night was dark and drizzly. He went on from Stemphleytown to Dry River. There he ran into a picket post, with camp fire burning low. He walked his horse very slowly until just opposite. Then the picket discovered him and called "Halt!" He then put his horse into a run up the river and through the Shickel ford. He was now outside of Sheridan's picket lines and had no more trouble.

Daylight found him near Ottobine, at the camp of the late Hiram Coffman, refugeeing with some of his livestock. He called Sandy, asked him where all the fires were towards Dayton (Coffman's home) and Harrisonburg. On being told that his property was not burned he seemed much pleased. He feared from the blazes seen during the night that his home had been burned.

Leaving Coffman's camp, Sandy went on to Sangerville, distant 15 or 18 miles from his home, by sunrise. There he met the late William T. Carpenter, who was also refugeeing stock, who wanted to know where the fires were and also where Sandy got the horse he was riding, saying, "Your father and I went down to Perry McCall's last evening to get a little whiskey, and the old gentleman drank a little too much. He got a quart more and started down the road on that horse. He said he was going home. I thought maybe the Yankees got him. Was he drunk when he got home?"

Sandy said "No, he was not; for father said the Yankee pickets drank all the whiskey he had with him."

When Shaver had learned the fate of Dayton, he and some officer of the 1st Va. went to the guard house and asked for the Federal prisoner, who had not yet been sent to Staunton, the railroad point for Libby at Richmond, and asked him whether, if he were paroled, he would go to Sheridan's headquarters at Harrisonburg (the home of Abe Byrd) and tell him that Meigs was killed by Confederate soldiers. He answered in the afirmative; was paroled and escorted back towards Bridgewater and the Federal pickets. This man lived up to his word and Sheridan revoked the order to burn Dayton.

I hope these facts will clear up the mystery that so many accounts heretofore published contain as to why Dayton was not burned, and will show also that Lieut. Meigs was not killed by bushwhackers.

The man Martin referred to in the forepart of this account, under the skilful hands of Dr. Brown and his nurses, was soon able to return to his home, but he did not see service again as a soldier. He always claimed that he had killed Meigs. About 1877 he learned that his pistol did not go off when it was aimed at Meigs's heart. When his pistol and belt were taken off they were placed on Meigs's white-faced horse and taken into Shaver's camp. Upon examination, it was found that his pistol contained all the loads, but the caps were all burst. Both Martin and Shaver had aimed at Meigs. Campbell fired at the soldier that surrendered and at the one that climbed the fence and ran into the woods.

Shaver never saw Martin again after leaving him at Robert Wright's, nor Campbell after they separated at Shaver's camp, until about 1878. Then the three met in Richmond by appointment.

Shaver remained in the army until the surrender. He was paroled, came home, and resumed work on his father's farm. The general amnesty granted to Confederate soldiers by the Federal government did not apply to him because he, Martin, and Campbell had gone inside the enemy's lines at the time Lieut. Meigs was killed; so they were considered as spies.

Accordingly, between the time of Lee's surrender at Appomattox and the reorganization of the state government of Virginia by Virginians, Shaver had several narrow escapes from the attempts made to capture him. One of the closest that I now recall occurred in this wise. One day a friend of his (I think it was Dr. J. N. Gordon) was in a barber shop in Harrisonburg, with one side of his face shaved, when in walked a Yankee soldier and inquired where Shaver lived. Mistrusting that the day was not healthy for Shaver, his friend asked the barber to excuse him for a moment. He stepped out the back door, hurried to a place where he had recently seen Mr. Levi Shaver, Frank's father, and told him the situation. Mr. Shaver forthwith mounted his horse and hurried home. He found Frank plowing, and told him to get out of the way.

Frank unhitched his horses, went to the barn, clapped saddle on a horse, and rode off. As he was going over the hill near where Frank Miller now lives, the Yankees turned in at the lane towards the Shaver home. At that time the lane left the Pike almost opposite the site now occupied by the Kaylor Park Garage, and led by the barn to the residence.

When the troopers rode up Mr. Shaver went out; and, in answer to their inquiry, he replied, "Yes, Frank is around somewhere. Get down, gentlemen; he will be in in a few minutes."

He then invited them into the house to have some cider and ginger cakes. They accepted the invitation and had a fair sample of "Virginia hospitality"; but all this time Frank was rapidly putting space between himself and the vainly waiting Blue-coats.

In March, 1875, my father, the late Louis W. Kaylor, bought
the Levi Shaver home, where Frank Shaver was born and reared. I
was 18 years old at the time. Frank married a Miss Byerly, daughter
of his nearest neighbor, who lived where Frank Miller now lives. He
was married after the war, and then lived on the Byerly farm. He
was our nearest neighbor for a number of years. We often exchanged
work on the farm, and frequently talked of the Meigs affair. He
personally showed me the spot where Meigs fell. An iron stake now
marks the place.

Some time in 1876 or 1877 a cousin of mine, William Shumate,
who lived in East Virginia, made us a visit. One night, during a
conversation, Cousin William asked my father if a Yankee officer
had not been killed in this neighborhood. Father answered "Yes,
just over the hill, back of the old house." Cousin said, "My nearest
neighbor killed him." Father said, "No, my nearest neighbor killed
him—a man by the name of Frank Shaver, who was born and raised
on this farm."

Cousin remarked, "Shaver was in the party, but my neighbor,
Martin, claims that when he wheeled his horse around it put him in
position to put his pistol against Meigs's breast, and when he fired
Meigs fell from his horse."

My father, turning to me, said "Pete, tomorrow morning after
breakfast you go down and tell Mr. Shaver to come up."

Well do I remember the errand and the ensuing conversation.
Frank came up and father introduced him to Cousin William; and
Frank described to him about examining Martin's pistol and finding
the caps burst, but the loads still in it.

Cousin Shumate returned home and told Martin that he had run
across Shaver and that he (Martin) was under the wrong impression
as to the killing of Meigs.

By means of Shumate's visit to my father Martin got into
communication with Shaver; and the three men, Martin, Shaver, and
Campbell, met at the state fair in Richmond that fall or the next.

I never saw or heard of any printed account of the killing of
Meigs until about ten years ago (1914 or 1915), while I was in the
state of Washington. I will make one exception. In 1895 the
Harrisonburg paper, in publishing an account of Shaver's death,
made mention of the combat in which Meigs was killed and stated
that Shaver was one of those engaged therein.

When I read the account in Dr. Wayland's history of Rockingham County (see pages 148-150 and 434, 435) I was surprised that
there was any question as to why Dayton was not burned. I thought
that every one who had ever heard of this occurrence knew that it
was not burned because the paroled prisoner (Federal) returned to
Sheridan and told him that Rebel soldiers had done the killing, and
that it was not done by citizens.

Dr. Wayland, on page 149 of his history of Rockingham,
publishes a letter from Col. Tschappat of Ohio, who was ordered by

Sheridan to burn Dayton. Col. Tschappat says that he had moved all the people out into the fields, when the order was revoked by Sheridan; and says that it was Gen. Thos. F. Wildes who prevailed on Sheridan to rescind the order because of its heart-rending effect upon the men in Col. Tschappat's regiment, which had been commanded at one time by Gen. Wildes.

This is not a reasonable story, for Wildes was one of Sheridan's staff and probably was present in consultation with Sheridan when the order was issued; and it is not likely that an officer would question the acts of a superior just because he did not want a regiment that he had once commanded to carry out a certain order.

Referring again to Dr. Wayland's history, page 434, he says that Shaver and his companions were planning to get on the high hills between the Warm Springs Pike and the Valley Pike to locate the Federals by their campfires. Shaver could have located the campfires easily enough without going inside the Federal picket lines to do so, from any high point south of the Pike Church.

In Governor O'Ferrall's "Forty Years of Active Service," page 128, he says that one of Shaver's men had fallen from his horse dead, and that Shaver and his remaining man had the two Federal cavalrymen prisoners. O'Ferrall also states, page 129, that General Sheridan, without stopping to investigate, issued and had executed his unjustifiable and cruel order.

The Harrisonburg *Daily News* of December 12, 1911, contained an article written by Capt. Foxhall Daingerfield and his wife, of Kentucky. They at one time were residents of Harrisonburg. This was a two-column article in which the facts were glaringly misrepresented. The statements cannot be verified, with two exceptions. These are that Lieut. Meigs was killed; and that the white-faced horse that was taken at the time of the killing was frequently seen after the war.

Captain Daingerfield says: "Three young men went to the home of a Mr. Shaver and had their haversacks filled and were watching their chance to cross the road and reach the ford by which they could return to camp, when they were charged by Meigs." This is not a plausible story, for it is at least three miles to the river. He further states, in the same paragraph, that the house at which the young Confederates had obtained food was one of the first reduced to ashes. This house was not burned, and is now the residence of Q. G. Kaylor.

Again the captain says: "The beautiful and hospitable home of Mr. John Herring was destroyed, the infuriated executioners of a dastardly order throwing back into the flames the cradle of a tiny baby against the pleadings of the mother, and all because in a great war six gallant soldiers had met in a fair and equal combat, in which two were killed and one wounded."

I am compelled to say that the great historian Joesphus was right when he wrote: "Some people write to show their skill in composition and that they therein acquire a reputation for speaking finely."

Sheridan was aware of the fact that there was a very bitter feeling in this neighborhood between the Confederate sympathizers and those who were opposed to war, or were Union sympathizers. The lives of the latter in some cases were in danger, and they had been threatened. Rev. John Kline was bushwhacked near Broadway on account of this bitter feeling. Sheridan had agreed to furnish one team and wagon to each Union sympathizer to transport his belongings and family beyond the boundaries of the Confederacy. In fact, the very day that Meigs was killed a number of persons, whose property was burned, had already loaded what they could take on one wagon and had moved as far as Harrisonburg. Among those that I can now recall were Florys, Sunafranks, Thomases, Halls, Blossers, Hinegardners, and some of the Wengers.

Noah Wenger owned the farm where John Dan Wenger now lives. It is near where Meigs fell. His barn was burned the same evening the conflict occurred. Mrs. Wenger was baking and getting ready to leave her home for an unknown destination, and Federal soldiers were encamped all about the premises. Some of them were not as polite as dancing masters, for they would go in where the cakes and pies were and help themselves. She or Mr. Wenger made complaint to an officer, and a guard was immediately put at the house. That evening Mr. Wenger and his family took what they could carry on one wagon and moved out.

When the party that did the burning arrived at the Wenger place they found there Andrew Thompson, now a well known resident of Harrisonburg. In 1864 he was a boy of 13, and made his home with Mr. Wenger part of the time. His mother lived in Dayton, and Andy, as his friends called him, had not come home—he was still at Mr. Wenger's. The Yankees went to the barn and took a portion of the hay that was therein. Then they tore off weather-boarding and broke it into small pieces to kindle the fire that consumed the building. It was raining that afternoon. Then they mounted their horses and rode away.

Another squad of Yankees came up to the house. They took the straw that had been emptied from the chaff ticks, piled it against a wooden partition and set fire to it. Andy Thompson then took a crock off of the paling fence (the buckets had been moved with the wagon), carried water, and put the fire out. This house was standing when Mr. Wenger returned home after the war. Andy was not molested by the soldiers who were at hand when he put the fire out.

About a mile down Cook's Creek from Dayton is the Squire Herring farm. Across the creek opposite the farm residence was a tenant house occupied by the late Valentine Bolton, who was then in the Confederate army. Mrs. Bolton was told to move out, that the house was to be burned. Some of the Federal soldiers were helping to remove the property when one of them picked up a Masonic manual. Turning to Mrs. Bolton he asked, "Is your husband a Mason?" She, feeling somewhat bitter at having the house burned, answered in no pleasant humor, "Yes, he is." Forthwith the men were ordered out of the house, and the property that had been removed was immediately replaced. A guard was left there. This house is standing today.

These same soldiers burned the main residence across the creek at the Herring farm, and this is the house that Captain Daingerfield speaks of, telling of the baby's cradle in connection. This story seems doubtful, in view of the conduct of the same men at the Bolton home.

At the home of Joel Flory, father of Jacob Flory, east of Dayton, on the Pike Church Road, old Aunt Betsy Whitmore was lying bedfast at the time the Yankees came to burn the house. After learning the condition of Aunt Betsy they went off and did no burning. A similar situation was found at Abraham Paul's, where the barn was burned, but not the residence, because in the latter was a sick woman (a Miss Paul).

The evening Dayton was to be burned (the day after Meigs's death), the Federal soldiers helped move the household goods from the dwellings into the surrounding fields and lots where it would be out of danger of the fires. That evening, when the order to burn was revoked, it was too late to move back into the houses; so the Federal officer in charge placed guards with each family to protect them from that class of rough-necks that are in all armies.

During the evening a drunken Yankee set fire to old Mr. Burnshire's straw rick. The soldiers of Col. Tschappat's regiment, who were protecting the families in the fields, extinguished the flames and punished the incendiary by kicking, beating, and rolling him out into the road.

When Sheridan received orders to destroy the grain and other supplies that were stored in mills and barns, and was carrying out the order by applying the torch, the burners came to the Burkholder farm, near Garber's Church, to destroy the barn, which contained grain. The wind being strong, and blowing towards the residence, they went away and left it, for fear of destroying the house. This occurred a few days after the burnings around Dayton, on the death of Meigs. Sheridan began his retreat and burning down the Valley about October 5.

Destruction of supplies was the object in the general burning, not the destruction of buildings. This was shown at the mill of Gen. Sam Lewis, at Lynnwood. This mill had a large quantity of wheat in it, but news was sent by "grape-vine telegraph" to General Lewis (who was a Union man) that if the grain were taken out before morning the mill would not be burned. He had his son, the late Sen. John F. Lewis, who was then superintendent of Mt. Vernon Iron Works, to send the furnace teams down and haul out the wheat during the night. This mill was not burned. Neither were some other mills and barns that were empty.

Tradition has it that the Yankees went to the Joseph Coffman place, just on the outskirts of Dayton, south, and set the barn on fire; then went to the residence to burn it. There they came across a Masonic apron belonging to Mr. Coffman; and so they did not burn the house. The Coffman place was headquarters of Gen. G. A. Custer. Some think that was the reason why the residence there was not burned.

It is my opinion, however, that the David A. Heatwole barn and the barn on the Joseph Coffman place were burned several days after the killing of Meigs, when Sheridan began his retreat down the Valley. It was at the Joseph Coffman place that T. R. Sandy saw the cavalry horses grazing when he passed there late the night of the destruction in the "Burnt District"; and the barn was standing at two o'clock that night.

Notes by J. W. W.—At Arcanum, Ohio, August 19, 1928, a Mrs. Baker, daughter of Abram Koontz, told Mr. P. C. Kaylor that the house of her father, Abram Koontz, near Dayton, Rockingham County, Va., was burned along with the others mentioned on page 189.

Anent the burning around Dayton, and the sparing of certain houses, the following is of interest:

On July 14, 1928, Mrs. Thomas Kille of Harrisonburg, whose old home was at or near Dayton, told me that when the "Yankees" came to the Joseph Coffman place to burn (see above on this page; also Wayland's History of Rockingham County, page 149) Mrs. Coffman met them and said, "I am a first cousin of Abraham Lincoln," and that this was the reason the Coffman house was not burned.

Mrs. Coffman was Abigail Lincoln, daughter of Lt. Jacob Lincoln; the said Jacob being a brother to Abraham Lincoln, the President's grandfather.

SHERIDAN'S HEADQUARTERS IN
HARRISONBURG

By P. C. Kaylor

The question having been raised, just where did General Sheridan have his headquarters in the fall of 1864, at Harrisonburg, Va., I have looked into all the evidence bearing on that subject that I could procure and have come to the conclusion that his headquarters were at the Abe Byrd residence on Red Hill.

Mr. John Taliaferro tells me that he was a small boy at the time, and lived near the Byrd residence. He says he remembers soldier guards walking back and forth before the headquarters. Mr. D. C. Reherd was then a boy about 14 years old, and his father, the late William Reherd, owned and lived on the farm that Hirsch Bros. now own. Mr. Reherd says a brigadier-general of Sheridan's army had his headquarters in their yard and house about the time the Yankees began to camp around Harrisonburg. They came to the Reherd place and took two cows. The brigadier-general told Mr. William Reherd to go to General Sheridan's headquarters and report the theft, which he did. Mr. D. C. Reherd (then about 14) went with his father to the Abe Byrd residence. His father informed the general of what had happened and the latter forthwith gave him a written order to take the cows wherever he found them.

C. R. Bush, a Confederate soldier, was captured on Sunday morning by the advance guard of Sheridan's army near Linville and brought into the town as a prisoner, and about three days later was sent to Point Lookout. Mr. Bush says that Gen. Sheridan's headquarters was on the hill near the old reservoir, and near where he was held a prisoner.

Mr. Hugh Morrison, then a young man, says that General Sheridan's headquarters was on Red Hill, and that the first troops came into town on Sunday morning, and that East Market Street was filled with caissons left there by General Early, but soon removed by the Yankees.

From the best information obtainable at this time (1925), I fix the date of the arrival of General Sheridan's army in Harrisonburg on Sunday, September 25, 1864, following the battle at Fisher's Hill on Thursday, September 22. This is confirmed by the Encyclopaedia Britannica, Vol. 24, page 837.

We the undersigned do certify that the above statements credited to each of us are substantially correct.

Signed by

JOHN W. TALIAFERRO
D. C. REHERD
C. R. BUSH
H. F. WAY

Notes by J. W. W.—It seems possible, probable indeed, that Sheridan at Harrisonburg had his headquarters at more than one place. If this be true, it is easy to understand how conflicting statements have arisen.

The Byrd home referred to above is now familiar as "Stoneleigh," or "Stoneleigh Inn." The present owner is Mr. A. R. Rosenberger.

Stoneleigh is becoming celebrated nowadays because of certain associations with Dr. Walter Reed, the famous surgeon and medical scientist. From about 1867 to about 1886 Rev. L. S. Reed, Walter Reed's father, owned Stoneleigh, and within that period Walter Reed was an occasional sojourner there. Rev. Mr. Reed's second wife was Mrs. Mary C. Kyle, widow of Robert M. Kyle. Before her first marriage Mrs. Reed (Kyle) was Miss Byrd, daughter of Abraham and Rebecca S. Byrd.

For a picture of "Stoneleigh" see Wayland's "Scenic and Historical Guide to the Shenandoah Valley," third edition, page 72.

Not very far beyond Stoneleigh, eastward, is a quaint old farm house which was for some time the home of Dr. William H. Ruffner, the "Horace Mann of Virginia."

HOOKE FAMILY DATA

*By (Mrs.) Audrey Kemper Spence, of Wytheville, Virginia
A Member of the Virginia Historical Society*

Captain Robert Hooke, Sr., born 1712, was alive on October the 16th, 1802, at which date he gave his deposition in Peter Sipe vs. Mary Gilmer. Ref. Judge Chalkley's "Abstracts of Augusta Co. Va." He stated that he was 90 years old and had known the walnut tree for 60 years.

He proved his importation at Orange Co. Va. Court, on May 22, 1740. "He brought his wife Jean and son William from Ireland to Philadelphia, and thence into this colony at his own expense." Ref. Orange Co. Court records, Scott's "History of Orange Co. Va." Waddell, in his "Annals of Augusta Co. Va." page 38, gives this same date and speaks of the heads of 14 families appearing at Orange Court to prove their importation.

He became a large land owner in Rockingham and Augusta Counties, Va. He received land by patent, 400 acres, from King George II, as early as June 30, 1743. Page 380 in Chalkley's "Abstracts." "December 3rd, 1750, Robert Hook, 100 joining his own land, the 5,000 acre tract and Williams' (c.g.c.p.), 17th June, 1752, Robert Hook, one right for the above. Wm. Hinds, vid. Robert McClenanchan, from Land Entry Book No. 1, Augusta Co. Va."

He served as one of the early Justices of Peace for Augusta Co. Va. Ref. Judge Chalkley and Summers's "Hist. of S. W. Va."; also, "Annals of Augusta Co. Va."

He saw active service in the French and Indian War, and succeeded Captain Robert Scott, as captain of the militia, May the 19th, 1758. Ref. Judge Chalkley, Court Martial Records, Staunton, Va.; Wayland's "History of Rockingham Co. Va."; also Va. Mag. of History and Biog. Vol. 30, No. 4.

He was a Presbyterian in religious belief, and was identified at different periods first with the Old Stone Church at Fort Defiance, Va., built 1740, and later with the Massanutten Church at Cross Keys, Va., built 1745. Ref. Journal of the Presbyterian His. Soc. Vol. X, March 1919.

Rev. John Craig's baptismal register which was in the possession of the late Gen. John E. Roller of Harrisonburg, Va., gave the following entries concerning the baptism of Robert Hooke's children: 1. Esther, Dec. 23, 1740; 2. Robert, Jan. 6, 1743; 3. Martha, Jan. 16, 1745; 4. George and 5. Jean (twins), Feb. 1, 1746.

In Sept. 1804, in Rockingham Co. Va., a will was probated of one Robert Hooke, in which the following children were named, viz: 1. Elijah; 2. Mary Murry; 3. Martha, $100.00 to her, or her heirs; 4. William; 5. Esther Belshey; 6. Robert; 7. Jean Read; 8. George; 9. James. He bequeaths one-half of his remaining property to his son, Elijah, and one-half to his daughter Mary Murry, for their life time, and at their deaths all of said estate was to go to his grandson, James Murry. The records show that James Murry died intestate, and his half-sisters and brother, Elizabeth Shanklin, Dorcas Graham, and John Huston, sold the land containing 200 acres on Jan. 18, 1816, to James W. Hooke and wife, Sarah (Pirkey) Hooke.

James W. Hooke, who was a brother of Robt. Scott Hooke of Highland Co. Va., was called, "Miller Jim," as he was a miller by trade; and there were others named James. He went west. Elijah Hooke, Sr., was still alive when this deed of sale was given. These 200 acres were sold on August the 24th, 1828, to David Huffman and wife Eliza by said James W. Hooke. One-fourth of an acre was reserved as a grave yard, and had formerly been used as such. File No. 26, 1868, Rock Co. Court Records, suit Flory vs. Hooke and wife.

James Hooke and wife Sarah made a deed for 200 acres of land three-fourths of a mile from Cross Keys, on the Port Republic Road, to Samuel Flory in 1837. The land adjoined Edward S. Kemper, Dr. Jennings's heirs, Wm. Van Lear, Solomon Berry, Wm. Rodeffer, a lot known as the Thompson lot, Sarah Pentz, and John Hough. Jas. Hooke and wife were non-residents of Va., in 1868, the date of the petition. This may have been the land sold to Huffman above and re-purchased by Hooke, then sold to Flory. It has always been common knowledge that an old Hooke grave yard was on the Flory farm near Cross Keys.

Robt. Hooke of the 1804 will made provision for his aged slave, Pondy. His son James was named as executor. Witnesses were George Snapp, George Huston and George Lung.

Chalkley, P. 69, March 21, 1759, Jno. Scott to Robert Hooke, £18. Bill of sale of a negro woman. Teste Robt. Breckinridge. Judge Chalkley quotes more concerning the Hookes, but lack of space prevents giving it all in this article.

Henry Pirkey and John Huston were the appraisers of the Robert Hooke estate; among the things sold at the sale were pewter bottle and tea kettle to Elijah Hooke. Candle snuffers, bread oven, reel, clock and looking glass to Polly Murry. Jas. Smilly, 1 pair of compasses. Daniel Mahoney bought 1 pair of knee buckles. Wm. Hooke 1 grey horse. George Hooke, 2 sickles and one bayonet. Geo. Compton, spoons and pewter. Other things listed in the inventory of Nov. 23, 1804, were 1 pot and hooks, pewter plates, basins, salt seller, 1 Psalm book and Testament, 2 old sermon books, 1 corner cupboard, knives, forks, spoons, flax, hemp, etc.

It is thought that either the mother or wife of Capt. Robt. Hooke, Sr., was named Scott, as that name appeared among his descendants.

It is thought that Capt. Robert Hooke, Sr., served in the Revolutionary War, by furnishing supplies etc. Wayland's "History of Rockingham Co. Va." pages 95 and 101.

Chalkley, Will Book No. 5, Nov. 17, 1772, Jane Hooke and Thomas McClullock's bond (with John Davidson and John Finley) as administrators of Robert Hooke, Jr.

Will Book No. 7, page 318, Vol. III, June 6, 1781, John Frazier's will, of Rock. Co. Va., to wife Jennett all estate whatsoever; to Jas. Walker, to Mary Anderson, to brother Jas. Frazier, to brother George Frazier, to sister, Molly Gallaway, to brother William, to Andrew Shanklin, son of testator's sister, Molly. Executors were wife Jennett and her brother, James Hooke. Teste, George Huston, Robert Hooke, William Hooke, Isabella Campbell, Elenor Campbell. Proved Feb. 15, 1791, by Huston, Robert Hooke, Wm. Hooke. Jennett qualifies.

Book III: Will Book No. 2, page 397, Oct. 22, 1783, William Hooke relinquishes to George Hooke his right to administer on the estate of James Hooke. Teste Geo. Frazier, Samuel Hill. Page 443, 7th of Oct. 1784, George Hook's estate sold at vendue to Martha Kennedy, Wm. Hooke, Wm. Hooke, Jr., Thomas Bleakley, Wm. Bean, Daniel Joseph, Daniel Fitzgerald, Robert Heslip, John Jasper, George Hooke Roe. (Possibly Roe was meant for Junior.)

Will Book No. 8, page 124, George Hooke witness to will of Martha Burnside, Jan. 20, 1794. Page 279, Dec. 16, 1794, Order Book 23, page 199, Joseph Hooke, aged 4 years 2nd of June, 1794, to be bound to John Read to learn the art and mystery of a weaver.

Page 224, March 16, 1784, Order Book No. 18, administration of estate of James Hooke, dec., granted George Hooke; Wm. Hooke, the eldest brother, having relinquished his right.

Page 7, Will Book No. 1, page 53, Aug. 20, 1747, John Taylor's appraisement by Robert Hooke, John Stevenson, Robert Scott.

1788, April 4th, vouchers in Capt. Geo. Huston's Co., Robert Hooke above 16 years of age; 170 acres; and son James (probably James Addison) above 16 years of age.

William Hooke, 4 horses; land 136, 70, 60, and 61 acres.

Robert Hooke, Sr., 2 sons, Elijah and George; 8 horses, 400 acres (Rockingham Court Records, Tax Books 1787). Robert Hooke, 400 acres; James, 200 acres; Robert Jr., 170 acres; William Hooke (Irish), 273 acres.

Deed Rock. Court Records. Wm. Hooke and wife Sarah to Peter Conrad, Mar. 6th, 1786.

(A) William Hooke, Sr., so designated by his grandson, Col. William Walker Hooke, in his manuscript, was alive on Nov. 2, 1824, the date of his brother John's death, according to File 302, in Chancery, Staunton, Va. His name has not been found on record after 1824, so he likely died in that year.

His will was drawn up on Sept. 25, 1817. He leaves all of his land, slaves and other property to his son, Captain Robert Hooke, who was to pay large sums of money to his sisters, Jennett, Martha, Ann, Catherine, and Rebecca. They were to be maintained on said plantation, have a riding horse and whatever household furniture they claimed. He had already portioned his son James. Capt. Samuel Linn was a witness to the will (which is in the author's possession). He said that payments should be made to some of his daughters one year after his death. One receipt is as follows: "Received of Robert Hooke, Executor of William Hooke, $100.00. I say received by me this 27th day of August, 1832, Rebecca Hooke." There is no proof that this is a first payment. A final settlement was concluded between them and their brother, Robert, on Sept. 15, 1837. Bonds were executed to them, the receipts of which show that they received their portion.

It is thought that he was the son of Capt. Robt. Hooke Sr., as his heirs owned the original 150 acres, patented to Robt. Hooke, Sr., on August 13th, 1743, and which was deeded to William on May 18, 1761, just 21 years after Robert Sr. gave in his declaration at Orange Court House. And it is possible William had just reached his majority, probably born in 1738 or 1739.

. Deed, dated June 26th, 1786, Rock. Co. Records, between Peter Coonrod and Wm. Hooke, 150 acres, which Wm. Hooke had sold to Coonrad on March 6, 1786, granted by patent August 13, 1743, to Robert Hooke and from him to the said Wm. Hooke May 18th, 1761. William Hooke repurchased the above 150 acres in two months and it is not likely that he ever gave possession to Conrad. This 150 acres was on a branch of the Shenandoah River called "Mill Creek." Also on Stoney Lick Branch, in Rockingham Co. Va., one and one-fourth miles from Cross Keys, Va. This land remained in the possession of the Hooke family from 1743 to 1904, 161 years.

William Hooke, Jr., owned land in a different direction from this 150 acre tract. Wm. Jr., 15 A. Va. Land Office. Wm. Jr., 112 A. Rock Co. Va. Records.

Page 76, in "Heads of Families 1784," Rock. Co. Va.: Robt. Hooke Sr., 5-1-4; Robt. Hooke Jr., 7-0-2; Wm. Hooke Sr., 9-1-0; Wm. Hooke Jr., 8-1-1; James Hooke, 6-1-1.

The above means that the Hookes had families of 5, 7, 9, 8, and 6 respectively, including father and mother.

The second and third rows of figures mean dwellings and other buildings.

Page 262 in Chalkley's Vol. (B.-21) August 18, 1790, Commissions for depositions of William Hooke and Robert Campbell, who are about to remove to Kentucky.

According to Wm. Hooke's memorandum book (in the author's possession), in which he recorded the number of the paper bills he received in payment, he was buying and selling goods in the Northern Neck as early as 1757, as the following will show: "No. 12643, June 8th, 1757, John Washington Staff." A three pound note, No. 236, received of Col. Tayloe, dated Nov. 7, 1769. "I promise to pay on demand to Wm. Hooke, eighty pounds, this 11th day of June, 1777, Joseph Frazier." £5, Bill No. 1545, dated May 24, 60. Received of Madam Lucy Alexander, 15th Dec., a bill of ten pounds. Pay to

Wm. Hooks, No. 652, 1757, Wm. Fitzhugh Mansion. "George Raymond, Richmond Co., I paid to Wm. Hooks one 37 pound bill No. 1186. Payed on the 11th July, 1771. This 8th of Dec., 1775, I Geo. Raymond do make the same good."

William Hooke, Sr., belonged to Capt. Hevitt's company of militia 1777 in the Revolutionary War. Ref. Wayland's "History of Rockingham Co., Va.," pages 90, 99, 100, 101, 102. Court records of Harrisonburg, Va. Courts Martial Records of Staunton, Va. See affidavit from said record in Corporation Court. Hening's Statutes at Large, VII: 181, 186, 187. Received pay for services rendered the Country in Revolution, Hening Vol. 7, page 186, 8 shillings. Va. State Library, Richmond, "List of Rev. Soldiers of Va. 1912" page 224, also Supplement, page 154. Boogher's "Gleanings of Va. History," pages 34, 39, 41.

See report of Ajutant General, War Department, Washington, D. C.

The application papers of Mrs. Audrey Kemper Spence, on the Revolutionary Services of William Hooke, Sr., were passed on and accepted on November 12, 1927, by the National Society of the Daughters of the American Revolution, Memorial Continental Hall, Washington, D. C.

As these papers have been accepted and approved by the D. A. R. Society, it makes all of his lineal descendants eligible; the female line for the D. A. R., and possibly the male line for the Sons of the American Revolution.

"Wm. Hooke Sr., built a large log house of hewen logs two and one-half stories high, with two floors, and one double door, divided across the middle, and hung from one side, and only one small window of four panes of small glass. Around the walls of the second story port holes were made, out of which to shoot if an attack was made by the Indians, who were still roving around in hostile bands. The site on which this house was built, was on the opposite side of the branch and 60 yards north of the spring. The said Wm. Hooke Sr., moved to this place and raised his family, and lived here during his life, and died here, and some of his descendants have owned and lived on some of these lands ever since up to this time 1899." Ref. Col. Hooke's manuscript.

Mrs. Wm. W. Hooke always planted cucumber vines around the fallen timbers of the old Fort House, mentioned above, because of the fertile soil.

The slaves were buried in a field near the branch.

Names of some of the Hooke slaves, as given by Mr. Jas. W. Hooke, in 1909: Pondy, or "Poney"; Tobitha and her husband; Hester Smith, married Temple, lives near Mt. Crawford. Mathias or "Mat," brother to Hester. He was a very fine athlete. He moved to Loudoun Co. Va., married. He accumulated a fine farm.

Issue of Wm. Hooke Sr., and wife, Sarah Hooke (her maiden name was Campbell). Married in 1772, she was alive on April 15th,

1790, as the following deed shows: "Deed dated April 15th, 1790, between William Hooke and Sarah his wife for $330.00 to Benjaman Bowman." Rock. Co. Court Records, Deed Book 26, page 42. Nothing further has been found concerning her, and she probably died near this date.

1. James Hooke born 1773, died Oct. 11, 1844, at 5 o'clock in the morning, Xenia, Green Co., Ohio. He was a Whig in politics. He married Mary (Polly) Lewis, Jan. 25, 1798, in Augusta Co., Va. They have descendants in Ohio and other states. Mary Lewis was the daughter of Anthony Lewis, sergeant of Inf. Revolutionary War. His will was proved May 25th, 1779. Wm. Campbell was the executor. Witnesses were Robt. and Ann Denniston. Probated at Harrisonburg, Va. Ref. for Anthony Lewis, Va. State Library, War 4, page 253, and Judge Chalkley, May 18, 1774, hemp certificate to Anthony Lewis. His wife was named Jean. She re-married to a Mr. Carr. Mary Lewis Hooke was a cousin of Gen. Samuel Lewis, of the Shenandoah River. Col. Hooke's Ms.

Mary (Lewis) Hooke born 1775, died 1861, age 86 years. They moved to Ohio near 1812. They went in a covered wagon; were six weeks on the road. He purchased 500 acres of land within three miles of Xenia. They built a handsome log house, finished inside with black walnut and walnut cupboards with brass handles. This house is occupied by Clinton Hooke, a grandson. The family burial ground was on his farm. James, his wife, their three sons, and his sisters are buried there. The oldest grandchild living in 1928 is Mrs. Nettie M. Herritt, Columbus, Ohio, 1044 McAllister Avenue, nearly 85 years old. Mrs. Grace Drake Hubble, 435 Riddle Rd. Clifton, Cincinnati, Ohio, is a great-grandchild, connected with the Y. P. work of Cincinnati.

Mrs. Jean Lewis Carr, with her Carr children and daughter, Mrs. Nancy Lewis Campbell, settled in Versailles, Woodford Co., Ky. There are living descendants of Nancy Campbell, who claim she was a half sister to the Carrs and was a Lewis. The letter of Miss Martha M. Drake, grand-daughter of James and Mary H. Hooke, Xenia, Ohio, dated Feb. 13, 1911, she stated (to the writer), "That the Carrs were half brothers to James Hooke's wife, and the mother of Mary Lewis Hooke had re-married to a Mr. Carr, and that Mary had a sister Nancy, who married Mr. Campbell, the half brothers were never married, the mother, and Mrs. Campbell and the Carrs had settled at Versailles, Ky. The families had exchanged visits in olden times."

Her descendants say that she was a half sister to the Carrs, who adored her and left all their property to her children, and it still remains in this family. They also remember hearing about the older members of their family visiting their relatives in Xenia, Ohio. Their estate is known as "Oakwood."

Dates taken from the family Bible of Mrs. Mary White Cary, "Oakwood," Versailles, Ky. A descendant of Nancy Lewis Campbell.

"Her mother's sister was named Nancy Lewis Campbell. Her great-uncle Thomas Carr was born June 13, 1787, in Rockingham Co. Va. He died April 7th, 1872, in Woodford Co. Ky., in his 84th year. N. M."

Samuel Carr born Sept. 19, 1789, in Rockingham Co. Va. He died May 31, 1866, in Woodford Co. Ky., in his 78th year. N. M.

Jane Carr born Nov. 18, 1792, in Rockingham Co. Va. She died Oct. 6, 1856, in her 64th year.

John Carr born June 1st, 1786; no record of his death in this Bible.

None of the Carrs mentioned were ever married.

Elizabeth Carr, born June 16, 1783. Tradition is that she married Mr. Hooke (?). Probably remained in Va.

Wayland's "Hist. of Rock. Co. Va." page 445 gives the marriage of Thomas Karr to Jean Lewis, Sept. 12, 1782.

Other children of Anthony Lewis, Judge Chalkley page 366; Sarah, daughter of Anthony Lewis, to be bound 1780, page 367. Jane, orphan of Anthony Lewis, bound.

Mrs. Jean Lewis Carr was 96 years old at death. The descendants of her daughter Nancy Campbell claim descent from Col. Lewis of Point Pleasant fame. It is probable Mrs. Carr's maiden name was either Lewis or Todd.

Extracts from a letter of Mrs. Richard P. Bell (Mary Grasty Bell) of Stonewold, Staunton, Va., to Mrs. Spence, under date of Feb. 2, 1928. The information was partly furnished by her uncle, Mr. Hubbard Carr White, deceased, of "Oakwood," Versailles, Ky.

Nancy Lewis, daughter of Anthony Lewis, Serg. Inf. Revolutionary War, and wife Jean, born 1779, died July 17, 1857, married David Campbell, Sept. 10, 1805, recorded in Rockingham Co. Va. Court Records; daughter of Anthony Lewis, William Lewis surety, who swears as to her age. (Was William Lewis a brother to Nancy?) David Campbell was born in 1780, died July 31, 1834. Their first child was born on November 10, 1806. They had eight children, most of whom died in infancy. Jean and Nancy Lewis Campbell are named.

David Campbell, born May 5, 1817.

Martha Mary Campbell, born March 10, 1816, married James White, April 28, 1840, by the Rev. Joseph Stiles (Styles). Issue, Elizabeth White married D. B. Price; lived in Alabama. David White married Addie Brown. Hubbard White, unmarried. William White, unmarried. Mary White married George Carry. Issue, Elizabeth Cary. Martha Virginia White married Thomas P. Grasty, parents of Mrs. Mary G. Bell of Staunton, Va., and Prof J. S. Grasty of Charlottesville, Va.

His descendants claim that Anthony Lewis or his family owned land near Port Republic, Va., and were related to the Lewis family of that section.

Dr. McElhenney was the former pastor of Mr. Thos. Carr, and on his 50th anniversary sent his sermon to Mr. Carr. The Lewis-Carr families went to Pisgah, Ky., near 1800; settled at Versailles in 1814.

Mr. White said that he thought one of the sisters of Nancy Lewis Campbell had married a Mr. Compton. Judge Chalkley gives the marriage license as follows: "1794, Sept. 5th, George Compton and Sarah Lewis, affidavit of Sarah's full age. Deed Book of Augusta Co. Va." Now if Sarah Lewis above was the daughter of the said Anthony Lewis, it makes her birth date near 1773; hence Anthony Lewis and Jean were probably married in 1772, as she must have been the oldest child, as she was named first when she and Jane were bound out, or adopted, in 1780. They were older children, and their mother likely kept Mary, born 1775, and Nancy, born 1779, who were of tender years.

Mr. Thomas Carr and niece, Elizabeth White, visited their relatives at Xenia, Ohio; went on horseback.

Notes from a letter of Mrs. Nettie M. Herritt, Columbus, Ohio, Feb. 20, 1928: "I cannot tell you my great-grandmother's name. When I was a young girl in college some of the Kentucky relatives visited us. My father's uncle, Tom Carr, a niece of his, Miss White, and her governess. It was just a year before the Civil War broke out. I promised to visit them the next summer. Instead we were fighting each other. I remember my father saying he had many cousins in Kentucky. Abraham Lincoln's wife was a fourth cousin of his. Her maiden name was Mary Todd."

Company 58, Reg. War 1812, War Dept. says "James Hooke served as a Lieutenant in the 58th Reg. Flying Camp, Rock. Co. Va., from July the 8th, 1813, to Sept. 28, 1813; to Jan. 16, 1814, in a detachment at Hampton. Rolls showed date of Commission, Dec. 2, 1811." It is believed that this James was the one who settled in Xenia, Ohio. His brother, Robert Hooke, was Captain of the 58th Reg. The writer has the Ohio Hooke Family History.

II. Robert Hooke born Oct. 10, 1776, died Oct. 9, 1852. He served as captain in a company of riflemen belonging to the 58th Regiment in the County of Rock. Va. Flying Camp (horses), McDowell's Va. Militia, War 1812. Ref. Wayland's His. Va., State Library, and War Dept. Washington, D. C. He was commissioned April 1, 1811, and commenced July 8th, 1812. Ended Jan. 16, 1814. Capt. Hook's minute book, War of 1812, is a cherished possession of his great-grandson, Wm. Robert Hooke of Penn Laird, Va.

Captain Hooke was very wealthy, had many slaves and many fine horses.

He built "Slate Hill" on the opposite hill from the old Fort House. It was very large, two and one-half stories high, walnut cupboards, etc. He planted coffee trees in front of the house, which grew higher than the house. It was very lovely when viewed from the road opposite. Captain Hooke inherited "Slate Hill" from his father, Wm. Hooke, Sr.

III. Jennett Hook went to her brother James Hooke in Xenia Ohio, in 1837, when past 55 years of age, N. M.

IV. Martha, N. M. went to James Hooke, Xenia, Ohio, when past 55 years of age.

V. Ann, N. M. went to Ohio when past 55 years of age.

VI. Catherine, married John Lyon, Jan. 25, 1794, by Rev. Wm. Wilson; went to Xenia, Ohio. Left descendants.

VII. Rebecca born near 1782, died 1861, went to Ohio with sisters in 1837. She had a very cheerful disposition, was so patient during her blindness, thus wrote her grand-niece, Miss Drake, to the author. She never married, was past 55 years of age when she left Virginia. In a letter to her niece, Elizabeth Jane Wilson, dated Jan. 2, 1855, she says that Samuel Drake, husband of Sarah Hooke, had died on last Thursday. Making the date of his death Dec. 28, 1854. She asked about Jane Walker (Elijah Hooke Sr.'s daughter); says that William Hooke's farm sold for $40.00 per acre; his eldest son bought it. He is living on his uncle, Wm. Lyon's farm. Wheat was worth $1.50 per bushel; pork was worth $4.50.

Captain Robert Hooke, son of Wm. Hooke Sr. and wife Sarah (Campbell) Hooke, married May 1, 1817, Miss Elizabeth Walker, born June 21st, 1792; died June 16, 1863; daughter of John and Sarah (Connelly) Walker, of Augusta Co. Ref. Walker and Connelly MSS. Issue: I. William Walker Hooke, born Feb. 5, 1818, died March 23rd, 1904; married Nov. 9, 1837 (by Rev. Jas. W. Phillips) Miss Maria Jane Dunn, born June 12, 1818, died April 20th, 1897 (daughter of Elizabeth Kephart and —— —— Dunn (an Englishman). Elizabeth Kephart Dunn was the daughter of Henry Kephart (War 1812) (?), and Magdalene Bargley, married April 16, 1798, by Rev. Paul Henkle. The author has this marriage certificate. The Englishman Dunn was a merchant, and was killed and robbed, while off on a buying trip, so his descendants believe. It is thought that he was a younger son of the nobility of England. The records concerning him have not come to the writer's hand.

The children of Mrs. Elizabeth Kephart-Dunn-Young (died Sept. 2, 1877, aged 75 years), by the Young marriage, were Sarah Ann Long (mother of Mrs. Sallie Wise of Bridgewater, Virginia) and her twin sister, Mary Ann, who left Virginia with her brothers, John, Silas and Henry (?) Young.

In a letter dated November 23, 1872, Bloomingburgh, Fayette County, Ohio, to his mother, John C. Young says that his wife had died September 26, 1870. He had three children, two sons and one daughter. His children were with their uncles, Leonard Bellinger and Hurman Crall, who had married his wife's sisters. He said, "You want to know something about Silas and Henry. Silas lives in West Virginia, twelve miles below Charleston, at the mouth of Cole River. His P. O. is Charleston ch. Henry lives in Charleston, the same post office. Mary lives in Braxton County, West Virginia, Braxton, ch."

John C. Young served in the Union Army during the War Between the States.

Col. Hooke served under Gen. Imboden, C. S. A., in the Old Reserves; was at the battle of New Market. He served under Capt. George Chrisman in the Va. Militia, when 5 battalions of reserves were sent to Fort Harrison below Richmond. No fighting. They disbanded during the winter.

He was commander of the "Big" Muster for Rock. Co. Va., sometime before the War Between the States. He took an active interest in church and civil affairs, was one of the trustees of the Massanutten Presbyterian church, and was a ruling elder at the time of his death. In boyhood he spent sometime with his uncle, Thomas Walker, near Mt. Sidney, in Augusta Co. Va. He was an extensive reader of the Bible, history and other literature. He wrote sketches of the Hooke, Walker, and Connelly families.

Muster Roll of 1844 of the Cavalry of the 58th Reg. of Militia of Va. commanded by Wm. W. Hooke, Captain, afterwards promoted to Colonel of the "Big" Muster of 1844. From original list:

John S. N. Keblinger, Lieut.—Sr.
Peter F. Earman, 1st Lieut.—Jr.
Jno. J. Rush, Lieut.—Sr.
Tom Jordan, 2nd Lieut.—Jr.
April, May, October.

Henry N. Argebright, James Crickenberger, Gebberton Ammon, John Debard, Jacob Earman, John Duniwin, John H. Austin, Daniel Eyler, Joseph Altaffer, Thos. Fletcher, Lewis Argabright, Wm. Floyd, Samuel Argabright, Richard P. Fletcher, John Earman, Robert Gibbons, Daniel Earman, Jas. M. Harnsbarger, Tipten Allstadt, Jno. Hedrick, Dr. Jno. G. Brown, David Hoffman, Adam C. Bear, Reubin Hoffman, Daniel Byerly, Henry Hulvey, Jno. Byerly, Bashiod Harshaw, Tom C. Bruffy, Jas. Hep, Jno. Bontz, Jacob A. Harnsbarger, Geo. Carpenter, Tom Johnston, Jno. Carpenter, Hyram Kyte, Samuel Carpenter, Joseph Kyte, Samuel Chandler, Tom Kyger, Wm. Kyger, Sam Ruebush, Eli. Kenen, Peter Ruebush, Jos. Eaton, Peter F. Keblinger, Wm. Reed, Jacob Kisling, Henry Roadcap, David Keller, Richard Runkle, Dr. H. Kyle, Peter S. Roller, Samuel Lewis, Francis Shipman, Wm. T. Miller, Jno. Shepler, Wm. J. Miller, Leanard Shefler, Robt. C. Miller, Martin Showalter, Frye Maupin, Amos Scott, Abner Moyers, Christian Swats, Wm. A. McGahey, George Saufley, Geo. Nicholas, Jno. Tutwiler, Albert Nicholas, Abner Trobough, Guncy Nicholas, Martin Tutwiler, Israel Minnick, Charles Weaver, Henry Null, Simon Whitsel, Daniel Miller, John Good, Annanias Pirkey, Peachey F. Hooke, Charles Rush, Levi Pence, Addison Royer, George Null, Samuel Royer, Michel Crawford, William Ruebush, Michael Meyerhoeffer, Lewis Meyerhoeffer, Joseph Eaton.

Issue of William W. Hooke and Maria Hooke:

1. Mary Elizabeth, born Aug. 6, 1838, died Jan. 4, 1897; married J. Stewart Slusser, born May 1, 1836, died March 9, 1898. Issue.

2. Robert, born Jan. 7, 1840, died Sept. 13, 1861, in a hospital at Fairfax Courthouse, Va., after the battle of Bull Run. He was a volunteer in the 1st Va. Reg. of Cavalry, commanded by Gen. J. E. B. Stuart. He enlisted April 17, 1861. Buried at Cross Keys, Va.

3. Sarah Ann, born March 26, 1841, died May 25, 1842.

4. William Franklin, born March 22, 1843, died Oct. 11, 1862, at 2 P. M. from a wound received at the Second Battle of Manassas. He enlisted in the Confederate service Jan. 12, 1862, and entered service at Winchester, Va., as a volunteer in the 2nd Va. Inf., Co. A, Stonewall Brigade. He was moved to the home of Mr. Wm. Foley near Lovettsville, Loudoun Co. Va., and nursed by members of his family, where he died, and was buried in the Foley graveyard on a high hill on their farm. He was wounded Aug. 28, 1862.

5. Martha Jane, born Dec. 19, 1844; married M. J. Meyerhoeffer. Both deceased. No issue.

6. John Calvin Hooke, born March 19, 1847, died July 27, 1923, at his residence in Pomona, California. Belonged to Co. A, 3rd Bat. Reserves (Chrisman's Boy Co.); mustered into service April 3, 1864; saw active service. Married first Emma Van Lear. Issue —1. Lena, dec. 2. Hattie Van Lear, residence, Washington, D. C. 3. Zarifa Bell, married O. Fred Carson,—issue, Howard Carson, residence, 3508 O. Street N. W., Washington, D. C. 4. Clyde Kemper, dec. 5. Infant, dec. Married second Mrs. Margaret Hepler Corder; issue, Lucy Maria Hepler, married Alfred Oakey; issue; Los Angeles, California. 2. Walker Williams, dec.

7. Rebecca Margaret, born Jan. 8, 1849, died Dec. 6, 1854.

8. Lucy Frances, born Feb. 5, 1851; residence Broadway, Va.; married Wm. D. Rodgers, Confederate soldier, dec. No issue.

9. James Walker, born Feb. 5, 1853, died 1912; married Dec. 27, 1885, Margaret Armentrout, born Dec. 27, 1858, dec. Infants dead. (1) Wm. Robert, born March 10, 1889, married Dulcie Collier. Issue Helen E., residence Penn Laird, Va.

2nd. Charles Marvin, born April 13, 1892; residence Penn Laird, Va. Married Ona Taylor, dec. Issue: 1st, Loraine; 2nd, Charles Jr.; 3rd, Ellwood. He has remarried.

10. Emma Melsina, born Feb. 24, 1855, died Oct. 16, 1861.

11. Charles McClung, born March 6, 1857, died Oct. 20, 1861.

12. Harvey Samuel, born March 28, 1860; residence, Roanoke, Va.; principal of Belmont School; married Sept. 3, 1902, Mary Lupton of Harrisonburg, Va. Issue—Alberta Lupton. She is a graduate of Randolph-Macon College, Lynchburg, Va., and is a teacher in the Roanoke schools.

13. Laura Bell, born Nov. 27, 1863, died April 4, 1903. Married Oct. 6, 1887, Arthur Lee Kemper, born Jan. 14, 1866, son

of Edward Stevens Kemper and Susan M. (Craig) Kemper of Rockingham Co. Va. Issue—1st, Audrey Lee, born Aug. 15, 1888; married Sept. 23, 1914, Philip Andrew Spence (son of Joseph M. and Sarah J. (Simmerman) Spence). Issue—1st, Philip Kemper Spence, born Oct. 12, 1915; 2nd, Laura Jean Audrey Spence, born May 9, 1923.

    2. Bertha Hooke, born November 25, 1889, died Sept. 28, 1893.

    3. Arthur Walker, born Oct. 23, 1891. Residence, Wytheville, Va. Former Chief Petty Officer in U. S. Merchant Marines. Served near the close of the World War.

    4. Harvey Ribble, born June 29, 1893; married Helen Floyd. Issue—1st, Virginia Lee; 2nd, James Authur; 3rd, Mary Elizabeth; 4th, Laura Hooke; 5th, Frances Craig; 6th, Harvey Ribble Jr.; 7th, Charles Edward; 8th, Helen. Residence Wytheville, Va. Merchant.

    5. Laura Marie, born March 13, 1897; sometime connected with the Veterans Bureau, Washington, D. C.

    11. Sarah Campbell, born Aug. 28, 1819; died June 20, 1847. Married James C. Williams, Sept. 20, 1838, by Jas. W. Phillips. Issue—

III. Ann, born Sept. 27, 1821, died March 5, 1899. Married Lewis F. Meyerhoeffer. Issue.

IV. Elizabeth Jane, born Sept. 1, 1823, died Aug. 23, 1887. Married Robt. K. Wilson, grandson of Rev. Wm. Wilson; served in C. S. A.; lost an arm at Gettysburg in 1863. Issue.

V. Rebecca, born Oct. 14, 1825, died Feb. 8, 1900. Married Rev. Samuel Filler. Issue.

VI. Martha C., born May 11, 1828, died July 30, 1907. Married John S. Meyerhoeffer, Jan. 21, 1851, by John E. Mapey. Issue.

VII. John Hooke, born April 23, 1830, died July 2, 1854; not married.

VIII. Lucy Margaret, born Oct. 19, 1835, died March 5, 1905; married Sept. 6, 1855, Charles A. Van Lear. Issue.

(B) George Hooke, the brother of Wm. Hooke, Sr., born Oct. 1750 or 1751 (as he states in application for pension); but if he was the son as we suppose of Capt. Robert Hooke, Sr., he was born near Feb. 1, 1746, according to Rev. John Craig's baptismal register. If he missed it by 4 years, he may have forgotten the exact date, and stated 1750 as did so many Rev. soldiers in their applications, so as to be sure to be 20 years of age or old enough for service. Died in Monroe County, Indiana, March 7, 1835. He married Jane or Jean Bleakley (born Mar. 17, 1762) Jan. 7, 1789, dau. of Thomas Bleakley (consent); surety, John Campbell; by Rev. Wm. Wilson, Rockingham Co. Va. Their names appear in a deed dated July 6, 1812, from Fleming Co. Ky., between John Hooke of Augusta Co. and George and Jane his wife for land they had formerly lived on in Augusta Co. Va. Deeded to James H.

Revolutionary War Pension claim W. 10112, Washington, D. C. states that, "Geo. H. was reared in Augusta Co. Va., about two years prior to the Rev. War, he went to Guilford Co. N. C., where he enlisted in 1776, and served two years as sergeant in Capt. Nelson's Company. In the Fourth N. C. Reg., was in the battle of Princeton, and was discharged May 7, 1778."

He returned to Augusta Co. Va., and after sometime he enlisted and served three months in the Va. Militia. Was in the Portsmouth Campaign. He also served three months in the Va. Militia at Yorktown; the officers in said two tours not named.

In 1801 he moved to Fleming Co. Ky. where he lived until 1830, when he went to Monroe Co. Indiana, where he was allowed a pension on his application executed Nov. 23, 1834.

The widow Jean was allowed a pension on her application executed Feb 19, 1841, while a resident of Monroe Co. Indiana.

In 1776 George Hooke's brother, James Hooke, was a lieutenant in Capt. David Stephenson's company, Col. Muhlenberg's Va. Regiment. There is no claim for pension on file on account of the services of said Lt. James Hooke. War Department No. E. S. S. O. R. D. says that "James Hooke served in the Rev. War as an ensign in Capt. David Stephenson's company, 8th Va. Regiment, Commanded by Col. Abraham Bowman. He was commissioned March 16, 1777, and resigned April 21, 1778."

Issue of George and Jean Hooke—1st, Ann R. A. H., born Sept. 26, 1789; married April 7, 1812, Gibson Baker; residence Brown County, Ohio; born July 22, 1790. 2nd, James Hooke, born Nov. 28, 1790; married April 4, 18—, Betty Patton. 3rd, Thomas Hooke; residence Davies County, Ind.; born Oct. 11, 1793; married April 21, 1830, Jean ————. Thomas was deceased on April 25, 1854. 4th, Betsy Hooke, born March 30, 1796; married Dec. 12, 1816, David Baker. 5th, John Hooke, born May 8, 1798; married March 28, 1822, Margaret White. 6th, Jane Hooke, born May 18, 1800; married John Fife (Phyffe). 7th, George or Geo. W. Hooke, born May 18, 1800 (twin to Jane); married Sept. 13, 1836, Sarah ————. Deceased before Aug. 17, 1844. 8th, John C. Hooke, born Jan. 11, 1803; married Sept. 7, 1826, Sarah Campbell. Will probated June 25, 1868. 9th, Rebecca W. Hooke, born Feb. 13, 1806; married Feb. 19, 1823, Andrew Vannoy. 10th, William D. Hooke, born Dec. 18, 1808.

Virginia State Library Notes: Rejected claim (for insufficient evidence): "August 17, 1844, John C. Hooke and David Baker made application for land bounty due their father and father-in-law. George HOOKE was before his death a pensioner of the United States. He heard that there was land due the soldiers. He then lived and served in Va. in County of Augusta, at the time of his enlistment, and entering service and served six years. He was entitled to 100 acres. The heirs of Col. George W. Hooke, died late of Monroe Co. Ind. The widow Jane received $120.00 per year.

George Hooke had a brother James H., who they believed was a Capt. in the Rev. War. Jas. H. lived and resided in Augusta Co. Va., at the time he entered service. James Hooke died about 1816, in Va. He gave his land bounty to his brother Geo. before his death. Capt. James never married and had no known issue. Capt. James served at the end of the Rev. entered service under a call, never sold or parted with his claim.

"The widow, Jane is yet alive, and the widow of George Minor-hears of Col. Geo. W. Hooke.

"John C. Hooke is Admr. of Geo. W. Hooke's children, also David Rodgers, Aug. 17th, 1844."

Virginia State Library record, Jas. Hooke, Lt. Inf. received of Geo. Hooke, March 21, 1785,—54—2—0.

Data furnished by Mr. Charles Hinkle, Clerk of Court, Bloomington, Monroe Co., Indiana, April 17th, 1924.

Will of John C. Hooke devises to his wife Sarah the east one-half fractional lot No. 21, in the town of Bloomington, Monroe Co. Ind. He also wills all money, rents, etc., to her as long as she lives. At her death he wills the same or what is left to William H. Stout, whom he has raised from infancy. June 25, 1868.

Thomas Hooke vs. Wallace Hight. Geo. W. Hooke vs. John C. Hooke, Jas. Jackson, guardian. Wallace Hight was gdn. of the estate of the minor heirs of Thomas Hooke, dec., on April 25, 1854. He asked permission to sell estate in Davies County, Ind. The real estate was sold to Oldham Trotter. The heirs were Charlotte M. Hooke and Sarah J. Hooke.

John C. Hooke (adm. papers taken out), appointed gdn. to David Rodgers and Aquilla Rodgers.

Eliza Ann and Martha Jane Hooke minor heirs of Geo. W. Hooke.

(C) John Hooke Sr., brother of Wm. Hooke Sr., served in Capt. Givens's company Rev. War. Ref. Court records, Staunton, Va., and Boogher's "Gleanings of Va. History." Died Nov. 2, 1824. John was not mentioned in the 1804 will, yet we are not certain that the Robert of the 1804 will was Capt. Robert Sr., and portions of the will were burned. Col. Hooke says that William Sr. and six brothers came from Ireland to America. He seemed so sure of his grandfather being pure Scotch; said Hooke was pronounced like Scotch "Huke." Capt. Robert Sr. says that he brought his son William from Ireland, thus he would be pure Scotch. He may have been an infant in arms. Esther was baptised Dec. 23, 1740, after settling in Rock. Co. Va., as were the other children.

The family tells of a song, or ditty, which Wm. Sr. sang to his grandson, Col. Wm. W. Hooke, as follows:

> "Willie Walker had a coo (cow),
> Black and white about the moo,
> Open the gate and let her thru,
> For she is Willie Walker's coo."

File 302, Staunton, Va., was a long drawn out suit between John Sr.'s heirs and others. This suit gives a great deal of information concerning the Hooke Family. He left 198 acres in Augusta Co. Va. (adjoining John Walker, Adam Long, David Golladay and Joseph Moon). He never married and had been a cripple (probably wounded in the Rev. War) for a number of years before his death. He was indebted to Robt. Hooke (his brother William's son) for board, washing and lodging from March 1, 1820, to November 2, 1824.

He willed one-half of his property to his grand-niece, Mary Ann Bleakley, wife of Alexander Bleakley; the other half (share and share alike) of his property to Jane, Martha and Rebecca, daughters of Wm. Hooke; Jane and Ann, daughters of his brother Robt. Hooke; Jane and Rebecca, daughters of his brother Geo. Hooke; Jane, daughter of Elijah Hooke; and Sally, daughter of Robert, William's son (Sarah Campbell). James Addison Hooke was the son of his brother Robert. Witnesses were Capt. Samuel Linn, Robt. Hooke, and Mary Ann Huston.

Deposition of Catherine Graham in home at Port Republic, Va., lived six years and two months in Robert's home, the funeral expenses were paid entirely by him and his family. John Hooke left no personal estate.

Robert Hooke paid James Hooke Sr. $80.00. Jennett Hooke said so. Her brother James and Martha Hooke also said so. Jeannett also said so. Major Golladay testifies.

John Bleakley Sr. was living with Robert Hooke at time of paying note for $70.00 to Jas. Hooke. Depositions taken July 12, 1828. Samuel H. Lewis attended four hours in taking depositions above.

Jane, Martha, Ann and Rebecca Hooke, daughters of Wm. Hooke, dec., are all alive and reside in Rockingham County, Va.

Ann Hooke, daughter of Robt. Hooke, the elder, dec., departed this life intestate, unmarried and without issue, before John Hooke (her uncle) her interest being one-tenth. Her parents died before her. She was survived by her sister Jane, and her brother James, and the descendants of two deceased sisters, Mary Ann Bleakley, daughter of her sister Mary, and the three children of her sister, Christine, viz: Martha, William and Jane Hatfield, who had removed many years ago to Indiana.

Since death of John Hooke above, Jane Hooke, daughter of Robert Hooke, the elder, had died, intestate, unmarried and without issue. Her interest to said land, under the will, lapsed to her surviving brother, James Hooke of Rock. Co. Va., together with the descendants of 2 deceased sisters, Mary and Christine. The devises, Jane and Rebecca, daughters of Geo. Hooke, are married and removed from the Commonwealth. Jane married John Fife and Rebecca married Andrew Vannoy. Jane, dau. of Elijah, married

Alexander Walker, moved away; but his wife resides at present in Augusta County, Va., October 1830.

From file 302, Staunton Va. Alexander Walker, Jane, his wife (dau. of Elijah Hooke), Martha, Wm. and Jane Hatfield (heirs of Christina and John Hatfield). John Fife, Jane his wife, Andrew Vannoy and Rebecca his wife were non-residents of Virginia on Aug. 30, 1830.

Alexander Bleakley died three months before Nov. 24, 1859. O. B. Rock. Court Records.

Alexander Walker and Robert Hooke, bound in the sum of $50.00, Nov. 1, 1824; Alexander Walker guardian of Jane Hooke, orphan of Elijah Hooke.

John Bleakley made oath that he moved to Capt. Robert Hooke's residence in the fall of 1817, at which time John Hooke Sr. was living there. August 25th, 1832.

(D) Robert Hooke, brother of Wm. Hooke, spoken of by Col. Hooke in his manuscript, also named in File 302, Staunton, Va. Col. Hooke says that Robert owned what was afterwards known as the Joseph Beery farm adjoining the old Hooke plantation, "Slate Hill," on the east. Probably died before 1806.

Robert Hooke served in Capt. Hevitt's company 1777, Rev. War. Court records, Staunton, Va. (Court Martial Records)

Col. Hooke names the four daughters of Robert, as follows: 1st, Mary—Issue: Mary Ann Bleakley, wife of Alexander Bleakley. 2nd, Jane, died near 1824. 3rd, Ann (died before 1824). 4th, Catherine. File 302 names fifth, Christina married John Hatfield, Nov. 25th, 1790. Issue: Martha, William and Jane Hatfield. Removed to Indiana many years before 1824. 6th, James Addison, served in 58th Va. Vols. War 1812, under his cousin, Capt. Robert Hooke. Ref. Wayland's History. Married Jane Campbell, daughter of William Campbell (dec.), June 19, 1810. William Campbell, surety, Rock. Co. Va. He adopted a nephew of his (probably Jermiah), and they located in Logan County, Ohio. One Jermiah left descendants in Ohio and Missouri.

(E) James Hooke. Col. Hooke says that he was a brother of Wm. Sr., and the only thing to disapprove it is the statement of Geo. Hooke's (Monroe Co. Ind.) children. See Rejected claim, Va. State Library in which they said "That their uncle, Capt. James Hooke, died 1816, was not married and left no issue." This claim was not allowed because of insufficient evidence, and as the Geo. Hooke family had been away from Virginia for such a long while it is reasonable that they might have lost sight of their relations and possibly had not known of James Hooke's family. Then again James (E) who was the ancestor of the Port Republic Hooke family, may have been of another family, and not been Lieut. James of Pension claim W. 10112, and not the brother of Wm. Sr. The Hooke family claimed that the three Roberts were first cousins, that is, "Robin" of Port Republic, Capt. Robt. War 1812, and Robert Scott Hooke of Highland Co. Va.

Col. Hooke names the children of James (E) as follows: James, John, Robert, Elizabeth, Mary and Ann. James (E) owned the place afterwards known as the William Rodeffer and Solmon Beery farms. James (E) may have been the son of Elijah or Elisha, as we know nothing of their issue, with the exception of Jane Walker, dau. of Elijah, who is spoken of in File 302, if he was not the son of Capt. Robert Hooke. One Elijah Hooke married Ann Allen, dau. of Richard Allen, May 16th, 1803.

Deed among the burnt records, Rock. Co. Va.

"William Byrd, from Mary Hooke and James Hooke, Sept. 1st, 1830, $1,552.50, 103 acres, same tract or parcel of land devised to them by his father, James Hooke, in his last will and testament, to have and to hold, the parcel of land adjoining lands of Robert H. Conrad, Rodheiffer, Benjaman Thompson and others." This will has never been found, probably burned during Federal raids.

D. B. No. 11, page 767, March 18, 1765, Robert Hooke to James Hooke, £5. 200 acres on south side of the land said Hooke now lives on, patented 1st of October, 1747. Teste, Wm. Hooke, Mathew McDowel, Samuel Scott. Delivered to Jas. Scott. Augusta Court, 1773. Judge Chalkley. Possibly Capt. Robt. Sr. gave James this land when he reached his majority or possibly 18 years of age. If so, this gives his birth date as 1747.

James Hooke was a soldier in Capt. Hevitts's company of militia; Court Martial Records, Staunton, Va.

Hening's "Statutes at Large" mentions James Hooke as being a Rev. soldier from Augusta County, Va.

Chalkley Vol. 3, Will Book 2, page 397, Oct. 22, 1783, Wm. Hooke relinquishes to George Hooke his right to administer on the estate of James Hooke. Teste, George Frazier and Samuel Hill.

Issue of James (E) Hooke, 1. James (of deed to Wm. Byrd) went west, probably Ohio. It is believed that he died unmarried.

2. John married Ann Chandler, dau. of Samuel Chandler Jr. (dec.) before 1830. See Deed Book 9, page 556, Harrisonburg, Va., for deed which John Hooke gave selling his daughter's and deceased wife's interest in the Chandler estate, September 13, 1830. Said John and dau. Mary Catherine moved to Freemont, Ohio. In a letter to his cousin Capt. Robert Hooke from Freemont, Ohio, he speaks of his dau. Mary having had twin babies. Letter dated Aug. 28, 1851.

3. Robert or "Robin" of Port Republic, Va., built a fine old colonial brick mansion on the North River, which is occupied by his grandson, Grover S. Hooke. Robin Hooke was born Sept. 5, 1780, died Jan. 25, 1858; married first Sarah Beard, Aug. 16, 1815; wife and infant died. Married second, Dec. 24, 1821, Elizabeth Fisher, dau. of Abraham and Elizabeth Fisher, born Aug. 21, 1801, died Dec. 13, 1882. Robert or Robin Hooke enlisted and served as

lieutenant in Capt. Adam Harnsberger's company, Va. Militia, from Aug. 30, 1814, to Nov. 19, 1814, Rock. Co. Va., War 1812. Ref. Pension claim widow certificate 10375 Washington, D. C.

Issue of Lieut. Robert and Elizabeth Hooke:

1. Sarah Beard, born Oct. 12, 1822, died Dec. 14, 1892; married David Trissel, Dark County, Ohio. Son, Randolph.

2. Elizabeth Louisa, born Oct. 19, 1825.

3. James Lewis, born May 25, 1827.

4. Mary M., born June 11, 1829, died April 2, 1890.

5. Abraham Scott, born Dec. 14, 1830, died April 20, 1912. Married S. Frances Null, October 29, 1865. Issue.

Sergeant A. Scott Hooke with his two brothers, Geo. W. K. and Robert J., were in the War Between the States, Company C, 6th Va. Cavalry. His brothers died during the war of typhoid fever at Charlottesville, Va.

6. Archibald H. Hooke, born April 20, 1824, died March 22, 1877. Married Thaney Mills, Dayton, Ohio. Issue—1. Robert W. Hooke, Brookville, Ohio. R. R. No. 4. Has one daughter, Rosella Hooke. 2. Cynthia, 3. George, 4. Olive.

7. Rebecca J., born October 1, 1832; married Mr. Batman. No issue.

8. Robert J., born April 1, 1835, died Nov. 22, 1861.

9. Amanda A., born Nov. 29, 1839.

10. George W. K., born Feb. 21, 1842, died Oct. 15, 1863.

11. Cynthia M., born March 25, 1837.

In a Chancery suit, 1840, in Staunton, Va., Lt. Robert Hooke signs himself "Jr."

4. Elizabeth probably went west with her brother James.

5. Mary (of deed to Wm. Byrd). It is thought that she accompanied her brother James and sister Elizabeth to Ohio or Mo. They went on horseback; were two weeks on the road.

6. Ann married Isaac Thompson, Aug. 7, 1807; probably went west. It is not known whether she had issue. The will of Robin Hooke is recorded in Harrisonburg, Va., court records; also a chancery suit, after his death. The writer has more data concerning the Port Republic family.

William and James Hooke were soldiers in the French and Indian War 1758. "Gleanings of Va. History." Chalkley P. 101, Nov. 17, 1762, James Hooke qualified ensign of militia.

(F) George Hooke, the ancestor of the Highland Co. Va. family. His widow, Mary Ann, and sons Jas. W. (Miller Jim), Elisha, Robert and Samuel, on March 27, 1830, sold 202 acres of land to Rodham Kemper, located near Cross Keys, Rock. Co. Va., being a part of the 400-acre tract granted to Robert Hooke, dec., on the 13th day of June, 1743; "relation there to will more fully appear."

Deed Book 7, page 126, Rock. Co. Va., Sept. 16, 1825, Elijah Hooke sold to his brother Samuel all his interest in the land of their father, Geo. Hooke, dec. The will is spoken of, and the money to be paid their sisters under this will. This will has never been found, and must have been destroyed during the Federal raids.

It is possible that George (F) was the son of Capt. Robert Hooke Sr., or the son of Elijah or Elisha. Col. Hooke says "Elisha was the father of Robert of Highland Co. Va.," but it is proven above that George was the father; yet Elijah (possibly called Elisha) or possibly Elisha was the father of George (F). It could be possible that Capt. Robert Sr. named two sons by the same name, as did George (B) of Indiana; and twins occurred in both George (B) and Capt. Robert Sr.'s families. This may have been some old Scotch custom, of naming two sons alike, when twins occurred in the family; however, if the wills of Geo. (F) and James (E) ever come to light they will likely prove their parentage. So far, we have not found any trace of Capt. Robert Sr. having had a son named Elisha. He could have had this son, who died or moved away, and was lost track of. It has been stated that an Elisha appeared in N. C. records.

Rockingham court records, Dec. 2, 1797: Robt. Hooke and Elijah Hooke his son and Richard Allen rent of land for 5 years, part of land said Robert and Elijah live on (his son Elijah), or being a piece of cleared land, with a small meadow adjoining the same, and being part of cleared piece that George Hooke formerly possessed, but now belonging to said Elijah Hooke as by "division made by said Robt. Hooke, father of Elijah and George Hooke."

Minute Booke No. 10, Rock. Co.: On June 30, 1823, an appraisement bill of the estate of George Hooke, dec., was returned and ordered to be recorded in said book. This is likely to be Geo. (F).

Land Book (of Rock. Co. Va.) for 1800: Robert Hooke, 198 acres; George Hooke, 202 acres; James Hooke, 200 acres; Robert Hooke Jr., 170 acres; Wm. Hooke, 253½ acres.

It could be possible that Capt. Robert Hooke Sr. had brothers to follow him to Virginia, and the early deaths recorded of the Hookes could have been of them or nephews or grandsons of Capt. Robt. Hooke Sr.

The following dates of the births of Geo. (F) Hookes's children were taken from an old Bible (published in Edinburgh, Scotland, 1793), owned by Mr. Sam H. W. Byrd, of Bridgewater, Va., a descendant of Jane Hooke Lite:

1. Jane Hooke, born Oct. 1, 1782; married Feb. 28, 1805, John Lite or Light, born April 9, 1771. Issue.

2. Esther, born April 6, 1785; married Samuel Harrison, Feb. 5, 1810. (Samuel Harrison belonged to the Harrisonburg, Va. family of that name.) Issue.

3. James W., born Feb. 17, 1790 (called Miller Jim); married Sarah Pirkey, April 17, 1811. Suit Hooke and wife vs. Pirkey, No. 19, Rock. records, shows that Sarah was the dau. of John

Pirkey, who made his will in 1794. Sarah was born July 15, 1791, as stated in the suit.

From suit No. 26, it shows that James and Sarah were non-residents of Va. in 1868. They settled in the west, probably in Mo., perhaps in Saline Co. Col. Hooke says that after the death of James's wife he married a widow lady of Rockbridge Co. Va., who lived only a few years. Then James and son Jacob went to Saline County, Missouri. Jacob died a few years later, but James was alive in 1875. (?)

One Jacob married Mary Hawkins, Sept. 19, 1850, by John Hopnokle.

4. Elisha, born Jan. 6, 1792, married Jane ————; went west, probably to Texas. This is probably the Elisha Hooke of the 5th Cor. in Capt. David Mathews's Company, 116th Reg. Va. Vol., War 1812. Wayland's History. An Elisha appears in the N. C. records.

5. Robert Scott Hooke, born Oct. 28, 1793, married Polly Erwin (Irvin), dau. of Benjaman Erwin, April 21, 1814. They settled in Highland Co. Va. Issue. See Morton's "History of Highland Co. Va." Robert S. Hooke acquired about 2,000 acres of land. He and his sons built fine colonial mansions, and they dispensed hospitality on a large scale. Robert S. was chief justice at one period, and he and his family were long holders of public offices. He dropped the final "E" of the Hooke name. Among his descendants is Miss Virginia Cobb, of Sapulpa, Okla., 211 S. Water St., who has compiled a history of the Highland Co. Va. Hooke family.

From pension claim, Sur. certificate, 15495, War 1812, Robert S. Hooke enlisted at Nicholas Tavern, Rockingham Co. Va., Sept. 2, 1814, as a private in Capt. Snapp's Company of Va. Militia, and was discharged Nov. 2, 1814.

There is a tradition in the Robert Scott Hooke family that their ancestor lived to be 101 years old, and that he walked one mile to visit his son on his birthday.

Another tradition is that their family was related to Gen. Winfield Scott, and that on one occasion one of the Hookes who resembled him (possibly Robert Scott Hooke) gave an order to the soldiers, who were so fooled by his resemblance to Gen. Scott that the order was carried out, probably War of 1812.

6. Elijah, born Nov. 28, 1795, married Phebe Reeves, dau. of William Reeves, dec. Married Sept. 12, 1818; moved elsewhere.

7. George, born July 2, 1797; nothing further known of him.

8. Samuel, born June 4, 1800, married Malinda Parks. Col. Hooke says "that Samuel's mother married an old man by the name of Warner, and that Samuel lived with him until October, when his mother died." A descendant of Samuel is Mr. James A. Hooke, 308 City Hall, St. Louis, Mo.

The records of Rockingham and Augusta counties, Virginia, show that one Geo. Hooke was married to Mary Warner, June 22, 1791.

The author has done a vast amount of research work concerning the Hooke family (from 1066 to 1927), in general, and has collected a great deal of material, which cannot be included in an article of this size. "The Hooke Family History," by Mr. James W. Hooke, New Haven, Conn., Blake and Valley Streets, treats of the family from its origin to the present time, and it is to be hoped those interested will consult his history, so as to go back to the founder and earlier history.

The motto of the English coat of arms is, "Be what you seem to be." Ref. Cong. Library, Washington, D. C., and Mr. James W. Hooke's History.

The Irish coat of arms is from No. 36, Page 427, O'Hart's "Irish Ped.": Wolf's head, forked tongue, blue stripe, red, black, red, black, red, b. blue, pale blue, bright red.

The author wishes to thank Dr. Wayland for the courtesy of publication; also to thank all who have helped in this work. And we hope to hear from all who are interested in any way, especially to obtain new or corrected data.

HISTORY AND REMINISCENCES OF THE CONNELLY AND WALKER FAMILIES

By Wm. W. Hooke, 1900

John Walker Sr. of Augusta Co. Va. married Miss Sarah Connelly of Augusta Co. Va. The Walker and Connelly families immigrated to America about the middle of the 17th century. They were Scotch-Irish Protestants, and in church connection Presbyterians. Alexander (Arthur) Connelly had four sons and one daughter, named Arthur, Alexander, Samuel, Williamson and Sarah.

Arthur was killed by Indians to procure his rifle, which he had refused to sell to them.

Alexander rode under a tree for shelter in a thunder storm. Lightning struck the tree, killing man and horse.

Samuel moved to Kentucky, married and raised a family.

Williamson went to Mississippi and engaged in surveying land for the government. He never married that his relatives knew of. Those Connellys were back to Virginia to visit relatives, the writer recollects them, about the year 1834. The writer also recollects seeing his old great-grandmother Connelly when she was nearly 90 years old, and living in her daughter's family.

John Walker Sr. and Sarah (Connelly) his wife raised eleven children, to-wit: Elizabeth, Alexander, John, Jane, Robert, Pollie, Sallie, Thomas, Patsie, James and Rebecca.

Elizabeth married Captain Robert Hooke, of Rockingham Co. Va., who had commanded a company of riflemen in the war of 1812.

The said Robert Hooke and Elizabeth his wife raised a family of eight children: two boys and six girls, viz: William Walker, Sarah Campbell, Ann Elizabeth, Jane, Rebecca, John, Martha Catherine and Lucy Margaret.

Alexander Walker (1794-1865) married Hannah Hinton, Dec. 2, 1830, of Rockingham Co. Va. They had seven children who lived to be grown, viz: Benjaman Franklin, Sarah Jane, John, Elizabeth, Hannah Mary, James A. and Silas H.

Dr. Benjaman Franklin married Mary Huston, daughter of Col. Archibald Huston of Rockingham Co. Va., by whom he had one child named Archie. His wife died some years later and the Dr. married a Miss Wright, had two children by her, lived only a few years, and he died.

Sarah Jane married Thomas Crawford, had one child, and lived but a few weeks and died.

John went to California to the gold diggings, returned broken down in health. He then went to Texas for a change of climate. Coming home he only got to Cincinnati and died there.

Lizzie married David Craig, had two children named Alexander, (better known as Sandy) and William. Sandy married Sue Butler, no children. Will married Miss Brownlee, no children. He is dead, as is also his father. Lizzie Craig is living.

Hannah Mary Walker not married (dec.).

Gen. James A. Walker married Sally Poage (daughter of Major Wm. and Peggy Allen Poage, a descendant of Gen. James Allen, Rev. soldier and officer. Another descendant of theirs was the late Hon. Waller S. Poage of Wytheville, Va.) of Augusta Co. Va. Issue—1. Alexander, 2. Frank, 3. James, 4. Allen, 5. Mrs. Margaret Jordan, Cincinnati, Ohio. Issue—1. Mrs. Annie Tiffany, Cincinnati, Ohio, 2. Mrs. Willie McFarland, Florence, Alabama; has issue; 3. Russell, 4. Marguerite, 5. Walker; has issue. 6. (dau. of Gen. Walker) Mrs. Willie W. Caldwell, Walker Hall, Roanoke, Va. See "The Abridged Compendium of American Genealogy," page 44. Educated at Mary Baldwin Seminary, Staunton, Va.; author: Donald McElroy—Scotch Irishman; also other romances. Past pres. Va. Federation Women's Clubs; mem. D. A. R., U. D. C. Residence: "Walker Hall," Roanoke, Va. Issue—1. Virginia, 2. Mrs. Sarah Butler, 3. James A. Walker Caldwell.

Gen. James Alexander Walker (1832-1901), Va. Mil. Inst. '52, Brig. Gen. Stonewall Brigade C. S. A., lawyer, lt. gov. of Va., mem. 54th and 55th Congresses. "The Abridged Compendium of American Genealogy" (First Families of America), page 44, says that Gen. Walker descended from John Walker who went from Scotland to Ireland, and to Penn. 1720, settled in Augusta Co. 1740. Mrs. E. Siggins White, in her "Walker Genealogy," page 643, says that Gen. Walker's great-grandfather Alexander, was a descendant of John Walker of Wigton, Scotland. (See sketch of Gen. Walker in the Richmond weekly *Dispatch* of Oct. 24, 1901.) Alexander Walker above mentioned had, so history states, 21 children, most of whom grew to manhood and womanhood and settled in Kentucky, Alabama, Missouri, Illinois and other states of the Union. Of these children the names of only two are known to us, John and Jane. John married Sarah Connelly. They were the grandparents of General Walker. He was made captain of a fine volunteer company at the beginning of the war; was promoted to the rank of lieutenant-colonel in April, 1861. In March 1862 he was promoted brigadier-general of the Stonewall Brigade. At the "Bloody Angle" in May 1864 he was severely wounded. In July following, his arm yet in a sling, he was put in command of the reserve troops guarding the line of the Richmond and Southside railroads, which roads were the feeders of General Lee's army.

In January 1865 he reported to General Lee for active service, and was assignd to the command of Early's Division, which he surrendered at Appomattox.

General Walker was with General Jackson in the famous Virginia campaign, and participated in all the battles of the Army of Northern Virginia. He was present at Bull Run, Front Royal, Winchester, Cross Keys, Port Republic, Gaines's Mill, Malvern Hill,

Cedar Run, Second Bull Run (Manassas), Ox Hill, Fredericksburg, Second Winchester, Gettysburg, Payne's Farm, Mine Run, Wilderness, Spotsylvania Court House, Fort Stedman, Petersburg, Sailor's Creek and Appomattox.

In 1869 he was elected to the Virginia House of Delegates from Pulaski County, serving two terms in that body. In 1877 he was elected Lieutenant-Governor of Virginia and served until 1881. He attended the three National Conventions of 1876, 1896, and 1900.

Silas Walker married Miss Laura Boon of Rockingham Co. Va. No living issue.

Jane, daughter of John and Sarah Walker, married Nathan Huston of Rock. Co. Va., when both past middle age. No issue.

John Walker never married; lived to be 83 or 84 years old and died at Silas Walker's home.

Robert Walker married Pollie Wonderlick, a sister of Gen. John D. Imboden's mother. Six children, namely: Susan Jane, Sally, John, Martha, Alphus and James. After their children were all about grown the parents and the children moved to Albemarle County. A year or two afterwards the mother came to Augusta Co. to visit her sister. She walked into the garden where there were bees kept. One honeybee stung her in the face about the temple, causing death in a few hours. The father and Susan Jane died soon after this. Sallie married Mr. Ballow of Nelson Co. Va. John married Daniel Murray's daughter. Mary Martha married Henry Clifton and all of them moved to Missouri. John died about ten years ago. Sallie and two of her daughters were once since on a visit to friends in Rockingham County. John's wife and one daughter were on a visit here from Missouri.

Sallie Walker, daughter of John Walker Sr., married Zacheriah Johnson of Augusta Co.; had five children, namely: James, John, Hester, Margaret Ann and Zachie. John lives in Madison County, Va. James and Zachie are dead. Hester married Sheriff Moore of Albemarle County. He died before the Civil War, and she married Henry Forner. No issue. Margaret Ann married a Mr. Melhorn; had two children; he died. She then married Mr. Peck and moved to Arkansas. Pollie Walker married Thomas Frame. Issue—five children, namely: H. John, Allen, Nancy Jane, Sarah Margaret, and Walker. They moved to Indiana, afterwards to Missouri. The parents both died a few years afterwards. The grandfather of the little girls, after their mother's death, brought them to Virginia. Nancy J. died a young woman grown. Sarah M. became Robert K. Wilson's first wife, and lived less than one year after their marriage.

Patsie Walker married John Johnson, had two children; one died quite an infant, not being named; the other daughter, known as Pett, became the wife of Oscar Perkey; after the war moved to Kansas. She died in 1890, leaving four children, all grown.

Major James Walker married Margaret Crawford (familiarly known as Aunt Peggy). No issue. She died a good many years ago. The Major never married again.

Thomas Walker, son of John and Sarah Walker, born Feb. 26, 1803, died 1866. Married Eliza Bourland, born Sept. 13, 1813, died Feb. 5, 1869. Their children were: 1. Mary Margaret, born Dec. 9, 1831, died May 6, 1866. Mary Margaret married John Whitmore; died without issue.

2. James Bourland, born March 27, 1833, died June 5, 1834.

3. George Samuel, born Mar. 22, 1836, died March 13, 18—. He married Margaret Malinda Huston in 1860. Their children were 1. Ann Huston Walker, married Mr. George St. Clair in 1891; residence Tazewell, Va. Mr. St. Clair is president of the Jewell Ridge Coal Corporation of Tazewell. Their children are: 1. Margaret Huston, who married Mr. Robert H. Moore of Tazewell, Va., in 1920. Their children are Robert H. Moore Jr., 4 years old, and George Walker St. Clair, age 3 years. 2. Katherine Bell, married Thomas H. Settle of Flint Hill, Rappahannock County, Va., in 1918. No Issue. 3. Samuel Huston, married Miss Janet McClure Hardy of Willmington, Del., on July 1, 1927.

2. William Bourland Walker, son of Dr. George Samuel and Malinda Walker, married Lucy Ashly Henry, daughter of Major Randolph Henry of Tazewell, Va. Issue—1. Margaret Henry, married Mr. Cochran Graves, son of John Temple Graves, 1925. Issue, Cochran Jr. 2. Ann Byrd Walker, married Aylette Coleman. No issue.

3. Miss Lucy Custer Walker, Tazewell, Va., daughter of Dr. George Walker above, furnished the dates and some other items concerning this family on Nov. 3, 1927.

4. Sarah Ann, daughter of Thomas and Eliza (Bourland) Walker, married Samuel Whitmore, brother to John above. Two children. After his death his widow married Rev. Osborne Ross. One daughter Girtie, who married a gentleman of Page County, Va.

5. Eliza Virginia, born Nov. 4, 1840, died Jan. 27, 18—.

6. Martha, married Stuart Crawford. Three children.

7. John Thomas, born May 14, 1846; still living in Texas. He married Miss Sally Crawford. No issue.

8. Rebecca Jane, born Nov. 16, 1848; died 46 years ago. Not married.

9. Amanda Melsene, born March 6, 18—; died about 12 years ago.

10. William Bourland, born April 19, 18—; died 1912. Not married.

11. Nannie McCulock, born Nov. 24, 1855; still living in Staunton, Va. She married Alexander Turk. One daughter, Mary Huston Turk.

12. Alexander, born Dec. 14, 1857; died seven years ago. He married Annie Kyle, daughter of Dr. Robinson. Five children.

13. Nellie Malina married Gilbert Zirkle of Page County, Va. Issue—six children.

"Rebecca Walker married Charles McClung of Greenbrier County, West Virginia. Eight children, as follows:

1. Thomas Walker, not married.
2. Sally Jane, married Griffin Rader of Greenbrier County, West Virginia. Seven children, three sons and four daughters, including Mrs. Laura Yager of Harrisonburg, Virginia.
3. James Crawford, married Molly Rosson of Louisa County, Va. Two daughters.
4. Samuel, died young.
5. Margaret, married Mr. Winters.
6. Charles William, not married.
7. John Franklin, married Jennie Patterson. Eight children, three boys and five girls.
8. Rebecca, married Robert Byers; two sons and three daughters. They owned and lived on the Major James Walker farm in Augusta County, Va. She is the only living member of her family."

Written by the eldest son of the Walker family and Robert Hooke family, in the 83rd year of his age; written from memory, but in the main correct, and is offered to those old families for reference by the undersigned, October 22, 1900.

William Walker Hooke.

Notes have been added to the above by Mrs. Audrey Kemper Spence, Wytheville, Virginia, 1928.

NOTES BY MRS. AUDREY KEMPER SPENCE OF WYTHEVILLE, VIRGINIA

Mr. William Elsey Connelly, Sec. Kansas Historical Society, Topeka, Kansas, has written an article on the Connelly Family and their Kin, which is published in "The Founding of Harman's Station and the Wiley Captivity." He treats of its early origin, and gives the coat of arms, the motto of which is "En Dieu Est Tout Fiat Dei Voluntas." It is to be hoped that parties interested will consult this book, either by purchasing from the author or calling for it at large libraries, as it is very interesting, and the article is too large to be reprinted here.

The Connelly Family, we are told, "Gen. of Irish Families," by John Rooney, is descended from Mileseus, King of Spain, through the line of his son, Heremon. The founder of the family was Eogan, ancestor of the Northern Hy Nials and son of Nial of the Nine Hostages, King of Ireland, A. D. 379. The ancient name was Conally, and signifies "A Light."

The possessions of the clan were located in the present counties of Galway, Meath and Donegal. The Connellys were also chiefs in Fermanagh. The names Connelly, Conally, Conneally, Connolly, Conneallan, O'Connel and other Irish families, are derived from the ancient Milesian name, O'Conghalaigh.

Reference, Judge Chalkley's "Abstracts of Augusta Co. Va."

Page 227, Will Book No. X, page 3, 12th of September, 1804, Arthur Connely's will, to wife Jean, to son Arthur, land on Eagle Creek in Ky.; to son James, sons John and David, daughter Jean, daughter Mary, son Robert, daughter Sarah, to grandson Arthur Williamson. Executors, sons John and David. Teste, William Johnston, Alexander Carns, Thomas Connely. Proved 25th of March, 1805.

1791, September 8, John Walker and John Connelly, surety, John Walker and Sarah Connelly, daughter of Arthur Connelly (consent); witnesses Thomas Connelly, Samuel Frame; by Rev. William Wilson.

Note—Col. Hooke says Sarah (Connelly) Walker was the daughter of Alexander Connelly. Here her father's name is given as Arthur.

1790, Arthur Conelly Jr. removed to Ky.; page 426.

Tithables. 1783, Arthur Conoly and sons Robert and James. Thomas Conoly and sons, Arthur and Thomas.

1798, Dec. 5, Samuel Thorp and Elizabeth Conally, daughter of Thomas Connally, dec. James Patterson swears that Elizabeth is 21 years of age. 1801, Jan. 3, Alexander Connelly and John Walker surety, Alexander Connelly and Nancy Jackson, daughter of ——— ——— Jackson, dec. Nancy is 22 years of age.

September 16, 1777, John Campbell, Thomas Connerley, guardians of Jane, Elizabeth and Alexander Walker, Jr.

Page 139, 20th November, 1774, Alexander Walker's will. To wife Elizabeth, to son Robert, Negro boy; to daughter Mary, Negro girl. To son Andrew, 90 acres, bought of Joseph Lindel. To daughter Martha, to daughter Elizabeth, to daughter Barbara, to son John, testator's home plantation, to daughter Isabel. (Many negro slaves are bequeathed.) To daughter Margaret, to son Alexander's two children, Jane and Elizabeth Walker. Executors, wife Elizabeth and son Robert. John Campbell to be guardian to children. Teste, Joseph Hannah, Robert Haslet, Thomas Conly. Proved March 21, 1775, by the witnesses. Executors qualify with John Hind, Arthur Connely, John Campbell.

May 19, 1778, Andrew Walker's appraisement recorded; Thomas Frame, Arthur Connly, John Campbell.

November 16, 1784, Rec. John Mahon's appraisement by Wm. Johnston, Arthur Connly, John Campbell, Hugh Donagh.

May 18, 1773, Alexander Walker and Elizabeth to Arthur Connly, part of 430 acres, patented by inclusive patent to Alexander April 6, 1769.

Page 417 in Will Book No. 1, May 21, 1752, James Connelly's (Conlys) appraisement by Thomas Ingles, Tobias Bright, Richard Hall.

Page 318 Will Book No. 4, August 21, 1770, Martha and Alexander Walker's bond (with Thomas Connly, John and Robert

Campbell) as administrator of Alexander Walker Jr.

Page 547 Will Book No. 5, Feb. 3, 1778, Andrew Walker's Will. To wife Margaret, to mother-in-law, to brothers and sisters. Executors, Thomas Connely and John Burnside. Teste, John Campbell, Robert McCormick, Mary Stevenson. Proved Feb. 17, 1778, by Campbell and recorded. Executor qualifies.

Page 375, Feb. 15, 1738, survey for Samuel Walker beginning at Alexander Walker's. Page 384, May 17, 1785, Alexander Reid guardian of John Walker; ditto, Alexander Walker.

Page 386, September 16, 1777, John Campbell, Thomas Connerly, guardian of Jane and Elizabeth Walker; ditto of Alexander Walker Jr.

Page 535, Will Book No. 6, June 24, 1785, Alexander Walker's estate settled, 1774, paid to legatees, Robert and Mary Walker, to Thomas Connelly, husband to Margaret, to Isabella Walker, paid to John Erwin for teaching the children. 1780. Paid John Young, ditto, 1785. Legatees Andrew and Martha are dead. Legatee Elizabeth is dead.

1789, Isabella and Barbara Walker, infants by Hugh Donaghe, against Robert and Elizabeth, et als. Oratrices were daughters of Alexander Walker, who died testate in Augusta. Will dated November 20, 1774. Bill for settlement. Administrators accounts show, 1774, cash paid Thomas Connelly, husband to Margaret (dau. of Alex.), May, 1793, abates as to Isabella by her marriage with Robert Reed.

Deed Book No. 17, Del. Arthur Connerly, May 9, 1773, 35 a. part of 230 acres patent to William Johnston, May 12, 1770.

Page 277, March 28, 1770, Alexander Walker to Thomas Connerly, bond to make title to one-half of a tract surveyed for Alex. and to be made as soon as the patent can be obtained. Delivered to Thos. Connerly, May 9, 1773.

Page 122, Fee Books of Augusta Court, Alexander Walker, Stone meeting house, Augusta.

Page 133, Alexander Walker, wheel-wright; Borden's land, May 17, 1767.

Page 415, Alexander Walker, constable. William Walker, twice charged. John Walker, gone to Carolina.

Page 433, April, 12, 1748, Alexander Walker, present; James Walker, present. Jan. 17, processioned Alexander Walker, John Walker, present for Jan. 27. Processioned for John Walker and James Walker.

Page 443, 1756, processioned by Henry Kirkum and Wm. Hall, viz: for John and Alexander Walker.

Page 178, 1756, processioned by Andrew Hays and Jacob Anderson, viz: Alexander Walker Jr. Alexander Walker Sr., for James Walker, for John Walker.

Copies of musters of Augusta County, 1742.

Capt. John Buchanan's list, Samuel Walker, Alexander Walker, Joseph Walker.

1787, August 20, Joseph McCauley and Mary Connelly, daughter of Arthur Connelly, with James Connely, Robert Connely, surety, Robert Connely.

1792, September 18, George Berry and Polly Connelly, daughter of Thomas Connelly (consent). Witnessed by Alexander Connelly, John Connelly, James Crawford, surety Thomas Connelly.

1787, Jan. 6, Arthur Connelly and James Levingston, surety, Arthur Connelly and Elizabeth Levingston.

Page 147, Will Book No. 8, July 28, 1794, Thomas Conally's Will. To wife Margaret, to three sons, Thomas, Alexander, and Robert; to each of my daughters, viz: Martha, Mary, Elizabeth, Barbara, Jean and Isabella; to son Arthur, 200 acres in Ky.; to son Thomas, 240 acres in Ky.; to Alexander, 200 acres in Ky.; to son Robert. Executors, wife Margaret and son Thomas. Teste, John Campbell, John Connely, John Hooke. Proved Jan. 20, 1795. (Presented by Thos. Connelly, surviving executor.) By Connely and Hooke. Thomas qualifies.

Robert Hooke and Elizabeth Walker, by Rev. Conrad Speece, lic., May 1, 1817.

Charles McClung and Rebecca Walker, by Rev. Samuel Kennerly, lic., Dec. 4, 1834.

Thomas Walker and Eliza Ann Boreland, by Rev. William Wilson, Dec. 2, 1830.

John Johnson and Patsy Walker, Dec. 29, 1827.

Page 15, Claim of John Walker, losses by Indians. File 19, 1845/6.

Old Augusta Stone Church graveyard, John Walker Sr., 1770, April 17, 1836.

Jacob Van Lear, Jan. 9, 1773, Feb. 28, 1845.

Nancy Van Lear, wife of Jacob, April 25, 1770, July 9, 1853.

Alexander Walker and Hannah Hinton, by Rev. C. Speece, Dec. 2, 1830.

Thos. Frame and Mary Walker, by Rev. C. Speece, June 3, 1830.

Robt. Conlly and Nancy Johnston, by Rev. McCue, July 20, 1796.

Page 2 in the "Walker Genealogy," by Mrs. E. S. White, 1. John Walker of Wigton, the first of the name that is known to us, lived and died we suppose in Wigton. He married Jane McKnight; of their children the names of only two are known to us: 2. John Walker, who married Katherine Rutherford and emigrated first to Scotland and from there to America. 11 children.

3. Alexander Walker, brother of the emigrant John, never that we know of left Scotland. He married, but name of wife not known. The names of only three of his children are known. These three came to America with their uncle John, and all married and left children.

John Walker (2) b. in Wigton, Scotland, m. Katherine Rutherford Jan. 7, 1702, in Scotland.   From Scotland he moved his family
and settled near the town of Newry, Ireland.   He and family and
three of his brother Alexander's children left Strangford Bay in May,
1726, (another record says 1728 or 1730) on board a vessel
commanded by Richard Walker, and landed in Maryland Aug. 2.
He transported his family and settled in Chester Co. Pa., where he
d. in Sept. 1734; his wife d. in 1738; both buried at Nottingham
Meeting House in Chester Co. Pa.

Most of the family left Penn. and settled in Rockbridge Co. and
adjoining counties in Va.   John Walker contemplated such a move,
and had been to Va. a short time previous to his death and selected a
farm upon which he erected a small building.

Katherine Rutherford was a daughter of John Rutherford and
Isabella Allein.   See sketch of Allein family.

Eleven children as follows: 4. Elizabeth Walker, m. John
Campbell; 5. John Walker, m. Ann Houston (or Hudson); 6. James
Walker, m. Mary Guffy; 7. Thomas Walker, (d. young); 8. William
Walker, (d. young); 9. Jane Walker, m. Jas. Moore; 10. Samuel
Walker, m. Jane Patterson; 11. Alexander Walker, m. Jane Hammer
(or Hummer); 12. Esther Walker (d. young); 13. Joseph Walker,
m. 1st Nancy McClung; m. 2nd Grizelda McCrosky; 14. Mary
Walker, no account of her, but one record states that she died young.
She may have been the Mary Walker who m. John Montgomery of
the Revolution, and after his d. she married a William Patterson;
she lived to be 104 years old.

Page 278, "The Walker-Rutherford Bible was printed in 1621.
The name John McKnight, born 1627, is written in the book.   It
was brought from Scotland by John Walker when he left for
Ireland, and from thence to America.   It is the property of Mrs.
Abba Beatrice Creel Walker, of Anaconda, Montana."

Page 282, "John and Katherine Walker emigrated to America
in 1726 or 1728; some descendants said 1726, others said 1728.   John
visited the Valley of Virginia, returned to Pa. expecting to bring his
family, but took sick and died.

"In the fall of 1734, Alexander with his 2 cousins removed to
Va., and later the most, if not all, of the family left Pa. and came
to Va.   Later some of them went to Ky. and some to what is now
Augusta Co.   Alexander, son of the emigrant, remained in
Rockbridge."

Page 625, Alexander Walker (3) (Alexander 1), was the nephew
of John and Katherine Walker, the emigrants.   He came to America
with them in 1728, with his elder brother (called Jack) and sister
Eleanor; first settled in Pa., then with his brother John and cousin
Alexander (8th child of John and Katherine) went to Va.; settled
on what was called Walker's creek, Rockbridge Co., then Augusta Co.
This was in the fall of 1734.   Alexander Walker lived on the farm
now owned by William Walker; his brother John settled about a

mile up the creek and their cousin Alexander pitched his tent near Jump Mountain, about one-half mile from his cousin Alexander's place, they being the first settlers there. The creek which runs parallel with the valley was called for them, still bears that name. Alxander, or "Shawney" as he was called, was killed by the falling of a tree, and was buried on a hill which is near and overlooks his farm. In this quiet "God's Acre" rest many of his kindred.

John Rutherford (See above book for the Rutherford and Allein coat of arms) lived on the River Tweed in Scotland; was m. to Isabella Allein. From Scotland he with his family moved to County Down, Ireland, where he died in his 84th year, and his wife in her 82nd year. Isabella was the daughter of Rev. Joseph Allein, author of "Allein's Alarm." See sketch of the Allein Family. John and Isabella had 8 children.

Genealogies of or remarks concerning the families mentioned in the foregoing sketches may be found in Chalkley's "Abstracts of Augusta County, Va.," Scott's "History of Orange County, Va.," the Kemper Genealogy, Morton's "History of Highland County, Va.," Boogher's "Virginia Gleanings," Wm. A. Connelly's "Harman's Station," Richard Mauzy's "Mauzy and Kisling Families," James William Hooke's "Hooke Genealogy" (New Haven, Conn.), Waddell's "Annals of Augusta County, Va.," H. M. Strickler's "Massanutten" and "Forerunners," Wayland's "History of Rockingham County, Va.," pages 60, 90, 95, 99, 100, 101, 102, 111, 239, 447, 450, 451, 454, 456, 459; J. Taylor Allen's "Early Pioneer Days in Texas"; the Virginia Magazine of History and Biography; the William and Mary College Quarterly, and "Genealogical History of the Descendants of John Walker of Wigton, Scotland, 1600-1902," by Mrs. Emma Siggins White, Kansas City, Mo. The last is listed in the Library of Congress, and a copy is preserved in the Library of Washington and Lee University, Lexington, Va.

NOTES BY J. W. W.

Mrs. Audrey Kemper Spence, author of the foregoing sketches, is a graduate of Plummer Memorial College, Wytheville, Va., a former student of the State Teachers College, Harrisonburg, Va., and the State Normal, Emory, Va.; and former teacher in the Wythe County, Va., schools.

She is a member of the Virginia State Historical Society, the National Society D. A. R. on Revolutionary services of Capt. May Burton, Jr., James Craig Sr., William Craig, William Hooke, Sr. (National No. 235190), and Jacob Kisling; also eligible on services of Capt. Benjamin Head, May Burton, Sr., and others. She is eligible for membership in the Colonial Dames, War of 1812, and Americans of Armorial Ancestry, etc.

She is a lineal descendant of Adam Miller, first white settler of the upper Shenandoah Valley; a member of the Taylor family, from which President Taylor sprang; also the same of the Gen.

Daniel Morgan family; a descendant from the Gascogne, Craig, Veazey, Medley, Sherman, Anderson and Kemper families, and those listed in the preceding paragraph, besides other notable families of Virginia and America.

Mrs. Spence is listed in the Social Recorder of Virginia; is a member of the Wythe Grey Chapter U. D. C.; of the Helen Trinkle Music Club, Wytheville, Va.; and of the American Red Cross. She is author of sketches of the Hooke, Walker and Connelly family genealogy; also of Spence, Simmerman, Cassell, and Keesling family of the Spence lineage.

LETTERS OF A CAVALRY CAPTAIN

1861-1862

J. Q. WINFIELD

Captain Company B, Seventh Regiment
Virginia Cavalry

COMPILED WITH ADDENDA

By

His Daughter

PAULINA SWIFT WINFIELD

LETTERS OF A CAVALRY CAPTAIN, 1861-1862

Foreword

In the history of a great upheaval such as was involved in the War Between the States, attention is usually centered upon the principals engaged in the struggle and the salient features of campaigns to the neglect of important and instructive details. Dazzled by the glory of victorious generals and able strategists, we overlook the captains and brave men who bore the brunt of battles, or else we regard them as mere pawns in the game of war, moved hither and thither at the will of superior officers. But in the Sixties there was room for the display of individual valor. And perhaps in no other period of the war and in no other branch of the army was so much ever left to the judgment, the authority and discretion of the captains, as in the one brief year of service under Ashby in the 7th Regiment, Va. Cavalry. Men of courage and character, they were worthy of the trust; and in these pages which follow mainly the fortunes of Co. B, should the old-fashioned terms "brave," "chivalrous," and "gallant" be used with frequent recurrence there shall be no apology as applied to the old-fashioned Confederate Captain and his men.

In giving my father's letters to the public I have suppressed as far as possible allusion to matters purely personal. They were written to his wife, with an intimate touch, often in haste and by the light of the camp fire after a day in the field. Yet, as containing many incidents hitherto unpublished, it is my hope not only that they may prove of general interest, but that they may help to perpetuate the memory of the Brock's Gap Riflemen with all who later swelled their ranks, and that another chapter not devoid of romance may be added to the history of Rockingham County and the Valley of the Shenandoah.

PAULINA SWIFT WINFIELD
Broadway, Va., 1928.

CHAPTER I

INTRODUCTORY

Adapting a quotation from an English poet, it might be said of John Q. Winfield, the author of the following letters,

> "His soul was pure and true,
> The good stars met at his horoscope,
> Made him of spirit, fire, and dew"—

so blended in him were these elements, the spirit of love, of truth, of patriotism, the fire of enthusiasm, the dew of kindness, as to form a winning personality, a man of force and action.

Or, borrowing the old Norse idea in which all life is figured as a tree, the roots of his ancestry are found to strike deep down in the three realms of England, Scotland, and France. And from each of these he received an endowment to enrich his nature.

Briefly, his father, Dr. Richard Winfield, came from Orange County, New York, to Mt. Jackson, Virginia, in the year 1817. In 1821 he married Katherine Salvage, daughter of Benjamin Salvage (originally De Seviege), a Huguenot, who came over with La Fayette, bore arms for the cause of Independence, and settled in the Valley of Virginia soon after the close of the war.

John Quincy Winfield was born at Mt. Jackson, Shenandoah Co., Va., June 20, 1822. When he was about twelve years old his father, who had lived for a time in Greenbrier County, removed to the Salvage farm on Linville Creek, several miles north of Harrisonburg, the county-seat of Rockingham.

Choosing the profession of his father and his grandfather, after graduating from Washington College, Lexington, Va., class of 1842, he pursued the study of medicine at Jefferson College, Philadelphia. He received his degree in 1845, and at once engaged in the practice of medicine in the neighborhood of his boyhood home. In 1852 he married Miss Sallie Neff, of Cootes' Store, Rockingham Co., and immediately took up his residence at Broadway, a few miles distant, where some members of his family still reside.

While a student at Washington College young Winfield took a course in tactics at the Virginia Military Institute, and it was then that he imbibed a taste for military evolutions and learned the first principles of warfare. In 1859, more as a matter of amusement than of serious thought, he gathered around him at Cootes' Store a band of young men, the nucleus of the famous Letcher Brock's Gap Rifles, afterwards known as Co. B of Ashby's Cavalry. These men, a complete roster of whom is given in the appendix of this volume, were drawn principally from the immediate neighborhood, and the company was named for Gov. Letcher and Brock's Gap, the latter a narrow pass in the little North Mountain, about one mile from

Cootes' Store. A mere gorge where the North Fork of the Shenandoah River breaks through the mountain barrier, this gap widens out into a valley of more than usual fertility, affording homes for a brave and hardy race of people. Robust of frame were these men, unerring marksmen, skilled in the chase, steadfast, devoted then and always to their captain, ready to do and dare to the end.

Cootes' Store, one mile from the Gap, was the rendezvous for the men of that section seeking companionship on a Saturday afternoon, or when the day's work was done. It was also the favorite haunt of the young doctor. Here in the hospitable home of Samuel Cootes he found a place of rest and refreshment after long rides on his professional rounds into the Gap and over the rough mountain roads. Here too he had come a-wooing the step-daughter of the house, pretty Sallie Neff, and here were most of his affections and interests centered at the beginning of his career.

Eager for action and an outlet for their energies, the young men of the Linville Creek neighborhood made haste to join with those of Brock's Gap and Cootes' Store in the proposed organization of a military company, and soon they mustered a force of sixty or more under the leadership of Dr. Winfield, as captain.

At that peaceful period perhaps they little recked of war's alarms, and though there were mutterings of the coming storm, even their captain scarcely dreamed that he was training a squad of men for the serious business of war. They were wiser after the John Brown raid, and the work of drilling the Letcher Brock's Gap Rifles was thence conducted with more system and precision. Lacking arms and uniforms, they were not called to serve at Harper's Ferry or at Charles Town, but measures were soon afterwards taken for their complete equipment.

Early in January, 1860, officers were elected and regularly commissioned. John Q. Winfield was elected captain, and his commission signed by his friend and classmate, John Letcher, governor of Virginia, gave him the official title of Captain of the Letcher Brock's Gap Rifles in the 116th Regiment, 7th Brigade, and 3rd Division of the Va. Militia, with rank from Jan. 21, 1860.

The summer of 1860, preceeding the Presidential election, was full of the signs of coming trouble. The election of Lincoln as a result of the division of political parties sounded the death knell of peace. Capt. Winfield was of the States Rights Democratic wing, supporting Breckenridge, and, while holding in common with politicans of three of the parties in the field the right of a state to secede, differed from many of his friends and associates as to the probability of being permitted to exercise that right peaceably.

The following extract from the *Rockingham Register* of January 25, 1861, will show the state of public feeling in the county at the period just preceding the war:

*MILITARY MEETING

"Monday was a proud day for old Rockingham. Notwithstanding the diversity of opinion which exists as to the best mode of settling our present difficulties, all are agreed on arming our Volunteer Regiment. The immense crowd was addressed by Messrs. Warren, Shands, Winfield, and Yancey, in patriotic and thrilling speeches." *****

In an old note book of J. Q. Winfield's the following brief extract from his impromptu speech on that occasion is found:

"There is scarcely an inequality of force that may not be compensated by intrepidity and resolution. Darius marched against the Athenians with one hundred and ten thousand troops. With 10,000 at his command Miltiades, the Grecian general, broke the ranks, put them to rout, and left upon the field of Marathon over 6,000 of their slain to give evidence that a people fighting on their own soil and in defense of their homes and firesides have little to apprehend from superiority of numbers.

"Rather than suffer the Black Republicans to take possession of the Capitol, rather than see them celebrate their triumph and hold their orgies in this temple of Liberty, I should prefer to see it washed from its foundation stone by a torrent of blood, and a statue of Nemesis erected from its ruins."

An occasion of more than usual interest to the Brock's Gap Riflemen at this time was the presentation of a flag by the ladies of the county.

The flag was presented by Dr. Samuel Coffman (father of Vice Admiral DeWitt Coffman, U. S. N.) in behalf of the ladies, and accepted by Capt. Winfield. The date must have been about February 1861, and it is to be regretted that only this fragment of Capt. Winfield's speech can be found:

"Sir: This splendid banner, the offering of beauty to these brave boys, I accept from your hands. The gift will ever be prized and long cherished in grateful remembrance of the fair donors. The interest which our countrywomen have manifested in the volunteer military organizations recently effected not only in the county of Rockingham, but in almost every section of the State is full of import. Without meaning for a moment to disparage the intellect or acquirements of woman, I would not give one of her instincts for all the reason and philosophy the world contains. While man is reaching his conclusions by long and tedious investigations, woman in an instant 'snuffs danger in the tainted breeze,' and gives the alarm. Let not her warnings pass unheeded. It is true we are at this moment enjoying an unexampled degree of prosperity"—Here the fragment breaks off.

---

*See Wayland's History of Rockingham County, page 130.

CHAPTER II

Secession

In March 1861 business of an important nature called Dr. Winfield to Texas. He was accompanied by his brother-in-law, the late J. N. Liggett, Esq., later 1st Lieut. Co. B.

From Dr. Winfield's notes on this journey the following extracts are culled:

Monday, March 25, 1861. Left Staunton. Arrived at Charlottesville at half past nine a. m. Secession feeling strong. Thirty or forty secession flags waving over the town. Supped at Liberty, Bedford County. All for secession.

March 27. Stopped at Charleston, a little village on French Broad river. Here saw first secession flag in Tennessee.

Supped at Chattanooga. Travelled all night, and lost opportunity of seeing country. Breakfast at Amite, Mississippi. Soldiers for Pensacola drawn up in battle array before the hotel. The men grounded arms at command of officers and huzzahed, while the eyes of sweethearts and wives filled with tears at the anticipated march. Officers fine looking soldiers, young, and apparently drawn from the middle classes.

Met with an old Mississippi planter on the cars. Says he doesn't want Virginia to secede yet. Feels confident that she will do so eventually. Says they will rush to her rescue when ever attacked by a common foe. Says no one in the Southern Confederacy wants to return to the Union. All that troubles them is the difficulty to keep the North from adopting their constitution, thereby coming into the Confederacy.

Thurs. March 28. At Grand Junction. 12 o'clock. Military enthusiasm. Several companies preparing to go to Pensacola. One company turned back. Disappointed. Old and young men in ranks, volunteering from all classes. No disaffection here. To-day witnessed here at Grand Junction an exhibition of that high-toned chivalry which impelled South Carolina, single-handed and alone, to hoist the banner of secession. We have heard the throbbings of the Southern heart. Mississippi, with an eager desire to serve her country which would have reflected credit on the Old Guard of Napoleon, concentrated at this point companies of brave and true men, all anxious to have a fray with the Black Republicans. If the submissionists whose serpent tongues are dispensing poison of malicious falsehood could have witnessed the enthusiasm of these chivalrous volunteers and seen the kindling eyes of the fair Southern maidens, even their mendacity would have shrunk from repeating the foul slander that *disaffection* prevails in the South. "Off for Pensacola!" shouts the brave youth of a company in time to fill the quota of the regiment. And "Oh, for Pensacola," sighs the sorrowful volunteer who arrives to find he was too late.

If the Black Republican government does not back out from every port of the South, the Confederate troops will drive them out in less than sixty days. The wailings of abolitionists and the croakings of submissionists cannot prevent their disgrace, perhaps annihilation.

Dined at Holly Springs, Mississippi. Pretty place. Men in uniform. Fine country, fertile for cotton. No grass. Weather warm, air fragrant.

Lake Caddo. Nearing Shreveport, La. Had on the boat yesterday a bevy of politicians. One a Col. Lewis, member of the recent La. Convention. Strikingly like William Seymour of Hardy Co. in manner and appearance, but not his equal in mind. Another member of the State Legislature resembled old Mathias of Hardy, uneducated, but a man of strong natural sense. Another was a Col. Somebody, a tall swarthy, black-haired, black stiff-mustached and bearded individual, who tried to palm off a certain air of superiority for sense. The position of the border states was alluded to during the course of the conversation. All expressed a strong desire to have them join the Confederate States, but felt confident of being able to care for themselves. The fierce and whiskered Colonel wanted a fight with the Yankees without assigning a very good reason for it. The rest of the party desired peace, if it could be purchased without dishonor. All, as everybody else here, regarded the Union as dissolved forever, without a wish for reconstruction.

April 7th. Pt. Pleasant, Texas. Spent the evening here with a young lawyer by the name of Hill, formerly from Madison Co., Va. He is pretty thoroughly tinctured with the "Union feeling," and is probably one of old Houston's adherents. We have not met with many disaffected individuals here. People here are not ignorant, but know nothing of politics of the country. Seem to be more interested in the "town ghost" than in the taking of Sumter or Pickens or the future of Texas.

Reached Henderson about four o'clock to-day. Place much injured by fire. Here is where Herndon, the Abolitionist, was hung, and where much apprehension was felt of insurrection. Forty miles from Gilmer. Passed yesterday the tree upon which Morrison was hung for tampering with slaves.

24th. Henderson. To-day heard first news of the stirring political events being enacted in the East. The joy and excitement of the people here extreme when learning that old Va. had seceded. The indignation against Republicans bitter. Heard at Marshall that a battle had been fought in Balto. between Mass. regulars and Baltimoreans. We impatient to get home. Will not lose a moment until we can reach Brock's Gap and rally around us the gallant mountaineers of that region.

Writing on S. P. Texas R. R. between Marshall and Shreveport. Left Shreveport for home about sunset on boat, in company with the Greenwood Guards commanded by Capt. Harney. Several rounds of cannon were fired in honor of their departure, a farewell address delivered by Judge Landrum. The company will receive orders where to march at Baton Rouge. The Captain thinks Washington will be their destination. The whole country here along Red river is in a blaze. Companies are being raised in every parish. The negroes on the large plantations drop their hoes, wave their hats, and hurrah to the troops on board. People assemble at the landings and give us salutes. Children and women hurrah and wave handkerchiefs. It seems to me now that I would give all that I am worth to be in Virginia at the head of the Brock's Gap Rifles, leading them on to victory or to death. If the North persists in their mad schemes, they may annihilate, but can never subdue this people.

April 28. Reached the Mississippi this morning. The military companies aboard have their flags unfurled from the upper decks, and at every town we pass are receiving salutes from cannon and other demonstrations of respect. Such waving of hats from men and boys and handkerchiefs from fairy hands! As the steamers pass each other the passengers exchange intelligence. The news we get every hour or two from New York makes our blood boil, and for a while we pace the deck like caged lions.

Company at Amite about to march to Missouri to-day. 2,000 troops to be concentrated at Jackson to-morrow. Destination not known.

Monday, 29. Arrived at Grand Junction about midday. Are now up in Tenn. in woods delayed by accident to train. At Grand Junction to-day met a fine company of Tenn. troops. Destination did not learn. Senator Clay of Ala. here addressed a large number of citizens from platform of cars. Made a handsome extempore speech. Said he was direct from St. Paul, Minn., and that but little disposition was manifested in the West and N. W. to fight the South; that great difficulty was experienced by the Black Republicans in raising troops. Most of the troops raised were foreigners of the lowest class, bought up for the purpose. "In the South," said he, "the question is not who shall go to war, but who shall stay at home." Gen. Clark of Miss. also delivered a short and patriotic address to the company and citizens.

The first intelligence we had of the secession of Va. was a rumor we heard in Henderson, Texas. At Marshall we heard it again. At Shreveport it seemed pretty well confirmed, but a beautiful little steamer, the Minnehaha, as she glided up the Miss. from New Orleans bore the intelligence on her flag. Then my heart leaped with delight. I waved my hat involuntarily and shouted "Three cheers for old Virginia!" This was heartily responded to by my fellow passengers as well as those on the Minnehaha.

May 1st. Three hundred Alabama troops on train to-day. Fifteen cars of Kentuckians and Alabamians passed us yesterday on way to Virginia. Fifty more will be on to-morrow or next day.

CHAPTER III

War

The Letcher Brock's Gap Rifles did not await the return of their impatient captain, but at the first call to arms, on April 18, assembled at Mt. Jackson. Here they were assigned to the 4th Va. Regiment of State troops, Col. Gibbons, afterwards as fully organized, the 10th Va. Infantry, C. S. A., and under the leadership of Capt. Isaac Coffman, of Rockingham Co., proceeded to Harper's Ferry. They carried with them the banner presented by the ladies of Rockingham, and bore as arms the old Mississippi rifles with which they had drilled. These being of short range, it was decided to give them to the incoming recruits and equip the Brock's Gap men with minie rifles. For a few days they were without arms, and being quartered in the old half burned armory, when the alarm of the advancing foe was given, as was a daily occurrence, every man seized a brickbat from the crumbling walls, and went out to meet the enemy. From this circumstance they were nicknamed the "Brickbat Brigade." How they were transferred to the cavalry and became a part of Ashby's brigade will be told later.

On May 7, Capt. Winfield, after a brief stay with his family, then at Cootes' Store, set out to join his company and take his place as their commander for the thirteen months following. He was accompanied as far as Mt. Jackson by his wife and his ward, Miss Lizzie Kratzer.

A letter signed by three of the boys and written before the arrival of their captain shows how the Letcher Brock's Gap Rifles enjoyed their first experience in soldiering:

Harper's Ferry, April the 22, 1861.

Mr. Michael Brock,

Dear Sir;

It is with pleasure that we have seated ourselves to drop you a few lines to inform you that we are well at present, hoping these few lines may find you well. Further, we arrived here yesterday about noon. We are stationed in the workshops. The Republicans didn't do any damage but bloody up the arsenal.

The whole town is full of Southern troops now. There are between 5,000 and 8,000 men in town. We hadn't been here half an hour until we were called out to face an army. Our men, the Gap crowd, rolled up, tumbled up, till we got to the bridge, and there was no more enemy there than we took along. They all thought the Letcher Rifles was some of the brave men in town. Our fare is as good as we can expect.

I wrote home yesterday. I wrote that we didn't expect to stay longer than to-day. But we don't know how long we will stay. It is likely we may be here several months.

We haven't been out sparking yet. We want you to take care of the girls.

No more at present but answer soon.

Yours with respects,

William F. Bowers,
Sylvanus Lindamood,
Wm. Toppin.

Address Harper's Ferry, Va.

P. S. April 23. We are at headquarters to-day standing till our backs are nearly broke.

We had three crackers for our breakfast this morning. We are well and hearty. Toppin is sometimes well and sometimes sick.

I want you to let them know at home all the news.

S. Lindamood.

Capt. Winfield writes from Harper's Ferry, May 10, 1861.

My dear wife:

I arrived here on Wednesday last, and immediately took charge of my company. The boys, as you may well suppose, were exceedingly glad to see me, met me at the depot, and greeted me with warmest demonstrations of welcome and regard.

We are quartered along with three other companies in one of the large armory buildings, near the railroad bridge and a little south west of the Wager House. A soldier's life is not as hard as many suppose. We have very good fare, the best bread I ever tasted, good fat beef, and bacon in abundance. The troops are generally in good health and fine spirits, and I believe ready, if not anxious, for an attack.

We have, I suppose, about five thousand men here. I have no data upon which to found an opinion as to the probability of an attack. A number of Baltimoreans reached here yesterday (by the way they are coming on every train, in squads and companies). They report that Maryland has been sold by Gov. Hicks to Abe Lincoln and that Federal troops will probably take possession of Baltimore to-day.

I have met here with a host of old friends and acquaintances. Strict military discipline prevails, and there is very little probability of any more desertions. My men are now perfectly satisfied and contented, and I believe as full of fight as any company on the ground.

I wish that you and Lizzie Kratzer would inquire into the wants of the families of the married men belonging to my company, and if you find them in need of anything, take steps to supply their necessities. Suggest this matter to the Home Guard forming at Cootes' Store.

I have not time to write more as the mail will leave in a few minutes.

The runaway boys in charge of Sergeant Joe Riddle have just this moment entered the barracks. They look lively and cheerful, and I think will give us no further trouble.

Your husband affectionately,

John Winfield.

Col. Harper of Augusta County, a graduate of the V. M. I., was first in command of the troops assembled at Harper's Ferry. He at once took vigorous measures to carry out the policy of the State to defend the border line. Moreover, Harper's Ferry, as a link between Washington and the West, was an important point. The Baltimore & Ohio railroad running through the place and the C. & O. canal on the Maryland side of the Potomac river afforded facilities for the transportation of supplies and the massing of troops. Hence the rushing of volunteers to this point.

On April 26 (1861) Major T. J. Jackson of V. M. I. was commissioned a colonel of volunteers, and assigned to the command of the forces at the Ferry. But when the Confederate government had been removed to Richmond and fully established, by orders of the War Department Gen. Joseph E. Johnston was put at the head of that division.

Among those who hastened to the support of Col. Harper was Turner Ashby, with his company of cavalry, the Mountain Rangers, a company formed and drilled by him before the John Brown raid. By order of Col. Harper, Ashby was sent to guard the Point of Rocks, lower down the Potomac river. Imboden with six guns followed, and Capt. Winfield, after his arrival at the gathering place of the Virginia troops, was dispatched to the same point with his company. Here began Winfield's acquaintance with Ashby, and here at Ashby's solicitation the idea of joining the cavalry service was first conceived.

In character, Ashby and Winfield had many traits in common, and it is not remarkable that a warm personal friendship soon sprang up between the two men. True sons of Virginia, loving her institutions, animated by the same spirit of courage and chivalrous honor, they were destined during the next twelve months to fare forth side by side in many a fray.

CHAPTER IV

WITH ASHBY AT POINT OF ROCKS

Point of Rocks, May 19th, 1861.

My dear wife; I write again this evening not because I have anything new or startling to communicate, but for the reason that I derive an inward satisfaction from sending fancy on the wings of affection upon even the most trifling errand to you.

I have spent most of this Sabbath day in my cozy little shanty. I have thought of you and the children fifty times, slept an hour or two, and have read several chapters in the Bible you gave me.

The enemy, I believe, are now no nearer to us than the Relay House. They have turned their big guns in this direction, evidently anticipating an attack from us. The small force we have here and the responsibility of my position have led me to think and be vigilant. I have a daily consultation with Captains Ashby, Imboden, and Johnson of Maryland, and my suggestions have generally been approved and adopted. We shall not be caught napping. Indeed, I am so well satisfied now with our plans that I confidently anticipate a brilliant victory against an odds of over five to one. I trust that we shall be able to rout them here for the moral effect of the contest. The County of Loudoun in which we are now stationed is by no means to be relied upon. We have enemies in front and rear, and therefore are compelled to be doubly vigilant. You can scarcely form an idea of the difficulties, responsibilities, and labors of a captain's position in times like these. To keep sixty or seventy raw, undisciplined troops in proper subjection, to instruct them, attend to their wants, to gratify and deny them, to keep up their spirits, to punish and reward and all the while retain their respect and regard is no easy task, I assure you. So far, however, I have succeeded beyond my expectations.

As soon as I reached Harper's Ferry I learned the cause of the desertions from my company: the want of a head first, and the desire of ——— ——— to get the whole company to bolt, in order that he might go with them, and thereby shield his own dastardly and cowardly heart. The men, however, soon returned, ——— assumed a penitent air, and I let the matter drop, keeping the while a close watch upon his conduct. Everything worked pretty well, until a few days ago, when business led me up to Harper's Ferry. Taking advantage of my absence, he commenced the old game of producing discontent among the Gap boys, by trying to operate upon their fears and by making misrepresentation. As soon as I returned to camp, I was informed of his conduct. I sprang out of my camp like a young tiger, caught him by the coat collar, shook him until I almost made his teeth rattle, denounced him as a contemptible coward, and told him that if he did not deport himself properly in future, I'd blow his brains out and be rid of him.

He is by far the greatest coward I have ever met with. Do not for the credit of the company make this public. I may be able to make something of a man out of him yet, bad as is the material.

It has just commenced raining, and the water is pouring through our shanty roof. Don't be uneasy. I have just nailed a gum coat on the inside of the roof and so inclined it as to run the water off into a crack in the floor about three inches from my right side. I shall have to-night, if not the lisp of my children and the affectionate tones of my dear wife, the lull of falling waters on my ear. The coat answers a good purpose, and is turning the rain drops most beautifully.

I have just been thinking perhaps I could procure you comfortable quarters in some private family, in Loudon say, a few miles from this, in order that I might have you near me. I was told by Capt. Ashby last evening that we should probably be retained here for some time. You and Lizzie Kratzer must make a flying visit at any rate to Harper's Ferry. A great many ladies visit the place. Some opportunity will present itself. If not, I think I will meet you in Winchester or send some one there to meet you. Say when you will be in Winchester, my heart beats high, and I allow myself to think I have a wife over the plan my fancy has suggested to meet with her once more.

I have sent Joe Riddle after a deserter. He may reach Cootes' Store. Send me some pickles to ward off scurvy. We have fresh fish, that is, John Barglebaugh and I almost every meal. Great fishing place here. My love to you all.

Your husband affectionately,

John Winfield.

Virginia Side of Point of Rocks,
May 23, 1861.

My dear wife: Peter Rader and Isaac Acker* arrived here this morning, the former bringing a very welcome letter from you, also the fox skin robe. The robe is the very thing I most needed at this time. The nights and mornings are quite cool, and it will answer for overcoat and blanket as well as serve to protect from rain.

This is a beautiful bright morning, and will be long remembered as the day on which the proud old Mother of States declared through the voice of her people for the second time in her history her independence. The twenty-third day of May, 1861, and the fourth of July, 1776, will mark two eras in our history.

At half-past five o'clock this morning the reveille was sounded in our camp, and soon we formed a line, unfurled our banner, marched to the polls on the Potomac Bridge, and cast a united vote

---

*Member of Winfield's company.

for secession. Let the friends of our boys know that every member of my company voted (except a union or two and two sick in the hospital) and voted for *secession*. We cast I believe fifty secession votes.

We had for the past week expected an attack at this Point and at Harper's Ferry on the day of the election, but everything passed off quietly, and to-night no sound is heard around me except the snorings of my comrades.

My health continues good, nowithstanding we have had some sickness in camp. Much of the ill health, however, has been occasioned by imprudence. Joe Hulva, Abe Wean, and Jerry Byrd have been very ill, but are convalescing. I shall send Hulva home though, as he will be unfit for service, being strongly predisposed to pulmonary consumption. We have an excellent physician here and clever fellow, by the name of Brandt. He was a classmate of mine in Philadelphia.

The citizens of Loudon and some on the Maryland side have been very kind to us. We have received some hams, butter, &c, and this evening from Mrs. Somebody in Maryland a monster pound cake, trimmed with flowers and sustaining a secession flag from its center.

There are no indications that we shall be attacked here soon. The Federal forces seem to be diminishing at the Relay House. As much as I desire to live for your sake and the children's, I must confess I feel somewhat chagrinned and disappointed at losing the opportunity to open the war.

Will you come down to the Ferry? You will, I think, be perfectly safe in doing so. Tell Mr. Cootes to come with you.

I think I will send for Sam* soon, and my two horses, as soon at least as I know where I will be permanently stationed. You can get some one to plough the little crop we have.

Have you heard anything of Charles and Frank?†

Send me some butter, eggs, pickles, and some of my summer clothes, white vests and trousers.

---

*Sam, a faithful family servant.
†Brothers Charles and Frank, living in Illinois.

CHAPTER V

BROCK'S GAP RIFLES JOIN McDONALD CAVALRY

Gen. Johnston had information that McClellan was advancing from Western Virginia to form a junction with Patterson, and convinced of the difficulty of holding Harper's Ferry against the combined force, decided to retire to Winchester. He gave orders that the munitions of war not destroyed by Lieut. Jones of the Federal army should be removed, and on Sunday, June 16, the troops concentrated at the Ferry took the line of march through Charles Town to Winchester.

There was then forming at Winchester a cavalry regiment under Col. Angus McDonald, a fellow graduate of President Davis at West Point. Col. McDonald, a brave and loyal Virginian, was now over sixty years of age and greatly afflicted with rheumatism. Yet, with true devotion to the cause, he bent his energies to the task of organizing a regiment, and to his skilled knowledge and untiring efforts is due much of the discipline that brought into being the effective body of men later to win renown as the Ashby Cavalry.

Col. McDonald with the consent of the War Department tendered the lieutenancy of the incipient regiment to Ashby, who, as has been said, was then commanding a body of cavalry at Point of Rocks. Ashby at once accepted, went to Winchester, thence immediately with McDonald to Romney.

The Letcher Brock's Gap Rifles remained to burn the bridge at Point of Rocks, and making a detour through the county of Loudoun, went on also to Winchester. Shortly afterwards they joined the troops who had gone in advance to the western part of the state.

Hanging Rock, Near Romney,
June 19, 1861.

My dear wife: As I anticipated when I wrote you from Winchester we marched directly West. My company spent one night in Romney, and was then ordered to this place, about three and one-half miles north west of the town, and on the main road leading to Cumberland. We are about twenty-three miles from Cumberland. I presume you are aware that the Federal forces marched upon Romney some days before we arrived and plundered the houses of some of the citizens. They remained but a few hours, stole some gold watches, shot a poor old deaf man, robbed a smoke house or two, and then left in double quick time.

We have a force here of about twenty-five hundred men, under the command of Col. A. P. Hill: Col. Gibbons regiment, a Tennessee regiment, Col. Hill's own regiment, with some cavalry.

The Tennesseans had a little brush last night with some Federal troops, about two hundred in number, who were stationed at the bridge over the North Branch, near New Creek Depot. Col. Hill, having been apprised of the enemy's position, dispatched the Tennessee regiment, lightly armed and equipped, to make a rapid night march and take them by surprise. The Yankees, however, fled precipitately upon the approach of our men. Some shots were exchanged resulting in the death of a Yankee or two, and slightly wounding a Tennesseean. We captured two pieces of their cannon, and frightened them prodigiously. The Tennesseeans returned to Romney to-day.

I am much pleased with our present location, which is in the midst of wealthy and hospitable people. The Inskips, Washingtons, and Parsons live around here in this valley. I am at present writing in the house of Mrs. Inskip. My men are all very well, not a sick man in my camp. My own health is about the same as when I parted from you in Winchester.

I have not time to say more. It is now about ten o'clock at night, and I have yet to ride around and visit the sentinels on the posts and see if all is going on properly. I have command of two companies here, and Col. Hill has left me to act at discretion and hold myself responsible for the defense or at least for any surprise upon this post. Consequently, I feel that I must be or ought to be doubly vigilant.

I should like to say more about the town of Romney, the pretty girls, the open generous hospitality of the people, the romance and picturesqueness of the country, but I have not time.

Good-night. My love to you all.

Your husband affectionately,

John Winfield.

In the mean time Col. McDonald, with headquarters at Romney, had been busy in completing the organization of his cavalry regiment.

The letter giving the circumstances of the transfer of the Brock's Gap Rifles from the infantry to the cavalry service is missing. As told by Sergeant Joseph Riddle and Lieut. Derrick Pennybacker, veterans living until recent years in Broadway, the occasion was a dramatic one. Urged by McDonald and Ashby to join the cavalry, pressed by Col. Gibbons of the 10th Va. Infantry to remain with their old friends and neighbors from Rockingham, Capt. Winfield resolved to leave it to the vote of the men. Orders had come for the return of the infantry to Winchester. They were already on the march. Jacob Liggett and Derrick Pennybacker limped wearily in the rear. "Wish I had a horse," said Liggett. "Never did like to walk." "Sun's pretty hot. My feet are gettin' mighty sore," rejoined Pennybacker. Suddenly down the line rang out the command: "Men of the Letcher Brock's Gap Rifles, fall out of ranks!"

What did this mean? They'd be court-martialed, wouldn't they? It must be right, though, if Captain said so. To a man they obeyed. For a moment there was confusion. Gibbons protested, but in vain. McDonald had the right to fill out his ten companies, and the Brock's Gap Rifles were needed.

Back they turned to Romney, with three cheers for the cavalry, Col. McDonald, and Capt. Winfield, and with laughter and goodbys for the Harrisonburg boys tramping on to Winchester.

The following companies formed the McDonald Regiment:

Co. A, Capt. Richard Ashby, Fauquier Co., Va.; Co. B, Capt. J. Q. Winfield, Rockingham Co., Va.; Co. C, Capt. S. D. Myers, Shenandoah Co., Va.; Co. D, Capt. Macon Jordan, Page Co., Va.;

Co. E, Capt. Walter Bowen, Warren Co., Va.; Co. F, Capt. G. H.
Sheets, Hampshire Co., Va.; Co. G, Capt. Frank Mason, Maryland.;
Co. H, Capt. A. Harper, Shenandoah Co., Va.; Co. I, Capt. E. H.
Shands, Harrisonburg, Va.; Co. K, Capt. Wm. Miller, Shenandoah
Co., Va.

With the following field and staff officers:

Colonel, Angus W. McDonald; Lieutenant-Colonel, Turner
Ashby; Major, O. R. Funsten; Adjutant, A. W. McDonald, Jr.;
Surgeon, Dr. A. P. Burns, Maryland; Assistant-Surgeon, Dr. T. L.
Settle; Chaplain, Rev. J. B. Avirett; Ass't-Quartermaster, Capt. T.
P. Pendleton; A. C. S., Capt. John D. Richardson.

CHAPTER VI

DEATH OF DICK ASHBY

Camp at Romney, June 26, 1861.

My dear wife: My mind has been so wholly occupied with the
duties pertaining to my position as scarcely to afford me at any time
sufficient leisure to write you anything like a graphic or interesting
letter.

We have not as yet had a shot at the enemy, though we have
experienced much of the romance as well as the reality of the war.
I have not now the time to give you any of the plans of our campaign,
or any general news. You must at present be content with the
assurance that I am in rather better health than when you saw me
last.

I am completely fascinated with the kind of service we are
now in. It is full of the spirit of wild adventure, and will no doubt,
furnish food for worms and novels.

A pretty well founded rumor reached us last night that the
Federal forces were reinforced by several thousand troops. We shall,
I think, have a fight within the next twenty-four hours. The citizens,
not the soldiers encamped here, are awfully alarmed.

We shall leave here as soon as we can become organized and
properly equipped. I think it probable that Moorefield will be our
next headquarters. We shall in a few days open communication
with Gen. Wise.

At present we are in a bad condition to fight, wanting in arms,
organization, ammunition, and discipline. My company and Capt.
Ashby's are the only effective force here, and my company is just now
much weakened by the number I sent home and to Hardy to purchase
horses. I have authority to buy ninety horses, and yesterday
dispatched Calvin Shoup and Joe Riddle to Hardy and Pendleton to
buy or press forty. I want you to send word to Giles Devier to send
on some of the men as soon as possible. Urge the matter on him.

Under the law, having been commissioned as Capts. and Lieuts. of infantry, the officers of my company were required to be recommissioned. On yesterday I tendered my resignation, and was reelected by my boys in a manner and with an enthusiasm that was indeed flattering to me. Lieutenants Rader (Derrick) and Fulk* also resigned, but did not offer for reelection, preferring for reasons of their own, to return home, which as officers resigning their commissions they had a right to do. They will probably return and attach themselves again to the company or join some other command. J. N. Liggett was unanimously elected 1st Lieutenant of my company, Joe Pennybacker 2nd Lieutenant, Hiram Devier Orderly Sergeant. The men are all well satisfied, and no discontent prevails in the camp.

I will write you again in a few days through the mail. Forward me the Richmond Dispatch, if you please, and request my friends not to take it out of the office. I can get to hear nothing from the East. Don't neglect this.

Love to all. Your dear husband,

John Winfield.

Camp at Romney, June 27, 1861.

My dear wife: Your letter was handed me about midnight by some one from Romney. I was then engaged in felling trees and making a barricade in a mountain pass with the view of defending the position against a large anticipated force of Federal troops. I read it by lighting matches. Soon after I received a dispatch from Col. McDonald to divide my command, leave a portion at the pass, and return with the remainder to town, in order to reinforce another point, if it became necessary. The old gentleman has retired, and left me in command for the night. I am now writing fast at daylight in his office. We shall not, I think, be attacked now, though we had every reason to apprehend that a sally would be made upon us.

I have been upon my horse almost all the while since yesterday morning, scouting through the mountains with a small party of my men. The last twenty-four hours have been to us eventful. Having learned that heavy reinforcements of Federal troops arrived yesterday at Cumberland, parties under different commands were dispatched in various directions to ascertain their movements. I took the road leading towards Cumberland, by way of a place called Bloomington, and then fell down Patterson's creek and crossed the mountain back again to Romney without meeting an enemy. Capt. Ashby, however, was more fortunate, having detached a small party headed by his brother Dick Ashby as an advance guard, in the direction of Patterson's creek bridge, he followed on with eleven men in the rear. The first party consisting of five were soon met by a large Federal scouting party, and fired upon. One of the party returned to the

---

*They never returned in the service. Went west.

reserve of eleven men, and stated that he thought his comrades were all killed. This stirred up the blood of the eleven gallant men headed by that brave and chivalrous man Capt. Turner Ashby. They put spurs to their horses, dashed ahead, and soon fell into an ambuscade of some sixty Federal troops, secreted by the road side in the bushes. Over forty fires were directed at Capt. Ashby alone, one shot wounding him slightly in the leg. A friend fell by his side, his horse was shot under him, and still they advanced. Dismounting they advanced, and drawing their bowie knives and revolvers, put the cowardly dogs to flight with a loss of ten or twelve of their men. A more daring feat has no parallel on record, eleven men charging upon sixty, and the latter in ambuscade! And yet to kill ten or twelve and put the rest to flight seems almost incredible. But it is true.

A messenger has just come galloping in and reports that Dick Ashby was not killed, but badly wounded, and is in the hands of friends. Thank God for that!

Two hundred of our force marched about two o'clock last night in the direction of New Creek Depot. At that place two companies of Federal troops landed yesterday. If our scheme succeeds, they will be cut to pieces. We know how and where they are quartered at that place, in a large factory building, probably drunk and asleep. They may be aroused by the dashing tramp of one hundred horsemen, and in a manner which I must not now trust to paper find every brick of the building tottering from its foundations around them. We have commenced work against our enemies in earnest. My dear wife, you will have no cause to complain of our policy.

I have been compelled to write in great haste, and while receiving and replying to dispatches for Col. McDonald. You can, however, gather the ideas and arrange them at your leisure so that you can make them intelligible.

We have sent to Gen. Johnston for reinforcements.

If you go to Orkney and we to Moorefield soon, I can visit you I think, though Col. McDonald will be reluctant to spare me for a night. I have been flattered by the Colonel's entire confidence, and trust I shall not prove unworthy of it.

Your dear husband,

John Winfield.

P. S. Alfred* is quite well and likes the service. He wants a uniform. I shall procure it for him, as I could scarcely do otherwise.

If you can conveniently take the children to Howard's Lick within ten days, and notify me, I think I can visit you and remain a few hours. Hard that it must be for so short a time! Is it not?

---

*His body servant.

Camp at Romney,
Sunday morning, June 30, 1861.

As to-day is one of quiet and of leisure to the soldiery, here at least, I have determined to spend a portion of it in giving you something more in detail of the doings and intentions of our little army in this section than my want of time has hitherto allowed me. My object in returnng to the West was simply to enter upon a theater where minie rifles in the hands of expert marksmen might soon be brought into service. I, like yourself, have become tired of delay and inaction. I did not want to be marched into the interior, to indulge in the luxury of dress parades to the inspiring strains of "Dixie Land" while the insolent foe behind us were polluting the soil of my native state. When I heard that Col. McDonald and Capt. Ashby had been commissioned to raise a regiment who were to have large discretionary powers, who were resolved to drive the enemy back, to pursue them even to their dens, into Maryland, Pennsylvania, or wherever they could be found, I made up my mind to join them, provided my boys approved of the project. As I had anticipated, my boys at once, when the matter was submitted to them expressed their entire willingness to follow me. Noble fellows! Their devotion to me,* is a double remuneration for all the pains and expense I have incurred for them. It seems that our fame as an efficient body of men had gone before us to Col. McDonald. He received us with demonstrations of the highest regard, took me at once into his entire confidence, gave me a splendid blooded horse, worth $300, and promised to mount and equip the company in the shortest possible time. Though we are far from being in a state of efficient organization, wanting in ammunition, and the regiment not half made up, we have already struck terror into the hearts of the abolitionists along the border, while we have driven off and arrested most of the tories (Union men) or brought about their reformation. We have the jail now full of spies and tories, and intend to send them on to Richmond. The leaders of the Tory party have mostly made their escape, leaving their families behind them. Such work as this had to be done, and must be done, before Western Virginia can be reclaimed from Yankeedom. Those who are in their hearts true to their native heath, but who are intimidated by the threats of the Union men, are now assuming a bolder front, and scarcely an hour passes day or night that some hardy mountaineer or usually quiet farmer does not come dashing up to Headquarters with intelligence from the enemy. I assure you we are rapidly putting this part of the house in order, and will have, ere long I trust, rendered efficient service to the cause in which we are engaged.

In my last I gave you an account of the fight between the Ashbys and the Federal troops. In the first skirmish Richard Ashby with five men was attacked by a body of Federal troops, from forty

---

*Private Dick Black years after the war wrote to a friend from Missouri that he would crawl thirty miles to see the old captain.

to sixty in number. After a desperate fight, Ashby's men retired. Two of the number were wounded, and Dick was left upon the field supposed to be dead. An inhuman wretch even thrust a bayonet into his abdomen, and beat him over the head with the heavy end of the gun after he was supposed to be in a dying condition. Every blow he gave him was followed by a pause, and in the interval Ashby was asked, "Are you a Secessionist or a Union man?"

In proud defiance the word "Secession" was hurled at the fiends as long as the lips of the gallant warrior could quiver a reply.

About two hours after the fight, Turner Ashby with eleven men fell into an ambuscade of the same party that had attacked his brother, and about one-half mile from the place where the first fight occurred. You see that Dick was proceeding up the railroad, and Turner Ashby reaching the road higher up, was going to strike the railroad at two points and effect a junction. The enemy through spies were aware of the movement, and set a trap for both. The Ashby parties were merely on a scouting expedition, and did not expect the enemy where they found them. They were taking observations of the mountains, the country, its advantages and disadvantages for an engagement. As I told you in my last Turner Ashby with eleven men routed the enemy, from forty to sixty in number minus those that Dick had sent to their long homes.

Turner Ashby had his favorite horse killed under him, lost two men, and had two wounded. With his own hands, having two naval revolvers, he shot down five of them, they firing at him all the while, with their guns on their hips, too much frightened to bring their pieces to their eyes, he taking deliberate aim, and bringing them down at every shot, remarking the while, "I brought you, did I?" "You have it," "That will do." His men that were not disabled followed his example, and after coolly firing off their revolvers, threw them down, drew their bowie knives, and made at the foe. The *valiant* foe could not withstand such intrepid bravery, but fled carrying off a number of dead bodies, and leaving the gallant Virginians in possession of the field. Turner Ashby then proceeded to the place where his brother fell, and found him still alive, bore him off, and astonishing as it may seem, Dick will in all probability recover. His attending physicians now entertain scarcely any doubt of his restoration.

It has been ascertained that in the two fights the Federal troops lost eighteen killed, and had some wounded, besides some horses. Our loss was two killed, two seriously wounded, and two or three slightly.

If I go to Howard's Lick, and you are not there, I will come on to Orkney, if possible Saturday night. This of course is contingent upon circumstances, and presumes that we shall not be moved from here before that time.

You would find no difficulty in obtaining a place here to stay among the most respectable and intelligent people, who would esteem it a favor to entertain the wife of one who is to his utmost endeavoring to defend their homes and firesides.

I have raised a hope in my own breast, a bright hope, and I know in yours also. May it be realized. Since I have allowed myself to think that I can see you, I wish that this message could fly to you to-night, and that I had appointed an earlier day to meet you. But I must give you time. You know how much joy it would give me to see you, the dear children, Lizzie, Ma, and Mr. Cootes, and every member of the family, white and black.

I must not forget to tell you that I expect before the week ends to have a turn at the Federal troops. A band of about sixty or seventy have been prowling around on the Virginia side. I have learned pretty well where they are in the habit of scouting, and I think I can capture the whole bunch of them. So when I reach Orkney Springs next Saturday or Howard's Lick, if you are there, I hope to bear the intelligence that I have won my spurs.

Wallace, the Col. who entered Romney before the arrival of our troops, is still at Cumberland, and has been reinforced by two Pennsylvania regiments. He says he intends to pay Romney another visit. He will be *warmly* received if he does, but he has no idea of doing so unless with an immense force, and then with slow approaches.

CHAPTER VII

First Battle of Manassas

Haymarket, Prince William Co.
July 22, 1861.

My dear wife: We reached here awhile before night in a heavy rain and concluded to rest until morning. We are within six miles of the place where the battle was fought on yesterday. I have seen quite a number of persons who were engaged in the fight and who have been down upon the battle field. The slaughter of men was very great on both sides. For three miles the road is strewn with dead bodies. The loss from the most reliable information I can obtain is about equal, twenty-five hundred on each side. The victory, however, perches on our banner. Our men drove them from the field, and pursued them to Centerville, a distance of six or seven miles, and captured sixty-two pieces of their cannon, among them Sherman's splendid battery. It is also said and believed here that we took thirty thousand stand of arms from them. It is certainly true that immense numbers of small arms and large ordnance were captured. It is thought that Gen. Paterson has been taken prisoner, and that Gen. Scott's carriage and four horses were captured. This may be true. The Yankees are terribly frightened. Their three months men are leaving, and their ranks are being thinned from disaffection and fear. Yesterday was doubtless the turning point of this unnatural contest. Jeff Davis and Scott were both upon the field on their respective sides. When Davis made his appearance a shout was sent to the very heavens, and the Yankees fell by hundreds at every fire. Many of our regiments have suffered very severely, among others Col. Gibbons'. I have not been able to learn who was killed or wounded in this regiment, but learned that they fought bravely, and suffered severely. I fear that many of our friends are among the killed and wounded. I trust that Frank Cootes is safe. I shall be on the battle ground to-morrow, and will at once see after him. I have many things to say to you, but have not the opportunity. Imagine, my dear wife, how my devotion to you and the children rises as there is a prospect of death before me, but console yourself with the reflection that no stain of cowardice or toryism or lack of devotion to my company will ever taint my memory.

Your affectionate husband,

(John Winfield.)

P. S. We report to Beauregard to-night.

Haymarket, 10 miles from Junction,
July 23, 1861.

My dear wife: While here awaiting orders from Gen. Beauregard I have concluded to drop you a line again this morning. I obtained pretty comfortable quarters last night, and feel better than I had a right to expect after a day's ride in the rain. The people all through the country shower their hospitality upon us. This is especially refreshing to those so recently accustomed to the cold if not traitorous countenances of our Western Virginia population.

The news received from the battle ground this morning is more favorable to our side. I will give it as reported: From 5 to 7,000 of the enemy killed, 1,000 of them taken prisoner, among the prisoners 70 officers of the grade of captain and above, 50 to 60 pieces of artillery captured, one piece with 16 fine horses attached, Gen. Scott's carriage and four fine horses taken, one hundred and fifty baggage wagons, from 5 to 7,000 small arms, and an immense amount of baggage.

Having just heard a shout of triumph in the street, I stepped out a moment and inquired the cause. It proceeded from a report brought from the battlefield by George Calvert, (son of John S. Calvert) that the enemy had retreated into Washington, that Senator Clingman had rode over the field, and from experience and observation gained in Mexico, felt justified in saying that not less than 7,000 of the foe are dead upon the field. Thousands of them were wounded and taken prisoner besides. Bonaparte in his palmiest day never had such fighting men as the Confederate States. Never was such a victory won. For several hours 4,000 of our men kept 60,000 of the enemy in check until reinforcements arrived.

It will take them two months to reorganize and supply the place of their lost ordnance and stores. The WAR IS ENDED, except for the enemy to skirmish a little while until they can most decently get out of the difficulty they are in.

I wish I might have been in the battle the day before yesterday, but I suppose Providence ordained otherwise. We have orders from Beauregard to come on to the Junction leisurely, so that we shall probably not have much to do at present.

The people here would be more rejoiced at the splendid victory we have won, were it not for the reflection that many of their friends and relatives are among the killed and wounded on our side. The last report from the battle field does not estimate our loss as any higher, that is, 500 killed and 1500 wounded. I have made inquiries of every one about Col. Gibbons, the 10th regiment, but cannot learn the names of any that were killed or wounded.

We shall leave here in about two hours.

Remember me to Mr. Cootes, and tell him not to be uneasy about Frank*. I feel almost sure he is safe. I wish I could relieve his anxiety. Col. Jackson was not killed, as at first reported. He is safe. Gen. Paterson (Federal) is probably taken prisoner.

The 7th Regiment Virginia Cavalry reached Winchester from Romney on the 19th of July. After obeying orders to scout along Paterson's line and ascertain the position of his army, they were marched to join Johnston at Manassas. Their failure to arrive in time to take part in the battle was partly occasioned by the condition of their leader, Col. McDonald, who was suffering greatly from rheumatism. But so great was his ardor and zeal for the cause that rather than commit the command to his lieutenant, though it were the daring Ashby himself, he determined to have himself conveyed in a covered wagon over the rugged mountain way, made almost impassable by heavy rains.

To oppose a threatened movement of Rosecrans against Staunton, the 7th Cavalry on July 24 was ordered to proceed to that point. But when it was discovered that Rosecrans had returned to the mountains of western Virginia, the 7th was at once sent back to the lower Valley as a guard to the border counties, and to protect the farmers in gathering the crops.

Upon reaching Winchester eight of the companies returned to the South Branch of the Potomac from which they had recently been recalled, accompanying Gen. McDonald. The rest of the regiment went into camp with Lieut.-Col. Ashby somewhere near Shepherdstown.

---

*Frank Cootes, stepbrother to Mrs. Winfield. He lived for some years after the war, and left two sons, Harry, now a colonel in the U. S. army, and F. Graham Cootes, the New York artist.

Camp Hollingsworth,
Sept. 2, 1861.

My dear wife: While you no doubt felt much disappointment upon learning that I had declined to take home on my route from Richmond, you will be gratified to learn that I have returned to my duties much improved in health.

I made but a short stay in the Capital, and of course scarcely looked beyond the immediate object of my visit. I met with some of my old friends, and spent some pleasant moments with them. There are but few troops in Richmond, everything having been attracted towards Manassas Junction. There are strong indications of another terrible conflict at Manassas, if it has not already occurred. I feel sure that we shall not remain here long. We ought not, at least, upon the eve of important events, and yet we are poorly armed and equipped. This fact may make us hesitate. As for myself, I am willing to go into the fight with a corn cutter, and I have not a man that would not follow me.

Dr. John Cootes* has no doubt already informed you of the running of the blockade by the English merchantman Alliance under cover of a British Man of War. Thus has England run the blockade, and in the most offensive manner proclaimed that she does not mean to regard it any longer. The Alliance was loaded with arms, ammunition, and many other things we need. The city of Richmond was much enlivened upon receipt of this news at the War Department, and more so when well confirmed rumors of a victory in western Virginia and in Missouri reached them. Gen. Tyler of the Federal army has no doubt been routed with much loss by Floyd and Wise at Gauly.

There are visible signs of a reaction in the Northern States, especially in Pennsylvania. The Democratic party are becoming alarmed at the high handed suppression of their journals, and the system of espionage that the Lincoln administration has adopted. The hand of the Almighty is plainly seen working the destruction of our enemies. While victory crowns our arms, while our troops are flushed with triumph, and at a time when unity of feeling and purpose is so much demanded in the North, the administration is widening the breach between parties, in its own section, trampling upon private rights, usurping all political power, and thereby raising up a secret and terrible enemy in their own bosoms. Thus they are working out their own destruction.

The war cannot continue long. Those who are spared will soon return to their homes and families to spend the balance of their lives in a land whose soil will still teem with the richest products, whose skies are bright, and whose history will have no parallel for brave and chivalrous deeds. This New Jerusalem, this people with high and noble instincts, with capacity for free

*Brother of Frank Cootes, of the 10th Va. Reg.

government, descended mostly from the cavaliers of Virginia, with the blessing of God upon them, *this, these* will ere long take their places in the galaxy of nations, and shine the brighter by its dark surroundings.   Long have I hoped and wished and prayed for this event, for a separation from this race that has been endeavoring to drag us back to despotism and destroy the last hope of free government.

I have four men sick with a mild type of fever, John Miller, Big Eph. Wean, William Bowers, and Henry Zirkle.   There is much sickness at the Junction.   It is thought about 10,000 men are sick in the army of Virginia.   The disease is now on the decline, and those sick are convalescing rapidly.   Upon the bare apprehension of a fight at the Junction hundreds of invalids left their rooms and tottered from Richmond and other points to join their commands. Can such a noble people be conquered?

It was a severe trial for me to forego the pleasure of seeing you on my return, and those dear little children.   What would I not give to fold them to my heart again!   Kiss them all for me.

Kindest regards to Mr. Cootes, and tell him that from what I can learn Col. Gibbons' regiment is in advance towards Arlington. Perhaps has had a skirmish.

Your husband affectionately,

John Winfield.

P. S.   Alfred* is down with a mild attack of fever.   He is at Col. McDonald's.

CHAPTER VIII

Brock's Gap Rifles at Shepherdstown

Shepherdstown, Jefferson Co., Va.
Sept. 13, 1861.

My dear wife: I was ordered here with a part of our regiment on Thursday last, and am now in command of this Post.   We are here in the very face of the enemy, and are firing at each other constantly across the river.   The Federalists have an encampment just one mile from here.   I can step out upon the street and see their camp without difficulty.   Pretty close, are we not?   I was out making a reconnaissance with my glass yesterday, and approached very near their camp.   They sent two minie balls towards me at last, but I found out all I wished, and returned to town.

We are getting up a scheme to rout the enemy by crossing the river and making a bold dash upon them.   They have not more than 250 men opposite this place, but can be reinforced from some encampments which are only a few miles distant.

------

*Body servant.

The people here are exceedingly hospitable. Spent last night with seventy-five of my men at Mr. Alexander Boteler's. He is the most accomplished gentleman I ever met. He has a very interesting family. His daughter entertained us with music, the old gentleman with his fine conversational powers, and the good lady with a most excellent breakfast. We had supped before we reached there.

I would give all the world to be with you to-night, but I must sacrifice the comfort of my home for a duty that is paramount to everything else.

Winchester, Va.
Sept. 16, 1861.

My dear wife: You observe from the caption of this letter that I am again back in Winchester. We were called here suddenly on yesterday from Shepherdstown to prepare for another wild goose chase in the mountains of Hampshire, called away from the face of the foe to seek one in the jungles and hills of a poverty stricken region. It is outrageous that brave men who entered into this war for their country's good and panting for an opportunity to distinguish themselves should see all their efforts and all their cherished hopes frustrated by a superannuated commander.

He now calls us away from a field of glory, from one of the most lovely sections of the state, from a land distinguished not more for its fertility, beauty, and resources than for its fair, intelligent and loyal daughters and brave and true men, I speak of the counties of Jefferson and Berkley bordering on the Potomac. We are to leave here to go to New Creek depot, among the unionists to starve, and perhaps to die "unwept, unhonored, and unsung." We must, however, obey orders for the present.

We had a considerable battle with the enemy at Shepherdstown day before yesterday. My company to which was attached a four pounder were alone engaged in the action. We fought about one hour across the river. The enemy fired at random. Concealed in rifle pits dug for the purpose, and behind the canal embankments, it was difficult to see them at all. Hence we could not do much execution. I gave my men orders to fire only when they saw them, and not to waste ammunition. Under all these disadvantages we saw a number borne off the field, killed or badly wounded. We had not a man touched, though many made narrow escapes. More than twenty balls at different times passed very near me. At one time I was in range of a platoon fire, and had I not squatted pretty low, would have caught it. My boys dodged the balls, and laughed at each other for dodging. George C. Fulk killed two Yankees during the engagement, Mike Bowman one, and others claim a similar distinction. The lumbering of the cannon early in the morning, the sharp crack of the rifles at intervals on our side, and by volleys on the other, made the scene quite an exciting one.

Do keep in better spirits. You do not know how it distresses me when I receive a gloomy letter from you. Trust that there is a brighter day coming, that there is sunshine behind the clouds that now darken our country, that there are years of happiness in store for us, years that will be entered upon with more wisdom and experience, more gratitude to our Creator, and with more rational views of the aims and objects of our existence.

Write to me at Romney, Hampshire Co., until further advised. When we go into winter quarters I intend to have you and the children with me. I trust that we may winter in Jefferson County, in or near Shepherdstown. They have the best society in the state. I should like for you to form the acquaintance of the people in that section.

We leave here this afternoon or in the morning. The lounging of my men about Winchester in obedience to the orders of our Colonel is the reason why so many importune me for leave of absence. When on active duty no one wishes to leave. I must set them an example of sticking close to my post, and therefore cannot hope to see you until we go into winter quarters, unless I have some business in Richmond. This is not improbable.

Romney, Va. Sept. 18, 1861.

My dear wife: We are again at Romney. Arrived here this evening, our destination New Creek Depot on the Baltimore and Ohio R. R., or perhaps some mountain or jungle in the moon.

This is a cold and inhospitable clime, compared to the section we so recently left behind us. The whole regiment are dissatisfied, and long to return to a land worth fighting for, and where the people are loyal and true.

There are, we have learned since we arrived here, about 1,000 Federal troops at New Creek Depot. We have about four hundred cavalry, four pieces of cannon, and several hundred militia, and if the enemy do not run before we get up, a fight will soon come off in this quarter. They have some cannon also, but we do not fear them, and hope they will be accommodating enough to remain forty-eight hours longer.

I gave you an account in my last of our skirmish at Shepherdstown. Since I wrote you, we have learned the result of our firing from a reliable source. We killed ten, and wounded severely a number. The distance we fired was about four hundred yards, with nothing but their heads peeking from pits dug in the ground to aim at. Pretty good shooting, and likely to establish the reputation we have won for marksmanship.

I am very tired this evening, and only write to let you know where I am.

Romney, Sept. 19, 1861.

My dear wife: I regret to have to say that I am suffering from a return of those irregular chills, with which I was attacked some time ago in Winchester, but I do not think they will be of long duration, as the mountain air of this region will be unfavorable to their continuance. Do not be foolish enough to be uneasy about me again. I hope to be able to be in the saddle in twenty-four hours, and could, if necessary, ride to-day. But as we shall probably not march as soon as I anticipated in my last, I have thought it best to lay up in the house of an old friend, and rid myself of these curious shakes. I am taking quinine heavily, and my head is in a sad condition to write. I mention this fact particularly that you may not apprehend that I have departed from my usual abstemious habits.

I trust that you arrived safely among your friends in Eastern Virginia, and that the change of climate and society will restore the bloom to your cheek.

Col. McDonald has just informed me that he had reliable information that we killed eight Yankees in our fight the other day, and that three wounded have since died. They report that they killed fifteen of my men and wounded a number more severely. If this report reaches you, I beg of you not to feel the slightest uneasiness in consequence. Not a hair of our heads was touched, though many shots passed whistling by our ears. You may scarcely credit it, but I assure you my men no more regarded the balls of the enemy than if they had been tow wads shot from the pop guns of playful urchins. When a ball would whistle pretty close to a fellow's ears, he would involuntarily dodge, while the group nearest would laugh, and in a moment dodge, and themselves become the subjects of laughter. Surely Providence protects your husband and his brave lads, or else so many deadly missiles aimed at us would have struck some one.

My company is at present much weakened by sickness. Most of those sent home were unfit for duty. About twenty-five are sick.

A pretty well authenticated rumor has just reached us that Gen. Lee is in possession of Grafton, and has torn up some seventeen miles of the railroad, and that Rosecrans is hemmed in between the columns of our army.

It is also rumored here that there are about 1,000 of our troops near Monterey, composed of infantry, cavalry, and artillery. This is probably Baldwin's regiment from Augusta. We have sent a courier in to learn if such be the case, and to solicit them to join us in the attack upon New Creek Depot. They would have but thirty miles to march, and we twenty to form a junction near the Yankee camp. We have four or five pieces of artillery, two rifled cannon among them, and if this junction can be formed, we shall do some work that will tell upon the general result. I shall be with them. Don't fear that a little shake will keep me back.

CHAPTER IX

Battle of Hanging Rock

Romney, Sept. 22, 1861.

My dear wife: An opportunity presenting itself to send you a line to be mailed in the Valley, and in advance of our regular mail from this place, I gladly take advantage of it to relieve any uneasiness which my last letter may have given you in regard to my health. As usual I have been speedily restored, thanks to quinine and the favor of Providence. I am very well indeed to-day. I trust that you and the dear children are equally blessed.

We have effected nothing of importance since our arrival here. Our Colonel promises us work to do before many days. No doubt we shall arrest some union men, and probably tear up some portions of the B. & O. R. R. What a splendid figure we shall cut in the history that is to be written of this war! Well, I must tell you that we are determined, as men valuing our reputations and desirous of doing our country service, to enroll under another banner. We have addressed the Secretary of War on the subject, and asked to be transferred to Stuart's Cavalry. We have a number of influential men in the State, backing us, and we shall succeed.

We shall, I understand, move to-morrow farther west, and you must not feel uneasy if you do not hear from me as frequently as usual, as all of our letters will have to be sent back to Romney to be mailed.

I am staying with my old college friend Andrew Kercheval. His sister is a nice lady, and has been very kind to me. But to-morrow, "I will mount my steed, and off to the wars again."

Romney, Sept. 28, 1861.

My dear wife: The last forty-eight hours have been the most stirring and eventful yet witnessed in this part of the grand battlefield. But before I attempt any account of our skirmishing, to relieve your anxiety let me assure you that I and all of my men are safe and unhurt.

On last Monday night between nine and ten o'clock our pickets came rushing into camp with the intelligence that the enemy were marching upon us in two directions. They had been fired upon by the advance guards, and seemed to be much excited, if not alarmed. In a few minutes the camp was in a furor, horses were saddled, swords and pistols buckled on, while the sharp comands of officers were startling the midnight air, as they ordered their respective companies to mount. Soon a part of the command were dispatched to the Hanging Rock or North West Pass about three and one-half miles from the town. Another part was sent to the West Pass, with orders to attack the enemy, and hold them in check, if possible.

I was ordered to remain near the town in command of three companies, and to act as circumstances might require. Our men and the Federalists reached both passes at very near the same time, and after some heavy firing at the North West Pass, our men gave way, and the Yankees entered the Valley. The fog was so dense that they did not advance.

The fog continued until near ten o'clock next day, and so thick that you could not see an object over fifty yards distant. The enemy, like ourselves, concluded to remain quiet until the sun's rays should have dissipated the fog. At last the curtain was lifted, and we stood opposed to each other.

About half a mile down the South Branch their cavalry were seen dashing from right to left, as skirmishers, while their infantry, about eight hundred or one thousand strong, were drawn up near by in line of battle.

I was ordered to make an advance with my company to draw them out. I sent nine or ten men under Lieut. Joe Pennybacker to give their cavalry skirmishers a round of minie balls. They lifted some of them from their saddles, and the rest soon disappeared into the pine thickets. I drew up my company after this in front of the infantry skirmishers, and drove them back to the reserve. The whole of them then disappeared for a time, but were soon seen crossing a mountain in our rear, with the view, no doubt, to reach the road to Winchester, and surround us. We dashed up the Winchester road to give them battle, but they observed our movements, and kept themselves in the mountain fastnesses. About this time we had to withdraw our forces from the West Pass in order to concentrate our strength. The enemy then approached us on the west side, sending their shell and cannon balls before them pretty near into the town. We soon discovered that this force was small, and only intended by loud demonstrations to draw us off. We kept a howitzer and small party to watch them, and employed our greatest force in skirmishes with the main body. The day was spent without any collision except an occasional encounter between the advance guards. The enemy kept bushed, and, of course, we could not charge upon them.

The sun was about setting. They were now all around us, and reported to be 5,000 strong. We had three hundred and fifty men (cavalry), and about one hundred and fifty militia to depend upon. We held a council of war and concluded to fall back five or six miles on the Winchester road. We did so, taking bag and baggage.

The next morning a message reached us that the enemy had entered Romney, and that a few of the militia were firing upon them. By common consent of the officers and men, and without many commands or words we soon saddled up, mounted, and in a few minutes were seen dashing back at the utmost speed of our horses, sending clouds of dust to the skies.

They by some means were apprised of our coming, a short time before we reached town, and took up the double quick.

We dashed into town with lightning speed, shouting at the top of our voices, and making the air ring with the clashing of sabers.

The Yankees were about half a mile from us. The head of our column dashed up within one hundred and fifty yards, dismounted and opened fire. I soon got up with the left wing, and took a position nearer and in front.

The first round from Brock's Gap made them take up the double quick again. They sent a volley or two at us, but no damage was done. The whole of our column now joined and pursued them to the West Pass. This is very much like the pass at Brock's Gap, except that the narrow defile is only one mile in length.

We had now ascertained their numbers not to exceed 1500, though the day before we stood our ground against the phantom of 5,000. But was it prudent to rush through such a defile with 350 cavalry against 1500 well armed infantry?

We sent a shell or two from our howitzer, and then at Major Funsten's command, I dashed through with my company as skirmishers. The enemy were just preparing to take a meal, not dreaming that we would follow them through the pass. Upon sight of us they took to double quick again. I followed up pretty closely, and arrested one of them, who had fallen back from fatigue, took his gun, and sent him back to the rear.

Soon the whole command came up, and on we pushed. A few minutes brought us again in sight of the retreating foe. They drew up in line of battle, and fired their volleys at us. These we answered in marksman style, bringing many of them to the dust.

They gathered up their dead, and off they took again. We pursued through the mountains, through narrow defiles and thickets until dark for miles, fighting them throughout the whole day. They were run to the verge of death, and had it not been for some misunderstanding of orders, which caused us at one time to fire on our own men, we should have flanked them, and in their tired condition captured the whole of them along with their baggage.

As it was, we killed and wounded great numbers. A reliable lady told us that they passed her house with three wagon loads of dead and wounded. Had not night overtaken us, we should have captured half of them in the woods completely helpless.

We brought off the field five prisoners, a number of guns, and five to ten horses, and chased the broken down enemy in sight of their camp at New Creek. As they had a reserve force there, we concluded to return to Romney, since we and our horses were also much fatigued and in no condition to encounter fresh troops. Thus ended an exploit of the much abused McDonald Cavalry, which has not been equalled in daring during the war.

Our loss was six horses killed and wounded, and three men wounded, two of them by mistaking friends for enemies. The enemy wounded but one of our men, Robert Fulton of Hardy, severely in the arm. He will recover.

Is it not astonishing how we are protected? A minie grazed my ear. I put up my hand to see if it had drawn blood. The wind of the ball I distinctly felt.

Some of our men took panic and fled to Winchester, reporting that we had been surrounded and cut to pieces. Much alarm was occasioned in consequence. Such cowardly dogs ought to be shot!

Alfred has recovered and is with me. My own health has improved.

Your dear husband,
John Winfield.

Romney, Sept. 29, 1861.

My dear wife: I wrote you yesterday giving somewhat of a detailed account of our battle with the Yankees. Upon reflection I can but regard it as a most rash and daring adventure, one from which we escaped being cut to pieces only by the cowardice of the enemy. Our force, between 300 and 350, pursued 1500 well armed men for sixteen miles through an almost continuous defile, from which they might at any point have mounted the sides and raked us fore and aft. But these difficulties did not deter us. We rode up and fired upon them and shot them down by scores. Providence sent their volleys aside or over our heads. Think of fifteen hundred shots being fired at us time after time within striking distance, and but one shot throughout the day taking effect in a man's arm.

Everything is quiet here now. The force at New Creek Depot have been completely demoralized by the rout they suffered. Their loss was very great. Night alone prevented us from capturing the whole of them and ascertaining their loss. We have found several of their dead in the river. They threw them in to conceal them from us in their hurry.

On the night the Yankees made their advance upon us they caught a party of twenty of our men under Lieut. Lincoln of Capt. Shands' company at Springfield. They were surrounded by three times their number, but fought gallantly. Lieut. Lincoln was taken prisoner, his hands bound and a gag put in his mouth, and in this condition he was left with a single guard. By some means he got his pistol from his case, and although his hands were tied he shot the guard and made his escape, coming into camp gagged and tied. One of our party was killed, and another taken prisoner. The rest escaped with the loss of ten or twelve horses.

The news reached here to-day that the Yankees have left New Creek. If they have not, we will attack them there soon, or perhaps at Cumberland.

We shall not, I presume, remain here a great while longer. But wherever we are do not feel uneasy about us. I have an abiding confidence that we shall triumph, and that your dear husband will return again to the peaceful shades of home without a scar. Do not believe the lying reports that are constantly being circulated of casualties occurring to us. If you do not hear from me as often as you desire, you may know that it is on account of irregularity of the mails, or because I have not the opportunity to write.

Romney, October 2, 1861.

My dear wife: Since my last nothing unusual has occurred in this quarter. The Yankees are still at New Creek, and rumor says heavily reinforced. Our scouts, however, report only 170 tents in their encampment. The tents are small, and probably do not contain more than eight persons each, so that the story of reinforcements having arrived is highly improbable. The truth is they have no forces to spare from other more important points.

We continue to receive information confirming previous accounts that the enemy sustained very heavy losses in their engagement with us last week. It is probable that their Col. (Cantwell) was killed or severely wounded. Reports from Cumberland say that their Major and several captains were killed. Their killed, wounded, and missing upon their hasty arrival at New Creek amounted to three hundred. Many of those missing, no doubt, found their way out of the mountains to their encampment.

They report our strength at 10,000, and say that we seemed to spring out of the ground suddenly, and that we did not fight them fairly, that we sheltered behind rocks and trees, that they had to fire against the mountain sides or in the air at random, and much more. These things are gathered from women living on the road and from farmers who are not in the army, and who were pressed with their teams by the Yankees for the day, and afterwards released. We hear something from these almost every day.

Col. McDonald in my opinion, and as I expected, is preparing to winter here. I am unalterably opposed to such a step.

You spoke of Col. Ashby as having been left in the lower valley. It is true, and the old Col. himself promised when we came up here to join Ashby in a very short time. Ashby was ordered by the Sec. of War to remain with 100 of our cavalry at or near Shepherdstown for the protection of the citizens of that quarter.

It is rumored that a fight is going on near Arlington. I hope so. To fight is to win a victory.

The weather is quite cool here at night, and I am afraid the winter will be upon us before we are prepared for it. I am very much in want of heavy flannels, but I sent to Rockingham, and may be able to procure them there.

Alfred has recovered, and is as well as usual. He came on here with me from Winchester.

The men we had wounded the other day are doing well, and will speedily recover. My men here are now nearly all well, and those at home rapidly convalescing will soon return to duty.

I am told that the report was taken to the Valley and elsewhere that my command was cut to pieces on last Tuesday and Wednesday, that I was killed, and Col. McDonald killed, &c, &c; that the militia alone triumphed over the Federal forces, that those of us who were spared ran off like cowardly dogs, &c. Doesn't McDonald's regiment catch it on all sides?

The friends of members of my company were no doubt uneasy until they received a correction of these lying rumors. And just here let me caution you not to believe anything you hear about me, no matter how good the authority, until you hear from me. If I am killed, time will reveal the truth, so don't be in a hurry about believing any such rumors.

Had you been at Cootes' Store you might have been alarmed, as one of my men fled home, and reported that I had been killed.*

*Mrs. Winfield was at that time visiting relatives in Eastern Virginia.

CHAPTER X

Ashby Promoted Colonel of McDonald Regiment

History and the testimony of survivors of Co. B must give the narrative of events occurring between October 2 and November 2, as no letters of Captain Winfield covering that period are found.

The following letter by Ashby is quoted in full, as it gives an account of the most important military incident of the month intervening in which Captain Winfield and his men were engaged:

"Camp Evans, Halltown, Va.
Oct. 17, 1861.

"My dear Sir:

"I herewith submit the result of an engagement with the enemy on yesterday at Bolivar Hill. The enemy occupying that position for several days, had been committing depredations in the vicinity of the camp. Having at my disposal three hundred militia armed with flint-lock muskets and two companies of cavalry,—Turner's and Mason's of Colonel McDonald's regiment,—I wrote to General Evans to cooperate with me, taking position on Loudon Heights, and thereby preventing reenforcements from below, and at the same time to drive them out of the Ferry, where they were under cover of the buildings. On the evening of the fifteenth I was re-enforced by two companies of Colonel McDonald's regiment (Captain Winfield), fully armed with minie rifles and mounted; Captain Miller's about thirty men mounted, the balance on foot and with flint-lock guns. I had one rifled four-pound gun and one 24-pound gun badly mounted, which broke an axle in Bolivar, and I had to spike it. My force on the morning of the attack consisted of 300 militia, part of two regiments, commanded by Colonel Albert of Shenandoah and Major Finter of Page. I had 180 of Colonel McDonald's Cavalry (Captain Henderson's men), under command of Lieutenant Glynn; Captain Baylor's mounted militia, Captain Hess, about twenty-five men. The rifled gun was under command of Captain Comfield. I made the attack in three divisions and drove the enemy from their breastworks without the loss of a man, and took position upon the hill, driving the enemy as far as Lower Bolivar. The large gun broke down, and this materially affected the result. The detachment from the large gun was transferred to the rifled piece, and Captain Avirett was sent to Loudon Heights with a message to Colonel Griffin. The enemy now formed and charged with shouts and yells, and the militia met them like veterans. At this moment I ordered a charge of cavalry, which was handsomely done,—Captain Turner in the lead. In the charge five of the enemy were killed. After holding this position for four hours the enemy were re-enforced by infantry and artillery, and we fell back in order to the position their pickets held in the morning. The position Colonel Griffin held upon Loudon was such as to be of little assistance to us, not being so elevated as to prevent them from controlling the crossing. My main force is now at Camp Evans, while I hold all intermediate ground. The enemy left the Ferry last night and encamped on Maryland Heights. My loss was one* killed and nine wounded. We have two prisoners and eight Union men cooperating with them. We took a large number of blankets, overcoats, and about a dozen guns. I cannot compliment my officers and men too highly for their gallant bearing during the whole fight, considering the bad arms with which they were supplied and their inexperience. I cannot impress too forcibly the necessity of the perfect organization of my artillery, and the forwarding at a very early day of the other gun promised. These guns are drawn by horses obtained for the occasion and are worked by volunteers. We are in want of cavalry arms and long range guns, and would be glad to have an arrangement made to mount my men. I herewith submit Surgeon N. G. West's report, and respectfully submit his name as one worthy of an appointment. He is temporarily employed by me as a surgeon. Casualties, thirteen wounded.

"Your obedient servant,

"Turner Ashby.

"Hon. Mr. Benjamin, Acting Sec. of War."[1]

In the mean time the Federal Department embracing the posts of New Creek and Cumberland was assigned to the command of

---

*Kline of Co. B, Capt. Winfield.
[1]Thomas, p. 40.

Brigadier-General Kelly. He had concentrated at New Creek a force consisting of about 5,000 men of all arms, and on Oct. 6 he advanced to attack the Confederates at Romney.

Col. McDonald's strength had been weakened by the loss of companies B and G under their respective Captains, Winfield and Miller, who had remained with Ashby after the battle of Bolivar Heights. Companies A and C had been acting with Ashby for some months, so Col. McDonald was left with only six of the ten companies composing his cavalry regiment. There was a regiment of militia commanded by Col. Monroe, and for artillery work a howitzer and a rifle-gun. With this small force Col. McDonald decided to try to hold his ground against an army of ten to one. The result of this unequal contest was a complete rout of the McDonald cavalry, with the loss of their baggage trains, guns, etc.

The following extract from a memoir of his father written by Capt. William McDonald* will explain the circumstances that led to the resignation of the brave old colonel, and the elevation of Ashby to the full command of the regiment.

"Previously to the defeat at Romney, there were many circumstances which conspired to make Col. McDonald unpopular with his command. He had reached that period of life when the infirmities of age incapacitated him from commanding a regiment of cavalry. He could rarely ride on horseback, and dared not expose himself to inclement weather, or to the ordinary inconveniences of a camp life. Every attempt to defy the dangers of exposure resulted in a painful attack of rheumatism; so that in a few months after he took command of his regiment he was more or less an invalid, with little hope of ever being otherwise. To secure discipline and efficiency in a regiment, especially one of raw troops, the constant presence and personal superintendence of the commanding officer is indispensable. Hence it was but a short time before the regiment were discontented with him, desiring, as was natural, a more active and vigorous commander. Their eyes, too, were turned upon Ashby, the next officer in rank. **********

"This being the condition of things previous to the disaster at Romney, it may well be supposed that this affair did not improve it. ********** Accordingly, Col. McDonald found upon his arrival at Winchester, where he attempted to reorganize his command, that the dissatisfaction among the men and officers was great, and would prove a serious drawback to his achieving on the field anything for the good of the country. ********** In an interview with Jackson, he requested him to relieve him from duty, if he thought the good of the cause required it. He was accordingly relieved, and placed in charge of the artillery defences of Winchester."

Hence from Oct. 15, 1861, Capt. Winfield and his mountain troopers were under the immediate command of Ashby, and were

---

*Memoir of Colonel McDonald, in Ashby and his Compeers, Avirett.

reckoned among his most trusted and efficient helpers. Says an admirer in a brief memoir of Capt. Winfield, "It was the gallantry of Capt. Winfield and his men that helped to achieve the glory which crowns the name of Ashby with an imperishable lustre. Whilst they acted together, Ashby looked to Winfield for support in his most perilous enterprises. In their enthusiastic devotion to country they were brothers, as they were friends in mutual regard."

CHAPTER XI

CAMPAIGNING IN THE LOWER VALLEY

Camp Evans, Near Charlestown,
Nov. 2, 1861.

My dear wife: Absence from camp on scouting duty for a day or two has been the cause of a wider gap than usual in my correspondence.

When the rain fell in torrents last night, and the wind blew, as if "twad blaw its last," I have no doubt that you were much concerned about our gallant soldiers; but you little dreamed that your husband at that moment was looking around for a rock whereon to lay his head and gathering the leaves round about him to afford something of a bed and shelter.

I left Shepherdstown about sundown yesterday evening, and by a circuitous route worked my way along the Potomac opposite Dam No. 4, where about 1,000 Yankees are encamped. I bivouacked my men in a dark woods, and intended remaining until morning and then making a dash from our retreat upon some of the scoundrels who come over the river at this point every day to plunder. The storm caused us to abandon the design. We mounted our horses and fell back to a big barn, some miles from the river. I obtained shelter in a house.

This morning we returned to camp, a distance of about fifteen miles. The day was one of the severest I ever encountered, and it has rained and stormed ever since without intermission. The men are leaving the tents like rats a sinking ship, and seeking shelter in barns and neighboring houses. If the Yankees venture out to-night they will find but little opposition from us, provided they could find us at all. But I do not apprehend any movement from them on such a night.

The approach of winter has again caused me to think seriously of resigning my commission. I shall determine in my own mind in a few days whether I shall engage boarding for you or return home. There is some difficulty likely to arise in obtaining a release. The surgeon may have to certify to my inability to attend to the duties incumbent upon me; Col. Ashby may be very unwilling to give me up

&c. But after all I apprehend that the most difficult part of the matter will be to obtain my own consent. I know that I cannot bear up under active duty during the winter, but then the Col. in the goodness of his heart and desire to retain me, will suggest that I had better obtain a furlough for a while, that we will go into winter quarters, and that my lieutenants can keep the company in proper discipline. But alas! I am afraid I have no one in the company who properly appreciates the difficulties and trials of a captain's position, and who would undertake to command the company. My lieutenants, though brave and ready for service at all times, have not the qualifications for this office. My company is, as you know, a hobby and pet with me, I have spent much time, pains, and money to render it efficient. Could I place it in competent hands, under a leader who would add laurels to those already won, I could retire satisfied and without hesitation. You understand now how I am situated, and the real difficulties that attend my resignation.

Tell Jake Liggett, when you see him again, that if he can return in a few weeks and take command, that I will leave on furlough indefinitely. But I will write him on this subject.

It is rumored here, or rather it comes from a reliable man who says he read the account in the "Baltimore Clipper," that McClellan and Cabinet have had a rupture, that Scott has resigned, that the peace party are giving the administration uneasiness &c.

The "Baltimore Clipper," the same gentleman says, has hoisted the flag for peace and a recognition of the Southern Confederacy. If this paper, and I don't doubt it, has done this in Baltimore, it plainly sees the props falling from under the Lincoln throne.

Gen. Jackson has been ordered to this region from Manassas with his brigade. He has been assigned command of all the country and forces between the Blue Ridge and Alleghanies.

I trust that the storm we are having will scatter the Yankee fleets and dash' them to pieces on our shores. It will probably injure the canal near here and stop transportation for a while. With the Potomac blockaded and canal drained, they would soon be pinched for supplies in Washington. If the winter is severe, they must build up the B. & O. R. R., or evacuate Washington. They will doubtless make an effort to possess themselves of Martinsburg and Charlestown to effect that object. They cannot succeed.

Give my love as usual to Ma and Mr. Cootes, and all the darkies. Tell Rose I miss her good coffee.

Your husband,
John Winfield.

Martinsburg, Friday, Dec. 5, 1861.

My dear wife: I learned through Lieut. Kennon that you had arrived safe in Woodstock, and that you had pretty nearly recovered from your recent illness, all of which intelligence, you may be assured, was highly gratifying to me.

Well, my dear wife, I cannot visit you to-morrow as I had fondly hoped to do, but I shall try to be with you one day next week.

I think I shall make arrangements when I go up to Winchester to board you there, and can bring you down when I visit you. I know that you are pleasantly situated at Mr. Shaeffer's, but it is inconvenient for me to visit you. At Winchester I can see you every week, at least.

My health is better again. Do not fear that I shall expose myself more than is necessary to a proper and conscientious discharge of my duty, and if I then fall, I trust that Providence will kindly care for those so near and dear to my heart.

Perhaps I told you in my last that Calvin Shoup was wounded. He is improving rapidly. Dr. Magruder was badly hurt some days ago by a fall from his horse. John W. West was also hurt by a fall of forty feet perpendicular on a bed of stones. Strange to say he is doing well and will recover without any deformity. He had a dislocation of the elbow, cut in the head, and a fracture of one of the bones of the forearm.

Dr. Magruder is getting well.

Martinsburg, Dec. 9, 1861.

My dear wife: I will now tell you the reason why I did not pay you the promised visit on Saturday last. I did not do so in my last because I thought I should thereby occasion you no little uneasiness.

On Thursday last I was apprised by Col. Ashby that an attempt would be made by his forces in connection with the militia and a portion of Gen. Jackson's brigade to break down Dam No. 5 on the Potomac and destroy the canal, and that the attempt would in all probability be stoutly resisted by the Federals. On Saturday morning accordingly we took up the line of march for Dam No. 5, about twelve miles distant from Martinsburg.

Our force consisted of six pieces of artillery,——— companies of cavalry, and some militia, besides two companies of Jackon's Stonewall brigade. We arrived upon the banks of the Potomac Saturday evening abut 3 o'clock, and opened upon the Yankees with the six pieces of cannon. The afternoon was a delightful one, and the scenery around picturesque. It was interesting to see every hill top around wreathed in smoke from our guns, to hear the shell and round shot rattling and hissing from the cannon's mouth, but more interesting than this was the speed with which the Yankees travelled from the river. The cannonading ceased about dark, and then a company was dispatched to attempt to demolish the dam. They were allowed to work on unmolested until about half past 10 o'clock at night, when the Yankees opened a terrific fire upon them from the canal which they had drained and now used as a breast work. The workmen escaped from the dam unhurt, and the firing ceased until daylight, when we opened on them again with cannon.

This time the Yankees, having erected fortifications and made themselves hiding places, were not to be routed. I dismounted my men and distributed them along the river bank. They fought throughout the day on Sunday with a few hours intermission. The firing extended at least a mile along the banks of the Potomac, and for hours not a moment was permitted to pass unbroken by the whistling of minie balls or the sound of cannon.

The river is narrow at Dam No. 5, and the more advanced portion of our men were within two hundred yards of the enemy. The enemy were well armed with Remington and Enfield rifles. Some of their balls known to have traversed a mile of space were picked up as they struck the ground completely flattened.

An interesting and novel feature of the fight was the delivery of a sermon by our chaplain, Mr. Avirett, on the battle field, or only a few hundred yards from the scene of actual conflict. A portion of us retired to a house to feed our horses and procure something for ourselves. We had eaten nothing for nearly twenty-four hours. While lying down upon the grass on this beautiful Sabbath with guns and sabres by our sides, our chaplain by request entered the group and preached a most eloquent impromptu sermon. He had concluded but a moment when an order came for us to go into the conflict again. We obeyed with alacrity. The engagement lasted until dark, when we drew off, and returned to Martinsburg.

The object of our expedition was not accomplished, and could not have been without crossing the river. Our force was not sufficient to risk crossing, besides I am inclined to think that Gen. Jackson had given orders not to cross.

I had one man severely wounded in the battle, Joseph Emswiler (Aly's son). He acted bravely in this action, as he has done in all that he has been engaged. He was shot through the head.* He is still alive, and there is a possibility of his recovery. Strange to say he is quite rational.

We had only two men wounded in the battle of Dam No. 5, my man, and two artillerymen. The Yankee loss was no doubt pretty heavy. My men alone know that they killed a number on this occasion as in every other contest. They were in the front rank, and stood first in gallant conduct, is the opinion of our leaders.

If there is no more fighting on hand, I shall certainly come up to Woodstock on Friday or Saturday next.

With love for you, Lizzie, and the children,

Your devoted husband,

John Winfield.

---

*Joseph Emswiler's wound was caused by a ramrod passing through the brain. He lost at least a teacup full of his brains, as I have often heard my father relate, but recovered, and lived some time after the close of the war.—P. S. W.

Winchester, Dec 12, 1861.

My dear wife: I dropped you a note to-day by Lieut. Liggett who passed up the Valley on his way to Richmond. I told you in that note why it was that my expectations of meeting you tonight were disappointed. Gen. Jackson will not let his officers pass Winchester unless on pressing business connected with the army.

I have, however, engaged boarding for you here at $50 per month for yourself and children and servant. Fuel and lights extra. They will charge Lizzie Kratzer $20 per month, and give her a room next to ours with door between the rooms. The boarding house I have secured is kept by Mrs. Tidball, a very agreeable lady. You will be pleased with her. She was a Baldwin, a niece of old Judge Baldwin.

I want you to come on immediately. I cannot bear to be separated from you so much. You had as well be in Brock's Gap as in Woodstock, the way matters now stand.

Nettie can go to school here. Mrs. Tidball has a daughter about her age and size who is going to school.

Several ladies board at the house I have selected, Mrs. Angus McDonald for one, and wife of our surgeon, Mrs. Burns another. Mrs. Burns is beautiful, and I dare say interesting. The society you will be thrown in and the situation of the place are no small advantages, and I would pay double the price to have you near me. So come right along.

I was at a wedding night before last in Martinsburg, and last night attended a reception given to the bridal party. By the way, I escorted Miss Belle Boyd to the party. She is quite a favorite with me, possessing an originality and vivacity, no-care-madcap-devil-of-a-temperament that pleases. Her mother who is much of a lady and had shown me much kindness asked me to take her daughter under my charge.

I have much to tell you when we meet of my adventures at Martinsburg.

I will send Pete Rader up on Saturday, and he can come down with you.

CHAPTER XII

Bath and Romney Expedition

The wider gap than usual in the letters is occasioned by the circumstance indicated that Mrs. Winfield spent the next four months at Winchester. Being in camp not far distant it was possible for the captain to see his family frequently, and visits took the place of letters.

Jackson's next expedition, after the unsuccessful attempt to destroy Dam No. 5, was the much execrated "Bath and Romney trip."

After the evacuation of Romney by Col. McDonald, Kelly took possession. The Federals had also considerable bodies of men at Bath and at Hancock, while Banks was busily drilling his host at Frederick City, Md., preparing for the spring campaign.

The Federals were committing depredations and acts of cruelty against the defenseless families in the valley of the South Branch, and the tender heart of Jackson was moved to deliver this his native section from the thrall of the enemy. To do this before Banks was prepared to invade the Valley of Virginia seemed sufficient argument for a winter campaign. For this purpose he was reinforced by Gen. Loring, and left Winchester on the morning of Jan. 1, 1862. His plan was to move swiftly on Bath and Hancock, and then on to Romney.

Of the sufferings of the troops on this expedition much has been said and written. We are concerned only with the movements of Ashby's cavalry, and especially with the part played by the Brock's Gap Riflemen of Co B.

On January 4 Jackson brought his wearied men to the vicinity of Bath. Here orders were given to Gen. Loring with the main force to enter the town from the south. The militia were sent to the west as a support, while Ashby with his column of cavalry and Chew's battery was sent by way of the east. But the wily foe were not to be caught in this trap. There were still two avenues of escape, and these they took with due prudence and without delay, leaving behind all their stores, camp equipages, and guns. Says Avirett:

"Their retreat was made by two roads, one down the Warm Spring Valley to Hancock, Md., the other leading to Sir John's Run. Ashby sending Capt. Winfield with a detachment to pursue them on the latter route, pushed on himself in hot haste with the remainder of his men, after those who fled toward Hancock. So rapid were his movements that, short as was the distance to the river, he overtook the rear guard of the enemy, which stood only long enough to enable the main body to cross. During the few moments fighting here, Lt. Lantz and three privates of Company C were badly wounded. The enemy escaped without material damage."

Capt. Winfield, in pursuit of the lesser number, came up with them at Sir John's Run. A skirmish ensued, but the Federals escaped and withdrew across the river, leaving no command in Morgan County.

On the morning of the 5th Colonel Ashby was sent blindfolded into Hancock to demand its surrender. This was refused, and Jackson gave orders to shell the town. His design to cross the river and enter Hancock was abandoned for the reasons given in his report:

"On the 6th the enemy were reinforced to such an extent as to induce me to believe that my object could not be accomplished without a sacrifice of life, which I felt unwilling to make, as Romney, the great object of the expedition, might require for its recovery, and especially for the capture of the troops in and near there, all the force at my disposal. **********

"The next day, the 7th, the command was put in motion.

*** "The enemy evacuated Romney on the 10th, and the town was soon occupied by Sheetz's and Shand's companies of cavalry. The Federal forces, abandoning a large number of tents and other public property, which fell into our possession, retreated to a point between the railroad bridge across Paterson's Creek and the northwestern branch of the Potomac, which was as far as they could retire without endangering the safety of the two bridges. Our loss in the expedition in killed was four; in wounded, twenty-eight. The Federal loss we did not ascertain. Sixteen of them were captured. After the arrival in Romney of General Loring's brigade, under Colonel Taliafero, I designed moving with it, Garnett's brigade, and other forces, on an important expedition against the enemy, but such was the extent of demoralization in the first-named brigade as to render the abandonment of that enterprise necessary. Believing it imprudent to attempt further movements with Loring's command against the Federals, I determined to put it in winter-quarters in the vicinity of Romney. *****

"I do not feel at liberty to close this report without alluding to the conduct of the reprobate Federal commanders, who in Hampshire County have not only burned valuable mill property, but also many private houses. The track from Romney to Hanging Rock, a distance of fifteen miles, was one of desolation. The number of dead animals lying along the roadside, where they had been shot by the enemy, exemplified the spirit of that part of the Northern army.

**** "On January 2nd there was not, from the information I could gather, a single loyal man in Morgan County who could remain at home with safety. Within less than four days the enemy had been defeated, their baggage captured; and by teaching the Federal authorities a lesson that a town claiming allegiance to the United States lay under our guns; Shepherdstown protected, which had repeatedly before, though not since, been shelled; the railroad communication with Hancock broken; all that portion of the country east of the Great Cacapon recovered; Romney and a large part of Hampshire County evacuated by the enemy without the firing of a gun; the enemy had fled from the western part of Hardy, had been forced from the offensive to the defensive—under these circumstances, judge what must have been my astonishment at receiving from the Secretary of War the following dispatch: 'Our news indicates that a movement is being made to cut off Loring's command. Order him back to Winchester immediately.' "

Thus did Jackson in his report sum up the results of the campaign, and express his surprise at the order for the recall of Loring.

Jackson in the meantime had returned to Winchester. His resignation speedily followed the order for the recall of Loring. The enemy changed again to the offensive and advanced upon Romney, drove the Confederate troops out of Moorefield on the 12th of February, forced the militia from Bloomery Pass, and came within twenty-one miles of Winchester.

After much correspondence with the Department of War and Governor Letcher, General Jackson was prevailed upon to withdraw his resignation and to remain in command of the troops in the Valley of Virginia.

Private Sylvanus Lindamood, Brock's Gap Rifleman, writes to the "girl he left behind him," and gives some incidents of the Romney campaign.

Martinsburg, Berkley Co., Va., Jan. 21, 1862.

Dear Miss: I have embraced the present opportunity of writing you a little letter to let you know I am quite well at present and hope this may find you well. Would have written to you before now, but we were kept so busy among the mountains and hills of the Potomac, I did not get the opportunity any sooner. But I still remember you, and hope that you may do the same. I have not received any letter from you either, but I hope you still think of absent friends.

We had a pretty hard time of it in the mountains. The snow was on the ground, and we laid on top of it while it was falling from above on us. But yet we all returned back safe and sound to Martinsburg, where I suppose we will remain. I do not think that our quarters will be moved, as we have just as good quarters here as we can find anywhere except our quarters at home. If we had some one to recollect us, this place could not be beat, as we are not exposed to the dangers of the iron sleet thrown amongst us from the Yankees' guns. But I would not care how soon they would play the game of quits, as we are getting pretty tired of this war. Although they have raised it, and they will have to end it.

The Rockingham militia are all here in Martinsburg. They look as if they had gone through some pretty tough times, too. They were along with us out in Morgan and Bath. From there they went to Romney, then to Winchester, and from there to this place, which they all appear to like very much. They marched 60 miles in three days.

We have had pretty rainy times since we came back, and the mud pretty near runs over a person, particularly when he gets a slip up and falls down. It has been raining here for three days with no signs of letting up. Everything looks so gloomy and desolate, a person cannot see many folks going about, nor neither can he do anything.

Jackson is still out among the mountains. He is putting his men through.

Your brother Casper and I took dinner together yesterday, and him and myself had a large talk about old times, he wishing he was home to go out to see the girls with Michael Brock.

William Bowers has been sick nearly all the time he has been down here, but is getting some better now.

I heard that Mike Brock come home a Saturday after we left. If I had known he was coming, I would have waited two weeks. Tell him I would like for him to come down and join our company.

We had a pretty high time a-coming down. The first night we staid at William Fanslers.

I must bring this letter to a close by asking you to write soon and let me know how you are all getting along.

Give my love to all inquring friends and reserve a portion for yourself.

I subscribe myself your ever true, faithful, and affectionate friend till death,

Sylvanus Lindamood.

Ashby and his cavalry returned to the Valley with Jackson on January 24. With headquarters at Martinsburg, his business was to guard the Potomac from the Blue Ridge to the Alleghanies. His cordon of pickets stretched from mountain to mountain, and his scouts were constantly on the alert. There were frequent skirmishes with the advance of the army, but Ashby and his little band could not withstand the mighty force that on February 27 was flung across the river. Major-General Banks with a vast army was at last on Virginia soil, his objective Winchester and the fair and fertile Valley of the Shenandoah. How could Jackson with his 5,000 patriots resist these overwhelming numbers? The answer has been well recorded, and the history of Jackson's Valley campaign has been the theme upon which volumes have been written, lectures have been delivered, and songs have been sung.

How Ashby and his cavalry and Chew's Horse Artillery harassed the enemy and protected Jackson's rear on the retreat; how they saved the day at Kernstown and prevented a complete rout of the infantry by Shields, how they lured Banks farther and farther from base until Harrisonburg in Rockingham County was gained, is known to every student of history. In all these skirmishes, engagements, and maneuvers Capt. Winfield and his Brock's Gap Rifles bore a conspicuous and gallant part.

In anticipation of the evacuation of Winchester, Mrs. Winfield, accompanied by her friend Miss Lizzie Kratzer, and with her three little children and servant, John, had taken refuge with friends at Frederick's Hall, Louisa Co.

Capt. Winfield's letters giving the story of his participation in the stirring events occurring in the interval were perhaps lost through the irregularities of mail service at that period.

Before giving the next letter dated April 24, 1862, written from Conrad's Store, what the writer believes to be the true account of the attempt to burn the bridge at Mt. Jackson is here introduced.

CHAPTER XIII

THE SHENANDOAH BRIDGE AFFAIR

Under this caption the following notes in Capt. Winfield's hand-writing are found among his papers. The narrative breaks off before it is well begun, but, fortunately, the incident is one that made an impression upon members of his family to whom it was related in after years, and the writer drawing upon these recollections and aided by the late Col. R. P. Chew and the late Cyrus Fetzer of Maurertown, member of Winfield's company and an actual participant in the attempt to burn the bridge, is able to complete the story.

According to Capt. Winfield: "On the morning of April 18, 1862, Ashby's cavalry force consisting of twenty-six companies and the gallant Chew's Battery, were, save an unusually vigilant picket line, slumbering quietly in the vicinity of the village of Hawkinstown. The enemy were in their immediate front. Suddenly before an overwhelming force the pickets were compelled to retire. The rattle of musketry and the clattering of hoofs upon the solid turnpike aroused the camp before a picket reached it. The bugle sounded the rally. Tents were prostrated as by a hurricane, baggage hurled into the wagons, teams moved to the rear, and the field cleared for action. Day began to dawn and soon revealed Ashby upon his white horse dashing towards the front, while his men were already formed and ready for the fray. In the turnpike by his guns stood the youthful but dauntless Chew. Having pitched my tent considerably in advance of the main encampment, I had just time to get my baggage loaded up, teams started to the rear and my company formed, when the enemy appeared in sight."

Here the fragment ends, but quoting from Avirett, Ashby's biographer; "Finding his position untenable, Ashby slowly fell back before the enemy's advance, turning upon them whenever too closely pressed, until he approached Mt. Jackson. Here he made his disposition to cross the river. Chew's Battery was ordered to move forward and take up its position on Rude's Hill, which commanded the bridge and the turnpike for some distance north of it. He then ordered his troopers across, he himself remaining some distance behind them."

Jackson had already been in camp a week or two at Rude's Hill, to which point he had gradually retired after Kernstown, leaving Ashby as a buffer between his worn and wearied regiments and the long line of Banks' mighty army. The river, too, greatly swollen by recent rains, poured its tawny waters between Jackson and the advancing foe. The bridge, an old wooden structure, a covered way with boxed sides, afforded the only crossing. This Ashby determined to burn, and Capt. Winfield and twelve of his men were selected to execute this order. After all had passed over this little band dismounted, tore up some of the planks from the floor and attempted to start a fire. It had been a month of rains. The timbers were water soaked and time pressed. Scarcely was a feeble flame kindled when the enemy's cavalry dashed forward at great speed. The river is narrow here, and only the span of the bridge separated the handful of dismounted men from the onslaught of a large force of Federal cavalry.

Capt. Winfield gave his orders coolly: "To the abutment, men, and hold your fire until they enter the bridge."

With bridle reins over one arm, they waited for a breathless moment. On came the charge. The captain's word rang out: "Now, boys, pick your man as you would a squirrel in a tree, and FIRE!"

They fired with deadly precision, and at the first volley the enemy fell back. Halting a few moments they came again. But Capt. Winfield and his men were ready. With deliberate aim the rifles cracked, and the second time the foe was repulsed.

Assuming that Col. Ashby had gone on with the cavalry to Rude's Hill, the men at the bridge thought only of the task in hand. They did not know that their colonel, seeing their peril, with a few of his officers who had remained with him behind the rest, was dashing to their relief. They awaited the third charge. But this time the impetuosity of the onset forced them to mount and fly.

The blaze that had flared for a little in the damp kindling had flickered out, but a friendly cloud of smoke now rolled through the narrow covered way, gathering in its folds both blue and gray. But Ashby on his milk white charger was still a shining mark. "Four troopers," says Avirett in this connection, "singling him out, made an attack upon him, ordering him to surrender. Firing they missed him, but one ball passed through the lungs of his horse, rendering him unmanageable. Just then a dismounted man shot the foremost assailant. Capt. Koontz of Shenandoah hastening up shot a second; Harry Hatcher, dashing forward, fired at a third, who also fell, and the fourth ran away. Ashby rode forward to Rude's Hill, where he got another horse."

Says Col. Chew, in a personal letter to the writer: "Hearing the firing, I rode back and met Col. Ashby coming up the road. His horse was bleeding profusely, and I remember I was uncertain whether it was Ashby or the horse bleeding. I asked him if he was hurt, and he said he was not. He seemed intent on calling back his cavalry which had gone in the direction of Rude's Hill under the command of Maj. Funsten."

Still unaware of Ashby's proximity and narrow escape from death or capture, Capt. Winfield and his twelve men spurred their horses up the pike. The Yankees pursued for a short distance, not more than a sabre's length behind. But not a shot was fired. "Blinded by smoke," was Capt. Winfield's conclusion in relating this incident, "they mistook us for their own men. Thus we made our escape."

Shells from Chew's Battery now began to fall around them, and the troopers in danger from their own guns were obliged to strike off into the fields. By dodging and sheltering whenever possible, they reached headquarters in safety without so much as a wound from either friend or foe.

Capt. Winfield found Gen. Jackson quietly sitting his horse and looking in the direction of the bridge. He rode up, saluted, and made his report: "We failed to burn the bridge, General," he sadly admitted. "And the enemy is coming." The general returned the salute, and showing no concern, replied soothingly, "Well, let 'em come, Captain. Let 'em come."

But they did not come. And deceived as usual as to Jackson's strength, permitted him to elude their grasp and to proceed in order with his small army to the next encampment at Conrad's Store.

In writing about this Col. Chew says further: "The burning of the bridge was interfered with by the unusual energy of the enemy, who charged with a large force. The small body of Ashby's cavalry there engaged behaved with remarkable courage, and were not at all disconcerted by the charge of the Federals, but were driven by largely superior numbers."

The only fatal wound on the Confederate side in this encounter was received by Ashby's beautiful white horse. It is said that the men plucked every hair from the mane and tail of the dead creature, and that watch guards and other charms woven from the same were cherished mementoes. And recalling the noble qualities of both horse and rider, well might the trooper think those a richer bequest than the one referred to by Mark Antony in his address over the dead Caesar, wherein he bids his countrymen:

"Beg a hair of him for memory,
And, dying, mention it in their wills,
Bequeathing it as a rich legacy unto their issue."

Henceforth it was the black stallion, a fierce and ungovernable animal that few besides Ashby could have managed, that was to carry the gallant rider. He carried him for the few remaining weeks of his life: at Buckton, in pursuit of Banks in his hurried exit from the Valley, and finally in his last skirmish near Harrisonburg on the fatal June the sixth.

CHAPTER XIV

BACK TO ROCKINGHAM

Conrad's Store, April 24, 1862.

My dear wife: I wrote to you some days ago from this place, giving you an account of my adventures up to this time. Hope you received the letter.

The Yankees are now in possession of our beautiful Valley, and are living upon the "fat of the land." We are here in a safe retreat, divided from the Yankees by the South Shenandoah river. What move we shall make in future I cannot say.

The vandals have been in Harrisonburg, Dayton, and various places in the Valley stealing and committing all kinds of petty depredations. They have at the same time picked up a number of our men who were straggling back around their homes. Tas Liggett was taken by them on yesterday. I am very uneasy about Lieut. Kennon and ten or twelve of my men, who have been cut off by the enemy. They started day before yesterday by a circuitous mountain route to reach Brock's Gap and look out for an apprehended Federal move in that direction from Moorefield. They were due on yesterday afternoon. Billy Funk, his son Tommy, and Wm. Miller were of the party. Peter Rader and Cal Shoup are also missing. When last seen they were on the Kratzer road below Harrisonburg, and were cut off by the enemy. They are, however, well acquainted with the country, and will most probably turn up in a day or two.

We scout out every day in the direction of Harrisonburg. Yesterday fifty-eight of the Yankee cavalry pursued our tracks to McGaheysville. I started upon the receipt of the news after them, but when I reached the place they had retraced their steps. I followed on after them until night overtook us, but saw only three who were probably lurking behind to steal a horse or something else. These escaped us by dashing into the mountains, and getting off under cover of night. They are becoming very bold.

I have not said anything about my health, a subject that gives you so much anxiety. My general health has very much improved. I am now capable of enduring almost any amount of labor.

The 10th Va. Regiment is here, but Frank Cootes is not with them. His wife is or was quite sick, and he was allowed to take Augusta in his route to the Valley. Frank will not likely succeed in obtaining a transfer. He is regarded by his commanders as an excellent soldier.

I will hold an election in my company for officers as soon as Lieut. Kennon returns, or his fate is known.

I long to see you and the dear children, and yet I hardly feel equal to the pain of parting from you. I am more myself, more of the soldier when you are away from me. I trust, and I somehow feel a strong confidence, that I shall come out of this war with a consciousness of having done my duty, at least, and shall yet live to enjoy years of unalloyed happines with my dear wife and children.

Direct your letters to Conrad's Store via Stanardsville. We have a mail here once a week. It reaches here every Thursday, and leaves Friday.

Conrad's Store, April 27, 1862.

My dear wife: An opportunity presenting itself to send you a letter to Stanardsville, I embrace it to drop you a word. Am much hurried, and cannot, I am afraid, interest you except to tell you that I am safe and well, though I was in much danger on yesterday. The enemy advanced upon our pickets in pretty strong force, and I was sent ahead from camp to support them. We charged up almost to the enemy's lines. Being unsupported we were compelled to halt. A brisk fire for fifteen or twenty minutes was then kept up between us. But I have not time to tell you all the particulars of this skirmish in which the Brock's Gap Rifles again set an example of desperate bravery to the regiment. Cal Shoup shot the commander of the Federals. We were so near as to hear him cry out as he fell from his horse, "Men, support me! men, support me!" We had no one hurt. Andy Dyer's horse was shot. Your husband was exposed to a very heavy fire all the while, but came off without a scratch.

Lieut. Kennon and party all returned to camp in safety, bringing with them two Yankees with their guns and equipments. These they captured near Brock's Gap. I received a letter from Ma Cootes by Phil Kennon. She is well, but low spirited.

It seems probable that a battle will soon take place about or not very far from Richmond. If you apprehend any danger of being cut off from me, you had better change your location. You can judge of this better than I.

The 10th Va., I understand, was ordered to leave here for Eastern Virginia again this morning. We may follow soon.

The Yankees have been pillaging at a round rate in Rockingham. They have been up as far as Dr. Moore's. Asked Mrs. Moore where I was, and if I had not a place in the Gap where my family was, also, if she thought I or any of my company was lurking around that region. Mrs. Moore told them she thought I was still about, and they turned upon the receipt of this information and left in a hurry.

The rainy season seems to be over, and the sun is shining brightly again. When will this cruel war be over, that we may return to our homes and enjoy the "merry, merry sunshine," the gladsome laughter of our dear children, and the society of our wives and friends?

Your dear husband

John Winfield.

CHAPTER XV

THE McDOWELL CAMPAIGN

Jackson remained in camp at Swift Run Gap near Conrad's Store (Elkton) about ten days. The cavalry, as stated by Capt. Winfield, had frequent skirmishes with marauding and pillaging parties sent out by Banks from Harrisonburg. In the intervals of fighting Jackson and Ashby bent their energies to the reorganization of the army. Many of the companies already full in the retreat up the Valley had largely increased their muster-rolls. This necessitated a division of several companies of Ashby's regiment of cavalry. Co. B, popular with the Valley men, now exceeded the limit. It was one of those divided and the rearrangement is given in a letter that follows.

Pursuing his habitual policy of secrecy, Jackson had his men here as much in the dark as to his future movements as the enemy. According to Capt. Winfield, the 10th Va., drawn almost entirely from Rockingham, was ordered to Eastern Va. on April 27. On the 30th Jackson broke camp at Conrad's Store and followed, crossing by way of Brown's Gap into Albemarle, leaving the impression with friend and foe that he had been called to the protection of Richmond. But to the surprise of the army, on striking the railroad at Mechum's Station, he swung around again, and reentering the Valley paused at Staunton.

Here at least he brought joy and comfort, where all had been gloom. With Banks reported as advancing from Harrisonburg, Milroy at McDowell, thirty-odd miles away, already reenforced by Schenck, and with Fremont on the move toward Franklin, Staunton, that Sunday morning, threatened by three armies, a force if combined of 40,000 men, was in a state bordering on panic. To oppose this advancing horde with Jackson on the road to Richmond, there was only Gen. Ed. Johnson with a handful of troops in camp seven miles to the west of Staunton.

When the troops found themselves on the cars headed for Staunton rather than Richmond they were wild with enthusiasm. With such a large proportion of Valley men among them there was a natural reluctance to have this section become the prey of the enemy, and all felt deep regret at leaving Banks in possession of the field without even striking a blow in defense.

The reasons for Jackson's secrecy soon became evident. His plan to mystify the enemy, to make a sudden attack upon Milroy before Fremont should come up, and thus prevent the threatened junction of these forces with Banks was a marvel of stategy, executed with vigor and dispatch. After a brief rest in Staunton, he united his forces with those of Gen. Johnson, and on May 8th led his army on to the victorious though hard fought battle of McDowell.

In compliance with Jackson's requisition for troops, Ewell had been sent from Gordonsville, and was then at Swift Run Gap. He was supported by Ashby with a portion of the cavalry, and both were watching Banks. The following order in connection with the cavalry movements is found among Capt. Winfield's notes.

"Send for 200 effectives. Balance to report to Ewell."

Hence it would appear that the cavalry force at McDowell was small, and Avirett has this to say of the part they played in the action: "Of the cavalry employed in this movement, the companies of Capts. Sheetz and Winfield must not be forgotten. ***** As soon as Milroy's retreat began, the Ashby cavalry under Winfield and

Sheetz pressed their rear; while other detachments were sent out to blockade every road by which Banks might come to the rescue."

As senior officer, and from other notes, it would seem that Capt. Winfield was in command of the cavalry forces at McDowell. He says further, in notes evidently made on the field: "Send Shoup with his command to Brock's Gap. Impress. Report to me. Send back Capt. Massie's Co. to blockade road from Shaver's (?) Fork to Franklin."

As the men of Co. B were well acquainted with every cattle track and mountain trail in the neighborhood, that portion of their number which had been assigned to Capt. Shoup as Co. H in the recent division was sent to blockade the roads leading to Harrisonburg by way of Brock's Gap. This they did by chopping down trees on each side of the road in such a manner that they fell across the narrow mountain way, and effectually blocked the pass, had Banks been bold enough to send a force in that direction. Years afterwards the trees thus felled, which had been thrown out of the road, were used in the manufacture of shingles, and hauled by peaceable citizens to the railroad at Broadway for shipment to Northern markets.

All these efforts at blockading were labor thrown away. For Banks, after McDowell, timidly withdrew to Strasburg, without hazarding battle or an offensive move.

Here he busied himself in fortifying his position, leaving a detachment under Kenly to guard his left flank at Front Royal and another at Buckton to protect the Manassas Gap railroad.

Capt. Winfield's letter from Franklin now follows:

Camp, Seven Miles from Franklin,
May 13, 1862.

My dear wife: Yours of the 10th reached me here in the mountains yesterday. I was as much surprised as delighted to hear from you, though we have daily communication with Staunton through couriers.

We fell back yesterday evening to this point, having pursued the enemy to within two miles of Franklin where they selected so strong a position that we found it almost impossible to dislodge them. We are this morning taking things very coolly. I do not know what Gen. Jackson intends to do. Perhaps he may make a flank movement upon them.

We have picked up quite a number of prisoners, and obtained baggage and plunder enough to fill a Swisher barn. Sam (black Sam, whilom of Brock's Gap) and Alfred are grieving that they have no means of carrying the coats, overcoats, hats, pants, shirts, &c. that they find strewn around.

I think it would be of service to you to take a little ride. So take the cars and come up to Staunton on Friday. I expect to be there by that time. If any change occurs in my destination, I shall inform you.

Have divided my company into two. Cal Shoup, Captain, Peter Rader 1st Lieut., Jake Shoup 2nd, Derrick Pennybacker 3rd. Phil Kennon has not been with us. I don't know where he is. Capt. Shoup with command is in Brock's Gap carrying on guerrilla warfare. Sent your letter by him to Ma Cootes.

My health pretty good.

CHAPTER XVI

Battle of Buckton

The letter from Franklin is the last in the series. In spite of Capt. Winfield's assurances to his wife, his health was rapidly failing, and the arduous labors of the next month were to tax his strength to the utmost limit of endurance. Whether his wife received no letters from him during the remaining period of service or whether they were not preserved cannot be determined. It is a matter of regret that the part played by himself and his men in this part of the Valley campaign cannot be given in his own words.

On May 21 (1862) Jackson reached New Market. He had within twenty days moved his army by a circuitous route from Elk Run Valley, near Conrad's Store, to Franklin and back again to the Shenandoah Valley, and in the mean time had fought and won the battle of McDowell. On May 22 he crossed the Massanutten Mountain at New Market and proceeded to Luray. Here he was joined by Ewell's division, and the cavalry reinforced by the 2nd and 6th Va. regiments under Gen. George Steuart, bringing the full quota of his forces up to 17,000, the largest number to that time under his command. The morning of May 23 found him about ten miles from Front Royal. Banks within his entrenchments at Strasburg, calmly awaited the approach of the Confederates by way of the Valley pike, while Kenly at Front Royal little dreamed of attack, so closely was the progress of the infantry screened by Ashby and his cordon of pickets.

Before making his surprise movement on Kenly at Front Royal Jackson ordered Ashby to diverge from the main road and make a covert sally upon the troops left at Buckton, a little station midway between Front Royal and Strasburg. Here there were two companies of Federal infantry quartered in the brick building used as a station, their mission to guard the army stores held here in reserve, to protect the telegraph line, affording communication between the two points invested, and to prevent the destruction of the railroad bridge.

Ashby with companies A, B, E, F, and G, commanded respectively by Captains Fletcher, Winfield, Buck, Sheetz, and Mason, regardless of the strong fortification of the enemy, ensconced within and behind walls of brick, made a cavalry charge upon the infantry in this apparently unassailable position. In the first onslaught they were met by a withering fire. Retiring and reforming, they advanced again, routed the foe from the station, set fire to their stores, cut the telegraph line, and drove the Federal troops to shelter behind the railroad embankment in rear of the bridge. In this second charge Capt. Winfield's horse was shot from under him. Freeing himself from the wounded creature, his favorite "Fancy," he swung his sword, and with the well known cry, "Come on, boys!" rushed into the station, followed by some of his dismounted men. Driving the Federals before them, the Captain emerged with a captured flag wound around his arm, seized another horse, and rallied his command.

The enemy, now under cover of the embankment, were pouring a hot fire upon Ashby and his exposed men. But Ashby had determined to burn the bridge over Passage Creek. "Forward, boys!" came the command. And away they dashed over fences, limestone boulders and rugged ground.

But unable to withstand such a volley of bullets, the cavalry fell back, and when almost up to the embankment, Capt. Winfield found himself alone except for a handful of his own men who still followed their leader. He gave the word to dismount and shelter in a low place affording a slight protection. But Ashby had drawn back only to lead another onset. He charged again with full force, but the enemy were too strongly entrenched, and the purpose to burn the bridge had to be abandoned.

In this charge Ashby lost two of his bravest captains, Fletcher of Co. A, and young Sheetz of Co. F.

In Co. B, private Coffelt, a youth of eighteen serving as a substitute, lost a leg. With blood streaming from his wounds he came up to Capt. Winfield and cried, "They got me, Captain, and I'll have to go home. But I'll come back when I get well, and try 'em again!"

CHAPTER XVII

EVENTS LEADING UP TO PORT REPUBLIC AND CROSS KEYS

The stampede of Banks, the brief stand at Winchester, resulting in further disaster, the race to the Potomac are familiar history. With Banks on the other side of the river, his army a disorganized mass, his wagons burned or abandoned, his vast stores estimated as worth $300,000 to the Confederacy in the hands of the victors, Jackson allowed his exhausted men a well earned rest at Winchester.

Ashby had pursued the enemy with a portion of his cavalry to the river. On May 27 (1862) he returned to Winchester, where he received from Jackson his commission as Brigadier-General, the crown of honor and authority which he was to wear in the service of his country for ten days only.

Jackson's well conceived plan of marching upon Washington had to be abandoned for lack of troops. He had not then more than 15,000. But to intensify the panic at Washington he made a feint upon Harper's Ferry, from which point the movements of the enemy were closely watched. The following order from Gen. Ashby to Capt. Winfield at Harper's Ferry will throw light upon the disposition of the forces at that juncture:

"Martinsburg, May 29, 1862.

"Capt. Winfield

"Dear Capt.—You will leave two companies with Gen. Winder and encamp the rest at some good point between Charlestown and Stephensons and inform the General where you are.

Respectfully,

Turner Ashby."

On May 30 we find Jackson's army again on the move with Winder bringing up the rear. Apparently the net was drawing around Jackson, and no wonder the government at Washington desired nothing so much as his discomfiture or capture in retaliation for the humiliation and rout of Banks. Shields by way of Front Royal was closing in on the east, Fremont with Milroy by way of the west; while Banks, screwing up his courage afresh, with the aid of Saxton, was ready to bring up the rear. Jackson realized the necessity for a rapid retreat. With his usual celerity and the added advantage of a march through a friendly and familiar country he was able to outdistance the ponderous columns of the cautious foe. By Monday, June 2, he had reached Mt. Jackson, and from this point proceeded more leisurely to Harrisonburg. Anticipating an attack from Shields by way of Luray through the gap at New Market, he dispatched a portion of the cavalry to burn the three bridges over the south fork of the Shenandoah, thus putting this stream, then at full flood, between him and the enemy.*

---

*An amusing incident is related by a lady of New Market, Miss Coffman: Jackson, with the bridges burned between him and his pursuers, and trusting to the swollen condition of the streams to halt their immediate advance, sent his army on at a leisurely pace in the direction of Harrisonburg. He with his staff stopped for a brief rest at the hospitable home of Dr. Joseph Strayer in New Market. A pitcher of his favorite beverage, lemonade, had been prepared, and he was beginning to make himself comfortable when the word came that Fremont's advance guard had crossed the river a few miles below, and were rapidly approaching. The pitcher of lemonade was left untasted (being Jackson's own pitcher it is still treasured by one of the family) and the general with thirst unquenched mounted his horse and made his exit with all speed. On came the confident Fremont with his host. Miss Coffman sitting in her doorway watched their advance. A little drummer boy stepping out proudly began a tattoo, and to the rhythmic patter of his drumsticks he chanted: "Jackson in a funnel, Jackson in a funnel, Got him in a funnel sure." Some days later on the return of the discomfited army, with Cross Keys and Port Republic behind them, Miss Coffman again sat in her door way. She looked out for the drummer boy.

"How about the funnel?" she inquired mockingly as he came along. The boy doffed his cap and replied: "I made a mistake, madame. It was a pepper box, and Jackson turned it around and gave us hell!"

When within a few miles of Harrisonburg, Capt. Winfield with another division of the cavalry was sent east to Conrad's Store to burn the bridge over the South River and watch the movements of Shields. In the skirmish that ensued with the advance of the Federals a considerable number of prisoners were captured. These were sent on under Sergeant Joseph Riddle of Co. B to be added to those marching in front of Jackson on their way to Staunton.

Here at last at Conrad's Store, Capt. Winfield sick, exhausted by the continuous marches, battles, skirmishes, and responsibilities of the past month, so weak that he had to be lifted to the saddle by his men, was compelled to resign his command. Stricken with grief at the news of the death of Ashby, his friend and adored leader, with a burdened heart he made his way to Staunton, thence to Frederick's Hall, Louisa Co., where he joined his family.

Staunton, which he reached on June 11, rang with the glorious victories at Cross Keys and Port Republic. A few days later Jackson went into camp near Mt. Meridian in Augusta County, and undertook the reorganization of his army. It seems probable that Capt. Winfield, if he had been able to remain in service would have received immediate promotion. He had frequently been in command of large divisions of cavalry, had acted as major or lieutenant-colonel on more than one occasion, and was confidently spoken of among the men as the one most likely to succeed Ashby as colonel of the regiment. It is a well known fact, however, that Jackson paid little regard to the wishes of the men in the elections that followed, and had Capt. Winfield been able to remain in the army his chief desire was not for promotion but for the high honor of serving his country where best he could further the cause.

With the resignation of their captain, we can no longer follow the fortunes of Co. B. Suffice it to say that under the leadership of Magruder and Humphries and incorporated with the Laurel Brigade they sustained the reputation for valor, good marksmanship, and devotion to duty won under their first commander. A portion of the original band followed that brave man Capt. Calvin Shoup until he fell on the field at Cedar Creek.

The devotion of these men to Gen. Ashby is shown by the following entry in a note book containing some records of both Co. B and Co. H:

"Amount subscribed to erect a monument in memory of our late Gen. Ashby, who fell on the battlefield June 6, 1862.

"In the hands of Capt. Jno. Calvin Shoup, July 28, 1862, $507.50."

CHAPTER XVIII

Conclusion

Dr. Winfield, as he must now be designated, returned in the fall of 1862 to Rockingham County. Deeming it unwise to remain within the track of straggling troops or Federal scouts he took refuge for about a year at "Clan Alpine," a small mountain farm which he owned in Brock's Gap, a few miles from Cootes' Store. In this quiet retreat his hope was that his health might be restored and that he would be able to return to the army. He was disappointed, and in the fall of 1863 came back to Broadway, and though never again free from suffering, rendered such service as was possible, as is shown by the following letters to Gen. Kemper, in command of the reserve forces of Virginia:

Broadway, Sept. 1864.

Gen. Kemper: I acknowledge the receipt of your order appointing me to organize the reserve forces of the county of Rockingham. You will please send me ten blank muster rolls.

Presuming that mounted companies will be preferred and accepted I shall endeavor to raise as many of such companies as is practicable, unless otherwise instructed. Will arms and ammunition be furnished a company as soon as a complete muster roll is forwarded?

Please answer these inquiries and give me any further information relative to my duties that you may deem important.

Yours most respectfully,

John Q. Winfield.

And this:

Gen. Kemper,

Dear Sir:

In compliance with your orders, I notified the local Reserve class of this county to meet at a stated point for the purpose of being enrolled. Before the day arrived, however, the enemy under Gen. Sheridan advanced to Harrisonburg, rendering a meeting and enrollment impracticable.

Immediately after the enemy retired from the county an order appeared calling upon the detailed men between the ages of eighteen and forty-five to report at Camp Lee. I then made arrangements to have the nitre and mining men enrolled at their respective places of business, and all gave due notice to the detailed men between seventeen and eighteen and forty-five and fifty, collectors of tax in kind, and exempts to meet me in Harrisonburg and enroll. Two collectors of tax in kind, one exempt, and one detailed man between forty-five and fifty appeared on that day and enrolled.

I next divided the county into three districts, and called upon the class mentioned to meet and enroll in their respective districts. At this district meeting which I attended personally one man appeared and enrolled. The results in the other districts I have not heard from.

I have given due notice to these men, have appealed and threatened without effect, and await your further orders in regard to them.

The detailed men between eighteen and forty-five I think would enroll promptly in this organization. They are of such numbers and material as to make a most efficient command under proper management. As the late order calling them into service has, I understand, been suspended, I desire to know if they will now be required to enroll in the Local Reserve Organization.

The roll of the nitre and mining men will be forwarded to you as soon as possible.

Respectfully,

J. Q. Winfield.

The following extract from an article by the late Dr. N. M. Burkholder, published in the Rockingham Register of July 13, 1900, shows the eagerness of the former captain to engage in repelling the foe whenever opportunity offered:

"While Sheridan occupied Harrisonburg his wagon-trains and their escorts were constantly harassed along the Valley pike by a small impromptu troop led by the gallant Capt. John Q. Winfield, of Broadway. This handful of men was composed of members of several cavalry commands who happened to be on furlough or cut off by Sheridan's advance. Some of these were McNeil's men, a number of them were Linville's Creek boys (members of the original Brock's Gap Rifles) the Pennybackers, Bowmans, Shoups, Sites, Showalter, and Houck of Harrisonburg, the Ackers, one of them being Jake Acker, kindhearted and gentle and true, but when aroused, brave beyond prudence.

"Rendezvousing always by appointment somewhere towards the Valley pike, they broke ranks every evening and retired for the night about the mouth of Brock's Gap, out of the way of the scouting parties of the enemy. One day we hung on the flank of a wagon train all the way from Mt. Jackson to Tenth Legion, but the guard was too strong and kept too well closed for assault. We usually had twenty-odd men.

"At another time we made a dash on a train and guard of apparently two hundred men down the lane from the hill just west of Sparta—now Mauzy. The wagons, going northward, had just gone over the little eminence in the road at the place and were barely out of view as we struck the pike, most of the guard with them. We had miscalculated a little. Four men were in Sparta. One was cut off by our movement, and was now in our rear, the other three made haste to escape—were chased hotly to the brow of the little eminence, losing their hats in the close run, and as we drove yelling into full view of the train, seeing and hearing confusion, the entire guard fell from their horses right and left and took to wagons and fences with their carbines to meet the sudden onset. Instanter we turn tail and gallop back to Lacey Spring, two miles distant. We were a mile away, before glancing back, and could see no movement to find out where the Yanks had gone. They then began to come back over the little eminence to Sparta.

"The prisoner rode with us to Brock's Gap. He evidently believed us to be bushwhackers. On the way he tremblingly asked if we were going to take his life. I told him that we did not make war that way. He talked about his wife and little children. We started him on foot through the mountains with the chance to escape. However, McNeil caught him over in Hardy, and he was brought back after Sheridan's retreat, and so got to Richmond after all."

The following verses written about this time would seem to have a place in this record:

Recruiting Song
for
Ashby's "Old Brigade"
Air: White Cockade

To the survivors of Gen. Turner Ashby's gallant brigade this song is affectionately dedicated by an old comrade in arms, J. Q. Winfield.

O come and wear the laurel leaf,
Won early by our fallen chief,
Whose life was brilliant, yet too brief.
Avenge him ere you bow to grief!

Chorus—

Then grasp a fallen hero's blade,
Fill up the place that death has made.
The trumpet sounds, our flag's displayed;
On! Charge with Ashby's Old Brigade!

Say would you live to feel and know
You did not strike the tyrant foe,
Nor dealt for liberty a blow?
Is there a man that breathes, so low?

There's darkness in the Southron's land,
There's light, 'tis from the foeman's brand;
And yet each breast with hope is manned,
And nerved with force is every hand.

Come, join us would you win a name,
We've Ashby's, Jones's, Rosser's fame.
They've made a hundred tyrants tame;
We can a hundred triumphs claim.

The souls of Ashby, Jones, have fled,
But Rosser charges where they led,
To bear its folds through storms of lead,
He bears the mantle of the dead.

Freedom, the boon our fathers gave,
The blood-bought purchase of the brave,
May find too soon, alas, a grave,
But must not leave one son a slave.

After the war Dr. Winfield resumed the practice of his profession, and whenever his own strength permitted it was his delight to minister to suffering humanity.

His death occurred at Broadway, July 29, 1892. One who stood near him all his life wrote of him at that time: "Captain Winfield died a Christian, in membership with the Presbyterian Church. The writer was with him often in his home, accompanied him on his travels and in the vicissitudes of war as one of his company; was with him in his dying hour, and can attest that his was an absolute faith. It would be well if his old comrades in arms could know this that they might follow him as they did in the troublous days of the War Between the States."

MUSTER ROLL

of Co. B, 7th Va. Regiment, C. S. A. Cavalry
1861-1865

Revised to 1902 by Corporal Edwin Taylor with notes.
Further revised by Paulina Swift Winfield.

1st Captain, J. Q. Winfield; Resigned on account of poor health, June 10, 1862. Died at Broadway, Va., July 29, 1892.

2nd Captain, Dr. John H. Magruder; Killed in battle near Liberty Mills, Madison Co. Buried Green Spring, Louisa Co.

3rd Captain, David Humphries; Charlestown man. Wounded at Greenland Gap. Disabled.

4th Captain, Jacob Acker; Promoted to Major 10th Va. Infantry; wounded Aug. 25, 1864, Reams Station. Died in Kansas after war.

1st Lieut., Jacob N. Liggett; Died in Harrisonburg, May, 1913.

2nd Lieut., Jos. S. Pennybacker; Died at Broadway, Jan. 24, 1894.

2nd Lieut., S. B. Jordan; Wounded at Ashland May 28, 1864. Disabled. Drowned in W. Va. after war.

2nd Lieut., George W. Fulk; Resigned at Romney, 1861.

3rd Lieut., Derrick Rader; Resigned at Romney, 1861.

4th Lieut., P. P. Kennon; Wounded. Died since war. Buried at Turleytown.

1st Sergeant, Erasmus Neff; Died at Timberville, July, 1921.

1st Sergeant, Henry Mason; Wounded at Reams Station. Died near Broadway, 1913.

1st Sergeant, S. F. Mullen; Went West after war.

2nd Sergeant, Aaron Fitzwater; ——————————————

2nd Sergeant, Joseph N. Riddle; Wounded at Reams Station. Died at old home in Brock's Gap, March 7, 1921.

3rd Sergeant, Thomas W. Funk; Wounded.

3rd Sergt., Phineas Stickley; Died in Mo. after war.

4th Sergt., Joseph Showalter.

5th Sergt., John W. Moore; Promoted to Lieut. Co. H, 7th Cav. Died at Broadway, 1913.

1st Corporal, D. D. Pennybacker; Died at Broadway April 16, 1916.

1st Corporal, W. F. Bowers; Died in Rockingham, July, 1913.

2nd Corporal, Isaac Ritchie; Killed in battle, May 29, 1864. Buried near Richmond.

3rd Corporal, Edwin Taylor; Wounded at Reams Station. Died in Rockingham, 1914.

4th Corporal, Isaac F. Ritchie.

Officers, 24; commissioned 10; non-commissioned 14.

PRIVATES

Isaac Acker—Died on Linville Creek July 25, 1908.

Peter Acker—Taken Prisoner March, 1862. Went to Indiana after war.

Richard Ashby—Died near Timberville since war.

Harvey Alger—Died near Broadway after war.

John M. Barglebaugh—Died since war near Cootes' Store.

Daniel S. Baker—Dead.

George E. Burkholder—Died after war.

Americus Vespucius Bull—Killed near Cootes' Store day of Sheridan's raid.

John Beam—Wounded at Mechanicsburg Feb. 1864. Died since war.

Jacob Beam—Died at Timberville since war.

Jerry Byrd—Dead.

Jacob Burns—Promoted to regimental bugler. Died in Rockingham, 1900.

David Barks ——————————————

George Bowman—Killed at Stony Creek. Struck on head by club in hands of ——————————

Michael Bowman—Died in Madison Co. since war.

Jacob Baxter—Living on Linville Creek. So far as known sole survivor of original Co. B. G. Rifles.

Henry Bush—Killed in Winchester. Buried there.

Charles Bush—Transferred to Co. H, 7th Cav.

Richard Black—Went to Troy, Missouri, after war. Died there, 1888.

Michael Brunk—Removed to Warwick Co. Probably dead.

David Bare ———————

John Bear—Dead.

Godfrey Brock—Died since war.

William Brock—Transferred to Co. H. Dead.

William Beam ————

Daniel Barb ————

Simon Barb ————

Noah Barb ————

Thomas Beach—Transferred to Co. H.

John Beach—Transferred to Co. H.

Samuel Cootes—Honorary member. Died at Cootes Store since war.

A. J. Correll—Wounded.

I. B. Coffelt—Young man acting as substitute. In service only a few days, when wounded severely at Buckton, losing a leg. Lived for many years in Staunton.

Isaac Custer—Taken prisoner. Died at Camp Douglas, Ill.

Henry Carnes—Died in Rockingham, 1899.

David R. Cromer—Died 1902 in Pendelton Co. Buried in Harrisonburg.

Newton H. Carpenter—Died in Frederick Co., 1914.

George Coffman—Wounded May 28, 1864.

John Carpenter—Transferred to Co. H. Dead.

Giles Devier—Former editor Rockingham Register. Died in Harrisonburg.

Hiram K. Devier—Died in Dayton, 1897.

Jacob Dingledine ————————————

Andrew W. Dyer—Died in native Co. Pendleton since war.

John W. Duff—Taken prisoner March 1862. Took oath of allegiance. Baltimore man. Remained in enemy's camp, but rendered no service after taking oath.

John Donnelly—Substitute.

William Effinger ————

Samuel Emswiler—Taken prisoner in Maryland, July 7, 1863. Died at Turleytown, 1902.

Wesley Emswiler.

Noah Emswiler—Killed near Cross Keys by accidental discharge of gun.

Joseph P. Emswiler—Wounded in brain at Dam No. 5 on the Potomac. Died at Turleytown since war.

John Fawley—Killed in battle.

Samuel Funk—Wounded. Thrown from horse and killed since war.

William Funk.

Hopkins Funk—Company blacksmith. Wounded severely several times. Died Moore's Store, 1901.

Milton Funk—Wounded on Bolivar Heights. Died in Charlestown of fever.

James Funk—Died in Texas, 1901.

A. Brown Funk—Wounded May, 1864. Died at Soldiers' Home, Richmond.

Adam C. Fulk—Killed. Buried at Capon Bridge, Hampshire Co., W. Va.

John G. Fulk—Killed in battle. Buried in Eastern Va.

George C. Fulk.

Harvey Fulk.

William Fulk

Cyrus Fetzer—Transferred to Co. H. Died at Maurertown, Shenandoah Co., 1927.

Samuel Fansler—Transferred to Co. H.

Henry Fansler—Transferred to Co. H.

Richard Finegan—Transferred to Co. H. Died near Timberville since war.

Richard Good—Went to Texas after war.

Jacob Good—Transferred to B. G. Rifles from Capt. Arehart's Co., Aug. 10, 1861.

John Good.

Cornelius Graybill.

Robert C. Graybill.

Samuel B. Hollar—Went to Texas after war.

William Helsley—Transferred to Co. H.

James Helsley—Transferred to Co. H.

Solomon Hulvey.

David Hulvey.

Jonathan Hulvey.

Peter Hulvey—Died after war in Pendleton Co. from effects of old wound.

Allen Hulvey—Son of widow. Killed. Body not recovered.

William Hughes.

Alrazi Horn—Went West after war.

John H. Harris.

Charles T. Hupp—Died in Shenandoah after war.

Rosin Hall—Transferred to Co. H.

Israel Jones—Wounded at Bolivar Heights. Taken prisoner near Darksville, Dec. 19, 1862. Died since war. Widow living near Miller & Wine's Store.

Evan Jones—Died at County Line since war.

Erasmus L. Keyes—Wounded severely. Died since war.

James Lindamood—Killed at Gettysburg.

Sylvanus Lindamood—Killed after surrender in raid on Yankee camp.

Rev. S. S. Lambeth.

William Leasy.

John Leasy—Died of consumption, 1898.

William Lee—Transferred to Co. H. Died 1903.

William Minnick—Taken prisoner Darksville, Dec. 11, 1862. Died at Soldiers' Home, Richmond.

Levi Minnick—Died in Rockingham, 1900.

George May—Wounded on Rappahannock River. Honorably discharged. Dead.

Alfred Morris—Taken prisoner July 1863. Went west after war. Kansas.

Isaac Miller—Shenandoah man.

John Miller—Killed in Battle. Ashland Station. Buried near Richmond.

William M. Miller—Died of fever during war.

William R. Messick—Wounded in cattle raid below Petersburg. Lost arm.

Emanuel McMullen—Went west after war.

David McMullen.

George Moore—Killed in battle.

Samuel Moore.

George Moffett—Transferred to Co. H.

Lincoln Maupin—Transferred to Co. H. Killed by explosion of dynamite in Arkansas, March, 1910.

Carter Minnick.

J. H. Minnick.

John H. Neff.

Michael Neff—Died in Missouri after war.

Erasmus Nicewarner—Transferred to Co. H.

Samuel Newham—Transferred to Co. H.

William P. Newham.

Isaac Orebaugh—Transferred to Co. H.

John S. Pennybacker.

Isaac Pennybacker—Wounded at Greenland Gap, and left for dead. Lived many years afterwards.

Benjamin R. Pennybacker.

Albert Pennybacker—At Soldiers' Home, Richmond.

Peter Rader—Died at Soldiers' Home, Richmond.

George L. Rader—Died in Mo. after war.

Charles C. Rader.

Jacob L. Rader—Died in Charlestown of fever.

Isaac Reedy—Taken prisoner at Mechanicsburg, Feb. 3, 1863.

Solomon Ritchie—Died at Broadway, 1924.

Jacob Roadcap.

James F. Scott—Wagoner, from Cross Keys. Died in 1900.

John C. Shoup—Promoted to Capt. Co. H, 7th Va. Cav. Killed in battle at Cedar Creek, Oct. 19, 1864.

Jacob L. Shoup—Promoted to Lieut. Co. H, 7th Cav. Killed at Gettysburg.

William Swanson.

Henry Showalter—Died in Rockingham, 1926.

Michael Showalter.

Abraham Showalter—Taken prisoner near Darksville, Dec. 11, 1862.
William Shultz—Lost his speech. Dead.
John Simmers.
Daniel Stickley.
Calvin Sprinkle.
William Sprinkle.
Uriah Silvius.
Moses Turner.
Jacob G. Turner.
Thomas Toppin—Died at home from fever, 1863.
George Toppin—Wounded in cattle raid below Petersburg.
William Toppin—Killed in battle.
John H. Thomas—Wounded in Maryland, July 3, 1863. Died at
    Broadway, 1902.
Benjamin Trumbo—Died in 1900.
Ephraim Wean, of C. Wean—Wounded at Ream's Station and died.
Ephraim Wean, of Isaac—Wounded at Ream's Station. Came home.
    Died.
Noah Wean.
Jacob Wean.
John W. West—Arm broken at Cherry Run.
George W. Woods—Discharged. Deaf man.
Charles B. Will—Transferred to Co. H, 7th Cav.
Henry Zirkle—Promoted to Corporal Co. H.
David Zirkle—Went west.

Sylvanus Lindamood writes again from

Camp Falling Springs Church, Va.
April 17th, 1864.

Dear wife: In the first place I will inform you that I received
your kind letter yesterday evening and was exceedingly glad to hear
from you. I will tell you that I wrote you a letter a few days ago,
but I don't expect you received it yet. Probably it has been mislaid
at some of the post offices. I will tell you that we are faring
tolerably bad at this time. Our rations are very short, besides we
don't get more than half enough feed for our horses. We get tolerable
smart corn, but don't hardly get any long feed at all. Our horses
are getting very poor.

I will tell you that our camp at present is about ten miles from
Lexington.

We have had a very wet, muddy time of it for the last few
weeks, but it is drying off considerable now.

I wrote to you in my other letter that you should pay Michael
Brock for shoeing my horse while I was at home. I sent the money
in the letter. I received the badge that you sent me, and I have

got it on my jacket a-walking about through camp as big as if I was somebody.

I will tell you that Ephraim Wean wants one of those hats that you have got there. He said that I should tell you that you should save him one until he comes home.

I will also tell you that I count on coming home about the 10th or the 15th of next month.

When you write I want you to tell me how my horse is getting along. I want to know if he will soon be fit to ride in service, for I expect I will have to bring him in service when I come home.

Now I have nothing of any importance to communicate to you at present, so will bring my letter to a close by asking you to write to me as soon as convenient.

Direct in care of Lieut. Jordan, Co. B, 7th Regiment, Va. Cavalry.

Nothing more at this time, but remain,

Your affectionate husband until death,

Sylvanus Lindamood.

N. B.   I also was glad to hear that Billy was still in the land of the living.   Take good care of him till I come home.

NEIGHBORHOOD HISTORICAL NOTES

By Charles E. Kemper

In these notes no great attempt has been made to write either complete or technically correct genealogies. The writer does not possess such information, except in the case of a few of the families, and they have long and formal genealogies already printed.

The genealogy in these notes is based upon the writer's personal acquaintance with the families and to some extent on the records of Augusta and Rockingham counties, Virginia. The chief purpose of the notes is to preserve some account of the families who settled early in Rockingham County, Virginia, chiefly in the eastern part of the county. An effort has been made, however, to locate the early homes of the first settlers as accurately as possible, so that their descendants, who live in distant states, when they visit Rockingham County, may find with little effort the places where their ancestors lived in colonial days.

As the notes are neighborhood history, they are to some extent gossipy, which is a wide departure from the writer's usual style. His excuse is that it has been a labor of love for his own county and his own people.

PEAKED MOUNTAIN CHURCH

This church, now called Upper Massanutten Church, dates back as a preaching place to 1742. In that year Reverend John Hindman, a native of Londonderry County, Ireland, was sent by Donegal Presbytery, in Pennsylvania, to the Valley of Virginia as a missionary. Among other places he preached at the "Head of Shenandoah." The Shenandoah "heads" at present at Port Republic, in Rockingham County, Virginia, but not until 1811 was there a Presbyterian congregation at that place. Cross Keys is the nearest point at which a Presbyterian congregation has existed continually since 1745, and that place was the "Head of Shenandoah," at which Mr. Hindman preached in 1742.

In May, 1748, John Craig, William Craig, Robert Hook and Robert Scott and others petitioned the county court of Augusta for a new road from the Mountain Road to the Court House Road, near the "New Stone Church," which petition was granted.

ANNALS OF CROSS KEYS

Cross Keys derived its name from an old book-store in London in 1650-1655. Who gave the name to the place in Rockingham County, Va., is not known, but a post-office was established there in 1804, and J. Hancock, probably an Eastern Virginian, was the first post-master. He cut his name on a plank weather board of the old Kemper homestead, at Cross Keys, in 1804, and so did John Braun (Brown), the Reformed minister, then a young man of 33.

John Harry was the owner of Cross Keys, in 1817, when the place was bought by Jacob Kisling, a soldier of the Revolution, and given to his daughter, Ann, the wife of John Pence.

In 1823, Rodham Kemper moved down from the old "Plow and Harrow Store," near Mt. Sidney, in Augusta County, Virginia, bought Cross Keys, and it remained in his family for many years.

Rodham Kemper was a merchant at that place from 1823 to 1845, the year of his death, and the business was continued by his sons, Edward S. Kemper and William Morgan Kemper. The latter was a private soldier in the Tenth Virginia Regiment and died in the service in 1862.

The oldest building at Cross Keys was a small one-story building called the "Tailor Shop." It stood in the angle of the Keezletown Road and the road leading to Pleasant Valley, probably built by John Harry; and his trade gave the name to the "Tailor Shop."

When the battle of Cross Keys was fought, on June 8, 1862, General Jackson's left wing rested on the Keezletown Road, about one-half mile south-west of Cross Keys; and General Fremont's right wing rested on the same road, directly at Cross Keys. The store of Edward S. Kemper and William Morgan Kemper was pillaged by the Federal soldiers and also Mrs. Ann Kemper's home to a considerable extent.

The home of Edward S. Kemper was made a Federal hospital during the battle of Cross Keys, in which eighty-odd soldiers were placed; and so was the Dovel house on the Rodham Kemper estate.

The Kemper house at Cross Keys, now owned by the Rogers family, was an ordinary or tavern before 1800. The house is built of hewn logs, weather-boarded and plastered inside, and to all appearances is a frame house of more modern days. In the hall-way was a latticed room, called the "bar," where liquors were served in the olden days.

The Dovel house on the Rodham Kemper place was burned upon the retreat of the Federals, and the wounded in the home of Edward S. Kemper were captured by Jackson's cavalry under Captain McNeil after the battle. After a stay of about one week, these wounded men were transferred to a hospital in Harrisonburg.

On the crest of a hill on the Van Lear place, about one mile south of Cross Keys, stood, until 1876-1877, the ruins of an Indian Fort, built there during the French and Indian War, in which the families of that section took refuge when the Indians invaded that part of the Valley.

Early Ministers in Rockingham County

Reverend John Hindman was the first settled preacher in the present county of Rockingham. He was a native of Londonderry County, and came to the Valley from Chester County, Pennsylvania, in 1742. He was the first pastor of the Peaked Mountain Church, in 1745, and died in 1748, and was buried probably in the grave-yard at Cross Keys

REVEREND ALEXANDER MILLER was the second pastor of the Peaked Mountain Church. He had been a member of the Londonderry Presbytery, in Ulster, Ireland, and was deposed from the ministry because of misconduct, and then came to America. He settled near Dayton, Virginia, in 1753, and the Peaked Mountain congregation made an application to Donegal Presbytery for his services in 1754, which was refused, but a second application in 1755 was granted and he was allowed to accept the call.

REVEREND JOHN CRAIG, of Augusta Church, was directed to install him, which he did in August 1755.

Mr. Miller was not a man of well regulated life, and so had trouble with his congregation. He tried to invade territory which belonged to Reverend John Craig and apparently committed other acts not agreeable to his people.

In 1763 he went on a missionary tour to North Carolina, and while there committed acts not creditable to him nor to his profession within the bounds of Orange Presbytery, which body ordered him not to preach within its jurisdiction. He was tried by Hanover Presbytery in Virginia and deposed as a Presbyterian minister.

Reverend John Brown, pastor of Timber Ridge Church, in present Rockbridge County, had investigated Mr. Miller's conduct in North Carolina and apparently upon his report, which seemingly was confidential, Mr. Miller was deposed from the ministry. He did not seem to have any knowledge of Mr. Brown's report until in 1768, when the latter told some of the Peaked Mountain congregation the facts of Mr. Miller's misconduct in North Carolina. This reached Mr. Miller's ears and he sued Mr. Brown for slander, alleging, among other things, that the slanderous utterances of Mr. Brown had caused him to lose a call to a congregation worth fifty pounds a year, which seems to indicate Mr. Miller had connected himself with some other denomination. Patrick Henry was Mr. Brown's counsel and the suit resulted in favor of the defendant.

When the Revolution came on Mr. Miller was a loyalist. He was indicted for treason in Augusta County Court, and found guilty, but he appealed to the General Court at Richmond, the records of which have been destroyed and the result of his appeal is not known. Mr. Miller died a year or two after the War of the Revolution.

(Note by J. W. W.—On pages 50 and 51 is recorded an incident which illustrates in a rather striking manner certain irregularities in Alexander Miller's conduct.)

REVEREND THOMAS JACKSON followed Mr. Miller as the Presbyterian minister in Rockingham County. He was a native of New York and much beloved by his people. He had four preaching places: Cross Keys, New Erection, Edom and Mossy Creek. He bought 240 acres of land on the divide between the waters of Muddy Creek and Linville Creek. He died in 1774. The records of Augusta County show that he owned a fine private library, but he died without known heirs and his estate was escheated to the Commonwealth.

Mr. Jackson served in the pastorate indicated from May 1769 to May 1773. In October 1773 Rev. Samuel Edmonson was installed and served the churches for a short period.

Reverend Mr. Campbell followed Mr. Saml. Edmonson as the pastor of Peaked Mountain Church and other Presbyterian churches in Rockingham County, but he remained only a year or two, and then removed to South Carolina.

After Mr. Campbell there is a hiatus of nearly fifty years in the history of the old Peaked Mountain Church at Cross Keys. New Erection was cut off from the old church and had its own minister; and so were Edom and Mossy Creek; but in 1824-25 the Presbyterians and Lutherans united and built a union church at Cross Keys. Even then the Presbyterians did not seem to have any settled pastor; but were preached to occasionally by the pastor of the Harrisonburg Presbyterian Church.

Reverend Philip Charles Van Gemunden was the first settled German Reformed preacher in Rockingham County, evidently a native of Holland, from his name. He came to the county in 1762; bought land on Fort Run in the Timberville neighborhood, and died in 1764. He preached at Rader's Church and at the Upper Peaked Mountain Church, now McGaheysville, Virginia. His will is recorded at Staunton, and he willed his two sons to Peter Scholl and Abram Bird.

Reverend Charles Lang followed Mr. Van Gemunden as a Reformed minister. He came from Frederick, Maryland, in 1768, and bought a farm in the Timberville section, and also one near McGaheysville. He was not a man of well ordered life and soon got into trouble in his congregation. In 1771 he was obliged to leave Virginia and thenceforth is lost to history. His Fort Run land was sold in 1771-1772, but his wife, Mrs. Ursula Lang, continued to live in the neighborhood of McGaheysville and was a woman much respected. The early name of the village, Ursulaburg, was given to it in her honor.

Frieden's Church appears first under that name in 1786 and Peter Ahl was the first pastor, who was succeeded by Reverend John Brown. The memory of the latter is still green and fragrant in Rockingham County and adjacent regions.

The records of Rockingham County in 1792 show that Frieden's Church was called the "Dutch Church" in that year.

St. Peter's Church, about five miles northeast of Elkton, was the Lower Peaked Mountain Church in colonial days, and was served by the same minister who preached at the Upper Church. In 1767 Henry Miller, the son of Adam Miller, and Jacob Bear, Mr. Miller's son-in-law, were Reformed elders in the church at St. Peter's. The present church was built and dedicated in 1777.

The land records of Augusta County, Virginia, show that Augustine Price, Jacob Herman and other families in the Shenandoah River section had first settled in 1749-50 in Southwest Virginia, on the New River, but were driven out by the Indians when the French and Indian War commenced.

John Madison, clerk of the Augusta County Court, states in a letter to his cousin, President Madison, that quite a number of families had been driven out of the New River country by the Indians. They sought refuge in present Rockingham County, in the strong German section of East Rockingham, and soon took prominent place among them.

Jacob Herman gave the land, in 1762, to the Lutherans and Reformed on which to build the Union Church, at present McGaheysville, Virginia. It is described in the deed as being on "Stony Run," which flows through McGaheysville.

THE LUTHERAN CHURCH AT McGAHEYSVILLE

The order book of Augusta County, Va., for the year 1758 shows that Rev. Lawrence Wartman was preaching at McGaheysville. A member of his congregation was naturalized by the county court of Augusta County, and Mr. Wartman came into court and testified as a Lutheran minister that the applicant had taken the sacrament as required by law, &c.

This shows that he was preaching at the Upper Peaked Mountain Church in 1758, and probably in 1757. He came from Lancaster County, Pa., and in a few years went to South Carolina. He seems to have been the first settled Lutheran preacher in Rockingham County.

A preceding note gives Rev. Lawrence Wartman as the first Lutheran minister at McGaheysville, but there is some confusion as to his Christian name. Rev. William J. Hinke, of Auburn, N. Y., a high authority on Lutheran and German Reformed church history, gives his Christian name as Lawrence, but this is probably not the case, as the following court record shows:

"Jacob Harman (Herman) produced a certificate from under the hand of the Reverend H. Wartman of his having taken the sacrament, took the usual oaths to his Majesties person and Government subscribed the abjuration oath and test which is ordered to be certified in order to his naturalization."

This was in 1758. (See Order Book No. 6, p. 180.)

This order shows that in 1758 Rev. H. Wartman was a minister at McGaheysville and gives to the Lutheran and Reformed Church that certain date; but since Mr. Wartman was not Rev. Lawrence Wartman it is an open question whether he was Lutheran or Reformed; but as he does not appear as a Reformed minister he must have been a Lutheran.

In 1762 the two denominations built a union church at McGaheysville, and in the contract agreement between them the Reformed elders and members precede the Lutherans.

But the weight of the evidence is that Rev. H. Wartman was a Lutheran minister and organized the Lutheran church at McGaheysville and Rader's Church, certainly as early as 1757.

The deed records at Staunton show that Jacob Harman (Herman) lived on Stony Creek at McGaheysville, and in 1762 owned a mill at that place.

OTHER MINISTERS

Charles Gallagher made his will Nov. 1, 1750, and in it gave £10 to Rev. William Wappeler and the same amount to Rev. Mr. Taylor, whose Christian name is not given, to be paid Nov. 1, 1752. To William Hopkins he left his rifle and other legacies. The rest of his estate he left to Ephraim Love, his friend and executor.

Hopkins is an old New Erection name, and Ephraim Love certainly lived in that locality. Diligent inquiry has failed to identify these early ministers in Rockingham, but they were probably either Presbyterian or Baptist.

SCHOOLMASTERS

The records of Augusta County, Va., show that prior to June 28, 1758, Thomas Opps taught a school in Pendleton County, Va., and in 1760-61 in the neighborhood of McGaheysville, Rockingham County. His name shows that he was a German; and probably he taught a German school.

The Augusta records (court papers 421) also show that Edward Sampson taught a school in 1766 in the vicinity of Andrew Bird and Thomas Moore. The school was on or near Smith's Creek.

EARLY DOCTORS

The Augusta court records show at least three doctors in Rockingham before the Revolutionary War. Dr. Conrad Knave practiced medicine in the Timberville neighborhood before 1760. About the same time Dr. ———— Housing was practicing in the Cross Keys section. About 1770 Dr. Michael Archdeacon was a physician in the vicinity of Port Republic.

THE KISLING FAMILY

Christopher Kisling settled in the neighborhood of the present McGaheysville in 1762 or earlier. He died in 1774, probably as the result of an accident, as the records of Augusta County show that an inquest was held over him. His inventory indicates that he was a dyer by trade. He left a widow, Christina, who married John Herdman in the Dayton neighborhood; and he had several sons and daughters, among them, John and Christopher Kisling. Reuben Kisling, who lived on the Lawyer's Road, was probably a son of John Kisling. The most prominent member of the family was Jacob Kisling, who was an orphan in 1778 and was bound to Philip Lingel to learn the trade of a wagon-maker. He served as a soldier in the

War of the Revolution in the campaign against Arnold in 1781 and
in the siege of Yorktown. He was a noted rifle shot, and after the
Revolution was a captain of Rockingham militia. He married
Barbara Lingel, widow of Philip Lingel, in 1782, and they had the
following children: Henry Kisling, who married his cousin, Miss
Miller; Christina Kisling, who married Colonel Joseph Mauzy, a
captain of the War of 1812; Ann Kisling, who married, first, John
Pence, and second, Rodham Kemper of Cross Keys; Mary Kisling,
who married Philip Hopkins, a merchant of Staunton, Virginia;
Elizabeth Kisling, who married Edward Stevens.

Henry Kisling had two sons: George J. Kisling, for years county
surveyor of Rockingham County; and Whitfield Kisling, a captain
in the Tenth Virginia Regiment and adjutant of that organization.
He was killed at the battle of Spottsylvania Court House in 1864.

THE CRAIG FAMILY

William Craig and Janet, his wife, came to America from
County Down or County Antrim, Ulster, Ireland, in 1732, with three
sons, Robert, James and John, and probably two daughters. The
family first settled in Chester County, Pennsylvania, near Kennett's
Square, and remained there until 1740, in which year they came to
Augusta County, Virginia.

James and Robert Craig settled permanently in 1745-46 in the
Mt. Meridian neighborhood, Augusta County, Virginia, while John
Craig, the youngest son, bought land from the Franciscos, in 1748,
on Cub Run, in Rockingham County.

William Craig died in 1759; his will is recorded at Staunton.
He signed a petition for a new road to the "New Stone Church" in
1748, and attended various sales in the McGaheysville neighborhood,
which indicates that he was a citizen of present Rockingham County,
and not of Augusta.

John Craig, son of William, married Sarah ————————, and
had the following children:

John Craig, who married a daughter of James Beard, and
removed to Kentucky;

Lieutenant William Craig, who also removed to Kentucky, and
was killed in a duel fought in the neighborhood of Danville,
Kentucky;

Captain James Craig, who served either as a captain in the
Revolution or in the Indian wars after the Revolution;

Mary Craig, who married Colonel John Cowan, of Rockingham,
and moved to Kentucky;

Margaret Craig, who married her cousin, David Laird, and lived
and died in Rockingham County.

THE HOUSTON FAMILY

In 1751 Archibald Houston patented land on Mill Creek,
immediately above John Stephenson, whose daughter he had married.

He had these sons: George, Nathan, John and Stephen; and daughters: Mary, Abigail, Jean, and several others. When the Revolution began, all of the Houstons belonged to Captain Thomas Hewitt's company of militia. Captain Hewitt lived at the Hiel place, later owned by the Saufleys, about one mile west of Cross Keys.

Archibald Houston died in 1774 and Captain David Laird was one of his executors.

During the Revolution George Houston served as a captain and was on the expedition against the Indians on the Ohio River in 1778 and 1779.

Among the later members of this family in Rockingham was George Houston who served as lieutenant-colonel of the 38th Virginia Regiment and was killed at the battle of Sailor's Creek on the retreat of General Lee from Richmond to Appomattox.

One of his daughters, Lavinia Houston, married Dr. William Bell of Mt. Sidney, Augusta County, Virginia; and still another daughter married Dr. Frank Walker of the same county.

The Taylor Family

James Taylor patented Taylor Springs, now called Massanetta, in 1751. He had a large number of children, one of whom, as stated elsewhere, was the second wife of John Stephenson. He died about 1765, and is buried probably at Cross Keys, where one of his sons, James Taylor, is interred.

The Good Family

The progenitor of this family in Rockingham County was Jacob Good. His wife is said to have been a Miss Garrett from Eastern Virginia, probably Albemarle County.

The late Samuel Good was a descendant of Jacob Good. He owned a mill and was the founder of the village of Good's Mill. His mill was burned by General Sheridan's army in 1864, and was rebuilt after the Civil War. Among the children of Samuel Good are the following: B. Frank, and several daughters. B. F. Good, County Surveyor of Rockingham County, is a grand-son of Jacob Good.

The Tyler Family

Colonel Charles Henry Tyler was born in Prince William County, Virginia, and educated at West Point. He served in the regular army of the United States as a lieutenant and a captain, and when the Civil War commenced, resigned and entered the Confederate Army. He was assigned to duty in the West and served as a colonel under General Sterling Price.

He married Miss Elizabeth Wright, daughter of Dr. Wright, of the regular army, and sister to Dr. Joseph Wright, also surgeon in the army.

After the Civil War Dr. Joseph Wright bought a portion of Rodham Kemper's place, about one-half mile northeast of Cross Keys, and on it Col. Tyler resided until his death.

After the death of Colonel and Mrs. Tyler, their only son, Johnston W. Tyler, resided on the property until his death. Johnston Wright Tyler was educated at the Virginia Military Institute and graduated in the class of 1880. He married Miss Robbie Turner, daughter of Dr. Turner, of Front Royal, Virginia. After the death of Johnston Tyler, his wife married a second time, Mr. James Stickley, of Harrisonburg. Colonel Tyler was a cousin of President Tyler, as stated by his family.

CHANGE OF KEEZLETOWN ROAD

Along in the 1830's Jacob Kiblinger, a worthy citizen of Rockingham County, who lived on the Van Lear place, just southwest of Cross Keys, decided to engage in the mercantile business. Rodham Kemper was then carrying on a prosperous mercantile business at Cross Keys, and Mr. Kiblinger wanted some of the business and some of the profits, but a difficulty confronted him: The Keezletown road, or "Indian Road," did not pass by his store, and a change was necessary in the location of the old Keezletown, or "Indian Road," in order to make it pass directly in front of his place of business.

He applied to the County Court and a change was made, probably without opposition. At all events, if any opposition was made, it was not successful. Before the change occurred, the old Keezletown, or "Indian Road," passed directly in front of the Kemper residence at Cross Keys, leaving the present store house of Thomas P. Yager to the left and crossing the Kiblinger farm about 250 yards west of its present location, until the residence of the late James Scott was reached, where it united with the old Keezletown, or "Indian Road."

The chief purpose of this note it to show that when at Cross Keys and directly in front of the Kemper residence, now owned by the Rogers family, one is on the "Indian Road." When a turn is made to the left in the road and passing in front of Yager's store, one is off the "Indian Road"; and one is not on the "Indian Road" again until the Scott place is reached, at a point near Hulvey's Shop.

THE STEPHENSON FAMILY

John Stephenson, according to the records at Staunton, was the earliest settler in the Mill Creek Valley. In 1741 he obtained a grant for 760 acres of land, embracing the present Herring and Conger farms. The name of his first wife is unknown to the writer, but his second wife was Esther Taylor, daughter of James Taylor of Taylor's Spring. John Stephenson died in 1776-77, and his lands descended to his son, Thomas Stephenson, who sold to John Snapp about 1790. In 1792 a tavern license was granted to John Snapp at his home on Mill Creek, and thus his house became a place of public entertainment.

David Kyle, the old merchant, at the intersection of the Port Republic and Keezletown roads, near Cross Keys, was the next owner of the Stephenson place until his death in 1845. In 1858 Edward S. Kemper and William M. Kemper bought the lower portion of the Stephenson place, including the old Stephenson residence. This land is now owned by the heirs of Dr. E. A. Herring, of Harrisonburg.

Some 240 acres of the Herring place and a portion of the Conger farm were included in the original 5000-acre grant to Jacob Stover in 1733.

The Laird Family

This family came to Augusta County, Virginia, prior to 1754. The Laird name first appears in the Augusta County records of that year. They seemed to be living then in the neighborhood of Mt. Meridian, Virginia.

In 1756, David Laird bought land on Naked Creek in Augusta County. In 1760 James Laird bought 400 acres of land near the base of Laird's Knob, now Rockingham County.

In 1769 David Laird bought land from Edward Beard on North River. He died there in 1802.

He is styled "David Laird, merchant"; and also as a captain in the Augusta militia in the Augusta records. Living on the line between Augusta and Rockingham counties, his interests and business were as much in one county as in the other.

In 1764 he appears as one of the executors of Archibald Houston's estate, and is called "Captain David Laird" in his will.

Lieutenant Laird was wounded in the fight at Point Pleasant in 1774, and he was probably a son of David Laird.

Captain David Laird commanded a company in the 10th Virginia Regiment, Continental Line, during the Revolution, and again it is uncertain whether it is the father or the son.

Captain David Laird married Ann —————, believed to have been the daughter of John Burton, of Henrico County, Virginia, but this is not certain.

Captain David Laird died, as stated, in 1802, and his will is recorded at Staunton. He left the following children: David, James, Samuel and Jean.

James Laird married Jean Anderson, daughter of Captain Anderson, of Augusta County, a soldier of the Revolution.

Jean Laird married Robert Cochran, of Augusta County.

The wives of David and Samuel Laird are unknown to the writer, if they married at all.

In 1803, Mrs. Ann Laird and her family removed to Jessamine County, Kentucky, and settled on land acquired by Captain David Laird in his lifetime.

Later Robert Cochran and his family also moved to Kentucky and settled in what is now Shelby County in that state.

In this line and also in the line of James Laird, his brother, and in the line of Mary Laird, their sister, who married James Craig of Augusta County, Virginia, Presbyterian ministers and elders have much abounded.

James Laird, of Laird's Knob, married Sarah ————, and they had the following children:

James, born in 1740, died in 1829; married Sarah King, daughter of John King, of Augusta County, Virginia. In 1806 he removed to Rockbridge County, Virginia, and settled at Loch Laird. From him descend the Lairds of Rockbridge and also the Lairds of Richmond, Virginia.

James Laird of Rockbridge, as he is called in his family, was a soldier of the Revolution in the militia and saw active service in the field, according to the records of Rockbridge County.

David Laird, probably the second son of James Laird, Sr., married his cousin, Margaret Craig, daughter of John Craig, of Cub Run. They had the following children: Margaret, who married Henry Bushnell; James Laird, who married his cousin, Jean Craig; Mary Laird, who married Alexander Hannah.

James Laird, Jr., had two children only, daughters, Sarah, who married Philip Thurmond, and Margaret, who married David B. Irick, of Harrisonburg.

The records of Rockingham County show, in 1781, James Laird along with Alexander Herring was a collector of the specific tax in that county, but whether it was James Jr. or James Sr. is uncertain.

The Miller Family

Adam Müller (Miller) was born November 17, 1703, at Schresheim, Baden, Germany. He was the son of John Peter Miller and Ann Margaretha Miller, his wife, and was baptized on that day by the Protestant evangelical minister of the place mentioned. His father, however, lived in Lamsheim, in the adjacent Palatinate, and in or near that place Adam Miller grew to manhood.

He married in early life Barbara ———— and removed to Pennsylvania about 1724.

In 1726-27 Adam Miller visited the Valley of Virginia and settled there in the year last named, according to his naturalization papers issued to him by Governor Gooch.

In 1742 Adam Miller bought 820 acres of land from Joseph Bloodsworth and made his home at Bear Lithia Springs.

Adam Miller had the following children: Adam Miller, Jr., said to have been killed by the Indians, probably when the Roads Massacre occurred in 1764; Henry Miller, who married Elizabeth Cowger (Cogar); Elizabeth Miller, married John Bear, of Brock's Gap; Ann Barbara Miller, married Jacob Bear, of the same place.

The family tradition is that Adam Miller was a Lutheran, but in 1767 his son, Henry Miller, and son-in-law, Jacob Bear, were elders of the Reformed Church at St. Peter's, and this seems to be evidence that Adam Miller was a Reformed and not a Lutheran. Adam Miller died in 1783, aged 80 years.

In 1745 Adam Miller and William Purce (Pierce?) were ordered by the county court of Augusta to "view and mark a way from the top of the Blew (Blue) Ridge at the head of Swift Run Gap to Capt. Downs place."

This was one of the old roads in Rockingham, and later on was called the Mountain Road.

Capt. Henry Downs lived in 1745 at present Port Republic.

THE KEMPER FAMILY

Rodham Kemper and Dr. George W. Kemper, Sr., were natives of Fauquier County, Virginia, and descendants of John Kemper, who came to Virginia in 1714 and settled at Germanna, in present Orange County.

Dr. Kemper came to the Valley in 1807-08, and settled at Port Republic. In 1809 he bought the Madison place, called Madison Hall, the home of John Madison, who was the first clerk of the Augusta County Court.

Rodham Kemper came to the Valley in 1811 or 1812, and took charge of the store of his uncle, Colonel Joseph Mauzy, who was a captain in the War of 1812. After the war, he was a partner with his uncle, Michael Mauzy, in the "Plow and Harrow Store," on the Keezletown Road, near Mt. Sidney, in Augusta County, until 1823. In the year last named he moved to Cross Keys and was a merchant there until his death in 1845. He married Mrs. Ann Pence, widow of John Pence and daughter of Jacob Kisling, a soldier of the Revolution, as stated elsewhere.

They had the following children: Margaret Elizabeth Kemper, who died unmarried; Edward Stephenson Kemper, who married Miss Susan M. Craig, daughter of James Craig, of Augusta County, Virginia; Frances Virginia Kemper, who married Robert A. Gibbons, of East Rockingham County; William Morgan Kemper, who married Miss Verlinda Mohler, daughter of Mr. Abraham Mohler, of Weyer's Cave, Va.

The Kempers of Cross Keys and Port Republic have an interesting line of descent back to two old English families—the Gascoynes and Veseys.

In 1625 Thomas Gascoyne came to Virginia on the ship *Nova Bena*. He brought with him Thomas, Elizabeth, Josiah, Mary, and Alice Gascoyne and a relative, Josiah Gambling.

Thomas Gascoyne died in 1629, and about 1650 his daughter Alice Gascoyne married John Taylor of Northumberland County, Va., who arrived in Virginia in 1648.

In 1652 John Taylor (1) was a vestryman in the Church of England in Middlesex County, Va., and also a vestryman in 1656 in Lancaster County, Va. He acquired a large estate in Northumberland and Lancaster—more than 3600 acres—on Corotaman Creek or River and its branches.

John Taylor (1) died in 1702 and his wife Alice (Gascoyne) Taylor died in that year also. He left a number of children, among them John Taylor (2), who married Ann Vesey, daughter of George Vesey, of Suffolk County, England, who came to Virginia about 1654 with his wife Joan, and died in 1666.

John Taylor (2) and Ann (Vesey) Taylor had a number of children, among them Benjamin Taylor, who married Elizabeth ——————, and in 1742 sold his land in Lancaster and Northumberland counties and removed to old Prince William County, Va. His home was near Bethel, about 3 miles north of Warrenton in the present county of Fauquier, Va.

Elizabeth Taylor, daughter of Benjamin and Ann (Vesey) Taylor, married James Morgan, a soldier in the French and Indian War, who died in 1763. Elizabeth Morgan (nee Taylor) married (2) Henry Mauzy. She was the grandmother of Rodham Kemper of Cross Keys and of Dr. George W. Kemper, Sr., of Port Republic, and the mother of Col. Joseph Mauzy of McGaheysville.

John Taylor (2) died in 1713. He seems to have been a member of the county court of Northumberland County, and he is called "John Taylor, Gentleman," in a deed recorded in Lancaster County, Va.

The Veseys, as the name indicates, were Norman-French in their descent. They were domiciled in three places in Suffolk County, England. George Vesey, who came to Virginia, seems to have belonged to the family whose home was at Aldham, about ten miles west of Ipswich, as his son, Thomas Vesey, was 7th in an unbroken line of Thomas Veseys who lived at that place.

Richard Bell, a member of the London Company in 1622, married Mary Vesey, daughter of Thomas Vesey, Gentleman, of Suffolk County, England.

The British Encyclopedia gives only one family of Gascoynes—Sir William Gascoyne, Lord Chief Justice of England under Henry IV; but Chambers, in the older edition of that work, gives Sir John Gascoyne, the father of George Gascoyne, a noted poet in the time of Queen Elizabeth.

The Gascoynes have their coats of arms, not necessary to be described. The home of the Gascoynes was in Yorkshire, England.

Burke in his "Landed Gentry" states that Sir William Gascoyne's branch is extinct, but the more modern Chambers in the work mentioned says that he left many descendants. Burke in his "Landed Gentry" gives coats of arms to three Gascoyne families. They vary, but all have the same crest, showing that they all belonged to the same stock.

In 1625 Thomas Gascoyne was the captain of a ship and living in Hull, England. He was apparently the Thomas Gascoyne who came to Virginia, or his father.

The British Encyclopedia states that the Gascoynes belonged to a noble Norman family, but the name points to an origin in

Gascony, a southwest province in France. As early as 1612 the Gascoyne name had been cut down to Gaskins in Essex County, England; and in Virginia the members of the family bear that name today.

The Gascoynes (Gaskins), Taylors, and Veseys have intermarried with the Balls, Conways, Lees, Hulls, Eustace and other families in the Rappahannock Valley. Richard Henry Lee, who moved the Declaration of Independence, married Annie Gascoyne (Gaskins), daughter of Col. Thomas Gaskins of Westmoreland County, Va.

The chief purpose of this incomplete sketch is to trace the Cross Keys and Port Republic Kempers back to their kindred in Eastern Virginia, from whom they have long been separated by distance and geographical divisions.

For much of this information the writer is indebted to Mrs. L. C. Anderson, of Bainbridge, Ohio, whose painstaking researches among the Virginia county records has done much to develop the family history of the Gascoyne, Vesey, and Taylor families, for which see recent issues (in 1927) of the Virginia Magazine of History and Biography.

For Thomas Gascoyne's emigration to Virginia in 1625 see Hatton's List of Immigrants to Virginia; and for a rather complete sketch of the Gascoynes (Gaskins) see William and Mary College Quarterly, Vol. II, pp. 276-280; and the same volume for a sketch of the Balls, Damerons, and other families related to the Taylors and Veseys.

When the writer was a boy of ten years of age he read in the family Bible of Rodham Kemper, his grandfather, the following entry relating to the father of said Rodham Kemper:

'John Kemper, born —— died —— He served six years as a soldier in the Continental Line.'

This Bible disappeared when the first child of Rodham Kemper, Miss Margaret E. Kemper, quit housekeeping and boarded until the end of her life; and search for it has been fruitless.

Saffell gives John Kem as a private soldier in Col. Alexander Spotswood's regiment, possibly an incomplete form for John Kemper.

TRADES AND OCCUPATIONS

Nearly all the early settlers of Augusta and Rockingham counties, Virginia, had trades, as was the custom in England and on the Continent of Europe in that day, and to some extent now.

Silas Hart, a member of the County Court of Augusta, and later of the County Court of Rockingham, was a stone mason by trade. This is given as an example that a trade was not a bar to the highest county offices.

In 1756 a boy was bound to James Laird, and, among other things, it was stipulated that he was to be taught the trade of a weaver, which shows that James Laird knew that trade, whether he practiced it or not. This appears in the vestry book of Augusta Parish, in which frequent articles of indenture are to be noted.

The early settlers were carpenters, black-smiths, weavers, stone masons; in fact, practically all the mechanical callings of that day were understood and carried on by the early settlers of Rockingham and the Valley. The court records of Augusta County and the vestry book quoted fully confirm this statement.

Philip Lingel was a wagon-maker and one of the most respected men in his section; and to him Jacob Kisling was bound in 1768 to learn that trade.

The descendants of the early settlers in Rockingham County to whom these facts do not quite appeal may find solace in the fact that the late King Edward of England was taught the trade of a master carpenter.

EARLY SETTLERS IN EAST ROCKINGHAM

Jacob Stover was the earliest settler in the present county of Rockingham. In order to obtain his upper grant of 5000 acres of land, it was necessary for him to remain on the land for three years after the grant by the Council, in order to obtain his patent, and to build a house after the "manner of Virginia building," which meant a log house at least 16 x 24 feet in dimension.

His upper grant was confirmed by patent to him in 1733, which shows that he had lived on the land, or had made the improvements, commencing in the year 1730.

The next river settler in East Rockingham was Joseph Bloodsworth. In 1738 Adam Miller bought the "uppermost" of the Massanutten lots from Jacob Stover and in the same year Joseph Bloodsworth bought 820 acres of land from Stover, which land he sold to Adam Miller in 1742.

In 1738 Christopher Francisco, Sr., came down from Lancaster County, Pennsylvania, and bought 3800 acres of land from Jacob Stover, including the Strayer farm, kown in more recent days as Bogota.

In 1734 John Landrum obtained a grant, quite a large body of land, apparently back from the river and bordering on the Stover Patent.

In 1745 Henry Downs, of Orange County, Virginia, patented land in and around present Port Republic, apparently within the bounds of Stover's 5000-acre grant.

A later sale by Jacob Stover, Jr., of his interest in his father's estate shows that Jacob Stover, Sr., had failed to pay the quit rents on his upper grant and much of the land had lapsed to the Crown, and no doubt the land acquired by Henry Downs was originally within the Stover grant.

Adam Hedrick and Henry Null came down from Lancaster County, Pennsylvania, and settled in the river country, the former near present River Bank, the latter on Mill Creek, almost immediately at its mouth.

Jacob Herman and John Mann settled on Stony Lick Run, near present McGaheysville, the former in 1756 or 1757, and the latter before 1748.

In the Mill Creek Valley John Stephenson was the pioneer in 1741. The first house he built was of logs, about 30 feet square. To this structure he added the main mansion house, which was about 80 feet long, two stories high and one story wide, built of logs, weather-boarded and lathed and plastered. This house was built prior to 1756, and represented a fair type of permanent homes built in Rockingham County prior to the Revolution. It stood until 1870.

The "Indian Road" of 1722 was changed to some extent before 1754. It originally bisected the Stephenson place and crossed the meadow in that farm about 150 yards below the ford over Mill Creek. The Stephenson farm is now owned by the Herring and Conger families.

In 1754 Henry Pirkey bought a large body of land on Mill Creek from John Wilson and another patentee, and made his home on the farm owned in more modern days by Abraham Bowman. On this tract he built a mill on the creek below the Herring farm.

In 1751, as stated elsewhere, Henry Null came down from Lancaster, Pennsylvania, and acquired a considerable body of land on Mill Creek, commencing at its mouth. On this tract Jacob Stover evidently built a mill before 1741, because in John Stephenson's patent of land for that year the creek is described as "Jacob Stover's Mill Creek." This mill stood on the creek near the road which leads from Port Republic Road to Shady Grove Church, and its remains were still visible as late as 1872-1873.

A deed dated Nov. 17, 1767, made by Francis Kirtley, attorney in fact for William Russell, contains the following words:

"Lying and being on Mill Creek and the branches thereof in the Parish of Augusta County in the colony of Virginia, being part of a larger tract of Five thousand acres of land formerly granted to Jacob Stover, part whereof being lapsed and forfeited was granted to William Russell Gent. [Gentleman] father of the said William Russell party hereto and contains two hundred and fifty acres, being the plantation whereon the said John Stevenson now lives."

(See Deed Book 14, p. 29 et seq., Staunton, Va.)

This was the land now owned by the heirs of Dr. E. A. Herring, on Mill Creek. As shown elsewhere in these sketches, the 5000 acres granted really contained 6600, and the survey in Russell vs. Francisco shows that William Russell, Sr., received 1600 acres of Stover's upper grant. The case was tried in the Augusta County court in 1754.

The land in the Mill Creek Valley, owned in modern times by the Miller, Long, Kyger and Yount families, was evidently embraced in the 3800-acre tract sold to Christopher Francisco, Sr., in 1738.

This about completes the holdings in the main Mill Creek Valley prior to 1765; but on its tributary streams were other landowners.

Robert Hook, whose home was in William's Run Valley, extended his holdings above into the Mill Creek Valley and owned a portion of the Rodham Kemper place and practically all of the Flory farm.

Andrew McCarrell, in 1743, patented the land around Cross Keys, and, in 1749, sold it to John Anderson, of Augusta County, who, in 1759, sold it to Mathew Thompson, who, in turn, sold to Robert Hite. This tract included the site and graveyard of the Peaked Mountain Church, now called the Upper Massanutten Church. The church first named acquired the legal title to its site and graveyard property in 1778 from Robert Hite.

In the Stony Lick Run Valley, now called William's Run, John Bumgardner settled in 1746, near its head spring; but in 1754 he removed to the river country and acquired the land in the great bend of the Shenandoah River, later called "Lethe," and owned by the Gilmers, Grattans and others. "Lethe" is the next farm on the river below the old Strayer place.

Robert Hook was the pioneer settler in the William's Run Valley. He settled there in 1739 or 1740, and acquired a large body of land on William's Run and its tributaries and in the Mill Creek Valley.

Dr. John Lynn, in 1746, acquired land not far from the mouth of William's Run.

In 1754 Thomas Hewitt acquired the Bumgardner property at the head of William's Run.

This completes the list of large landowners in William's Run Valley prior to 1765, except, in 1763, Captain David Laird came over from Augusta County, Virginia, and patented land on Collin's Branch, but continued to live in Augusta at Beard's Ford.

In the Cub Run Valley Samuel Scott was the pioneer. His patent for 400 acres of land is dated 1742. It gives 1739 as the date of his location in the Valley mentioned. His home was near Peale's Cross Roads.

Valentine Pence bought land at the mouth of Cub Run from the Franciscos in 1754-55; he came from Lancaster County, Pennsylvania.

James Beard came over from the Grottoes section in 1755 and acquired holdings near Penn Laird, probably the old Earman farm.

Jacob Persinger settled on the Keezletown Road prior to 1765, just below Peale's Cross Road, on the farm owned in modern days by Albert H. Eiler, deceased.

James Laird, Sr., as shown elsewhere, settled near the base of Laird's Knob in 1760. This land was patented by Henry Downs, Sr., in 1747, which shows a settlement there in 1744. A small section of the Sheets home is evidently the improvement cabin built by Henry Downs or his agent, in 1744, and is evidently the oldest house standing in Rockingham County.

In 1754 George Carpenter, Sr., and George Pence settled in Cub Run between present Keezletown and the Laird farm.

In 1754 John Francisco entered land on the "Indian Road," in the neighborhood of present Keezletown.

In 1754 Jacob Stover, Jr., made an entry of a tract of land in Cub Run Valley; and this about completes the records of the land-owners in the Cub Run Valley in 1755.

Felix Gilbert, a merchant, was conducting a store at Cross Roads in 1765, in the store house which stood near the intersection of the Keezletown Road and Swift Run Gap Road; and, in 1768, Joachim Van Fersan, "The Dutch Lord," as Thomas Lewis, the county surveyor, called him, and as he is styled in the court records of Rockingham County, settled in the neighborhood of Keezletown. His heirs removed to Wilkes County, Georgia.

In the neighborhood of Mt. Crawford, John Grattan settled prior to 1765 and carried on a store, probably at the site of Mt. Crawford. He was a prominent citizen of Augusta County and afterwards of Rockingham County when that county left her mother county in 1778.

John Brewster, probably a brother of James Brewster, settled in the Burketown neighborhood prior to 1760; and John Hanna, who settled on Naked Creek in 1745, went over to the South River country and acquired a considerable body of land on the opposite side of the river in Rockingham County.

In 1754 George Trout settled on land afterwards acquired by James Craig of Augusta County, and later by Stephen Harnesberger.

The Slusser family settled in the Frieden's Church neighborhood prior to 1760 and the Earmans came at an early date to the Cross Keys section.

Going back to the river country, Jacob Bear, who had married Barbara Miller, daughter of Adam Miller, went over from Brock's Gap in 1764 and bought 260 acres of land from his father-in-law, including the Bear Lithia Spring. A contract of record at Staunton, Virginia, between Adam Miller and Jacob Bear shows that Mr. Miller was building a new house in 1764. It was a support contract and provided that Jacob Bear was to furnish Adam Miller with a certain quantity of beef, flour, pork, etc.; and among the items of support, which Mr. Miller thought necessary for his well being, was 30 gallons of whiskey a year, which indicates that Adam Miller was not an ardent prohibitionist.

In 1751 Gabriel Jones bought the Bogota farm from the Franciscos; and in 1754 Thomas Lewis, his brother-in-law, settled at Lynnwood, across the river.

Jacob Cogar was an early settler in the neighborhood of St. Peter's Church, and his son, Michael Cogar, was a captain of militia during the Revolution and commanded a company of Rockingham troops in the siege of Yorktown.

CAPTAINS IN THE REVOLUTION

Courts-martial records of Augusta County in the office of the clerk of the corporation court of the city of Staunton, Virginia, show the following captains, whose homes fell into Rockingham County when the county was organized in 1778:

Captain Peachey Gilmer;
Captain George Pence;
Captain John Hopkins;
Captain Abraham Lincoln;
Captain James Boggs;
Captain Anthony Rader;
Captain ———— Teter.

The latter's home was in the vicinity of present McGaheysville. There were two John Stephensons in Augusta County, and one of them, Captain John Stephenson, lived in the general neighborhood of Burketown and probably commanded a portion of the Rockingham militia in the Revolution.

When the war of the Revolution commenced actively throughout the colonies in 1776, the Virginia Convention passed laws organizing militia. The companies consisted of 60 men, rank and file, each commanded by a captain, and they were required to appear at muster places once a month fully equipped. If they failed to appear at a muster, they were reported to the courts-martial; if they had a good excuse, they were acquitted; if not, they were fined a small amount. In busy seasons many of the farmers preferred to pay the fine than to lose the time. In this way the name of nearly every militiaman appears in the courts-martial records.

The status of the militia in Virginia and the other colonies is not now fully understood or appreciated. They were the armed forces of the various colonies, regularly organized, officered and equipped, and were liable to be put into active service by the governors of the states at any time. They were the reserves, the men in the second line, and the courts-martial records show that the Augusta militia were ordered out thirteen times by the governor; and although there were flaws in the manner in which they were placed in the field, even under that system, practically every man enrolled in the militia in Augusta County or Rockingham County, Virginia, was at one time in active service.

A part of the Rockingham militia were at Yorktown and in the campaign of General Green against Cornwallis in North Carolina. They were in the expeditions against the Ohio Indians in 1779, and in the campaign against Arnold in 1781.

Captain Teter, who commanded the militia of the present McGaheysville neighborhood, at one time had in his command members of the Rush, Kisling and other families who resided in that vicinity.

There was still another captain, George Haynes, who commanded a militia company from the Elkton neighborhood, and in this company were Henry Miller and others of that vicinity.

Persons in Rockingham County who are interested in tracing the records of their Revolutionary ancestors will find the courts-martial records in the office of the corporation court of the city of Staunton a source of valuable information.

THE KYLE FAMILY

David Kyle, a native of Ireland, came to the Valley about the year 1800, and commenced his business life in Virginia as a peddler with his pack. His fortunes improved and he opened a store on the Keezletown road, near Cross Keys, where he continued in business for many years. While in business as a merchant he bought from the Snapps John Stephenson's place on Mill Creek and died there in 1845. He was a very successful merchant, farmer and stock raiser, and died, in 1845, the wealthiest man in Rockingham County. The mill on his place, now owned by the Conger heirs, he called the Brackey Mill, probably from some place of that name in his native county in Ireland.

Among the children of David Kyle were Dr. Harvey Kyle, deceased, of Bridgewater, who married Miss Elizabeth Eiler; William P. Kyle, who married Miss Spangler; Joseph Kyle, who left the Valley and settled in Culpeper County, Virginia; and a daughter, who married Mr. Dowdell; and another son, Jeremiah Kyle, who died without issue.

THE GORDON FAMILY

James Gordon first settled on Lewis Creek, a few miles below Staunton; but, in 1754, sold his farm to the Reverend John Craig, and made his home on Muddy Creek, now in Rockingham. He was one of the vestrymen of Augusta Parish. This family of Gordons are connected with the Lairds; and the late Dr. J. N. Gordon of Harrisonburg was a descendant of James Gordon.

THE RALSTON FAMILY

An ancestor of the Ralston family in West Rockingham was Charles Ralston, a school-master by profession, who died in 1760. This family has long been prominent in Rockingham.

THE FLORY FAMILY

This family lived about one mile south of Cross Keys, and the key to Jackson's position on June 8, 1862, was on the Flory hill. This house stood between the opposing battle lines on that day and was under the artillery fire of both armies throughout the fight; the family remained in the house and not one of them was injured.

THE SCOTT FAMILY

Samuel and Robert Scott were among the early settlers in East Rockingham. Samuel Scott patented land in 1742 on Cub Run, near present Penn Laird, as shown elsewhere.

Robert Scott also settled in Cub Run Valley and, in 1747, was captain of the Augusta County militia. During the French and Indian War he commanded a company of militia, including the men of military age in the Cross Keys neighborhood and in the northeastern part of Augusta.

A suit record at Staunton shows that Captain Scott and his company were in an expedition against the Indians in the South Branch Valley of the Potomac in 1755 or 1756.

THE BOWMAN FAMILY

This family settled rather early in the Mill Creek Valley. They acquired the Brewster and Pirkey lands. James Brewster sold his farm in 1804, and that was about the time when the Bowmans came up from the Linville Creek section.

Noah Bowman lived at the intersection of the Keezletown Road and the Lower Road from Port Republic to Harrisonburg, on the farm now owned by Reverend Charles Long.

Abraham Bowman, his brother, bought the Pirkey farm, about one mile down the Port Republic road, below his brother.

SPORTS AND GAMES

Horse-racing was carried on and witnessed in Rockingham County as early as 1745-46 on the Herring place, on Mill Creek, by the Reverend John Hindman and his neighbors; among them the Craigs, on Cub Run, the Lairds, Stephensons, Houstons, Brewsters, Pirkeys, Hooks, Scotts, and other families in East Rockingham.

Fox-hunting was one of the early sports in Rockingham County. In 1766-67 Henry Miller sued Francis Kirtley for damages, because the latter's dogs had injured Miller's wheat crops by running through the fields. This sport long survived in Rockingham and probably is carried on to a certain extent to this day.

The mother of the writer was Susan M. Craig, the daughter of Mr. James Craig, of Augusta County, Virginia, who lived at "Meadow Dale" in the forks of Middle and North River; and she stated that as late as 1845 flocks of wild turkeys, numbering 25 to 30, would come out of the woods into the wheat fields after the crop was harvested. This was just across the line from Rockingham; and no doubt similar game conditions existed in the county last named.

THE GILMER FAMILY

This family came over from Eastern Virginia prior to the Revolution and settled at "Lethe," the beautiful river farm, owned in more recent years by Mr. J. M. Weaver.

Captain Peachey Gilmer, a member of this family, commanded a company of militia for several years during the Revolution. He was succeeded by Captain George Pence.

John Gilmer, his brother, married a Miss Bear, of the Elkton neighborhood, and lived and died at "Lethe."

George Rockingham Gilmer, who was governor of Georgia, was born at "Lethe." He wrote a book called "The Georgians," and in it gives an amusing account of the efforts of the early settlers around the foot of Peaked Mountain to discover a traditionary silver mine in that mountain. This tradition seems to be well founded.

THE EILER FAMILY

Peter Eiler acquired a large tract of land in east Rockingham, bordering on the Page line, prior to 1755.

George Eiler, whose home was in the Mill Creek Valley, below Massanetta Springs, was a descendant of Peter Eiler; and so was William Eiler, whose home was on the Keezletown Road, a short distance below Peale's Cross Roads.

James A. Eiler, of this family, was a gallant Confederate soldier; and Mrs. Dr. Harvey Kyle was a daughter of George Eiler.

The late A. H. Eiler of Harrisonburg was a son of Mr. William Eiler.

THE HERRING FAMILY

Alexander Herring settled in the Dayton neighborhood prior to 1755, and the family has long been prominently identified with the history of Rockingham County. Some of them were officers in the Revolution; and, in 1781, Alexander Herring and James Laird were collectors of the specific tax in Rockingham County.

The Christian name of Captain Abraham Lincoln's wife was Bathsheba, and as this name occurs only in the Herring family in Rockingham County it is believed that the grandmother of President Lincoln was Bathsheba Herring, a daughter of Alexander Herring.

THE BREWSTER FAMILY

James Brewster patented land adjoining John Stephenson and Archibald Houston in 1754. His home was at the intersection of the Keezletown Road and the Lower Road, leading from Port Republic to Harrisonburg; and for many years the Bowmans and then the Harrisons lived at this place, now owned in more recent years by the Reverend Charles Long.

The Brewster house was one of the ancient structures in the Cross Keys vicinage and stood until about 1880, or later. It was built of logs, weather-boarded, ceiled and plastered within, and the eaves of the house came down within about seven feet of the ground.

James Brewster served as a soldier in the American Revolution, according to the Rockingham County records, and was a prominent member of the Peaked Mountain Church; and the deed for that church was recorded by his son, Thomas Brewster. After the Revolution James Brewster sold his Rockingham lands and moved to Jessamine County, Kentucky, where the family became prominent.

THE KEEZELL FAMILY

George Keezell came to Rockingham County, probably from one of the southeastern counties of Pennsylvania, prior to the Revolution, and settled near the village which bears his name. For many years the Keezletown Road, which, as shown elsewhere, was the "Indian Road" of 1722, was called the "Great Road"; and over it passed the trade of Southwest Virginia and Eastern Tennessee to Baltimore and other northern markets. This trade became so heavy that many ordinaries, or taverns, became a public necessity. For this reason George Keezell took out a tavern license. As shown in these sketches, John Snapp also kept a tavern at Mill Creek on the farm belonging to the heirs of Dr. E. A. Herring, and the old homestead of the Kempers at Cross Keys was an ordinary, or tavern.

George Keezell married Mary —————————, and had at least one son, Bernard Keezell, who was a soldier in the War of 1812.

Honorable George B. Keezell, for many years prominent in the state government of Virginia and also in the county government of Rockingham, is a descendant of George Keezell.

TORIES

In 1778 there was a Tory uprising near the Peaked Mountain, due probably to the influence of Felix Gilbert, the old merchant at Cross Keys, who was considered at one time a Tory during the Revolution. The uprising probably occurred in the Penn Laird neighborhood. Apparently the Tories were few in number and were soon suppressed by the Augusta militia. These facts are recited in McAllister's History of the Virginia Militia in the Revolution.

THE CURRY AND ALLIED FAMILIES

Dr. Robert Curry settled in Augusta County, Virginia, in 1748, and his brothers, Nathan, David and Isaiah, came at about the same time to the Valley from Lancaster County, Pennsylvania. The Augusta County Currys descend from Dr. Robert Curry. One of them, Robert, married Margaret Anderson, daughter of James Anderson, of Rockingham County.

Isaiah Curry settled on War Branch in West Rockingham; and one of this family, James Curry, was a captain in the Continental Line during the Revolution, and after the War postmaster of Harrisonburg.

James Anderson married Margaret, daughter of William Blain of the Dry River section; and the Currys are allied by blood and by marriage with the Stuarts, Henrys, Chestnuts, Herrings and other prominent families of Rockingham County.

THE UNION CHURCH

In 1823 Reverend Lewis Mayerhoeffer, a native of Frederick County, Maryland, came over from Madison County, Virginia, to preach to the Lutherans of the Cross Keys section.

In 1823 or 1824 the Union Church was built jointly by the Lutherans and the Presbyterians, to be used by them on alternate Sundays. This church stood on the site of the present church at Cross Keys and continued to be used by the two denominations mentioned until 1864, when General Sheridan encamped a portion of his army in the Cross Keys section. While the Federal cavalry were there they stabled their horses in the Union Church, tore up the floors and wrecked the church to such an extent that the Lutherans abandoned it and went to Frieden's Church and the Presbyterians went to Cross Roads and rented the old Felix Gilbert store house and continued to use that as a place of worship until 1871, when the present Presbyterian Church at Cross Keys was built, the Lutherans having conveyed to the Presbyterians all their right, title and interest in and to the church and graveyard, reserving, however, the right to bury in the graveyard and to preach funeral sermons and solemnize marriages in the church.

The "New Stone Church," mentioned in a preceding note, as having been built in 1748, was probably the second church structure at Cross Keys, the first church having no doubt been constructed of logs as was the custom of the early settlers in the Valley when they built their first places of worship. The "New Stone Church" of 1748 stood about 75 yards nearly due south of the present frame church near Cross Keys, and its foundations were still visible as late as 1872-73.

THE CONRAD FAMILY

Stephen Conrad bought land in the Elkton neighborhood in 1763. This family has long been prominent in Rockingham County and they have intermarried with the Millers, Bears and other families of East Rockingham.

George O. Conrad was for many years an active business man in Harrisonburg, and his son, Honorable George N. Conrad, has been commonwealth's attorney of Rockingham County and has represented the county in the state senate.

Edward S. Conrad, another son of George O. Conrad, was a prominent lawyer of Harrisonburg; and Dr. Charles E. Conrad and Laird L. Conrad, attorney-at-law, in Harrisonburg, are his sons. He married Miss Margaret Irick, daughter of Andrew B. Irick, of Harrisonburg.

THE HOOK FAMILY

Robert Hook was one of the early settlers in the Cross Keys neighborhood. He was living there in 1740 when he proved his coming into the colonies at his own expense in the Orange County, Virginia, County Court. His home was about one mile south of

Cross Keys, and he became one of the large landowners in that vicinity. He was captain of militia in the French and Indian War and also a member of the county court of Augusta in 1760. A history of his descendants is now in course of preparation by Mrs. Audrey K. Spence, of Wytheville, Virginia.

THE VAN LEAR FAMILY

The Van Lears were among the good old people living near Cross Keys. The progenitor of this family seems to have been Jacob Van Lear, who settled near Tinkling Springs prior to the Revolution and was a soldier in that war.

William Van Lear was the head of the Cross Keys branch of the family. He married Miss Baskins, of Augusta County, and among his children were the late Charles A. Van Lear, a gallant soldier of the Confederate army, who married a sister of Colonel W. W. Hook. A daughter, Miss Amanda Van Lear, married Mr. James Murray, of Port Republic; and still another daughter, Miss Emma Van Lear, married John C. Hook.

THE LONG FAMILY

Reverend Isaac Long before, during, and after the Civil War, was a man of prominence in the Mill Creek Valley. He married Miss Sauffley and had, among other children, David, Benjamin, John, William and Daniel.

Reverend Isaac Long was for many years a leader in his church (Dunker), not only in the Mill Creek section, but also in Rockingham County. He was a man of sound judgment, the strictest integrity and was known and loved by all who ever came in contact with him.

GEORGE ALFRED

Among the early school teachers in Rockingham County was George Alfred, as he was called, as late as 1840-5. The name, however, appears in the courts-martial records of Augusta County as Alford, where John Alford, probably the father of George Alfred, appears as a soldier of the Revolution. John Alford's home was about one mile north of Cross Keys. His farm adjoined the Simon Whitesell land, and this indicates that his place of residence was in the immediate vicinity of the home in recent years of the Kennedy family.

He taught a school for at least four years at Cross Keys, and about that time published an Arithmetic. He seems to have been an accomplished mathematician, probably the best of his day in Rockingham County.

(Note by J. W. W.—I have before me, Dec. 21, 1927, a copy of Alfred's book. The title page reads: "The American Student's Guide, containing a Compendious System of Theoretical and Practical Arithmetic, compiled for the use of Schools and Private Students in the United States. By George Alfred, a schoolmaster

in Virginia. Winchester: Printed at the Republican Office. 1834."
It is a 12mo. of over 300 pages.)

THE PIRKEY FAMILY

Jacob Burki (Pirkey) founded this family in the McGaheysville
neighborhood prior to 1755, and from there they have widely
dispersed themselves into the western states.

One of the last of the name living in the Cross Keys neighborhood was Ananias Pirkey, whose home was about one mile northeast
of Cross Keys.

The Pirkey graveyard on the Keezletown Road is at the
intersection of the old road leading from Port Republic to
Harrisonburg, and is well known to travelers on the road first named.

THE HARNSBERGERS

The ancestor of this family in Virginia was John Harnsberger.
He came to America either in 1717 or 1719, although there is a
family tradition that he came earlier. But he was not a member of
the 1714 colony of Germans who settled at Germanna in that year,
and therefore he must have come in 1717 or 1719. He located near
Germanna and in 1725 removed with the Lutheran colony to the
present county of Madison.

Stephen Harnsberger seems to have been the first of the family
to come to the Valley. The entry book of Thomas Lewis, county
surveyor of Augusta County, Va., shows that about 1760 Stephen
Harnsberger located land near the present town of Elkton; and
from that place his descendants have largely dispersed themselves.
One of them, Henry Harnsberger, settled on the North River, in the
Bridgewater neighborhood.

The Harnsbergers intermarried with the Bears of the Elkton
section, and one of them, Jeremiah Harnsberger, was the father of
Capt. J. Samuel Harnsberger, deceased.

Stephen Harnsberger, Sr., settled on South River, just across
from Port Republic. He married a daughter of Michael Baker, a
prominent citizen of the Brock's Gap neighborhood and a captain in
the Rockingham militia in the Revolutionary War. One of their
daughters married Major Thomas G. Miller.

A son of Stephen Harnsberger, Sr., Capt. Henry B. Harnsberger,
was for many years a prominent citizen of Rockingam. He was
educated at Dickinson College, Pa.; was county surveyor, and
represented the county several terms in the Virginia House of
Delegates. He was the captain of a company in the Civil War, and
a good officer. His brother, J. M. C. Harnsberger, was a gallant
soldier in the 10th Va. Regt., volunteer infantry, and badly wounded
at Gettysburg.

Another son, Stephen Harnsberger, Jr., married Miss Fauntleroy
(?) of Eastern Virginia, and was the father of William and Charles
D. Harnsberger of Grottoes.

Capt. H. B. Harnsberger married Miss Fannie Hopkins, and of their children as follows:

1. Elizabeth married Mr. Rousseau, a civil engineer from New Jersey.

2. Catherine married her cousin, William Harnsberger, a son of Robert S. Harnsberger, another son of Stephen Harnsberger, Sr., who lived near Mt. Meridian, Augusta County.

3. Jennie married Charles G. Harnsberger, her cousin, who is now (1928) president of the Rockingham National Bank of Harrisonburg.

4. John I. Harnsberger, who married (1) Adaline and (2) May, daughters of Dr. George W. Kemper, Jr., of Madison Hall, near Port Republic.

5. Annie, who married John F. Lewis, Jr., son of John F. Lewis, U. S. Senator from Virginia 1869-1875.

The Harnsbergers are of Swiss descent, and each succeeding generation has lived up to and well maintained the best traditions of the Valley people.

This sketch is written entirely almost from memory, and momentarily the writer failed to recall Miss Fannie Harnsberger, the eldest child of Capt. H. B. Harnsberger and his wife. Miss Fannie was a charming woman, of splendid character, and married John W. Blackburn, father of J. Frank Blackburn, the present efficient clerk of the circuit court in Rockingham.

Miss Lizzie Blackburn, a daughter of John W. Blackburn and Fannie (Harnsberger) Blackburn, married Dr. Albert S. Kemper of Bogota, near Port Republic.

IN DUNMORE'S WAR

On Jan. 18, 1775, Jacob Bear, of Bear Lithia Spring, presented a claim which was ordered to be certified to the General Assembly along with many others, growing out of the Point Pleasant expedition, which shows that he had some connection with it.

Capt. William Nalle commanded a company from the Elkton neighborhood in the battle with the Indians fought at Point Pleasant October 10, 1774. A partial list of his company has been printed. A member of the Harnsberger family was in this company. (See Wayland's History of Rockingham County, pages 449, 450.)

EARLY MERCHANTS

There were not many stores in Rockingham before the Revolution. Andrew Johnston was a merchant in the Dry River section before 1755. Felix Gilbert kept a store at Peale's Cross Roads; and John Grattan at or near Mt. Crawford, before 1770.

Most of the every day trade centered around Staunton before 1760, except when they marketed their produce in Fredericksburg or Richmond. Sometimes they went "far afield" for their trading.

In 1755 or 1756 William Craig and John Craig of the Cub Run section and James Craig, brother of John Craig, were trading with William Beard, a merchant in Urbanna in Middlesex, far down in Tidewater Virginia.

The Augusta records show that the first settlers in the Valley traded back to Christiania in Delaware and to Lancaster and Lititz in Lancaster County, Pa.

Stock Raising

Rockingham and Augusta have from early times been fine centers of stock raising. The records of Augusta County show that they had horses in large numbers and allowed them to run almost wild in the woods and on the public lands. Settlements of estates recorded at Staunton show that men were paid for days and days of service searching for the half wild horses of the decedents.

They also raised cattle in large numbers, which were driven to and sold in Pennsylvania.

They bred some good horses, too. Bald Eagle was a noted stallion, evidently a thoroughbred, as he stood at £7 and more before 1760.

Robert Harrison owned a "trotting stallion" in 1761, the predecessor by many years of the famous Sam Purdy.

The term thoroughbred as applied to horses has not come under the writer's observation in his search of the Augusta records, but as late as 1872-73 evidences of a thoroughbred or well bred ancestor now and then cropped out in the horses of Rockingham.

On the Meadow View Farm, the home of the writer, two mares used as work horses could without training trot a mile in about four minutes; and William Clatterbuck's gray Buck Rabbit evidently had thoroughbred blood in him.

Henry Bowman's Ride

On June 4th or 5th, 1864, Gen. David Hunter's army passed "Meadow View," then the home of Edward S. Kemper, now owned as before stated in these notes by the heirs of Dr. E. A. Herring.

A little group of five persons sat on the steps of the porch enjoying the soft June air and sunshine; and then three horsemen rode by.

The group mentioned consisted of Mrs. Kate Bullock, the widow of a Confederate soldier; her two children; James R. Kemper, now of Staunton, Va., a lad of nine; and Charles E. Kemper, just then on the eve of his fifth birthday.

The horsemen consisted of Thomas Adams, of Baltimore, Md., a paroled Confederate soldier; Samuel Wampler, a member of the Brethren Church; and Henry Bowman, a youth just about 16 years of age, a son of Abraham Bowman. All three were, of course, noncombatants.

They rode quietly up the Keezletown Road and disappeared from view. The little group at "Meadow View" kept their places on the steps, when suddenly the thunder of a horse's feet rang out upon the air, and Henry Bowman, with pale face, swept into view, riding as if death were close upon his rear. As he rode at full speed past the group, Mrs. Bullock cried out, "Henry, what is the matter?" He made no reply, but went on with impetuous speed.

And then more and louder other horses' feet smote the echoing air, and three of Gen. David Hunter's scouts burst into view in swift pursuit of Henry Bowman. Just before they reached the little group they drew their pistols. Mrs. Bullock cried out to the scouts, "Don't shoot! He is a neighborhood boy, and not in the army"; but in vain.

They fired one or more pistol shots at Henry Bowman, who was then just about to reach Mill Creek. Fortunately they missed him. One of the soldiers drew rein, revolver in hand, and spoke quickly to Mrs. Bullock about as follows:

"Madam, who is that young man? We are General Hunter's scouts and met him and his companions in the road. Upon our demand they surrendered, but he turned his horse and fled. We did not understand the cause of his flight and therefore pursued him."

Mrs. Bullock said she did not know the cause of his flight and repeated the statement that Henry Bowman was not a soldier; that he was a neighborhood boy, and not in the army.

All this quickly passed between them, and then the soldier thanked Mrs. Bullock and rode swiftly after his comrades.

Meanwhile the two soldiers who had not halted continued the race after Henry Bowman, but fortunately for him they ceased firing. Mrs. Bullock's woman's cry to the soldiers probably saved his life.

When young Bowman reached the lower, or Port Republic road, owned today by Rev. Charles Long, he turned and rode for home. An intervening piece of woods shut out for a time any view of the race; but soon young Bowman rode in sight, but his horse was flagging. The Federal scouts were splendidly mounted and were fast overtaking the youthful fugitive.

When young Bowman reached his home he saw that further flight was useless, and he surrendered. They did him no harm, to their honor and credit be it said, but took him to Port Republic and led him before Gen. Hunter himself, who asked Master Bowman why he had fled from his scouts; and Bowman frankly told him in order to save his horse.

Gen. Hunter considered this a valid reason, and gave him and his horse a pass through his army, and Bowman returned to his home. He told the writer of this sketch the facts about his interview with Gen. Hunter years after the Civil War.

Henry Bowman lost his life afterwards from a premature explosion of dynamite near Harrisonburg. He was a good man and a good citizen.

A Fox Hunt in Rockingham in 1873

On a bright clear morning in October, 1873, the writer, then a sturdy boy of some fourteen summers, left his home at "Meadow View" on Mill Creek with a small pack of four hounds to enjoy a fox chase. The destination he had in mind was the range of hills beyond Friedens Church, but events changed his purpose.

He was trotting along rather leisurely on the old Port Republic Road, with the pack training contentedly behind him, when suddenly Lead, the oldest dog, put up his nose and trotted into the woods. The other dogs followed and suddenly all of them broke into full cry—and the chase was on.

The fox had slept late that morning, and was almost caught napping in his leafy bed; but he heard the dogs in time to get about 200 yards the start.

Down Oak Ridge he went, with the pack in full voice in swift pursuit. He went almost to Mill Creek and then turned and went over the old historic Houston farm. Away they went, across the open fields, the pack tuning their voices in the chase almost from the high alto to the lowest bass.

Reynard then headed for the Maple Swamp near the Whitesell farm, his object being to gain Oak Ridge once more.

The young master of the fox hunt could not follow: fences 10 and 11 rails high checkered the country everywhere, and the best mounted and most skilful rider then in Old England could not have followed. All the youthful rider could do was to go back to the open road and watch, and wait, and listen.

Soon he heard the music of the pack as they took the fox across one of his father's fields near Maple Swamp, and on Oak Ridge they went again. Then the fox turned and started towards the jumping point. Suddenly the hunter saw a red fox, full form, at one bound clear the fence and leap into an open field on the Kennedy place; and then came the pack over the fence at one jump, looking like a long chain.

Little Speed, the smallest but the swiftest dog, was in the lead; but then they saw the fox about 150 yards ahead. The pack gave a cry which all fox hunters will understand, and it was a sight race for nearly a quarter of a mile. The fox still had his tail straight out behind him, but the dogs were setting the pace fast enough to bring the gamest fox in Rockingham to earth.

Once more the hunt went down Oak Ridge, over the Houston farm, over the fields for Maple Swamp. The young master of the hunt heard the music of the dogs, but they were not "talking" very much. Apparently they were running again by sight, and close upon the fox. Up Oak Ridge they went again, when all at once the cry of the pack stopped. The chase was ended, and it seemed as if the fox had run his last race. The huntsman threw down fences and opened bars and galloped rapidly to the finale of the chase.

Presently he came upon the dogs lying quietly in the wood road which led across the hill. The dogs looked up and wagged their tails as if to say, "We have finished the work." But no fox was in sight, dead or alive. The hunter dismounted, looked around, and found the key of the puzzle. The fox, pressed beyond endurance, had sought refuge in a large upright hollow tree. The hunter tried to twist him out with a switch, as boys twist rabbits out of hollow logs, but in vain. The fox snarled, but clung to his place of refuge.

The only solution was to cut him out with an axe. The tree stood on land which had once belonged to the grandfather of the hunter, but it had passed into other hands and the owner lived near by. To him the hunter went and politely asked the loan of an axe to chop out a fox. He was told, not quite so politely, that he was not believed; and besides if there was a fox in the tree he did not want it spoiled.

The hunter simply said, "You may regret this, as you have some ducks," and went back to his pack. He pulled away every stick and stone which stopped up the fox, got on his horse, told the dogs that the hunt was over, blew his horn, and went back to "Meadow View," where a good dinner awaited him, his horse and pack.

In this way passed into the history of sports in Rockingham one of the fastest races ever run in the county, after a red fox which was run down in a course about six miles long, with about 200 yards start on the dogs, and through an open and wooded country.

Next day when the young huntsman was quietly riding up the Keezletown Road to Cross Keys, not on but near the true course of the Indian Road of 1722, he saw the owner of the tree sowing wheat. At his hail the boy drew rein and awaited his approach. When he reached the fence the tree owner and *former* duck owner said, "I am sorry I did not lend you an axe yesterday to cut out that fox." "Why?" the rider asked. "Because," the other said, "something came to my house last night and killed twenty-five of my ducks."

The young rider said, "I told you that you would be sorry"; and then went his way.

This tells a truthful story of a fox hunt in Rockingham more than fifty-five years ago, and also points the moral to the breeders of its splendid poultry that a fox hunter and his pack may after all serve a useful economic purpose.

Since that eventful day in his varied life the writer has had the privilege and pleasure of hearing some of the best public speakers in the United States, and some fine voices on the lyric stage. He has heard the Marine Band of Washington and the 7th Regiment Band of Baltimore at their best, but never has he heard sweeter music than the cry of his pack in that clear autumnal day. Tom Moore's Irish Middies alone are comparable.

EXTRACTS FROM THE AUGUSTA CO. VA. COURT RECORDS

By Mrs. Audrey Kemper Spence

(See pages 199-230, above)

Will Book No. 8, page 147, will of Thomas Connelly, July 28, 1794, wife Margaret, sons Thomas, Alexander and Robert, daughters Martha, Mary, Elizabeth, Barbara, Jean and Isabella, son Arthur. Signed by John Campbell, John Connelly and John Hooke.

File No. 39 in Chancery, Connelly vs. Connelly, Dec. 9, 1803. Settlement of estate. Thomas, Alexander, Robert, Jane, and Isabella, children of Thomas Connelly, deceased, who departed this life on August 7, 1794. His wife, Margaret, died three months after his death. Barbara died about nine months after her mother's death, intestate. Robert was 12 years of age at death of his father. Thomas was the oldest child and was about 29 years of age at death of his father. He was married in March, 1803, about nine years after the death of his father. Thomas had made a business trip to Kentucky. Thomas said "that he had sent Robert to school to James Laird for about two years." Alexander St. Clair deposes July 22, 1808, that Robert Connelly removed to Kentucky some years ago.

Suit between David Connelly and John Connelly, November 14, 1800, speaks of John Connelly having owned 400 acres of land in Kentucky.

Will Book 8, page 322, will of John Connely of Xenia, Green County, Ohio, names his nephew Samuel Connely as his sole heir and as his executor, dated Sept. 27, 1830. The witnesses were John Haines, Frederick Burner and Hourace Hawkins. Probated in Green Co., Ohio, Nov. 26, 1830.

Deed Book 32, page 49. Oct. 25, 1802, deed between Alexander and Robert Connelly of Augusta Co., Va., and Thomas Connelly, 100 acres on Little Run, being 1/3 of land of Thomas Connelly, deceased. Recorded Dec. 23, 1805.

Deed Book 33, page 291.

Alexander Connelly and wife Nancy of Bourbon Co., Kentucky, also Robert Connelly of same place, to William Bell, 2/3 of 150 acres willed to said Connelly by Thomas Connelly, deceased, adjoining lands of David Laird. Deed recorded Nov. 25, 1805.

Will Book 12, page 137.

This day Alexander Walker came before me James Rankin, a Justice of the Peace for the County of Augusta, and took the oath as prescribed by law as Commandant in a company of horse in the third Regiment and third Division of the militia of Virginia. Certified under my hand this 30th day of Sept. 1815.

James Rankin.

Addenda

On December 12, 1928, twin boys, Theodore Hughes and William Walker, were born to Mr. and Mrs. Alfred F. (Lucy Hooke) Oakey of California.

On Aug. 31, 1928, a daughter, Margaret Louise, was born to Mr. and Mrs. Harvey Ribble Kemper. Mr. Kemper is a brother to Mrs. Audrey Kemper Spence.

Mrs. Spence has recently been elected one of the Founder Members of the Institute of American Genealogy.

NEWSPAPER ARTICLES ON ROCKINGHAM AND ROCKINGHAM PEOPLE

On pages 464-467 of Wayland's History of Rockingham County, published in 1912, is a list of newspaper and magazine articles of interest in connection with the history of the county. The following list was also made out at the time but was omitted from the printed volume for want of space. It is presented here as of interest and value.

In the *Harrisonburg Daily News*

Judicial Charity, July 23, 1903

Is the Date Wrong? Four articles by W. J. Showalter, the first one July 25, 1903

Sketches of G. B. Keezell, H. M. Rogers, C. L. Hedrick, E. W. Carpenter, G. N. Conrad, D. H. L. Martz, J. S. Messerley, and J. A. Switzer; September 22, 1903

Auld Lang Syne, December 29, 1904

Virginia Conference of United Brethren, 106th Session; at Dayton; March 21, 1905

G. O. Conrad Obituary, January 24, 1907

Tribute to Timothy Funk, January 28, 1907

J. P. Houck Obituary, June 14, 1908

3000 Temperance Petitioners, August 20, 1909

Work Begins at Normal, October 1, 1909

A. H. Snyder Obituary, January 19, 1910

C. A. Sprinkel Obituary, February 15, 1910

Final Link Gone, by L. J. Heatwole; February 25, 1910

R. H. Sheppe Obituary, March 6, 1910

How Cynthia Hooke Saved the Horse, May 18, 1910

Fifty Years Ago, by S. T. Shank; February 27, 1911

William Ott Building Torn Down, April 1, 1911

J. H. Ralston Obituary, September 29, 1911

J. S. Harnsberger Obituary, May 3, 1912

New Erection Cornerstone Laying, July 11, 1912

In the *Harrisonburg Daily Times*

J. S. Harnsberger Obituary, May 3, 1912

In the *Harrisonburg Free Press*

J. W. Howe Obituary, June 25, 1903

In the Harrisonburg *Old Commonwealth*
Musical Convention, November 20, 1867
Harrisonburg, A Growing Town, September 9, 1868
Report of Township Commissioners, May 4, 1870
A. B. Irick Obituary, December 6, 1877
    In the *Rockingham Daily Record* (Harrisonburg)
J. H. Ralston Obituary, September 29, 1911
J. S. Harnsberger Obituary, May 3, 1912
New Erection Cornerstone Laying, July 11, 1912
    In the *Rockingham Register* (Harrisonburg)
Violent Tornado, April 27, 1866
Brock's Gap, September 6, 1866
Sabbath School Convention, November 8, 1866
Allan C. Bryan Obituary, November 15, 1866
Colored Church Dedication, November 29, 1866
Township Commissioners' Report, May 5, 1870
Re-Division of County into Townships, May 3, 1872
Breaking Ground for the North River Railroad, July 11, 1873
Donors to the Harrisonburg Catholic Church, September 5, 1873
Union Springs, August 26, 1875
A. S. Gray Obituary, October 3, 1878
Rockingham Teachers' Institute, November 21, 1878
The Viriginia Rustics, Nov. 28 and Dec. 5, 1878
Our Public Schools, November 6, 1879
Eventful Career of Jesse Fry, February 2, 1882
Business Interests of Harrisonburg, October 16, 1884
Robert Johnston Obituaries, Nov. 12 and 26, 1885
Samuel Shacklett Obituary, July 8, 1886
Among the Schools, by G. H. Hulvey; Dec. 9, 16, 23, 1886
Muster Roll Co. B, 7th Va. Cavalry, April 18, 1889
Harrisonburg Boom, April 11, 1890
New Election Districts, December 26, 1890
A Young Confederate, June 19, 1891
Synagogue Dedicated, March 4, 1892
A Rockingham Boy's Experience, February 24, 1893
The Giant's Grave, by Ella Broadus; September 29, 1893
Rockingham Figures, December 15, 1893
Provost-Marshal Bowen, by C. W. Boyce; May 11, 1894
Confederate Reunion, October 12, 1894
James Kenney Obituary, October 19, 1894
Peter Roller Obituary, November 2, 1894
Harrisonburg Fire Patrols, 1828; November 23, 1894
Beginnings on Chesapeake & Western Railroad, June 14 and
July 5, 1895
Burke Chrisman Obituary, July 12, 1895
Judge Paul's Address at Dayton, August 2, 1895
John F. Lewis Obituary, September 6, 1895
Bridgewater Celebration of C. & W., September 20, 1895

George W. Berlin Obituary, November 15, 1895
More about Meigs, November 29, 1895
Opening of the C. & W. Railroad, May 1, 1896
Muster Roll of Valley Rangers, June 26, 1896
Mrs. Bryan's Painting in Richmond, July 10, 1896
S. H. Moffett Obituary, August 7, 1896
$16,000 Fire in Harrisonburg, September 11, 1896
New Courthouse Cornerstone Laying, October 16, 1896
C. C. Strayer Obituary, April 30, 1897
Architect's Report on Courthouse, August 20, 1897
S. B. Gibbons Obituary, reprint, February 11, 1898
Mutual Telephone System, May 6, 1898
Harrisonburg Guards off for Cuba, May 13, 20, 1898
W. B. Compton Obituary, July 29, 1898
John Burkholder Obituary, July 29, 1898
Muster Roll Co. H, 12th Va. Cavalry, March 9, 1900
B. G. Patterson Obituary, March 9, 1900
A. M. Newman Obituary, March 30, 1900
A. E. Heneberger Obituary, August 10, 1900
N. M. Burkholder Obituary, December 14, 1900
Charles Eshman Obituary, March 22, 1901
J. R. Jones Obituary, April 5, 1901
Philander Herring Obituary, August 23, 1901
Emanuel Sipe Obituary, September 27, 1901
John Paul Obituary, November 8, 1901
A. H. Wilson Obituary, November 15, 1901
Charles Grattan Obituary, June 27, 1902
Big Spring for Sale, June 27, 1902
Harrisonburg Sunday War Panic, by J. I. Miller; Aug. 22, 1902
Emanuel Suter Obituary, December 19, 1902
A Rockingham Hero, April 3, 1903
Alfred C. Rohr Obituary, January 5, 1904
W. W. Hooke Obituary, March 25, 1904
Locating the County Seat, April 22, 1904
H. B. Harnsberger Obituary, September 6, 1904
A. S. Kieffer Obituary, December 2, 1904
S. R. Allebaugh Obituary, April 3, 1906

THE CUSTER FAMILY

By Milo Custer

Custodian of the McLean County, Ill., Historical Society

(Written from Bloomington, Ill., January 11, 1911)

Richard Custer (Sr.), son of Paul Custer (Küster), of German descent, was born in Pennsylvania June 1, 1757. His family settled in the north part of Rockingham County, Va., in 1762. Early in the year 1781 (as appears from his and his widow's applications for pensions), Richard Custer, Sr., enlisted in the Virginia troops under Colonel Nall for service against the British in the War of the Revolution. He served as a private soldier three months under Capt. George Huston and three months under Capt. Anthony Rader. He was in the skirmishes at Williamsburg, Va., and Hot Water Creek.

On March 18, 1788, he married Jane Humble, daughter of Conrad Humble. She was born in the year 1771. They were the parents of Richard Custer (Jr.), Mrs. Sarah Fulk, Susan Custer, Gabriel Custer, Mrs. Johanna Wevner, Strawder Custer, and George Custer.

Richard Custer, Sr., received a pension for his service in the Revolution and his widow also received a pension after his death. He died February 14, 1837. The date of his wife's death is not known, but she was still living in Rockingham County, Va., and drawing a widow's pension as late as the year 1841. The remains of Richard Custer, Sr., and his wife are buried on the Custer homestead near Cootes's Store.

Richard Custer, Jr., son of Richard Custer and Jane Humble, was born on his father's farm in Rockingham County about the year 1790. The farm is located about four miles north of Cootes's Store. Richard Custer, Jr., was a gunsmith by trade and also farmed to some extent. He also owned a sawmill. His sawmill was located on the farm of his son-in-law, Isaac Ween, and was situated about 13 miles northwest of Cootes's Store, in the valley of the Dry River.

On March 28, 1810, Richard Custer, Jr., married Elizabeth Trumbo, daughter of Jacob and Hannah (Hess) Trumbo. She was born August 21, 1791. Their wedding ceremony was performed by the Rev. William Bryan. Both the Trumbos and the Hesses were of Pennsylvania-German descent.

Richard Custer, Jr., and his wife Elizabeth were the parents of eight children, namely: Sarah Custer (Mrs. George Riddle), born August 21, 1811; George Custer, born September 9, 1813, married Margaret Ritchie; Jacob Custer (the writer's grandfather), born January 25, 1817, married Isabella Miller (a great-granddaughter of Rev. Alexander Miller); Deborah Custer (Mrs. Isaac

Ween), born September 29, 1819; Hannah Custer (Mrs. Absalom Ritchie), born February 5, 1823; Conrad Custer, born February 10, 1825, married Nancy Shoemaker; Amanda Custer (Mrs. Abram Hess), born November 28, 1829; and Berryman Custer, born February 2, 1833, married Margaret Shoemaker, a sister of the wife of his brother Conrad.

Richard Custer, Jr., was a soldier of the War of 1812, having served from August 29, 1814, to December 8, 1814, in Capt. Thomas Hopkins's company of Virginia militia. He died June 4, 1858. His wife died in the year 1871. Their remains are buried on the old Custer place four miles north of Cootes's Store. This farm is now owned and occupied by their son-in-law, Abram Hess.

In personal appearance Richard Custer, Jr., was a small stoutly built man about five feet six inches in height, weighing about 150 pounds. He was light complexioned, had light hair and blue eyes. He never wore a beard or mustache, but was always smooth shaven. Elizabeth Trumbo Custer was a large strongly built woman, with dark hair and eyes. Her mother, Hannah Hess Trumbo, was once taken prisoner by the Indians. This occurred when she was a young girl about 12 years old. She was captured by a band from some of the Ohio tribes and was taken by them to their village where she was kept for several years, until finally released in some exchange of prisoners. She often related her experiences as a captive to her family and said that she was never mistreated by them save upon one occasion, and that was when she was set to the task of cleaning some entrails of a deer, which she did by carefully slitting and washing them instead of merely turning them and scraping them out, as was the Indian style. For this breach of savage custom the old squaw who had charge of her gave her a severe whipping.

Jacob Custer (the writer's grandfather), son of Richard Custer, Jr., and Elizabeth Trumbo Custer, was born on his father's farm four miles north of Cootes's Store, January 25, 1817. His early life was spent among the mountains of his native county and was in many respects typical of that rugged locality. In 1838 he married Isabella Miller, daughter of Alexander Miller 3d and Ann Matthews, his wife. Her grandfather was also named Alexander Miller, and her great-grandfather was Rev. Alexander Miller, a pioneer Scotch-Irish Presbyterian minister, who settled on Cook's Creek in Rockingham (then Augusta) County, Va., about 1750.

Jacob Custer and Isabella Miller Custer were the parents of five children, born as follows: Mary S. Custer (Mrs. Martillons Miller), born April 20, 1839; Samuel Custer (the writer's father), born October 8, 1842; Amanda Custer (Mrs. Winfield McFee), born April 7, 1845; Nancy B. Custer (Mrs. John Steele), born January 24, 1848; and Nettie Custer (Mrs. Lee Scogin), deceased, born April 9, 1850.

Jacob Custer owned a farm of 400 acres in the valley of Dry River, near Pendleton Mountain, in Rockingham County, Va. He lived on this farm about fifteen years. Most of his land was covered with a fine growth of pine and poplar timber. Some of the trees were over 100 feet high, and logs 60 feet long and entirely clear of limbs were cut from many of them. In the fall of 1852 he sold his farm to Anthony Rhodes for $800 and moved with his family to McLean County, Ill. He also owned one Negro slave, a young man named Wesley, whom he sold to Samuel Cootes, the founder of Cootes's Store, for $200.

Jacob Custer died in Bloomington, Ill., September 10, 1892. His wife, Isabella Miller Custer, died December 19, 1870. Their remains are buried in the Scogin Cemetery, four miles southwest of the city of Bloomington, Ill.

Richard Custer, Jr., the father of Jacob Custer, was a gunsmith as well as a farmer, and the site of his gun shop is still known as one of the old landmarks near Cootes's Store.

Sarah Miller (*nee* Crawford?), wife of the second Alexander Miller, came of good Scotch-Irish stock and was possessed of a good share of temper. Her son, William Miller, had become enamored of a certain Pennsylvania-German girl who lived with her parents somewhere in the mountains of Rockingham, very much to his mother's disgust, as she had little liking for anyone not of her "ain fowk." Her Billie's visits to his sweetheart becoming more and more frequent, the old lady determined to put a stop to the matter. One day when Billie had been gone from home an unusual length of time, she, well surmising where he was, requested her husband to go after him and bring him home. Receiving an evasive reply she said, "Then if ye'll not gae after heem, I'll gae myself, an' I'll fetch him!"

Suiting the action to the word, she put on her bonnet, tied its strings firmly beneath her chin, went out and caught up a small riding horse which she owned, saddled, bridled, and mounted it, and with riding whip in hand rode away, over the mountain, in pursuit of Billie. Arriving at the home of the Yeakels, where she found Billie's horse tied, and disdaining to dismount and enter, she called out, "Billie! Billie! Coom out here!"

Receiving no answer, she called again, this time in no uncertain tones: "Billie! if ye don't coom oot here this minit an' gae hame wi' me, I'll coom in there an' I'll lick the hide aff ye!"

Billie came out promptly, mounted his horse, and very dutifully rode home with his mother. But he did not allow her prejudice to defeat his purposes, and eventually he married the girl of his choice and moved to McLean County, Ill., where some of their descendants still reside.

Hessian Baker (Becker?)

Philip Baker, Sr., lived about two miles west of Brock's Gap, prior to the year 1853. His father was a native of the German province of Hesse, and was one of the Hessian soldiers who were hired by the British to fight against the Americans in the Revolution. Like many others of his comrades, he decided after a term of service under his British employers that the cause of the Americans was best, and so taking "French leave" of the former he joined the colonial troops. While he was in the service his company one day came to an orchard, and Baker, like the rest, being tired and hungry, reached up to a low-hanging limb to pluck a fine-looking apple. But before his fingers could close around it a bullet from the enemy came whizzing along and knocked the apple from him.

He was long known among his neighbors as "Hessian Baker." He had three sons, Philip Jr., Jacob, and John. The last-named settled in McLean County, Ill., where he died and where some of his descendants still reside.

WILLIAM MATTHEWS

William Matthews (a brother-in-law of the 3d Alexander Miller), left Rockingham sometime shortly after the Revolution (?) and took up his abode with a tribe of Indians somewhere north of the Ohio River. He once visited his relatives in Rockingham, and went among them decked out in a fine savage costume; then returned to the Indians and was not heard of again.

The foregoing items are from information furnished by the writer's father, Samuel Custer, and his sister, Mrs. Mary Custer Miller.

ON PENDLETON MOUNTAIN

By MILO CUSTER, of Illinois

A Grandson of Virginia

The sunrise bright on Pendleton Mountain
Gives promise of a fine, clear day,
Its beams shine out o'er the Valley wide,
Through pines and poplars flit and play.

The hunter takes down from the gun rack high
His flint-lock rifle worn and old,
Yet ever ready for service good
When in his hands so strong and bold.

"Sling o'er one shoulder a bullet-pouch,
And o'er the other a powder-flask;
Take knife and horn, call up the dogs;
With gun in hand, get to the task,
On Pendleton Mountain."

Far up among the tall old pines
The deer is grazing, unaware
Of dogs or human enemy,
Till startled by the horn's loud blare.

Then down the mountain-side afar
　　Swift feet will follow dogs and deer;
And soon, perchance, down in the vale,
　　The ending of the chase draws near.

"Sling o'er one shoulder a bullet-pouch,
　　And o'er the other a powder-flask;
Take knife and horn, call up the dogs;
　　With gun in hand, get to the task,
　　　　On Pendleton Mountain."

The chase is o'er; the hunter has
　　His game at last; the deer is down,
Its life-blood flows out at his feet,
　　And stains the thick leaves sear and brown.

Then with the game slung on his back,
　　His weary feet are homeward turned;
His dogs, strong faithful friends, leap up
　　To hear his word of praise well-earned.

"Sling o'er one shoulder a bullet-pouch,
　　And o'er the other a powder-flask;
Take knife and horn, call up the dogs;
　　With gun in hand, get to the task,
　　　　On Pendleton Mountain."

The sunset glow on Pendleton Mountain
　　Brings memories of bygone days.
'Tis many years since my fathers there
　　Were wont to see its glorious rays,—

Ran deer across Dry River plain,
　　Or up some mountain steep and lone,
And then tramped homeward with the prize
　　To rest beside their own hearthstone.

But glowing lure of western lands,
　　So far away, called to the brave;
Gave promises of greater wealth
　　Than ever they could hope to have
　　　　At Pendleton Mountain.

Dame Fortune's smiles are sometimes false;
　　Bold ventures do not always win;
Yet we shall never plain the loss
　　Or failures of our own blood-kin.

A welcome hand we'll offer you,
    Across the chasm of the years;
We'll hope for better things to come,
    Though come they may through toil and tears.

Perhaps we'll meet in some fair land,
    Beyond the evening sunset's glow;
Or e'en perchance we'll meet some day,
    For aught that each of us may know,
        At Pendleton Mountain.

A REVOLUTIONARY SOLDIER

February 4, 1841, died in Rockingham County Henry Hammer, Sr., aged 88. His first service as a soldier was against the Indians on the northwest frontier under Captain Cravens of Rockingham County. Subsequently he was engaged in the "wars of the Revolution."—From *Rockingham Register,* Harrisonburg, Va., date of February 20, 1841.

DR. JESSEE BENNETT, PIONEER SURGEON

In the *Virginia Medical Monthly* of January, 1929, appears an article under the above caption by Dr. Joseph Lyon Miller of Thomas, W. Va., which is of interest to the medical profession of the world generally, and to the people of Rockingham County specially. In 1794 Dr. Bennett, a pioneer surgeon, with primitive equipment, performed in Rockingham County an operation involving most serious risks, with complete success, and thus set a precedent in this field for North America and in some respects for the world. The following account is condensed from the most valuable article by Dr. Miller.

Jessee Bennett, of Norman-French ancestry, was born July 10, 1769, in Philadelphia County, Pa. He died at his home, Riverview, Mason County, Va. (now West Virginia), on July 13, 1842.

He read medicine with a physician in Philadelphia and then continued his education in the University of Pennsylvania. He was regarded as a thorough anatomist and a most excellent surgeon. In 1792 he located for the practice of his profession in the Shenandoah Valley of Virginia, and on April 8, 1793, married Elizabeth Hog, daughter of Peter Hog, first clerk of Rockingham County.

In due course of time Mrs. Bennett came to her first and only confinement. Owing to a contracted pelvis, or other obstruction not definitely determined, parturition appeared difficult or impossible. Dr. Bennett called to his assistance Dr. Alexander Humphreys of Staunton. After consultation and an unsuccessful attempt at a forceps delivery, it was decided that only two courses were open to them—either craniotomy or Caesarean section. The first, of course, meant death to the child; the second might mean death to the mother or the child, or to both. There was a third course, to be sure—to do nothing; but that was certain death to both mother and child.

Mrs. Bennett, expecting to die, insisted that the child be saved. Accordingly, over the protest of Dr. Humphreys, Dr. Bennett made ready for Caesarean section, a thing that was almost unheard of at that time, on a living mother, anywhere in the world. Dr. Humphreys refused to undertake so formidable an operation. It was up to Dr. Bennett, the young mother's husband, himself. The details as recorded here were given later by persons who were present.

Mrs. Bennett was given a large dose of laudanum which, in her weakened condition, quickly put her to sleep. She was then placed on a long, narrow table, made of two planks laid side by side on two barrels. Two Negro servant women held her, and Dr. Bennett with one quick sweep of the knife laid open the abdomen and uterus. Enlarging the opening in the uterus with his hands, he quickly lifted out the child and the placenta. Remarking, "This shall be the last one," Dr. Bennett removed both ovaries by excision. He then closed the wound, sewing it up with some stout linen thread of the hand-made variety then common.

Much to the surprise of everyone, both Mrs. Bennett and her child, a daughter, survived, Mrs. Bennett dying many years later in Mason County, and her daughter at the advanced age of 77. The latter was the wife of Dr. Enos Thomas.

Dr. Miller secured his information regarding this remarkable case from Dr. A. L. Knight (1823-1897), and the latter obtained the facts chiefly from Mrs. William Hawkins, a sister to Mrs. Bennett, and one of the Negro women above mentioned, both of whom were in the room during the entire time of the operation. Dr. Knight also knew Dr. Bennett, being about twenty years old when Dr. Bennett died.

In 1795 Dr. Bennett joined the army as a surgeon and served with the troops in putting down the Whiskey Rebellion. See page 122 above. In 1797 he, in company with his wife's brother, Thomas Hog, and sister, Mrs. Nancy Hawkins, and their families, removed with his wife and daughter to the Ohio River, about six miles above the mouth of the Great Kanawha River. In that region his father-in-law, Major Peter Hog, had secured a grant of 9,000 acres of land. At that time Dr. Bennett was the only doctor within fifty or a hundred miles of Point Pleasant. So great was his reputation that in later years, after competition was strong, he was still called for over a wide field, specially in surgical cases.

In 1804, when Mason County was cut off from Kanawha County, Dr. Bennett was one of the justices of the first county court. He was also a major in the county militia; and, in 1808 and 1809, he represented the county in the Virginia General Assembly at Richmond. In the War of 1812 he was a surgeon in the 2d Virginia regiment.

In 1794 a Caesarean section with living mother and child was practically unknown anywhere in the world, even in the chief medical and surgical centers. One performed by Dr. John Richmond at Newtown, Ohio, in 1827, is generally credited as the first in America; but, as we have seen, the one by Dr. Bennett, in Rockingham County, Va., antedated Richmond's by 33 years.

Dr. Knight asked Mrs. Hawkins why Dr. Bennett had never reported his operation to the medical profession at large. She replied that she had heard Dr. Bennett say that no strange doctors would believe it, and he did not intend to give them the chance to call him a liar. At another time she heard him say that no doctor with any feelings of delicacy would report an operation that he had performed upon his own wife.

Dr. Bennett was a small active man, with reddish hair, and a temper to correspond. He was an enthusiastic huntsman, and owned some fine race horses. He was fond of a joke, even when it was on himself. One time he mounted a big strong horse, took a preacher behind him, and forded him across Oldtown Creek, which was high. The water was so deep that the big bay had to swim. As they came out they met on the bank an old Negro servant belonging to Col. Charles Lewis.

"Kyger," said Dr. Bennett, "if we had drowned, which one would Old Nick have grabbed first, Mr. Smithers or me?"

"Marse Smithers, sah," laughed Kyger, "caise he done sho' o' you now, sah."

In his later life Dr. Bennett took much delight in telling the following story. On one occasion a neighboring practitioner had a very difficult labor case and sent for Dr. Bennett in consultation. After examination he advised forceps. While the two learned gentlemen were on the front porch completing their discussion they saw approaching "Old Root and Yarb," a well known Thompsonian ("yarb") doctor of the vicinity, carrying his bulging saddlebags over his shoulder.

The case was at an urgent stage, but the two regular doctors could not forego a little fun at the expense of "Old Root and Yarb." Gravely they called him in and asked his advice. One of them had a pair of forceps in his hand. "Old Root and Yarb" glanced apprehensively at the instrument of torture. "Gentlemen," he said, "have you sneezed her? Before using them hurtful things I'd sneeze her."

Feeling that he could do no harm they said, "Suppose you try it." He did. From a large old pewter box, which he carried, he presented to the sufferer's nostrils a generous portion of snuff, and to the unbounded surprise of the two doctors who had so cleverly set their trap for a joke a new citizen of the growing republic was, in a few minutes, laying claim to recognition with vociferous squalls— and "them hurtful things" had not been needed.

(Note by J. W. W.—Records published at Richmond show that Jesse Bennett represented Mason County in the Virginia House of Delegates from 1805 to 1807.)

Dr. Joseph Price

The foregoing article on Dr. Jessee Bennett is of unusual interest, and it suggests the fact that many other eminent surgeons have lived in Rockingham County or have gone out from it as native sons to win distinction elsewhere. A notable example is Dr. Joseph Price, born near Tenth Legion on January 1, 1853. He received his early education at Fort Edward, New York, and later attended Union College. He obtained his medical degree from the University of Pennsylvania in 1877. He married Louisa Troth by whom he had seven children, Marian, Phoebe, Louise, Anna, Joseph, Henry, and Thomas.

The following paragraphs are taken almost verbatim from a paper written by Dr. W. Kennedy and published in the American Journal of Obstetrics and Gynecology.

Dr. Price began his work in the Philadelphia Dispensary in 1877. There his fertile brain, skilful hand, and tireless energy were soon conspicuous. In this work, and at the dawn of abdominal surgery, he attained the unequaled record of 100 operations with only one death. With the courage of a Spartan, with matchless skill and judgment as an operator he forged to the front and made an aggressive figure. During the period from 1885 to 1900 he was prominent in the medical profession of America. He impressed the profession more by the spoken than by the written word. He attended county, state, and national societies and in almost every state of the Union and in Canada he discussed the surgical problems of the day.

But his teaching was most inspiring and forceful at the operating table. For years his clinic was thronged with young, ambitious, and progressive surgeons from every part of the United States. He did magnificent work at Preston Retreat. In 1891 he opened his private hospital at 241 North 18th Street, Philadelphia. His simple technic and masterful work in this institution is world-wide in reputation. He made no undue attempt at speed, but the system and economy of his manipulations and movements gave him the greatest dispatch in his work. He was so definite in his touch that many of his operations were done with the skill of a juggler. On account of his dexterity he was often spoken of as "The American Tait." His capacity for work was unlimited, and it is doubtful if any operator has done as much difficult abdominal surgery.

He never picked his cases and never refused to give any patient the last chance. In pelvic surgery he was a pioneer. His finished enucleation of tubal ovarian abscesses was classical and he was acknowledged master of this work. In plastic surgery he was an artist and a beautiful demonstrator. He was one of Dr. Emmet's most ardent followers. It can be truthfully said of him that he had the combined qualities of an Emmet and a Tait.

Dr. Price was president of the American Association of Obstetricians and Gynecologists in 1895. A month prior to his death he was given the degree of LL. D. by Union College. He died June 6, 1911.

Thus far from Dr. Kennedy's paper.

Although notably charitable, Dr. Price was not averse to a good round fee when the conditions warranted it and the means of the patient were adequate. On one occasion he confided to an old friend that his biggest fee had been $6,000.

Dr. Price had two brothers, also natives of Rockingham, who made their marks in Philadelphia, Reuben Price, lawyer, and Mordecai Price, physician and surgeon. Dr. Joseph Price asserted that his brother, Dr. Mordecai Price, was just as good a surgeon as he was. Dr. J. E. Lincoln states that Dr. Mordecai Price performed the first appendix operation in Rockingham County, on Dr. Jennings of Lacey Springs. Dr. Lincoln was the local physician in charge of the case.

Acknowledgments are made also to Mrs. Wornom of Dare, Va.. for a copy of Dr. Kennedy's paper. Mrs. Wornom was Miss Annie E. H. Moore, whose old home is near the birthplace of Dr. Price.

Dr. Walter Reed

It has been stated by some that Dr. Walter Reed was born in Harrisonburg. This is a mistake. He was a native of Gloucester County, Va. However, his father, Rev. L. S. Reed, married his second wife in Harrisonburg and had a home there for a number of years. Within that period Dr. Walter Reed was an occasional sojourner in Harrisonburg.

THE CASSELL FAMILY
By
Mrs. Audrey Kemper Spence
of
Wytheville, Va.

The Cassell Family History by David K. Cassell of Morristown, Pa., says that "The first family of Cassells to emigrate to this country came from Kreisheim in the Palatinate in the year 1681, Nov. 20th, in the ship *Jeffries,* and settled at Germantown, now Philadelphia, Pa."

History mentions a number of later immigrants, among whom were many pious ministers of the Gospel, writers, poets and others.

The Cassell family of Maryland say that they are descended from a Cassell who came from Pennsylvania early in 1700. He had three sons, Jacob, Abraham and Martin.

Abraham Cassell and Martin Cassell moved to Kentucky in early life, and the grandchildren of Abraham are living there today. Nothing more is known of Martin. Jacob had 11 children, and the 10th was Rev. Leonard Cassell, born April 1, 1784, died Sept. 1808. He was a Methodist preacher and was such an eminent man that a book was written on his life.

A Michael Cassell came to Wythe County, Va., in the latter half of 1700, he being born in 1772. His mother was a Miss Rick, and it is said that he married a Miss Simmerman. This Michael came from Pennsylvania and was evidently a grandson of Hupert Cassell who came over from Germany in 1715 or 1720. He was probably a son of Yelles Cassell of Henry of Hupert. This Michael Cassell is buried at the old St. John's Church about one mile north of Wytheville, Va., near the center of the graveyard. He is lying by the side of William Cassell, who died in 1844.

Another Michael Cassell moved to Wythe County, Va., at the close of the Revolutionary War, and it is said that he was present at the surrender of Cornwallis.

This Michael Cassell was born in 1763 or 1764, and had three brothers, Frederick, Jacob and Immaniel. His father was named Jacob Cassell, and it is believed that this Michael was a first cousin to the other Michael Cassell.

Michael Cassell, son of Jacob Cassell, settled in the western end of Wythe County, about one mile north east of the old Kimberlin Lutheran Church (organized 1797). He married Mary or Katherine Dobler (Dobbs), daughter of Jacob Dobler, about the year 1786. His children were Jacob, William, John, David, Joseph, Mathias, Mary and Ann. Joseph Cassell married Mary Foglesong Dec. 23, 1823; children, Sophia (who married Mr. Neff), Michael and Margaret. This Michael Cassell, son of Jacob, is the ancestor of Mr. S. Sidney Cassell on Black Lick, Wythe County, Va., also Rev.

C. W. Cassell of Luray, Va., pastor and historian, and who is living at the present time. The above is from Cassell family data, collected by Dr. William H. Cassell, of Wytheville, Va., who is a descendant of Michael Cassell who lived east of Wytheville, Va. Dr. Cassell has one of the oldest Cassell Bibles with dates in it.

David Cassell lived near Bethel Church, in the eastern portion of Wythe County, Va. Mrs. Johnston, deceased, said that Michael Cassell of east Wytheville had three half brothers, John, David and Andy. Mr. W. H. Simmerman, deceased, said that these families were related. He gave the David Cassell line as follows: David Cassell, born Jan. 7, 1784; died April 11, 1869. Married Catherine Keesling, born April 15, 1795; died July 29, 1865; daughter of Conrad and Rebecca Keesling. Issue: 1. David, moved to Carroll County, Va., married twice; issue. 2. John, married Mary F. Umberger June 10, 1858, aged 32 and 18 years, both single; son of David and Catherine Cassell; daughter of Michael and Nancy Umberger.

3. William, married Sarah Kegley, Sept. 23, 1858, son of David and Catherine Cassell, daughter of John and Catherine Kegley, aged 21 and 22 years. They moved to Missouri. Issue.

4. Thomas, married Catherine Matilda Johnston, Feb. 10, 1853, resided on Cripple Creek, Va. His son John owns and resides on the farm of the late Joseph Cassell near Bethel Church. See dates.

5. Sophia, married Joel Umberger, June 15, 1858. She was his second wife. He was aged 43; she 39 years. He was a son of Sarah and Henry Umberger. No issue.

6. Katherine A., born 1829, married William Kinzer of Carroll County, Va., Aug. 21, 1851. Issue.

7. Rebecca, born June 16, 1817, married Aerhart Simmerman, son of George, son of Arehart Simmerman. Issue, Susanna who married Wylie A. J. Spence, Mar. 3, 1859, and others. See Spence History. Rebecca Simmerman, married (2) Dec. 7, 1853, Henry Shrader. Issue Letitia Agnes, who married V. Shelton; issue.

8. Elizabeth A., born Nov. 21, 1831; died Feb. 18, 1915. Married Thomas H. Ott of Carroll County, Va., May 5, 1857, son of Elizabeth and William Ott. They were aged 22 and 25 years. She married (2), Aug. 18, 1867, Calvin R. Shortt of Chesterfield County, Va., son of Reuben Shortt; a widower, age 67. Bride was 36, daughter of David Cassell. Issue.

9. Rosanna, married Andrew Felty, Oct. 1, 1857. They were 32 and 37 years old. Issue.

10. Senah, married Stephen Umberger; went to Texas. Issue.

Dates from the Cassell Family Bible, owned by Mr. W. A. Williams of Max Meadows, Va.:

Thomas Cassell, born Sept. 1, 1823.

Catherine Matilda Johnston, his wife, was born Aug. 3, 1834.

Their children:

William A. Cassell, born June 26, 1855.

John Fenton Cassell, born Oct. 14, 1857.

Florence Alabama Cassell, born Sept. 8, 1859.

Mary Lutitia Cassell, born Sept. 5, 1867.
Jefferson Davis Cassell, born June 10, 1861.
Gustavus Adolphus Cassell, born May 10, 1864.
James Kincannon Cassell, born Feb. 15, 1869.
Thomas Drake Cassell, born July 21, 1873.
Deaths: Jas. K. died Sept. 24, 1876.   Gustavus Adolphus died—
no date.   Florence A. died Feb. 26, 1905.   Matilda, their mother,
died July 3, 1919.

Register of deaths of Wythe County, Va.:
Ephriam Cassell, son of Andrew, died Oct. 10, 1866, aged 85
years; born in Wythe County, Va.   Shoemaker; married.   Information given by Mrs. Bell, his sister-in-law.   *Wythe County News,* "Ye
Old Days": Died in the Cove, on Thursday, the 3rd March, 1870,
Andrew Cassell, age 84 years.   (Born in 1786.)   Andrew was
probably the ancestor of the Crockett Cove Cassells.

Will of John Cassell, Sr., Will Book No. 10, page 383, bequeaths
to his son, Joseph Cassell, the plantation where his son Joseph now
resides, lying in this County, on Reed Creek, Black Lick settlement,
supposed to contain upwards of 200 acres.   Son-in-law, George
Keesling.   Son-in-law, Michael Umberger.   His daughter Letitia
Neff.   Grandson, Emory Adkins Neff; Elizabeth Cassell, Almeeda
Cassell, Eliza Cassell.   Sons, Abraham and Reuben Cassell.   Robert
Saferight, husband of my daughter, Malvina.   Will was made Nov.
25, 1853.   Proved at April court in 1863.   Witnesses, Michael F.
Davidson, Thomas Hoofnoggle, John S. Meyers.   John Cassell's
mark.

Abraham and Reuben refused to take the oath, so David A.
Whitman did so, together with Stephen Porter and Thomas Sanders,
and probated will.

Deed Book No. 20, page 372: John Cassell to Harrison Baylor,
Christopher S. Holston, Michael Meyers, Elijah Dyer and William
H. Foster, trustees, for $5.00, and in consideration of the love he bears
to the Methodist Episcopal Church, 80 perches of land on the Peppers
Ferry Road, for the use of the Church.   Jan. 10, 1856.   (Probably
Bethel Church.)

Deed Book No. 7, page 61: June 10, 1817, John Cassell and
Margaret his wife, to John Doak, for $175.00, grant and sell 14½
acres, on Reed Creek in Wythe County, Va.   Speaks of Kinder's
corner.

Dates from the John Cassell Bible, Bethel Church neighborhood:
Margaret Cassell departed this life Dec. 27, 1847.
John Cassell departed this life ——— 9, 1862.
Abraham N. Cassell departed this life Oct. 4, 1875, aged 73.
Rueben Cassell departed this life July 16, 1886.
Lucretia Simmerman Hoback departed this life June 28, 1894.
Emory Akins Neff was born Oct. 23, 1842.
James Hoback was born July 16, 1832.
Letitia Neff was born July 15, 1824.

Robert Levi Hoback was born Aug. 13, 1859, son of Letitia and James Hoback, above.

John was the father of Lucretia and others. She was a sister to Abraham and Reuben Cassell. It is not known what relation John was to the other Cassell families, but he might have been a brother to David, above.

Mr. Thomas Wingate of Independence, Grayson County, Va., says that his grandfather, John Cassell, had a brother David (who was Mr. Wingate's great-uncle), who had 11 sons, raised them, and one was named David, for himself, one also named Mike. He remembers hearing his mother tell him that the Cassells came from Germany. John Cassell married a woman named Etter, who had come across the ocean, and who was six weeks crossing over. He has an old trunk which belonged to her, which has an old newspaper pasted in it, with items dated 1739 in it. His father was Wright Wingate, who married Eliza Cassell, daughter of John Cassell and Margaret (Etter) Cassell, their youngest child, April 21, 1864. She was born June 24, 1824. The marriage record says that she was 36, but he says she was 40 years old at her marriage. Wright Wingate was aged 47, a widower, born in Irvin County, N. C. Residence of husband was Grayson County, Va. Son of John Wingate.

Mr. Wingate said that John Cassell was over 80 years of age at death. Wright Wingate was born June 24, 1824. Mrs. Eliza Wingate died in 1905.

Children of John Cassell and wife Margaret (Etter) Cassell: Abraham, unmarried; Reuben, unmarried; Joseph, no known issue; Lettie Hoback; Elizabeth Whitman; Allie Bryant; Eliza Wingate; ———— Neff. List as given by Mr. Wingate.

Mr. Wingate says that he always heard that the Cassells came from Germany, and that there were the two brothers, John and David.

From the Whitman Bible:

Elizabeth Cassell to David Whitman, Sept. 30, 1854. She died Oct. 13, 1898. She was his third wife. No issue.

From Wythe County Court records:

Married Sept. 27, 1854, on Peppers Road, David Whitman and Elizabeth Casel; husband a widower; wife single; place of their births was Wythe County, Va.; she a daughter of John Cassell.

Nov. 8, 1858, James Hoback and Luticia Neff; groom 28, bride 29; widow and widower; son of Peter and Elizabeth Hoback; daughter of John and Margaret Castle; husband a carpenter; by John Walsh.

Rufus Naff and Letitia Cassell, Nov. 16, 1841. Wythe County, Va., March 20, 1834.

Thomas Dean to Nancy Cassell, Dec. 24, 1833.

John Sharret and Mary Cassell, June 3, 1792; married by John Cassell, minister of the Gospel of Wythe County, Va.

The above shows that there was a John Cassell who was a preacher in Wythe County, Va., in 1792. Probably Mary Cassell and Henry Castle were his children.

Oct. 20, 1797, Henry Castle and Christine Pickle.

Henry Cassell and wife Christina to Joshuah Hammond, survey of 100 acres, granted to Henry Cassell by patent bearing date Sept. 9, 1802, on Cove Creek, on line with Cassell's tract; 33 acres.

Dec. 12, 1815, between Michael Cassell of Wythe County, Va., and Henry Cassell of the County of Warren and State of Ohio, sold to Henry Cassell land lying on Cove Creek, 100 acres.

Michael Cassell and William Daugherty were in the 100th Regiment, 1st Battalion, of 1802. It met at William Inglelow's.

Oct. 10, 1797. Deed. Michael and Elizabeth Cassell to Columbus McDonald, 180 acres in Rich Valley, Wythe County, Va., on North Fork of the Holston; granted to Michael Cassell by patent bearing date Sept. 6, 1793.

Jacob Gross and Bezy Witten, Mar. 1, 1798.

Tavern license to Jacob Gross in May 1799. See Simmerman notes for Jacob Gross (probably Gose), perhaps intermarried into Keesling, Cassell or Simmerman connections.

Mr. Charles E. Bryant of Marion, Va., states that he formerly had a paper with items on it relative to his Cassell ancestors, which was given to him by his mother over 40 years ago, which paper has been either lost or distroyed. He further states that the records which were brought from Pennsylvania to this state, and which contained dates of births and deaths of the family, were destroyed in a fire 80 or 90 years ago, in the little log church that stood on the Pepper's Ferry Road, four miles from Wytheville, Va.

He thinks that it was either his great-grandfather or great-great-grandfather who was born in Cassell, Germany, and who came to this country in early manhood.

Mr. Bryant is a son of Mrs. Allie (Cassell) Bryant, daughter of John and Margaret (Etter) Cassell.

Bethel Cemetery: R. B. Saferight, born 1825; died Oct. 10, 1900; erected by his son, J. W. Saferight, of Pueblo, Colorado.

Deed book No. 23, page 160: Reuben and wife, Margaret Cassell, daughter of John Schweigart, son of Christian Schweigart, who owned land in Wythe County, Va., at his death. A large number of heirs, all residents of Carroll County, Maryland. Aug. 20, 1866.

Rev. C. W. Cassell of Luray, Va., says his father gave him the following record of the Cassells of the east end of Wythe County, Va.

Michael: issue, I. Adam; issue, Col. Joseph, William, Major Samuel, Capt. J. L.; II. John; issue, Reuben and Joseph; III. Catherine, wife of Peter Yonce.

Half brothers to Adam, John and Catherine: IV. David; issue Thomas, John, William, Sophia Umberger, Rosana Felty, Catherine Keesling, Rebecca Simmerman, Lizzie Utt, Senah Umberger; V. Andrew; issue John, Hiram (killed by falling tree), William and Ephriam.

Land Entry Book No. 1, pages 33 and 34.

1791, Michael Brown, by the last mentioned warrant, enters 200 acres. Beginning on John Finley Patent line, on the west side of the Sally Run, and joining the lands of Stophel Brown and an entry made by William Neel and the lands of John Harkrader, to include the vacant land whereon Nicholas Castle now lives, for a quantity.

Michael Castle by virtue of the last mentioned warrant enters 200 acres upon a branch of Reed Creek, joining the lands whereon said Castle now lives, on the south, and Jacob Toblar, Laurance Kettering, David Vaught and John Rouse.

1790, Frederick Castle, by virtue of the last mentioned warrant, enters 60 acres, joining his lands on the south and Daniel Pirkey, David Vaught and John Mangle.

Frederick Castle withdraws this entry and assigns the warrant to William Ward (?), Oct. 25, 1794.

Register of deaths of Wythe County, Va.:

Andrew Cassell died March 3, 1869, of paralysis, aged 84; names of parents not given; born in Virginia; name of consort was Catherine Cassell. Information given by John Cassell, Sr., his son. He was a farmer. See notes from "Ye Old Days," probably Cove Andrew Cassell.

East Wytheville, Michael was born in 1772.

Ephriam Cassell, son of Andrew, born in 1781.

One John Sr. born in 1782.

David C. born 1784.

Crockett's Cove Andy Cassell was born in 1786.

From these dates we know that they could not have been sons and father. They were probably brothers; and we find Andrew, probably brother of Jacob, Sr., named as the father of Ephriam; so Andrew must have been their parent or the parent of some of them, if not all. A grand-daughter of David says she heard her mother speak of Uncles Andy, John, Mike; and of Adam and Abram, but not as uncles.

Early historians speak of one Jacob Castle as having been a very early settler in Southwest Virginia.

Some of the earliest known Cassells of Wythe County, Va., were Jacob Sr., Andrew, Rev. John, Henry, Mary, Nicholas and Frederick. Probably Jacob Sr., Andrew and Rev. John were brothers.

THE KEESLING FAMILY
By
Mrs. Audrey Kemper Spence
of
Wytheville, Va.

Mr. Harold C. Keesling, P. O. Box 126, Fredonia, Kansas, is compiling a Genealogy of the Keesling Family. He invites correspondence on the subject.

He contributes a part of the following:

Tradition has said there were three Kisling brothers who came to this country, and from whom we all are descended. In this case, tradition seems to be substantiated by fact and record.

On Oct. 17, 1749, the ship *Fane* docked in Pennsylvania having sailed from Rotterdam, via Cowes, and carrying 596 passengers. Among those listed were Jacob Kelling (Jacob Kisling, from Pa. Archives). Again, the same route with apparently an unlisted number of passengers, among whom was Christopher Ensling, from Rupp's Thirty Thousand names, Christoph Kistling—or Kisling, from Pa. Archives.

The item next in order, I think, is the following, copied verbatim: "In Pursuance of an act of Parliament made in the thirteenth year of the Reign of his present majesty King George, the second, Entitled an Act for naturalizing such Foreign Protestants, and others there-in mentioned, as are settled or shall settle in any of his Majesties Colonies in America.

"At a Supream Court held at Philadelphia, before William Allen, William Coleman and Alex. Stedman, Esquires, Judges of the said court, on the twenty-fourth day of Sept. in the year of our Lord one thousand seven hundred and sixty-six, between the Hours of nine and twelve of the clock in the forenoon of the same Day, the following persons, being Foreigners and having inhabited and resided the space of seven years and upwards in his Majesty's Colonies in America, and not having been absent out of some of the said Colonies for a longer space than two months, at any one time during the said seven years, and having produced to the said court Certificates of their having taken the Sacrament of the Lord's Supper in some Protestant or Reformed Congregation in this Province within three months before the said court, Took and Subscribed the Oaths, and did make and repeat the Declaration prescribed by the said Act, to entitle them to the benefit thereof, and thereby became natural born Subjects of Great Britian, as the same is certified into this office by the Judge of the said Court, viz.:

	Berks County		
Jurors' names	Township	Sacrament	When taken
Jacob Kiesling	Bern	22 Sept.,	1766
George Kiesling	Bern	22 Sept.,	1766

Edw. Shippen, Jr. Probably from the Pa. Archives, Series 2, Vol. 2, pages 164-5.

These two are all the items I have been able to locate up to the present having to do with our forefathers and their immigration. However, I do find the following, which may serve to carry the line farther:

Page 187—Christofull Kislin's will, of Lick Run, Will Book No. 5, Augusta County, Virginia; of Chalkley's Record of Augusta County, Va.

Page 190—Jacob Keslinger, orphan of Christian (probably his mother was named Christina) Keslinger, to be bound to Philip Lingle. From Augusta County Records, Order Book No. 16.

Christopher Kisseling and wife Christina mentioned as standing sponsor for a Lingle baby.

From William and Mary College Quarterly, Vol. 13, page 253:

Private Conrad Kisling listed in the roll of Col. Hiesters' Battalion, Capt. Baldy's Company of Sixth Berks Company Militia in the service of the U. S. from Aug. to Sept. 7, 1780.

It is my opinion that Hugh Conrad (of Wythe County, Va.) was a son of George Kisling. This George Kisling was brother (supposedly) of one Jacob Kisling. The two brothers were naturalized in 1766, in Reading, Pa. Jacob Kisling had a son John, whose services in the Revolutionary War have been proven. His is the only branch of that particular family of which we have any considerable trace.

Hugh Conrad Keesling was one of the first children of George, hence old enough for service at the time of the Revolutionary War, which would be attested by the last reference. He died in Virginia prior to the pensioning of the Revolutionary soldiers, and hence we have not, as yet, been able to verify his service, other than shown.

Shortly after the Revolution (about 1785) the Keeslings seem to have been smitten with a trans-migratory urge. We find that some of them settled at Max Meadows, Va., and some at Cedar Springs, Va. John and Conrad settled east of Wytheville, and George (a brother of Conrad) stopped about an equal distance west of the same place.

Hugh Conrad Keesling was born at Reading, Berks County, Pa. He married Rebecca Ann ———. She was buried at the Rees Cemetery, near Muncie, Indiana. Their children were 1. John, drowned in the Arkansas River in Arkansas, left Jacob, Joseph, Conrad, daughter and David.

2. Catherine, married David Cassell; see Cassell Data.

3. Jacob Keasling, born April 11, 1796; died Jan. 12, 1848, Johnson County, Ind. Buried at the Miller Cemetery. Married Anna Deck; issue, Jacob, Abraham, Rebecca, Elizabeth, Mary, Susan.

4. David, married a Lewis.

5. Sarah.

6. George Keesling, married twice, both wives were Cassell sisters, the daughters of John Cassell of Bethel Church. His first wife must have been Anna or Ameda Cassell, whom he married Nov. 29, 1825. They had three children, Mary, John and Eliza Jane.

By his second marriage, to Matilda Cassell, he had the following children, James H., Ephriam, Melvina, Mariah, Almeda, Gustavis, Martha, Joseph, Robert Thomas, Virginia. This George Keesling remained in Virginia and resided near Keesling's Bridge in east Wythe County, where he has descendants today. See Bible dates for the family.

7. Martin, born May 11, 1802; died Dec. 16, 1867, at Muncie, Ind. Buried in Rees Cemetery; married Coracy Rees, who was born April 3, 1810, and died Aug. 10, 1880, at Muncie, Ind. Buried at Rees Cemetery. Issue, Morrison H., Lewis, Sophia, infant, Mary, Mahala, George, Lee C., Henry, Clay, Stephen C. "A native of West Virginia, he came to Delaware County (Ind.) with his mother, brother (Daniel) and sister (Sophia), being comparatively poor; but he was a shrewd, hard working man, and owned at the time of his death 756 acres of land."

8. Barbara, died before 1865, in Pike County, Ind.; married John Penner, died 1868 in Pike County. Issue, Peter, Joseph, James, Hugh, infant son, infant son, Polly, infant daughter.

9. Christena, born Sept. 28, 1809; died May 16, 1871; married Peter Doty, Feb. 17, 1831, who was born Nov. 13, 1800, and died May 1, 1871. Issue, William, Rebecca, Elizabeth, Mary Margaret, Jacob, Sarah Ann, Harrison, Jane, Christena, Peter, Morrison.

10. Joseph, married Betsy ———; issue, Joseph, Susan. This man moved to Delaware County, Ind. Later he went to Kansas, where I understand he designed the state bank notes.

11. Daniel, born Dec. 28, 1810; died April 2, 1882; married Elizabeth Keesling, daughter of Jacob Keesling, Feb. 6, 1834, who was born Oct. 1, 1814, and died Sept. 10, 1890. Married in Delaware County, Ind. Issue, Sophia, John, Sara Ann, Martha, Isaac, Jacob, Hugh, Mary C., Daniel, Anna, Elizabeth, Lutitia, Clarissa, Rosanna.

12. Rebecca Keesling, born May 13, 1813, in Wythe County, Va.; died Aug. 13, 1863; married David Keesling, Jan. 1, 1833, son of Jacob Keesling, born Aug. 7, 1811, died Oct. 12, 1892, buried in Wayne County, Indiana.

13. Sophia, married Bowen Rees. Issue, Rebecca Ann, Samantha, Mahala, Morris, William, Hiram, Charles, Robert.

Dates from the Keesling Bible, owned by Mr. Charles Keesling at Keesling's Bridge, near Fort Chiswell, Wythe County, Va.:

Mary Keesling born Oct. 22, 1826, married John Fink. She died Feb. 5, 1867.

John born Sept. 22, 1827. Killed in the War between the States, Sept. 20, 1862.

Eliza Jane born May 30, 1830, married Mr. Blessing. She died Sept. 19, 1860. Henry Blessing died July 1, 1873.

James H. born Jan. 30, 1832, married ——— Umberger.

Ephriam born June 11, 1833, not married.

Melvina E. born Nov. 16, 1836, married David Fink.

Harriet A. born M—— 10, 1838.

Almeeda C. born Aug. 17, 1839, married Mr. Umberger.

Gustavus, born Mar. 11, 1840.

Martha E. born Dec. 15, 1841, married Jas. L. Repass.

Virginia Martha Repass died Sept. 23, 1872.

Joseph E. born July 15, 1843, died Aug. 30, 1864.

Robert T. born May 10, 1845, married Julia Fisher; one child, Charles.

Virginia E. born Aug. 5, 1852, married James Perkins.

Maria A. died unmarried.

Dates from the Keesling Cemetery:

Robert F. Keesling, born May 16, 1845, died May 13, 1921, aged 76 years and 3 days.

Julia A. (Fisher) wife of Robert F. Keesling, born ——, died ——, 52 years, 3 months, 29 days.

John F. Fink, born March 21, 1829, died April 23, 1921.

Malvini E. wife of David V. Fink, born Nov. 16, 1836, died Nov. 15, 1905. Aged 68 years, 11 months, 29 days.

Mary Keesling (daughter of George) wife of John F. Fink, born Oct. 22, 1826, died Feb. 5, 1867.

George Keesling, born March 31, 1801, died July 2, 1876. Aged 75 years, 3 months, 1 day. Buried with a wife on each side of him (both wives were said to have been Cassells).

Matilda, wife of Geo. Keesling, born July 8, 1814, died May 1, 1887.

Maria A. Keesling, born Mar. 10, 1838, died Sept. 19, 1900, age 62 years, 6 months, 9 days.

Wythe County Court records:

Nov. 22, 1791, George Kisling and Mary Gooss.

Feb. 13, 1798, Jacob Gost and Susanna Cesling.

Feb. 13, 1798, John Miller and Christena Keesling.

Dec. 20, 1804, Jacob Keesling and Caty Phillipi.

Deed Book 4, page 56: Feb. 8, 1803, Koonrad Keesling and Margaret, his wife, to Daniel Lockett, on Mine Mill Creek, in Wythe County, Va. Signed in German.

Feb. 10, 1807, Bargain and Sale, Conrad Keesling and Rebecca to Stephen Sanders, Jr.

George Keesling and Anna Cassell were married Nov. 29, 1825, by Samuel H. McNutt.

Joseph Keesling and Polly Moyer, Feb. 24, 1825.

May 28, 1807, John Keesling and Barbara Stailey.

Feb. 2, 1808, John Raper and Elizabeth Keesling.

1818, John Kisling and Barbara Sprecker.

July 26, 1823, William Keesling and Dicy Smith.

Sept. 29, 1825, David Kesling and Harriet Butler.

Stephen Keisling and Anna Painter, June 9, 1825.

William R. Buchanan and Catherine Keesling, Mar. 4, 1830.

May 14, 1799, Jacob Keesling and wife Phebe to George Keesling, 14 acres on Peak Creek, a branch of New River.

Also a deed for 23½ acres, same date, being a part of the tract the said Jacob Keesling now lives on, lying in Wythe County, on Roberson's tract fork, a branch of Peak Creek; $100.00.

Nov. 11, 1817, Bargain and Sale. Peter Keesling et al. Jas. and Nancy Williams.

June 2, 1796, Bargain and Sale from John Baxter and Jean, his wife, to John Keasling.

"The Mauzy-Kisling Families," by Col. Richard Mauzy, can be procured from Mrs. Ella M. Bader, of McGaheysville, Va. This history deals with Jacob Kisling of Rockingham County, Va., and his descendants. Said Jacob Kisling was a soldier of the American Revolution, and his services have been proven and papers accepted by the D. A. R. Society. Mrs. Audrey K. Spence of Wytheville, Va., is one of those descendants whose papers have been accepted.

The following notes are by another descendant of his, namely, Mr. Charles E. Kemper of Staunton, Va.

Christopher Kisling appeared in 1759 at a sale.

His widow, Christena, married second John Hindman and lived near Dayton, Rockingham County, Va.

Jacob Kisling, the Revolutionary soldier, is said to have been the son of John Kisling, son of Christopher, but of this I am not certain.

Jacob Kisling was bound to Philip Lingell and taught the trade of a wagon maker, and married, in 1782, Lingell's widow, who was about 18 years older than himself. He owned and resided till his death on the farm, known as "Cave Hill" farm, one mile east of McGaheysville, Va.

Jacob Kisling was a Lutheran, and his children were reared as Lutherans. His wife was Barbara Bear, daughter of Jacob Bear and Barbara (Miller) Bear. She was a grand-daughter of Adam Miller, who was born in Schrisheim in Baden, Germany, on Nov. 17, 1703. He died in Rockingham County, Va., in the year 1783. Miller was the first white settler in the Shenandoah Valley of Virginia, in 1726.

John Bear, brother of Jacob Bear, was not naturalized until 1774. The court order states that he was a native of Switzerland.

Of the other descendants of Christopher Kisling, I have little knowledge.

The family undoubtedly came from Pennsylvania.

What became of Frederick Kisling's descendants, I do not know.

Christopher Kisling left sons, Christopher, Jr., Mathias (?) and John, also one daughter Christiana or Christena.

Jacob Kisling Mauzy, grandson of Jacob Kisling of the Revolution. once sent me a description of his grandfather. He stated that he was rather low in stature, inclined to be corpulent, had blue eyes, and very fair complexion.

An old tax ticket was found loose in Will Book No. 11, of Wythe County, Va., court records, of George Keesling. He was taxed for 5 slaves, 1 tithable, 755 acres, 1 clock (metal), in the year 1845.

Wythe County, Va., court records.

Nov. 22, 1856, near Fort Chiswell, William M. Umberger, Ameda Keesling, 20 and 16 years old, both single, of Wythe County, Va. Both born near Fort Chiswell. Son of Andrew and Peggy Umberger; daughter of George and Ameda Keesling; farmer; by Jas. A. Brown.

THE SIMMERMAN FAMILY

By

Mrs. Audrey Kemper Spence

of

Wytheville, Va.

In Scott's History of Orange County, Virginia, there is a list of names of "German Protestants" who proved their importations and who were naturalized Jan. 28, 1743. Among these names is that of John Zimmerman (alias Carpenter).

In 1717 a second colony came to Germanna, in Orange County, from Alsace, the Palatinate, and adjacent districts of Germany. They were Lutherans. They became involved in litigation with Gov. Spotswood, of whose treatment they more than once complained. The record shows these names, as being among them: Christopher Zimmerman, wife Elizabeth, children, John and Andrew.

This colony seems to have remained in that neighborhood (of Germanna) until 1725 or 1726, when they removed to the Robinson River section, in Madison County, where they acquired lands. They built Hebron Church, near Robinson River and Madison C. H.

In another place it speaks of Christopher Zimmerman being appointed by the court to survey the "German Road to Potatoe Run."

Page 258, Appendix F. Commissions 1734-1738, 1740, Lieutenant Christopher Zimmerman.

From the Orange County court records John Zimmerman (alias Carpenter) and others took the oaths of allegiance on Jan. 28, 1742.

The records further show that John Zimmerman paid a tithable in John Mitchell's precinct in the year 1739. He was in the census of Orange County, 1734-1739.

The will of Christopher Zimmerman was recorded in Orange County court on Thursday the 23rd day of March, 1748. He speaks of his wife Elizabeth, his son John, daughter Barbara Zeighler, son Frederick, son Christopher, daughter Elizabeth, daughter Katherine.

In the year 1729, in Spotsylvania court records, there is recorded a deed from Christopher Zimmerman, a cooper of St. George Parish, said county, to one Francis Cohler.

In the year 1730 the said Christopher Zimmerman and wife Elizabeth, deed to William Johnson; the same land which was patented to him on Sept. 28, 1728.

Frederick and Reuben Zimmerman also mentioned in the deed records of Spotsylvania County either as witnesses or adjoining land owners, the same date as above.

In the original record of Soldiers and Sailors of the Virginia State Line who were entitled to Bounty Land for Revolutionary services on said record are found the names of Christopher and Frederick Zimmerman as soldiers of the infantry.

In Sept. 1740 Christopher Zimmerman was commissioned a lieutenant, and again in August, 1742.

Extract from Virginia State Library notes. From Dunmore's War, Capt. Pauling's list of Botetourt troops names George Simmerman.

Judge Chalkley and other historians of Augusta and Rockingham Counties, Virginia, speak of the Zimmermans or Simmermans of those counties.

Mr. W. C. Barrickman, of Allen Building, Dallas, Texas, is a descendant of Christopher Zimmerman (Carpenter), an early immigrant to Virginia whose descendants lived in Culpeper and Madison Counties; and he has collected data concerning same.

Nothing has been found by which the Wythe County, Va., family of that name can be traced to any family named in the foregoing, only the similarity of names, and a very remote possibility of such a connection, because the will of Stophel Zimmerman of Wythe County, Va., was written in German.

Christopher or Stophel Zimmerman of Wythe County, Va., gave 90 acres toward the town of Wytheville. Mr. Davis gave 10 acres. The first court was held in the house of Stophel Zimmerman on June 22, 1790.

He died Feb. 4, 1813, age 56 years, and was buried in St. John's Cemetery.

In his will Christopher Zimmerman speaks of his wife Margaret, seven sons, Christopher, Erhart, Thomas, Peter, John, Henry, and Philip. His daughters, Sarah Holston and Polly Saufley. He also speaks of his grandson, Henry Simmerman, the son of Philip Simmerman, deceased. So this shows that he had at least seven sons.

He and his wife Margaret were married long before 1790, when the first records began to be kept. See chancery suit.

Philip died in December, 1810, age 35 years (see tombstone in St. John's Cemetery). He was a merchant. See court records. His wife Katy is spoken of.

Philip Simmerman born 1775, died 1810. Married Mrs. Katy (?) Clyse (a widow, who had one son, John Clyse). Their son Henry Philip Simmerman, born 1805, died 1891. Henry P. married Sophia Wolford, daughter of Jacob and Rebecca (Myers) Wolford, son of Ludwig Wolford and Anna Margaretta (Hoeg) Wolford. Issue of H. P. and Sophia Simmerman, I. John, 2 sons, 1. Charles, issue, a. Thomas, b. Mary (2 daughters, Eleanor and Mary Alice), c. Edward, d. Boyd.   2. Lincoln.

II. Charles.

III. Emily, married David Gates.

IV. Henry, issue 1. Anna E., 2. Iva Grace, 3. Fred, 4. Otto, 5. Ernest, has son Paul.

V. Thomas Joseph Simmerman, 48 Adams Ave., Huntington, W. Va., age 85; wife is 75. Issue 1. Oscar, resides in Pittsburg, Pa., son Marion.   2. Gertrude, 3. William, 4. Charles, resides in Charleston, W. Va.

Mr. T. J. Simmerman says that his parents moved from Wytheville, Va., to Gallipolis, Ohio, in 1830, and that his grandmother Simmerman accompanied them.

Mrs. Margaret Zimmerman, wife of Stophel Simmerman, died June 3, 1821, age 78.

Mrs. Jennie Holston Sutherland of Wytheville, Va., a descendant, has the certificate of baptism of their daughter, Clara. The translation is as follows: "In the year 1781, the 25th of Oct., there was born Clara. The father is Christopher Zimmerman, and the mother is Etna Margaretta, whose maiden name was Rei-handten," one letter missing in the name. (Probably "Reinhardten.")

Probably Clara was meant for Sarah, from whom Mrs. Sutherland descends.

There are a large number of descendants of Stophel Simmerman, among whom is Ex-Gov. E. Lee Trinkle, formerly of Wytheville, Va., now of Roanoke, Va.

It is believed and claimed that Stophel Simmerman had brothers, Arehart and Charles Simmerman.

Charles and wife Catherine owned a large estate north east of town, and they left their property to their nephews, which tends to show that they left no issue.

Arehart Simmerman owned a large estate at Cedar Hill. He took up one survey of 573 acres of land on Oct. 10, 1791. He owned 1000 acres or more of land.

The graves of him and his wife were found on Mr. David Blair's land, which was formerly a part of Simmerman's estate. The inscriptions were as follows:

"In memory of Arehart Simmerman, Died August 31, 1827, ae. 65 years. Precious in the sight of the Lord is the death of his Saints. By J. A. and M. Simmerman."

"In memory of Mary Simmerman, Died Nov. 28, 1834, ae. 70 years. Precious in the sight of the Lord is the death of his Saints. By J. A. and M. Simmerman."

The old Muster Roll of Col. Joseph Kent's Company, dated Oct. 8, 1796, contains, among other names, that of Arehart Simmerman. This list was published by the *Southwest Virginia Enterprise* on Nov. 26, 1926. The paper is owned by Mr. Joseph G. Kent of Bluefield, W. Va.

The following children are spoken of by Arehart Simmerman in his will (wife Mary). 1. Jane, 2. Nancy, 3. Samuel, 4. George, born before 1797, 5. John A., born Aug. 18, 1798. 6. Joseph, 7. William, 8. James, 9. Arehart, 10. Elizabeth Pierces, 11. Polly Stalls (?), not plain, 12. David.

1. Jane was born March 21, 1810; died Feb. 6. 1873; married James Yerian. July 4, 1837; no issue. Above dates were taken from the Yerian Bible, which is in the possession of Mr. Sidney D. Gray, of Ivanhoe, Va.

3. Samuel probably died unmarried, as he was an invalid.

4. George, born near 1797, died in Aug. 1841. See File No. 8206 in Chancery. His wife was named Mary Ann; her maiden name is unknown, unless it was Montgomery or Fuqua. The following marriage bond is from the records of Hustings Court, Richmond,

Va., by W. Mac Jones, and was published in a list with other bonds in the *Virginia Magazine of History and Biography,* April 1926:

Married by Rev. John Lindsey, George Zimmerman and Mary Montgomery, 4 Jan., 1810.

It is not known which of their children was born first.

Issue of George and Mary Ann Simmerman, 1. John D., 2. Catherine, wife of John Williams, who went to Anna, Ill.: 5 sons, 1 daughter.

3. Arehart, born July 4, 1811.

4. Henry, born 1814.

5. Polly, wife of James P. Graham, married Oct. 17, 1837: 3 sons, 2 daughters. Married second Mr. Carr, no issue. Settled at Anna, Ill.

6. Sarah Ann.

7. George Washington, 8 children.

8. Peter Fuqua.

9. Jane E., born 1828; died Dec. 11, 1875; married first Henry Harkrader, Mar. 2, 1848; issue. Married second Rufus Hedrick, born 1810, son of Jacob Hedrick, June 13, 1872, no issue.

10. Noah, 2 daughters, Rebecca Pruitt and Katherine Treace, Catersville, Ill.

5. John A. Simmerman and wife Margaret had a daughter, Mary Ann G., who married her second cousin, J. P. M. Simmerman, son of Thomas and Polly (Saunders) Simmerman of Cripple Creek. They were the parents of the late Col. S. S. Simmerman of Wytheville, Va. Thomas was the son of Stophel Zimmerman.

John A. Simmerman bought out the rest of his father's heirs and became very wealthy. He was buried on what is now Mr. Mason Bourne's farm. Inscriptions from stones on said land: "In memory of John A. Simmerman, born Aug. 18, 1798, died June 1853, age 54 years, 9 mo., 30 days."

"Sacred to the memory of William D. Simmerman, son of J. A. and Margaret Simmerman, born Aug. 17, 1822, died Aug. 18, 1846. Ae. 24 years, 1 day."

On Aug. 26, 1839, Joseph Simmerman and Elvina, his wife, William and Eliza Caroline, his wife, James, wife Margaret, Arehart, wife Mahala, are mentioned in deeds to their brother John A. Simmerman.

Issue of George and Mary A. Simmerman: 1. John D., died Jan. 26, 1880; thought to have been 75 years of age; not certain. Moved from Cedar Hill to Berea, where he resided till his death. He was buried at Evergreen Church. He was a nurseryman, also a school teacher, and the writer has seen the handmade books of both him and his brother, Areheart, all copied in splendid handwriting. The list included an arithmetic and a dictionary.

John D. Simmerman married Patsy Gilpen, daughter of Rodham Gilpen of Patrick County, Va., on Oct. 19, 1837. She died the same day on which her second son, Wylie Winton, was born. She was about 21 years of age. Died in 1840.

John Gilpen, her brother, was a very large man, and was a great wrestler.

Betsy Gilpen, their sister, married Mr. Ackin, and went to Tazewell County, Va.

Peggy Gilpen, their sister, married Mr. Puckett, went to Tennessee. These Gilpens resided at Cedar Hill, Va. From old marriage book of Wythe County, Va., George D. Findey and Nancy Gilpen, Aug. 16, 1853.

Issue of John D. and Patsy Simmerman: 1. Andrew Jackson, born July 21, 1838, died July 3, 1927.

2. Wylie Winton, born 1840. After the death of his mother in 1840, he was taken to Anna, Ill., by his grandmother, Mary A. Simmerman, and raised by some of his relatives.

An official statement from the Adjutant General of the War Dept., Washington, D. C., states that he enrolled Aug. 26, 1861, at Anna, Union County, Ill., and was mustered in Sept. 18, 1861, at Cairo, Ill., as a private, Co. E, 31st Ill. Inf. in the Federal Army, to serve three years, and died Sept. 13, 1863, at Vicksburg, Miss., of disease, a private. His age at enrollment is shown as 21 years, height 5 ft. 8¼ in.; complexion light, eyes blue, hair light; occupation farmer.

Andrew J. Simmerman married Mary J. Daugherty, Sept. 12, 1859. Issue 1. Alice, married Joseph Thomas; issue. 2. Sarah Jane, married her cousin, Joseph M. Spence; issue. See Spence History. 3. James Harvey, married Nannie Kegley, daughter of Geo. Kegley; issue. 4. Jennetta, married W. L. Grubb. 5. Joseph L., married Frankie Wisely, now deceased. 6. John, married Cordella Etter; issue. 7. Tilden, married Lula Fry; issue. 8. William H., married Elizabeth Irvine; issue.

Mary J. Daugherty was the daughter of John Daugherty, born Dec. 1819, died Jan. 6, 1879, and wife Catherine Corvin, daughter of Joseph Corvin, born Nov. 1817, married Oct. 8, 1840.

Joseph Corvin had a large number of children. He was very wealthy and owned over 2000 acres of land. He gave a large farm to each one of his children.

John Daughterty was the son of William and wife, Margaret (Etter) Daugherty, died Oct. 14, 1879; married Sept. 8, 1818; daughter of John Etter. See marriage bonds of Wythe County, Va.

Issue of John and Catherine Daugherty: 1. Mary Jane Daugherty Simmerman, born Feb. 28, 1841; died Dec. 16, 1926. 2. Margaret Daugherty, born Feb. 29, 1844; married Mr. Heldreth; had son Thomas Heldreth and others of Tazewell County, Va. 3. William Daugherty, born Oct. 24, 1846. 4. James Harvey Daugherty, born June 9, 1850.

Order Book for Wythe County, Va. A deed of bargain and sale from Robt. Daugherty, Exor. of Michael Daugherty, dec'd, to Jno. Cregar was acknowledged in court and ordered recorded, at an early date.

Andrew J. Simmerman belonged to Co. H, 63 Va. Inf., C. S. A. Served gallantly four years; was in many battles.

John D. Simmerman married (2) Amanda Knipp, Oct. 17, 1852; no issue.

3. Aerhart, born July 4, 1811, son of George and Mary Simmerman, married Rebecca Cassell, born June 16, 1817, daughter of David and Catherine (Keesling) Cassell, daughter of Conrad Keesling (his wife Rebecca is spoken of in will), May 23, 1837.

Buried in St. John's Cemetery, David Cassell, born Jan. 7, 1784; died April 11, 1869.

Catherine (Keesling) Cassell was born April 15, 1795; died July 29, 1865.

Another grave in the cemetery bears this inscription: Margaret Cassell, died Dec. 27, 1847, age 67 years, 2 months, 9 days.

Issue of Aerhart and Rebecca Simmerman:

1. Ephriam W., born Sept. 30, 1838, died 1868. 2. Susan or Susanna, born Mar. 19, 1840; died Feb. 20, 1903; married Wylie A. J. Spence, March 3, 1859; parents of Joseph W. Spence and others. See Spence History. 3. Robert Thomas, born Sept. 5, 1847; married Sarah Fry; issue, Rev. Hickman, Riley, Mrs. Cena Hornung, of Honolulu, and others.

Robert Thomas served in Co. C, 51st Va. Regt., C. S. A.

John Smith, father-in-law of Mr. Riley Simmerman, served in the 61st Va. Regt., Co. G, C. S. A.

4. Catherine, married Robert Jackson; issue.

5. John, born Dec. 6, 1842; died 1918; married Mary Hollandsworth.

6. George David, born Nov. 21, 1843. Killed at Gettysburg, 1863.

7. William Henry, born July 4, 1845; died June 28, 1922; married Susan Felty, who was born April 24, 1837, daughter of William and Christina (Gressel) Felty.

William Henry Simmerman served in the 51st Regt., Co. C, Floyd's Brigade, under Wharton and Breckenridge, C. S. A., two years in the Valley of Virginia. He was captured at Winchester, taken to Point Lookout on the Chesapeake Bay; six months in prison, under negro guards. They had no fire all winter; other privations; only the strongest survived.

4. Henry, son of George and Mary A. Simmerman, born 1814; died Aug. 12, 1904; married Eliza Calaway, July 15, 1841, who was born Oct. 23, 1815; died April 17, 1878. No issue. He resided in East Wytheville, was a merchant, and was very wealthy. He served as mayor of the town for a number of years. He married (2) Mary Crockett, gave his age as 78, bride's age as 40; widower and widow; son of George Simmerman; married by E. H. McDonald, Nov. 3, 1892. No issue.

Mary C. Simmerman, above, died Jan. 14, 1914, age 74 (?).

7. George Washington, the son of Geo. and Mary A. Simmerman, born May 7, 1820, died Dec. 10, 1885; married Elizabeth Beasley,

born Aug. 16, 1824; died Jan. 19, 1860. He settled in Anna, Ill., before his marriage. Their son was George W., born June 15, 1848; died Sept. 23, 1921; his wife was Emma Brown, died Oct. 26, 1925. Daughter-in-law is Mrs. Cora Simmerman of Anna, Ill. She has children. Mr. Grover Simmerman is a son; also Columbus Simmerman of Anna, Ill.; Mrs. Lillie Hill (Anna, Ill.) is a daughter.

    8. Peter Fuqua, born Jan. 23, 1823; died Aug. 25, 1888. Born near Wytheville, Va., buried in the Williams Cemetery at Anna, Ill. Married twice. By first marriage 1. Mrs. Mary A. Hunsaker, 220 West 8, Oklahoma City, Okla. She was 75 years old on Dec. 14, 1926. 2. Charles, born Mar. 2, 1847, buried in the Williams Cemetery. 3. A son, born Oct. 10, 1865; resides in Kansas City, Mo.

    By second marriage, Robert E. Lee Simmerman of Hartford, Ky., born April 25, 1872, at Hartford, Ky. Married April 18, 1894, Jessie Rowan Ford, daughter of Mr. and Mrs. James W. Ford; one daughter, Mrs. Winnie Davis Barnhill of Hartford, Ky.

    Mr. A. J. Medlin of Anna, Ill., is a descendant of Nancy Simmerman. Name of parents is not known to the writer, but thought to be daughter of Mary A.

    Mrs. Mary Anna Simmerman died before 1851. She and some of her children settled at Anna, Ill., after the death of husband George. She was buried in the Williams Cemetery, 5½ miles from Anna, Ill.

    Mr. A. J. Simmerman said that his grandmother came from Pennsylvania and that she was of Dutch descent. He probably meant German.

    Extracts from letters in possession of Mrs. Jennie H. Sutherland of Wytheville, Va.:

    Richmond, Ray County, Mo., March 8, 1842. From F. F. Holston to his brothers. Speaks of going to Nashville, Boone County, Mo. "William Simmerman of Richmond has lost all of his negroes except 3, namely, Harry, Permelea and Sam."

    David Simmerman, his son David, and family are out here.

    Brunswick, Mo., Mar. 4th, on back of letter. Thomas F. Holston of Chillicothe, Livingston, Mo., to Mr. Jas. H. Holston, Aug. 18, 1844:

    Asks when Stephen and John Simmerman are coming to that place. Also whether George Simmerman's family moved to Illinois last fall. The Missouri river was at flood tide, causing great destruction, and he had not heard whether Mr. Simmerman's plantation had been washed away or not.

    Rogersville, Tenn., June 28, 1857, from Sarah S. Hounshell to her uncle, Christopher S. Holston, of Wytheville, Va.:

    Speaks of her Aunt Lucy Holston, who lived with one of her daughters in Grainger County, Tenn.

    On back of a note:

    Christopher Holston was born Oct. 31, 1812. Alexander P. Holston was born May 11, 1818.

    To Chris. S. Holston, from his brother, 1841:

Visited Clinton City, 55 miles from where the widow Simmerman had settled. She paid over $800.00 for her farm.

William Simmerman had settled near Ray. Christopher Simmerman Holston was born Oct. 31, 1812; died May 15, 1890. He was the son of Benjamin and Sarah (Simmerman) Holston.

Joseph H. Holston born 1815, died Aug. 4, 1880. From the Holston Bible, owned by Mr. Walter M. Holston of Wytheville, Va.

Translations from a German Bible, owned by Mr. Riley Simmerman, and once the property of his grandmother, Rebecca (Cassell) Simmerman:

March 31, 1790, was born into the world to Jacob Gross, a son, at thirty-two minutes after eleven o'clock in the forenoon; his sign was "The Balance," in the full moon, Martin H. Cassell.

1766, July 2, morning, Catherine Hepstin came into the world.

1800, Aug. 22, was born a son to Jacob Gross between eleven o'clock and twelve, the sign was "The Virgin" in the full moon.

Wythe County, Va.:

Recorded marriage, also bond, Daniel Shafer and Nancy Simmerman, daughter of Aerhart Simmerman, Nov. 13, 1827.

From Register of Deaths of Wythe County, Va.:

Amanda Simmerman died Oct. 18, 1870, from a fall, aged 43 years, 3 months, wife of John D. Simmerman.

John Simmerman to Ann Montgomery, Sept. 28, 1831.

Erhart Zimmerman and Mahala Ramsy, Oct. 26, 1820.

Summers's "Annals of Southwest Virginia," page 151: At a court held for Botetourt County Sept. 9, 1772, Cornelius Dougherty, assignee of John Lusk, who was assignee of Hans Zimmerman, against Jacob Young, for debt. The jury was composed of John Dailey, John Looney, James Gilmore, John Jackson, John Potts, Wm. Dale, Jas. Hays, Archibald Hanley, Jas. Allcorn, Geo. McCoun, Wm. McMurray and John Hanley, who returned a verdict in favor of the plaintiff. Judgment accordingly and damages of £18 Pa. money and costs. But the debt may be discharged by the payment of £9 with interest from May 27, 1763, till paid, and costs.

Page 789: At a court for Montgomery County June 29, 1785: Ordered that Stophel Symmerman be allowed in the next levy £5 for boarding and clothing Katura Symmerman, a blind girl, one full year from the 20th day of May past—his wife have undertaken for the same.

Page 1367: Wythe County, Va., court minutes, March 13, 1798: Wm. Gleanes qualified as captain 35th regt., 17th brigade, Va. militia. Earhart Simmerman and Joseph Evans, Jr., qualified as ensigns in the militia.

Page 1358: June 22, 1790: Christopher Zimmerman and John Davis assign 100 acres, on the south side of the New Road, for the erection of public buildings.

Reference to the Daugherty family may be found in Judge Chalkley's Abstracts of Augusta County, Va.; also in L. P. Summers's Annals of Southwest Virginia.

THE SPENCE FAMILY

By

MRS. AUDREY KEMPER SPENCE

of

Wytheville, Virginia

"The Scotch-Irish," by Charles A. Hanna, Vol. I, page 345, says,

"A faint clue exists in Fife through the old privileges of the Clan MacDuff which were certainly claimed by the families of de Spens and de Arbuthnot, whilst the Seneschalstrep was held by de Blair and de Balfour. The latter office seems to have been invariably conferred upon a near kinsman, though in either case it may of course have been acquired by marriage."

From Spens of Lathallam:

"The family of Spens is of very high antiquity in Scotland, descended from a younger son of the Earl of Fife, as it had been in use of carrying in its armorial bearing the lion rampant of the great McDuff, which denotes descent from that ancient house."

Spens of Lathallam (page 169, Burke's Com.) : Thomas de Spens, who in the reign of Robert Bruce, is mentioned in a charter of donation to the monastery of Loltray, together with Sir Robert Keith, great Marshal of Scotland, Sir Richard Keith, his brother, and John Keith, his son, &c. This charter has no date, but appears to have been granted about the year 1320. He is a witness in another charter to the same monastery, with the said Robert Keith, &c. This charter also wants a date, but must have been in or before 1332 in which Sir Robert Keith lost his life fighting in defence of the liberties of his country at the disastrous battle of Duplin. Thomas de Spens died shortly after, and was succeeded by his son William de Spens, who is mentioned in an authentic writ in favor of his son, William, etc. —— Lathallam had been their chief seat and title ever since the reign of Robt. II.

Hanna, Vol. II, page 404: The English name of Spencer is steward or butler, from Spens a butlery, whence the Scotch name of Spence.

The roll of Battle Abbey, A. D. 1066, contains the name of De Spencer along with others.

The Virginia State Library has compiled within its indexes a list of the Revolutionary soldiers by the name of Spence.

David Spence, wife Esther, lived in North Carolina. See North Carolina notes. David Spence married Esther Lambord, Jan. 27, 1804, in Randolph County, N. C. Miles McDaniel, witness. David was born in Rowan County, N. C.; lived for awhile in Guilford County, N. C.; and died in Surry County, N. C.; but was buried on top of the Blue Ridge mountains in Alleghany County, N. C. It is thought that he was one of five brothers. The writer and others have more data concerning the early history of this family, but lack of space prevents giving it. Esther Spence died and was buried in Surry County, N. C.

Issue of David and Esther Spence: I. Joseph Perry, born April 14, 1809, died Dec. 11, 1875. Buried at Allen's Chapel, Texas. Went to Texas in 1838. At his death he left a large estate at Honey Grove. His wife survived him, but no children. See "Early Pioneer Days in Texas," by J. Taylor Allen, of Honey Grove, Texas.

II. David, died in Surry County, N. C. Three children.

III. Henry, two children, Frances and Baxter.

IV. Wylie, died in Surry County, N. C.; wife Martha. W. A. Moxley of Boonville, N. C., is a descendant.

V. James. Issue at Cumberland Gap, Kentucky.

VI. Malachi, born before his brother Joseph Perry, who was born in 1809. Died Dec. 6, 1880; buried in Wilkes, County, N. C. He married Elizabeth Minerva Ramsower (or Ramsu, Dutch); see North Carolina notes. They were married Aug. 23, 1820, in Randolph County, N. C. Jeremiah Allred, witness. She was born in Randolph County, N. C., and died March 8, 1876. Was buried in Wilkes County, N. C. Issue, 1. John David, last heard from in 1859 in Aurora, Ind.

2. William Madison, born Feb. 29, 1833 (?), in North Carolina. He went to Texas with his uncle, Joseph Perry Spence, in 1854. They were 38 days on the road. They rode horseback, and carried no arms with them for protection. By his first marriage he had a daughter Virginia, who married George Finley; residence, Ravenna, Texas. He married (2) Virginia C. Baker, Mar. 24, 1869. She died March 24, 1903. Their only child is Mr. William M. Spence, county surveyor of Windom, Texas. William M. Spence, the father, died July 24, 1905. He was buried in Allen's Chapel, Texas. Allen's Chapel was the first church organized in Fannin County, Texas.

3. Wylie Andrew Jackson Spence.

4. James Perry, died at six years of age.

5. Henry Benjamin, died in Texas; buried at Honey Grove, Texas. Issue.

6. Nancy, married T. E. Blackburn of Roaring Gap, N. C. Their son is Mr. J. J. Blackburn of Glade Valley, Alleghany County, N. C.

7. Huldah, married Houston Darnell; issue in Bluefield, W. Va.

8. Stephen Franklin, died during the War between the States, June 29, 1865; buried at White Oak, N. C.

9. Richard Columbus, of Troutdale, Va. Issue.

10. Charlotte, married William W. Woods; lived in Asheville, N. C., but died in Spartansburg, S. C. Issue.

VII. Nancy, married Mr. Wingate.

VIII. Betsy, married Wylie Nixton; issue Frances and Nancy; and lived at Capes Mills, Surry County, N. C., on Mitchell's River.

Richard Columbus (9) married Minerva Jane Ayers, the daughter of Dr. Elikan Ayers. Nine children.

Malachi II was born in Rowan (?) County, N. C.; removed to Surry County, N. C.; died in Wilkes County, N. C.

When Perry came back from Texas at one time he persuaded his brother Malachi to sell out 1200 acres of land and get ready to start to Texas with him the next day; but when they got up the next morning Malachi changed his mind and didn't go. They were going across the country in covered wagons. Perry offered to give him a part of his land after getting to Texas, but he wouldn't go.

Wylie A. J. Spence (No. 3), the son of Malachi and Elizabeth (Ramsour) Spence, was born Feb. 14, 1833, in North Carolina, and died March 2, 1875, in Wytheville, Va. He was married to Miss Susanna Simmerman of Wytheville, Va., on March 3, 1859; the daughter of Arehart Simmerman, son of George, son of Arehart I.

Wylie A. J. Spence belonged to Co. D, 45th Va. Regt., C. S. A., 1861; Floyd's Brigade; Capt. R. H. Gleaves; Major W. C. Sanders. He was captured and imprisoned at Camp Morton, Indiana, in 1861.

His brother Henry Spence was in the same company. He was captured and taken to Camp Chase, Ohio.

Issue of Wylie A. J. Spence:

1. William.

2. Mary, married H. L. Byrd. No issue.

3. Joseph Malachi, married his cousin, Sarah J. Simmerman, daughter of A. J. Simmerman. Residence, Wax Pool, Loudoun County, Va. Issue. 1. Jeanetta, married Clarence Headrick. 2. Philip Andrew, married Audrey Lee Kemper, daughter of Arthur and Laura (Hooke) Kemper, son of Ed. S., son of Rodham, son of John K. III. Issue, Philip Kemper and Laura Jean Audrey. 3. Susie, married William Hilton. 4. Wylie Joseph, married Vada Walker. 5. Malachi G.

4. John Spence, married Virginia Byrd. Issue, Richard and Minnie.

5. Sarah Spence, married Reece Doak of Chatham Hill, Va. Issue, three children.

Mr. Richard C. Spence, age 87, gives the following as the order of birth of David's children, 1. Malachi, 2. Joseph P., 3. James, 4. David, 5. Henry, 6. Wylie, 7. Betsy, 8. Nancy. And the following for order of birth of Malachi's children, 1. John D., 2. William M., 3. Joseph, 4. Wylie A. J., 5. Henry Benjamin, 6. Nancy, 7. Huldah, 8. Stephen, 9. Charlotte, 10. Richard C.

Joseph C. Spence is clerk of court of Pasquotank County, N. C.

Mrs. E. C. Kirk of Albemarle, N. C., and her brothers, who are lawyers of note, viz., U. L. Spence of Carthage, N. C., J. A. Spence, Asheboro, N. C., J. B. Spence, New London, N. C., and John B. Spence, Pawhuska, Okla., are children of Daniel Spence of Pasquotank County, N. C., and are interested in collecting the genealogy of their family.

SPENCE on the Revolutionary Army Account Books, in the North Carolina Historical Commission, Raleigh, N. C.:

Judge, Israel, Isaac, Jabez, James, John, Sam, William, David, Solomon.

Mrs. Spence, Vol. 10, p. 809.

Alexander, vestryman in Perquimans Co., N. C., 1715; Vol. 2, p. 209.

Alexander asks aid of Va., Vol. I, p. 837.

Alexander imports persons, Vol. I, p. 488; proves rites for five sons into this county (Perquimans) in 1697, whose names are under written, viz., himself, Dorety Spence, John Spence, David Spence, James Spence.

Alexander Spence Juror in Perquimans Co., 1713; Vol. 2, p. 89.

Alexander road overseer in Perquimans Co., 1699; Vol. I, p. 523.

Alexander in Militia, in Capt. Nehemiah Jones Co., Pasquotank Co., in 1755; Vol. 2, p. 357.

Alexander in Militia, in Capt. Wm. Abercrombie's Co., Vol. 22, p. 352.

Alexander Juror 1723, Pasquotank Co., N. C.; Vol. 25, p. 188.

Alexander pays quit rents 1729-1735 on 380 acres land in Pasquotank Co., Vol. 22, p. 250.

Alexander vestryman in N. E. parish, Pasquotank Co., 1741; Vol. 23, p. 7.

Alexander Sr., juror in Perquimans Co., 1723; Vol. 25, p. 187.

Cathron, imported by her husband John Spence, also 3 sons; Vol. 1, p. 488.

David, imported by father Alexander in 1697, Perquimans Co.; Vol. 1, p. 488.

David in Militia in Capt. Griffen Jones Co., 1755, Pasquotank Co.; Vol. 22, p. 349.

Dorety, imported by father Alexander, 1697; Vol. 1, p. 488.

Ed., in Militia, in Capt. Nehemiah Jones Co., 1755, Pasquotank Co.; Vol. 22, p. 347.

Greve, in Militia, drummer in Capt. Nehemiah Jones Co., 1755; Pasquotank Co.; Vol. 22, p. 347.

Insell, Army pay, received by B. McCulloch. £26 s.16 d.1. Army Line settled by Commissioners at Halifax, Sept. 1, 1784, & Feb. 1, 1785; & at Warrenton 1786; Vol. 17, p. 247.

Jabez, paid by B. McCulloch, £108 s.3 d.8; Vol. 17, p. 248.

Jabez, Army rank, pt. in Pointer's Co., 1777; omitted 1777; Vol. 16, p. 1157.

James, Army pay £65 s.1 d.4; rec'd by Arch. Little; Vol. 17, p. 247.

James, imported by father Alexander, 1697, Perquimans, Co.; Vol. 1, p. 488.

James, in Militia, pt. in Capt. Alex. Whitehall's Co., 1st N. C. Regt., commanded by Col. Sam'l Jarvis, June 2, 1780; Vol. 17, p. 1054.

James, in Militia, drummer in Nehemiah Jones Co., 3rd regt., Nov. 26, 1784; Vol. 22, p. 347.

James, land lapse 1719; obtained patent for 640 acres in Pasquotank Co., N. C., which is not cultivated; therefore land lapses; 1724; Vol. 2, p. 523.

James, pays quit rents on 300 acres land in Pasquotank Co., N. C., Sept. 1729; Vol. 22, p. 250.

James Jr. was juror, 1723, Pasquotank Co.; Vol. 25, p. 187.

James Sr. was juror, 1723, Pasquotank Co.; Vol. 25, p. 187.

John imported in 1697, Perquimans Co.; wife Cathron; & Robert Spence; Vol. 1, p. 488.

John, juror, 1723, Pasquotank Co.; Vol. 25, p. 187.

John, in Militia, in Capt. Richard Pierce's Co., Oct. 7, 1766; Vol. 7, p. 263.

John Sr., pays quit rents on 400 acres land in Pasquotank Co., 1729; Vol. 22, p. 250.

Joseph Spence, in Militia as drummer, in Wm. Abercrombie's Co., Pasquotank Co., 1755; Vol. 22, p. 352.

Robert, imported by father John Spence 1697; Vol. 1, p. 488.

Robert, in Militia, in Capt. Jos. Nash's Co., 1755, Pasquotank Co.; Vol. 22, p. 347.

Sam., in Militia, pt. in Alex. Whitehall's Co., 1st regt. N. C., commanded by Sam Jarvis, June 2, 1780; Vol. 17, p. 1054.

Samuel was juror 1740, Pasquotank Co.; Vol. 4, p. 518.

Simon, in Militia, in Capt. Henry Delon's Co., 1755, Pasquotank Co.; Vol. 22, p. 353.

Truman, in Capt. Jos. Nash's Co., 2d regt., 1755, Pasquotank Co.; Vol. 22, p. 347.

COPIED FROM GRIMES'S ABSTRACTS OF WILLS

Alexander Spence, Aug. 2, 1734—Apr. Court 1735; Pasquotank Co.: Sons: James (240 acres on Eastern Shore in Md.), Alexander, Joseph (land on Pasquotank River), Robert (land adjoining Rich'd Ferrell, Abel Rose, John Trueblood), Truman (appointed Ex.); Daughters: Jane & Catherine Sawyer. Witnesses, Jeremiah Munden, Thom. Sawyer, Evin Lurry.

James Spense, Mar. 20, 1739-1740, Oct. Court, Pasquotank Co.: Sons: Alex., David, James; Daughters: Bridget Spence, Betty Mardrum; Wife & Ex. Sarah. Witnesses, John Jones, Bud Bangor, Elizabeth Perisho.

James Spense, Nov. 9, 1753; April Court 1755; Pasquotank Co.: Sons: Alex., John, James; Daughters: Sarah Cook, Lettesha, Arey & Dorothy Spense. Wife & Ex. Elizabeth Spense. Witnesses, Sam. Smith, Sam. Ednye, David Davis.

John Spence, Mar. 14, 1735-36; Apr. 13, 1736; Pasquotank Co.: Sons: David, Alex. (land divided between them); Daughters: Dorothy Davis, Elizabeth Spence; grand daughter, Reachell Sawyer; Exrs., Chas. Sawyer & John Davis.
Witnesses, Geo. Rowe, Alex. Leflear, Elizabeth Leflear. Device on Seal, Letters S. S., three circles and square.

Alex. Spence & James Spence witness Mary Relf's Will Jan. 13, 1724, Pasquotank Co.

Alex. Spence witnesses Wm. Wood's will, Pasquotank Co., Nov. 4, 1732.

Jeremiah Symon's will, Nov. 1, 1740, Pasquotank Co., mentions daughter Ann Spence.

Joseph Spence witnesses Robt. Ednye's will, 1752, Apr. 4; Pasquotank Co.

Lymon Spence witnesses Thos. Hamlin's will, Dec. 31, 1737; Pasquotank Co.

Jeremiah Munden, will, Aug. 3, 1745, Pasquotank Co., mentions his granddaughter, Mary Spence.

Samuel Spence witnesses Matthias Ellegood's will, Sept. 10, 1773.

Wm. Spence, Guilford Co., N. C., Will; 1808: wife Sarah; children: George, Ely, John, William, Quinton, Joseph, Thomas; Sarah Strain, married daughter.

COPIED FROM OLD'S ABSTRACT OF WILLS, IN NORTH CAROLINA

Esther Spence, 1785, Pasquotank Co.; Miriam, Nancy, Ely, Mary.

COPIED FROM HATHAWAY'S GENEALOGICAL REGISTER,
VOL. 3, PP. 351-352

Wm. Spence died 1816, Perquimans Co.; wife, Margaret H. Skinner, daughter of Joshua Skinner; 1. Joseph Skinner; 2. William.

David Spence, Surry Co., N. C.; wife, Mary Ann McElyed, daughter of Lodowick McElyed; 1. Thomas; 2. David.

MARRIAGES

Alex. Spence married Fanny Satterfield, d. of John, who died 1836.

Betty Spence, daughter of James Spence m. ———— Mardrum.

Caleb Spence m. Elizabeth Simmons, Apr. 1, 1797; Tyrrell Co., N. C.

Catherine Spence m. John W. Kruger, May 31, 1848; Stokes Co., N. C.

Elizabeth Spence m. Arthur Glison, Apr. 13, 1780; Bertie Co., N. C.

Dorothy Spence m. John Davis (Grimes Abstracts, p. 355).

Isaac Spence m. Elizabeth Bowden, Apr. 27, 1789; Duplin Co., N. C.

Polly Spence m. John Donaldson, May 14, 1799; Guilford Co., N. C.

Quinton Spence m. Sarah Tate, Apr. 18, 1791; Orange Co., N. C.

Rebecca Spence, of Wm., m. John Anderson, who was born 1803 in N. C. See History of Tenn., p. 94.

Wm. Spence m. Hannah Morris, Surry Co., N. C.; witness David Spence.

Joseph Spence m. Lavenia Elliott, Nov. 16, 1837; Perquimans Co.; witness Wm. Albertson.

Sam Spence m. Julian Gray, Aug. 19, 1786; Pasquotank Co.; John Sawyer witness.

Daniel Spence m. Elizabeth Williams, Feb. 2, 1854; Pasquotank Co.; by Wilson Spence, J. P.

Almon Spence m. Mary Williams, Dec. 10, 1853; Pasquotank Co.; James Hunter witness.

Hunter Spence m. Martha Williams, Oct. 2, 1854; Pasquotank Co.; James Hunter witness.

Alex. Spence m. Adeline Manning, Jan. 14, 1828; Chowan Co.; Jos.
　C. Skinner witness.
Robt. Spence m. Sabra Broughton, May 1, 1833; Chowan Co.; Henry
　Scott witness.
Wm. Spence m. Margaret Skinner, Jan. 14, 1812; Chowan Co.;
　Richard Muse witness.
Alex. m. Frances Satterfield, May 10, 1830; Chowan Co.; Geo. Blair
　witness.
Wm. Spence m. Catherine Middleton, May 23, 1835; Chowan Co.
Malichiah m. Elizabeth Ramsower, Aug. 23, 1820; Randolph Co.;
　Jeremiah Allred witness.
Robt. Spence m. Frances Hill, Sept. 29, 1829; Randolph Co.; Jesse
　Gibson witness.
Willis Spence m. Sally Hall, Oct. 31, 1827; Randolph Co.; Jos.
　Spence witness.
Wm. Spence m. Elmora C. Kearn, Sept. 30, 1849; Randolph Co.;
　B. W. Galmore witness.
David Spence m. Esther Lambord, Jan. 27, 1804; Randolph Co.;
　Miles McDaniel witness.
Miriam Spence m. Malachi Brothers, May 15, 1770; Pasquotank Co.
Sarah Spence m. Busby Manning, June 10, 1793; Duplin Co., N. C.
Media Spence m. David Prince, Sept. 23, 1829; Cumberland Co., N. C.
Nancy Spence m. John Prince, Aug. 23, 1815; Cumberland Co., N. C.
Sidney Spence m. Jacob Jester, Mar. 17, 1798; Guilford Co., N. C.
James Spence m. Nancy Pate, Jan. 1, 1825; Johnston Co., N. C.
Dudley Spence m. Richmond Harris, Feb. 6, 1782; Wake Co., N. C.
Demsey Spence m. Mary Davenport, Dec. 22, 1799; Tyrrell Co., N. C.

Copied From The Census of North Carolina, 1790

Ann Spence, Tyrrell Co., 1 m, 2 boys, 4 females.
Cary Spence, Currituck Co., self.
Charles Spence, Dobbs Co., 2 males, 0 boys, 1 female.
David Spence, Camden Co., 1 male, 2 boys, 1 female.
David Spence, Pasquotank Co., 1 male, 0 boys, 1 female.
David Spence, Surry Co., 1 male, 2 boys, 3 females.
Grieves, Camden Co., 1 male, 0 boy, 3 females.
Isaac Spence, Duplin Co., 1 male, 1 boy, 2 females.
Isaac Spence, Pasquotank Co., 1 male, 0 boy, 3 females.
James Spence, Pasquotank Co., 1 male, 1 boy, 3 females.
James Spence, Bertie Co., 1 male, 1 boy, 2 females.
John Spence, Camden Co., 1 male, 2 boys, 1 female.
John Spence, Camden Co., 1 male, 0 boy, 2 females.
John Spence, Dobbs Co., 3 males, 0 boy, 3 females.
Joseph Spence, Northampton Co., 1 male, 2 boys, 1 female.
Lemuel Spence, Pasquotank Co., 1 male, 2 boys, 3 females.
Malachi Spence, Currituck Co., 1 male, 1 boy, 1 female.
Mark Spence, Pasquotank Co., 2 males, 1 boy, 2 females.
Mark Spence, Camden Co., 1 male, 0 boy, 4 females.
Noah Spence.
Reuben Spence, Pasquotank Co., 2 males. 0 boys, 8 females.

Robt. Spence, Tyrrell Co., 1 male, 0 boy, 3 females.

Sam Spence.

Thomas Spence, Surry Co., 2 males, 1 boy, 1 female.

Thomas Spence, Camden Co., 1 male.

Thomas Spence, Jr., Camden Co., 1 male, 0 boy, 1 female.

Samuel Spence, Pasquotank Co., 1 male, 0 boy, 3 females.

Daniel Spence of Elizabeth City, Pasquotank County, N. C., married Lovie Sexton, and they moved to Randolph County, N. C. Their son Daniel was born in Pasquotank County, N. C., January 30, 1808. He died March 26, 1882, and was buried in Randolph County, N. C.

Daniel Spence, the father, was also buried in Randolph County, N. C.

Daniel, the son, was married twice. Mr. J. B. Spence, of New London, N. C., is the only child now living of the first marriage, while the following are by the second marriage: Mr. J. A. Spence of Ashboro, N. C.; John B. Spence of Pawhuska, Okla.; Mr. Union L. Spence of Carthage, N. C.; and Mrs. E. C. Kirk of Albemarle, N. C., who has one son, Spence Kirk. Three of these men have been very prominent lawyers, and one has been a member of the legislature of North Carolina. They were born in Stanley County, N. C.

Daniel Spence, the father, had the following known issue: Daniel Spence, Robert Spence, Randolph County, N. C.; John Spence, Ill. Either he or his brother Mark was an officer in the War Between the States.

Willis Spence, Missouri.

Thornton Spence, went to California during the gold rush.

Mark Spence, Illinois.

Albert Spence, Georgia.

Joseph Spence, Arkansas.

John Spence, probably left North Carolina.

See notes from Historical Com. for data.

The North Carolina Historical Commission data give the marriage of David Spence and Esther Lambord as of January 27, 1804, Randolph Co., N. C. Miles Daniel witness. Esther was probably the daughter of John and Miriam (Spence) Lambert and the grand-daughter of Esther Spence of the 1785 will. If Malachi was the son of David and Esther above, he may have been born in the last part of the year 1804, and so he would have been old enough to have been married in 1820 to Elizabeth Minerva Ramsu (Ramsours). Mr. Richard C. Spence gave from memory his father's birth date as 1806, which is a mistake, as the marriage date proves.

As Alex. Spence of 1735 will leaves land on the Eastern Shore in Maryland, he must have been related to the Spence family of Maryland.

The Sawyers, Mundens, and Lamberts seemed to have been among the families who inter-married with the early Spences.

Esther Spence, Pasquotank, will 1785: son Isaac, daughters Miriam Lambert, Alif Sawyer, Elizabeth Forehand, Mary Sawyer,

Jane Sikes. Sons-in-law, James Forehand, John Lambert, Wm. Sikes, Isaac Sawyer. Grand-daughter, Esther Lambert. Mentions Nancy Sawyer, daughter. Probated at August court, 1785.

William Spence, Pasquotank, Co., 1785: wife Judah; children, Thornton, Joseph, Sarah and Elisha Spence. (These two "Wills" are here in the Historical Commission.)

Jeremiah Symons, wife Rachel, daughter Ann Spence. Will in Pasquotank Co., 1749.

Henry Spence m. Dec. 1, 1829, Huldah Herring, Duplin Co.

Cary Spence m. Martha Fulford, Dec. 31, 1861, Currituck Co.

Additional counties searched, Tyrrell, Bertie, Currituck, Duplin, Caswell, Northampton, Rowan, Orange, and Pasquotank.

John Spense m. Sally Burney, Feb. 19, 1822, Guilford Co.

Alvis Spense m. Isabella Shelrutt, Jan. 28, 1826, Guilford Co.

James Spense m. Peggy Lester, Feb. 21, 1820, Guilford Co.

Witness Wm. Lester.

Malachi (I) Spence was born March 5, 1806; died Dec. 6, 1880.

Elizabeth Minerva (Ramsour) Spence was born Sept. 15, 1808; died March 8, 1876.

Additional Lewis Items

In reference to the Lewis and Bell items on pages 204-206 of this volume, Mrs. Spence wrote March 25, 1929: "I am in receipt of a letter from Mrs. Richard P. Bell, Staunton, Va., who says that Dr. (Richard Preston) Bell is a lineal descendant of William Lewis, son of John Lewis, pioneer. I do not remember whether I stated the fact in my notes on Anthony Lewis or not."

Kephart Items

Mrs. Spence supplies the following Kephart items, which should be read in connection with statements on page 207 of this volume.

"Tradition is that Henry and Magdalene (Bargley) Kephart had the following children:

1. Peggy, married Mr. Owens.
2. Kate, married Mr. Losch.
3. Elizabeth, married (1) Mr. Dunn, (2) Mr. Young.
4. Polly, married Mr. Ray; had daughters Harriet and Rachel.
5. Henry Kephart, of the War of 1812 (?).

"The Kepharts resided on Dry River, in Rockingham County, Va."

Kemper Item

On November 1, 1929, Mrs. Kemper reported the following death of her niece: "Mary Elizabeth Kemper, daughter of Harvey R. and Helen Floyd Kemper of Wytheville, Va., was born August 2, 1918, and died September 20, 1929."

See page 210 of this book.

ADDITIONAL ITEMS FROM MR. CHAS. E. KEMPER
January 8, 1930
McGAHEYSVILLE LUTHERAN CHURCH
(See pages 305, 306, above)

A survey of the Peaked Mountain Church record (German) gives 1745 as a probable date for the founding of this congregation, and August 15, 1753, as a certain date for its existence, as shown by three baptisms.

George Henry William, son of Henry Wilhelm and wife Anna Elizabeth, born April 8, 1747; baptized July 21; year not given.

Michael Wilhelm was the first child baptized in the Peaked Mountain Church; his brother George the second; Susanna Price the third; and her baptism gives us 1753 as a certain and positive date for the Lutheran and German Reformed Peaked Mountain Church; but since the baptism in 1745 appears in the church records for that year it seems to be clear that 1745 was the year in which the congregations, Lutherans and German Reformed, commenced their existence at McGaheysville; and 1753 is a certain date to assign to them.

The record of baptisms at the Peaked Mountain Church:

Michael William, son of Henry Wilhelm and wife Anna Elizabeth, born June 25, 1745; baptized Dec. 20; year not given.

Susanna, daughter of Augustine Preiss (Price) and wife Anna Elizabeth (*nee* Scherp), born May 9, 1750; baptized Aug. 15, 1753.

These baptisms coincide with the presence of Rev. Lawrence Wartman, a Lutheran minister, in the McGaheysville neighborhood in the year 1747, as shown elsewhere in this work.

Rev. Lawrence Wartman was certainly there in 1747; but since a minister had to perform the baptismal rite, he seems to have been officiating in 1745 at McGaheysville. This nearly ranks the German Peaked Mountain Church in age with the Presbyterian Peaked Mountain Church at Cross Keys.

ADDITIONAL KEESLING ITEMS
By
MRS. AUDREY K. SPENCE
(See pages 352-357)

The will of Conrad Keesling was made Oct. 24, 1817; probated May 12, 1818. See Will Book 2, page 245, Wythe County, Va., court records.

On January 23, 1930, Mrs. Spence was referred by Mr. Harold C. Kesling of Fredonia, Kansas, to Penna. Archives, Series Five, Vol. V, page 234, for Revolutionary services of Conrad Keesling.

FROM PENSION BUREAU—KEISLING OR KIESLING, JOHN
S. 16434

App. for pension, May 16, 1833. His claim was allowed. Age, born March 23, 1758, was the son of Jacob Kiesling. Residence at date of application, Fall Creek Township, Henry Co., Indiana. Residence at date of enlistment, Reading, Berks Co., Pa. Soldier enlisted Sept. 1776 and served 2 months as a private under Capt. Jacob Whetstone, Pa. troops; enlisted November 1776 and served 2 months under Capt. Lindemoot and Col. Hiester; enlisted in 1777 and served 2 months under Col. Hiester; enlisted in 1779 and served 2 months as wagoner under Capt. John Lindemoot. He died about Dec. 25, 1840 leaving a widow, name not stated. There is no further family data on file.

ADDITIONAL SIMMERMAN (ZIMMERMAN) ITEMS
(See page 358-365)

On January 26, 1930, Mrs. Spence had a letter from Mrs. Mary Zimmerman Herndon of "Bonnie Brae," Prince George County, Va., giving information about her father, George Henry Zimmerman; her grandfather, William Zimmerman, of Augusta County; and her great-grandfather, David Zimmerman, born 1801.

David Zimmerman married Susan Catherine Perkins, born 1804. William Zimmerman married Sarah Elizabeth Williams of Wytheville. Mrs. Spence states that the record is in the Wythe County Marriage book, date February 12, 1857. George Henry Zimmerman married Mary Frances Mullins of Giles County, Va.

CASSELL ITEMS

Under date of January 31, 1930, Rev. C. W. Cassell of Luray, Va., wrote:

"See page 346, third line from the bottom: Sophia, daughter of Joseph Cassell, married Ransom Hubble of Smythe County. Margaret married Wallace Cecil of Pulaski County. In the second line from the bottom of the same page it is said that Michael Cassell was son of Jacob Cassell. He was the son of Joseph Cassell, as is shown in lines 3 to 5 from the bottom of the page."

ANOTHER MEMORIAL TABLET

On November 11, 1928, the Rion-Bowman Post 632, V. F. W., presented a bronze tablet which is affixed to the big German cannon in Harrisonburg. The big gun first stood for a while at the south corner of Court Square in the city; but later it was removed to its present location near the new high school building.
(See pages 184, 185)

SOURWINE, BOWMAN, KISLING AND OTHERS

Notes from MRS. JOHN S. MACY

3353 N. New Jersey Street, Indianapolis, Indiana

Jacob Kiesling came to America in 1759 or earlier. He owned a small farm on the west bank of the Schuylkill River in Berks County, Pa., north of Reading. He married Walburga Miller in 1754. She came to America in 1749. He was drowned in the Schuylkill February 4, 1784. The story goes that during a flood he was trying to save some of his stock when his boat upset and he was drowned. His wife witnessed the tragedy. His body was found the next day.

The children of Jacob Kiesling and Walburga Miller were: Martin, John (born 1758 or 1759), Jacob, Sebastian, Agnes (?), and Barbara (?).

The first census taken in Pennsylvania (1790) lists the name "Widow Kiesling" in Reading Township, Berks County. Tradition has it that the Widow Kiesling and her sons went to Wythe County, Va.

One historian lists Jacob Kiesling's children as Jacob, Conrad, George, John, Priscilla, and Catherine; states that the sons George and Conrad lived and died in Wythe County, Va.; also that Priscilla married a Miller and lived in Boston Township, Wayne County, Ind.; that Catherine married Abe Fillinger; that she died March 19, 1832, and was buried on Daniel Keesling's farm, west of Mechanicsburg, Henry County, Ind.

Others affirm that Priscilla and Catherine were not Jacob's daughters, also that Conrad (Hugh Conrad) and George were sons of George Kiesling who took the oath of allegiance September 22, 1766.

Penna. Archives, 5th series, give the names of Jacob, Conrad, George, Martin, and John Kisling as soldiers of Berks County, Pa., in the Revolutionary War. Joseph Hiester was colonel of Berks County militia.

An enlistment qualified one for the war even if he did not participate in battle.

Conrad Kiesling, Maxatawny Township, Berks County, Pa., single, appears on the 1785 tax list.

Conrad Kisling was in Joseph Hiester's company and on the pay roll of Capt. Jacob Bauldy's company.

From Pennsylvania Archives.

John Keesling, son of Jacob Kiesling, was born March 23, 1758 (tombstone record 1759), in Berks County, Pa.; died December 31, 1839, in Berks County, Pa. Died December 31, 1839, in Henry County, Ind., a pensioner of the Revolutionary War.

John Keesling married first Eve Miller, who was born April 12, 1765, and died in Preble County, Ohio, about 1806; second, Barbara Staley, widow, about 1807.

Children of John and Eve (Miller) Keesling: Jacob, 1789, m. Catherine Shaffer; Elizabeth, 1791, m. John Raper; Catherine, 1792, m. Daniel Shaffer; Polly, 1795, m. Benj. Fisher; John, 1796, m. Melinda Bulla; Daniel, 1797, m. Catherine Zeek; Peter, Feb. 9, 1800, m. Nancy Bosworth; George, 1804, m. Elizabeth Miller; Susannah, 1806, m. Rice Price, Jr.

Children of John and Barbara (Staley) Keesling: Dorotha, born in Preble County, Ohio, Dec. 15, 1808; m. Adam Carter.

Some of John and Eve (Miller) Keesling's children were born in Wythe County, Va. They left Wythe County after 1800.

The Keeslings, Millers, Shaffers, Zeeks, and Rapers all lived in Wythe County, Va., before coming to Preble County, Ohio, and Wayne County, Ind., 1801 and later. Several of Christopher Kisling's descendants settled in Wayne County, Ind., and other Indiana counties after leaving Preble County, Ohio.

Following is the lineage of Mrs. John S. Macy, a member of Caroline Scott Harrison Chapter D. A. R., through service of John Keesling:

(1) Jacob Keesling and Walburga Miller
(2) John Keesling and Eve Miller
(3) Peter Keesling and Nancy Bosworth
(4) Martin Keesling and Adaline Moore
(5) Sarah M. Keesling and N. W. Sourwine
(6) Alma E. Sourwine and John S. Macy

Following is the lineage of Harold C. Keesling, Fredonia, Kansas:

(1) George (?)
(2) Conrad Keesling, Wythe County, Va.
(3) Martin Keesling, Muncie, Ind.
(4) Morrison H. Keesling
(5) Charles E. Keesling, Kansas
(6) Harold C. Keesling

Personal data concerning some of the foregoing:

(1) Jacob Kiesling, naturalized Sept. 22, 1766
(2) John Keesling, Revolutionary soldier
(3) Jacob Keesling, settled in Wayne County, Ind.
(4) Elizabeth Keesling, m. "Muncie" Dan Keesling
(5) Martha Keesling, m. Morrison H. Keesling
(6) Charles E. Keesling
(7) Harold C. Keesling, Fredonia, Kansas

Note—John Keesling, Revolutionary soldier, had a son Daniel Keesling who settled in Henry County, Ind., about 1825. "Muncie" Dan Keesling lived in Delaware, a county directly north of Henry, near Muncie, therefore the appellation "Muncie" Dan, to distinguish him from the other. It is said that "Muncie" Dan was a son of Conrad Keesling of Wythe County, Va.

John Keesling, Revolutionary Soldier

John Keesling was a private soldier in Col. Hiester's company; enlisted at Reading, Berks County, Pa.; applied for a pension May 16, 1833. His claim was allowed. At date of application he resided in Fall Creek Township, Henry County, Ind. Age at date of application—born March 23, 1758. Was a son of Jacob Kiesling.

Remarks. He died about Dec. 25, 1840, leaving a widow, name not stated. There is no further family data on file.

The above statements follow an official report. See page 376.

Rockingham County, Virginia
Lineage of Alma E. (Sourwine) Macy

(1) Peter Souerwein and Maria Bouer (Bowers)
(2) John Sourwine and Elizabeth Bowman
(3) William Sourwine and Elizabeth Gentry
(4) Noah W. Sourwine and Sarah Keesling
(5) Alma E. Sourwine and John S. Macy

John S. Macy is a lineal descendant of Thomas Macy, first settler of Nantucket, Mass., in 1639, and of John Howland (?), Mayflower passenger, 1620.

(1) Jacob Miller and Charlott Catherine
(2) Matthias Miller and ——— ———
(3) Margaret Miller and George Bowman
(4) Elizabeth Bowman and John Sourwine

Bowman Line

(1) George Bowman and ——— ———
(2) John Bowman and Mary M. Zarvus (Surface)
(3) George Bowman and Margaret Miller
(4) Elizabeth Bowman and John Sourwine
(5) William Sourwine (6) N. W. Sourwine (7) Alma E. S. Macy

The Souerweins (Sourwines), Bowmans, Millers, Surfaces, and Bowers, lived near Timberville, Va., and were communicants of Rader's Lutheran Church. Some of the Bowers attended Solomon's Lutheran Church, in Shenandoah County, Va.; also the Surfaces.

Elizabeth Gentry, who married William Sourwine, was the daughter of Ephraim Gentry and Elizabeth Foland. The latter was a daughter of Valentine Foland of Rockingham County, Va. Accordingly, Alma E. S. Macy is an offspring of the Sourwines, Bowerses, Bowmans, Millers, Surfaces, and Folands of Rockingham.

Personal Notes

Mrs. Macy had bound typewritten copies made of the translations of Rader's Church (German) records. The said records were translated by her cousin, Mr. Leslie A. Miller, Cheyenne, Wyoming. Mr. Miller presented a copy to the Virginia State Library, Richmond; another to the D. A. R. Library, Washington, D. C.; one to the Newberry Library of Chicago; one to the Library of Philadelphia; and still another to the officials of Rader's Church.

Mrs. Jesse L. Bowers, McGaheysville, Va., has written up the genealogy of the Bowmans and Millers.

KISLING OR KEESLING, CONRAD
(To Mrs. Spence, January 29, 1930)

"Referring to your letter of January 27, the name Conrad Kisling with reference to Vol. 5 in the Pennsylvania Archives, Fifth Series, appears to be the only reference to Keesling, with various spellings, that we have on our lists of Revolutionary Soldiers.

"This name appears as having been taxed as a single man in Maxatawny Township, Berks County, 1785. The name George Kisling appears upon the same list.

"Conrad does not appear in the Census of 1790 as the head of a family in Pennsylvania. The name Martin Kisling appears as the head of a family in Berks County 1790. The fact that Conrad does not appear in this Census of 1790, if he was the head of a family at that time, may show that he had left Pennsylvania, and the Census records of Virginia would probably contain his name. I would suggest that you write to the Census Bureau, Washington, D. C., and if he located in Wythe County you would probably find some court records that would aid you.

"Very sincerely,
"H. H. Shenk,
"Archivist, Harrisburg, Pa."

(See pages 352-357; 375, 376)

MORE REVOLUTIONARY SOLDIERS

Mrs. Audrey K. Spence of Wytheville, Va., sends the following letter, written March 4, 1930, by her cousin, Jasper Newton Keesling, of New Castle, Ind.

I began in 1906 to gather our family history, and have gathered a bushel basket full of real "dope." About three years ago Harold C. Keesling of Fredonia, Kans., took up the work and is going ahead with it. We expect to put into print our combined effort.

Of course, we have many riddles which remain unsolved. Some of the original data has been proven wrong.

Daniel Webster Keesling is a farmer and a first cousin to my father. His address is Shirley, Ind., R. F. D. No. 2. Yes, Mrs. Macy of Indianapolis sent me some items of Wythe County, Va., which she got of you. I have a letter from Charles E. Kemper, written in 1906, which gives some main facts of the early Kislings or Keeslings in Augusta and Rockingham County, Va.

Some of the main facts (and supposed facts) of the Kislings are as follows: Charles Kissling, who came from Erlach, Switzerland, at the close of the Civil War, says:

"One of my school mates who had access to the old records there informed me that during a Hun raid at Erlach, which came out of Sweden about the year 1372, for some cause one fellow was left behind when they departed. During the next 300 or 400 years the descendants of this raider scattered over Austria and Germany and Switzerland."

He then gave an account of his own people. His Uncle Abraham marched with Napoleon Bonaparte when he went against Moscow, Russia, and was lost.

About 1700 there were Kieslings of Swiss blood living at or near Dresden, Saxony, where many still live. (Those German Kieslings of Illinois and New York City are from Dresden.) Among others, there was a family at Dresden in 1700 who had four sons. These sons joined the Reformed Church movement and were banished by royal decree from the kingdom. Two came to America and two went to Bavaria, Germany.

The two brothers in America were Christopher and George Kiesling—also spelled Kisling and Kissling. Later Jacob, a younger brother, came over from Bavaria and joined his brothers at Reading, Berks County, Pennsylvania. Jacob married Walburga Miller in 1754. She came over in 1749. Jacob was born April 12, 1714, and was drowned in the Schuylkill River, near his home. He settled in Bern Township, Berks County, Pa., and owned some live stock and over 100 acres of land. His death happened on February 4, 1784. His wife was a witness to the capsizing of his canoe. His body was found the next day in some drift. It was during high water.

His children were: Martin, Revolutionary soldier. John, born August 31, 1759; Revolutionary soldier. Jacob, born 1764. Sebastian, and two girls.

Jacob and his brother George took the oath of allegiance to King George III of England, September 24, 1766. (Signed Kiesling.)

The son, John Kisling, married Eve Miller in Pennsylvania. His first child was Jacob, born 1789. Some time prior to 1797 John and Eve settled in Wythe County, Va., and about 1802 to 1808 came to Preble County, Ohio; and in 1828 or 1829 to Henry County, Ind., where he died Dec. 31, 1839. He was given a pension in 1833. Eve died in Virginia. He then married Barbara Staley, who had one girl.

John and Eve had Jacob, Daniel, John, George, Peter, Catherine, Polly (Mary), Elizabeth, Susanna, and Dolly (Dorothy). Dorothy was a half sister. All came here.

Now Jacob, son of John and Eve, had 14 children. One was Samuel, who had one son, Clinton, and two girls. Clinton was my father. I was born Oct. 29, 1882, and have a brother Thomas and a sister Alvada.

Now, just who George the immigrant's children were is a guess, but I say that when John and Eve came to Wythe County, Va., he had at least four first cousins then, viz., Conrad, who was a Revolutionary soldier of Berks County, Pa.; George, living at Cedar Springs, near Rural Retreat, Wythe County, Va.; Christena (Kisling) Miller, wife of William Miller; and Mrs. Abe Fillinger, who died here in 1834.

The above George of western Wythe County had a large family. Some came here. Peter lived there; had a large family; and one, Emory, has not been dead very long. He had Basil (at the old home), Peter, Minnie, and another daughter. The descendants of Jacob and George, the immigrants, have always lived neighbors in Pennsylvania, Virginia, and here. And of these I know most.

Conrad probably had a brother Peter in Pennsylvania. I do not know what became of those who stayed there. They never came here.

Christopher Kisling, the immigrant, was early in the Shenandoah Valley of Virginia. He was there in 1763 and sooner. He died in 1773 or 1774. He had five or six boys and two girls. A grandson Jacob, was present at Lord Cornwallis's surrender at Yorktown, 1781. Jacob was Charles E. Kemper's grandfather. This Jacob had a brother Teter who settled in Ohio in 1805 and founded the Kesling Clan of Ohio, etc.

Conrad Kisling of Wythe County, Va., died near Max Meadows. His wife died here. She came here with sons Daniel and Martin and daughter Sophia.

Conrad's children : 1. Rebecca, married Daniel Keesling, a grandson of John and Eve Miller Kisling. 2. George, married Matilda Cassell of Wythe County. 3. Daniel, married Elizabeth Keesling, granddaughter of John and Eve. 4. Martin, married a Miss Reese. 5. Joseph, married Betsy ————. 6. John, married ————. 7. David, married ———— Lewis. 8. Christena, married Peter Doty of Johnson County, Ind. 9. Sophia, married Bowen Reese. 10. Jacob, married Anna Deek, or Dock. 11. Katy, married David Cassell. 12. Barbara, married John Penner.

Now, what became of this even dozen? Well, Daniel, Martin, Sophia, and their mother came to Delaware County, Indiana, about 1830 or 1834. Conrad was dead then. Joseph came about 1833, but went to Kansas. He had sons Samuel, Joseph, Daniel, and a daughter Susan. John and his oldest boy were drowned in the Arkansas River, Arkansas. He had sons Jake of Missouri, and Joe, Conrad, Daniel, and David, who was killed in the Mexican War.

David went to Tennessee. Jacob settled in Johnson County, Ind. He and his son Abraham were killed while cutting timber. Abraham's brother Jacob settled in Iowa in 1853. He married a Kegley, and had Mike (and John) Keasling of Nashua, Chickasaw County, Iowa. Jacob Keasling, Sr., had also these girls: Rebecca Haugamier, Elizabeth, Mary Steffler, and Susanna Shipley. All have descendants. Some of them are in Iowa, others in Montana,

Washington, and Oregon. Mike had a sister Melissa Krause, Ionia, Iowa. Maybe she or Mike still lives.

George Keesling, the son of (Hugh) Conrad Kisling, lived and died near Max Meadows, Wythe County, Va. He also had 12 children. They are: 1. John, died single of typhoid fever in Johnson County, Ind. 2. Mary, married John Fink; lived at Max Meadows. 3. Melvina, married David Fink, and lived at Max Meadows. 4. Harvey, married Katy Umbarger, and went to Lyons, Kans. He had two sons, James and George, still living. 5. Mariah, died single. 6. Ephraim, married Matilda Umbarger, sister to William. He was in the Civil War, Va. troops. 7. Almeda, married William Umbarger, Johnson County, Ind. Write his son James, Greenwood, Ind. 8. Gustavus, came here with his brother John (to Johnson County, Ind.) about 1860. Gustavus married Martha A. Rush, Sept. 17, 1863. He was born March 17, 1840; she, March 21, 1843. They have three children dead, six living, thus: George and Mary, who died infants, and James, when 31, single; Charles, Emma, Cora, Everett, Otis, and Carl; all married. Write Carl Keesling, Greenwood, Ind., R. R. He lives at the old home and is the "baby."

9. Joseph, was not married. 10. Robert, married Julia Fisher, and died at Max Meadows a few years ago. 11. Martha, married James Repass. Lived at New Augusta, Ind. Write her son, Grover Repass, Farmers Trust Building, Anderson, Ind. He is a dentist. 12. Virginia, married Jim Perkins.

Now, Harvey Keesling's wife, Katy Umbarger, was a cousin to William Umbarger. The Robert Keesling of this set died at Max Meadows, Va., only a few years ago. But I know nothing of his family, if he had one. I suppose he had a family. I have a letter that he wrote me.

The George Kisling who lived west of Wytheville had a large family. John and William came here in 1826, and located north of Greensburg, Ind. John was a Methodist preacher of some note and delivered his sermons in German. He went to Iowa, but William and his wife, Ludicy Smith, died here. He was born January 25, 1803; died December 1, 1884. She was born January 10, 1801; died March 22, 1872. He spelled his name Keisling, and has many descendants here. Some of this set went to Arkansas, others to Missouri, Texas, and elsewhere.

I have a letter from Emory, the son of Peter, son of this George, which tells much, and states that the Keeslings at Max Meadows are cousins to his set—his father said so.

From papers in the Revolutionary War pension claim, S. 16178, it appears that Ditrich (the name also appears as Teter) Kesling, while residing in Rockingham County, Va., enlisted, date not given, and served 3 months as private in Capt. Wm. Knawl's (Nall's) Virginia company.

He enlisted in the fall of 1780, and served 3 months in Capt. John Rush's company, Col. Smith's Va. Regt.

He enlisted in the summer of 1781, and served 3 months in Capt. Reagan's Va. company.

He stated that he also served other short tours, details not given.

He was allowed pension on his application executed October 3, 1832, at which time he was aged 75 years and resided in Clear Creek Township, Warren County, Ohio.

For other Keesling items see pages 352-357; 375.

ADAM MILLER LINE

Miller Lineage of Martha Leftwich Terry-Goodwin

(Mrs. J. H. Goodwin, Roanoke, Va.)

Manuscript furnished by MRS. JOHN S. MACY

Indianapolis, Ind.

First generation—Adam Miller. Adam Mueller was born in Shresheim, Germany, son of Johann Peter and Maria Margaretta Mueller. Came to America in 1704; removed from Lancaster County, Pa., through Maryland to Yorktown, and settled in Orange County, Va., 1726. Naturalized in 1741.

Second generation—Catherine Miller. Catherine (some authorities say Elizabeth) Miller, daughter of Adam Miller, married John Baer, son of Jacob Baer, a native of Switzerland, who located in Pennsylvania about 1728; later removed to Virginia. Catherine's sister, Barbara Miller, married Jacob Baer, brother to John Baer. Barbara Miller Baer's daughter, Barbara Baer, married (2) Jacob Kisling.

Children of John Baer and Catherine Miller

Anna Baer, married Jacob Miller

Barbara Baer, Andrew Andes

Mary Baer, married (1) Harpine; (2) James Kennerly

Jacob Baer, married Mary Karns (Carns)

John Baer Jr., married Elizabeth Miller

Henry Baer, married Catherine Karns (Carns)

Elizabeth Baer, married Michael Trout

Third generation—Elizabeth Baer. Married Michael Trout, son of George Trout and Mary ————. Their children, as copied from the Rader Church records, page 12: Henry, born March 10, 1786; John, born January 1, 1784; Maria, born October 2, 1788; a daughter, born in January 1791. From other records: Elizabeth, born August 13, 1793; George, born January 11, 1782.

Fourth generation—George Trout, son of Michael and Elizabeth Baer, married March 16, 1809, Mary Miller, daughter of Matthias and Mary (Moyer-Schaeffer) Miller.

George Trout and Mary Miller were parents of several children:

Elizabeth, married John Noffsinger

John, married Eliza Jane Shaver

Catherine, married Benjamin Keagy

Anna, married Michael Airhart
Sallie, married John Gish, Salem, Va.
Susan, married Berryman Shaver
Jacob, married Magdalen Etzler
Daniel, married Susan Persinger
Hannah, married John Gussena

George Trout and Mary Miller were married in Rockingham County, Va. Removed to Roanoke County, Va., in 1814. George Trout's sister Elizabeth married Michael Miller, brother to Mary Miller (wife of George Trout). George Trout and Michael Miller were devoted to each other and were prominent in Roanoke County. Their sons, John Trout and Jacob Miller, contributed largely to the building of Roanoke College. Mary Miller Trout was born February 4, 1792.

Fifth generation—John Trout, son of George and Mary Miller Trout, was born in Rockingham County, Va., in 1813. He married Eliza Jane Shaver. He died in Roanoke, Va., a very prominent man.

Children of John Trout and Eliza Jane Shaver: Henry S. Trout and Mary Susan Trout, both of Roanoke, Va.

Sixth generation—Mary Susan Trout, daughter of John and Eliza Jane Shaver Trout, was born in Roanoke, Va., in 1839. She married Peyton Leftwich Terry. Died in Roanoke. She had a daughter, Martha Leftwich Terry.

Seventh generation—Martha Leftwich Terry resides in Roanoke. She married J. H. Goodwin. She has a son and a daughter, Mary Goodwin.

Miller Lineage of Martha Leftwich Terry-Goodwin
(Mrs. J. H. Goodwin, Roanoke, Va.)

(1) Jacob Mueller, married Catherine Charlotte ————
(2) Matthias Miller, married Mary Moyer-Schaeffer, widow of Peter Schaeffer
(3) Mary Miller, married George Trout
(4) John Trout, married Eliza Jane Shaver
(5) Mary S. Trout, married Peyton Leftwich Terry
(6) Martha Leftwich Terry, married J. H. Goodwin

Genealogy of Michael Miller, brother to Mary Miller, wife of George Trout:

(1) Jacob Mueller, married Catherine Charlotte ————
(2) Matthias Mueller, married Mary Moyer-Schaeffer
(3) Michael Mueller, married Elizabeth Trout

Michael Miller was born June 13, 1790, in Berks County, Pa.; died in Roanoke County, Va., April 18, 1862. He married, March 17, 1811, Elizabeth Trout, daughter of Michael and Elizabeth Baer Trout. Elizabeth Trout was born August 13, 1793, and died December 23, 1855. Michael Miller and Elizabeth Trout were married in Rockingham County, Va.; removed to Botetourt County (now Roanoke) in 1816.

Children of Michael Miller and Elizabeth Trout Miller
(Fourth Generation)
Dates of Births at Left

1812 Mary, married Rev. Samuel Sayford
1813 Hannah, married John P. Kizer
1816 Ephraim, died in infancy
1817 Jacob C., married Mary Jane Dyerle
1819 Leannah, married John M. Shirey
1822 Edmund, married Jennie Gilfillan
1824 Michael, died in infancy
1826 Sallie Agnes, married George Kisling, Harrisonburg, Va.
1828 Luther M., died in infancy
1829 John Trout, married Mary Malinda Foutz
1831 George Henry, married Susan Higgins
1833 Elizabeth, died in infancy

Michael Miller was a Tory, George Trout a Whig. Both were Lutherans. They lived about half a mile apart—built substantial brick houses which are now standing. There is a Trout Hall and a Miller Hall in Roanoke College.

Miller lineage of Alma E. S. Macy (Mrs. John S. Macy, Indianapolis:

First generation—Jacob Mueller, came to Philadelphia September 19, 1732. According to his tombstone inscription, at Little Tulpehocken Church, he was born October 22, 1697, and died December 18, 1772. He was married to Catherine Charlotte ——— 55 years. The inscription states that he "left a good name, a sorrowing widow and four children."

His wife Catherine Charlotte was born October 11, 1699, and died April 15, 1777.

Children of Jacob and Catherine Charlotte Mueller
John Jacob, born Sept. 24, 1728, in Europe
John, born Nov. 9, 1733
Mary Elizabeth Barbara, born Sept. 9, 1736; m. Hess
Matthias, born Oct. 18, 1743; baptized by Rev. Joh. Casper Stoever
(Ten children in all—others deceased)

Second generation—Matthias Miller, son of Jacob and Catherine Charlotte Mueller, was born in Berks County, Pa. (near Bernville), October 18, 1743, and moved to Rockingham County, Va., in 1794-5. He was a Revolutionary War soldier. He married (1), about 1760, Susanna Catherine Mueller, daughter of Michael and Mary Catherine Mueller; (2) Catherine Aulenbach, widow.

From Christ Lutheran Church records, Stouchsburg, Berks Co., Pa.: "May 17, 1777, Matthias Miller, widower, and Catherine Aulenbach, widow, married." This wife died in 1782, July 14.

(3) No data.

(4) Anna Maria Schaeffer, *nee* Moyer, widow of Peter Schaeffer. Matthias Miller was a communicant of Rader's Lutheran Church, near Timberville, Va. He died in December 1805 and is buried in the old cemetery of Rader's Church. His 4th wife, Anna Maria, born 1753, died in 1815 and is buried beside him. He was the father of 17 children.

Children of Matthias and Susanna Catherine Miller
(Susanna Catherine born 1740, died 1777)

1762 Maria Barbara, married Ludwig Peiffer (Phifer), 1779
1764 Maria Magdalena, married Frederick Meier (Moyer), 1779
1766 John, married Maria Salome Gilbert
1769 Catherine Charlotte, married Philip Meglin; moved to Ohio
1771 Maria Elizabeth, married George Miller (mason)
1772 Anna Maria, married Matthias Lynder
1774 Susannah Catherine, married Simon Shell
(Two others)

Children of Matthias Miller by second and third marriages, including probably two by the first, as only 7 of the 9 are listed above.

1780 Jacob, married Mary Kipps, 1802
Matthias, married Martha (Massa) Painter, 1808
Philip, married Catherine Painter, 1806
Sevilla, married Abraham Pope, 1796; moved to Ohio
Christina, married David Miller
Second wife, Catherine Aulenbach, died July 14, 1782.
1783 Margaret, married George Bowman, 1803
1784 George, married Rachel Shoemaker, 1808
1789 Conrad, married Mary Bowman, 1810

Children of Matthias Miller and his 4th wife, Mary Moyer-Schaeffer:

1790 Michael, married Elizabeth Trout, 1811
1792 Mary (Polly), married George Trout, 1809
Both moved to Roanoke County, Va.

Third generation—Margaret Miller, daughter of Matthias Miller and his third wife, was born in Berks County, Pa., December 23, 1783; married George Bowman, son of John and Mary Magdalena Surface Bowman, January 20, 1803, in Rockingham County, Va. Fifteen children. Died September 24, 1824; buried in the old cemetery of Rader's Church, near Timberville, Va.

Fourth generation—Elizabeth Bowman, daughter of George and Margaret Miller Bowman, born in Rockingham County, Va., November 25, 1805; married John Sowerwine, son of Peter and Mary Bower Sowerwine, August 8, 1825. Moved to Indiana in 1834. Mother of three children. Died near Cicero, Ind., June 11, 1876. Buried at Cicero.

John Sowerwine, her husband, was born in Rockingham County, Va., Sept. 17, 1796; died June 14, 1876.

Fifth generation—William Sowerwine, son of John and Elizabeth Bowman Sowerwine, was born in Rockingham County, Va., June 17, 1826, the eldest grandchild of George and Margaret Miller Bowman. Married October 9, 1850, Elizabeth Gentry, daughter of Ephraim and Elizabeth Foland Gentry, of Wayne County, Ind. Died November 5, 1906, at Cicero, Ind. His wife, Elizabeth Gentry, was born October 2, 1833; died January 22, 1895. Seven children.

Sixth generation—Noah W. Sowerwine, born February 12, 1856, married Sarah M. Keesling, daughter of Martin S. and Adaline Moore Keesling, August 26, 1877, of Deming, Ind. He resides in Cicero, Ind.

Seventh generation—Alma E. Sowerwine, born Sept. 15, 1880, married John S. Macy, Oct. 4, 1905. One daughter, Margaret E. Macy, born in Indianapolis, Oct. 15, 1906.

Miller Lineage of Laura R. Pence-Bowers
(Mrs. Jesse L. Bowers, McGaheysville, Va.)

(1) Jacob Miller and Catherine Charlotte ————
(2) Matthias Miller and his 3d wife
(3) Margaret Miller and George Bowman
(4) Abram Bowman and Rebecca Bowers
(5) Elizabeth Bowman and Joshua Pence
(6) Laura R. Pence and Jesse L. Bowers

Mrs. Bowers's husband, Jesse L. Bowers, is a descendant of Jacob and Catherine Charlotte Miller through the marriage of Margaret Bowman (daughter of Margaret Miller Bowman and Shem Bowers). Jesse L. Bowers is a lineal descendant of Adam Miller, who settled in the Valley of Virginia in 1726, and of John Bear. John Bear's daughter, Barbara, married Andrew Andes. Mr. Bowers's lineage is through the Andes marriage: Susannah Andes, daughter of Andrew Andes and Barbara Bear, married Jacob Bowers in 1815.

Miller lineage of Leslie A. Miller, Cheyenne, Wyoming, who translated the records of Rader's Church:

(1) Jacob Miller and Catherine Charlotte ————
(2) Matthias Miller and his 3d wife (name unknown)
(3) Conrad Miller and Mary Bowman (moved to Roanoke County, Va., in 1820)
(4) Jacob Bowman Miller and Martha Ann Kelly
(5) Andrew Early Miller and Annabell Z. Orr (moved to Laramie, Wyo.)
(6) Leslie Andrew Miller and Margaret M. Morgan

Reside in Cheyenne, Wyoming. Children, Katherine and Jack.

Mr. Miller's Bowman lineage: (1) George Bowman (2) John Bowman (3) Mary Bowman-Miller (4) Jacob Bowman Miller (5) Andrew Early Miller (6) Leslie Andrew Miller.

Mrs. Macy's Bowman lineage: (1) George Bowman (2) John
Bowman (3) George Bowman (4) Elizabeth Bowman-Sowerwine
(5) William Sowerwine (6) Noah W. Sowerwine (7) Alma E.
Sowerwine-Macy.

For other Miller items see pages 311, 312.

Note On Lacey Spring

(See note by J. W. W. on page 57)

In a letter of December 7, 1929, Mr. J. Frank Blackburn of
Harrisonburg states:

"You will observe that in all the records down to August 15,
1849, mention is made of the spring as 'Big Spring' and not Lacey
Spring. I have examined the records carefully, but failed to find
any reference to any Laceys in this county; however, the deed from
Lacey, if he owned this property, might have been destroyed. I
have been told by Mr. Arch Brock, who owns land adjoining, that
he has seen a deed among Prof. Taylor's papers signed by one Lacey,
which, coupled with the fact that one Samuel Lacey was a witness
to the will of Reuben Harrison, makes it almost certain as to where
Lacey Spring got its name."

ROCKINGHAM WILLS

ABSTRACTS OF BURNT RECORDS

WILL BOOK A

The records of Rockingham County, Va., were partly burned in 1864. The remnants of wills that had been recorded prior to 1864 have been collected from the burnt records and recopied in Will Book A. On the pages here following are abstracts of all the wills, so far as preserved, in the said Will Book A. All personal names are given, and all personal relationships are shown, as far as possible; and many other items of interest are included.

The names of the testators are here arranged in alphabetical order. The date after the name of the testator is, in each case, the date when the will was written. In a few cases the dates are missing.

ALDER, BARBARA; MAY 24, 1848

Plantation on both sides of Smith Creek, adjoining lands of Jacob Rhodes. I give to Deliah Alder widow . . . . John Michael M. Alder dec'd and her two infant children Elizabeth and Mary Michael Alder one equal third . . . . . . her deceased sister. My daughter-in-law Delilah the mother of the children, and David P. Alder and my grandson David Stephens, as he calls himself, a base born child of my daughter Elizabeth Stephens. My son . . . Alder. My son John M. M. Alder's dec'd fami . . . . My son David P. Alder; advancements to him by me in the state of Ohio, some years since. My son John . . . . dec'd. My daughter Elizabeth, wife of Lewis Stephens of Ohio. My daughter-in-law Delilah Alder. My grandson David Stephens and my two granddaughters, children of my son John M. M. Alder, dec'd. My friend Isaac Thomas exr. Witnesses, J. M. Hunter, Isaac Thomas. Proved June 1848. Bond $20,000.

ALTAFFER, JOSEPH; OCT. 25, ——

Wife Margaret. Son Joseph. Daughter Mary. To the missionary society of the M. E. . . . . $300. My sons John and Rubin; daughters Nancy, Catherine, Betsy, and Margaret. . . . Sally Eckard . . . . Witnesses, Stephen Harnsberger, James O'Brien, R. W. Palmer. Proved May 1852. Bond $1200.

AMON, CHRISTOPHER; —— 24, 1830

Pay one dollar to my . . . . Peter and the remainder to be equally divided among my children Jacob, Mary, and Elizabeth. Witnesses, Conrad Marica, Jacob Runkle, Michael Rhinehart, Jonothan Sipe. Proved July 1842 by Jacob Runkle and Jonothan Sipe. Jacob Ammon exr.

ANDERSON, MARY; MAY 10, 1847

Mary Bridges who now . . . . me have $100. My brothers and sisters: George; my brother Jacob Pehtle; heirs of Elizabeth

Andrews; and . . . . of my brother Samuel. My part . . . . .
Pehtles Estate is included in these devises.   . . . John H. Funk-
houser exr. Witnesses, John H. Campbell, George Crawford.
Proved May 18 . . . . by oaths of John Heatwole and George
Crawford. James Anderson, husband of Mary Anderson, dec'd,
granted admr.

ARMENTROUT, ANANIAS; AUG. 1, 1850

David Armentrout to be paid for his trouble and services during
my illness at his house; a decent pair of tomb stones to be put at
my grave. John Sibert to be exr. Balance, if any, to be equally
divided between my 3 brothers. Witnesses, Riley Armentrout, David
Armentrout (Dry Fork). Proved Dec. 1850.

ARMENTROUT, HENRY; JULY 9, 1806

Wife Elizabeth. My children, namely, William, Barb . . . ,
Molly, Elizabeth, Susanna, Henry, Jacob, Ann, Sally. My brother-
in-law Jacob Eargabright and my wife Elizabeth exrs. Proved in
September —— by oaths of John Koontz and Henry Sipe.

ARMENTROUT, HENRY, SR.; APRIL 17, 1847

My son David. Henry Armentrout Jr. Spring branch. My
daughters Henrietta and Delilah Bo . . . . My wife and D . . . .
Anna. My 5 children. My deceased son Samuel (his heirs). My
friend Philip Miller exr. Witness, Wm. P. Richards. Proved April
1848 by George Overholt and Henry Armentrout Jr.

BAKER, MICHAEL; JANUARY 10, 1801

Wife Elizabeth to have home plantation and be exr. Youngest
son Joseph under 17. Sons Henry and John to have house, lot,
tanyard, slaughter house, and lot in Georgetown, Md.; also to have
use of my store in Rockingham till Joseph is 17. Son Michael to
have 400 acres in Green Bryer Co. Michael is under 24. Sons Jacob,
Abraham, and Isaac to have all my lands "on the western waters,"
estimated 1400 acres; these three sons all under 24. Daughters
Catherine, Elizabeth, and Sarah. Son John and son-in-law Jacob
Claypole exrs. Witnesses, Andrew Shanklin, George Dove, Richard
Custer.

By codicil, fifty pounds to be taken from son Michael's part and
given to Isaac, son of Catherine Fulk, if Michael does not marry
Catherine before distribution. Witnesses, A. Shanklin, Richard
Custer, John Folk, Richard Hughes, Probated December 1803.

BARE, ALESABETH; Nov. 16, 1842

To William Southens and his wife Elithabet for their kindness
to me. My wiring eperel or clothing to be eculeey divided amonst
my three sisters, Sue Bore (Bare) and Margaret Bore (Bare), Polly
Fry and my nease Alisabeth Swartz. Witnesses, Henry Burtner,
Samuel Bachtel. Proved Dec. 1842. Henry Burtner qualified as
admr.; bond $100.

BARNS, CHARLES T.; SEPT. 23, 1851

Wife Elizabeth Barnes. My brother and sister. To Lucretia Kennedy, sister of my first wife. My brothers and sisters. My friend DeWitt Coffman exr. Witnesses, Richard Winfield, John Etinger. Proved Nov. 1851.

BARRET, REBECCA T.; NO DATE

My son John W. Barret. My daughter Mary Ann Gorden. Witnesses, Joseph Good, John Billhimer, Isaac Billhimer. Proved Feby 1861.

BAUGHER, NICHOLAS; APRIL 11, 1848

Being old. My wife Ellinor. Son Samuel. Daughter Nancy Long. My daughter Margaret Lawson. The mill tract. Negro woman Clarcey and her daughter Margaret Ellen to be free after death of my wife. My son Samuel Baugher and son-in-law Lewis Long exrs. Witnesses, Joseph Mauzy, Joseph Baugher. Proved Feb. 1849.

BAZZLE, MARGARET; OCT. 5, 1852

To be buried in family burying ground on the premises. My nephew Michael Bazzle, son of Daniel Bazzle. To Jacob Lee, one of the trustees of the meeting house on land conveyed by Richard Pickering for that purpose, $15. To Bro. Daniel the right to convey the water in pipes as it is now conveyed from Spring run through my land, to his house. My sister Ann. My nieces, Margaret, Jane, Rachel, and Amantha, daughters of my brother . . . niel Bazzle. I request my friend Andrew Henton to take my bound boy Algernon Greenwood. Andrew Henton exr. Proved by . . . . and P. P. Koontz. Bond $5000.

BEAR, ANDREW; APRIL 28, 1832

Wife Frances Bear. Son David Bear. Coffee, sugar, wool, money, stove wood for Frances. Son John Bear. Springhouse. Lands I hold in Rockingham County adjoining lands of Rader and Hopkins. My son Samuel Bear. Three grandchildren, namely, Mary Ann, Frances, and Andrew Heneberger, children of my deceased daughter . . . . Watering ditch through the meadows. My son Christopher Bear. My daughter Esther, wife of Wm. Hopkins. My son Jacob Bear. My daughter Anna, wife of David Irick. My daughter Frances, wife of Eli Longnecker. My daughter Mary, wife of Thomas Wayte. My son Joseph Bear. My son Michael Bear. My son Andrew Bear. My son Christian Bear. Witnesses, Joseph Funk, John Gordon, Archibald Hopkins, Jr. Proved March 1842 by John Gordon and Arch Hopkins Jr. David and John Bear exrs.

BEAR, HENRY; JAN. 17, 1851

Son-in-law Dr. Alfred S. Wolfe; a writing of April 15, 1847. Henry Bear has since died, leaving children. My son Jacob Bear to Thomas Kennerly. My son Henry Bear, now dec'd. My deceased son Alexander H. Bear. My son-in-law, Jacob Brubaker. Witnesses,

Wm. C. Lauck, James T. Graves, Peter C. Lauck. Proved June and August, 1852.—Henry Bear Sr. evidently lived near Elkton and Shenandoah City.

Bear, John K.; Dec. 29, 1857

Mercantile business at Mt. Clinton to be continued until expiration of time agreed upon by myself and partner, March 1, 1856. (One of the dates possibly in error.) To my 3 daughters, D. E. Bear, C. A. Bear, S. W. Bear, $1000 each. My wife Nancy C. Bear. Proved (no date) by William R. Warren.

Belin, Jane; March 16, 1852

My sister Gemima Galihu. Remainder equally divided between . . . . ave, Hannah Suthard, and Eliza Galihu. I appoint my friend . . . . Burkholder exr. Witnesses, Reuben Kingree, Wm. Swecker, Wm. Fletcher. Proved April 1852. John Burkholder refused to qualify as exr. Wm. A. Cave granted admr.

Berry, Kenly; July 18, 1842

My daughter Margar . . . My son A . . . R. Berry . . . . all the oats that falls to his shear in the Cr . . . he has on the land of Levi May. My daughter Pheby Jane, wife of John D. Freed, one fall leaf table, one washing tub, one flatiron, etc. My widow Catharine Berry. My four daughters, namely, Margaret A . . . ., Phebe Jane, Elizabeth Mary, Julia Catharine. Witnesses, John H. Rolston, Abraham Haugh, Abraham Vance. Proved Oct. 1842. Levi May exr.

Bierly, Joseph; Sept. 28, 1850

My wife Sarah. Youngest child under 21. I appoint Jacob Bierly exr. Witnesses, Solomon Garber, Jonah S. Roller, I. G. Brown. Proved Nov. 1850. Bond $40,000.

Bierly, Sarah; Nov. 5, 1839

My three sons, Daniel, Jacob, and Peter. Daniel exr. Proved (date missing) by Robert M. Kyle and John Sanger.

Billhimer, Joseph Sr.; June 27, 1842

. . . . Mary Madaline. My land on east side great road leading from Harrisonburg to Ru . . . . being part of the land deeded to me by Mary Beask, to be sold. My son Joseph. My wife Mary Magda . . . . My youn . . . . Sarah Ann arrives at 18. My son John. Two children of my son Jacob, dec'd. My son Abraham. My four other children, namely, Amandus Isaac G. William Mana Sarah Ann. Al Jarnon (Algernon) Gray exr. Witnesses, John C. Cookley, Lewis Lane. Proved Dec. 1842.

Bilhimer, Joseph; Aug. 20, 1851

My wife Mary. My son George, who is afflicted in his eyes. My other sons. My friend John Allbright exr. My daughters, Harriet and Elizabeth. Witnesses, A. Huffman, Wm. Eiler, George Secrist. Proved Sept. . . .

BILLHYMER, HENRY; APRIL 15, 1861

My daughter Polly Trissel (wife of Jacob). My daughter Elizabeth T . . . . . . Gouchenour as (or?) her heirs her full and equal share. My son Jacob Billhymer dec'd, his heirs. To Mary Shumaker $100. She is a kind and affectionate girl to myself and wife in our old and infirm age. My friend and neighbor Lewis Will exr. Witnesses, Samuel K. (H?) Wine, George Brunk. Proved Aug. 1861. Abraham Funk a surety. Bond $2400.

BLACK, WILLIAM; MARCH 14, 1857

My wife Elizabeth exr. No witnesses. Will holographic. Wm. C. Whitmore testified to Black's writing and signature. Elizabeth Black refused to qualify. Adam Showalter, with Jacob Moyers surety, granted admr., April 1861. Bond $200.

BLOSER, JOHN; APRIL 1, 1852

My wife Barbara. My sister's daughter, Maria Runion. My friend David Bowman, son of Samuel, exr. Witnesses, Abraham Knopp, Sr., Sampson Turner. Proved April 1852.

BOSWELL, BETSY; NOV. 14, 1843

My daughter Harriet Peters. My son Thurston Boswell. To William Peters, husband of my daughter Harriet. I appoint David H. Gambill exr. Witnesses, Aug. Waterman, A. St. C. Sprinkel. Proved August . . . .

BOWMAN, ESTHER; JAN. 16, 1837

My daughter Elizabeth. My daughter Esther Miller. My daughter E. Yount. My two granddaughters, they being the daughters of my daughter Magdaline Bright . . . liza Virginia being the elder and Sallie Bright the younger (both under 10). Item, to my grandchildren, viz., Isaac, Magdaline, and David Bright, children of my daughter Magdaline Bright. Item, to my son Samuel Bowman. My daughter Mary Tresset and her husband David Tresset (Trissel?). Item, my two granddaughters Esther Tresset and Anna Tresset, daughters of Mary. To my daughter Esther Miller and her husband Martin Miller. My daughter Magdalina Bright and her husband Peter Bright. My two grandsons, David and John Bowman, sons of Samuel. My grandson Jacob Bowman, son of Samuel; Jacob under 21. My granddaughter . . . . becca Bowman, daughter of Samuel. Witnesses, Benjamin Solomon, W. B. Smith, Samuel Kline. Probated June 1841.

BOWMAN, GEORGE W., SR.; APRIL 5, 1850

Farm I own in the county of Hardy, 120 acres, either of my sons . . . . at the price I paid. My sons Ephraim and William Bowman. My son Noah. Remainder among my children. Fiftee . . . . member (number?) namely Jacob Bowman, Elizabeth Lowerwine (Sowerwine?), Abrah . . . . man, Margaret Bowers, George Bowman, Solomon Bowman, ... Bowman, Shun (Shem?) Bowman, Eliat Bowman, Ephraim Bowman, M . . . Bowman, William

Bowman, John Bowman, Noah Bowman, Sarah . . . . share and share alike. My friend and neighbor Wm. G. Thompson exr. Witnesses, Peter Paulsel, Philip Reedy. Proved May 1850.—George Bowman probably lived near Timberville.

BOWMAN, SAMUEL, SR.; JUNE 22, 1861

My 11 children. On April 21, 1852, I made them all equal (each $1052.13). All gave their receipts except my daughter Cathren, Peter M. Whitmore's wife. She is not living in this Co. I just entered her receipt. I paid David Whitmore Sr. for 100 acres in Botetourt County, Va., which I bought of him for my daughter Cathrin. My son Joseph (I paid the 3 last payments to his wife Mary). My daughter Hetty Crawford. My son William Bowman. My grandchildren. Now my son Joseph's wife might die and he may marry again and have children. They shall have no claim on . . . . estate. Cathrin Whitmore's 3 children. My son Daniel. My sons Benjamin and Samuel. My son Simon. My son John. Lizzie Hopkins. I have a note on James Crawford. Witnesses, Jacob Miller, Jackson Showalter. Proved Jan. 1862. Bond $10,000. Simon Bowman exr. Sureties Michael Whitmore and Wm. R. Hopkins.

BRANNER, GEORGE; MARCH —, 1861

My wife Rebecca C. Branner. My son Franklin Branner. My children under age to be supported, &c. Youngest will be 21 in 1872. My slaves. My daughter Eliza and her husband Dr. Homan. In 1872 my home farm (except the E end which has been surveyed off by J. J. Bowman and attached to the Knopp land), about 200 acres, to my wife. The house and lot I own in Timberville to be sold, within six months after the M . . . . Road is completed to Timberville. My wife Rebecca and my son Fran . . . Branner exrs. Witnesses, John H. Thomas, Abner K. Fletcher, Wm. G. Thompson. Proved by John H. Thomas and Wm. G. Thompson. Isaac F. Branner and Rebecca exrs. Bond $7000.

BRENEMAN, CHRISTIAN; NO DATE

My wife Anna: No other names remain.

BRENNER, JOHN; JANUARY —, 1859

Wife Elizabeth. To Rebecca Bare. My nephew and namesake John . . . . Bare, son of Rebecca and Naason Bare. My Miller land and the Stoner farm. To Mary Branner and her heirs. She is . . . . wife of Franklin Brenner. The Pomfrey land and . . . land, the Reuben Bare farm and the Brocks Gap L . . . . Give to my Brothers Sisters. Witnesses, Wm. M. Sibert, Benj. Hoover, Martin Garber. Proved April ————. Bond $15,000.

BRIGHT, PETER; JANUARY 13, 1803

Of the county of Shenandoah. My tract of land in Rockingham, 13½ acres, joining Sheetz and Altz land. (This may be in Shenandoah.) My wife. My 3 children, minors: George Bright, Peter Bright, and John Bright. . . . and her two youngest John Billhimer and Mary Billhimer, minors. My friends Joseph Bowman and Frederick Kline exrs. Witnesses, Peter Cook, Lawrence Speagle, Martin Garver. Proved March 18— by Peter Cook and Lawrence Speagle.

BROCK, ELIZABETH; FEB. 3, 1860

My servants to be freed (certain ones named); others to Erasmus Rinker. To Isaac, freeman of color by my father's will, $400. Graveyard to be purchased and to remain as such. My nieces Mary Douglas (?), widow of D . . . . Douglas, and Elizabeth Stickley. My nephew Erasmus Rinker exr. Witnesses, J. N. Gordon, George Keezel. Proved Jan. 1862. Sureties Daniel Stickley, J. Milton Moore, Wm. Quick.

BROCK, FANNIE E. C.; MAY 8, 1852

My mother. My brother John P. Brock exr. Witnesses, Georg Fausette, Isaac Thomas. Proved October 1852. Bond $3000.

BROWER, JOHN; OCT. 24, 1842

My land on beaver Creek . . . . Mill on said land and my interest in the carding and . . . . machine be sold. My farm on which I now reside on Silver Creek. My wife Hannah. My youngest child Lydia, under 21. My land in Ohio. My son Samuel. My three sons Daniel, David, and Enock. My son David the NE quarter of section 4 in Allen Co., Ohio, 176.15 acre, to be valued at $3.50 per acre. My son David the SE quarter of section 4 in Allen Co., Ohio, 160 acres, to be valued at $3.50 per acre. My son Enock the south half of the NW quarter . . . . My land lying in the North Mo . . . . in mines, hollar or all my interest in said land. Witnesses, Martin Miller, A. W. Brown. Proved Nov. 1842. David Brower exr.; bond $14,000.—One "David" above should probably be "Daniel," in land division.

BROWN, JOHN; FEB. 22, 1848

I John Brown of Bridgewater. Old. My wife Elizabeth. Son John G. Brown. Son Daniel . . . . Son I. G. Brown. H. Daniel Brown. Son H. D. Brown. Son Daniel's wife Mary. H. David Brown. My daughter Mary Coyner, wife of Arch'd R. Coyner, land on which she now resides . . . . in the county of Harrison, Va. My daughter Elizabeth Coyner, wife of Addison H. C. . . . . And I believe it was old Father Marton Coyner dec'd desire and will that the bond which H. Dan . . . hold against David Coyner should be paid out of his estate, and so it is my . . . . John Sellers, husband of my daughter Catharine, dec'd. Lydia, wife of Harry H. Waynand. Priscilla Deal, wife of Saml. C. Deal. My son Herman Daniel Brown. Codicil of May 5, 1849, witnessed by Wm. R. Speck, John Williamson, A. W. Brown. Appendix Dec. 7, 1849, provides $100 for Marshall College, Pa., of German Reform Church. Witnesses, A. W. Brown, Christian Hoover. Proved Oct. 1850 by Wm. R. Speck and Allan W. Brown. John G. Brown exr. Bond $5000. —"Father Brown," noted Reformed preacher. Buried at Friedens Church.

Burner, Isaac; Feb. 1, 1862

My wife. My son-in-law, Samuel Niswander. My daughters. The children of my daughter Elizabeth Cool. Anna Wine, wife of John Wine. Sarah, wife of David Roderock. The names of Elizabeth's children: Henry Cool, Lydia (wife of Henry Sheets), Isaac Cool, Jacob . . . ., Samuel Cool. My daughter Susannah, wife of Abraham Young. Barbara, wife of Samuel . . . . Lydia, wife Henry Niswander. My friend Benjamin Miller exr. Witness, John Burkholder. Proved by David Rolston and Eli Andes. Bond $6000. Sureties Jacob Miller and John H. Cromer. L. W. Gambill clerk.

Burtram, Julius; (No Date)

Wife Eve. To my daughter Polly the loom, &c. To my daughter Lydia a loom, with all the guns, spools, warping bars, and all the apparatus belonging to it, &c. My son Andrew. Andrew exr. Signature of Julius proved by Philip Miller Sr. and Philip Miller; in the origin . . . . being in the German language. H. J. Gambill, clerk.

Byrd, Andrew (?); 1823(?)

Sick and weak in body. My wife Ruth Byrd. . . . . land that I own in Shenandoah County it b . . . . . nds of her father's estate that fell to her share . . . My friend Isaac Sam . . . Witnesses, . . . ham Byrd, ... Byrd. Proved August 1823. Isaac Samuels exr. Daniel Zirkle, Lewis Zirkle, David Brookhart, Henry Miley appraisers.—Evidently lived near the Fairfax Line, vicinity of New Market.—N. B. The clerk's note states, "the last will and testament of Abram Byrd, Jr. dec'd was presented," &c.

Campbell, John H.; —— 30, 1850

My wife Dorcas. To my grand daughter's children . . . . . . daughter Lavinia R. Hopkins, dec'd. Land called the Bowman farm. All my grand children. My grandson Wm. C. Hopkins. My daughter Margaret Erwine. My daughter Elizabeth Shumate. My daughter Nancy Bare; also 203 acres called the Berry Farm. My grand children, children of my daughter Margaret, $3000; to wit, John H. and Andrew Erwine. To my wife, lan . . . . Hopkins daughters, Margaret Erwine, Elizabeth Shumate, and Nancy Bare. The children of my four daughters. Witnesses, Jos. Burkholder, James Flick, Henry E. Rexrodes, B. D. Bowman. Proved June 1850. David R. Hopkins and Francis M. Erwine exrs.; separate bonds, $42,000 each.

Carpenter, John; July 13, 1841

All my lands in the state of Kentucky, and my tract of land in the county (Rockingham) Known as the Allford tract. My wife Sarah. Her daughter Eliza, wife of Enos Keezel. My said daughter Eliza. My son William Carpenter, all my lands . . . . mills on Smiths creek in this county and also my two . . . of land called and known as the "Step" and the "Fridley" tracts. I also give my said son William Carpenter $4700. My daughter Eliza Keezel. Witnesses, S. H. Lewis, Charles Nicholas, Peter Koontz. Proved Jan. 1842.

Carr, John; Oct. 23, 1861

My 10 children: John, Jacob, Samuel, Joseph, Betsy, Frances, Caty, David, Fredric, Abraham; some living north, out of the Southern Confederacy. Caty's husband, Eli Spitzer. My friend John Zigler exr. Witnesses, Abraham Knopp Sr., Levi Helbert. Proved Dec. 1861. Bond $5000.

Click, Frederick; May 7, 1821

My sister Elizabeth Shaultz. My sister's daughter Peggy Moore. My mother Margaret Click to hold possession of the plantation where we now live. At her death the land to be sold and divided equally among Elizabeth Click, Peggy Moore, John Click, and Michael Click. Witnesses, Joseah Smith (?), John Homan, Sr. Proved August 1821 by oaths of Josiah Smith, John Zommers. John R. Homan made admr. with will annexed, Margaret Click and Betsy Click having refused to qualify.

Click, John; March 14, 1851

My 2 sons Isaac and Joseph. Click's Mill works. All my children. My son Jacob; son Abraham; daughter Catharine Swartz; daughter Elizabeth Burner; my sons David and Samuel. Jacob Burner, husband of Elizabeth. Son (?) John. To Dunkard Church $100. Witnesses, Jacob Wine, David Garber, John G. Brown.—Probably lived near Bridgewater.

Coe, Lucy; Jan. 19, 1839

My just debts . . . . those I am due to Freeborn Garrison Bryan . . . . my trusty friend Freeborn Garrison B . . . . out of my estate I may be entitled to in the states of Kentucky or Tennessee . . . . . to my son James Coe. John Chrisman exr. Witnesses, Johothan Funk, Daniel Garber, John Brown. Proved Feb. 1843 by Jonothan Funk and Daniel Garver.

Coffman, Christian; June 20, 1848

My wife Catharine. My daughter Elizabeth Lincoln. My other daughter. My daughter Elizabeth's children. My grandson Christian C. Bear, under 21. Samuel Bare exr. Witness, . . . Bowman. Proved . . . by . . . Bowman and Joel Funkhouser. Bond $15,000.

Coffman, Samuel; Feb. 1857

My 3 children . . . . son Benjamin, my daughter Polly and her heirs . . . . and my daughter Katharine and husband. . . . rother and Polly wife of Will . . . Wikle . . . . Equally divided between Rebecca Thomas wife of . . . . and my daughter Katharine Miller, wife of John M . . . . Provided said Sarah . . . . Hoover gets married or have any issue before the abo . . . . time the said legacy is to be paid to her husband . . . . My friend Abraham Knopp exr. Witnesses, Jacob Hoover, Wm. Knopp, Wm. Bull. Proved Jan. 1860. Joseph Miller and Jacob Miller sureties. Bond $7000.

CONROD, BARBARA; Nov. 16, 1847

To my grandchild Elizabeth Fry $20. .... y Fry shall have my burough (bureau). Sally Fry shall have my sadle. Polly Fry shall have a good bed. Jacob Fry shall have all my outstanding moneys. .... in my long illness and he is to pay . . . my Doctor bills and funeral expenses. Note I hold against Andrew Coffman. Witnesses Michael Huffman, Henry Billhimer. Proved May 1848 by Michael Huffman and Burto . . . Seever. Jacob Fry granted admr. Bond $400.

CONRAD, SUSAN; AUG. 24, 1801 (1861?)

My daughter J. E. Conrad. My daughter Virginia C. Conrad. My granddaughter Emma Nettie Bear, to be hers at the death of her mother, Margaret A. Bear. Residue of my estate to be equally divided among . . . . nine children, Jennetta E., William A., J. Mitchell, Margaret A., Elizabeth S., Martha C., Mary F., George O., and Virginia C. My negroes, part of the estate of my late husband. Witnesses, Geo. O. Conrad, J. E. Harnsberger. Proved Nov. 1801 (1861?). Bond $2000. L. W. Gambill, clerk.

COOK, JOHN; Nov. 3, 1859

. . . . y Cook and his heirs. Witnesses, Jacob Miller, J. I. Kite, S. B. Jennings. Proved July 18—. On motion of Robert B. Cook, Joseph H. Conrad and . . . . W. Miller, who made oath . . . . Derick Pennybacker, Samuel P. H. Miller, Charles . . . ., Edward S. Yancey, John C. Walker, John H. Wartmann, ... B. Borst their securities . . . a bond in the penalty of one . . . . and thirty-five thousand dollars . . . . .

COONTZ, MARTIN; MARCH 12, 1805

My wife Christena Coontz. To Mary Bargle 50 acres of land, adjoining John Lemon's land by the lick Hill beginning at the lower corner of P. Lemon's land, her natural life time and the sum (?) of her Henry Bargle maintains her he shall after her death have the land. To Barney Whetebaker and Christian Whetebaker 25 pounds apiece. Philip Coontz and Peter Coontz exrs. Witnesses, John Reeves and Franklin Hancefora (her mark). Proved June 1805.

CRATZER, CATHARINE; DEC. 17, 1855

To John Miller or Samuel Wine, trustees or deacons of the Church . . . . Dunkerts or German Baptists, being the church of which I am a member, for the benefit of the poor, $17. Every instalment being in all the sum of $51. To the heirs of my brother Joseph Cratzer dec'd, viz., John Crotzer, Simo . . . and Catharine Panabaker or their heirs. To the heirs . . . Sister Rosina Simons dec'd, viz., Anthony Simons, Benjamin . . . . Christian Simons, and Susana Simons. To Elizabeth Burgholder or her heirs. Heirs of my sis Susana Bowman dec'd, viz., Joseph Bowman . . . . Bowman, Simon Bowman, Anna Whitmore, Catharine W . . . ., Hetty Crawfort, Benjamin Bowman, Elizabeth Hopkins . . . . Bowman, Samuel Bowman, and William. My brother Christian Crotzer. . . . Cratzer,

heir of my brother John Cratzer . . . . Witnesses, John Kline, John
B. Kline. Codicil March 1, 1859. Sister Elizabeth Burkholder and
brother Christian Cratzer now dead. Heirs of Elizabeth Burkholder,
viz., Joseph . . . . holder, Jacob Burgholder, Anthony Burgholder,
Jessy Burghol . . ., Simon Burgholder, and John Burgholder. Heirs
of brother Christian, viz., Anna Christman, Lidia . . . ., Gideon
Kratzer, Catharine Shaver, Elizabeth Jennings, Susan . . . . hart,
and George Kratzer. My brother Joseph Kratzer dec'd. I will that
Jessy Burgholder be my exr.

DASHNER, CATHARINE; JAN. 6, 18—

Am old and weak in body but of perfect mind. My daughter
Cristenia Dashner to have my land if she pays the payment and
further pays Anna Sholtz 3 pounds that I owe her. Also I give my
daughter Anna Sholtz one bed and half my kitchen furniture.
Witnesses, Philip Miller and Peter Miller. Proved August 1821 by
Philip Miller, Peter being dead. Translation of memorandum
written on back of the will proved by Michl. Myerhoeffer.

DAVIES (DAVIS), ROBERT; SEPT. 11 ——

Wife Nancy Davis to have my negro woman Aemy with her
issue; also my negro man Harry; also house and plantation, &c. My
negro man Tom to be sold. My children James, Nancy, Anne, John,
R . . ., Samuel, Ruth. My brothers James Davies and Walter
Davis exrs. Witnesses, Ben Erwin, Ruth Davis. Proved November
1804.

DEAVER (DEVIER), NANCY; OCT. 20, 1853

My son Hiram K. Deaver $1000, when he is 25, if he has used
well what he received from his father. My daughter Martha Jane
Bruffy. My daughter Lucy Catlet (widow). To her son George
Allen and her daughter Ady Wiloby Catlet (both under 21). My
sons, Ewin Deaver, Hugh Deaver, Giles Deaver, William Deaver,
Allen Deaver, and . . . . . daughter Elizabeth Dinkle. My friend
John A. Herring exr. Witnesses, Daniel F . . . ., Jackson Rhodes,
M. H. Harris. Codicil Jan. 28, 1861. Granddaughter Aida Catlet.
My daughter Martha Jane Bruffy. My daughter Lucy Catlet.
Catharine Deaver, my daughter-in-law. Grandson George Catlet.
My daughter Elizabeth Dinkle. Witnesses, J. O. Hensell, Wm. P.
Byrd, M. H. Harris. Proved May 1861. Saml. Dinkle granted
admr. Bond $6000.

DEEDS, PHILIP; DEC. 9, 1846

My son Adam Deeds. My daughter Amy Armentrout. My
daughter Patsa Armentrout. My daughter Sallamy. My wife.
Witnesses, James Botton, John Shumaker, Isaac Botton. Proved
Nov. 1851.

DEKEY (DECKEY), ROBERT; JANUARY 7, 1804

"I Rober . . . being old." To my wife Eme . . . Dekey; my
six sons and three daughters, towit: Adam, Robert, James, Solomon,

Willia . . . , Mar . . . , Rebeakah and Emelia. Adam and Robert (sons) exrs.

Witnesses, John Armentrout, ——— Armentrout, Junr. Probated 1816. Jacob Roads gave bond to administer, with will annexed; exrs. refused to qualify.

Denton, Benjamin; No Date

His will proved by John Blain and John Weast. John H. Funkhouser, one of the exrs. named therein. Bond $15,000. Sureties, Simon S. Harmon, James R. Crawford, Allen C. Bryan. . . . . G. Denton, the other exr. named in the will, refused to qualify. L. W. Gambill clerk.

Depoy, Christian; January 1860

My brothers Philip and Charles and . . . . Brother John Widow shall have equal shares of my real estate. I direct that brother Charles Son David Harvey shall . . . . Proved Feby ——— by Jacob Bowman and Abraham Wenger. L. W. Gambill clerk.

Depoy, Mary; June 7, 1853

My sister C . . . . My brothers John . . . . Philip Depoy. Witnesses, Solomon Messerley, Abraham Wenger, Henry M. Wenger. Proved Feby ———.

Detrick, Adam; Sept. 7, 1847

Wife Elizabeth. Her brother, Peter Brown. . . . . The residue of my estate to my brother . . . . . ters, or their heirs (if they my brother and sisters are not living) my full brothers and sisters . . . . also my half brothers and . . . . My brother Jacob's son William. My friend Michael H. Harris exr. Witnesses, David Wise, Michael, Daniel Feete. Proved July 1849. Bond $24,000.

Dever, Sarah; Dec. 15, 1848

My niece Martha Ann. My land on North River and in the counties of Orange and Pendleton and which was inherited from my father and mother . . . . her and Margaret Dever. It is my will that she Martha Ann Dever have one of my beds. My brother Francis C. Dever. My two sisters Polly and Melinda. My niece Sally Dever, daughter of John Dever. Sally under 15. Witnesses, Wm. C. Blakemore, C. R. Harris, Wm. Robertson. Proved April 1849.

Dingledine, Balser; Jan. 28, 1862

Wife Margaret. My two sons, Jacob . . . . . Samuel. Until Samuel is 18. Nine children, viz., John, Margaret, Adam, Mary, Balser, ... , Peter, Jacob, and Samuel. To Cather . . . , a daughter of my first wife, $20. Witnesses, Jos. A. Mitchell, N. Britton. Bond $5000. Sureties Jacob Zircle and Christian Brunk.

Duff, James; 1843

Advanced in life. My friend Isaac Hardesty . . . in trust. . . . . . in event of Strothers death without legal heirs. My four daughters. I give to Strother my Negro man Daniel. I give to Strother a bed . . . . he will know the one . . . it is the one his mother selected for him. My four daughters . . . . Francis Smith and Elizabeth Kenney of Rockingham, and Mildred Relfe and Harr . . . . of the state of Missouri. Son Strother. My daughter Harriet Luc . . . . I appoi . . . . . in law the Hon. Daniel Smith and John Kenney of Harrisonburg esquire exrs. Witnesses, John Ebersole, John Long, Aug Waterman. Proved July 1843. Bond $12,000.

Dundore, Mrs. Catharine; Mar. 19, 1850

What her will was was certified by John Dundore and Geo. W. Kemper on the above date. She called the said John Dundore and Geo. W. Kemper on March 16, 1850; Told them her will. To her daughter Maria Jones. Bequest to Fountain, son of Benj. F. Kemper, $50. Balance of her property equally to her six living daughters, Matilda Kemper, ... Jones, Minerva Holt, Virginia Farra, Columbia Fry, and Huldah Has . . . . The said Catharine Dundore died the next morning. Writing presented to August court 1850. Admitted to record. Nuncupative will.

Ebert, Andrew; May 22, 1804

To my wife Mary Elizabeth the plantation whereon I now live, her bed, furniture, and $100 in money. To my sons John, Enoch, Philip, Frederick. Daughter Elizabeth. Witnesses, Jacob Kiser, Daniel Kiser. Proved July 1804.

Eiler, Margaret; March 24, 1850

The estate of my son Samuel, dec'd. My nephew John Pirkey. My following nephews and nieces: Rebecca A. Michael, Solomon A. Pirkey, John Pirkey, Claressa Kern, Nancy Pirkey, David I. Pirkey, Benj. T. Pirkey, Alex. E. Pirkey, Mary E. Pirkey, Oval Pirkey, and Harvey Pirkey. Witnesses, William Briwt, Addison H. Paine. Proved June ————. John Pirkey and Jonathan Peale exrs.

Ervin, Jacob C.; June 29, 1842

My wife Jane . . . . Clements and my daughter Harriet. My daughter Anna Scott. My granddaughter Eliza Jane Poage of Ohio. My son Clements. Harriet single. Eliza Jane Poage of Highland County, Ohio; her grandfather Francis. Witnesses, J. G. Brown, . . . hn Dinkel Jr., ... Shickel Jr. Proved April 1848. Bond $15,000. Clerk E. Coffman.—Jacob C. Ervin lived near Bridgewater.

Ervin, John; Feb. 16, 1811

My wife Phob . . . . My son William. My wife to have as many of my books as she may choose. My daughter Ann Shanklin . . . her husband Thomas Shanklin. Children of the said Ann. My daughter Mary Pence . . . her husband John Pence. My daughter Hannah Mall . . . My son John Ewin. My son John Ervin. My daughter Elizabeth Nichols. My granddaughter Adella Ervin, under 21. In hands of . . . . James Ervin for the use of my daughter Anna Shanklin. My daughter Hannah Mallary. My son William Ervin and my friend Daniel Smith exrs. Witnesses, Margaret Berry, Reuben Harrison, Philip B. Harrison. Proved June

1822 by oaths of Reuben Harrison and Philip B. Harrison. William
Ervin (Ewin) qualified; Daniel Smith refused.—It is probable that
this testator was John Ewin rather than John Ervin.

Evers, George; April 4, 1846

My wife (Margaret), my 3 daughters, Elizabeth Mary, wife of
George Niffner (Hiffner?); Margaret Ann and Sarah Catharine.
My son George W. Evers). Witnesses, Abraham Breneman, Peter
Breneman. Proved Nov. 1849. Margaret Evers and George exrs.

Eversole, Jacob; April 8, 1804

To my wife Mary her choice of two cows, the oldest of the two
sorrel mares, one of the two smaller iron kettles, her saddle and bridle,
2 chairs, her spinning wheel, &c. My 5 oldest children namely, Peter,
John, Christian, Jacob, and Barbara. My four youngest children,
Mary, Joseph, Samuel, David. My friend H———, two sons John
———exrs. Witnesses, John Berry, Aron Solomon, Robert Shanklin,
Samuel Bowman. Proved April 1804 by oaths of Robt. Shanklin
and Samuel Bowman. John and Jacob Eversole, exrs., give bond in
sum of $15,000.

Flook, Elizabeth; April 30, 1857

My daughter Phebe Flook. My son Daniel Flook. My husband, Henry Flook, dec'd. My daughter Catharine Armentrout, wife
of Henry. Witnesses, Wm. W. Carpenter, Jacob Hoster (Hosler),
Harriet Whitmore. Proved June 1861. David Flook, John Sibert,
and Samuel Sheets granted admr. Bond $5000.

Flook, Henry; Aug. 12, 1841

My son David. My wife, children, and grandchildren. My
daughter Molly Armentrout, wife of Ph . . . . Armentrout, of the
State of Ohio. My daughter Sally, wife of Philip M . . . . My son
Jacob Flook. My grandchildren, Daniel Arm . . . trout Lydia Ann
May (formerly Lydia Ann Armentrout) M . . . . Armentrout and
Augustin Armentrout, children of my daughter Elizabeth and her
former husband Augustin Armentrout 1 give and bequeath one-tenth
part of my estate, but as one of my grandchildren Daniel Armentrout
is of unsound mind I give and bequeath h . . . portion to my exrs. as
trustees for his use. My son Daniel. My daughter Catharine, wife
of Hen . . . Armentrout, one-tenth, &c. For benefit of my daughter Phoebe, who is of unsound mind. My daughter Dianna, wife of
Michael. My sons David and Daniel exrs. Witnesses, George Kar-
eckhoff, Lewis Karickhoff, Thomas Clarke. Proved Nov. 1841.

Flory, Jacob; Feb. 14, 1842

Wife Catharine. My children, Soloman, Joel, John, S . . . .
Michael, David, Ann, Sarah, Lydia, Mary, to be put out to good
people. Soloman the oldest. Son Samuel. My exr. to see that they
can read rite and un . . . . the arethmatic tolerably well; that is, the
boys; the girls ow . . . . read well. I wish my daughter Sarah to
be put out to So . . . suitable place until she is 18. My friend

Soloman Garber exr. Witnesses, Saml. Cline, Samuel Coffman, Michael Flory. Proved April 1842.

FOWLER, WILLIAM; APRIL 8, 1796

My mother A . . . . her and Easter Towler my sister all my land goods . . . . . William Herring Esqr. and John Guin exrs. Witnesses, John Guin, Henry Hansbarger, Mary Hansbarger. Proved May 1823 by oaths of Henry Hansbarger and Mary Hansbarger. Daniel Kysor granted adm. with will annexed.

FRANCIS, CALUP (CALEB?); JUNE 7, 1856

My children, Mary Augustus, Albert, and Douglas. I appoint Hiram A. Kite exr. Witnesses, Henry C. Hammer, W. D. C. Covington, Wm. C. Kite.

FULK, CATHARINE; JUNE 17, 1851

To Magdalena Fawley, my mother. To . . . . niece Deanna Huffman $25. My late husband. To Catharine Hulva, wife of Solomon Hulva, 1 red heifer, &c. Lands of which my father G . . . . died seized. The residue of my estate . . . . Adalena Ritchie, Susan Fulk, and my . . . . Witnesses, ... Newham, Isaac Fulk, Joshua Fulk. Proved March 1852 by W. T. Newham.

FULK, GEORGE; APRIL 12, 1850

My wife. To Lilas Fifer $100. To Catherine Hulvey (formerly Catherine Richey) . . . . dollars. To my nephew James Fulk. My friend Wesley T. Newham exr. Witnesses, Levi Hess, John Riddle, Isaac Riddle. Proved April ———.

FULS, JOHN; JULY 18, ———

Lower part of my tract, 119 acres, adjoining the County line to an agreed line made between him and his brother Sebastion. To my son Sebastian. The agreed line made between him and his brother John. Another line made between him and his brother Philip. His brother David. His sisters. My son Jacob. My son George to get the place he now lives on on the other side of the river, 93 acres. My son Sebastian exr. Witnesses, several in German. Proved June 1806. The exr. having refused the execution, Reuben Fuls was made admr. with the will annexed.

FULTON, ELIZABETH; JUNE 21, 1805

To my brother James Fulton. My sister Margaret Johnston to have one black gou ———, one pair of stockings, one striped Cotton petticoat, one handkerchief, &c. My sister Hana Deuston. My sister Quency Magell to have one dark Calligo gound and one cross bard Calligo gound, one shift, one pair of stockings, one Yellow petticoat. To James Fulton, son of my brother Thomas Fulton. To Maria Fulton. To Elnor Little. To Elizabeth Cochran. My brother-in-law James Magell exr. Witnesses, John Black, Thomas W. Collough, Samuel Cochran. Proved March 1806.

GAINES, JAMES; FEB. 28, 1852

Wife Rebecca. Son Robert B. Gaines; daughters Mary, Elizabeth, Catharine, and Lucenda Gaines. Witnesses, Samuel Nisewander, John Swartz, Adam Thomas. Proved May 1852.

GAMBILL, HENRY J.; NOV. 7, 1847

Wife Margaret. My 5 children, Charlott Sn . . . W. Gambill, D. Holmes Gambill, Isabella, and Richard Ga . . . . in the proportion of 3 to 5 Charlott, Littleton, and Richard . . . . Slaves; farm. My son Littleton. My son-in-law, Abraham Smith, and my sons Littleton, Holmes, and Richard exrs. Witnesses, Isabella L. Gray, Margaret D. Effinger, Annie Gray, Robert Gray.——The date (Nov. 7) was corrected to Dec. 7, 1847. This correction was made Dec. 8, 1847, and witnessed by Robt. Gray and Isabella L. Gray. Agreement between D. H. Gambill and Isabella B. Gambill, in reference to the will, made Feb. 20, 1848. ——Large estate. E. Coffman, clerk.

GARBER, CHRISTIAN; JUNE 18, 1849

My daughter Anny Snell . . . . her husband Hen . . . . Henry Snell. My son Solomon exr. Witnesses, Samuel Miller, Joseph Miller, Abraham Sager. Proved Aug. 1850.

GARBER, DANIEL; FEB. 17, 1842

Wife Elizabeth. My books. My son Daniel Garber. Cellar under the old house. My carryall. Land between the stage road and Turn . . . . joining the lands of George Kyle and others; also my plantation in Augusta Co., on Thorny Branch, joining Christian Huddle, dec'd, and Christian Clines and others, on which Rubin Folly Sr. now resides. Land in Rockingham, south side of Dry River, joining Martin Speck and Andrew Rogers, 58 acres, to Joseph Miller, John Wine, Daniel Shickel, and Jacob Miller, in trust, income to be used for the poor members of the German Baptist church. Witnesses, John Brower, Isaac Long, Martin Miller, John Bowman. Proved Dec. 1849.

GARVER, SOLOMON; AUG. 20, 1848

To be buried according to the rites and ceremonies of the Dunkard Church. To my nieces and nephews my sister Sally's children Catharine Mary Sally John, Noah, ... Jacob, Elizabeth excepted all children of my sister . . . . The said . . . . Mary Sally, John Noah Daniel and Jacob Kife (Rife?). My nephew (by marriage) Peter Richy. Witnesses, John Arehart, Elias Nave, Levi H. Byman (Ryman?). Proved November . . . . Peter Richy exr. Bond $9000.

GILMER, LUCY; SEPT. 25, 1838

Three neat tombstones at the graves of my father and mother and of my brother George at Lethe. To my nephew Robert Grattan. My sister Mrs. Grattan. My nephew Peachy R. Grattan. My nephew George Grattan. My niece Lucy G. Harris (formerly Lucy G. Grattan). My sister Mary Peachy Gilmer my Scott . . . . mily Bible and to my sister, Elizabeth Grattan, my Davies sermons and my clock. My niece Elizabeth Gilmer (wife of my nephew). My nephew George Taliaferro 12 neat silver table spoons. Witnesses, S. H. Lewis, John F. Lewis, Samuel H. Lewis, Jr. Proved Jan. 1850. Robert Grattan (her nephew) exr. Bond $12,000.

GILMER, MARY; OCT. 1, 1805

To my son George Gilmer 5 negro men; 5 horses. The remainder of my horses to my four daughters, Peachy Gilmer, Lucy Gilmer, Francis Walker Talliaferro and Elizabeth Grattan. To my son Thomas Gilmer a negro boy Henry, &c. Other negroes disposed of; cattle, sheep, &c. To son George $300 out of the debt due from the estate of George Nichols. My late husband P. R. Gilmer. My son-in-law, Robert Grattan. Witnesses, Christian Kyger and Jacob Nicholas. Proved November 1805.

GOOD, DANIEL; 1849

My son Henry Good. His brothers and sisters. His sister Mary Good. My granddaughter Susanna Good, daughter of my deceased son Daniel of the state of Ohio; Susanna under 18. His two brothers and sister. Jacob Good, David Good, and Mary Good. Witnesses, Joseph Funk Sr., Jonathan Funk, Christian Burkholder. Proved Feb. 1850.

GOOD, ELIZABETH; NOV. 28, 1844

To the church which I belong to . . . . at Garber's meeting house. To my friend Jacob Ritchie. Solomon Garber exr. Witnesses, Joseph Byrd, Isaac Burner. Proved Nov. 1848. Bond $700.

GOOD, PETER; DEC. 26, 1821

Wife Anna. My two sons Peter and David. My two sons Peter and Daniel. Their two sisters Anna and Elizabeth. My son Daniel shall have the plantation whereon he now lives. My son Daniel to have 4 acres of the old tract whereon I now live. My sons Peter and Daniel exrs. Witnesses, Jacob Burkholder, William Dunlap, Jacob Knisely.—It seems evident that "David" as first written above should be "Daniel."

GRAY, ROBERT; MARCH 17, 1859

On account of death of my son John W. Gray (Jan. 12, 1835), of my afflicted daughter Rebecca I. Gray (Jan. 9, 18—), and of my wife Isabella L. Gray (April 4, 1857), I change my will. Algernon S. Gray has rec'd his portion. To his daughter Rebecca I. Gray. My daughter Sally W. Gray to be her guardian. To Ora Anne D. Gray and Henrietta Gray . . . . of Alg. S. Gray $9000 (for both). I appoint Algernon guardian for his 3 last named . . . . without security. My son Douglas Gray. My son Jouette Gray. My son Robert A. Gray . . . . my big meadow. Hill Top, which includes the Cedars and the woodland purchased of the Liskeys. My daughter Harriet . . . . her husband William . . . . To Robert A. Gray my law books. All my other books to my daughter Sally W. Gray. Proved Dec. 18— by Allen C. Bryan and James Kenney. Bond $20,000.

Grove, Abraham; March 17, 1855

I have commenced to build a dwelling—I wish it finished. My Mole Hill timberland—about half of it to be sold. My son David. My wife Sophia. Youngest daughter, Hannah Margaret. My daughter Elizabeth, wife of Daniel Heatwole. My daughter, Catharine Mary. Witnesses, Gabriel Heatwole, Albert Long, Joseph Coffman. Proved June 1855. Daniel Heatwole (son-in-law) exr. Bond $20,000. Sureties, John S. Heatwole, Peter Whitmore, Peter Swope Jr.

Grub, Peter; Jan. 9, 1849

My wife. . . . . until my youngest child is 21. My neighbor John Sibert exr. Witnesses, Michael Bazel, James Botton. Proved Feb. 1849.

Haines, Frederick; Jan. 9, 1811

My wife . . . . My three sons.

Daughter Barbara. John Kaylor should have $50 as his wifes . . . . Daughter Barbary Kaylor. Son Frederick. Son Peter. My blacksmith's tools. My son John. My sons John and Frederick exrs. Witnesses, Samuel Sellers, John Sellers, Michael Rhinehart, Joseph Mauzy. Proved April, 1812, by oaths of John Sellers and Michael Rhinehart.

Halterman, George; Sept. 2, 1858

My wife. My son Jacob J. Halterman. My son Adam Halterman. My land in Hardy County. My land in Rockingham County. My line to the county line; near foot of North Mountain, with Adam Tusing's line to C. Tusing, crossing the Lost River road to the West Mountain, &c. My rifle gun. From Jacob J. Halterman's line to James Fitzwater's line. My son George Halterman. My daughter Judy Halterman. My son William Halterman. Witnesses, George W. Dove, Moses Moyers, George Halterman, William Fitzwater. Proved Dec. 1861.

Hamer, Henry Sr.; Aug. 22, 1831

My wife Molly. As I have heretofore given and deeded to all my children (except Isaac and William) the lands that I have allotted them, . . . Isaac and William to have the balance. . . . . pine corner . . . . me and Bennet Raines. Isaac and William exrs. Witnesses, James Dean, Jacob Conrad, John Fray. Proved April 1841. (Will of Henry Hammer, Sr., deceased.)

Hansberger, Emanuel; July 25, 1844

My brother John Hansberger . . . . William I. Hansberger. To Mary Conrad, now living in Boomville, Cooper Co., Mo. To brother John Hansberger that portion of my estate in Va. and Wm. I. Hansberger that portion in Mis . . . . Witnesses, Jacob E. Hansberger, Adam Hansberger. Proved Nov. 1849.

Harnsberger, Jacob; March 25, 1852

Part of the home farm on which I now live, on west side of the public road leading through said farm from the Iron Works to

Brock's Gap. My wife Elizabeth. To my granddaughter, Mary Young, child of my dec'd daughter Mary, $1000. My children. My dec'd son John. His children, some under 21. My slaves. My son George Harnsberger exr. Witnesses, John W. G. Smith, Wm. Henry Tams. Codicil March 25, 1852. Same witnesses. Second codicil July 20, 1860. My son Daniel has since died, without issue. My daughter, Jane Koogler, wife of John Koogler. Nicholas K. Trout exr., with my son George. Witnesses, W. H. Tams, N. K. Trout. Proved Oct. 1861. Sureties, Wm. Claton, Peter Wise, Joseph Click, Henry H. Peck, Samuel Whitmore, W——— Howell, John Dinkle, Wm. Patterson, David Garber, and John Harper. Bond $80,000. —The Iron Works referred to were probably those on Mossy Creek, above Bridgewater.

HARNSBERGER, NANCY; FEB. 27, 1847

To buried in the burying ground at Elk Run Church. I give to Marg . . . . Keter, formerly Margaret C. Miller, daughter of Henry Miller, Jr. To Sar . . . Miller (woman). To Martha viz. Miller. To Susan H. Miller. To P. Henry Miller. To Robert C. Miller. To G. H. Miller, Hiram Harise Miller and Mary Seg Miller. To Henry Miller Jr. Witnesses, Wm. P. Roudabush, Daniel Harlin, Joseph H. Kile. Proved Aug. 1848.

HARRISON, DAVID; FEB. 27, 1846

Wife Elizabeth. Son William. Son Reuben. Land which my son William purchased of my son Reuben, beginning at Daniel Harrison's corner in the middle of the Valley Turnpike road . . . . crossing Dry Fork . . . . two pines Wenger's corner, &c. My 4 daughters. My sons John, Nathaniel, Daniel. My stock in the Valley Turnpike. The heirs of my brother Josiah Harrison. My son Reuben N. Harrison exr. Proved by Michael Sellers and Geo. W. Gaither. E. Coffman clerk.

HARRISON, GEORGE W.; 1821

My negro boy Henry who now is in the possession of my father Ezekiel Harrison in the state of Kentucky shall be sold into good hands until he is 21—then be free. Also my negro men Cason and Tom Setty. Catherine Harrison, daughter of my Unkle Reuben Harrison of Harrisonburg. Reuben Harrison, Joseph Cravens, and Philip B. Harrison exrs. Witnesses, Joseph Thornton, Peter Effinger, Robt. Harrison. Proved November (year missing).

HARRISON, HANNAH; SEPT. 12, 1803

Widow of John Harrison. My eldest son, Wm. Harrison. To my second son, Zebulon Harrison. Daughter Phebe Harrison. Sons Henry, John, Isaac, Abraham. Abraham under 21. "My two well beloved brothers Jacob Lincoln and Lincoln my soul Executors." Witnesses, Nathaniel Harrison, Josiah Harrison, William Tallman. Probated December 1803.

HARRISON, JOHN; APRIL 17, 1806

Wife Betcey to have my negro girl named Nell, my sorrel horse with a bald face, 2 milch cows, &c. My daughter Sifselah to have one good bedstead, furniture, my dark bay horse I got of Dorman Sofland (Lofland?), one milch cow, &c. All my children except Thomas who has already received his full share. The three children of my daughter Pheby to take share as if—mother was alive. House and lot I now live on in Harrisonburg to continue in possession of my wife Betsy. My daughter Pheby Regan's children. Reserve from Isaac Kiser and his wife's share $125; also from Michael Dashner and his wife's share $98; also from James Campbell and his wife's share $108; also from Henry McEttee and his wife's share $46. My son Thomas and my brother Reuben exrs. Witnesses, And. Shanklyn, Robert Rutherford, Benjamin Tinder, Nancy Tinder. Proved Sept. 1806.

HARRISON, PEACHEY; FEB. 26, 1848 (?)

My son Peachey Rush Harrison, my medical library and medicines. I wish my son Peachey Rush to continue his practice. My daughter Margaret, Frances (one person). My library of miscellaneous and other books not medical to be distributed after my death among the members of my family . . . . excepting Watson's Tracts and Barrows Sermons, which I give to my son Gessner. My wife. Her daughter Margaret Fran . . . . Stevens. My daughters Mary Jane or . . . . Elizabeth (both single). Should the title be deci . . . . . of the Methodist Episcopal Church South shall re-fun . . . . sums paid by members of the M. E. Church . . . . pur-chases of the property intended to me made of me, and pay the . . . . from Dr. Michael H. Harris and Jacob Rohr, as agent of the M. E. Church . . . . clair Kyle, and the balance of the purchase money due me . . . . . . property shall be held by my heirs for the use and benefit of the tra . . . . eachers of the M. E. Church South; &c. My daughter Caroline Elizabeth. Witnesses, Jacob Rohr Sr., John Daugherty, J. R. Stevens. Proved May 1848. William G. Stevens and Peachey R. Harrison exrs. Bond $22,000.

HAUK, GEORGE; MARCH 20, 1822

My . . . .Carbrand hanke . . . . as long as . . . . will remain my widdow . . . . My children Christtean Elizabeth George Catharine Jo . . . . Baggy Henry. My son Chr . . . . My son Henry. Daughter Catharine. Daughter Elizabeth. Sons Henry and . . . . John exrs. Witnesses, Henry Sipe, Jesse Thompson, John T. Kerickhofe. Proved May 1822.

HEAD, URIAH; SEPT. 3, 1849

Franklin Taylor and Harvey Taylor shall have my land whereon I now live, 134 acres. Erasmus Taylor and Mary Catherine Taylor to have $600, when they come of age. Jacob B. Houck to be my exr. Witnesses, Dewit Grada, Siles Taylor, Ambrose Grada. Proved Nov. 1849.

HEASTON, JOHN; SEPT. 5, 1861

My wife Isabela the Peterfish tract I now live on. My children, under 21. Witnesses, Lewis F. Gaither, Charles W. Dovel, A. G. Segler. Proved Nov. 1861.

HEATWOOLE, DAVID; 1842

Son Shem Heatwool. Another tract near the Mole hill. My heirs, namely, Gabriel Heatwoole, Francy Hildebrand (formerly Francy Heatwoole), the heirs of Elizabeth Shank, dec'd (formerly Elizabeth Heatwoole), Christian Heatwoole, David Heatwoole, Abraham Heatwoole, Shem Heatwoole (being the same that is to possess the lands and pay over to the balance of the heirs), John Heatwoole, the heirs of Anna Suder (formerly Anna Heatwoole), and Henry Heatwoole. My several children. My son Abraham Heatwoole exr. Witnesses, Jacob Rohr Sr., Daniel Thomas, Jacob Thomas. Proved April 1843.

HELFREY, JOHN; AUG. 11, 1804

My wife Christnina. My son Daniel. Two daughters, Elizabeth and Charlott, to have equally the plantation lying on Kinel's Ridge after my wife's decease. And to my two daughters Dolly and Cat . . . . "one Shillings." Wife Christnina and son Daniel exrs. Witnesses, Jno. Armentrout Jr. and ———. Proved December 1805.

HENRY, SAMUEL; JULY 1, 1846

I am advancing in life. My son, Stewart Henry. My daughter, Maria G. Shacklett. My daughter, Frances S. Lam. My trusty friend and son-in-law, Samuel Shacklett, exr. Witnesses, Allen C. Bryan, John Kenney, Alg. S. Gray. Samuel Shacklett refused to qualify. Henry Shacklett granted admr. Bond $25,000.

HENTON, BENJAMIN; APRIL 16, 1804

Wife Sarah. Son David, minor. Each of my two Eldest sons and my daughter Gean. David second and Gean third choice and . . . . shall take the horses at the appraisement at part . . . . their devide and they shall assist themselves to their horses to move the family to Kentucky or to any other place their mother shall choose. Two of my daughters. . . . Ohio river 200 acres I give to my sons over and above their divide with my daughters. I allow John the land at 300 pounds with paying the others their equal part. Thomas Hopkins and David Rolston and my son John exrs. Witnesses, Archebald Hopkins, Mary Rolston, Ruth Hopkins. Proved March 180—. Exrs. give bond of $25,000.

HENTON, MARGARET; APRIL 28, 1860

Her natural life and after his death. To all the lawful children of David H. La . . . . Witnesses, Jacob Dundore, Joshua A. Ruffner, Joseph Burkholder. Proved May ———.—A fragment.

HERRING, ELIZABETH; 1820 (?)

. . . . ter Elizabeth Herring one bed, &c. . . . . ter Rebecah Davis a Chest drawers, &c. My daughter Edith Shanklin. My daughter Margaret Porter. My son William S. Herring. . . . . . presented to me by the late Gabriel Jones Esqr. My grandsons Wm. H. Porter Wilson Porter, they being children of m . . . . Margaret Porter. To my . . . . Elizabeth S. Shanklin a child of my daughter Sarah Huston dec'd. My granddaughter Ca . . . . the second

daughter of my last daughter Sarah Huston dec'd. My grandsons
. . . . H. Huston and Wm. H.Huston and my granddaughter Sarah
Husto . . . . of my late daughter Sarah Huston dec'd. To my
grandson Wm. Benja. Chipley, son of my late daughter Abegail.
To my G . . . . ter Elizabeth H. Chipley. To my granddaughter
Elizabeth S. Herring, daughter . . . . Alexander Herring one white
counterpine to her and her heirs. To my daughters Elizabeth
Herring and Rebecah Davis. My children Alexand . . . Elizabeth
Herring, Edith Shanklin, Rebecah Davis, Margaret Porter, and
Willi . . . . . Herring and the children of my daughter Sarah Hus-
ton, dec'd, and the . . . . . of my daughter Abegail Chipley, dec'd.
My son William . . . . and my son-in-law Walter Davis exrs.
Witnesses, . . . Lockridge, . . . Lockridge, ... S. Smith, ...
Smith. Proved February 1821 by oaths of William Lockridge and
Daniel Smith, motion of Walter Davis and Wm. S. Herring exrs.

HESS, PHILIP; ——— 13, 1850 (?)

My two daughters Fanny Gordon and Betsy Minigh. To my
wife. My son John Hess. Witnesses, T. H. Erwine, John Fleming,
Jacob Simmers. Proved Aug. 1850.

HINTON, MARGARET; JULY 11, 1859

My son Joseph Henton, to him the Taylor land; then to his
children. All my children to have bonds from Joseph. Witnesses,
Wm. Eiler, R. C. Mauch. Proved July 21, 1863, by Wm. Eiler and
A. C. . . . . The other witness (Mauch) dead.

HOMAN, JOHN R.; MAY 22, 1861

My wife Mary Homan. My plantation lying west of the M. G.
(Manassas Gap) Railroad. My son Wm. D. Homan. My lands
east of the M. G. Railroad. My house and lot at Orkney Springs.
My slaves. My youngest child under 21. My daughters: Dorcas,
Frances, Margarete, and Mary. My son John C. Homan. My
daughter Dorcas Jenkins. Witnesses, B. Rust, J. F. Branner, Wm.
G. Thompson. Proved Jan. 1862. Bond $12,000. Surties, B. F.
Lincoln, Henry Neff, Wm. A. Pence.

HONER (HARNER ?), CHRISTOPHER; MARCH 1806

Wife Catherine Honner to have 12 bushels of good wheat sent to
the mill and brought back to her yearly, &c. My children Christenah
Catherine Adam Mary Philip, John, Michael and my son Christopher's heirs; except my son Philip which is to have 10 pounds more,
and my sons John and Michael 6 pounds each more; &c. My two
well be . . . sons Adam Howard and John Howard exrs. Witnesses,
Nathaniel Harrison, David Harrison. Proved April 1806. Here the
name is written as Christopher Howard.

HOOKS, ROBERT; JULY ———

To my son Elijah Hook. To my daughter Mary Murry. To
my grandson James Murry. To my daughter Martha Hook. My
other children, namely, William Hook, Easther Belshey, Robert Hook,

Jean Read, and George Hook. Witnesses, James Rutherford, John Snap, Geo. Huston, George Hawk. Proved Sept. 1804.

Hord, James; March 6, 1806

Wife Mactabna. My eldest son John, minor. His sisters Sally and Elizabeth. My second son William. My wife and Benjamin Kite exrs. Witnesses, Jacob Kysor, Peter Runkle, Michael Lormia. Proved April 1806.

Huffman, Anthony; June 26, 1861

My wife. My daughter Asberina Cornelia. My daughter Caroline Matilda Link. My daughter Ann Elizabeth Lowenback. My daughter Frances Koontz, My son John's share to his children, he to be their guardian. Deed of trust against John Koontz to be null and void. My son David. Negro slaves. My son-in-law, Jonas Lowenback, and my son John W. M. Huffman exrs. Witnesses, Joseph Lowenback, Robert Cox, Abraham Koontz.

Huffman, Barnett; April 16, 1846

My daughter Julia, wife of Abraham Nisewander, and her children; house and lot she now occupies, the land I purchased of Michael Howard. My daughter Elisa, wife of Joseph Flick, and her children; house and 10 acres she now occupies, part of my father's old place. My wife Peggy. Witnesses, Edwd. H. Smith, Adam Andes, John Andes. Codicil May 28, 1850. Witnesses, E. H. Smith, Abraham Byrd, John Andes. Proved Dec. 1851.

Hummel, Frederick; March 12, 1850

My 2 oldest daughters. My daughter Catharine. I want Wm. E. Coffman to settle my estate. Proved July 1860 by John Bowman and William E. Coffman. —— Fred Hummel signed in German.

Hurley, Sarah; Nov. 3, 1851

I Sarah Hurley, a free woman of colour, of Rockingham County, &c. To my husband, though a slave by the name of Banaster. . . . sister and brother. I appoint my friend M . . . . Lofland exr. Witnesses, William Gaither, Nelson Keysair. Proved March 1852. Smith Lofland granted admr. with will annexed. Bond $250.

Irvine, Harriet S.; Feb. 10, ——

My sister Anny Scott of th . . . . of Indiana $600. To . . . . . Frances Harriet Scott $200 and my breast-pin. To foreign missionary society of the Presbyterian Church $100. To the 3 little daughters of George R. Gibbons each one bed quilt. To Harriet Adaline Wynant $100, &c. I appoint my old friend J. G. Brown exr. Witnesses, John Dinkel Jr., John Williamson. Proved March 1852. —In vicinity of Bridgewater.

Jones, Gabril; Dec. 1, 1804

My wife Margarett. Land in Rockingham; in Bath; slaves; stock; &c. Son-in-law John Harvie of Belvadier. My daughter Ha . . . . the wife of John Hawkin and to her son Wood Hawkins who I understand is entended for the profession of the law. All my law books I give to William Herring. To Gabriel Lewis and Warner Lewis, my grandsons. Their father John Lewis. Their late grandfather Fielding Lewis in the town of Fredericksburg. My wife's nephew Andrew Lewis and son of my late friend and brother-in-law, Thomas Lewis, who had the misfortune to lose his arm in his country's service, an annuity of 12 pounds. To Mrs. Jane Doughthat, formerly Miss Jane Price, the same that lived with . . . . and sister to the present register of the State, 100 pounds, in regard to her own merits and the great respect I bear to the memory of her late mother at whose house I lived during my sickness and the operation of my eyes. My other grandchildren. I owe no debts, if there be any they must be very trifling. I cannot recollect at this moment so much as a dollar. Residue to be equally divided among my grandchildren— this not to extend to my great-grandchildren, not to my grandson Wm. Strother Jones; his father-in-law Dr. Buckner. My daughters Harvie and Hawkins (my daughter Lewis being dead). My wife and my friend James Allen of Shenandoah County, atty. at law, exrs. Written with my own hand. Proved Nov. 1806 by oaths of Jonathan Shipman, Charles Lewis, Daniel Smith, Tobin R. McGahey.

Keezel, Henry; April 20, 1859

My wife Mary, ... with the exception of stone house and lot in Keezletown, which is at present occupied by my . . . . ter Amanda Jane Long, her husband and family. To George Keezel, as trustee for my daughter Am . . . . Jane Long, the house and lot she occupies. My son Enos. Daughter Mary Ann Sheets. Daughter Elizabeth Dud . . . . Son-in-law, John Long. George Keezel my exr. Witnesses, Allan C. Bryan, John C. Woodson, Benj. B. Ewing. Proved March 1861. George Keezel exr. George P. Burtner surety. Bond $4000.

Keezel, Pheby; 1821 (?)

My lands to my 3 brothers, William Keazol, George Keazol, and Andrew Keazol, which is an undivided share, in my father's land. To Jacob Roalston's 2 children, namely, Margaret Rolston and George Roalston $50 each, after they are 21. To my mother all the money now . . . . Witnesses, Henry Sipe, Richard Ragin. Proved August 1821 by Hy Sipe and Richard Ragan.

Keller, Catharine Ann; Feb. 22, 1849

To be buried according to rites of Presbyterians. My brother Henry Keller. My sister Teny Arginbr . . . . . I also will that my two gilt pitchers, the largest one, be the property of Margaret Keller and the smallest one be the property of Mary Dobill. . . . . . my esteemed . . . . laws Jacob Earman and Samuel Slusser. Witnesses, Franklin Pence, Edw. S. Kemper. Proved Aug. 1849. My brother Henry Keller exr.

Keller, Philip; May 4, 1849

My brother Henry Keller. My nephew, Philip Keller. Land on Foughts Run . . . . stream that runs by Freedons Church. My brother William Keller. My nephew Lewis Argabright. Also I leave Philip Boon, son of Abram Boon in the state of Indiana, $400. Also John Boon, son of Abram Boon, in Indiana, $100. Also Elizabeth Boon, daughter of Abram Boon, $100. To Lewis Argabright, son of John Argabright, $200. To Freedons Church $100. To the Union Church $10. Witnesses, Franklin Pence, Edward S. Kemper, Henry Pence. Proved June 1849.

KIBLINGER, CATHARINE; FEB. 6, 1822

My daughter Margaret Nicholas, as formerly Margaret Kiblinger, to have $200, also one counter pane of a blue and white color and one bead quilt. Jacob Kiblinger, John Kiblinger, Anny Keller (formerly Anny Kiblinger), Polly Kiblinger, and the aforesaid Margaret Nicholas. Witnesses, Samuel Hersher, Thomas W. Darnall, John Earman. Proved March 1822. John Nicholas and Jacob Kiblinger granted administration.

KIRTLEY, ST. CLAIR D.; JULY 23, 1849

Wife Catharine, half of the tracts known by the old farm, and bounded by Henry Miller . . . . the River, Daniel Dovel, John Peterfish, the Deck slipe (?) and John Cook, including the mansion, &c. Machinery, negroes. An issue in expectancy. If it be a son it is to be educated on the eastern side . . . . the Blue Ridge after it attains the age of 12; . . . . but if it should be a female my wife may control it. My brother Francis W. P. Kirtley is deranged . . . . . Debt due to the heirs of Henry Conrad, dec'd, from my brother Frances W. P. Kirtley shall be paid. After death of my wife, the oldest nearest male relation by the name of Kirtley . . . . shall have the estate I have given to her. I should like the old tract always kept in the Kirtley name. My wife Catharine and my brother-in-law Henry . . . . Lofland exrs. Witnesses, A. S. Wolf, Thomas Dolin. Proved Feb. 1852 by Joseph H. Conrad and . . . . . Kite. Henry M. Lofland exr. Bond $20,000.

KITE, JOHN, SR.; AUG. 18, 18—

Wife Christena. My son John. My children. Philip Kite the heirs of Daniel Kite, dec'd. Michael Kite Chri . . . . . of John Fultz Adam Kite Susanah wife of Benjamin . . . . . . Wife of Simeon Lucas Elizabeth wife of Jacob Steep Mary . . . . . Henry Peterfish . . . . give Simeon Lucas the house and other improvements where he . . . . . . lives . . . . Except my . . . . Adam who have rec'd $42 and Simeon Lucas who . . . . rec'd $392, which are to be deducted out of their legacies. My son . . . . . Kite and my friend Jacob Strole exrs. Witnesses, Joseph Sampson, Reuben Foltz, ... Cob Foltz. Proved . . . . by . . . . John Kite and other exr. refused to qualify.

KITE, WILLIAM; SEPT. 22, 1798

My children, John, Martin, Adam William and Elizabeth. My wife Catharine. My two youngest sons Reuben and Benjamin. Reuben and Benjamin to maintain my son John. My son William.

My daughter Elizabeth, married to Philip Kisor. Witnesses, Philip Lohng, Jacob Kiser, John Kite. Proved July 1806.

KNOPP, PHILIP, SR.; FEB. 15, 1845

My son John the farm (167 acres) which I purchased of Jacob Good. My son Andrew the tract I now reside on. My son Philip. My 3 daughters, Mary, Magdalana . . . . Sarah. Witnesses, Daniel Crist, John Crist. Proved March 1850. Benj. F. Reed admr.

KOOL, JOHN; JUNE 8, 1852

My daughter Mary Kool, by my last wife; under 21. My other children. Witnesses, Jacob Cool, Samuel Flory. Proved August 1852 by Samuel Flory and Samuel Cool exrs. Bond $2500.

KOOL, PHILIP; MARCH 11, 1805

Also my plantation, 105 acres, where the Widow Bright now lives. Remainder of my money to be divided among two of my brothers and one of my sisters. My sister Catherine. My brother John Kool. My brother Ernest Kool. My friends John Kool and Jacob Garber exrs. Witnesses, John Roler, Martin Garber, Peter Lohr. Proved April 1805 by oaths of John Roler and Martin Garber.

KOONTZ, JOHN; MARCH 22, 1852

My daughter Hannah, dec'd; her children. My daughter Christina. My daughter Catherine. My daughter Mary. My son Joseph. My friend and nephew, Eli H. Koontz, exr. Witnesses, Wm. C. Jennings, Lewis Sayton. Proved May 1852. Bond $500.

KOONTZ, PETER P.; JUNE 12, 1861

My wife Elizabeth Ann. My negroes, not to be sold into the hands of traders unless it be for a fault. If I die before the house I have commenced is completed, my wife may finish it. My seven children, David Edwin, Reuben Franklin, Ann Eliza, Mary Elizabeth, Philip Peter, Wilson Eli, and William Abraham. My son David Edwin, having left home long before he was 21, against my will, and married without my consent, has received his share in advance (to be so considered). Witnesses, Jacob P. Rhodes, Henry Layman, Eli H. Koontz. Proved Aug. 1861. John Cowan security on bond.

LAIR, CATHERINE; JULY 9, 1799

To Rader's Church 5 pounds. To son Joseph Lair. Daughter Catherine Newman. Son Andrew Lair. Son Matthias Lair (dec'd). Daughter Elizabeth Trumbo (dec'd). Daughter Mary Ruddle. Daughter Margaret Custer. Son John Lair. My friend Henry Stolp exr. Witnesses, Jno. Barnett, Benj. Yount, Frederick Frizer. Probated January 1804.

LAMB, JEREMIAH; 1842 (?)

My wife. Augustine Coffman to have use of my . . . . as long as my wife Nancy lives for taking care of my wife Nancy. She to have interest on money, two beds, four hogs, and all the Bee Scalps, &c. At the death of my wife my Plantation to be divided by a line running from the Poin . . . . the branch crosses the fence between me and Leonard Tutwiler to the Door of th . . . . House and from thence by a strait line to where the branch crosses the fence . . . . . me and Steven Roadcap, and that Augustine Coffman have all the land on . . . . . , on which the said Coffman lives. . . . . between the said Augustine Coffman, Annie Lee, and Jacob Shaver in equal porti . . . . Witnesses, R. Gratton, Henry Bushong. Proved March 1843.

LARD (LAIRD), JAMES; MARCH 1, 1789

To my son James Laird 200 acres, part he now lives on, from Miller's line; &c. To Mary Lard, daughter of James Lard, one red cow, &c. To son David 200 acres, part he now lives on. To my daughter Mary Lard. To "my neffew Sarah Laird one red and white cow." To "my neffew James Lard son to David . . . . Mallatow boy named Sam." Sons James & David exrs. Witness, David Tayler. This will of "James Laird Senr." was probated December 1803. Proved by oaths of Adam Carpenter and Adam Faught.

LAYMAN, MICHAEL; DATE MISSING

Wife Elizabeth. Friend Abraham Fisher, exr. Will proved by oaths of George Huston and John Kite. ——— S. W. Williams, clerk.

LEWIS, BENJAMIN

Only a fragment; no date; no other name; no significant statement, except that he is of Rockingham County.

LEWIS, DELIA M.; AUG. 5, 1857

Intending in a few days to leave Harrisonburg for Richmond to place myself under treatment of a physician for the cure of a sore on my breast supposed to be a cancer, I make my will, &c. My daughter Ann T. Lewis my gold watch and chain. My sister Susan E. Fletcher all the remainder of my property. My brother Abner K. Fletcher exr. Proved Feby 1861 by Samuel Shacklett and M. Harvey Effinger. Bond $1200.

LEWIS, THOMAS; JULY 21, 1845

To Delia M. Lewis. Decree in chancery against Samuel H. Lewis, admr. of Thos. Lewis Jr. To Richard P. Fletcher my black mare, &c. My friend Rich'd P. Fletcher Sr. exr. Proved by Robt. R. Fletcher and . . . . . Thomas C. Fletcher granted admr. Bond $500. E. Coffman clerk.

LINCOLN, ABRAHAM; MAY 14, 1851

My wife Mary. The Vanpelt tract, purchased by me from Joseph Coffman, John Strayer, and others. My daughter Elizabeth Maupin and her husband D . . . . Maupin. Land on which I reside, on the west side of the road leading from Christian Kratzers to Timberville, including . . . . my father gave me west of said road, &c. My 3 single daughters Caroline Amanda, Josephine Rebecca, and Dorcas Sarah. My lands lying east of said road leading from C. Kratzer's to Timberville, called my pine land. My interest in the Rader Mill property in partnership . . . . . . ck Pennybacker. My daughter Mary Elizabeth Maupin and Re . . . . her husband my entire interest in the land they live on. Said interest . . . . three of the heirs of Jacob Lincoln, John, Dorcas and Rebecca. Numerous negro slaves. My 4 daughters. My land in Brock's . . . . Each of my four named children. My wife Mary and my son-in-law . . . . Maupin and Michael Homan exrs. Witnesses, C. C. Spears, Jacob Lincoln. Proved July 1851. Bond $20,000.

LINCOLN, JACOB; FEB. 7, 1822

Land which I purchased of Tunis Va . . . . My yellow girl Jane and her two children . . . . also negro man Jerry son of Kate . . . . one mare . . . . three cows. My son David. My son Jacob. My tract adjoining Custer and Strock, also about six acres . . . Eyman tract which was deeded to me by Benj. Bryan. Tract which I purchased of Thomas Lincoln whic . . . . . willed to him by his Father. . . . . Which I purchased of John and Handle . . . . . Land patented to me adjoining . . . . the lands of John Morris. Bond which I assigned . . . on the Revd . . . Bryan. My daughter Dorcas Strayer . . . . in law Mathew Dyer . . . . in the county of Pendleton . . . . Daughter Rebecca. My daughter Hanner Evans. My daughter Polly Hinton now a resident of Kentucky. My daughter Abegal Coffman. A negro boy called Sam and a negro girl named Emily. My daughter Elizabeth Chrisman. Negro girl named Ann. My wife. My pine lands. My three sons-in-law, John Strayer, Joseph Coffman, Joseph Chrisman, exrs. Witnesses, Joseph Bywaters, John Rader.

LINCOLN, PRESTON; APRIL 26, 1848

My wife and children. My friend Samuel Bare exr. Witnesses, John H. Funkhouser, Jacob Bowman, John H. Campbell. Proved June 18—. E. Coffman clerk.

LISKEY, ROBERT; APRIL 15, 1858

My wife. To Franklin Liskey $150. To Harvey Liskey $50. All my children, including Franklin and Harvey. Witnesses, John T. Harris, Allen C. Bryan, Samuel Shacklett. Presented to court Feby 1861. On motion of Abraham Liskey and Martin Liskey, a commission was issued. Later admitted, the same month. James J. Miller and William Liskey sureties. Bond $100.

LOFLAND, DORMAN; MAY 23, 1849

Wife Peggy. Slaves, &c. My four daughters, Polly Lofland, Jane Ann Lofland, Catharine Lofland, and Caroline . . . . . d, each $3000. My children, excepting my son Hazlett Lofland and my son-in-law William Smith—they already paid. William Smith, husband of my daughter Eliza. My mountain tract, known as Shepps Spring Tract. Quarter-acre (present burial ground) on my home plantation for a burial place. My son Henry M. Lofland exr. Witnesses, Robert M. Kyle, George Keezel, Philip Cole. Proved Aug. 1849. Bond $75,000.

Long, Issac; ——— 1849 (?)

My son Isaac Long, the tract I purchased of Daniel Long and the said Long purchased of Daniel Fisher. My wife Barbara. To the church of which I am a member $150. My six children—son John; daughter Frances; son Daniel; son Samuel; son Isaac; another daughter, perhaps "Any." Witnesses, Alexander Kyger, William Kyger, Daniel Miller. Proved Dec. 1849.

Ludy (Leedy?), John; Sept. 12, 1849

My son Abraham part of farm on which I reside as surveyed and plotted by George Conrad, 1849; also 20 acres I purchased of the Liskies. My son Hohn (John?). Also 20 acres I purchased of James Clarke, which is woodland. My 5 oldest children. My son John. My wife Mahola. My sons Jacob and Daniel. My 3 daughters, Betsey, wife of Daniel Brown; Catherine, wife of Christian Myers; and Peggy, wife of Henry De . . . . . baugh. My seven children. A man by the name of John Moyers has long lived with and worked for me for his victuals and clothes; he is now old and infirm—each of my children to pay him $5 a year as long as he lives; and he is to choose which of them he will live with. Witnesses, L. M. Hunter, John Kenney. Proved May 1850. Bond $8000.—A long will. John Ludy (Leedy) probably lived near Harrisonburg.

McAtee, Jane; Nov. 19, 1847

To my daughter Betsy McAtee. Witnesses, M. H. Harris, W. M. McAtee, Abner Smith. Proved August . . . . Elizabeth McAtee exr. Bond $800.

McCausland, William; Oct. 5, 1841

The whole of my estate . . . . shall be divided into three equal shares, one share of which shall belong absolutely to my slave Abraham, and the other two shares equally is my slaves Rachael and Mitilda, in the manner hereinafter described: . . . to Rachael all the beds and bedding which she has been in the habit of using and calling her own . . . . . and $200 for her unwearied attention and fidelity to my sister for years, and especially in her last illness; to Mitilda beds, &c.; to Abram beds, &c.; to Jim beds, &c.; also his freedom and $100. To the son of Balsey Armentrout (I think his name is Branson), who is supposed to be my illegitimate child, $500. Algernon S. Gray trustee for Rachael and Matilda. Branson under 21. I am the last of my race of all the kindred who come with me from a far . . . . . Algernon S. Gray and John Rush exrs. Witnesses, Sam'l Shacklett, Henry Brown. Codicil Oct. 19, 1842, John Nicholas appointed exr. in place of John Rush, dec'd. Witnesses, Jacob Sherry, Joseph Good. Proved March 1843. Exrs. bond, $20,000.

Manning, James; Jan. 14, 1849

My mother and three children John, Robert and Julia. My said 3 children, to wit, John, Robert, and Julia. My friend Joseph Billhimer exr. Witnesses, E. H. Smith, William Gather. Proved Feb. 1849.

MARTZ, HIRAM; OCT. 7, 1861

My eldest son, Benjamin Franklin, dec'd. To his 3 children.
My 3 sons, Addison B., Daniel G., Michael J. My daughter Adaline
(single). My youngest son Julius (under 21). My five children
. . . . . . Henry Lee, to make his legacy equal with theirs. My
brother Jackson Martz and my son Addison B. Martz exrs. Witnesses, Daniel B. Reid, Dorilas Martz. Proved Nov. 1861. Dorilas
Martz and Madison West sureties. Bond $50,000.

MARTZ, JACOB; FEB. 16, 1850

My son Dorilas Martz. My daughters—some married, some
unmarried. My smith tools and old irons. Ann Homan, Mary
Homan Bathsheba I Orts, Catharine Martz, Grace Martz, Lydia
Martz and Dorilas I Martz my six daughters and son my only heirs
except two grandchildren Crawford and Elizabeth Rosenbarger to
whom I will $300 each. Witnesses, Madison West, Curtis Yates,
Dorilas Martz. Codicil Feb. 16, 1850. Same witnesses. Proved
April 1851. Jackson Martz and Dorilas Martz exrs. Bond $40,000.

MATHENY, STEPHEN; AUG. 7, 1848

My wife. My granddaughter Elizabeth. My 12 children. My
son Elijah Matheny exr. Witnesses, John Blain, Eugenia Anderson,
Abner Blain. Proved May 1849.

MATHEWS, DANIEL; DEC. 21, 1841

For the recovery of against Robert and Cyrus McCormick . . . .
Chancery at Staunton. One other suit against Edward Bryan heirs
and others in chancery at Lexington. My wife Ester. The children
of my daughter Agnes F. Hines, they under 21. To my daughter
Hannah Martz. My wife Ester exr. and Henry A. McCormick of
Rockbridge Co. exr. Witnesses, Jacob Lincoln, Abraham Lincoln,
William Looker, David Lincoln. Proved Feb. 1842.

MAUPIN, MARY C.; FEB. ——, 1848

My son James C. Maupin. My daughter Cathar . . . . W.
Miller, wife of William Miller. The children of my said daughter.
Witnesses, John Daugherty, C. A. Burnett.

MEFFERD, GASPER: NOV. 28, 1805

Wife Mary. Benjamin my son, to live with his mother on the
home plantation as long as she lives. After my wife's decease my
daughter Leaney Hannah to have Rachel my Black woman, if she
lives. My daughter Caty Kite to have my black girl Hannah. As
for my son John Mifford it is my wish for his son George Mifford to
have his part. As for Casper my son he shall have one dollar.
Another son (name missing). Benjamin my son shall have equal
part, &c. W. George Heuston and W. John H—— exrs. Witnesses,
Holland Forguson, Anthony Ginger (?), Samuel Moore, W. George
Heuston, W. John Heuston. Proved December 180—.

MICHAEL, PETER; SEPT. 6, 1859

Three pewter basins; 6 pewter plates; 10 split baskets; 3 stone jugs; 1 wool wheel; 1 flax wheel; 2 copper kettles; 1 fat firkin; 16 crocks; 1 pair cotton cards; 2 stand of bees; money due me from Henry Miller, Geo. Haynes, and John . . . . . Harnsberger. My wife. My son Elicous Michael. His 3 sisters and brothers $2000 in the following manner $500 to Christina May or her children; $500 to . . . . Simmers, $500 to Malinda Si . . . . My son Peter Michael. B. F. Michael, son of Chr . . . . shall receive one-sixth of her entire legacy. My 5 children . . . . heirs, viz., Elicous, Christena, Mary Ann, Malindas children . . . . Peter. I appoint Y. C. Ammon exr. Witnesses, Christopher Wetsel, Henry Michael. Proved Nov. ———.

MILEY, HENRY; OCT. 20, 1——

. . . . son-in-law Benjamin Hakings. My hereafter named children a . . . . heirs, Barbara being dead her children shall have her share; John Elizabeth of Daniel Hoff Polly the wife of Peter Roller Susana the wife of David Cris . . . . my insain son, Jacob, Rebecka the wife of John Guire alia the wife of Benja . . . . kins Sally the wife of Samuel Car and Henry . . . . except my son Marten. My son-in-law Benjamin Hawkins. If Hawkins refuses to keep Martin or mistreat him . . . . My friend Reuben Moore exr. Witnesses, Michiel Roller, Daniel Driver. Proved June ———. Bond $18,000. E. Coffman clerk.

MILLER, ADAM; FEB. 3, 1812 (?)

Wife Eve Miller. My wife and children Geo . . . . . . beth, Joseph, Madalene, and my grandson . . . . . My daughter Eve. Joseph Gonvey (?) as soon as he arrives of lawful age. . . . . ter Elizabeth, Henry Dirmon's wife. . . . and son Frederick Miller. My friends Martin Witmer and Adam Wise exrs. Witnesses, Jacob Kiser and John Pence (tanner). Proved May 1812. Exrs. refused to qualify. Daniel Ragen made admr. with will annexed. Robert Grattan, Adam Wise, Jacob Shank, and Peter Roler to appraise estate.—This Adam Miller probably lived near Mt. Crawford, judging from the names of his neighbors.

MILLER, AGNESS; APRIL 21, 1840

. . . . . Dollars to remain in hands of my exr. during the lifetime of Mary Long (my . . . . the wife of George Long) and for her benefit. . . . to be divided equally among the child . . . . my granddaughter Manah Long and wife of James Long. My son Benj. A. Miller. Balance to Mariah Long . . . . of James Long, my granddaughter . . . . among her surviving children. My friend and relation Abr . . . . Smith exr. Witnesses, O. C. Sterling, Isaac Ackin, Rob. H. Smith. Codicil Dec. 31, 1842. Proved May 1843.

MILLER, CATHERINE; JUNE 9, 1821

My four daughters, Catherine Dovel, Mary Argent . . . . Smith, and Barbara Miller. My brother Peter Conrad, deceased. My grandchild Nancy Fye. The heirs or (of?) . . . . my son Christian Miller, dec'd. . . . . Stephen . . . . My grandchildren, namely, and

Joseph Moyers and Christian Eaton and Catherine Sellers. My daughter Mary Argenbright. My son Adam. My daughter Elizabeth Smith . . . excepting $20 came out of her share my grandchild Nancy Fye her daughter. My son-in-law Iac . . . . Argabright exr. Witnesses, Geo. Conrad, . . . Marshel, . . . Boyer, . . . S. Purkey.

MILLER, CHRISTIAN; FEB. 1, 1821

Being old. My only son Henry Miller. My daughter Catharine Sellers . . . . her husband John Sellers. My daughter Sharlotte Burnside . . . . her husband James Burnsides. My wife Doutha. My daughter Elizabeth McVey. My daughter . . . . Pickering. . . . . Hannah . . . . Witnesses, Philip Koontz, Thomas Hinton, John Walton. Proved May 1822.

MILLER, CHRISTIAN; JUNE 28, 1851

Wife Susanna. Sons John and Samuel. My 5 daughters now living. Heirs of my deceased daughter, Betsy Click. . . . . . . on which I live lying on Long Glade, 515 acres. I appoint Solomon Garber exr. Witnesses, Abraham Sager, Samuel Miller, Jacob Shickel. Proved April 1852. Bond $10,000.

MILLER, JOSEPH; JULY 16, 1850

My children. My minor children. My son Joseph the lower end of my . . . . saw-mill, where he my son now lives. My son Peter a tract of land on N E side of Dry River, 147 acres, and joining lands of John A. Herring, Daniel and Abram Miller, and is the tract I purchased of the . . . . Daniel and Abram Miller. My two sons John and Henry my homeplace. Henry under 21. My fourteen children. Witnesses, Martin Miller; Daniel Thomas; Joseph Miller, son of Martin. Proved Dec. 1851. Sons Abraham, Daniel, and Joseph exrs. Bond $20,000.

MILLER, PETER, SR.; FEB. 10, 1821

Wife Barbary. My sons George . . . . . my son Nicholas a Horse. My daughter Sally a Bed, &c. . . . daughters have already got a bed each. All my children my son John Mill . . . . viz. Polly Susannah and Peggy Miller. My sons Peter and Nichol . . . . son John Miller's children to have likewise a child's part. My son Peter Miller . . . . Pense, Felty Pense and John Pense exrs. Witnesses, Joseph Mauzy, Christian Argenbright, Henry Argenbright. Proved June 1 . . . . by oaths of Christian Argenbright and Henry Argenbright, and recorded on motion of Miller, Jacob Pence, Felty Pence, and John Pence.

MILTENBERGER, CONRAD; ———

My wife Elizabeth. All my children.—No dates remaining.

MOFFETT, HENRY; AUG. 28, 1836

To Mary Newman $150. To Elizabeth Moore $150. To Samuel Moffett $150. To Catherine Moffett $500; in event of her death without heirs, her legacy to be divided equally between George, Anderson and Isaac Moffett. Balance of my property, both real and personal, to George Moffett, Isaac Moffett, and Anderson Moffett. Witnesses, John Moffett and William Bryan. Proved November 1841.

MOORE, JOHN; JULY 13, 1833

Nephew, Reuben Moore, to have all; and to be executor. Lands and negroes in Rockingham. Witnesses, Samuel Coffman, Mathias Hillyard. Proved September 1841.

MOORE, REUBEN; AUGUST 1807 (?)

Wife Phebe, exr. "Her three daughters, Elizabeth, ... , Sarah." Son Thomas. To son Reuben all of the plantation purchased of David Harnet. My daughter Elizabeth Walton. My daughter Ann. Wife Phebe exr. with John Moore and Thos. Moore Sen. Disposed of much land, many slaves, &c. Witnesses, Jacob Pirkey, Solomon Kingree, Josiah Harrison. Proved November 1803 (?).

MOYERS, HENRY; AUG. 11 ——

To the mother for her life, ... during the daughter's life, ... between the children of my brother G . . . . brother David, my sister Barbara Smith, my brother Abraham . . . . Henry, Margaret Paulsel, wife of John Paulsel, and Levi Hols . . . . his children, if he be dead. If my wife's daughter shall have issue . . . . The death of my wife. My wife Margaret Moyers, E . . . . and my friend DeWitt Coffman exr. Witnesses, Erasmus Coffman, Henry Ott, John S. Effinger, Allan C. Bryan. Proved Feb. . . . . . .

MYERS, SAMUEL; MAY 26, 1861

My wife. Any two of my sons.—Only a fragment remains.

NAVE, JACOB; APRIL 14, 1852

My plantation on the River. My son Jackson Nave. My son Jonathan Nave. My daughters Catharine and Rebecca. My daughters Sarah, Catharine, and Rebecca. Land devised to me by my uncle Mathias Nave. My children, Jonathan, Jackson, Catharine, Rebecca, Leanna, Sampson, Joseph, Mary, and Elias. My friend and neighbor Wm. G. Thompson exr. Witnesses, John M. Bargabaugh, Geo. Branner, David Reedy. Proved ————. John Zigler Jr. granted admr. Bond $15,000.—Evidently lived near Broadway and Timberville.

NAVE, MATHIAS; JAN. 6, 1842

To my Beloved . . . . . Nave son of my brother John Nave, late of Rockingham County. My daughter Katharine. . . . . the . . . . . Jacob Nave. My friend George Branner exr. Witnesses, John Linebaugh, George Fits Moyers. Proved Dec. 1842.

NEFF, HENRY; JUNE 4, 184—

Of Rockingham County. My wife Barbary. My personal estate, with the Sugar Camp on Skidmore's Fork and the land back of the mountain to be sold. The home plantation to be rented out till Feb. 2, 1845. My children. Mary Susan Ann and Barbary married before the age of 21. Elizabeth and Lydia to be allowed $20 a year for their services after the age of 21. . . . and Martin Neff exrs. My land in Knox Co., Ohio . . . . be appraised . . . . that John . . . . the Liberty of keeping it at the appraisement if he will. John Neff . . . . living on the land and Isaac K. Burkholder exrs. Witnesses, Joseph Burkholder, Joseph Swank, Westley Tailor. Proved August 1842 by Joseph Burkholder and Joseph Swank. John and Martin Neff exrs.; $16,000 bond.

Noland, William Alfred H. P.; —— 15, 1851

My mother Rebecca Pool; all her children. My friend and brother-in-law William Wright exr. Witnesses, W. N. Miller and others.

Oarbaugh, Rebecca; Oct. 29, 1849

My son-in-law . . . . than Hulva. Samuel, son of my daughter Regina, whose . . . . father is Joseph Good. Samuel under 21. My five children, Elizabeth, Isaac, Lydia, Regina, and Leana. My son-in-law, Jonathan Hulva, exr. Proved Feb. 1850.

Palser, Henry; 1845 (?)

My son Frances. My wife. My daughter Elizabeth Rogers. My daughter Lydia. Daughter Adeline. My son Joel to have a set of blacksmith's tools. I have sold to David Weaver a piece of timber land . . . . on the west side of the Peaked Mountain, being the same purchased of John S. Calvert of New Market. My friend Isaac Hardesty exr. Witnesses, Adam Wise, John Faught. Codicil July 12, 1845. Left Joel other things in place of the blacksmith tools. . . . . My granddaughter, May Jane, the child of my Daug . . . . . which she had previous to her intermarriage with Wills . . . . but it is my wish and desire that my Daughter Lydia shall . . . . enjoy the benefit of the said property until my said G . . . . ter shall arrive of age. . . . To my granddaughter May Jane, the chi . . . . Daughter Lydia. Witnesses, Jacob Rhodes, Adam Wise. Proved March —— by Adam Faught, Adam Wise, Jacob Rhodes. Clerk E. Coffman.

Pence, Catherine; June 30, 1803

My daughter Catharine Long; the heirs of Jacob Pence, my son now dead; Sarah Pirky, Barbary Propst, Henry Pence, John Pence, and Mary Swartley. My son Adam Pence's children—to each of them 25 cents except his eldest son Henry Pence (to him my stove and Window that is now in the house wherein he lives). My son John Pence exr. Witnesses, John Sites, Jeremiah Cross, Geo. Huston, Christian Kyger. Proved June 1803 (?) by oaths of Huston, Kyger, and Cross.

Petefish, John; June 10, 1859

. . . . Adam Petefish my son Isaac Petefish . . . . . y daughter Lucy Nauman, ... on Jeremiah Petefish $420 in the year 1836, and if my son Jeremiah is willing . . . . My above named children,

and as Reuben Petefish has already received the plantation he
n . . . . on . . . . I consider Jennetta Sampson has received her
portion. My land warrant of 120 . . . . My grandson John Petefish,
son of my son Reuben. My friend Wm. Sigler exr. Witnesses, Geo.
W. Harnsberger, John Welfley. Proved July 1859.

PETERFISH, JOHN; Nov. 20, 1802

To wife Anna Mary the dwelling house I now live in, garden,
spring house, &c. My mother still living. Sons, Jacob, John,
Christian, George, Henry I bought land of Peter Coonrad, ———
Hammer, and Vogel. My daughters Molly, Elizabeth, Catherine,
Salome. Youngest daughter under 18. Several of the boys in their
teens or younger. My son Jacob and my friend William Pence Sr.
exrs. Witnesses, Philip Long, Simeon Snider, and two signing in
German. Will proved March 1804 by oaths of Simeon Snider and
Adam Price.

PIFER, ANN MARY; MARCH 16, 1806

My husband Augustine Pifer, dec'd. My son Godlove. Witnesses, R. Gratton, Geo. Gilmer, Eve Stromback. Proved April 1806.

PIRKEY, CHRISTENA; MAY 28, 1842

My negroes—all to be free. I appoint Abram Mohler exr.
Proved June 1855 by Joseph Beery and others. Benj. Showalter, one
of the witnesses, being dead, his signature was proved by Joseph
Beery. Abram Mohler refused to qualify. Alexander Kiger granted
admr. Bond $10,000. Sureties, Joseph Beery and George Null.

PIRKEY, HENRY S.; MARCH 4, 18—

To my nieces, Clerisa and Nancy Perkey. Also my lot in Port
Republic. My lands in Kentucky. 500 acres in Lovin . . . . and
about 530 . . . . Christian County. Three slaves to be liberated.
My brother Solomon Perkey; also $100 to each of his children, viz.,
Julian, Harry, and Elizabeth Pirkey. My sister Margaret Eiler;
remainder to h . . . . Samuel Eiler. To my sisters, Catharine
Pirkey, Elizabeth Fisher, M . . . . Eiler, and Mary Ann Miller.
My nephew Oral Pirkey. Bro. Jacob Pirkey's children, viz., Rebecca
Pirkey, Solomon Pirkey, John Pirkey, Cla . . . . Pirkey, Nancy
Pirkey, David I. Pirkey, Benj. T. Pirkey, Alex. A. Pirkey, Mar . . . .
and Oral Pirkey and Samuel Eiler, son of Margaret Eiler. My
friend Jonathan Peale exr. Proved by Chas. Weaver and William
Hiden. Bond $20,000.

PIRKEY, MARY ANN; MAY 1, 1849

The daughters of my sister Ann Weller. The children of my
sister Janetta Kyger. Lands now held jointly by Alexander Kyger
and myself. My brother-in-law Alex. Kyger exr. Witnesses, Geo.
W. Kemper, J. P. Hook.

POINDEXTER, ROSEANNA; MARCH 11, 185—

My son George Poindexter. Daughter Margaret and my son
St. . . . My son John and my daughter Eliza. Robert Grattan
exr. Witnesses, Edwd. H. Smith, Abraham Byrd, Philip Cole.
Proved April ———. E. Coffman clerk.

QUINN, JAMES; NOV. 16, 1821

My Daughter . . . My Daughter Elizabeth . . . My Daughter
Sarah . . . My Daughter Nancy . . . My son James F. Qu . . .
My son Si . . . My son Benj. F. Quin . . . and the fo . . . towit
Nelly Tom Aimy Ester George Simon Eliza and Fanny (probably
negro slaves). I also give my son Benj. F. Quinn Daniel Joseph
Jude and . . . . During his step mother life at which time Daniel
and Joseph to be sold . . . . My daughters Anna Harrison and
Eliz . . . . Miller . . . . My son Benj. F. Quinn exr. Witnesses,
George Arey, Jacob Koogler, Jacob Snell.

REED, JACOB; MAY 25, 1848

My brother Isaac, my partner. My wife Sarah. $200 to each
of the 3 children which I had by Sarah Kiser, namely, Elizabeth,
Abraham, and Amanda (all under 21). My interest in my mother's
estate to a child which I had by said Sarah Kiser, by the name of
John, which is now living with me (under 21). My brothers Isaac
and Daniel B. Reed exrs. Witnesses, Abraham Knapp Linear.
Proved Aug. 1848.

REID, ISAAC; NOV. 4, 1861

To my illegitimate child, born of Maria Sprinkle, March 20,
1851, whose name I call Matrona Reid, all my lands. To my
brot . . . . $6000 (apparently in trust for Matrona). The Meadow
farm. I give my daughter with her mother the privilege of living
(on) either the Hupp and Reid farm or the Long Meadow farm.
Money to pay for Matrona's schooling, to give her a good education.
My brother Daniel Reid. To my nephew John F. Reid $2000, after
the death of his father Jonas Reid. John F. under 21. My brother
Peter Reid. My brother Ephraim Reid. To my exrs. $100 to
improve the family graveyard. My brother-in-law Cyrus Spitzer.
If Maria Sprinkle should marry she is to be excluded from the fore-
going requisitions. My brother Daniel Reid and friend Jackson
Martz exrs. Witnesses, Isaac Huffman, Edmon Minnick. Proved
Nov. 1861.

RHODES, HENRY; NO DATE

My wife Elizabeth. My son David. My daughter Anna. My
son-in-law, John Heatwole. My son-in-law, Joseph Heatwole. My
son Henry. To David all my interest in the McAdamized road
between Winchester and Staunton. My daughter Anna, widow of
Samuel Rhodes. My daughter Elizab . . . . . married to John
Heatwole.

RICE, THOMAS; NOV. 21, 1849

Wife Martha. My oldest son Bram . . . . (under 21). Black
boy Jerry to be freed at 21; after 21 to be hired out until he earns
enough money to take him to Liberia, Africa. If he is unwilling to
go, the money to be paid to the Colonization Society. The house
which I lately . . . . of Harvey Piercey; rents to go to missionary
society of M. E. Church. My youngest child. All my children.
Wife and children commended to the friendly counsel of Michael H.

Harris, I. G. Brown, William Rice, Jacob Shickle. Witnesses, I. G. Brown, Hugh Fairburn. Proved Feb. 1850. Bond $14,000.

RITCHIE, PHILIP; FEB. 19, 1841

"I Philip Ritchie of Brocks Gap in the County of R" . . . . . My son Isaac. My son Jacob. My son Adam. My son Philip. Son Abraham. Son William. Daughter Elizabeth Bible, wife of Jacob Bible. Daughter Catharine Hoover, wife of John Hoover. Daughter Margaret Hulvey, wife of John Hulvey. My wife Margaret. Witnesses, ... Fulk. Proved October ———. Philip Ritchie Jr. exr. H. J. Gambill, clerk.

RODE, ANTHONY; JAN. 27, 1806

To Anthony Rode. Henry ——— to Anthony Rode (John Rodes son) ——— ——— ——— (. . . . daughter) to Ann German to Elizabeth German to John Branaman to David Branaman and to my cousin Christian Burkholder. And to Anthony Rode (Frederick Rhodes son) to Anthony Showalter (John Showalter's son). Mill and saw mill in Augusta Co. to be advertised in one of the Gazetts in Richmond and in one in Staunton. Two lots in Waynesborough. My brothers Henry Rode and Frederick Rode exrs. Witnesses, David Birer, Solomon Hoffman, John Bierer, Daniel Branaman. Proved March 1806.

RODEHAFER, MARY; AUG. 24, 1859

Mary Rodehafer, widow of Conrad . . . . Rodehafer Sr. My stepson Conrad Rodehafer. Christian Myers my exr. Witnesses, Joseph W. Kratzer, Isaac C. Myers, Catharine Myers. Proved Jan. 1861. Bond $1200.

RODES, DAVID; NO DATE

Proved October ——— by Frederick Rodes, Henry A. Rodes, and David G. . . . . Rhodes, exr. named, refused to qualify. Joseph Burkholder granted admr. Bond $15,000. Sureties, David Bear, David R. Hopkins, Peter Whitmer Preston . . . . . . holder, and Henry B. Harnsberger. L. W. Gambill clerk.

ROLSTON, BENJ. H.; JULY 13, ———

Tract on which I reside is owned by my father Jesse Rolston and myself. Henry Beery and DeWitt Coffman to choose a third person and make division. I wish my debts first to be paid, giving preference to the debt due from me as admr. de bonis non . . . . of Henry Neff dec'd. My wife. My children. I appoint David R. Hopkins exr. Witnesses, Isaac Deavers, Allan C. Bryan. Proved August ———. Bond $12,000.

ROLSTON, DAVID; APRIL 21, 1849

My sons-in-law living and dead. My negro woman Lydia to be free. I desire tha . . . . Fielding Rolston may remain on my home farm on the same terms. My son Jesse Rolston and my grandson John H. Hopkins exrs. Witnesses, John Burkholder, Joseph Miller. Codicil April 21, 1849. My sons David and Benja . . . . F. Rolston . . . . Samples farm. Proved . . . . . E. Coffman clerk.

RUEBUSH, GEORGE; JUNE 30, 1849

My body to be buried at Friedens Church. My wife. My daughter Mary Whitmore, Peter Whitmore's wife. . . . . children then living of my daughter Margaret Baker, dec'd.; daughter Catharine; daughter Susanna; daughter Elizabeth. My sons, George, Samuel, and William Ruebush, exrs. Witnesses, Samuel P. Dagg, Edward S. Kemper, Wm. M. Kemper. Proved Feb. 1851. Bond $25,000.

RUNKLE, JACOB; JAN. 12, 1850

My daughter Nancy. My daughter Janette. Land whereon I now live adjoining John Conrad, John Cook, and others, on both sides of Boon's Run; another tract adjoining Jacob Ammon. My daughter Mary. My daughter Margaret. My 11 children: Nancy, Susan, Joseph (dead) . . . . Richard, Elizabeth, Margaret, John Oliver, Franklin, Jacob. My friend Isaae Thomas exr. Witnesses, Abram Moyers, Isaac Thomas, Layton I. Moyers. Proved October ——. Bond $20,000.

RUNKLE, LEWIS; DEC. 10, 1804 (?)

Wife Catharine. All my children, Jacob Peter, John Lewis, Frederick William, Elizabeth Catharine, and Bekah Runkle. An acre and a half is surveyed out of the said 128 for the use of the Church, for which my exrs. are to make a deed. To my son Peter all the Blacksmith's tools. Adam Kite, my son-in-law, to be sole exr. Witnesses, James Hoard, ———. Proved April 1805 by oaths of James Hoard and William Oler.

RUNKLE, PETER; 1821

Wife Margaret. My children. My daughters Mary Price and Christina Sellars. . . . . . . Children by their first husbands. The land that was willed to my son Jacob Runkle by his grandfather Jacob Runkle. Jacob Runkle and Daniel Sellars exrs. Witnesses, Philip Moyers, Michael Snyder, T. R. McGahey. Proved August 1821 by Philip Moyers, Michael Snyder, and Tobias McGahey.

RUSH, CHARLES; APRIL 4, 1806

Wife Elizabeth. . . . . . John Rush, George Rush, Peter Rush, and my daughter Anliss Lear. My granddaughter Elizabeth Hanger now married to William Steel. John Rush exr. Witnesses, Peter Nicholas, Jacob Rush, Jacob Nicholas. Proved June 1806.

RUTHERFORD, ROBERT; 1811 (?)

My wife Marth . . . . Town lots. Alley. Proved March 1811 by oaths of George Huston, Daniel Smith, John Hall. Appraisers, George Sites, Joseph Thornton, Henry Tutwiler, and Jacob Rohr. Probably lived in Harrisonburg. A mere fragment of the will remains.

SANGER, CONRAD; DEC. 7, 1821

My son John. My wife. Eggs, salt, fruit, coffee, sugar, wool, two pair shoes, flax, clean hemp, firewood. My wife shall have half of my Spring . . . . one-third of my Garden. Sheer plow, Cutting

Box, ten plated stove. My thirteen children . . . . daughter **Magda-**
line, daughter Barbara, my daughter Nancy, my son John, my
daughter Elizabeth, my daughter Cath . . . ter Mary, my son Jacob,
my son Daniel, my son Henry, my son Sa . . . . daughter Susanna.
My sons Jacob, Daniel, Henry, Samuel, under 18. **If John and my**
wife can't agree in the said house then my son John is to build my
wife a lik . . . . house to live on the place. My son Conrad. My
friends John Flory and my son-in-law Samuel Miller exrs. Witnesses,
Isaac Long, Jacob Spader. Proved March 1822.

SELLERS, HENRY; AUG. 30, 1841

Wife Mary Magdalene. Among all my children except Mary
. . . . , and that part my exrs. shall keep and put out on interest and
pay it as I sha . . . . My sons John and Henry. My daughters
Molly and Elizabeth. Beginning at a Poblar tree near the River
. . . . all my lands on the south side of the main road leading from
Portrepublic . . . . Run Gap. To pay unto Anna Maggott, married
to Reuben Mag . . . . My daughter Mary Sowers, after the decease
of Jacob S . . . . her husband. One steel trap. One Negro named
Tom. A Negro woman Sealy. My loom house. Little wheel and
big wheel and Jack Reel. (Mary Sowers and "Molly" seem to be
different persons.) Witnesses, John Rhine, Wm. Brown, George
Pence. Proved June 1843. Wm. B. Yancey granted admr.

SELLERS, JOHN; JANUARY 17, 1804

To wife ——— her spinning wheel and big wheel, the reel and
all the pewter, my horse, her saddle and bridle and two cows, &c. To
my sons John, Daniel, Henry. To my daughters Catherine, Elizabeth, Molly, Margaret, Christena. Witnesses, Philip Long, Michael
Rinehart, Jacob Yancey, and others. Proved March 1804.

SESSER, SARAH JANE; MAY 7, 1862

My daughter Mary. My two sons, Isaac and David. My sister,
Nancy Hashbarger. My son Abraham. My neighbor John Wine
exr. Witnesses, Jos. A. Mitchell, Joseph McMullen, Levi Reedy.
Proved July 21, 1862.

SHACKELFORD, ZACHARY; APRIL 27, 1822 (?)

Provides for freedom of Negroes; they to have horses, &c.
Apparently his estate is to be used wholly for them—to purchase
western lands, &c. . . . . eek (creek?) near to William Bryans.
(Perhaps on Linville Creek.) Witnesses, ... therford, ...
Burkholder, ... tian Moyers. Proved May 1822 by oaths of
Archd. Rutherford, Martin Burkholder, and Christian Moyers.—Some
of the Negroes named in the will were Bauston, Sela, Sarah, Samuel,
and Daniel.

SHAVER, GEORGE; 1810 (?)

Son Philip. My other sons. . . . . . ge Shaver, $133. My
son Jacob, $133. My son John. Proved Oct. 1810 by oaths of
George Huston and John Huston. Appraisers, John Huston, John
Pence, Thomas Pain, Peter Pyler.

SHEETS, SAMUEL; Nov. 10, 1846

My wife Elizabeth. To Mary Elizabeth Sheets, daughter of Strother and Frances Sheets (under 21) $1000. To Elizabeth Huffman, daughter of John Huffman and the niece of my wife, $200. My nephew Strother . . . . who married Frances Sheerly niece, to my wife The tract I now reside on, &c. Witnesses, Edward H. Smith, Wm. T. Hill, John Willard. Proved Nov. 21, 1859. Bond $15,000.

SHEPP, JOHN; JULY 2, 1842

Daughter Pheaby Shep exr. Wife Margaret. Rest of my children, Catharine and Sarah and Chr . . . . Reuben and . . . . shall receive an English shilling. Witnesses, Jacob B. Houck, Henry Keezel. Proved Sept. 1842.

SHERFY, BENJAMIN; MARCH 27, ——

My wife Ester. Two Bibles, together with my other books, &c., be divided between my two daughters, Leah Richey and Rachel . . . . My son-in-law Jacob Richey exr. Witnesses, John Braner, David Garber. Proved February court 18—.

SHICKEL, DANIEL; AUG. 7, 1852

My wife Elizabeth. My son Jacob. Rest of my four children. My four daughters. Witnesses, Daniel Thomas, John Wine, Solomon Garber. Daniel Thomas exr., with Daniel Bowman surety. Bond $4000.

SHIPMAN, JONOTHAN; JAN. 30, 1848

To Lucy R. Shipman $2000, single. Mary A. Shipman $2000, single. To Saraan Turk $250. To James C. Shipman Daughter Mary, the granddaughter of Dr. John Wills, $1000. Mary under 21. Residue to Frances W. Shipman and Jonothan M. Shipman. I appoint Robert Gratton, Givens Fulton, and Frances W. Shipman exrs. Proved June 1848. Signature of Jonothan Shipman proved by James Moore and Littleton W. Gambill. Givens Fulton and Frances W. Shipman qualified exrs. Bond $50,000.

SHLOSSER, BARBARA; OCT. 19, 1836

I, Barbara A . . . . , old, weak, and infirm, but of sound mind. My G . . . . Son Samuel Sloesser. Witnesses, Frederick Hoffman, Samuel Hoffman, John Brown. Proved June 1842. Samuel Sloesser exr.

SHOEMAKER, CHRISTIAN; MARCH 16, 1850

Wife Eva. My sons, Levi, Joshua, and Christian Shoemaker. My son Isaac. My daughters, Gevina Deannah, Susan, Elizabeth Sarah and Deborah. Witnesses, Wm. G. Thompson, Isaac Ruddell, Henry C. Shickel. Proved June 1861. Bond $500.

SHOWALTER, GEORGE; APRIL 12, 1855

Wife Mary. Friend David Holler exr. Witnesses, Cornelius Grabill, Wm. Howdyshell, Saml. Eaton, W. G. Newham. Proved May 1855. Giles Devier surety on Holler's bond.

Showalter, Jacob; April 10, 1847

Advanced in life. All my children, except my 3 daughters, Elizabeth Bright, Nancy Coffman, and Polly Parrot, the wifes of Amos Bright, Reuben Coffman, and Branson Parrot. They to have interest from money in trust. The names of my children are as follows: Elizabeth Bright, Ca . . . . Peter, Margaret, Whitehouse, William, Hannah Byrd, David Sophia Grace, Jacob Nan . . . . . Adam, Polly Parrot, Henry and Leannah Carpenter. My son-in-law John Evers and my son Peter exrs. Witnesses, Sam'l Shacklett, Geo. Bruffy, J. G. Coffman. Codicil ———— 28, 1850. Same witnesses. Proved (no date). Bond $30,000.

Shultz, Adam; Feb. 16, 1842

Wife Susanna. My daughter Hannah. My four above children. My son-in-law Daniel Brillhart. First note which Abraham Young gi . . . . me. My son-in-law Abraham . . . . My friend Abraham Knopp exr. Witnesses, Benj. Bowman, Samuel Miller, David Bowman, Daniel Miller. Proved May ————. Bond $16,000. E. Coffman clerk.

Sims, Elizabeth; Jan. 29, 1850 (?)

No name of legatee preserved except that of Charles, a Negro slave apparently, and "my . . . . H. Austin," exr. Witnesses, A. Davisson, Wm. L. Leckie, Mary Murray. Proved March 1850. John H. Austin exr. Bond $500.

Sipe, David; 18th ——

My 5 children, Susan, Sa . . . . Delila and Jacob each have an equal share with my other 4 children N . . . . Emanuel, and George. My nine children. My wife. My sons-in-law John . . . . Rosenberger exrs. Witnesses, Geo. F. Johnson, Wm. F. Dyer, Noah Wansturf. Proved July ————. On motion of John Zirkle and Gedeon Rosenberger, exrs. Bond $15,000.

Sipe, Peter; March 24, 1806

Wife Margaret. My children, Jacob, Michael Henry and Nancy or Ann. My daughter Elizabeth Fritts. Rosena Shaver, my second daughter. My daughter, Catharine Crist. My son George Sipe. My daughter Mar . . . . Harthey. My son John Sipe. My daughter Marga . . . Blauzer. My daughter Mary Magdal. My son Michael Sipe. Daughter Ann Sipe. ———— Margarett and my nephew Henry Sipe exrs. Witnesses, R. Gratton, Geo. Gilmer, David Sipe, Geo. Huston. Proved June 1806.

Smith, Ann; Dec. 10, 1850

My body to be buried in the burying ground near Robert . . . . . Creek, where my parents and friends are buried, according to the custom of Me . . . . . Two sisters and brothers daughter Sarah Right. My sister Margaret . . . . my part of the farm. My sister Maria Rodes. My sister Margaret Smith. Pay to the Missionary Society in New York of the M. E. Church $500. My sister Sar . . . .

Adam Rodes, my brother-in-law, exr. Witnesses, John Long, John
B. Lindsey, P. H. Snyder. Proved Jan. 1850.

Smith, Daniel; March 10, 1848

My wife. My son Daniel, under 21. A tract I purchased of
Alexander Herring, 1823. My plantation on Dry River. My
daughter Margaret . . . . Dollars to her son Robert Craig . . . . .
My daughter Elizabeth . . . . not subject to the . . . . of her
husband. My daughter Francis E. Beirno. My son Luceius. The
old barn, orchard, and spring near thereto and the road from Samuel
Liggett to Dayton and joining Shaver's land. My daughter Maria
Antinnette. The said Maria Antionette Tams and not subject to
the mantal (marital?) rights of her husband. My two youngest sons,
John W. G. Smith and Daniel Smith. My friends John Kenney and
Edward H. Smith exrs. Codicil Nov. 29, 1849. Second codicil
April 19, 1850. In lieu of the 90 acres directed to be laid off for my
daughter Maria Antionette Tams, only 50 acres shall be laid off for
her joining Shavers and Nisewangers . . . I also give her my house
and . . . . in Harrisonburg purchased of Joseph C. Braithwaite.
My daughters Margaret D. Effinger and M. Antion . . . Other items.
Third codicil —— 2, 1850. I appoint my sons John Green and
Daniel and Herring Chrisman exrs. in place of John Kenney and
Edward H. Smith. Pay all the debts of Lucius Q. Smith in Rockingham and Augusta. To my . . . . Margaret and Harvey Effinger
during their coverture . . . . then divided between her two children
Robert Craig and John F. E. Effinger. My daughter Francis . . . .
her two children Mar . . . . Plunket. My daughter Elizabeth Scott.
My Waverly farm. Witnesses, John James Williams, Erasmus
Coffman, Herring Chrisman. Admitted to record Nov. 1850. Again
presented Jan. 18, 1858.

Smith, Dorotha; December 1822

My daughter Reashe . . . . to m . . . Joseph Smith. My son
Joseph Smith. Daughter Eliz Smith, wife of Shealton Stockel. One
women saddle, one large copper kettle, one small detto, one set of
copper leatles (ladles), one half dozen pewter plates, one half of
pewter spoons, one pladed coffee bott, &c.; one little spinning wheel
and my beck (big?) wheel. My children, namely, George Smith,
Joseph Smith, ... daughter Eliz (wife) of S. Stockel. Witnesses,
Henry Sipe, John Carpenter, . . . tian Doreman. Proved March
1823 by oaths of John Carpenter and Chas. Doreman. Henry Life
(Sipe?) qualified. John Carpenter, James Laird, Anthony Huffman,
Peter Koontz, appraisers.

Smith, Edw. H.; April 24, 1852

I appoint Robert M. Kyle exr. and Julia my wife admr., to act
jointly. My 13 nephews and nieces, it being understood that —rom
Wm. Smith's children there is to be deducted such debts as I hold
against their mother and father. Witnesses, Wm. B. Johnson, John
W. G. Smith, Mary Kyle. Proved June 1852.

SMITH, JOHN; JUNE 4, 1834

My wife Barbary. My children, John Smith, William Smith, Augusten; daughter Polly, now the wife of John Mills; daughter Rebecca, wife of Michael Newman. Witnesses, Peter Hinton, Peter P. Koontz, Andrew Sellers, Reuben Sellers. Proved February 1842 by Peter Hinton and Andrew Sellers. Reuben N. Harrison certified for obtaining letters on the estate with will annexed.

SMITH, WILLIAM; OCT. 3, 1806

Wife Dianna. My children. Son Edward.

My executors to build a small comfortable house near the head of the Spring in which the pipes are laid for the use of my wife and children. Wife Dianna exr. with my brother-in-law Edward H. W. Donaghe and Daniel Smith. Certain Negroes to serve a term of years and then be emancipated. Witnesses, Arch'd Rutherford, Benja. Smith, Elizabeth Smith (?), Elizabeth Benson, Elizabeth Rogers, Hy. I. Gambill, D. Lofland. Proved Nov. 1806.

SNELL, HENRY; FEB. 13, 1860

Wife Ann. The 100 acres next . . . . Bridgewater. My friend David Garber (brother-in-law) exr. Witnesses, Isaac Wright, John Garber, Joseph Coffman. Proved March ———. Jacob Thomas and Daniel Forrer sureties. Bond $8000.

SONEFRANK, JACOB; SEPT. 5, 1855

My wife Mary. To Selimy, the daughter of my wife before our marriage, who goes by the name of Selimy Sonefrank. Witness, I. Hardesty. Proved Dec. —— by O. C. Stirling and I. Hardesty. Benj. Wenger exr. Jonas Blosser surety.

SPADER, CATHERINE; MARCH 25, 1841

My brother Jacob Spader. My sister Mary Baker, wife of John Baker. My sister Elizabeth Spader. My sister Susannah Crickenbarger. My brother Jacob Spader and sister Mary Baker to erect a brick wall around the graveyard, which is upon the land I now live on, 50 feet wide, 60 feet long, 5 feet high, &c. Witnesses, Rev. Henry Wetzel, Christian Blose, George Bowman Jr. Proved Nov. 1851.

SPEERS, GEORGE; OCTOBER 14, 1796

Wife Christenah. Daughter Elizabeth, wife of Asher Morrison. Son Jacob. Daughter . . . . Daughter Hannah, wife of . . . . Newman. Son John. Son David. Daughter Sarah, wife of John Rader. Land in Rockingham and in Lincoln Co., Ky., on which son Jacob Speers now lives. Son Daniel. Daughters Catherine Carpenter and Mary Rife. Wife Christenah, friend John Rader, and son David Speers exrs. Witnesses, Jno. Barnett, Christian S. Sites, Elizabeth Sites. Probated November 1803.

STALB, JOHN; AUG. 22, 1849

Farm on which I reside on the Shenandoah River, same descending to me from my brother, dec'd; 180 acres. I bequeath to my Friends and Relations as . . . . Rodes my housekeeper, $2000, to

Cathe . . . . . and $75, to Mary Hess, formerly M . . . . . Mary
Miller formerly Mary . . . . . with Peter Sheets in Indiana $50, to
Solomon . . . . . of Andrew, $30, to Lobias Shull $30, ... To
William and Strough son of Mary Him . . . . and his heirs. To
each of my grave diggers and witnesses to my will $1. My friend
and neighbor Wm. G. Thompson exr. Witnesses, G. H. Copp, I.
N. Messick, John C. Homan. Proved Nov. 1850.

Steele, David; April 4, 1860

My estate to be divided equally among the following persons,
James Steele, Isaac Steele, Wm. Steele, John Steele, Elizabeth
Roadcap . . . . . . my deceased sister Mary Steele . . . . . . My
brother John, when John is old enough to own a horse. The share
coming to Mary's child John and to Elizabeth Roadcap shall be
placed in the hand of Jam . . . . Steele as trustee. The husband of
Elizabeth Roadcap. A share on lot in Woodbine Cemetery near
Harrisonburg to be bought—I wish to be buried there. Francis W.
Shepman my exr. Witnesses, John C. Woodson, John McQuaide,
W. T. Fisher. Proved Feby 1861. Bond $1200.

Stockard, Charles; Nov. 23, 1820

Wife Elizabeth. My two children. Margaret and William,
under 21. Wife exr. Witnesses, James Planno, David Swazzo,
Elkena Walters. Proved at Lancaster, Fairfield Co., Ohio, January
1821, by Elkena Walters and David Swazzo. Hugh Boyle, clerk.

Stoner, Abraham; ——— 6, 1850

Wife Sally. Daughter Hannah a tract in Fairfield County,
Ohio . . . . to her children. My five children, Jacob, Amas,
Abraham, Daniel, and Susannah. I appoint Peter Whitmore and
John Swope exrs. Witnesses, Joseph Coffman, Benj. S. Byerly,
William Herring. Proved Feb. 1851.

Strine, Hannah; June 12, 1852

My son John. Land now in the possession of my father and
mother, Jonas and Margaret Strine. I appoint John Long Sr. exr.
Witnesses, I. Hardesty, Robert Wright. Proved August 1852.

Stuart, Alexander; June 6, 1822

To the offspring, if any then be, of my Al. Stu . . . . Second,
to my son John Stuart. My son David Stuart. My son Christopher
Stuart . . . . plantation . . . . old survey occupied by me and John
Stuart's plantation. My daughter Margaret Sims. My 3 grand-
children, Jane, James, Sarah Sims, my Negro woman and her increase
to be equally divided between them when the youngest comes of age.
My two grandchildren . . . and John Stuart, $100 each. My grand-
. . . . David Stuart's two children Jane and John Stuart and James
Sims . . . . My son Christopher Stuart, John and James Sims exrs.
Witnesses, John C. Hamilton, Charles Berry, David D. Berry.
Proved October 1823.

Swank, Joseph; Oct. 17, 1860

My wife Elizabeth. Until Ann Eliza is 21. Forty dollars a year respectively for Lydia Frances and Louisa Virginia till they are 21. All my children Sarah's interest Particularly to her and her children. I select Joseph Harvey Swank exr. Witnesses, Isaac W. Bowers, James P. Rolston, John H. Rolston Jr. Proved Nov. 1860.

Taylor, James; June 3, 1843

I, James Taylor, of Dayton, Rockingham Co. My wife, Elizabeth Taylor. My house and lot in the town of Dayton, for herself and family. My five children. My friend Wm. K. Gailey exr. Witnesses, Thomas Lenden (Linden?) Dav Stinespring, ... ham Coffman.

Taylor, William; July 18, 1848

Of Taylor Springs (Massanetta). I emancipate my man slave Bob. I give Bob the choice of my horses and my saddle and bridle. I confirm to the Negro woman Sally McMahon the cow Beck. $500 to enclose with a stone fence the graveyard at Union Church, where my father, mother, brothers, and other friends are buried, and where I wish my body to be interred. My exr. to purchase for Bob $1000 in land in some free state, &c. I had 3 sisters who married— Margaret (Carter), Catharine (Tratchet), Elenor (whose husband's name I do not remember). My friend Robert M. (Kyle) exr. Witnesses, John Kenney, Evan Henton, Edwd. Smith, Robert Cox. Proved August . . . .

Trout, Michael; April 12, 1819

My children . . . . George . . . . . Catharine, Elizabeth, ... Jacob, Michael, ... Hannah, to all her children . . . . My son George Tro . . . . my son-in-law Samuel Yount exrs. Witnesses, Anthony Rhodes, Sam'l Rhodes, Jacob Weaver.

Trumbo, Jacob; 1833 (?)

My son . . . . the plantation I now live on and also my Miller pla . . . . . on the south side of the river . . . . blacksmith tools, &c. . . . . Hannah Trumbo to occupy and possess the mansion house, &c. My s . . . . Jacob Trumbo. Jacob to maintain . . . . mother. Children and co-heirs of my son John Trumbo. My son Andrew Trumbo, 100 acres of land I own in Ohio (Licking County). Heirs of my deceased daughter Dorothy Baggs. My daughter Elizabeth Custer. My son Mathias Trumbo. Witnesses, Simon Nicholas, Jacob Snyder, John Rader. Codicil, July 19, 1833. My son Jacob hath this day paid my son-in-law Richard Custer $154.18; said Jacob to be relieved from this in settlement with daughter Elizabeth, wife of Richard Custer. Witnesses, Geo. H. Chresman, S. H. Hopkins, John Rader. Proved Feb. 1842 by Philip Tussing, John Rader, and Geo. Chrisman. Jacob Trumbo, Jr., exr.

Tutwiler, Leonard; June 25, 1804

To my wife Catharine. To my son John, under 21. Land I bought of Widow Long. To my sons Henry and Jacob. To my daughter Mary Whitesel. To my daughter Elizabeth Brock. To my daughter Catharine s . . . . . To my daughter . . . . MClough. To my daughter Susanna Tutwiler. My children John, Fanny and Johnathen. My daughter Fanny Keester. My son and son-in-law John Tutwiler and John Keesner exrs. Witnesses, Geo. Huston, Henry Lott, H. Butt, G. C. Huffman. Proved September 1804 by Henry Butt and George Huffman.

WAGGY, PHILIP; FEB. 6, 1812 (?)

"Philip Weggy sinor" (Sr.?), being frail by old age. My wife Susannah. My . . . . . braham Weggy and Isaac Weggy and their heirs. My two sons . . . . ggy and Isaac Weggy exrs. Proved at March court 1812 by oath of William Cockran Jr. and at June court 1812 by oath of Emanuel Tillman.

WAMPLER, ANNA; OCT. 17, 1851

The following heirs I acknowledge—Harrison Ross, Mary Ross, Henry Ross, Andrew Ross, Eliz . . . . and David Ross, all children of my sister Barbara Ross, dec'd; next Regina Rodcap, . . . Rodcap, Franklin Rodcap, Emanuel Rodcap, all children of my sister Elizabeth R . . . , now wife of Reuben Rodcap, and Anna Kline, daughter of my sister Mary, now wife . . . . Samuel Flora. I appoint John Kline exr. Witnesses, Samuel Wampler, Martin Wampler. Proved Feb. 1852.

WEDECK, HENRY; FEB. 6, 1822

My wife Rachael. My daughter Barbary Roadcap. My daughter Molly Markey. The children of my daughter Pakey Brince, dec'd. The children of my daughter Elizabeth Pence, dec'd. My daughter Christina Good. My daughter Mary Deeds. My daughter Aimy Weddeck. My daughter Eve Good. Eve Good's children. Jacob Bear and Jacob Ammon exrs. Witnesses, Joseph Samuels, Abram Strickler.—"Weddeck" is now probably "Wittig."

WETZEL, JOHN, SR.; AUG. 29, 1849

Wife Sarah. My two sons, John and Peter. I have not mentioned my son Jac . . . . because I have heretofore made him a title to his land, &c. Witnesses, Ro. Grattan, C. Grattan. Codicil Jan. 6, ——. No new names. Witnesses, Ro. Grattan, George Sherman. Proved Sept. 1855. John and Peter Wetzel exrs. Bond $1500.

WHISLER, DANIEL; DEC. 11, 1847

Wife Sarah. Son Joseph. My Brother Henry's estate. Son Joseph's part of the land lying on . . . . ap Creek, adjoining Peter Moyer, Jacob Early, and others. Samuel Hedrick has rented my farm. Samuel Hedrick an heir. My son Henry. Adam Shank an heir. My son David. My son Daniel. Samuel Wine an heir. Samuel Huddle an heir. My son . . . . her rec'd $77. My son-in-law Samuel Wine and my friend Martin Miller (on Beaver Creek) exrs. Witness . . . . Coffman.

WHITEZELL, WILLIAM; DEC. 18, 1860

To Jacob Burkholder my entire interest in my father's (Abraham Whitezell's) estate in the county of Rockbridge. To Jacob Burkholder also my entire set of tools, embracing joiner, carpenter, shoemaker, and cooper tools. To Jacob Burkholder also accounts due me from Silas Hinton, Michael M. Miller, David Fry, Christian Myers, Peter Good's estate, and Gasner Messick. Witnesses, Samuel Nisewander, Jacob B. Niswander, Michael Lohr. Proved Jan. 1851 (1861?).

WHITMER, DAVID G.; NO DATE

My wife Frances. Witnesses, Henry A. Rhodes, John Frank, Anthony Showalter. Proved Jan. 1861. Widow Frances granted admr., with Benj. F. Byerly and Henry G. Brunk sureties. Bond $1000.

WHITMORE, MARTIN; OCT. 31, 1835

My four sons, Jacob, Daniel, Samuel, and John. My three daughters, Elizabeth, wife of John Roller; Susanna, wife of Benjamin Berrly; and Anna, wife of David Hatrick. My daughter Sarah. . . . . then . . . . Sons Martin and Ephraim shall pay her. My sons Martin and Ephraim. Witnesses, John Brown, George Rubush, Daniel Whitmore. Proved Jan. 1843.

WILHELM, POLLY; OCT. 20, 1851

My sister Elizabeth Fifer (widow). My Cousin Jacob Deatrick and Elizabeth Fifer exrs. Witnesses, D. Wilkins, Stephen I. Few, P. A. Clarke. Proved Nov. 1851.

WILL . . . . (MILL . . . . ?), HENRY; JAN. 26, 1840

My son Philip. Wheat-fan, 2 log-chains, 1 wagon, my tools now on the place. My wife Barbary, his mother. My son Solomon. My son-in-law Wm. Jones. My son David. My friend Charles Nie . . . and my son Philip Miller exrs. Witnesses, George Hosler, Enos Keezel. Proved July 18—.

WILLIAMS, WILLIAM PINKNEY; FEB. 14, 1852

. . . . other (mother?) Mrs. Elizabeth Pinkney Williams, making her sole heir to all I possess. My brother-in-law, Chas. D. Gray exr. Holographic will. Proved by . . . . Gambill and Joseph H. Shere . . . . Chas. D. Gray exr. Bond $10,000.

WILLIAMSON, JAMES; JANUARY 16, 1804

My land in Rockbridge Co. To my wife a horse, her saddle, one cow, &c. My son Thomas is to be put out to school immediately; then to choose a trade. If I have any more sons, they are to be treated the same way. My daughters are to go to school till they can read and write. Archibald Hopkins Thomas and John Baxter exrs. Proved March 1804.

WILLIAMSON, THOMAS; JUNE 14, 1806

Wife Elizabeth. My son William McCleary Robison Williamson. His three sisters. His brother John, minor. My daughter

Irene McCleary Williamson. My daughter Nancy Williamson. Other daughter (name missing). My wife and my friend William Beard exrs. My waggon cover, stretchers, and two pairs of gears I direct to be sold, &c. Witnesses, Geo. Huston, ————— —————. Date probated missing.

WISE, ADAM, SR.; JAN. 10, 1852

My sons Harvey and Samuel. My wife Elizabeth. My daughter Catharine. Timber lands by . . . . . he lands of David Wise and Mrs. Susan Kersh. My sons Adam and Peter exrs. Witnesses, ... Hoffman, John Wise Jr., Wm. H. Black.

WITMER, JACOB; SEPT. 18, 1800

My 4 sons, Martin, Jacob, John and Daniel. My 3 daughters, Anna, Mary, and Elizabeth. My large German Bible to my youngest son Daniel. None of my books to be sold. Witnesses, T. Paul Kenkle, Adam Long, and others. Proved March 1803 by oaths of Jacob Spader and Adam Long. Martin and Jacob Witmer exrs.

WITTS, DANIEL; NOV. 20, 1850

My son John Witts all right and title in lands that have accrued or may accrue to me under Act of Congress of Sept. 28, 1850, by reason of my having served as a soldier in the war declared by the U. S. against Brittain on June 18, 1812, in Co. commanded by Capt. Wm. Harrison, and which went from Rockingham County in 1814. Witnesses, Francis S. Moore, John Messerly. Proved Dec. 1851.

WOODLEY, JACOB; MARCH 6, 1802

To my son John Woodley's two sons Jacob and John all my old plantation that I now live on. Quarter acre excepted for burying ground. My . . . . Hannah. John Harrison's wife Grace Harrison . . . . Abram Pickering excepted in the above division. . . . . Barbara Pickering or her heirs . . . . Nathaniel Harrison and John Philips exrs. to make over all my movable estate to Ulrich Philips, Barbara Pickering, Grace Harrison, and Polly Harrison. Witnesses, Samuel Marks, Jacob Spohr, David Cummins. Proved Sept. 1804.

YANCEY, CHARLES L.; NOV. 23, 1850

Mountain land in Madison Co., Va. My farms on Elk Run. Line . . . . self, Solomon and Elias Merica near the house and run with the foot of the mountain divi . . . per corner of the 5 acres formerly owned by John Embey, thence a south course across . . . . tain to a run corner near Hawkings house. That purchased by Bennet Rains by Jacob Conrad except the piny land lying . . . . northside of Wolf Run and joining the lands of Wm. Kite, Henry Wenger, &c. My mills. My wife Lucinda Yancey. My father, Layton Yancey Sr. Various Negro slaves named. My children, Elizabeth F. Hudson, Charles B. Yancey, Ann V. Yancey, Nancy C. Yancey, Mary C. Yancey, and Alexander F. (T?) Yancey. My exrs. to have a family graveyard walled in with brick, where I have directed . . . be buried, 40 feet square, 5 feet high, and of good thickness. I appoint Maj.

Joseph H. Conrad and . . . . exrs. Witnesses, Wm. H. Perry, A. L. Wolf. Proved Feb. 1851. Bond $20,000.

YOUNG, CHAS. A.; FEB. 22, ——

I, Charles A. Young of the town of Harrisonburg. My wife Catharine Elizabeth. My friend Erasmus Coffman exr. Witnesses, Geo. O. Conrad, Jos. C. Braithwaite. Proved May 185—. Bond $600.

ZETTY, PETER; DEC. 10, 1838

My . . . . Susannah (wife). Daughters Susannah and Lydia. Daughters Fanny and Rebeccah. My son-in-law John Sh . . . . . My son-in-law Jacob Fl . . . . My son-in-law Peter Weaver. My son-in-law John Blosser. Anna Blosser. My son-in-law David Carver. My son-in-law Benjamin Zetty. My son Peter. My exrs. to pay to John Shoemaker $60 to make his amount $500. The six first named heirs, children of my first wife. My plantation on which I now live, southeast side of the dry fork of Smith's Creek, to be rented out till my daughter Lydia is 16. Susannah and Lydia under 21. My granddaughter Piggy, a . . . . born child of my daughter Barbara Shoemaker. My six children by my first wife. Overplus to be equally divided between the ten children by my first wi . . . . . My son Peter Zetty Jr. and my friend Isaac Thomas exrs. Witnesses, Isaac Thomas, Michael Sellers. Codicil July 11, 1840. Same witnesses. Proved February 18—.

ZIRKLE, DANIEL; JAN. 13, 1850

My 3 sons, Jacob, Perry, and William; the place on which reside and the place lately purchased of Reuben Moore, exr. Henry Myle (Miley). My wife. My daughter, Malinda Kline they must pay the note I executed to Abraham Kagy for $1500. My daughter Mary Hinkle. My daughter Catherine Koyner. I have advanced to my sons John and Lewis $11,000. My sons John D. Zirkle and Jacob W. Zirkle exrs. Witnesses, Jacob D. Williamson, Samuel G. Henkel, Reuben Zirkle. Proved Jan. 1850. Bond $10,000.

KEESLING AND SIMMERMAN ITEMS
See pages 352-365, etc.

Under date of May 29, 1930, Mrs. Philip Spence writes:

"The Wythe County, Va., court records show the second marriage of Henry Simmerman—that he stated her mother's maiden name was M. A. Helvey. Also Mrs. Mahala Pence of Alexandria, Ind., says that her grandparents were Conrad and Rebecca (Kegley) Keesling of Wythe County, Va.

"Conrad Keesling's will was probated May 12, 1818, in Wythe County, Va.

"Montgomery County, Va., court records state that George Keesling, Jr., was appointed administrator of George Keesling, Sr., June 3, 1788.

"Mary Ann Helvey was the wife of George Simmerman, born 1797, died August 1841. They were the parents of Henry and others.

"The Montgomery County, Va., court records have a marriage bond dated February 6, 1787, Jacob Keesler to Phillipina Keesler, daughter of George Keesler of that county. 'Keesler' was meant to be 'Keesling.' There are other records, as the appraisers of the estate of George Keesling, Sr., July 30, 1788, supposed to be the father of Conrad Keesling of Wythe County, Va."

INDEX

Aaron 75
"Abe Lincoln" 242
Abdominal surgery 344
Abercrombie, Capt. William 369 370
Abolitionists 239
Abright (Albright?) 17
Abstracts of wills 391
Acars 158
Acers 156
Achins 109
Acker, Capt. Jake 293
Acker 245 291 294
Ackin 362 421
Ackletree 12 (See Ochiltree)
Aclen 156
Acort 45 106
Acre (Acker?) 30
Adams 34 35 39 140 158 328
Adams's Geography 124
Addimson (Adamson) 19
Adkins 348
Adler 10
Aged 104 228
Agle 7
Ahl, Rev. Peter 304
Airhart 45 385
Airmon 109
Airy 115 116 138 143
Akerd 20
Akins 19
Alabama troops 240
Albemarle barracks 89
Albemarle Co., Va. 222
Albemarle, N. C. 368 373
Albert 15 268
Albertson 371
Albright 18 26 30 394
Alce 42 98 (See Aulse)
Alder 391
Alderson 48 49 51 52 54-8 153 156 160
    162
Aldersons in Rockingham and Greenbrier
    153-163
Alderson, W. Va. 153
Aldham 313
Aldir 9
Aldorpha 42 101 (See Altaffer)
Aldorphats 9
Alexander 101 142 146 162 202
Alexandria, Ind. 440
Alford 10 11 34 35 42 101 137 325
Alfred, Geo. 325
Alfred's Arithmetic 325
Alger 14 21 27 28 294
Allborphes 38 (See Aldorpha)
Allbughs 41
Allcorn 365

Allebaugh 135 140 172 335
Alleghany Co., N. C. 366, 367
Allein 228 229
"Allein's Alarm" 229
Allen, James (of Shen. Co.) 414
Allen, Gen. James 221
Allen, J. Taylor 229 367
Allen 15 35 39 40 93 96 106 137 140
    215 217 352
Allen's Chapel 367
Allen Co., Ohio 397
Allford tract 398
Alliance, ship 257
Allorphes 39 (See Aldorpha)
Allred 367 372
Almon 142
Alsace 358
Alsie 154
Alstatt 28 36 45 97 143 208
Alstoff 112
Alsup 161
Altaffer 33 208 391 (See Aldorpha, &c.)
Althair 161
Altorpher 35 (See Altaffer)
Altz land 396
Amend 38 42
"American Genealogy" 221 333
American Hotel 174
American Legion 184
"American Tait" 344
Americans of Armorial Ancestry 229
Amite, Miss. 238 240
Ammon 14 20 27 35 45 115 136 141
    145 208 391 421 428 436
Amusing incident 288
Anaconda, Mont. 228
Anderson, Capt. 310
Anderson 18 22 90 156 201 226 310
    314 317 323 371 391 392 420
Anderson family 230
Anderson, Ind. 383
Andes 9 10 24 25 28 107 384 388 398
    413
Andres (Andrews?) 7
Andrews 18 23 38 45 145 392
Angle 106
Anglin 157
Anna, Ill. 361 362 364
"Annals of Augusta" 229
Annon 30
Apburt 15
Apler 42 90 102
Aply 36 41
Appomattox 221 222 308
Arbaugh 161 162
Arbuckal 161
Arbuthnot 266